THE
EXECUTIVE'S
GUIDE TO
INFORMATION
TECHNOLOGY

THE
EXECUTIVE'S
GUIDE TO
INFORMATION
TECHNOLOGY

Second Edition

John Baschab

Jon Piot

Foreword by Nicholas G. Carr

BICENTENNIAL
1807
WILEY
2007
BICENTENNIAL

John Wiley & Sons, Inc.

Foreword

I know what you're thinking. What's the guy who asked *Does IT matter?* doing writing the Foreword for the *Executive's Guide to Information Technology?* If it doesn't matter, why should executives care? It's a good question, and I have what I think are two pretty good answers, one professional and one personal.

As I argue in my book *Does IT Matter?* I believe information technology has lost most of its power to provide a business with a meaningful competitive edge. Valuable new innovations in computer hardware and software are so rapidly copied today, either by competitors or by vendors, that an IT innovator rarely gets more than a fleeting advantage. And since the costs and risks of being a technological pioneer are so high, it hardly ever makes economic sense to be out in front. It's better to be a smart follower, waiting for prices to come down and technology standards to emerge.

But if IT itself isn't much of a differentiator anymore, IT management still is. About half the capital investments of the average company go into IT today, and ongoing IT costs usually represent somewhere between 3 and 10 percent of a company's overall expenses. Big IT projects, moreover, continue to be afflicted by very high failure rates. The risks are as high as the costs. Improving the management of your IT assets and operations can thus translate into big and immediate cost reductions and profit gains. And because successful IT management is *hard,* an advantage here can last for years.

What John Baschab and Jon Piot do in the pages that follow is take IT management out of the data center and put it into the executive conference room. That doesn't mean they give short shrift to the technical aspects of IT management. In fact, the source of much of the value of this guide resides in the breadth and depth of the authors' technical expertise. What they're able to do, though, is translate technical issues into a context and a language that will make sense to any executive. Their guide helps span the divide—and it's often a deep and pernicious divide—between the technology and the business. Spanning that divide is the essential first step in improving the management of IT.

Understanding the business implications of technology decisions (and the technology implications of business decisions) has never been more important than it is today. Information technology is going through its biggest transformation since the personal computer invaded the business world in the early 1980s. More and more IT resources and capabilities are supplied over the Internet rather than residing within a company's own IT organization and equipment. The way companies manage the transition to on-demand, or utility, computing model—the way they coordinate their internal resources with those supplied over the new computing grid—will determine whether IT works for them or against them in the marketplace.

That's why this second edition of the *Executive's Guide* is so welcome. Much has changed since the first edition came out four years ago, and the authors have added rich new material on such pressing topics as IT governance and compliance, outsourcing and offshoring, open source software and server virtualization. It's hard to think of a contemporary IT challenge that this book won't help you tackle—whether you're an IT manager, a business-unit manager, a functional manager, a student, or a CEO.

That's why the *Executive's Guide to Information Technology* matters from a professional perspective. And now for the personal answer. The first edition of this guide appeared in 2003, just as I was beginning to write *Does IT Matter?* and it quickly became an invaluable resource to me. In fact, over the next few months, the guide was a permanent fixture on my desk, serving as an ever-dependable source of clarity and insight on all kinds of complex matters.

And so it gives me great pleasure to introduce the second edition of the guide. I feel like I'm paying back at least a little of the debt that I owe John Baschab and Jon Piot.

NICHOLAS G. CARR

Preface to the Second Edition

It has been four years since the publication of the first edition of *The Executive's Guide to Information Technology*. It is with great pleasure that we introduce the second edition.

Since its introduction, the *Executives Guide* has experienced great success, joining the top 30 on Amazon.com's business bestsellers list. It has been adopted as the main text for both undergraduate and graduate courses at nearly a dozen leading colleges and universities. We use it in our courses at Southern Methodist University as well. It received favorable reviews in a variety of publications, including new media outlets such as Slashdot.org. It was even translated for the Chinese market by the Publishing House of Electronics Industry. Most importantly it seemed to please readers, who called and e-mailed us with thanks and suggestions over the years.

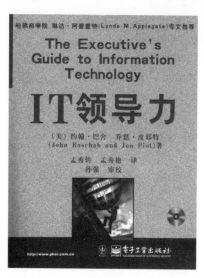

***Executives Guide:* Chinese Translation** (*Source:* Publishing House of Electronics Industry, www.phei.com.cn.)

We believed a second edition of the book was in order for several reasons. First, like many disciplines, and probably more than most, the information technology (IT) field is constantly in flux. The challenges and opportunities for IT have changed significantly in the intervening years and are worth a new look. Second, as we use the book continually in our own business and in teaching, we have identified areas that will benefit from additional clarification and illustration. Third, we have identified and added a number of new areas that are important for IT managers and organization senior executives. Fourth, we wanted to add some organizational features to the book that make it easier to use both as a reference guide and in the classroom. Finally, the industry statistics used in demonstrating its concepts were ready for an update.

We have added two new chapters, dozens of new exhibits, and expanded the book by over 100 pages. In all, we have added or revised over 35 percent of the first edition. A sampling of the major topic areas that we have expanded in this edition includes:

- IT governance and compliance.
- IT scope and strategy.
- IT auditing.
- Outsourcing.
- Offshoring.
- Data center management.
- Server virtualization.
- Security management.
- Problem management/Helpdesk.
- Disaster recovery/Business continuity.
- Development methodologies.
- Developer effectiveness.
- IT policy management.
- QA testing.
- Risk management and decision making.
- IT asset management.
- Application release management.
- Free and open source software (FOSS).
- IT organization design.
- Application performance measurement and management.
- The terminology list.

We are excited to have built what we believe is the leading comprehensive treatment of IT management, and, as always, invite and welcome your feedback. We can be reached at:

John Baschab—jbascha@chicagogsb.edu
Jon Piot—jpiot@mba1995.hbs.edu

Please also visit our weblog at www.exeguide.com. There you will find up-to-date IT management thinking and tools.

Preface to the First Edition

The bulk of our experience in the technology field has been in consulting to companies of all sizes and across a wide variety of industries, and helping them to improve the effectiveness of their IT departments. We have worked with many struggling information technology (IT) departments and have been fortunate enough to help many of them transform themselves into highly effective, fine-tuned organizations, which deliver the highest return on investment to the companies in which they operate. We have observed a consistent pattern of symptoms and causes in the IT departments experiencing difficulties. We have captured these lessons learned and the tools, techniques, and practices that can revive a struggling IT organization.

This book is a sophisticated and comprehensive guide to running a cost-effective and efficient corporate IT unit. While we spend time describing the challenges facing IT departments, our primary aim is to prescribe a course of action for senior managers and IT staff. To that end, we provide sharply defined, specific policies, approaches, and tools for each important aspect of managing the IT function, from human resources to operations to vendor selection to project prioritization.

The techniques covered in this book facilitate a detailed assessment of current operations, and development of a step-by-step improvement plan designed to save companies significant IT expenditures, while providing measurable productivity improvements. Further, the book will help IT managers and directors improve individual performance in their organizations or consulting companies by identifying common areas of friction and miscommunication between IT departments and the business, and addressing ways to overcome these dysfunctions.

The reader will gain valuable skills, including:

- Understanding the main sources of wasted IT dollars and identifying specific areas where IT managers can reduce costs.
- Identifying the industry average IT spending.
- Identifying the main management areas of a successful IT operation.
- Distinguishing the *business* of managing IT from the technical aspects.

- Understanding symptoms and sources of IT department inefficiencies.
- Learning critical improvement steps in each of the main IT management areas.
- Learning how to make better decisions in technology direction setting, project management, human resources management, risk management, and technology strategy setting.

In addition, consultants can build new consulting services for companies who are in need of these practices and cost reductions; they will be able to propose additional engagements and services to clients based on the techniques they learn in this book, as well as bring new thinking to existing projects. Companies can attain higher utilization from their existing IT assets and avoid unnecessary IT expenditures in the future. CEOs and CFOs can gain a better understanding of how to work with their top IT executives.

How This Book Is Organized

Each chapter in the book stands on its own. Therefore, some minor overlap of content from chapter to chapter occurs. We work to be prescriptive and specific instead of conceptual and theoretical. We attempt to show not just *what* to do but also *why* to do it. We also try to follow each *should* with a *because*. The book is arranged in three parts and an appendix.

Part I: The Effective IT Organization

Part I examines the ongoing dilemma that effective management of the IT function has presented for both technical and nontechnical managers. IT management is consistently considered a "neither fish-nor-fowl" business area. Few of the constraints or management considerations that apply to a normal business functional area, such as finance or human resources, apply to IT, but neither do the natural efficiencies and incentives that affect the practices of a P&L-driven business unit.

This situation has been exacerbated by the fact that nontechnical managers are confounded by the combination of business and technical skills required to manage IT, and many IT managers lack the business training and experience to bring the P&L mind-set to the function. The result is long-term dissatisfaction from all concerned—senior managers, business users, and the IT department. In many cases, businesses have an ongoing dysfunctional, mildly hostile relationship with their IT departments, and, in the worst cases, IT departments spin out of control, damaging the business with inappropriate spending, squandered opportunities, and other forms of waste.

Part II: Managing the IT Department

Part II explains in detail the key practices, policies, and strategies for effectively managing the IT department across all activities. Unlike many other treatments of this topic, we focus on the *business* of managing an IT shop, rather than focusing on a specific technology area or a niche topic. This section is geared to the IT manager, director, or CIO who wants to understand how to get the best out of their people, vendors, systems, and budget. This comprehensive, detailed guide provides concrete, specific approaches for all aspects of managing IT, as well as real-world "war stories" from a variety of organizations.

Part III: Senior Executive IT Management

Part III covers executive decision-making tools and processes for senior executives and IT managers. The traditional difficulties managing the relationship between IT and the business users can be overcome. Similarly difficulties setting company-wide priorities and ensuring that IT is executing against these priorities is critical to the executive team's success. These topics are discussed including working with the business, IT budgeting and cost management, risk management, IT demand management, effective IT benchmarking systems, and the IT steering committee. The topics and processes described will assist the executive in managing those areas that are critical to IT success and its alignment with the company both financially and strategically.

Terminology

We use specific terminology repeatedly throughout the book. These terms are used inside IT departments at many companies:

TERM	DEFINITION
Agent	Small software application that runs on a server, desktop computer or other network hardware to facilitate reporting of status, often for monitoring or CMDB purposes.
Application	Software used for any business functions.
Back-office	Applications which support internal business functions such as finance and human resources; typically accounts receivable, accounts payable, general ledger, fixed assets, payroll.
Blog	Weblog; a running commentary on a specific topic (or variety of topics) usually operated by an individual. Sometimes affiliated with a company or organization.

(continued)

TERM	DEFINITION
The business	Business managers and users who are part of the company but are not part of the IT team.
Business continuity	Similar to disaster recovery, but focused on providing systems that are available regardless of hardware, network or software failures (versus natural disasters).
Business units	Units within the corporation whose functions are in line with revenue- and profit-generating activities.
CFO	Chief Financial Officer; in an organization the top finance executive; sometimes VP of Finance. In smaller companies the CIO may report to the CFO.
CIO	The top information technology officer in the company.
CMDB	Configuration Management Database; inventory of all IT hardware systems, their configuration and the applications and services running on them.
COBIT	Control Objectives for Information and related Technology; a set of standards and processes for IT governance and management.
CRM	Customer Relationship Management; applications for tracking sales and business development efforts.
Data Center	Physical location of IT department servers and network equipment. Also known as server room, network equipment room, or equipment room.
Demand management	The process of determining which projects the IT department should execute.
DR	Disaster Recovery; processes, plans, infrastructure and systems outlined and tested in advance in the event of an unplanned natural disaster or other system outage.
ERP	Enterprise Resource Planning software; large-scale software that provides a significant portion of the functionality required to operate a business; typically has back-office capabilities (accounts receivable, accounts payable, general ledger, fixed assets, payroll) as well as core business functions, which will vary according to business type and range from order entry, inventory management and manufacturing planning to time-keeping and customer management.

TERM	DEFINITION
Firewall	Network security device which monitors and manages traffic between a wide area network (usually the internet) and the local area network belonging to the organization.
FOSS	Free and Open-Source Software; software that is either provided free of charge (gratis) and/or has no or few restrictions on its distribution, modification and deployment (freedom of usage).
Front-office	Applications which support core business functions which will vary according to business type and range from order entry, inventory management and manufacturing planning to time-keeping and customer management.
Functional group	Overhead departments in the company that support operations, not including IT, for example, human resources, finance, marketing.
Help desk	IT department sub-organization tasked with being the first point of contact for IT problems and requests.
IM	Instant Messaging; software that allows messages to be sent over the local network or internet to other users; typically in real-time but can be on a delayed basis; often used as an alternative to phone calls or e-mail.
Infrastructure	Used synonymously with the term *operations* (see definition for *operations*). Infrastructure is the breadth of utility services an IT department provides, for example, e-mail, network access, file storage, printing. Infrastructure can be contrasted with *applications,* which are software-based business transaction and analysis systems.
ISACA	Information Systems Audit and Control Association; a certifying body for IT auditors and co-contributor to the COBIT standard.
IT	Information Technology or the IT department itself.
IT department	The main IT unit in the company. Also called *information systems* (IS) *group, IT group, IT, MIS department.*
IT director	Often used interchangeably with Chief Information Officier (*CIO*).

(continued)

TERM	DEFINITION
ITIL	Information Technology Infrastructure Library; a set of standards and processes oriented to effective O&I management.
IT initiatives	Information technology improvement programs that include multiple projects for completing a single goal.
IT management	The group of top managers in the IT department, usually the IT director and his or her direct reports.
ITSC	IT steering committee; Governing body for IT decision making, strategic direction setting and prioritization; usually composed of non-technical organization senior executives.
ITSM	IT Service Management; O&I oriented processes and procedures but without the certifying component of ITIL.
Middleware	Applications which facilitate the transfer of transactions, entity data and triggering events between systems.
O&I	Operations and Infrastructure; the activities, systems, staff and policies which provide hardware, systems software and networks upon which applications run and rely.
Operations	The full breadth of utility services in an IT department includes the entire infrastructure. Chapter 8 and 9 are devoted to this subject and contains a comprehensive definition.
OS	Operating System; the core systems that operate a server, desktop, laptop computer and some network devices. The OS provides a platform of systems services on which applications run.
Patch	Update to software applications (and sometimes hardware devices) that provides enhancements, bug-fixes, updated data or new capabilities.
PMO	Project Management Office; in large IT departments the coordinating body that manages reporting, status and cross-dependencies between independent project teams.
ROI	Return on investment, a method of financial analysis to estimate financial impact of an investment.

TERM	DEFINITION
SAAS	Software as a Service; a mechanism for providing application capabilities to an organization without the related acquisition of hardware and software to operate it; software is instead provided by the vendor on a per-usage or other basis.
SDLC	Software Development Life Cycle; the steps in defining requirements, specifying functions, establishing technical architecture, developing, testing and implementing and deploying software.
Senior management	Everyone who manages a business unit or function and senior managers executive officers. Typically includes the top two layers of management in an organization and all C-level officers, for example, CEO, CFO, COO.
SNMP	Simple Network Management Protocol; a network protocol used to interrogate systems regarding their status and configuration; used in CMDB and IT monitoring systems.
SOA	Service Oriented Architecture; a methodology of systems development that promotes code re-use and modularity, thereby reducing future development and enhancement costs.
Spam	Common synonym for UCE.
System	Computer systems and applications.
TCO	Total Cost of Ownership; the cost of an activity or element of the IT department that accounts for all related expenses (e.g., TCO for a server includes costs of electricity to power it as well).
Technology	The full range of hardware, software, infrastructure, and telecommunications systems that the IT department has control over. The broadest sense of items and services that the IT department controls and is responsible for.
Tier-1	Synonymous with help desk.
Tier-2	IT department sub-group tasked with solving application and O&I requests and problems escalated from Tier-1.
Tier-3	IT department sub-group tasked with solving application and O&I requests and problems escalated from Tier-2.

(continued)

TERM	DEFINITION
UCE	Unsolicited commercial email; email sent to organization staff advertising commercial products or opportunities (nearly always unsolicited and undesirable).
UPS	Uninterruptible Power Supply; a device (usually, but not always battery powered) that provides electricity to IT equipment when the main power supply fails.
Vendor	Any outside provider of hardware, software, products, or services to the IT department.
VOIP	Voice-Over-Internet-Protocol; set of standards, hardware and software which allow voice phone calls to travel over data networks.
VPN	Virtual Private Network; networking protocol which provides to wide-area-network (internet) based connectivity to the organizations local-area-network; used to connect remote locations as well as individual remote computers (laptops and home devices).
VTL	Virtual tape library; software and hardware which simulates magnetic tape hardware but in reality consists of magnetic disks; used in high-performance data backup systems.
WMI	Windows Management Instrumentation; Microsoft implementation of protocol for systems management and interrogation.

Acknowledgments

An endeavor of this type is the result of countless investments by mentors, clients, friends, family, and teachers. We thank our readers, for making the first edition a success. Thank you to our clients, staff, and students as well for your suggestions, feedback, ideas, and interest.

Many individuals have had an important impact on the process and content of this work including Matt Holt our editor at John Wiley & Sons, Neil Salkind and his team at Studio B, and John Rosenbaum. Their support through our prior books as well as the update of this book was invaluable.

We would also like to thank our teams at Technisource and our previous companies who made many client successes possible.

Thanks also to Dr. Brad Jensen, Dr. Leon Kappelman and Dr. Jack Becker of the University of North Texas, Dr. Dick Barr of Southern Methodist University for their help in making this book useful in academia. We are also grateful to our endorsers, Dr. Lynda Applegate of Harvard Business School, Neal Aronson of Roark Capital Group, Dr. Erik Brynjolfsson of MIT, Gary J. Fernandes, and Tom Nealon, and especially Nick Carr for his Foreword.

Last, and most important, we thank our families, Mary, Emily, and Will Baschab; and Susan, Lauren, Allison, and Will Piot. Without their patience, support, and sacrifices of time, neither this book, nor the careers that provided its content, would be possible.

About the Authors

The authors have a combined 40 years of experience in information technology management at *Fortune* 500 companies and middle-market companies operating in industries ranging from retailing to services to manufacturing. They have combined their real-world experience with academic business education on dozens of consulting engagements focused on IT effectiveness and strategy.

JOHN BASCHAB began his career with a degree in MIS from the University of Alabama. He received the prestigious Seebeck award for achievement in computer science. John continued his career in the IT department of Bell-South and in the technology and finance department of computer hardware and software manufacturer, Intergraph Corp. After receiving his MBA with honors in behavioral science from the University of Chicago Graduate School of Business, John worked as a technology consultant to Fortune 500 companies in the Chicago office of Booz-Allen & Hamilton. Along with Jon Piot and John Martin, John cofounded Impact Innovations Group, a $100mm privately held IT services firm. Impact was acquired in 2005 by Technisource, where John is currently president of Technisource Management Services. He is also an adjunct professor of management information systems at Southern Methodist University. E-mail: jbascha@chicagogsb.edu.

JON PIOT received his degree in computer science from Southern Methodist University and joined Andersen Consulting, developing computer applications and providing technology-consulting services to Fortune 500 companies. Jon continued his career as vice president of DMACS International, a software company whose international software rights of Fox Software products were later acquired by Microsoft. After receiving his MBA from the Harvard Business School, Jon joined the information technology strategy group of management consultancy Booz-Allen & Hamilton. Jon is a cofounder of Impact Innovations Group, a $100mm privately held IT services firm. The company was acquired in 2005 by Technisource, where Jon is currently president of the Technology Solutions Group. E-mail: jpiot@mba1995.hbs.edu.

Contents

xxiii

PART I

The Effective IT Organization

1

The IT Dilemma

Dilemma: A situation that requires a choice between options that are or seem equally unfavorable or mutually exclusive.

—American Heritage Dictionary[1]

You're damned if you do, and damned if you don't.

—Eleanor Roosevelt[2]

Several years ago, we were taking a brief vacation with our families. Like any good technology consultants, we were never far from our mobile phones. The call came from an acquaintance, the chief operating officer of a mid-size company based in the Southeast. He knew we were on vacation, but he really wanted to talk . . . now. His story came out in a rush:

> I tell you, I've completely had it with my IT department. We have a tremendous number of business initiatives that rely on technology projects in the IT department. Not only have we lost the chance to get ahead of the competition, but we are falling behind because the IT department can't seem to finish anything. We have a list of over 150 projects and no one seems to know what the status is or who is in charge. I can't remember the last time one was completed. The entire executive team has lost confidence in IT.
>
> Every time I ask how I can help the IT department, they come back with additional headcount or capital expenditure requests. Now the IT budget is twice what it was two years ago, and the headcount has doubled, too. I think our costs are way out of line. I can't see a light at the end of the tunnel, but I don't know enough about technology to understand the issues and get out of this mess either.

We responded with some anecdotes from previous work with clients in similar situations. After listening to a few of these, the COO responded, "It's almost like you were here. This is a relief—the fact that you are so familiar with the symptoms means you probably know the cure. See you Monday."

This was not the first, nor the last, call that we received from an exasperated senior executive whose IT department had grown into an uncontrollable tar pit of backed-up projects, miserable staffers, and frustrated business users—all set against a backdrop of never-ending spending increases for additional staff, services, equipment, and software. This scenario, with no light at the end of the tunnel, is usually when we hear from senior managers who later become our best clients.

This call resulted in an engagement that allowed us to help the client dramatically, measurably improving the company's IT operations and project completion rate, while, at the same time, reducing their overall IT spending significantly. That project, and the multiple similar engagements that preceded and followed it, were the basis for some serious contemplation. We had been fortunate enough to help lead a variety of clients through the improvement of their IT departments. Our client base covers a disparate array of geographies, industries, and technologies. Nevertheless, in each case the symptoms and causes of problems in the IT department are common.

Our experiences begged the questions: What is it about IT departments that seem to so often result in such unproductive relationships with senior management? Why do successful corporate senior management teams, who manage every other aspect of their businesses with incredible acumen and ability, turn into confused neophytes when it comes to managing IT? Why do IT managers have so much trouble communicating with the senior management team? If IT departments are so bad, why are they tolerated and even given enormous spending power? And, most important, how can IT managers learn to avoid being the victims of this phenomenon, and how can senior managers learn to work with the IT team so that the organization can avoid all of the torment and pain we have observed?

Our insights on these questions, and a set of specific, actionable prescriptions, are the subject of this book. We have based this book on our experiences working with clients with 1,000-member IT departments and 10-member IT departments; from industries ranging from retailing, to manufacturing, to services; and from IT budgets ranging from under $1 million to well over $100 million. We are fortunate to have had smart, forward-thinking, action-oriented clients who have moved aggressively with us to implement our recommendations; therefore, we can assert with field-tested confidence that our methods produce real, quantifiable results. We hope that you derive as much enjoyment and value from our findings and approaches as we have had in creating, executing, and documenting them.

What Good Is Information Technology?

Most companies ought to use technology in their business and have an IT department to support it. This appears to be an obvious statement. However, it is worth recognizing that, in the memories of more than half the working population of the United States, a company department organized solely around information technology was unheard of. The IT department has evolved from a narrowly focused data processing element of the accounting department to a function that supports and, in many cases, drives, nearly every area of a company. This has happened in a mere 45 years. Stand-alone IT departments are a relatively recent development. The number of people working in technology-related jobs grew six times faster between 1983 and 1998 than the U.S. workforce at large. Information technology-related industries doubled their share of the U.S. economy between 1977 and 1998. Practically overnight, technology-related services have become a global, trillion-dollar industry.[3]

The principal driver behind this remarkable, rapid creation of a vibrant, sophisticated, and enormous industry and the attendant inclusion of a department dedicated to it in every credible company, is the quest for business productivity improvement. Susan Schmidt Bies of the Federal Reserve Board put it well: "Productivity growth receives a considerable amount of attention . . . because its rate is an important determinant of a nation's standard of living."[4] Better productivity means that businesses can produce more with the same or fewer labor and capital inputs.

The notion of technology investments as a driver of U.S. business productivity has a controversial history. The benefits of technology investments (and IT departments) were not always so apparent. Productivity growth in the United States faltered from the mid-1970s through the early 1990s,[5] in spite of large technology investments from most major U.S. corporations. The disconnect between heavy capital and expense investment and the theoretically associated improvements in productivity led to a so-called *productivity paradox*. In reaction to the failure of large IT capital investments to produce the expected productivity gains, MIT Nobel Laureate Robert Solow famously remarked in 1987, "You can see the computer age everywhere but in the productivity statistics."[6] More recent research suggests that the productivity benefits from the deployment of technology have had a massive, albeit delayed, impact on the U.S. and world economy.[7]

A variety of researchers have concluded that investments in IT have been instrumental in the improved productivity seen in the U.S. economy beginning in the mid-1990s, and accelerating starting in 2000. In early 2000, the Federal Reserve gave information technology investments credit for approximately $50 billion in productivity improvement, which represents more than 65 percent of the total $70 billion in productivity gains seen by businesses in the United States in the last half of the 1990s[8] (see Exhibit 1.1).

The Federal Reserve staff report, by Kevin J. Stiroh, concluded, "Industry-level data show a broad productivity resurgence that reflects both the production and the use of IT. The most IT-intensive industries experienced significantly larger productivity gains than other industries." The report went even further, attributing most of the productivity improvement to technology. "Results show that virtually all of the aggregate productivity acceleration can be traced to the industries that either produce IT or use IT most intensively."[9]

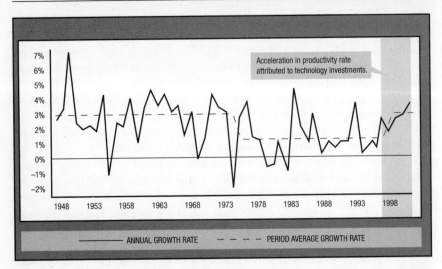

Exhibit 1.1   U.S. Productivity Growth, 1947 to 2000 (*Source:* Federal Reserve Bank of New York, staff report, no. 115, January 24, 2001.)

Business 2.0 magazine summarized the turnabout in top economic thinkers' viewpoints on the productivity gains from technology, saying that those gains:

> materialized in force beginning in 1995. What followed was a five-year run in which productivity grew an astonishing 2.8 percent a year, or double the rate of the previous two decades. (The numbers may sound small, but at 2.8 percent, living standards double every 25 years; at 1.4 percent, they double every 50.)[10]

In 2002, Solow went on record saying " . . . the paradox has dissipated in part"[11] and a Federal Reserve white paper noted that " . . . the U.S. economy has become highly dependent on information technology as the driving force in continued growth."[12]

Laura D'Andrea Tyson, dean of the Haas School of Business at the University of California, and former National Economic Advisor in the Clinton administration, emphasized the point as well, writing in *BusinessWeek:*

> The productivity numbers tell the most convincing story. According to a recent study by the Council of Economic Advisors, labor productivity accelerated by 1.6 percentage points from 1995 to 2000, compared with its growth from 1973 to 1995. The lion's share of this acceleration stemmed from more investment in information technology and the efficiency improvements made possible by this technology.[13]

In a speech before the Boston College Conference on the New Economy, Federal Reserve Chairman Alan Greenspan, a former skeptic, remarked that the "source of [the U.S. markets'] spectacular performance [is] the revolution in information technology."[14] Former Secretary of Labor Robert Reich says that it should now be obvious that "the extraordinary productivity improvement [is] generated primarily by information technology," which has been "the driving force behind this economy."[15]

Leading researcher Erik Brynjolfsson of the Massachusetts Institute of Technology has spent nearly a decade researching the link between technology investment and business benefit. Along with Lorin Hitt of the Wharton School at the University of Pennsylvania, Brynjolfsson has also concluded that investment in information technology has been responsible for major productivity improvements in corporate environments. Brynjolfsson says that "firms that invest more in IT have greater productivity improvements, and productivity continues to improve over time."[16] Additional evidence came in a 2003 study by O'Mahoney and Van Ark that concluded that industries that were intensive technology users improved their annual growth rate from 1.2 percent in the early 1990s to 4.7 percent from 1995 to 2001. Non-technology sectors experienced a net negative 0.5 percent change during the same period.[17] Use of technology appeared to be a significant differentiator.

More recent data from 2000 through 2005 continue to support this notion. The Bureau of Labor Statistics shows that the 2000 to 2005 period not only showed sustained productivity increases, but that productivity continue to accelerate, moving from the mid-2-percent range to 3.3 percent, and a whopping 5 percent in the manufacturing sector, which is arguably one of the biggest beneficiaries of the extensive IT capital investments of the 1990s (Exhibit 1.2).

In the past few years, research has continued on IT's productivity impact. Attribution of economic productivity gains to IT is not without some controversy. Recent work has attempted to evaluate productivity improvements at a more detailed level than economy or industry sector. While the macrolevel numbers seem to support IT as a driver of productivity increases, research at the firm level and further examination of the overall data have been somewhat

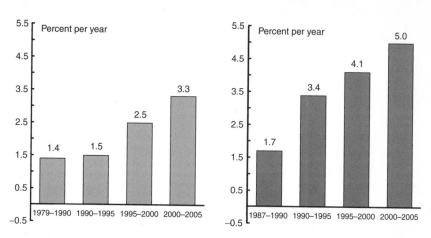

Exhibit 1.2   U.S. Productivity Improvement Statistics (*Source:* U.S. Bureau of Labor Statistics, http://www.bls.gov/cps/labor2005/chart1-18.pdf.)

less conclusive. Martin Bailey, senior fellow at the Institute for International Economics and senior advisor to McKinsey & Company, in a late-2003 retrospective on 1990s IT spending said "to a degree, it may have been the economic boom that created the big wave of IT investment rather than the wave of IT investment that created the boom." He also encourages caution linking IT investment to the 1995 turnaround because "the growth accounting framework did not do very well in tracking productivity movements prior to 1995."[18]

Earlier, Paul Strassmann, former CIO of Xerox and a leading IT effectiveness researcher and consultant, took an even tougher stance, observing of productivity statistics that "corporate management cannot make practical use of this data. It is by the economists, for the economists and is of use only for engaging in unresolvable disputes." Strassmann advocates the more detailed research that has followed saying that "only measures that can be explicitly related to corporate financial performance can settle the arguments whether the U.S. is either losing or gaining on productivity growth in the private sector."[19]

The large body of research attempting to further clarify the issue by examining more granular data is best summarized by Bailey in another 2003 report that concluded that "counting both the productivity growth within IT-producing industries and the productivity growth enabled by IT in using industries, IT did contribute to productivity growth in the 1990s and to the acceleration."[20]

The amount of the productivity improvements in the U.S. economy due to IT spending is still a matter of debate. However, researchers, academics, and economists all appear to agree on two points: First, that U.S. labor productivity started improving in 1995, and that improvement has accelerated since 2000. Second, certainly some, if not most, of the improvements are the result of the creation, deployment, and effective use of IT in organizations.

We do not have to rely merely on academia, economists, or on abstract concepts such as productivity gains in the U.S. economy for confirmation that IT investments produce results for corporations. According to the World Information Technology and Services Alliance (WITSA), "Global reliance on [technology] is growing . . . and [Information and Communications Technology] has become the indispensable technology for social and economic growth in developed and developing countries alike." The WITSA analysis found that global spending on information and communications technology grew by $1 trillion between 2001 and 2006, topping $3 trillion in 2006. They project spending to reach $4 trillion by 2009.[21] Clearly, business decision makers are voting with their budgets on the value of technology.

The quantitative, specific results that companies who invest in information technology have enjoyed are easy to identify. Significantly improved sales forecasting, rapid month-end closings, shortened supply chains, tightened inventories, streamlined customer communication, and better information for business decision making are just a few of the results of the combination of hardware, software, and effort expended over the past 25 years, for example:

- General Electric (GE), through a systems-based push to monitor all of its business activities more effectively, has created capabilities and reporting systems that allow it to respond quickly to events. Business managers have real-time dashboards or "digital cockpits" that highlight important aspects of their operation—sales results, inventory levels, and order status. Overall, systems implementations have helped GE achieve impressive savings numbers: $100 million from inventory, accounts payable and receivables, $680 million saved in procurement through on-line auction purchasing. GE estimates total savings as a result of "digitization" at a staggering $1.6 billion.[22]

- Weirton Steel, a $1.3 billion steel manufacturer, has lowered labor hours per ton of steel from 6.5 hours to 1.3; the CEO attributes the cost improvements directly to the deployment of technology.[23]

- Roadway Express, a $2.8 billion freight hauler, implemented systems that provided detailed tracking for all internal operations. This allowed the systems to track the true cost-to-serve for all processes using Activity Based Costing (ABC). The system not only helped them identify process improvement and cost reduction opportunities, but also understand the true cost of serving customers, allowing them to turn away unprofitable business. Based on these IT initiatives, the company was able to improve their operating yields, with revenue-per-ton up 4 percent in 2001, in an environment where their competitors were struggling to merely maintain existing margins.[24]

- United Health Group, an $18-billion insurer, used technology-driven reengineering to produce large productivity gains and reduce overhead costs by more than $300,000 annually.[25]

- KIAH, a financial services firm, reduced its mortgage approval process from four days to 10 minutes, all based on technology deployment.[26]

- Tsutaya, Japan's largest CD and video retailer used a combination of customer relationship management systems, data warehousing, and wireless technology to begin offering new services to customers through their subsidiary, Tsutaya On Line (TOL). By taking advantage of the large number of wireless phone subscribers in Japan, TOL achieved a subscriber base of over 2.5 million in a few short years. TOL builds an assessment of subscribers personal entertainment preferences and provides content to their wireless phones, including music clips, movie reviews, and film recommendations. TOL customers who use the mobile service spend 9 percent more with Tsutaya than non-TOL customers. Based on their sophisticated delivery of personalized content, TOL has grown profits by more than 48 percent, in a challenged Japanese economy.[27]

- CSX, an $8 billion rail and intermodel transportation company, implemented a "black box" system for trains that records operational information. The wirelessly downloaded data provided information on engineers' performance to their supervisors for evaluation. Supervisors in turn were able to provide helpful feedback. The resulting improvement in engineer driving is projected to save $6.8 million in fuel costs annually. These savings are only likely to increase as fuel costs rise.[28]

- Dell computer, a $50 billion computer hardware company, used a combination of Oracle software and Linux systems to replace and enhance its existing order processing capability. The result was a doubling of Dell's order handling ability with estimated annual benefits of over $18 million.[29]

- Baptist Health South Florida, a nonprofit hospital, implemented a system that monitors patients and provides information regarding patient condition to health care workers. The system reduced Intensive-Care-Unit stay duration by 20 percent, and most importantly reduced mortality rates by 25 percent.[30]

- Atmos Energy, a $5 billion natural gas provider to residential and commercial users, implemented Oracle technology to improve asset management. The resulting productivity gains reduced manual data management by over 100,000 hours as well as improved worker deployment.[31]

For dozens of additional positive anecdotes, look at the "Top 100" awards from *CIO* magazine, given annually to innovators who improve their organizations through the use of the technology. Commercial enterprises from every industry—nonprofits, state, and federal government agencies alike—are enjoying the improved productivity that accompanies effective technology use.

The benefits of IT-enabled innovation don't stop at the office. New technologies for mobile computing, wireless networking, Internet search engines, and even entertainment continue to improve peoples lives. BlackBerries, iPods, wireless networks, and high-speed Internet access have all been enabled by continued capital investments in IT infrastructure and capabilities in homes and businesses.

In short, no reasonable person today contemplates a life without corporate systems supporting every business function, from manufacturing, to finance, to sales and customer support, to say nothing of desktop office-automation products such as spreadsheets and word processors and even IT-enabled consumer electronics such as MP3 players and console games.

Corporations have adopted technology to increase productivity, reduce costs, drive revenues, offer new capabilities to customers and suppliers, and improve competitive positioning. Researchers, educators, economists, pundits, and, most importantly, business managers and consumers agree that investments in information technology are not only unavoidable, but, in fact, are undisputedly and universally beneficial. What is immensely perplexing, then, is that studies of business satisfaction with IT and IT initiatives have produced surprisingly negative results.

Information Technology Misery

In spite of the impressive results from business investment in technology, the IT department is the source of tremendous frustration, missed opportunity, and inefficiency in companies. Corporate management is at odds with the IT department more often than not. The revolving door in the top IT management spot at so many companies has led to the only half-joking interpretation by some that the CIO title stands for "Career Is Over." This level of cynicism is not something you generally hear directed at the individuals who have risen to similar levels of responsibility in a corporation in other functions or business units. Something is clearly amiss with IT departments.

A host of evidence backs this position. One important snapshot of the failures of IT is provided by the Standish Group, a technology research group and consultancy, which has performed an exhaustive analysis of the outcomes of more than seven years of corporate IT projects. The researchers at the Standish Group have performed periodic studies on the results of corporate IT initiatives since 1994. In their widely publicized, groundbreaking research, they found that IT initiatives had surprisingly high failure rates. They found that more than one-half (53 percent) of IT projects had overrun their schedules and budgets. Thirty-one percent of IT projects were cancelled. The average time overrun on projects was 222 percent of the original estimate. It is impossible to calculate the opportunity cost of the failed projects.[32]

Incredibly, the initial Standish survey in 1994 found that a scant 16 percent of projects were completed within the original time frames and budget constraints. The group found that the percentage of completion in larger companies was even lower, at 9 percent. Of projects that were completed, only 42 percent delivered the original planned benefits.[33]

A decade later, Standish found the success rate increasing to 29 percent, an improvement but still surprisingly low.[34] The investment stakes for projects and information technology initiatives are high. Standish has estimated that the average cost of a development project for a large company is well over $2 million, and even small companies invest over $400,000.[35] Others confirm a high level of investment in IT. In their long-running annual survey of IT costs in companies, *Information Week* finds that IT budgets run from two to nine percent of revenue, averaging between three and four percent.[36]

Standish is not alone in its findings. Consultants KPMG found that 87 percent of projects surveyed went 50 percent over their budget. They also found that 45 percent of projects failed to produce the expected benefits and that nearly 90 percent went over schedule.[37] A 2001 Gartner Group survey found that that approximately 40 percent of IT projects do not produce their intended results. They further found that a cancelled IT project lasted about half the time originally intended, and cost companies an average of at least

$1 million per year. Gartner showed that 10 percent of a typical company IT team worked on efforts that had no business benefit.[38]

A 2001 survey by Robbins-Gioia of over 230 firms found that over a third of them were implementing an enterprise system. Fifty-one percent of those companies viewed the ERP system as unsuccessful. Nearly 50 percent said their organization understood how to use the system to improve the business.[39] A similar survey by the Conference Board found that only 34 percent of companies implementing ERP systems were "very satisfied." The survey also showed implementation costs were 25 percent over budget, support costs were 20 percent higher than expected, and 40 percent failed to achieve their anticipated business benefits within a year of launch.[40]

A survey presented at the Joint Aerospace Weapons Systems (JAWS) symposium found that 75 percent of the software budget spent by the U.S. Department of Defense was for systems that were never used or cancelled before completion—a price tag of nearly $27 billion. Worse, the JAWS work found that a paltry 2 percent of projects were successful upon launch.[41] The government is not alone is this. Gartner Group estimates that IT project failures in companies accounted for $75 billion in losses, attributing 60 percent of the failures to poor project management.[42]

If statistics and research results aren't proof enough, observers need look no further than some of the high-profile IT failures of the past few years. A review of a few of these provides ample empirical evidence of how difficult IT projects can be and the tremendous amount of damage they can cause when they go awry:

- *Denver International Airport:* A new state-of-the-art automated baggage handling system was approved to improve baggage management speed, accuracy, and throughput. The sophisticated system was to be controlled by more than 300 computers and be composed of more than 4,000 unmanned baggage cars running over 21 miles of track. Difficulties with the project, which required an investment of more than $230 million, delayed the opening of the airport by 11 months. The delayed opening of the airport cost the city more than $1 million per day while system shortcomings were corrected, with a net result of costs higher than the original investment in the project over the course of the delay. Ultimately, the airport installed a $51 million conventional baggage handling belt system so that the airport could open for business.[43] Much of the new system was later sold for scrap.[44]

- *Hershey Foods:* Three up-to-date programs designed to increase productivity, cut costs, enhance customer-relations management, and improve logistics were arranged to replace Hershey's legacy system simultaneously. Despite that, glitches during peak buying season resulted in sales decreases of 12.4 percent, yielding a dismal third-quarter report.[45]

- *Nike:* New software was implemented to manage Nike's supply chain production line. However, the software failed to adequately match supply with consumer demand, resulting in shortages in some product lines and overproduction in others. Nike blamed its $100 million quarter-to-quarter revenue drop on i2 Technology's software, a part of a larger software project, which ultimately cost Nike more than $400 million.[46]

- *Washington State Department of Licensing:* A new program was implemented to provide a fully automated system for vehicle registration and renewal. The program was expected to cost $41.8 million and take five years to execute. However, difficulties after only three years increased the cost to more than $51 million. The project was terminated seven years after its initiation. Consequently, $40 million had been wasted because of bad management and poor guidelines.[47]

- *Mississippi Department of Information Technology Services (ITS):* The original $11 million contract called for a consulting firm to build an automated tax system to collect 36 taxes for the state's tax commission during a 40-month period. However, "not a single tax was implemented during the 64-month term of the contract," according to an ITS statement. Settlement attempts failed, the case made it to trial, and a jury in August 2000 awarded the state of Mississippi $475 million in actual and punitive damages. Post-verdict negotiations between the parties reduced the settlement to $185 million over several years.[48]

- *Cisco Systems:* A modern forecasting system was produced as a major strategic competitive advantage. However, management's trust in the system allowed a large economic turndown to go unnoticed, which, in turn, led to write-offs totaling $2.2 billion, 8,500 layoffs, and a decrease of $68.37 per share in its stock.[49]

- *FoxMeyer Drug:* A top-of-the-line enterprise resource planning (ERP) program, anticipated to cost $65 million, was facilitated to boost the drug distributor's productivity. Release of the software was pushed forward 90 days, sacrificing valuable module test time and eliminating the opportunity to reengineer business processes. Software glitches and inaccurate inventory forecasting resulted in bankruptcy.[50]

- *Tri Valley Growers:* A modern software program was designed to cut costs and improve productivity. The system cost more than $6 million; however, no expectations were met and some of the software could not even be installed. After investing $20 million in the implementation, Tri Valley refused to pay its vendor and stopped using the software. When Tri Valley filed a $20 million lawsuit, its software provider countersued for breach of contract.[51]

- *W. W. Grainger Inc.:* A software system was implemented to optimize profit and cut costs. The system, costing at least $9 million, repeatedly overcounted warehouse inventory, which led to inventory shrinkage. As a result, Grainger experienced $23 million in reduced earnings and a loss of $19 million in sales.[52]

- U.K. food retailer J Sainsbury wrote off a $526 million supply chain system that failed to deliver merchandise properly from the companies warehouses to its stores. The company ultimately hired 3,000 temporary workers to get items on their shelves.[53]

In late 2005, the IEEE published its software "hall of shame" highlighting some of the major systems implementation failures of the previous dozen years (Exhibit 1.3). Total costs for failed projects were over $5 billion in just these incidents alone, not to mention billions more in damages, lost revenue, or other costs highlighted by the survey.[54]

These high-profile IT project failures are simply those highlighted in the technology press. The Standish Group statistics imply that such anecdotes are the rule, not the exception.

Dissatisfaction with the IT department, however, extends beyond these high-profile project flameouts. There is also well-documented dissatisfaction with all levels of corporate IT departments, from help desk support, to operations, to management. Marcy Lacity and Rudy Hirschheim documented this in their research for *Information Systems Outsourcing: Myths, Metaphors, and Realities,* finding that "only 2 of the 13 companies that participated in the study agree that their IT departments are critical to corporate success. The remaining 11 companies all see their IT departments as a necessary, but burdensome, cost pit."[55]

The proverbial surly, supercilious, and contemptuous "tech guy" from the IT department has become such a common corporate stereotype that *Saturday Night Live* immortalized the character in the form of "Nick Burns: Your Company's Computer Guy."

The character of Nick certainly goes over the top, with comments such as "They teach this kind of stuff on *Blue's Clues*"; "[so] it's the e-mail that's stupid, not you, right?"; "I was trying to help those morons on the third floor. They're trying to run RealPlayer behind a firewall without the proxy set—can you believe that?"; and (responding to his ever-beeping pager) "It's those goofs over in Organizational Development—they make you guys look like brainiacs over there." Much of the effectiveness and humor of the skit comes from the fact that everyone seems to know a Nick Burns in his or her own organization.

The image of technology workers is so negative that even the federal government got into the act. A U.S. Department of Commerce publication concluded, "Many people have a distorted, negative image of IT workers," and recommended remediation in the media of the IT profession image to attract additional workers to the field.[56]

The result is that IT has, in many companies, been relegated to a backwater operation, in spite of its clearly recognized importance to operations and productivity. As a former CIO writing under the pseudonym "Anonymous" writes

YEAR	COMPANY	OUTCOME (COSTS IN US $)
2005	Hudson Bay Co. [Canada]	Problems with inventory system contribute to $33.3 million loss.
2004–2005	U.K. Inland Revenue	Software errors contribute to $3.45 billion tax-credit overpayment.
2004	Avis Europe PLC [United Kingdom]	Enterprise resource planning (ERP) system canceled after $54.5 million† is spent.
2004	Ford Motor Co.	Purchasing system abandoned after deployment costing approximately $400 million.
2004	J Sainsbury PLC [United Kingdom]	Supply-chain management system abandoned after deployment costing $527 million.
2004	Hewlett-Packard Co.	Problems with ERP system contribute to $160 million loss.
2003–2004	AT&T Wireless	Customer relations management (CRM) upgrade problems lead to revenue loss of $100 million.
2002	McDonald's Corp.	The innovative information-purchasing system canceled after $170 million is spent.
2002	Sydney Water Corp. [Australia]	Billing system canceled after $33.2 million is spent.
2002	CIGNA Corp.	Problems with CRM system contribute to $445 million loss.
2001	Nike Inc.	Problems with supply-chain management system contribute to $100 million loss.
2001	Kmart Corp.	Supply-chain management system canceled after $130 million is spent.
2000	Washington, DC	City payroll system abandoned after deployment costing $25 million.
1999	United Way	Administrative processing system canceled after $12 million is spent.
1999	State of Mississippi	Tax system canceled after $11.2 million is spent; state receives $185 million damages.
1999	Hershey Food Corp.	Problems with ERP system contribute to $151 million loss.

(continued)

Exhibit 1.3   IEEE Project Failure "Hall of Shame"   (*Source: IEEE Spectrum,* September 2005, http://www.spectrum.ieee.org/sep05/1685/failt1. © 2006 by IEEE.)

YEAR	COMPANY	OUTCOME (COSTS IN US $)
1998	Snap-on Inc.	Problems with order-entry system contribute to revenue loss of $50. million.
1997	U.S. Internal Revenue Service	Tax modernization effort canceled after $4 billion is spent.
1997	State of Washington	Department of Motor Vehicle (DMV) system canceled after $40 million is spent.
1997	Oxford Health Plans Inc.	Billing and claims system problems to contribute to quarterly loss; stock plummets, leading to $3.4 billion loss in corporate value.
1996	Arianespace [France]	Software specification and design errors cause $350 million Ariane 5 rocket to explode.
1996	FoxMeyer Drug Co.	$40 million ERP system abandoned after deployment, forcing company into bankruptcy.
1995	Toronto Stock Exchange [Canada]	Electronic trading system cancelled after $25 million is spent.
1994	U.S. Federal Aviation Administration	Advanced Automation System canceled after $2.6 billion is spent.
1994	State of California	DMV system canceled after $44 million is spent.
1994	Chemical Bank	Software error causes a total of $15 million to be deducted from 100,000 customer accounts.
1993	London Stock Exchange [United Kingdom]	Taurus stock settlement system canceled after $800 million is spent.
1993	Allstate Insurance Co.	Office automation system abandoned after deployment, costing $130 million.
1993	London Ambulance Service [United Kingdom]	Dispatch system canceled in 1990 at $11.25 million; second attempt abandoned after deployment, costing $15 million.
1993	Greyhound Lines Inc.	Bus reservation system crashes repeatedly upon introduction, contributing to revenue loss of $61 million.
1992	Budget Rent-A-Car, Hilton Hotels, Marriott International, and AMR [American Airlines]	Travel reservation system canceled after $165 million is spent.

Exhibit 1.3 *Continued*

in *CIO* magazine, "As far as most people at your company are concerned, [the] IT staff operates . . . somewhere apart from the 'real' company."[57]

In their article, "IT's Rodney Dangerfield Complex," *CIO* magazine highlighted the result of business frustration with IT, quoting a CIO from a major corporation: "[IT] gets no respect [from the other departments]." The article goes on to say that IT was "left out of business process or technology-related discussions" and that the department "was fragmented and the organization lacked consistency in project management, processes, and production."[58]

The Standish Group goes one step further, saying that in the computer industry, "failures are covered up, ignored and/or rationalized."[59] The unfortunate reality is that the "Rodney Dangerfield complex" describes the position of the IT department in all too many organizations.

A Burning Platform

For more than a decade, *Information Week* has conducted a survey on IT spending in top U.S. corporations. The results are telling. Most U.S. companies spend between 2 percent and 9 percent of their annual revenues on IT-related expenditures. The rate varies by industry, but median spending is somewhere between 4 percent and 5 percent.[60] Exhibit 1.4 outlines the average spending by industry, as a percentage of corporate revenue. Although the benchmark IT spending as a percentage of revenue varies from industry to industry, the majority of industries spend between 2 percent and 5 percent of revenues on technology.

Exhibit 1.5 shows the trend in the *Information Week* data over the past few years. The average spent on technology by companies has risen steadily, in spite of the well-known pullback in 2001.[61]

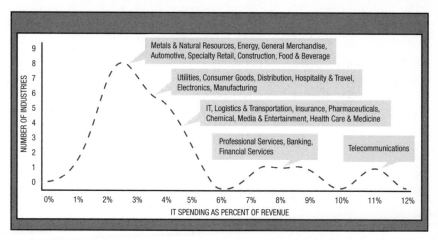

Exhibit 1.4   IT Spending as a Percent of Revenue by Aggregate Industry Group

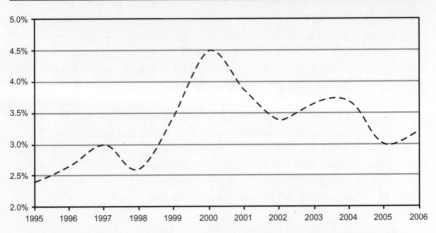

Exhibit 1.5   IT Spending in *Information Week* 500 Companies (1995–2006)
(*Source: Information Week,* http://www.informationweek.com/iw500.)

The problems outlined in the previous section should be of material interest to corporations. The amount of spending and investment by corporations, even those investing in IT at the low end of the scale, means that the problems in IT have to be addressed. At 4 percent to 5 percent of revenues, the IT costs in a company must be managed effectively. At this average range, IT costs are usually one of the largest nondirect expenditures in a company. In comparison, according to studies performed by the Hackett Group, world-class companies on average spend only 0.67 percent of revenues on finance.[62] Both the benefits to be achieved, and the high investment required by IT justify close attention from senior management to ensure that IT is effective and producing the right results.

Information Technology Satisfaction?

One useful way of rating corporations' effective use of IT is to plot their level of overall satisfaction with IT—the sum of customer service levels, cost reductions, improved business operations, or other relevant aggregate measures of benefits produced by the IT department. Exhibit 1.6 compares this satisfaction with the level of cost relative to peer companies.

Companies with limited IT operations begin in the southwest quadrant. While their satisfaction with IT is low, it is not surprising given their low level of investment. To improve IT operations and achieve the benefits outlined in this chapter, the company begins investing in technology. This migrates them northward on the matrix. The senior management team generally has the intention of finding a way to migrate to the southeast corner where IT costs are kept at reasonable levels expected for the company, and higher satisfaction is achieved.

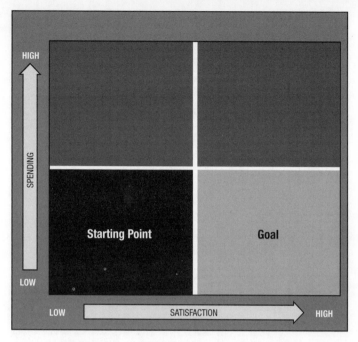

Exhibit 1.6   IT Satisfaction versus IT Spending

In many companies, the increased investments in IT do not produce the expected benefits. Satisfaction stagnates, or even diminishes, based on the high expectations set from the incremental investment. Often, at best, companies achieve large improvements in their level of satisfaction, but the baseline steady state of IT investment never levels off, or it goes back to previous levels. As Exhibit 1.7 demonstrates, the fate of many companies is at best a permanent residence in the northeast quadrant and, at worst, the northwest "high-spending, low-satisfaction" corner.

This combination of IT dissatisfaction and high spending has created a burning platform for the improvement of the IT department.

The Information Technology Dilemma

Why, then, if IT is an absolute requirement in any company today, is corporate senior management's satisfaction with such a critical function so startlingly low? Why is the actual and perceived satisfaction of the end customer so low? Why is the IT department's satisfaction with consultants, applications providers, and hardware vendors similarly low? How can IT shake the "Nick Burns" stereotype and thrive as an integral, vital function in a company?

Why do companies spend as much as 9 percent of their annual revenues on a function that didn't exist 40 years ago and, while achieving incredible

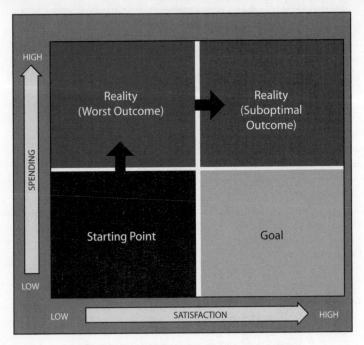

Exhibit 1.7 Typical Company Progression

benefits, still so often fail to derive full value or satisfaction from their investment?

These are intriguing questions, and, more importantly, ones that senior management teams ignore at their peril. Many companies appear to be caught in a perplexing dilemma. They must invest in information technology, if not for productivity gain, at least for competitive parity. Technology investments have created major productivity gains over the past two decades.

Research and anecdotal evidence, however, also make it clear that the failures of IT departments to produce cost-effective, satisfactory results have produced misery on a massive scale for corporations and IT department personnel alike.

Every company spending money on an IT department has no choice but to grapple with these issues. Many organizations continue to throw money at the problem, escalating the issue even further. Ignoring the issues, or treating them with superficial infusions of additional investment, does not change the underlying problems. In fact, it is the primary reason companies find themselves in the northwest corner of the IT spending and satisfaction matrix.

Chapter 2 outlines some of the symptoms and causes of the IT dilemma. The remainder of this book presents the building blocks of effective IT management that we have used to help many of our clients move to the southeast corner of the matrix.

NOTES

1. Copyright © 2006 by Houghton Mifflin Company. Adapted and reproduced by permission from *The American Heritage Dictionary of the English Language, Fourth Edition.*

2. Eleanor Roosevelt, *Ladies Home Journal, 61* (November 1944), pp. 155–171.

3. C. A. Meares and J. Sargent, U.S. Department of Commerce, Office of Technology Policy, Update: The Digital Workforce (Washington, DC: U.S. Government Printing Office, September 2000).

4. Remarks by Governor Susan Schmidt Bies before the Tech Council of Maryland's Financial Executive Forum, Bethesda, MD (January 18, 2006), http://www.federalreserve.gov/boardDocs/Speeches/2006/20060118/default.htm (accessed December 7, 2006).

5. Kevin J. Stiroh, "Information Technology and the U.S. Productivity Revival: What Do the Industry Data Say?" Federal Reserve Bank of New York, staff reports, no. 115 (January 24, 2001), http://www.newyorkfed.org/research/staff_reports/sr115.pdf (accessed December 9, 2006).

6. R. Solow, "We'd Better Watch Out," *New York Times Book Review* (July 12,1987), p. 36.

7. See note 5.

8. Marianne Kolbasuk McGee, "It's Official: IT Adds Up," *Information Week* (April 17, 2000). All rights reserved. Reprinted with permission. http://www.informationweek.com/782/productivity.htm (accessed December 10, 2006).

9. See note 5.

10. Jerry Useem, "And Then, Just When You Thought the 'New Economy' Was Dead," *Business 2.0* (August 2001).

11. Douglas Clement, Federal Reserve Bank of Minneapolis, "Interview with Robert Solow," *The Region* (September 2002), http://www.minneapolisfed.org/pubs/region/02-09/solow.cfm (accessed December 10, 2006).

12. Jorgenson and Stiroh, Federal Reserve Bank of New York, "Raising the Speed Limit: U.S. Economic Growth in the Information Age" (May 1, 2000), http://econweb.fas.harvard.edu/faculty/jorgenson/papers/dj_ks5.pdf (accessed December 10, 2006).

13. Laura D'Andrea Tyson, "Why the New Economy Is Here to Stay," *BusinessWeek* (April 30, 2001), http://www.businessweek.com/magazine/content/01_18/b3730032.htm (accessed December 10, 2006).

14. Alan Greenspan, "The Revolution in Information Technology" (March 6, 2000), http://www.federalreserve.gov/BOARDDOCS/Speeches/2000/20000306.htm.

15. See note 8.

16. See note 8.

17. M. O'Mahoney and B. Van Ark, *EU Productivity and Competitiveness, An Industry Perspective*, Report to DG Enterprise, European Commission, 2003 (pp. 82–83), http://www.ggdc.net/pub/EU_productivity_and_competitiveness.pdf (accessed December 10, 2006).

18. Martin N. Baily, Senior Fellow, Institute for International Economics, "Recent Productivity Growth: The Role of Information Technology and Other Innovations,"

FRBSF Economic Review, 2004 (p. 36), www.frbsf.org/publications/economics /review/2004/er35-42bk.pdf (accessed December 7, 2006).

19. Paul Strassmann, "Facts and Fantasies about Productivity" (1997), http://www .strassmann.com/pubs/fnf/factnfantasy.shtml (accessed October, 2006).

20. Martin N. Baily, "Information Technology and Productivity: Recent Findings," presentation at the AEA Meetings (January 3, 2003), www.petersoninstitute.org /publications/papers/baily0103.pdf (accessed December 10, 2006).

21. ITAA Press Release (May 2, 2006), "Global ICT Spending Tops $3 Trillion," http://www.itaa.org/newsroom/release.cfm?ID=2338; WITSA can be found at www.witsa.org (accessed October 2006).

22. Dave Lindorff, "General Electric CO's Drive to Real Time," *CIO Insight* (November 2000).

23. See note 8.

24. Edward Cone and David F. Carr, "Unloading on the Competition," *Baseline* (October 2002), http://www.carrcommunications.com/clips/roadway.pdf.

25. See note 8.

26. See note 8.

27. Alexandra Harney, "Always On," *CIO Insight* (February 2002), http://www.cioinsight.com/article2/0,1540,122780,00.asp (accessed December 10, 2006).

28. "2006 Top 100," *CIO*, http://www.cio.com/archive/081506/winners.html (accessed October, 2006).

29. See note 28.

30. See note 28.

31. See note 28.

32. "The Standish Group," *The Chaos Report* (Yarmouthport, MA: The Standish Group International, Inc., 1994), http://www.standishgroup.com/sample _research/chaos_1994_1.php (accessed December 10, 2006).

33. See note 32.

34. Deborah Hartmann, "Interview: Jim Johnson of the Standish Group," (August 25, 2006), http://www.infoq.com/articles/Interview-Johnson-Standish-CHAOS (accessed December 10, 2006).

35. See note 32.

36. "Multiyear Comparisons of InformationWeek 500 Survey Data Reveal IT Trends," *Information Week* (September 12, 2006), www.informationweek.com (accessed December 10, 2006).

37. KPMG Project Risk Management and Information Risk Management (1998), http:// www.kpmg.co.uk/kpmg/uk/IMAGE/PRMFINAL.PDF (accessed August 2003).

38. "Research Shows High Failure Rate on IT Projects," *Journal of Accountancy* (February 2001), http://findarticles.com/p/articles/mi_m6280/is_191/ai _70423157 (accessed December 10, 2006).

39. Robbins-Gioia press release (January 28, 2002), "ERP Survey Results Point to Need for Higher Implementation Success," http://www.robbinsgioia.com/news _events/012802_erp.aspx (accessed December 10, 2006).

40. The Conference Board, "ERP Trends," (June 2001), http://sloanreview.mit.edu /smr/issue/2001/winter/1e/ (accessed December 10, 2006).

41. Stanley J. Jarzombek, "The 5th Annual Joint Aerospace Weapons Systems Support, Sensors, and Simulation Symposium (JAWS S3)." Proceedings (1999), http://www.stsc.hill.af.mil/crosstalk/2002/04/leishman.html.

42. Jennifer Mateyaschuk, "Training Address Project-Management Needs," *Information Week* (October 25, 1999), http://www.informationweek.com/758/project.htm.

43. See note 32.

44. "Braunagel: United stuck with baggage system," *Denver Business Journal* (December 2, 2004).

45. Polly Schneider, "Another Trip to Hell," *CIO* (February 15, 2000). Copyright © 2002 CXO Media, Inc. Reprinted with permission. http://www.cio.com/archive/021500_hell.html.

46. Christoper Koch, "Nike Rebounds," *CIO* (June 15, 2004), http://www.cio.com/archive/061504/nike.html.

47. Tom Field, David Pearson, and Polly Schneider, "To Hell and Back," *CIO* (December 1, 1998). Copyright © 2002 CXO Media, Inc. Reprinted with permission. http://www.cio.com/archive/120198/turk.html.

48. Ann Bednarz, "IT Malpractice," *Network World* (April 8, 2002), http://www.networkworld.com/careers/2002/0408man.html.

49. Scott Berinato, "What Went Wrong at Cisco," *CIO* (August 1, 2001). Copyright © 2002 CXO Media, Inc. Reprinted with permission. http://www.cio.com/archive/080101/cisco.html.

50. Malcom Wheatley, "ERP Training Stinks," *CIO* (June 1, 2000). Copyright © 2002 CXO Media, Inc. Reprinted with permission. http://www.cio.com/archive/060100_erp.html.

51. Dawn Kawamoto and Wylie Wong, "Case Study: Oracle Customers Pay the Price," *ZDNet News* (June 28, 2001), http://news.zdnet.com/2100-9595_22-530193.html.

52. Craig Stedman, "ERP Woes Cut Grainger Profits," *ComputerWorld* (January 7, 2000), http://www.computerworld.com/news/2000/story/0,11280,42976,00.html.

53. Robert N. Charette, "Why Software Fails," *IEEE Spectrum* (September 2005). Copyright © 2006 IEEE. Used with permission. http://www.spectrum.ieee.org/sep05/1685.

54. See note 53.

55. Marcy Lacity and Rudy Hirschheim, *Information System Outsourcing: Myths, Metaphors and Realities* (Chichester, England: John Wiley & Sons, 1993), p. 190.

56. See note 3.

57. Anonymous, "No Satisfaction," *CIO* (January 15, 2001). Copyright © 2002 CXO Media, Inc. Reprinted with permission. http://www.cio.com/archive/011501/confidential.html.

58. "IT's Rodney Dangerfield Complex," *Information Week* (March 28, 2002). All Rights Reserved. Reprinted with permission.

59. See note 32.

60. See note 36.

61. See note 36.

62. Press release "Hackett Book of Numbers Analysis" (November 16, 2006), The Hackett Group. www.hackett.com press releases.

2

IT Ineffectiveness Sources and Causes

I think it is an immutable law in business that words are words, explanations are explanations, promises are promises—but only performance is reality. Performance alone is the best measure of your confidence, competence and courage. Only performance gives you the freedom to grow as yourself.

Just remember that: Performance is your reality. Forget everything else. That is why my definition of a manager is what it is: one who turns in the performance. No alibis to others or to one's self will change that. And when you have performed well, the world will remember it, when everything else is forgotten. And, most importantly, so will you.

—Harold Geneen, CEO, ITT[1]

In the previous chapter, we outlined the fundamental IT effectiveness dilemma facing both the CIO and the senior management team in a corporation. This chapter focuses on the symptoms that manifest themselves in ineffective IT departments, the proximate causes of those issues, and the ultimate cause of IT dysfunction: the leadership gap caused by inadequate preparation for the management responsibilities a career in IT gives to future managers.

We been fortunate to have worked in dozens of IT departments, in a variety of roles—technical support staff, developers, managers, consultants, and advisors. We have observed a common set of symptoms of an ineffective, struggling IT department. Most of these phenomena have very little to do with the specific technology deployed, the industry the corporation participates in, the external market conditions, or the size of the organization. Instead, the same sets of issues emerge repeatedly.

In this chapter, we broadly categorize these indicators and inventory them. With these identified, we begin to answer the question raised in Chapter 1: What are the ultimate causes of ineffective IT departments?

Symptoms of IT Distress

We have identified four main categories of symptoms of trouble we have seen in distressed IT departments. A brief description of the four areas follows:

1. *Business satisfaction:* Level of satisfaction and confidence in the IT department on the part of the business.
2. *Budget problems:* IT spending, including internal resource costs, services, and capital expenditures.
3. *Project effectiveness:* IT support for business projects; internal software and hardware deployments.
4. *Staffing problems:* IT human resources management, team morale, and IT organization.

This chapter covers some of the symptoms we have seen in each of these categories. While this list is lengthy, it is certainly not comprehensive. The symptoms of a distressed, ineffective IT department show up in many ways. However, most manifest themselves in one of these four categories, particularly business satisfaction, which is the ultimate arbiter of the effectiveness of the IT department.

Business Satisfaction

The most important category by which to measure IT is business satisfaction rate. This measure presumes a well-run company where members of the senior management team and business unit heads are motivated to run their businesses with the best efficiency to produce economic gain for the company and shareholders. This "invisible hand," which keeps the business units motivated toward the right goals, in turn, puts pressure on the IT department to provide infrastructure, applications, service levels, and initiatives to help the business drive revenues, reduce costs, or achieve better control. It also assumes that business unit managers understand how IT can be used to drive those goals and generate business value. Given the statistics in Chapter 1 on level of investment in IT for the past 30 years, this is also a reasonable assumption. Therefore, if the business unit managers are motivated to drive company revenues and profits, and they clearly understand how IT can help them do so, the business will recognize if the IT department is not living up to those goals.

Many companies suffer from an enormous disconnect between the IT department and the business. This often results in a negative image of IT departments and staff as covered in the previous chapter. This disconnect and overall lack of satisfaction with IT services manifest in a variety of common symptoms:

- Business unit leaders (and functional heads) are dissatisfied with the performance of IT and the support for their initiatives and day-to-day requirements.
- Business managers lack confidence when IT commits to a deadline.
- Business users are frustrated by their lack of control over IT; they perceive that IT "doesn't listen."
- Business managers don't believe that IT has the same goals as they do, most easily evidenced in the perception that IT "doesn't care about helping" the business succeed.
- Business users either don't know or don't understand priorities in the IT department.
- IT claims the business "doesn't respect them" and/or "ignores IT" and leaves IT out of decision-making processes.
- In response to IT shortcomings (real or perceived), business units hire their own, separate IT teams, which they control.
- Business units blame IT shortcomings for missed business opportunities or failed projects.
- Business units create and implement systems without input or help from IT.
- Business units bring IT into decision making that affects systems at the last minute (or not at all).
- IT department insulates itself from the rest of the organization and does not communicate or socialize with business units or other functional areas.

Budget Problems

The second potential area of weakness in the IT department relates to budgeting. Properly managing IT investment (and measuring the return on the investment) is treated in several chapters in this book. In discussing IT budgeting, we include not just the actual IT budget but all spending on technology in the company, including technology spending in the business units, on any technology-related labor, technology consumables, outside technology services, hardware, software, and other capital.

We have observed that often IT managers and staff have trouble showing sensitivity to the effect of cost on the bottom line. The "customer" of the IT department, usually a business unit manager, is quite familiar with assessing costs in terms of how they affect the bottom line profitability of their division or organization. This means, given average profit margins of 10 percent for a company, that the business unit manager, intellectually and, most importantly, viscerally, understands that spending a dollar on something "costs" approximately $10 in revenue to cover it. This P&L-focused view of costing means that incremental investments in staff, services, or equipment are carefully and clinically scrutinized, and that the business unit manager makes the investment only after he or she is convinced that it is essential and that it will return more to the business than it costs. Further, they will monitor the investments and projects to be sure that the promised business returns are realized.

We have not found this keen awareness of the "cost of costs" to be present in IT managers and staff, who have generally not had experience in a line role where they are responsible for managing both the costs and revenue sides of a profit-and-loss statement. For example, a junior manager over a 15-person IT shop had submitted a requisition for a server that cost more than $20,000. Although it was clear that a less robust, less powerful model would suit just as well, her response to the notion of a downgrade was "Look, its only $20,000; we have millions and millions in revenues." This, unfortunately, is often the perspective from IT. We reminded the manager that to "cover" the cost of the server would require a sales team to sell (and successfully deliver) more than $200,000 in products and services.

There is ample evidence of this behavior at the end of the fiscal year in many companies in the mad scramble by IT personnel to spend unused IT budget dollars on items that may or may not be good investments for the company. Typically, the money is consumed in overpurchasing goods and services from vendors who are trying to make year-end sales goals. The vendor entices the IT staff with discounts and incentives on items like disk storage and software licenses that have only marginal benefit for the company. These funds are also used on training that may have little or no relevance to the skills needed to run IT or complete upcoming projects. Unfortunately, the IT budget is viewed as "Monopoly money" and not real dollars that might be better spent in other parts of the company, for instance, funding for an additional salesperson or dollars sent back to the company treasury to preserve operating cash.

This behavior leads companies to see IT as an endless sink for resources. As observed in the previous chapter, this spendthrift flippancy by IT concerning costs has contributed to the attitude of many companies. In an IT satisfaction survey by researchers Lacity and Hirschheim, the majority of the companies "see their IT department as a necessary, but burdensome, cost pit."[2]

Although less common, the reverse problem can happen as well. IT departments can underinvest. This is often caused by timidity on the part of the IT managers who do not work to push their agendas through, or by business unit managers and a senior management team who do not see the value of technology. The effect of underinvestment on a company can be just as corrosive as out-of-control spending. Companies can fail to achieve the benefits attendant with the quality use of technology; after all, investments in technology have accounted for more than two-thirds of the productivity growth in the past half decade. Companies who consistently underinvest in technology are at risk for higher than necessary operating cost structures, missed opportunities in new markets, and erosion of share in existing markets by aggressive competitors who find ways to serve their customers better with technology. Ironically, companies in this position often get caught in a downward spiral; their unwillingness to make smart technology investments drives away the talented technology professionals who could potentially help them realize gains from well-executed IT spending.

Symptoms of an IT department that is out of control on spending or is underinvesting include:

- Spending more than peer group companies on IT (percentage of revenue or other relevant measure).
- Large quarter-to-quarter or year-to-year expansion of IT budgets without associated expansion of business volumes.
- Large quarter-to-quarter or year-to-year expansion of capital expenditure without associated business imperative or retirement of capital being replaced.
- High levels of outside purchasing, particularly services or consultants.
- Company failing to cover or exceed cost of capital on IT projects or other capital spending (IT dollars not achieving same value as they could in other parts of the company).
- Continuous flow of "emergency" requisitions from IT for headcount, services, equipment, or software.
- IT management has difficulty forecasting IT costs annually or quarterly.
- Ongoing large budget variances (positive or negative) in IT department; high budget variances in top-level categories of IT budget (staff, services, capital expenditures). Chapter 3 outlines the key drivers of IT spending and provides a starter set of benchmarks by which companies may measure themselves.
- Technology infrastructure does not have capacity or capability to support business initiatives.

Project Effectiveness

One of the best measures of the overall competence of an IT department is its ability to successfully manage projects. Poor project execution by IT is one of the largest complaints from business users. Although many IT managers and team members are often exposed to, or are even well versed in, the mechanics of project management, the actual results do not reflect their supposed capabilities.

IT departments usually are part of projects that are internal to IT (they involve no one outside the department, e.g., server upgrades, e-mail system rollouts) or external (involve some level of coordination with areas outside IT; e.g., financial package implementations, sales force automation software implementations). We have not observed any appreciable differences between the success rates of these internally directed projects and those that involve significant external coordination. This implies that IT managers struggle with the fundamentals of good project management.

We have found that these struggles are not specific to any particular piece of the project management discipline, but instead run the spectrum from project scoping, ROI calculation and business value justification, requirements gathering, business process mapping, team building, planning, execution, tracking, and completion.

A major source of project ineffectiveness is the overall management of project demand within the IT—creating potential project inventories, prioritizing the projects, determining the baseline project capacity of the IT department, and ensuring that only the number of projects supported by that capacity are allowed to be open simultaneously.

Some of the trouble concerning project completion, is due to the notion, propagated for quite some time, that the business is a "customer" of the IT department. While there is some merit to this notion, it has led IT teams to adopt a "customer is always right philosophy." Without negotiation (or even protest), the IT team continues to absorb a barrage of project requests and to-do items from the business. Business managers quite reasonably assume that the capacity to complete the projects is available, or the IT management would reject the request. Instead, IT signs up for yet another project that, as 200th on a list of 200, is doomed before it begins. Four months later, on the project due date, a very unhappy business manager reminds the IT department that they are the "customer" and the cycle continues.

The typical IT department we are asked to assist easily has more than 100 projects "on the books." These projects are at every level of magnitude (with projects such as "repair the system clock on the backup server" aggregated at the same level as "migrate servers from Windows NT to Windows XP"). IT managers often confuse their to-do lists and their projects lists, hopelessly commingling both.

Most often, there is significant overlap in the project inventory. What may be listed as a project in one part of the inventory is actually a substep of yet another project in the inventory. In one client engagement, just based on overlap elimination alone, we reduced the project list from more than 160 projects to fewer than 50. For example, auditing and purchasing server licenses and upgrading server memory could both be substeps in a larger project to migrate the servers to a new operating system.

Aggravating matters further, the projects have widely varying creation dates, or worse, no date. Rarely has the business rationale, or business owner, for the project been documented, to say nothing of a cost benefit or return-on-investment analysis. This makes culling projects whose relevance has long passed challenging.

Finally, each of the projects is underway, each in varying stages of completion, but far from 100 percent. In a misguided effort to please the business, IT departments often fail to complete one project before starting another. The result is a quagmire of multiple, often contradictory, efforts that, in aggregate, never seem to be completed.

Common symptoms of an IT department struggling with project management issues include:

- No clear successes to point to on the project front; no record of the last successful project completed.
- Multiple project inventories; no consolidated project list.
- No distinction between "internal" IT projects versus those that must coordinate with the business.
- Confusion between to-do lists and projects.
- Large numbers of projects (greater than 100).
- No project charters for projects underway.
- Slight progress on the entire list of projects in inventory instead of substantial and real progress on a limited subset of priority projects.
- No relationship between IT team capacity to execute projects matched to the number of projects (and required labor capacity) allowed to be underway simultaneously. IT team capacity to execute projects has not been calculated.
- Multiple, simultaneous, uncoordinated projects underway.
- No framework (or even attempt) to prioritize projects based on business value, risk, existing system adequacy, ease of completion, or other relevant factors.
- No clearly set individual responsibility for project management or completion (responsibility at team level only or responsibility split between two or more people).
- Project documentation (scope, requirements, work plans, and deliverables) incomplete or missing.
- System projects that are completed have poor quality and reliability and require constant patching and rework.

Staffing Problems

Often, the first refuge of a beleaguered IT manager in charge of a distressed IT department is the addition of staff.

As so famously outlined in Brooks' classic text on technology project management and organization, *The Mythical Man-Month,* adding capacity to any late projects (even well managed ones) does not improve their timing.[3] We believe that adding resources to an already disorganized, chaotic, mismanaged environment is simply the recipe for more cost, not beter results. The addition of capacity in these cases often obscures the issues even further. It is difficult for organizations to absorb a high number of new staff in a short period and still be productive.

Because the CIO in a distressed department is, by definition, having difficulty managing, he or she most often, ironically, also has trouble identifying the very talent most likely to be of use in turning the situation around. The result is that new staff are of average or below average quality, or at best, deficient in the very skills and knowledge most needed. Often, the IT managers turn to their social circle for sourcing of new candidates. This complicates matters even further because of the negative consequences from the mixing of business and personal agendas in the office.

Because the capacity additions are made as part of a panicked response, they are not part of a clear, well-thought-out plan and, therefore, do not have clearly defined roles and responsibilities. The resulting distorted organization chart creates responsibility gaps and overlaps that lead to even further chaos. Inexperienced new managers struggle with the inherent ambiguity of a rapidly changing organization, and seasoned staffers have trouble keeping track of the rapidly changing plan.

The final blow to the IT departments comes as the best players realize that the situation is hopeless. Morale among those seasoned staff that are in the know sinks rapidly. High morale is found only among the newest team members who have not yet had time to grasp the situation. Those with options outside the company (again, ironically, the very team members who are most likely to have the highest positive impact) begin to flee. The resulting replacement hiring continues to lower the average ability in the department and contributes further to the issues attendant with large numbers of new staff.

The CIO begins spending more time behind closed doors hoping for a miracle. Eventually, the issues in IT become a burning platform for senior management, and a major housecleaning ensues.

This pattern of failure, reflected in the following staffing symptoms, is one that we have observed in multiple clients struggling with IT challenges:

- No ownership of results by IT, particularly IT management.
- Worried IT staff.
- Large number of recent hires (greater than 30 percent of staff members have less than one year of tenure).
- Organization chart not clearly defined (or entirely missing) as to operations support and application support.
- Disparate titles; no standardization of roles and responsibilities; no clearly documented job responsibilities at any level of the IT organization.
- High (or no) attrition in IT department; attrition disproportionately high among tenured staff.

- Large volume of gossip in IT department.
- Inadequate (or unsatisfying) interaction between IT staff and rest of company.
- Strong morale dichotomy: newest staff members with adequate or high morale; exceedingly low morale among staff with most tenure.
- Inexperienced IT managers (no previous management experience, or experience in only a subset of the disciplines within IT).
- Little or no screening of new hires to department (in-person interview screening only).
- Sourcing of candidates from social circles (friends and family members of managers or other IT team members; from same neighborhood or other nonbusiness association).
- Excessive consumption of vacation time or sick leave by tenured staff.
- Inordinate number of team members "working from home."
- Disengaged management (CIO or managers difficult to find, behind closed doors, taking excessive vacation, or other offsite activities).
- Constant infighting and bickering between business and IT and within IT.

Proximate and Ultimate Causes of IT Ineffectiveness

In most departments, there are nearly as many obvious causes of IT ineffectiveness as there are symptoms. With every failure, it is easy to spot a multitude of potential causes (e.g., "The implementation project failed because the team never clearly defined scope and didn't do requirements gathering before selecting a vendor").

The most common categories of causes of ineffectiveness are:

- *Business turmoil:* Changes to the business because of external or internal pressures that manifest themselves in radical changes in demand on the IT department:
  —Changes to the business model: New lines of business, new operating models, new sales and distribution channels.
  —Changes to external entities: More customers or suppliers, or more transactions with customers and suppliers.
  —Merger and acquisition activity: New business units to be integrated, along with associated staff, applications, data, customers, and suppliers.
  —Divestiture: Business units being carved off; disaggregating of data and separation of systems.

—Changes to business profitability: Higher profitability driving investment in IT and increased pressure on increased IT capability; lower profitability driving cost pressures to IT.

—Rapid revenue growth of the company requiring new/rapid response to changes from IT.

—Additional support for disparate geographies required from IT, particularly requiring international support.

—Multiple technologies in place for operations, development, and database creating "technology chaos" and slowing down every initiative.

- *Vendor management:* Use of hardware, software, and services vendors not capable of supporting the business; poor selection and weak ongoing management of vendors:

  —Vendors and service providers that were appropriate for a smaller company, but have not scaled with growth in the company.

  —Poorly performed vendor selection and implementation.

  —Weak management of vendors.

  —Weak or nonexistent standard setting; wide variety of disparate technologies and vendors creating a chaotic, heterogeneous environment.

- *Staffing and communications:* Inexperienced and insular management style alienates the IT team and business; business uses IT ineffectiveness as an excuse for its own shortcomings:

  —Business unit leaders take no interest in IT and use it to finger point and lay blame.

  —IT makes little or no effort to socialize with the business.

  —IT leadership is usually in the role for the first time; CIO has limited experience managing people, growth, and setting technology direction.

  —CIO is unable to identify good new hires and resorts to personal contacts for sourcing.

  —Department lacks ability to attract the "right" talent; issue goes beyond technical capabilities to inability to recruit team-oriented achievers.

  —Poor staff management, hiring; unclear organization and roles/responsibilities.

  —Rapid growth in IT department—large numbers of staff with fewer than one to two years with the company and/or fewer than two to three years in technology.

  —Each decision approached as a one-off proposition resulting in suboptimal decision making for the department at large.

- *Financial and risk management:* Team does not understand the critical link between expenditures on IT and the benefits, cost-reduction, or incremental revenue; team does not make (or even contemplate) effective cost-benefit trade-offs:

—No attempt to calculate or document return on investment for projects or other IT expenditures.

—No record of ROI for previous projects; no analysis of ROI for proposed projects.

—No understanding of cost of additional expenditures to company profits; no comprehension of marginal-spend versus marginal-benefit.

—IT managers consistently "overinsure" system engineering at significant expense.

—IT managers engage in "sunk cost fallacy" and continue to plow additional money into clearly losing projects or technologies.

—CIO focuses on optimizing each project on a one-off basis instead of the overall company.

All of these causes provide some level of explanation for failings in the IT department. However, they also share a common thread. It is important to distinguish *proximate* causes—the most obvious explanations for behavioral phenomena—and *ultimate* causes—root causes that are the behind-the-scenes driver of the proximate causes.

This behavior model is particularly relevant in the case of the dysfunctional IT department. In attempting to "fix" the IT department, the senior management team (and sometimes IT leadership) gets caught up in chasing the proximate causes to problems, such as those previously inventoried. This can be confusing and demoralizing, because new proximate causes continually emanate from what we believe are the ultimate causes—lack of experienced leadership from IT management and lack of engagement from senior management.

Most new IT managers are woefully inadequately prepared to begin taking on their new responsibilities. The skills and competencies required to survive, let alone excel, at managing a functional department in a corporation are quite different from those required to excel as a staff member in that same department. In few professions is the gap between doing and managing so profound as in IT.

One of the primary causes of this difficulty is the internal split between the functions that the IT manager must successfully oversee. As Chapter 4 shows, most IT departments are organized into two large activity areas split between operations and applications. IT managers usually have been trained in and promoted from one or the other of these two areas and, therefore, have had little experience managing (or even interacting) with team members outside their subfunction.

In addition to lacking experience with half of the IT functions that the novice manager is newly responsible for, the skills and knowledge required to be effective are vastly different. Exhibit 2.1 summarizes the skills developed and mastered by IT professionals before promotion to IT management

PRE-PROMOTION SKILLS
System requirements gathering and analysis.
Programming and systems development.
Application design and management.
System configuration.
Business process documentation.
Technology implementation.
Systems administration.
Systems performance management.
Technical, data, and applications architecture design and management.
Limited project management.
Upward reporting relationship with technical manager.

Exhibit 2.1   Skills Developed Pre-Promotion

levels, as contrasted with the list of skills required for success as an CIO or manager shown in Exhibit 2.2.

This gap between the pre-promotion skills learned as an applications manager, developer, or operations specialist and the skills required to succeed as an CIO is the root cause of many of the woes discussed in this and the preceding chapter.

Newly minted CIOs find themselves in an entirely different role, with high expectations from their senior management team. To exacerbate matters, the new manager is usually reporting to a nontechnical professional, most often the corporate CFO. This means that at the very moment the CIO needs the most guidance and support, it is unavailable.

This finding has been the primary diagnosis in many of the IT turnarounds that we have completed in the past few years. For many of the senior managers we work with, the notion that something as simple as leadership can be the ultimate cause of problems in the IT department can be difficult to swallow. A simple answer to what seems to be an impossible-to-solve knot of issues is particularly tough to believe when many of the issues, at the surface, appear to be technical in nature.

If these arguments are not compelling enough on their own, we usually point to the empirical evidence we have gathered as part of the IT effectiveness. We have seen repeatedly that most of the proximate issues resolve themselves quite rapidly once the IT leadership challenges have been solved. Two client examples illustrate this:

1. Our client, a software development company, relied on the IT department for not only internal applications support, but also development

POST-PROMOTION SKILLS
Management of both applications and operations portions of IT function.
Vendor selection, negotiation, and management.
Hiring, evaluating, managing, motivating, developing, promoting, and firing team members.
Decision making.
Cost containment.
Cost/benefit estimating; project economics estimation.
Budgeting.
Risk management.
Communications with business units and senior management.
Resource and project prioritization.
IT organizational design.
Standard setting and enforcement.
IT measurement and effectiveness.
Coordination of multiple, disparate projects, and initiatives across business units and internal functions.
Determining best use of scarce economic resources (staff, budget, time).
Maintenance of *steady-state* service levels for basic IT services.
Upward reporting relationship to nontechnical business manager, COO, or CFO.

Exhibit 2.2   Skills Required Post-Promotion

of the company's core product. Over the year before our work with the client, the IT department had trebled in size. Many projects were at a standstill, with little hope of near-term completion. The product itself was producing inaccurate results, and even outright operating failures. The internal and external customer frustration with the IT group had reached a fever pitch. In response, IT had become defensive and belligerent. The impasse between business and IT seemed truly unbridgeable.

Working with the client senior management team and the technical team, in short order, we implemented the leadership, cost-containment, organization, demand management, and vendor management principles outlined in this book. Within three months, the IT staff had been reduced by more than 70 percent, containing the out-of-control costs. Not only had the product accuracy and failure issues been fixed, but also the performance of the product itself had been measurably improved, much to the delight of the customer base.

2. A mid-sized manufacturing company, already under intense cost pressure, was informed by IT management that the hardware on which all of the corporate systems were running had to be replaced due to capacity constraints. The company's peak order season was threatened. System capacity issues from previous seasons had nearly capsized the business, and the anticipated increases in order volumes might very well result in complete systems failure. The company could ill afford the nearly $1 million in capital expenditures it would take to completely replace its systems hardware, to say nothing of the business disruption and risk that are part of any major systems overhaul.

   When the client retained us to assume management of the IT department, our first task was to identify opportunities to reduce systems load. In the previous four years of systems capacity issues, many ideas had been considered, but no testing or attempts at implementation had been made. Within a few short weeks, the IT team had identified a combination of data purging, database tuning, tight-loop code rewrites, and usage smoothing that reduced the overall system load by more than 40 percent, creating more than enough room to make it smoothly through the peak season and beyond.

What makes these client examples both interesting and highly relevant is that the fundamental changes were made in the leadership and management of the IT department. In every case, the major elements in the IT department remained the same: the same systems, the same technology, the same hardware, the same infrastructure, the same business users, and most important, the same technical staff. The only variable introduced was the management of the IT staff, which produced measurable and dramatic results in surprisingly short order.

Support for this theory can be found in IT effectiveness research that has emerged in the past few years. Because the stakes are so high for organizations, the dilemma of what root causes are behind IT failures has proven attractive as a topic. The research supports our conclusion that the root causes of IT failures lie in IT leadership quality.

Paul Strassmann, former CIO of Xerox and a leading industry thinker, performed an IT spending analysis on nearly 3,000 U.S. companies (see Exhibit 2.3). He plotted IT spending per employee (which normalized the data for company size) against return on equity for the company (which measures business success). The result? No clear correspondence between IT spending and financial results. Instead, companies that have succeeded in using IT to advantage are those with quality IT (and other) leadership. Strassmann writes:

> What few people take the trouble to do is to correlate spending with actual economic outcomes, such as profits after taxes, or even better, economic value added (EVA). I have done such analyses for 2,865 U.S. industrial corporations. In each

Return on equity

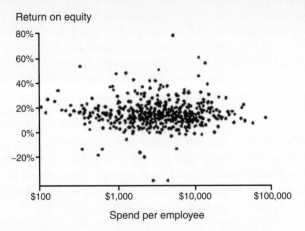

Exhibit 2.3 Return on Equity versus IT Spending per Employee (Courtesy of Paul Strassmann.)

case I plotted IT outlays per employee against rates of return on equity (ROE) producing a completely random distribution. Clearly such a scatter plot shows that there is zero correlation between IT spending and economic outcomes. . . . The essence of leadership lies in how an individual leader balances and mixes the ingredients of strategic influence to deliver the most effective results.[4]

Other analysts have similar findings. Research from the London School of Economics and McKinsey & Company "found that major increases in IT intensity were associated with 20 percent higher productivity in the best managed firms . . . but the same increase in IT intensity only raised productivity by 2 percent for the poorly managed (defined as firms in the bottom quartile of managerial good practices)."[5]

In a 2004 Gartner, Inc. interview, Erik Brynjolfsson, of MIT said:

[N]ine-tenths of the cost and nine-tenths of the benefit of big IT projects are not in computer hardware or even software. They're in the organizational and human capital changes. And so, if you want to have a big impact, you need to be able to understand those organizational and human capital aspects of the business process change. . . . Historically too many CIOs have thought of productivity just as how they can deliver more gigabytes of disk storage or megabits of communications capacity. Those aren't the productivity measures that really matter to the organization; it's how satisfied your customers are, how you're saving cost on the supplier side, and have allowed for more creativity and added value at all levels of the organization.[6]

Martin Bailey, senior fellow at the Institute for International Economics writes "the examples where businesses were successful in their IT investment were ones where the companies had already identified a specific problem to be solved or opportunity to be exploited. . . . Successful IT applications also typically occurred where outcomes could be quantified and monitored."[7] Working on the right things and driving them to quantifiable conclusion are clearly contingent on appropriate leadership from IT.

While laying most of the responsibility for IT ineffectiveness at the feet of CIOs (or more accurately, at the lack of preparation most CIOs receive), it would be remiss to remain silent on the contribution of senior management to the situation.

We have found that, although IT is rightly considered a *function*, along with departments such as human resources, finance, accounting, and marketing, it also has hallmarks of a business unit. More so than any other functional department, IT is required to interact with, and understand the processes of, every business unit and every functional unit. IT departments are, in many ways, the nerve center of the entire company.

Further, as outlined in Chapter 1, technology, as deployed by corporate IT departments, has been the largest driver of productivity for corporations. It is a key component for most company initiatives focused on cost reduction or revenue building. At best, IT is a source of competitive advantage, productivity gains, and new capabilities and, at a minimum, the largest nondirect expense for most companies. In every case, it cannot be ignored. Yet, in many cases, senior management refuses to engage with IT, and so it remains managed as neither a function nor a business unit. This happens for a variety of reasons, including disinterest, uncertainty of how to manage technology issues, or no understanding of how IT can help the business. In every case, it is demoralizing to IT and produces a resentful, marginalized IT management team.

In working with one client, we were having particular difficulty convincing the senior team to pay attention to IT issues. To draw their attention to the importance of the IT department, we took the budgets of each of the eight strategic business units in descending order of size. We then inserted the IT department into its proper part of the sequence according to budget size. If considered a business unit, IT would be fourth largest in the company, well ahead of the smaller business units. Faced with this analysis, all agreed that, in proportion to its cost to the company, IT did not receive enough attention from senior management.

Steps to Effective IT Management

Although our complete prescription for implementing effective management of the IT department is covered in this book, we are often asked for the short version of our program. A checklist of specific steps across five broad areas that can be taken in dysfunctional IT departments to improve performance and begin reaping the rewards of a productive relationship with the business follows:

1. Improve IT management:
   - Implement an IT steering committee as a "virtual CIO" to provide advice and leadership to the CIO and help speedily resolve issues between business and IT.
   - The committee should be composed of the top 5 to 10 senior managers in the business; they should be required to attend every meeting.
   - Upgrade management talent in the IT department by hiring the right director.
   - The IT steering committee should source the candidates and hire the new director as a senior manager instead of a senior programmer.
   - Clean up the IT organization chart; this means no "floating boxes" and clean, clear lines of responsibility between applications management and operations without gaps or overlaps in coverage.
   - Every staff member should have a shorter-than-one-page roles and responsibilities document posted at his or her desk.

2. Add basic project management disciplines:
   - Establish a single, well-documented master inventory of projects.
   - Determine the ROI or business benefits for each project.
   - Projects that do not improve revenues, reduce costs, or improve control over the business should be ignored.
   - Prioritize projects by their benefits, difficulty, and adequacy of the current systems, generating a force-ranked list.
   - Determine the intrinsic project capacity of the IT department.
   - Limit the number of open projects to that capacity.
   - Expect this number to be shockingly small and disconcerting, but be comforted by the notion that the projects will actually be accomplished.
   - Assign a specific person from the IT department to be responsible for the management and execution of the project, and have him or her report progress in a five-minute update to the IT steering committee on a weekly basis.
   - Each team lead must develop a clear work plan for accomplishing the assigned project, with work tasks, time lines, deliverables, dependencies, and required resources clearly defined.

3. Manage vendors:
   - Determine which vendors are good, productive partners and which are sapping the IT budget with bloated fees and unproductive products, services, or billable hours.
   - Migrate business to the former and dismiss the latter.

- Insist on favorable contracts and pricing in return for vendor exclusivity.
- Migrate the technology platform in the department to homogeneity to facilitate ease of management and project execution.
- Negotiate hard with vendors for best pricing, and aggressively manage them after the sale.
- Ask vendors how they measure their own client-satisfaction performance internally, and require them to produce a report card on themselves at reasonable intervals.
- If they don't know how to measure themselves internally, get them out.
- If they do, hold them to the periodic reporting and help them improve their services with clear feedback.

4. Fiscal management/budgeting:
   - Recognize that most companies must generate $10 in revenues to cover every $1 spent in IT.
   - Build a reputation for saving the company money by "making do" and reserve capital expenditure requests for must-have items. Although more difficult, CIOs must become a business resource for the senior management team by suggesting ways to lower the company's overall operational costs through use of IT.
   - If budget variances appear, proactively explain them to senior management and provide fair warning for surprise capital or operating expenditures.
   - Build trust with the CFO by avoiding typical agency issues that accompany the budgeting process that give IT teams a bad reputation for being focused on the constant acquisition of new toys.

5. Improve relationship with the business:
   - Reduce finger pointing between IT and business users by initiating a "seat rotation" that has key IT staff members sitting with the businesses they support one to two days per week.
   - CIO should have a quota of two lunches per week with business unit managers, functional managers, or members of the IT steering committee.
   - Add effective business-user relationship management to the appraisal process for all IT team members.

With the right leadership in place and enthusiastic engagement from the senior management team, the IT department can lead the company in management excellence.

As evidence that the IT department can lead the entire company toward excellence, we share a note received from the CFO of a client for whom we had previously completed an extensive IT effectiveness engagement:

> We are a totally different company today than when you were here last year. It all started with the IT area. [Based on the work completed there,] we have reorganized every phase of our operations and continue to refine our processes.

NOTES

1. Harold S. Geneen and Alvin Moscow, *Managing* (New York: Doubleday, 1984), p. 285.
2. Marcy Lacity and Rudy Hirschheim, *Information System Outsourcing: Myths, Metaphors and Realities* (Chichester, England: John Wiley & Sons, 1993).
3. Frederick P. Brooks, Jr., *The Mythical Man-Month* (Reading, MA: Addison-Wesley, 1995).
4. Paul Strassmann, *Leader to Leader Magazine* (Winter 2002), Peter Drucker Foundation.
5. John Van Reene and Raffaella Sadun, "Information Technology and Productivity: It Ain't What You Do It's the Way That You Do It," (September 2005), p.6. Centre for Economic Performance, London School of Economics, www.statistics.gov.uk/articles/nojournal/sadun_bvr25.pdf (accessed December 10, 2006).
6. Erik Brynjolfsson, interview with Gartner Fellow Ken McGee, (October 13, 2004), http://www.gartner.com/research/fellows/asset_124138_1176.jsp.
7. Martin N. Baily, Senior Fellow, Institute for International Economics, "Recent Productivity Growth: The Role of Information Technology and Other Innovations," *FRBSF Economic Review*, 2004 (p. 38), www.frbsf.org/publications/economics/review/2004/er35-42bk.pdf (accessed December 7, 2006).

3

Information Technology Costs

You cannot ask us to take sides against arithmetic.

—Winston Churchill[1]

There are only two qualities in the world: efficiency and inefficiency, and only two sorts of people; the efficient and the inefficient.

—George Bernard Shaw, John Bull's Other Island, 1904, Act IV[2]

This chapter outlines the process for benchmarking IT spending in a corporation. It suggests general determinants and targets for IT spending and presents multiple methods of calculating benchmarks as well as the pros and cons of each. It also introduces historical IT spending trends in aggregate and by industry.

The chapter is organized around the IT cost benchmarking process. First, we introduce some of the historical spending levels of U.S. corporations. Second, we outline the various methods for benchmarking and discuss key IT cost drivers, which can affect IT spending, and the subsequent attempt to benchmark spending. Finally, we analyze scale economies that can be achieved as a company grows and then provide recommendations for aligning IT spending with the corporate business strategy.

Benchmarking approaches discussed here are intended to be guidelines for spending—not a specific recommendation as to the precise amount for a given company to spend on IT. First, the data provided by industry group is a blunt metric. The Chief Information Officer (CIO) must perform some independent analysis to gather peer group information to add additional meaning and context to the data. Second, the analysis provided here is best used as a reasonableness test. That is, is the current level of spending reasonable in light of factors such as industry, peer group spending, and other company-specific attributes? The bottom line is that the CIO must justify all spending on technology in relation to the benefits it generates for the business.

This chapter highlights the importance of the proper management of IT expenses, as one of the largest components of spending in organizations, yet one of the most mismanaged areas.

Why This Topic Is Important

In the final analysis, the CIO is evaluated on the level of output from the IT department compared to the input required to produce the results. In this case, the output is effective technology that drives productivity, profits, user satisfaction, competitive advantage, and new revenue streams. The input is capital in terms of labor and dollars.

Unfortunately for the CIO, the measurement of both variables has traditionally been poor. The input in terms of expenses required to fund the IT department is generally readily available; however, the true total input requires some investigation of IT spending outside the IT department and is typically overlooked. The output is also not measured rigorously. The result is a seemingly clear but understated knowledge of IT spending paired with almost no knowledge of benefits (output), making justification of the spending, or a precise linkage between the spending and business benefits difficult.

The next step in the process is a justification of IT spending based on the industry benchmark, but as we discuss later, this process can be flawed and result in widely different ratios and recommendations for IT spending.

Compounding the issue is the fact that peer spending information on IT is difficult to find. As a result, companies are often left with no basis to create or adjust the IT budget and resort to the baseline set by the previous year's budget. Meanwhile, the company is challenged by a technologically advanced competitor that is reaping huge cost savings from being fully integrated with its customers and suppliers.

It is vitally important that the CIO understand how to benchmark IT spending and develop recommendations for general spending levels to achieve the company's strategic objectives.

Chapters 17 and 19 further outline calculating the business value of projects or IT initiatives based on their costs and benefits.

Introduction to Benchmarking IT Spending

By any measure, U.S. corporations make substantial investments in information technology. Approximately 40 percent of nonresidential business investment is in IT. The real IT investment by U.S. corporations grew 16 percent per year since 1959.[3] This is a staggering growth rate by any account. At the same time, executives are attempting to determine the benefit of this spending in terms of productivity, profits, and competitive advantage. As Chapter 1 illustrates, after years of questioning the linkage between IT spending and business productivity, the economic data finally shows a causal link between IT spending and higher productivity.

The frustration with increased costs and the lack of a clear correspondence between IT expenditures and profits as well as the proportionally large operating expense outlays, are the reasons IT costs are a major concern for senior executives in U.S. corporations and have led to the IT dilemma outlined in Chapter 1. IT spending can range anywhere from 1 percent to 10 percent of overall company revenues, depending on the dynamics of the industry and the specific situation of the company. For example, a company turning $1 billion in annual revenue might spend anywhere from $10 million to $100 million on information technology each year. This order of magnitude difference in what is the "right" level of IT spending is explained by a variety of macroeconomic factors, including industry, size, competitive environment, and customer concentration.

In spite of significant expenditures and corresponding financial exposure, many companies do not have a clear understanding of actual dollar amounts of direct IT costs, much less hidden IT costs scattered throughout their organization. Further, there is a lack of understanding of how to benchmark their IT spending—whether they are overspending or underspending in the area.

Company senior managers do not generally know how to determine what their IT costs should be. What should be considered reasonable expense in information technology? What are the key predictive variables that drive IT costs? The senior manager in a company often has only the historical IT budget and trends as a test of reasonableness of spending.

The operating budget for IT is not only one of the largest expenses for companies, but also is becoming the single largest capital expense for corporations. Information technology was 30 percent of the capital expense budget in 2000, according to Gartner, Inc. and the U.S. Department of Commerce reports that IT spending is 50 percent of the capital expense budget.[4]

Major drivers of increased spending in the past decade include client-server conversions, Year 2000 remediation, enterprise resource planning (ERP) package implementations, e-commerce, Internet, customer resource management (CRM), and mobile computing and wireless initiatives. Over the past decade, savings in declining hardware prices have been outweighed by increased spending on personnel, increased software costs, and spending on outside service providers, as the benefits from IT have increased and the IT operating environment has become more complex.

Understanding current spending on IT is critically important as a first step for assessing whether a company is overspending or underspending on IT. Developing appropriate benchmarks is difficult and takes careful analysis and context setting. A simple benchmark such as the average IT spending-to-revenue ratio, should serve only as a starting point for further study.

There are multiple factors that should be considered, and we highlight some of the most important ones in this chapter.

Paul Strassmann, a leading thinker on the valuation of business IT investments and a regular columnist in *ComputerWorld*, emphasized this point:

> IT spending is not a characteristic of an industry, but a unique attribute of how a particular firm operates. CIOs should stop taking an easy (and easily manipulated) path for explaining their spending plans. Don't ask what others tell you is the "right" spending, but commit to what profits you can deliver for the company, whatever the cost.[5]

However, based on these top-level benchmarks, the CIO can at least determine some ranges of spending in which the IT department should be operating.

IT Spending—Trends, Comparisons, and Benchmarking

We next examine IT investment trends and spending comparisons from leading IT research companies. We present historical IT spending of sample companies and make predictions on future spending. As we have noted, CIOs should determine the applicability and relevance to their companies and specific situations.

Additionally, we present an approach for benchmarking IT spending within a company. We discuss multiple methods, including comparisons versus peer groups based on revenue, employees, expense ratio, and other factors.

We also examine how to measure the return on IT spending, identifying hidden IT costs, and present average IT spending metrics by budget category (hardware, software, services, resources).

The IT Capital Budget

The capital budget is used for allocating the costs of long-term outlays for assets that depreciate over a long period of time to the periods over which the asset is used. For example, a piece of manufacturing equipment, which may have a useful life of 15 years, is a capital budget item that affects cash and the balance sheet. Capital budget items affect the income statement only as the asset is depreciated over time. Capital assets are usually long-term assets that are not bought or sold in the normal course of business. In general, the term includes fixed assets, such as land, building, equipment, furniture, and fixtures.

For the IT department, capital expenditures could include hardware, equipment, purchases of packaged software, and, in some cases, application development. In many cases, accounting rules allow most of the expenses for large projects, whose value will be realized over a long period of time, to be capitalized. Chapter 17 discusses this process in further detail.

Because these are large cash outlays for corporations, it is worth examining the trend in spending for capital assets. Further, the IT portion of the capital budget is usually associated with large projects, such as hardware replacements, desktop rollouts, or other systems renewal efforts.

The percentage of IT spending devoted to the IT capital budget varies by industry. Exhibit 3.1 covers a period of 8 years—from 2002 to 2010—and shows that capital spending on IT in the U.S. economy is projected to nearly double by 2010, rising from $300 billion to $500 billion. Corporations are obviously anticipating large payoffs from investments in technology and systems—and are allocating their expenditures correspondingly.[6]

While capital spending trends by industry provide some benchmarking information, CIOs should treat each purchase hitting the capital budget as they would any other corporate investment. That is, it must generate financial value for the company and generate benefits in excess of the costs, producing a rate of return greater than the hurdle rate set for company investments, or for other possible projects or investments within the company. If the investment cannot stand on its own merit, it should not be an investment in your portfolio. The fact that a competitor is spending significant dollars on new hardware or an ERP system has only tangential relevancy to the company's needs. It is useful to know where competitors are investing, and what they believe their outlay will mean for their costs, pricing, and services they can

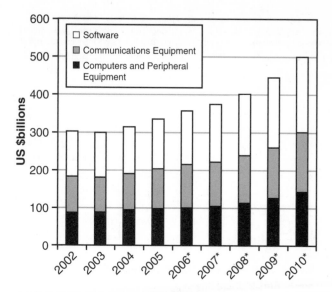

Exhibit 3.1   U.S. IT Capital Budgeting (*Source:* Forrester.)

deliver to customers. However, the company may or may not need to make and equivalent investment given the employee base, specific services offered, vendor services, and so on.

Total IT Spending

IT spending over the past two decades has risen dramatically for North American companies (Exhibit 3.2). Over time, this growth in spending has been driven by continuing advances in technology that have enabled IT departments to deliver new capabilities to their companies.

In the early 1980s, personal computing, office automation capabilities on the desktop, and the advent of client server systems drove large investments in IT spending. This was followed by enormous spending in enterprise resource planning (ERP) software in the mid-1990s (e.g., SAP, Peoplesoft, Lawson, JD Edwards, Oracle); remediation for the year 2000 technical problem; the rush to the Web; and the frenzy in spending on e-commerce, CRM, and wireless platforms in the late 1990s and early 2000s. Spending dramatically dropped in 2001 to 2003 and began to recover thereafter due to over investments in IT in the late 1990s. After the tremendous waves of investment over the past two decades, the downturn was probably to be expected. At the end of the market gains of the 1990s and the following economic doldrums, companies needed time to fully absorb the impact of the previous IT investments and retrench. However, the productivity improvements from IT are undeniable and IT spending recovered and is projected to continue increas-

Exhibit 3.2   IT Investment and Major Technology Industry Advances
(*Source:* Christopher Mines, Forrester Group, "The Seeds of the Next Big Thing," June 24, 2005. Copyright © 2005, Forrester Research, Inc.)

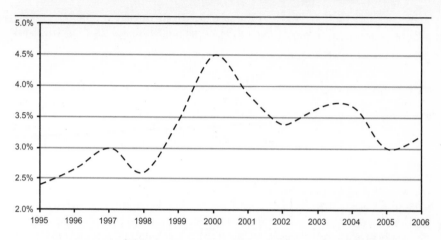

**Exhibit 3.3   IT Spending as percent of revenue in *Information Week*
500 Companies (1995–2006)** (*Source: Information Week,*
http://www.informationweek.com/iw500.)

ing throughout the remainder of the decade. The best estimate is that the
percent of spending as a percent of gross domestic product (GDP) will increase throughout the decade.

Supporting this assertion is the data from *Information Week,* showing that
IT spending may have peaked in 2000–2001 (Exhibit 3.3).

Because large companies, particularly in industries such as financial services, traditionally have heavy IT spending that elevate the averages, it is important for the user of these statistics to control for industry and size effects
to properly analyze the information. Most surveys in 2005 and 2006 show IT
spending grew at 5 to 10 percent per year. This trend is expected to continue
but at a slower pace through the end of the decade.

Further validation appeared in a survey of CIOs conducted by Merrill
Lynch released in mid-2006. CIOs showed confidence in a yearly growth target for IT of 5.2 percent in 2006 and 4.8 percent in 2007. CIOs are spending
their larger budgets on "laptops, applications software, networked storage,
networking equipment, and security." The survey also forecast salaries for IT
positions would increase 3 percent to 5 percent.[7]

The Quality of IT Spending

Clearly, IT spending cannot be assessed in a vacuum. There must be some return for the dollars spent on IT. The ultimate goal is to spend IT dollars as
long as each incremental dollar generates an appropriate return for the business. To help benchmark IT spending effectiveness, a variety of analyses
may be undertaken, including:

- *User satisfaction:* Are users satisfied with the level of support?
- *Financial cost/benefit analysis:* Do the benefits justify the investments?
- *Financial performance versus peer group:* Are you spending more or less than competitors?
- *Return on investment/return on assets (overall and for specific projects):* Do the projects generate sufficient return in an appropriate amount of time?
- *Level of senior management objectives met:* Is IT meeting senior management imperatives qualitatively and quantitatively?

IT spending mapped to the IT effectiveness score illustrates the quality of your IT spending (Exhibit 3.4). It is acceptable to be very efficient (low cost) and have relatively lower user satisfaction if there is a conscious strategic underinvestment decision made by the company. It is unacceptable to have high costs and low user satisfaction and effectiveness. There should be a correspondence between IT spending and overall user satisfaction (e.g., points A and C in Exhibit 3.4). Companies that find themselves off of this linear relationship (points B and D in Exhibit 3.4) may either have unusually effective or ineffective IT departments.

Understanding where your company currently falls on this matrix is a worthwhile exercise. Ensuring that a tight linkage between IT spending and user satisfaction and the levels that are either required or acceptable to the company are critical in building an overall strategy for IT.

Other benchmarks for ensuring that IT spending is generating the proper return for the company are covered throughout this book. Other chapters specifically addressing the topic of return on IT investment include Chapters 12, 15, and 17. Chapter 18 addresses issues in measuring quality of service, user satisfaction, and other performance metrics in IT.

Defining IT Spending and Identifying Hidden Costs

Making IT spending comparisons and trend analyses even more challenging is the fact that the assessment of what comprises IT spending varies substantially from company to company and even within companies. Should the measure of IT spending include capital expenses or just income statement expenses? Does it include the IT department costs and business unit IT spending? What are the hidden costs of technology spending? Are technology-related expenditures such as telephony included?

In this analysis, we include the following when we refer to *IT spending:*

- Capital expenditures for IT projects, hardware, software, and services.
- IT services and outsourcing: Expenses for external IT services (IT consulting, research services, hosting, etc.).

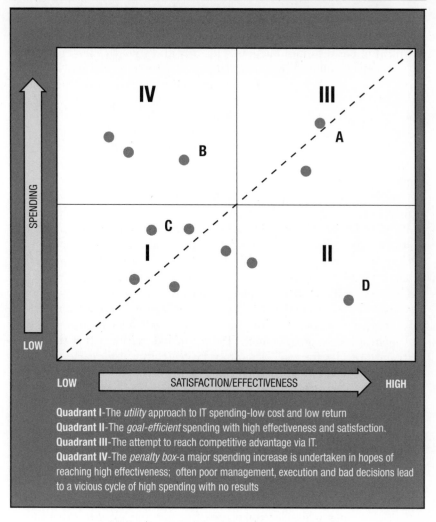

Quadrant I-The *utility* approach to IT spending-low cost and low return
Quadrant II-The *goal-efficient* spending with high effectiveness and satisfaction.
Quadrant III-The attempt to reach competitive advantage via IT.
Quadrant IV-The *penalty box*-a major spending increase is undertaken in hopes of reaching high effectiveness; often poor management, execution and bad decisions lead to a vicious cycle of high spending with no results

Exhibit 3.4   IT Satisfaction versus IT Spending

- Salaries and benefits.
- Applications: Cost of implementing and enhancing application systems that support existing business systems.
- Maintenance and administration: Cost of IT staff functions plus baseline costs of running and maintaining systems.
- Voice telecommunications are usually not included except in small companies (less than $100 million revenues).

The next factor that makes analysis difficult is hidden IT spending. As much as 10 percent to 20 percent of IT spending occurs outside the IT department in business unit budgets. This may also equate to 0.50 percent to 1.0 percent of company revenue. This occurs because ineffective IT departments cause a bottleneck for projects and technology investment. Business units go around IT to complete their critical initiatives, often creating mini IT departments within the business unit, additional IT vendor spend, as well as investments in hardware and software that do not show up in the IT budget. This hides a portion of IT spending and aggravates the IT ineffectiveness issues because of inconsistent technology choices across the company.

Overall, the IT budget, plus the hidden IT costs buried in the business units or functions, provides a good measure of the total IT spend in a company.

We were involved in assisting a $400-million media company in calculating their IT budgets. After combing through the centralized information systems budget, we ascertained that IT spending was roughly 5 percent of revenue. We then embarked on a mission to discuss IT spending with each of the business units. During the fact-finding effort, we asked one question of the business unit general managers that would prove enlightening: "What percent of your business unit revenue do you spend on technology, for example, applications or programming? Do not include services that the IT department provides for you." Almost every general manager came back with the following answer: "About 5 percent." After sifting through business unit organization charts and financial statements, we determined that the general managers were right at about 4 percent to 5 percent of spending on various services, applications, and hardware. The final result was a company with a central corporate IT budget of only 5 percent of revenue, but a total IT spend of about 9 percent of revenue. The 9 percent measure was definitely outside the range of reasonable spending for their company and drove them to take a hard look at the effectiveness of their IT spending. The analysis ultimately resulted in a successful cost reduction effort.

This effect pervades most companies. Gartner, Inc. estimates that the average spent outside the IT budget for IT-related products and services is 10 percent of the companies' total IT spending.[8]

There is a wide variety of these hidden expenses that should be considered as part of the IT budget to get an enterprise-wide view of total IT spending. A sampling of these include:

- IT staff embedded in business units or functional departments (e.g., web developers working for the marketing department, report writers working in the finance department, desktop support staff within a business unit).
- Outside service vendors (e.g., IT contractors, web site hosting, technology consulting company implementing systems or software within a business unit or function with no reliance on IT).

- Software (e.g., salesforce automation software purchased by the sales function and photoshop software and Apple computers purchased by the marketing group on credit cards and purchase orders).
- Hardware/IT fixed assets (e.g., vice president of manufacturing doesn't like the standard laptop and orders them via credit card or purchase orders).

There are several drivers of "hidden" IT spending. Hidden IT spending will be higher in companies where these characteristics are present:

- Loose integration between IT and business units; infrequent communication of needs and priorities.
- Subpar service levels delivered by IT, forcing business to seek alternatives.
- Slow decision making and purchasing processes in IT, creating a bottleneck for projects, hardware acquisition, and other business requests.
- Poor adherence to corporate standards for technology (software, hardware, desktops).
- Loose corporate procurement processes and standards.
- Decentralized, geographically disparate business operations.
- Weak leadership in IT.

Well-managed companies work diligently to aggregate IT spending within IT, or at least ensure that all components of IT spending can be identified and, therefore, managed.

How to Estimate Appropriate IT Spending Levels

The popular IT press is filled with spending survey results. Reviewing these generalized IT investment trends is helpful to understand the macroeconomic activity occurring at large, however, trends are of limited use in helping determine what each individual company should plan on spending. Measurement against peer groups of companies or other methodologies, as well as incorporating idiosyncratic company information, will help arrive at a more accurate answer.

While there is no industry consensus on a single correct way to estimate the appropriate level of IT spending, there are several different industry-accepted approaches that can provide a starting point for the executive:

- Comparison of IT spending as a percent of revenue against peer group of companies (industry or other comparative).
- Comparison of IT budget by company size (revenues).

- Comparison of IT spending per employee against peer group of companies (industry or other comparative).
- Formula developed by leading IT investment researcher Paul Strassmann based on key drivers of IT spending.[9]

Regardless of the approach used, the initial steps to estimating target IT spending levels for a company are the same:

1. Baseline current IT spending. Because this analysis is based on current expenditures, it can be thorough and should include:
   a. Baseline IT costs: Current fixed portion of the IT budget.
   b. Variable IT costs: The variable portion of the IT budget—that changes depending on the level of business demand, service level requirements, and project work currently approved.
   c. All IT costs borne by the business units and functions in the company (see previous definition of hidden IT spending).
2. Allocate the costs to budget categories. The high-level major categories of spending may include hardware, software, staff (salaries, benefits, training), and outside services. Other breakouts may be appropriate, depending on the specific company and IT department situation. Costs aggregated in major categories will facilitate analysis of appropriate ratios between categories (e.g., hardware to software spend ratio, staff costs to hardware spend ratio). (See Chapter 15.)
3. Select a peer group of companies based on similarity across relevant factors such as company size, industry, geographic footprint, or business operations. Where possible, selecting public companies will often provide for better revenue and spending data, as it may be disclosed as part of the companies' required financial filings.

After this preliminary data gathering is complete, any of the previous four comparison methods may be used. We address each of these in turn.

BENCHMARKING USING IT SPENDING AS A PERCENT OF REVENUE. IT spending averages about 3.5 percent of revenue across all industries. However, results show "for a particular industry, there does not exist a required ratio for IT spending to remain competitive."[10] Various research groups, most notably *Information Week,* Gartner, Inc., and Forrester Research, have put significant effort into determining IT spending as a percent of revenue by industry group (Exhibit 3.5). This type of high-level estimate is useful as a starting point for determining appropriate IT spending for a specific company; the specific situations for a given industry, competitive landscape, and financial position have a significant impact on the actual number. If the peer group developed in the previous step can be used as a comparison, instead of the industry as a whole, more precision can be achieved. Senior management

Forrester Industry groups	Medium (100–499)		Medium–Large (500–999)		Large (1,000–4,999)		Very Large (5K–19K)		Global (2K–20K+)		
	IT "lights-on" ops. as pct. of rev.	IT spending as pct. of rev.	IT "lights-on" ops. as pct. of rev.	IT spending as pct. of rev.	IT "lights-on" ops. as pct. of rev.	IT spending as pct. of rev.	IT "lights-on" ops. as pct. of rev.	IT spending as pct. of rev.	IT "lights-on" ops. as pct. of rev.	IT spending as pct. of rev.	Total per empoyee
Manufacturing	2.5%	3.3%	2.2%	2.8%	1.9%	2.4%	1.5%	1.9%	1.3%	1.6%	$6,274
Retail	3.1%	4.1%	2.7%	3.6%	2.3%	3.1%	1.4%	1.9%	0.9%	1.2%	$1,439
Wholesale	1.5%	2.1%	1.5%	2.0%	1.2%	1.6%	0.9%	1.2%	0.5%	0.7%	$2,936
Trans. and logls.	3.5%	4.5%	3.1%	3.9%	2.7%	3.4%	2.1%	2.7%	1.5%	1.9%	$4,370
Professional services	3.7%	4.8%	3.5%	4.5%	3.3%	4.3%	3.0%	3.9%	2.4%	3.1%	$8,996
Construction and eng.	1.7%	2.1%	1.5%	1.8%	1.0%	1.3%	0.6%	0.8%	0.4%	0.5%	$2,724
Media, art, and leisure	2.0%	3.7%	1.9%	2.5%	1.5%	2.5%	2.3%	3.1%	2.7%	3.7%	$4,351
Utilities	1.6%	2.3%	1.6%	2.2%	1.5%	2.1%	1.3%	1.8%	1.0%	1.4%	$7,985
Telecommunications	4.7%	6.4%	4.3%	5.8%	3.9%	5.3%	3.4%	4.7%	3.0%	4.1%	$18,469
Finance and insurance	5.8%	8.2%	5.9%	8.3%	4.9%	6.9%	3.8%	5.4%	3.3%	4.7%	$21,396
Financial services	6.4%	8.8%	6.4%	8.8%	6.3%	8.7%	5.7%	7.8%	4.5%	6.2%	$29,498
Insurance	3.0%	4.3%	3.0%	4.2%	2.8%	4.0%	2.0%	2.9%	1.2%	1.7%	$7,677
Overall	3.1%	4.2%	3.0%	4.0%	2.8%	3.8%	2.7%	3.6%	2.6%	3.5%	$5,753

Exhibit 3.5   IT Spending as a Percent of Revenue by Industry (*Source:* Forrester Research, Copyright © 2005, Forrester Research, Inc.)

should not automatically increase or decrease IT budgets based on these calculations, but instead use them as a general benchmark for understanding why the right spending should be more or less in their company.

The overall industry average IT spending as a percent of revenue from this information is about 3.5 percent. Some industry-level trends are shown in Exhibits 3.5 and 3.6. Note that the columns in Exhibit 3.6 correspond to the number of employees (e.g., size of company by number of employees). Differences in percentages can be attributed to the company size in the comparison. Exhibit 3.6 includes only companies with $1B in revenue and above.

Several observations are worth noting:

- Industries with heavy concentration of knowledge workers have higher IT spending as a percent of revenue.
- Conversely, industries with a large number of physical labor employees have lower IT spending.
- Industries that are data analysis or technology intensive have high IT spending as a percent of revenue (e.g., financial services).
- High profit margin industries (financial services) have higher IT budgets than lower profit margin industries (e.g., distribution).
- Industries that depend on technology to deliver their products and/or services have higher IT spend as a percent of revenue (e.g., media).

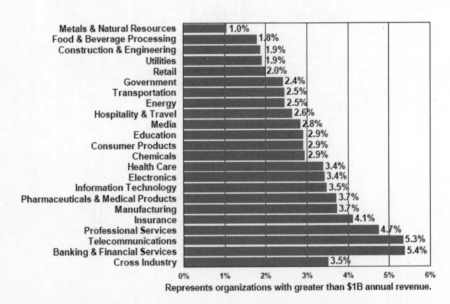

Industry	IT Spending (% of revenue)
Metals & Natural Resources	1.0%
Food & Beverage Processing	1.8%
Construction & Engineering	1.9%
Utilities	1.9%
Retail	2.0%
Government	2.4%
Transportation	2.5%
Energy	2.5%
Hospitality & Travel	2.6%
Media	2.8%
Education	2.9%
Consumer Products	2.9%
Chemicals	2.9%
Health Care	3.4%
Electronics	3.4%
Information Technology	3.5%
Pharmaceuticals & Medical Products	3.7%
Manufacturing	3.7%
Insurance	4.1%
Professional Services	4.7%
Telecommunications	5.3%
Banking & Financial Services	5.4%
Cross Industry	3.5%

Represents organizations with greater than $1B annual revenue.

Exhibit 3.6   IT Spending Revenue Percent by Industry and Company Size
(*Source:* Howard Rubin and Jed Rubin, "Worldwide IT Benchmark Service Trends and Findings for 2006," Gartner, Inc. www.gartner.com/teleconferences/attributes/attr_140228_115.pdf. The data contained in this exhibit may not represent Gartner's current view.)

BENCHMARKING USING IT SPENDING PER EMPLOYEE.   This approach assumes that IT costs are driven by the number of knowledge workers, professionals, or individuals who use computing resources in your company.

Exhibits 3.7 and 3.8 show IT spending per employee by industry, which provides the IT team another basis for comparison of existing or planned IT spending.[11]

Forrester Industry Group	IT Spending Per Employee
Manufacturing	$6,274
Primary production	$2,999
Consumer products	$5,372
Chemicals and petroleum	$17,671
High-tech products	$13,563
Industrial products	$4,302
Retail and Wholesale	$1,727
Retail	$1,439
Wholesale	$2,936
Business services	$6,836
Transportation and logistics	$4,370
Professional services	$8,996
Construction and engineering	$2,724
Media, entertainment and leisure	$4,354
Utilities and telecom	$14,627
Utilities	$7,985
Telecommunications	$18,469
Finance and Insurance	$21,396
Financial services	$29,498
Insurance	$7,677
Public sector	$5,187
Public services	$2,512
Government	$12,498
Overall	$5,753

Exhibit 3.7   IT Spending per Employee by Industry
(*Source:* Forrester.)

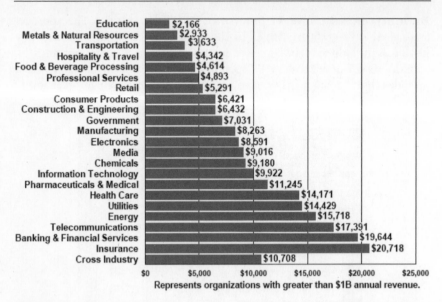

Exhibit 3.8 IT Spending per Employee by Industry—Large Companies (*Source:* Howard Rubin, Jed Rubin, "Worldwide IT Benchmark Service Trends and Findings for 2006," Gartner, Inc. www.gartner.com/teleconferences/attributes/attr_140228_115.pdf. The data contained in this exhibit may not represent Gartner's current view.)

Several observations are worth noting:

• Industries with heavy concentration of knowledge workers have higher IT spending per employee.

• Financial services is by far the heaviest spender of IT per employee.

• This metric does take into account the fact that, in many industries (e.g., retail), the majority of the workers provide physical labor and are not knowledge workers. Calculating on an end-user basis can be more relevant.

• The average spending on IT per employee across most industries is between $10,000 and $14,000; the average is heavily skewed by the large spenders.

Another related analysis is to calculate the ratio of IT employees in your company as a percent of the total employee count. While this should not drive any spending considerations, it gives you a rough idea of the number of IT employees it takes to support a company. There are a number of caveats, especially as they relate to outsourcing. Many companies outsource functions, including IT. Outsourced employees are not included in the calculations shown in Exhibit 3.5 and, thus, skew the analysis. We have seen averages for this ratio across all industries range from 2.2 percent to 4.6 percent (Exhibit 3.9).[12] Also noteworthy is the clear staff scale economies for the IT function in larger companies. Exhibit 3.10 shows this ratio grouped by

Forrester Industry Group	SMB (6-999 employees)	Enterprise (1,000+ employees)
Manufacturing	2.4%	2.2%
Primary production	1.1%	1.0%
Consumer products	2.9%	2.5%
Chemicals and petroleum	2.0%	1.7%
High-tech products	4.7%	3.9%
Industrial products	2.6%	2.2%
Retail and Wholesale	1.8%	1.6%
Retail	2.1%	1.7%
Wholesale	1.6%	1.4%
Business services	3.7%	3.3%
Transportation and logistics	3.0%	2.5%
Professional services	4.4%	3.7%
Construction and engineering	2.0%	1.4%
Media, entertainment and leisure	3.3%	2.5%
Utilities and telecom	1.5%	4.3%
Utilities	2.1%	2.0%
Telecommunications	5.5%	4.9%
Finance and Insurance	7.7%	6.7%
Financial services	9.6%	8.5%
Insurance	3.7%	3.3%
Public sector	5.6%	5.1%
Public services	5.4%	5.0%
Government	4.7%	5.1%
Overall	4.0%	3.4%

Exhibit 3.9   IT Staff as a Percent of Total Staff by Company Size
(*Source:* Forrester.)

industry; as expected, information-intensive industries, such as financial services and insurance, have a high ratio.

BENCHMARKING AGAINST PEER GROUP USING COMPANY SIZE. As the company being assessed diminishes in size, it gets more difficult to compare industry averages as a measure of correct IT spending, because most of the data is driven by public companies. Public companies are generally large

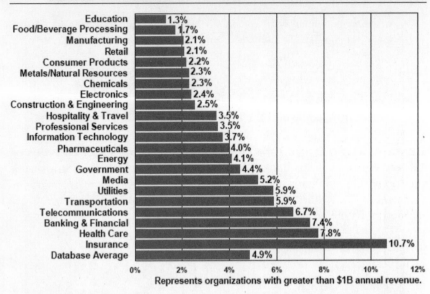

Represents organizations with greater than $1B annual revenue.

Exhibit 3.10   IT Employees in Organization as a Percent of Total Employee Population (*Source:* Howard Rubin, Jed Rubin, "Worldwide IT Benchmark Service Trends and Findings for 2006," Gartner, Inc. www.gartner.com /teleconferences/attributes/attr_140228_115.pdf. The data contained in this exhibit may not represent Gartner's current view.)

in terms of employee count and revenue. As IT budgets and staff increase with company size, the company begins to enjoy economies of scale across a wide variety of IT spending categories, as well as the ability to leverage fixed costs over a larger pool of employees and operations. This makes comparison of the data presented earlier more difficult for a mid-size company that has, for example, $30 million in revenue or less.

Measuring against a peer group using company size is generally more applicable for small companies. The data presented in Exhibit 3.9 show some benchmarks for spending at a variety of business sizes.[13]

Several observations are worth noting:

- Most of the industry surveys on IT spending are made up of Fortune 1000 companies (small businesses cannot achieve economies of scale in IT spending); this measure may be more applicable.
- Small- to mid-size businesses have different spending patterns and IT needs and therefore company size should be considered in any benchmarking exercise.
- Companies begin to see benefits of economies of scale in IT after they reach approximately 500 employees.
- The average company with fewer than 20 employees spends approximately 1.7 percent of revenue on IT.

- An average company with 100 employees spends approximately 4.7 percent of revenue on IT. The number of employees drives increased IT spending.

- Companies between 251 and 500 employees spend approximately 6.7 percent of revenue on IT.

- Companies between 501 and 1,000 employees spend approximately 5.4 percent of revenue on IT.

BENCHMARKING USING LINEAR EQUATION BASED ON KEY DRIVERS OF IT SPENDING. In his book, *The Squandered Computer,* Paul Strassmann, the former CIO of Xerox and a leading thinker on the value of corporate investment in IT, outlines an alternate method for calculating IT spending. His method is based on regression analysis of specific business attributes that drive IT spending.[14] Strassmann proposes that a small number of variables can actually predict appropriate levels of IT spending when companies have common characteristics and similar employment structures. Employment structures include ratios of professional, clerical, and factory workers.

Strassmann's linear equation method is:

$$\text{IT Budget} = K + (A \times \text{SG\&A}) + (B \times \text{Profit after tax}) + (C \times \text{Desktops}) + (D \times \text{Professionals}) - (E \times \text{Officials})$$

In this equation, the estimated IT budget can be calculated based on the variables:

K = Fixed IT budget—that which is nonvariable.

A B, C, D, E = Weighting of each category appropriate to the peer group.

SG&A = Company's sales, general, and administrative expenses.

Desktops = Number of desktop computers (includes laptops for this purpose) deployed throughout the company.

Professionals = Number of knowledge workers (e.g., professional, administrative, and clerical workers) employed by the company.

Officials = Number of executive officers in the company.

This equation implies a number of conclusions. First, supplying computers to all information professionals in the company, and supporting them, is a major driver of IT cost. Second, officers can be heavy users of IT and thus their costs (salaries and bonuses) are included in the SG&A calculation. Officials receive a "already large allotment of IT funds because their high salaries represent a disproportionately large share of SG&A. Since the expense for officials is always in SG&A accounts, this line item generates excess funding for supplying the officials' computing needs. The negative entry then corrects for such excess funding."[15] The "negative entry" in the calculation is − (E × Officials). Additionally, cost for Officials is embedded in the Desktops and Professionals calculations as well.

CIOs must determine the values of the variables required by the formula to calculate for the applicable IT budget, which may pose a challenge. However, Strassmann's methodology is based on extensive research and is worth investigation. Before using this method, or to investigate further how companies can derive optimum benefit from their IT spending, we recommend Strassmann's book.

Key IT Cost Drivers

We touched on a few key IT cost drivers earlier in the chapter. Exhibit 3.11 highlights some of the many factors to consider when analyzing corporate IT spending and attempting to understand what factors should drive the appropriate amount of IT expenditure for the company.

Scale Economies

Scale economies have a major impact on spending levels and are therefore an important consideration when estimating appropriate IT spend. Economies of scale occur when size provides efficiencies and purchasing power, which drive down costs. This is important to the IT spend estimating process for several reasons. First, when planning an IT budget, it is critical to know if and when the company will achieve economies of scale in spending. Second, company growth (and therefore IT growth) can help lower overall spending as a percentage of revenue, but it will likely increase overall spending. Technologies and IT activities with scale economies include:

- *ERP systems:* These systems have high entry costs. As companies grow, the systems can support the increased volume of activity with little or no incremental costs, reducing IT cost as a percentage of total spending. Additionally, vendor discounts on enterprisewide licenses help lower costs further as you get larger.
- *Help desk infrastructure:* In large organizations, the help desk fixed cost—particularly the infrastructure—is spread across a larger user base. Incremental growth in support representatives is the only variable cost component as the company grows.
- *Management team:* As the firm produces more goods and revenue increases, the fixed cost of the IT management team is leveraged across a larger organization.
- *Purchasing:* Larger firms gain benefits by consolidating purchasing and receiving deeper vendor discounts in return for volume.

IT COST DRIVER	COMMENTS	AREAS AFFECTED
Industry	• Some industries dictate higher IT spending e.g., transportation—airline reservation systems	• General spending
Company size (sales, profitability, number of end users, type of end users)	• Company revenue • Number of knowledge workers • Number of professionals	• General spending • Support • Capital items
Number of computers per knowledge worker	• IT costs rise with the number of personal computers deployed	• Purchase of PCs • Support
Complexity of internal operations	• Outsourcing functions should lower IT costs since no longer have to support. Cost will show up in services • Computational intensive environments will increase IT costs	• Personnel • Hardware • Maintenance • Integration
Historical capital spending	• Historical CapEx spending does not drive increased cost however increased depreciation expense will affect the IT budget, e.g. purchasing Mainframe will affect depreciation for 3–5 years or useful life of the equipment	• Depreciation • Capital expenditures
Current economic/ marketplace condition	• Economic pressures will increase need to cut IT spending • Profitable companies tend to spend more on IT	• Personnel • Overhead
Competitive initiatives	• Major business transformation projects such as supply chain reengineering will precipitate major IT expenses to support	• Personnel • Software • Hardware
Demands from customers or suppliers	• Pressure from customers or suppliers for electronic information flows and other types of computer related messaging can drive up IT expenditures in the short term	• Software

(continued)

63

IT COST DRIVER	COMMENTS	AREAS AFFECTED
Merger and acquisition activity	• Acquisitions and mergers acquisitions will drive IT integration costs • Potential economies of scale in the long term	• Personnel • Integration
Age of infrastructure	• As age of infrastructure increases, cost to support generally increases	• Maintenance
Central versus decentralized IT operations	• Decentralized IT operations tend to increase IT spending due to lack of controls and volume discounts	• Personnel • Software • Hardware
Number of platforms	• Costs increase in relation to the number of supported platforms • Standardization of environments lowers IT costs	• Personnel • Maintenance
Application complexity	• Application complexity drives higher support costs	• Maintenance
Application age	• Application age drives higher support costs	• Maintenance
Central versus decentralized purchasing	• Decentralized purchasing tends to increase IT spending due to lack of controls and inability to leverage purchasing volume	• Personnel • Software • Hardware
Standardization	• Standardization of environment, technical platform and tools reduces IT spending	• Hardware • Support/Maintenance
Chargeback mechanism employed	• Chargeback mechanism can lower IT spending by driving more rationale behavior with business units, e.g., market pricing	• General spending

Exhibit 3.11   Key Drivers of IT Costs (Continued)

64

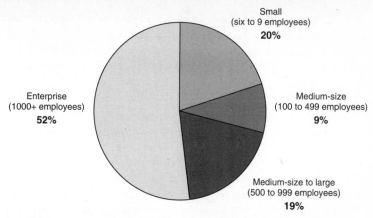

Exhibit 3.12   Allocation of U.S. IT Spending by Size of Organization
(*Source:* Forrester.)

- *Tool sets for development and infrastructure management:* Development tools and their infrastructure are leveraged for a larger team with little or no incremental costs.

The following variable cost items are worth noting since they usually do not experience scale economies, and most often grow with employee headcount:

- *Desktops:* Prices may drop because of discounts, but the company will still acquire additional equipment for employees.
- *Network:* As the employee base grows, the network will require additional capacity and investment.
- *Telecom:* Additional phone lines, bandwidth, and voice mail capacity may be required as employee count increases.
- *E-mail servers:* Additional server, bandwidth, and backup capacity required.
- *End-user license fees:* New licenses or seats required as employee count or business volume increases.
- *End-user desktop support:* New IT capacity for end-user desktop support required as employee base grows.

It is also important to note that diseconomies of scale can occur (e.g., average costs go up) if the IT environment is overly complicated (e.g., multiple complex platforms and lack of standards, Exhibit 3.12). Chapter 7 covers these issues in detail.

Aligning IT Spending with Business Strategy

An important reason for benchmarking is to provide context from which measurements and recommendations can be made to senior management and the IT steering committee. One of the main considerations should be the business strategy executed by the senior leadership of the company and endorsed by the board of directors and shareholders.

An assessment that indicates that corporate technology spending is low compared to competitors who are in build mode, while the company strategy is harvesting profits mode, does not necessarily indicate that IT spending should rise in response. A minimal spending approach may make the most sense for a company in low-growth mode, regardless of what competitors are planning.

Therefore, the CIO, when presenting benchmarking data, should consider the business strategy of the company and attempt to compare spending with companies with similar business attributes and, ideally, similar business strategies. In any case, the CIOs should adjust their benchmarking to account for specific business strategy. Exhibit 3.13 shows how IT spending can change in relation to business changes in revenue or capital expenditures. When revenue is growing faster than IT spending, either the company is obtaining value (scalability) from IT assets or penalizing the IT department for not delivering value (e.g., in effect, reducing funding). Be aware of where your department stands in the investment quadrant and understand why spending may be set as a particular level. If you are in the penalty box, it is time to take appropriate action to increase the value created by the IT department.

Taking Action Based on Spending Benchmarks

After accounting for all the caveats outlined previously, the CIO, in conjunction with the IT steering committee, can begin to take action based on the benchmarking results. If the ranges of spending computed are close to the current spending levels, no action may be necessary. If the ranges of spending are significantly higher or lower than the current spending, further action should be investigated:

- If benchmark spending is significantly higher, the company may elect to undertake an aggressive review of technology requests or potential investments on the basis of their business value. Clearly, every technology investment still must stand on its own merit. However, senior management and IT may have been slow to approve technology initiatives or additional capacity in the past, which may explain why the company is significantly outside the peer group.

- If benchmark spending is significantly lower, senior management should begin a detailed analysis and prioritization of IT costs, while investigating ways to improve productivity and eliminate excess spending. While it may be tempting for companies to begin chopping IT costs rapidly, a higher-than-peer benchmark simply indicates that there may be

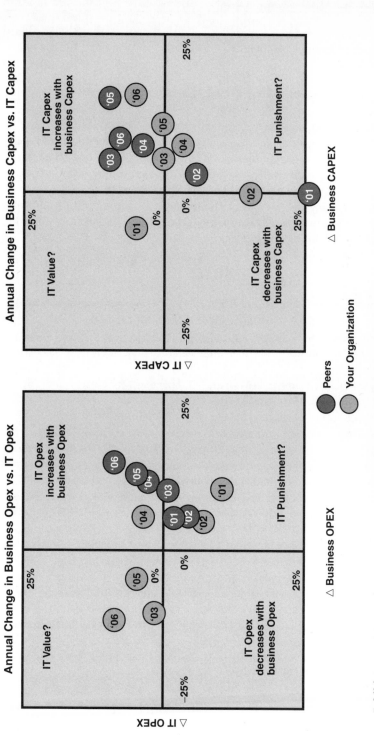

Exhibit 3.13 IT Spend versus Company Revenue Growth and CapEx Spending (*Source:* Howard Rubin, Jed Rubin, "Worldwide IT Benchmark Service Trends and Findings for 2006," Gartner, Inc. www.gartner.com/teleconferences/attributes/attr_140228_115.pdf. The data contained in this exhibit may not represent Gartner's current view.)

opportunities to reduce spending, and the company should take a hard look at its technology spend.

IT Spending Decisions: Summary

Estimating and benchmarking IT spending provide focus and validation of an organization's IT spending and investment strategy. It also educates IT management and the steering committee on the spending levels and strategies of peer companies. Additionally, it provides deeper insight into company-specific IT spending and puts into clear focus the actual total dollars spent on IT in your company. Regardless of the outcome of the exercise, companies should only invest in projects that meet all the criteria for business value and prioritization laid out in Chapter 17.

NOTES

1. Winston Spencer Churchill, speech in House of Commons (August 31, 1926).
2. George Bernard Shaw, *John Bull's Other Island*, Act IV (1904).
3. Kevin J. Stiroh, "Information Technology and Productivity in the "New Economy" Federal Reserve Bank of New York, presentation to London Business School (June 1, 2006).
4. Kurt Potter and Carolyn LeVasseur, "IT Spending: Its History and Future" (Stamford, CT: Gartner Inc., 2002).
5. Paul Strassmann, "Misleading Metric," *ComputerWorld* (July 1, 2002).
6. See note 4.
7. Mary Crane, "Market Scan: Survey Suggests Higher IT Spending in 2006," *Forbes* (May 31, 2006), http://www.forbes.com/markets/emergingmarkets/2006/05/31/hewlett-packard-ibm-0531markets02.html (accessed January 1, 2007).
8. Jeff Relkin, "10 ways to effectively estimate and control project costs," *TechRepublic* (May 31, 2006), http://articles.techrepublic.com/5102-10878-6078705.html (accessed January 1, 2007).
9. Paul Strassman, *The Squandered Computer* (New Canaan, CT: Information Economics Press, 1997), p. 320.
10. See note 9.
11. "IT Spending per Employee by Industry" (Metricnet a Division of META Group, 2001).
12. "Percentage of IT Employees in a Company" (META Group and Rubin Systems, 1998).
13. Barbara Gomolski, *Mid-Size Company Summit* (Stamford, CT: Gartner Measurement Services, 2002).
14. See note 9.
15. See note 9, pp. 319-327.

4

IT Scope and Strategy

However beautiful the strategy, you should occasionally look at the results.
—Winston Churchill[1]

A pragmatist . . . turns away from abstraction and insufficiency, from verbal solutions, from bad a priori reasons, from fixed principles, closed systems, and pretended absolutes and origins. He turns towards concreteness and adequacy, towards facts, towards action and towards power.
—William James[2]

IT scope and strategy are inextricably linked topics. It is impossible to set a strategic plan for IT and participate in the overall strategy of the organization, without having a clear definition of the scope of activity and responsibilities of the IT department. This chapter is focused on outlining that scope. The chapter also covers IT strategic priorities. This is a different discipline than strategic planning, which is typically done in conjunction with the entire organization. It will be dependent on overall organization plans and goals, and will be highly specific to the organization and IT department. Instead, there are a number of strategic issues within all IT departments that should be understood and managed by the CIO. We cover those here. Finally, this chapter discusses the utilization of various IT-industry strategic methodologies such as the Information Technology Infrastructure Library (ITIL) and IT Service Management (ITSM).

Why This Topic Is Important

Building a model of the major components that compose an IT department and identifying their scope and relationship to each other is a critical step in understanding and managing the department. CIOs must have a clear conceptual model of the IT department activities to set and execute IT strategy.

While IT strategy varies from organization to organization, a similar set of IT strategic priorities applies to all IT departments. CIOs and IT departments

69

who ignore these priorities at their peril, generally find themselves suffering the woes described in Chapter 2. This chapter builds the case for our idea and presents specific recommendations for building the strategic priorities into the daily activities of the department.

Scope of IT Activities

Having a good understanding of the scope of IT activities is the foundation for decision making in IT. A conceptual model for IT scope will in turn inform decision making on all aspects of IT: organization, staffing, spending, projects, and most importantly, management attention. Exhibit 4.1 contains our model. We cover each of the components of the model in turn.

Governance

Governance includes the decision-making and policy-setting activities within IT. All other IT sub-components derive their priorities from the governance function. Governance answers such questions as:

- What are the appropriate service levels for the business?
- What staffing levels and staff skills are required to maintain systems based on those service levels?

Exhibit 4.1 Conceptual Model for Scope of IT Activities

- What is the best portfolio of software and hardware to accomplish organizational goals?
- What outside hardware, software, consulting, and staffing vendors will serve the organization best?
- Are we managing those vendors to our best advantage?
- What projects shall IT execute?
- How many simultaneous priority projects should IT take on?
- When should IT augment existing staff to move projects forward?
- What organization or external obstacles are impeding IT success and how should they be dealt with?
- What should the IT capital and operating budget be?
- What metrics will IT use to measure performance?
- What policies regarding IT operations should be set for all constituencies within and outside the organization?

Governance also includes the hiring, management, appraisal, and training of IT staff, and internal department and external organization communication. Governance activities are primarily the CIO's responsibility, along with the IT Steering committee (ITSC). The ITSC is covered in detail in Chapter 19. Prioritization activities are covered in Chapter 17 and Risk Management is covered in Chapter 16. Chapter 18 covers IT measurement metrics. Chapter 5 outlines organization design for IT and Chapter 14 discusses internal communication with the business.

Problem Management

Problem management is the day-to-day process of aggregating and executing against issues and requests from organization end-users. It is also known as Tier-1 or help desk. It includes the processes for acquiring the problems via phone calls, e-mail or other communications, solving the issue or fulfilling the request or escalating the issue to a different part of the organization for resolution. It also covers systematically tracking the issue to ensure final resolution and producing reports to manage organization performance, perform root-cause analysis, quantify service levels, and determine appropriate staffing levels.

Chapter 9 covers problem management process, systems, staffing, and approaches in detail. Chapter 5 outlines staffing roles and responsibilities.

Operation and Infrastructure Baseline Support and Projects

Operations and Infrastructure (O&I) refers to the acquisition, upkeep, and management of the hardware and systems software that is used by the organization. This covers a wide diversity of equipment, including servers, desktops, laptops, mobile devices, routers, switches, cabling, disk and tape storage, physical facilities (data center), and software tools used to manage these.

There is an important distinction between baseline support and projects. Baseline support activities are the minimum required to run a well-performing, secure, and effective infrastructure. This includes such things as keeping current backups, systems software updates, desktop maintenance, network monitoring, and asset management. Projects are distinguished by their discretionary nature or by the level of effort and/or the discrete, infrequent nature of the task. For example, a network upgrade to improve performance is a discretionary O&I project. A desktop replacement project to update all end-user computers over 5 years old qualifies as a project (although likely nondiscretionary).

This distinction is an important one. It helps the IT department understand the bare minimum staffing levels required to run. All staffing levels in excess of this should be justified by ROI-generating projects chartered by the business. The level of effort required each year for baseline support informs the budgeting process as well. IT must have accurate processes for tracking hour spent on baseline and project activities. A number of things impact the baseline level of effort required. Good standards adherence, updated equipment, and effective O&I management practices reduce the amount of baseline support required. A disparate IT environment, large numbers of locations, end-users and equipment will increase it. Year over year, the two biggest drivers of change in the level of baseline support required is the outcome of the projects IT completes and the change in business volume. Some projects reduce complexity and reduce the amount of effort required, while others necessarily increase IT labor effort needed. Likewise, business volume changes (larger revenue, more staff, more locations or the opposite) impact baseline support. The CIO must track labor information throughout the year as well as the effect of these changes to determine the right level of support for the coming year.

Within O&I, usually the majority of the labor effort will be baseline support activities (about 60% to 80% of the total effort); maintaining infrastructure tends to naturally take more effort and projects are oriented toward periodic upgrades, replacement, and growth.

Setting IT staffing levels is covered in Chapter 11. Chapter 7 discusses IT standards. The scope of responsibilities for O&I baseline and project support is detailed in Chapter 8. IT budgeting is discussed in Chapter 15. Chapter 5 covers organization structure, roles, and responsibilities.

Application Baseline Support and Projects

In the application area, the same bifurcation between baseline support and project labor exists. Typically, the baseline support required for applications will be equal to or smaller than the labor for O&I, especially for stable, long-term applications with little change. Most of the focus within the application support area will be on projects, which are most often the source of high-ROI opportunities within IT.

Application baseline support activities are focused on ensuring application stability, periodic cleanups of data, upgrading software via periodic vendor-supplied patches, and performing updates to external lookup-data such as tax tables and shipping rates.

The tracking, budgeting, and staffing implications for application baseline support and projects are the same as outlined earlier for the O&I area. Likewise, the drivers of year-over-year change are similar. One refinement in the application area is that the volume of labor for application projects is more flexible; high ROI projects and/or rapid company growth typically justify bringing on temporary labor and expertise in the form of consultants and contractors.

Scope of IT

All of the IT responsibilities and activities covered in the remainder of this book fit within one of the categories listed. Each chapter is focused on best practices in one of the specific areas. The CIO should use this conceptual framework for explaining the roles and responsibilities of IT as well as managing activities in each area and interactions between areas. Exhibit 4.2 shows the relationship between the content of each chapter and the IT scope areas.

Setting IT Strategic Priorities

The topic of IT strategy gets a lot of ink in popular industry publications. Endless coverage of how IT should "align with the business" and "be strategic" or "treat the business as a customer" highlight how difficult this topic must be. We have evaluated dozens of IT departments and interviewed hundreds of IT staffers and senior executives. We have identified the common actions and priorities that differentiate the most successful operations. This section outlines our model for those actions and priorities.

IT Pragmatism

The best CIOs use a tough pragmatism to ensure well-functioning baseline operations in IT at lowest possible cost. Trouble-free basic operations give them the freedom to focus on effective working relationships with the senior executives in the organization, building an in-depth understanding of the business, recruiting the best talent to their team, and keeping their eye on industry and technology developments of value to their company. Their focus

Exhibit 4.2 Coverage of Area by Chapter

74

on these things in turn ensures that the CIO is able to identify, advocate, and execute meaningful, business-changing initiatives. CIOs who fritter their time and budget away on firefighting or the wrong priorities invariably preside over the worst-run departments, the lowest end-user and senior management satisfaction, and are exposed to the career jeopardy immortalized in the cartoon that follows:

Bamaland **by Walt Guthrie (Used with permission of the author and the Crimson White, www.cw.ua.edu.)**

Building a solid trouble-free baseline of IT operations (infrastructure, core applications, problem management, O&I, and application baseline support area) is the top priority for the CIO. If these areas are not operating effectively, the organization will have little interest in strategic projects or other high-value areas. Unfortunately, CIOs are often prone to distractions and will get these priorities out of order, worrying about strategic alignment before stabilizing the basics. As illustrated in the cartoon, the CIO must foremost be a pragmatist and make sure he is worried about the "fish food." Senior executives love pragmatists, especially in the IT realm. A pragmatist with vision will find an eager audience. A visionary without pragmatism will not.

Abraham Maslow identified the familiar hierarchy of priorities for human needs.[3] At the base level are physiological needs, such as air, food, water, and clothing. Next up is the need for safety and shelter, then love/belonging, esteem, and finally self-actualization. Implicit in the hierarchy is the notion that each of the needs must be fulfilled in order; achievement of each level of need is contingent on the reasonable realization of the prior need. If you don't have air, food and water don't mean much. If you don't have food and water, then shelter isn't important, and so on.

We have designed a conceptual model for thinking about IT priorities similar to Maslow's hierarchy. Exhibit 4.3 shows this hierarchy, mapped to Maslow's original. The hierarchy is divided into five ascending levels. Levels I through III (the bottom three levels) are internally focused on operations, infrastructure and applications. The top two levels are governance oriented and externally oriented.

Exhibit 4.3   IT Hierarchy of Needs

Level I: Operations and Infrastructure

The base level of hierarchy is all of the systems, staff, processes, and infrastructure required to provide the basic utility services for the organization. These utility-level services include such things as:

- Desktop and laptop computers.
- Desktop software (basic office productivity—word processing, spreadsheets).
- E-mail.
- Printing.
- File transfer.
- Network access/Internet access.
- Network infrastructure devices (firewalls, routers, switches).
- Mobility (mobile e-mail).
- Application servers and operating system (OS) software.
- Facilities for appropriately housing computing hardware.
- Telephones.
- Effective remote office support.
- Reasonably secure networks and systems.
- All hardware of a recent enough vintage to operate reliably.
- Enough staff to do problem management, O&I baseline support, and very limited O&I projects (1 to 2 projects per year).

These are considered "lights-on" applications; like any utility, if you cannot deliver these, no one cares about anything else on the hierarchy. This means that the CIO must build robust level I capabilities, from a hardware, software, process, and staffing standpoint. Until these are covered, it is futile to spend time on the other issues.

There are staffing and budgeting implications to level I. First, the CIO should find a highly effective person to run the O&I portion of the IT department. A weak player in this role will prevent any progress in the high value areas. Second, the CIO should ensure that proper budget allocations are available to implement a capable infrastructure. If the budget is not available, the CIO will be constantly defensive. In these cases, we recommend at a minimum getting express agreement from the ITSC that utility functions will be suboptimal, and at the extreme case, consider finding a different position. It is career limiting and frustrating to work from a constant position of weakness brought on by inability to invest properly in the basics.

Level II: Business Supporting Applications

Once the need for stable basic infrastructure is satisfied, the next level of the IT hierarchy is concerned with establishing the basic applications that support the business. These are usually referred to as "back-office" and "front-office" systems.

Back-office systems provide functions for basic accounting and other internal administrative functions. Basic capabilities include accounts receivable (AR), accounts payable (AP), and a general ledger (GL). These usually come as a single package because of their tight integration and need for a common database.

The front-office systems are used to operate the business. Their functions vary widely depending on the industry or type of organization they support. For instance, typical functions for a manufacturing company would include order entry, customer database, manufacturing planning, inventory management, and distribution. Service companies might require time-keeping systems. Financial services companies will include credit decision making and loan processing. Occasionally the accounts receivable portion will be part of a front-office system due to its close relationship to customer management and order entry.

At level II, the functions on both the back-office and front-office area provide rudimentary functionality. If they are provided by packaged software applications, they will be implemented with the minimum of customization and configuration. The system capabilities will be the minimum required to operate the company, and will be considered minimum par for industry participants. There will be little or no competitive advantage in these systems.

If packaged software, the front-office and back-office systems will usually be from different vendors; the front-office package may even be from two or more suppliers. The systems will usually not have built-in communication between front-office and back-office systems, or between modules of front-office system (i.e., system integration). If the systems are integrated, the integration will be in the form of periodic batch-based data transfers instead of real-time integration. The systems will usually have disparate pools of similar data. Systems will be used reasonably well, but may not be used to their full capacity.

In the O&I area, at level II there will be good documentation (run books), solid vendor contracts, well-built data, network and system security. On the staffing front, there will be adequate people to provide problem management, O&I and application baseline support, as well as limited O&I and application projects. Limited governance will be focused on cost control, limited demand management, and vendor management. Governance will usually have limited attention from organization senior management.

Level III: Competitive Parity Plus

The focus of level III is improving the usefulness of applications to the business. Organizations operating at level III will have the following characteristics:

- The package or custom systems will provide full coverage of core front-office and back-office needs. The organization will be fully exploiting package capabilities, as well as using customization and configuration to create additional unique functionality.
- Additional helper applications for both administrative support and to augment the core front-office and back-office systems have been implemented. Administrative activities include such functions as human resources (HR) support, marketing systems, asset management, contract management, intellectual property management, document management. Core business capabilities include such things as forecasting, advanced inventory management, forecast exchange, supplier/customer integration, distribution planning, route optimization. Business driving systems such as customer relationship management (CRM) and sales management systems are in place.
- All applications are well integrated, using either frequent batch data transfer, real-time asynchronous data transfer, or sophisticated middleware messaging systems. For common entities such as customer, product, or inventory information, a common database is used. Applications have global access to lookup and transaction data.
- Overall applications will be industry or market leading through the incorporation of strategic, proprietary capabilities that are used effec-

tively throughout the organization. IT exceeds competitive parity when compared to other firms in the same industry.

- Supporting systems infrastructure will be robust and redundant. O&I function will be well advanced: effective disaster recovery, data center management, run books, systems monitoring, configuration management, and systems management tools in place. Proper problem management process and associated reporting is implemented.
- Staffing levels will provide full baseline support for O&I and applications, as well as the ability to do multiple concurrent applications and O&I projects.

Level IV: Business-IT Alignment

At level IV, all IT decision making is made congruent with business priorities. This is reflected at all levels across staffing, budgeting, project, application architecture, and O&I support decisions. Business priorities should pervade all decisions. For example, the capacity, expandability, and reliability required of a piece of networking hardware varies greatly depending on whether it is a slow-growth small manufacturing firm or a large-scale financial services company. The business priorities provide a backdrop for answering such questions as:

- What hardware to purchase.
- What staff to hire.
- What staffing levels are set.
- Which vendors to partner with.
- How capital and operating budgets are deployed.
- Which projects are done.
- How many concurrent projects are appropriate.

The IT department will also demonstrate the additional following characteristics:

- IT has developed management and project management capabilities. Demand management is taking place in a methodical fashion and focuses IT efforts on high-return initiatives. The appropriate number and size of concurrent projects are underway. Project completion rate is reasonable and no long-term projects are lagging unnecessarily. Demand management process is eliciting and completing projects with business relevance and high ROI.
- IT department has implemented an IT steering committee for governance and will be meeting with reasonable frequency. All of the

disciplines regarding IT governance outlined in Chapter 19 are in place and effective.

- IT has implemented all important policies required. IT is aware of and has successfully complied with any relevant industry regulations or internal company requirements.
- The CIO has an effective relationship with senior management; senior management rates the CIO as responsive and effective.
- IT budget is within ±20 percent of industry averages and is spent on appropriate activities.
- Periodic IT end-user customer satisfaction surveys consistently provide satisfactory or above ratings for IT problem management, systems availability, and systems quality.
- Staffing levels are industry appropriate; low turnover in staff due to high job satisfaction and relevant training and development programs. Staff are of higher-than-average caliber compared to average compensation and skills.

One of the most difficult challenges of achieving level IV for the IT department is understanding precisely what the business needs and what will make it most productive. Doing this requires a deep understanding of how the business operates and what the executives who are running the business care about. This in turn requires the CIO and IT department to have effective working relationships with the business users and to spend significant time with them. What many CIOs discover in attempting to align IT with the business is that there is often conflicting information and conflicting priorities within the business. One of the myths of business-IT alignment is that the business side of an organization has a coherent, well-defined strategic plan, and that if IT could simply understand it, they will be on their way to level IV. On the contrary, organizations often have numerous disparate priorities, or even no plan at all. The CIO should be aware of this when attempting to achieve full IT alignment and make the appropriate adjustments in his or her plan.

Level V: Setting the Agenda

In popular IT management press, level IV is considered the highest aspiration of the CIO. We believe that there is an additional level in the hierarchy to be achieved. Level V elevates IT from a model in which it exists to ascertain and then carry out the wishes of the business, to one where IT is helping the business by spotting opportunities to use technology and IT services to improve both IT and business performance.

This is a critical difference. IT departments have been told for many years that "the business is their customer." This notion implies a host of other corresponding behaviors such as "the customer is always right," "customer appreciation," and other service orientation. It is appropriate because IT should always seek to provide the best quality service possible within budget. However, it ignores IT's ability to lead as well as follow.

Organizations that achieve the best value from IT have CIOs who not only understand and serve the business, but also combine that understanding with deep technology and application expertise to drive high ROI initiatives within the organization. In these companies, the CIO is a peer of senior management and a critical part of the executive team. The CIO frequently sets the agenda for governance and brings ideas from competitors, suppliers, customers, and firms outside the industry that improve the business.

Level IV organizations invariably have the highest satisfaction and benefit from the IT department and are attractive to the top performers in the industry. They achieve the highest possible benefit from their IT spending and derive significant competitive advantage from technology.

In Summary

We have found that our prescription is sometimes met with distaste by IT practitioners. Accomplishments at the base level of the IT hierarchy are often considered uninteresting, mundane drudgery. However, walking before you attempt to run is advisable in IT. The common thread in the troubled IT departments we have worked with is ineffectiveness in the first three levels of the IT hierarchy, preventing any meaningful achievement at the top two.

Methodologies for IT Management

This chapter highlights two conceptual models for thinking about the scope of IT operations and for setting the priorities for decision making within that scope as well as a number of popular methodologies for IT management that have emerged in recent years and deserve some attention by the CIO.

Those relevant specifically to the governance function and are covered in Chapter 19.

Information Technology Infrastructure Library

The Information Technology Infrastructure Library (ITIL) has its roots in IT management processes beginning in the 1980s. It is a set of best practices and IT management concepts developed over the intervening years. It originated with the Office of Government Commerce (OGC) in the United Kingdom. It is a comprehensive, process-oriented framework for the management of information technology services. It is generally O&I focused, with some applicability to software management (change management, release management). It is also most appropriate for baseline support activities as defined in our conceptual model. It defines best practices and processes for IT functions. It also defines a common tightly defined vocabulary for IT operations. It is currently available in a series of eight books. Each book is oriented to a separate ITIL topic area.

A number of software vendors have integrated ITIL principles and processes into their software. As expected, these tend to be O&I baseline support-oriented systems tools. Individual IT professionals can receive an ITIL certification from the ITIL Certification Management Board, which is comprised of the OGC and other examining bodies. Training companies focused on providing preparation for ITIL certification and associated consulting services are available. Three levels of certification (foundation, practitioner, and manager) are defined. This certification is not one that we have seen in common use in the United States. As of this writing, just over 200 ITIL Foundation certified professionals were listed on a third-party (voluntary) ITIL registration site (www.itlibrary.org).

ITIL does appear to be gaining ground as of this writing. *Computerworld* magazine and the Gartner Group report that over 85 percent of surveyed respondents rate ITIL as somewhat or very critical of IT management. Thirty-nine percent of respondents claimed to use ITIL for managing internal processes.[4]

Because it covers such a breadth and depth of IT services, and because it takes an academic slant, it is often regarded by some IT practitioners as overly cumbersome for full usage. This has led to partial or hybrid adoption of the principles in many departments. A specific publication from the OGC covers *ITIL Small Scale Implementation* (ISBN 0-11-330980-5). The framework is also sometimes regarded as too generic to be useful for off-the-shelf usage. We believe that ITIL principles can be useful in achieving competence at level I and II activities as defined in this chapter, but do not have as much relevance for levels III and above. We recommend that CIOs evaluate which portions of ITIL have relevance for pragmatic improvement of O&I baseline application support operations.

IT Service Management

IT Service Management (ITSM) is a philosophical approach to IT management that focuses on the end-user (customer) viewpoint. ITSM has no governing body or specific set of documented standards, and therefore suffers from a looser definition than competing methodologies. While ITSM shares nomenclature with some sub-parts of the ITIL framework, and covers some of the same scope, the two frameworks are not the same. Like ITIL, ITSM corresponds to the O&I and application baseline support and level I and II areas of the frameworks in this chapter. ITSM has the most relevance in setting service level agreements (SLAs) and determining budget, staffing, and operating priorities in the context of end-user needs.

ISO/IEC 20000

ISO 20000 is an international set of standards for IT management processes from the International Standards Organization (ISO). The ISO is a non-governmental international organization composed of over 150 member countries, which provide one representative per country. Its mission is to provide a common set of standards that promote international commerce and management. The ISO 20000 standard has considerable overlap and reliance on the ITIL standards, but provides the additional benefit of an international certifying body. The standard replaced a previous ITSM standard known as BS15000. It consists of two subparts, ISO 20000-1 that defines 10 key areas of IT service management, and ISO 20000-2 that contains best practices for implementing the areas defined in ISO 20000-1. The formal charter for ISO 20000-1 is to "promote the adoption of an integrated process approach to effectively deliver managed services to meet the business and customer requirements."[5] In both cases, the ISO standards seek relevance to organizations regardless of size and organization structure and provide measurement of adherence to the standard.

International standards for core O&I and application baseline support activities have some applicability for improving those activities. However, due to the diminishing marginal returns from rigorous adherence to ITIL, ISO, and ITSM standards, the primary benefit to complete adoption is primarily found in compliance and auditing.

ISO/IEC 17799

ISO 17799 provides audit standards for IT security from the ISO. It covers a dozen areas of information security and confidentiality, ranging from risk assessment and access control to compliance and policy. The standard has a related certification ISO 27001 that covers the implementation and improvement of the recommendations of ISO 17799. Because the 17799 standard is entirely focused on security, it is an incomplete mechanism for overall IT management. Security topics relevant to ISO 17799 are covered in the security management section of Chapter 8 and compliance topics are covered in Chapter 19.

Control Objectives for Information and Related Technology

Control Objectives for Information and Related Technology (COBIT) is a product of the Information Systems Audit and Control Association (ISACA) and the IT Governance Institute (ITGI). It provides a framework for ensuring the best use of IT in an organization as well as guidelines for compliance with best practices for IT processes and controls. It was created in 1992 and has undergone a number of revisions since.

The most recent version, the fourth edition, released in late 2005, contains four major areas: Plan and Organize, Acquire and Implement, Deliver and Support, and Monitor and Evaluate. The four areas are in turn comprised of 34 sub-areas. COBIT is an accepted standard for Sarbanes Oxley (SOX) compliance, which is covered in Chapter 19. The COBIT standard is geared to ensuring regulatory compliance, delivering best value from IT, and operating IT effectively. We believe the COBIT is one of the most complete of the frameworks relevant to the CIO, and is the framework that most closely corresponds to the views on effective IT management outlined in this book.

Zachman Framework for Enterprise Architecture

The Zachman framework was first developed in 1987 by John Zachman and has been updated numerous times since (Exhibit 4.4). The framework captures an approach to IT architecture in a single 36-cell chart. The chart has six rows: scope, business model, systems model, technology model, components, and working system, and six columns: who, what, when, where, why, and how, corresponding to data, function, network, people, time, and motivation. The framework provides for defining business processes that need to be supported by enterprise systems, and categorizing and aligning them appropriately. While the framework is focused on enterprise architecture, typically an application-oriented area, its scope includes non-IT components such as people, processes, and time, making it an appropriate addition to the overall IT strategy toolkit for CIOs.

There are numerous models and frameworks for the pursuit of management of best IT. New models and buzzwords continually emerge. We recommend that all of these be viewed through the filter of pragmatism and appropriate priorities as defined in this chapter. Numerous resources are available on the Internet that provide detailed information on these IT management frameworks. A few of these include:

- Good coverage of ITIL, COBIT, and ITSM: www.wikipedia.org
- The official U.K. Office of Government Commerce (OGC) site for ITIL: www.itil.co.uk
- IT Service Management Forum, a not-for-profit organization for ITIL practitioners, vendors, and companies; there are over three dozen country-specific chapters of the group: www.itsmf.com

Exhibit 4.4 Zachman Framework for Enterprise Applications (*Source:* The Zachman Institute for Framework Advancement. Reprinted with permission.)

- Abstracts and purchasable standard documents for ISO 20000 conformity and auditing: www.iso.org
- Special interest group dedicated to ISO 20000, ITIL, and ITSM issues: www.15000.net
- IT Governance Institute: www.itgi.org
- Information Systems Audit and Compliance Association; organization of over 170 chapters and 50,000 IT professionals focused on governance issues for IT; works with ITGI to define and promote COBIT: www.isaca.org
- The Zachman Institute for Framework Advancement: www.zifa.org

NOTES

1. Winston Spencer Churchill (b.1874, d.1965), widely attributed.
2. William James (b. 1842, d.1910), *Pragmatism: A New Name for Some Old Ways of Thinking*, (New York: Longman Green and Co.,1907).
3. Abraham Maslow, "A Theory of Human Motivation," *Psychological Review*, vol. 50 (1943), pp. 370–396.
4. Gary Anthes, "ITIL Catches On," *Computerworld* (October 31, 2005), p. 42, http://www.computerworld.com/managementtopics/management/story/0,10801 ,105761,00.html.
5. International Organization for Standardization, www.iso.org.

PART II

Managing the IT Department

5

The IT Organization

You will find that the State is the kind of organization which, though it does big things badly, does small things badly too.

—John Kenneth Galbraith[1]

This chapter identifies the organizational components of the IT department and defines the roles and responsibilities of the IT staff and the interdepartmental and intradepartmental interactions necessary to complete IT projects on time while successfully running the existing systems and applications. While there are a wide variety of ways to structure an IT organization, we recommend a specific structure that has proven successful across many companies. This chapter addresses two major aspects of the IT organization—the structure of the organization and the division of labor within the structure.

The wide variety of roles and responsibilities in an IT organization can be difficult to fully understand for those in the organization and completely baffling to those outside the IT department. The myriad of technologies and their complicated interactions require a complex organization that can support the business while managing sophisticated technology environments and achieving the highest levels of service. Creating an organization that can achieve this is a daunting task. The inputs to this organization come from every direction, ranging from the IT organization working to maintain the systems day-to-day and solve customer problems; the business from user questions to system problems to the endless stream of requests to enhance the systems; and externally through vendor-driven software or hardware upgrades, maintenance and security requirements, and new technology evaluations. This can make priorities difficult to establish, and the balance between maintaining existing systems and satisfying perpetual requests from the business a significant challenge.

Why This Topic Is Important

The organization of the IT department directly impacts the success or failure of IT to meet the mission-critical business needs. An IT organization that is well structured and coordinated can manage the complexities and adapt to new business requirements, while maintaining service levels and successfully completing priority projects. On the other hand, a poorly structured and uncoordinated IT organization is a major liability because of its inflexibility for rapidly solving problems and its inability to deliver new capabilities to the business.

One of the most common symptoms we have seen in underachieving IT departments is a poorly designed organization. The result is a confused staff and confused business users. The overlaps and gaps in roles and responsibilities present a disorganized face to the business and cause endless turmoil within the IT department. The organizational chaos hampers the team's ability to effectively execute projects, prioritize demand on the IT department, manage vendors, or even maintain the most basic service level commitments to the business or external partners.

Inevitably, the confusion and fuzziness of roles and responsibilities leads to multiple staff members' providing overlapping coverage for similar unclear duties, resulting in unauthorized pet projects, slack time, and coverage gaps. Unfortunately, this leaves fewer resources for the most important duties. It also destroys any form of accountability.

Understanding successful organizational structures, establishing well-defined roles and responsibilities, and actively managing and measuring performance are the same approaches used by other parts of the business. All too frequently, IT managers are promoted because of their technical expertise, and few have developed the managerial skills needed to lead an organization. The result is a CIO who understands the technologies but fails to understand the business; how to communicate with the business; how to organize, manage, and motivate teams; and how to organize the department. Chapters 2, 6, 12, and 19 discuss this phenomenon further.

Further complicating matters is the fact that many newly promoted IT managers have come from either the operations or applications area of the department and do not have enough exposure to the subtleties required to skillfully manage all parts of the department. While it is common for a manager to have an extensive knowledge of one or two areas and a general understanding of others, it is very uncommon for an individual to have an extensive knowledge of all IT areas. In addition, maintaining detailed knowledge in one or two areas requires considerable reading, training, and on-the-job experience with new technologies. It is common for a manager to change positions in the IT organization and no longer be considered an expert in his or her previous area of expertise in fewer than 18 months. Systems hardware, applications, and networks are continuously changing, and it is difficult for managers to have more than a limited understanding of all the technologies deployed in a large department, putting even more pressure on achieving an effective organizational structure.

This chapter focuses on the organizational structure of the IT unit in a company. Roles and responsibilities must be clear so that the team can work together effectively to deliver all of the IT capabilities required by the business.

IT Organization Overview

A major source of IT department inefficiency is poor organization of staff and lack of clear roles, responsibilities, and accountability. The resulting chaos causes responsibility gaps and overlaps, unclear roles, and difficulty holding individuals accountable for their results. This section highlights a standard approach to organizing IT and delineates key components in an IT department: management, operations, applications, development, help desk, infrastructure support, and administrative support. We then discuss how each of these areas should interact with the others and the business and describe optimal ways to organize each area.

The costs of an ineffective IT department are high. As discussed in Chapter 2, while a disorganized department is another symptom of poor IT leadership, the symptom can lead to a variety of other failings. One of our most memorable client anecdotes occurred while we were restructuring a particularly poorly organized IT department. Because of the multiple overlapping responsibilities and unclear role definitions, it was difficult to account for which staff members were actually responsible for any given project or system. The cost to the client was driven home for us during a lunch meeting with an acquaintance who happened to own a small business in the same town. He remarked that we must be quite busy making changes at the client, because the three IT staffers from the client who usually came to his office several afternoons a week to moonlight for him had not had time recently for their extracurricular activities.

Missed project deadlines, frequent unplanned system and "maintenance" outages, unmanned help-desk lines, abundance of slack time, and pet projects are symptoms of poor organization and accountability.

IT Department Organization Structure

Exhibit 5.1 provides a standard structure for the major components of the IT department. Depending on the size of the business, the CIO may report to a senior vice president, CFO, COO, or directly to the CEO.

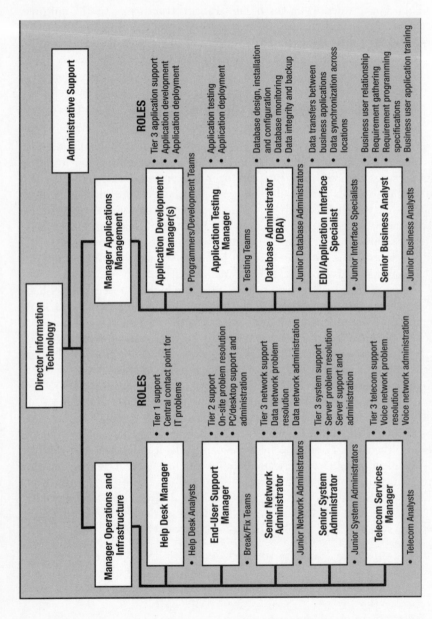

Exhibit 5.1   Standard IT Department Organization Chart

92

At the simplest level, the IT department consists of two areas: infrastructure (called IT Operations and Infrastructure, or O&I) and applications (called Application Management or Applications Development and Support). Correspondingly, the IT organization structure relies on two managers with a direct reporting relationship to the CIO: the manager of operations and infrastructure and the manager of applications management. The structure assumes strong leadership and managerial skills, in addition to technical acumen for the people in these two key positions. The operations manager is responsible for all day-to-day management of the computing environment, maintenance and upgrades, and security. The application manager is responsible for all work associated with the business applications, enhancements, and upgrades.

We have observed a tendency for the CIO to maintain too many direct reporting relationships. Often we will, as part of an IT assessment, find an CIO with five or more direct reports, such as application development, user support, operations, network administration, and telecommunications administration. A CIO with too many direct reports typically spends a disproportionate amount of time dealing with day-to-day "fire drills" and very little time working and communicating with the leaders of the other business organizations (e.g., sales, manufacturing), setting the long-term architecture and strategy for the IT organization, and monitoring and reporting the status of projects with significant long-term business benefits to key executives. While the director may feel busy, he or she is working on the wrong issues.

Within the operations and application organizations, specialized groups exist around specific technologies or functions. The operations group consists of the help desk, end-user support teams, data network administrators, system administrators, and telecommunications network administrators. The applications group has application development teams, testing teams, database administrators, electronic data interchange (EDI) specialists, and business analysts. Each of these roles is examined in detail in this chapter.

The organization outlined here establishes a clear division of labor, but because of multiple touch points between the two main component organizations, over time, the organizational boundaries often become blurred. Monitoring and measuring each of the groups is critical to ensure that each is accomplishing its stated goals and not simply passing responsibilities to other groups. The managers and members of the specialized groups must understand that they are accountable for the success or failure of their teams. Variable compensation and other incentives can be used to reinforce accountability.

Roles and responsibilities of each of these two subgroups are discussed in the remainder of this chapter.

IT Operations and Infrastructure Group

The IT Operations Group is responsible for maintaining the day-to-day functionality of the IT systems. Because of the utility nature of these systems (desktops, e-mail, file and print services, networks), this group has an enormous impact on the overall satisfaction level of the business user. The IT operations group is typically organized into five major areas: help desk, end-user support, network management, systems administration and operations, and telecommunications services. Each of these groups focuses on either a function or a technology in the IT organization. Larger companies (i.e., greater than 1,000 employees) may further segment the group into additional areas. Some commonly split out functions including operators, security management, change control, disaster recovery, and demand management.

Help Desk

The help desk is the IT group that company employees initially contact when they have a computing question or a problem. From a business perspective, the help desk represents the IT department's face to most employees and is closely identified with the customer experience—regardless of whether this should be the case. From an IT perspective, the help desk is the first line of defense to address and resolve as many problems and questions from users as possible. It is the central point where most business user problems are identified and tracked. It facilitates communication between the users and other components of the operations group, resulting in a rapid response to major outages and critical problems and a timely, coordinated response to less important problems. The help desk is frequently referred to as the *first tier* for problem management and resolution.

Broad-based skills are required of the help-desk staff to triage the wide variety of questions that inundate any help-desk team. The staff must adhere to a methodology that systematically eliminates the possible causes of a problem. After the help-desk staff member understands and isolates the problem, he should have the ability and authority to resolve it or assign it to the next tier of support for resolution. Frequently, this requires interaction and cooperation with another IT operations group, as well as the end users.

In a typical service request, a business user might call the help desk and report, "I cannot access the customer order system." What appears to be a simple request—fix the customer order system access—actually requires a fairly complex diagnostic process to understand which one (or more) of a host of interacting systems components might be causing the problem.

The problem may be with the PC on the business user's desk, it may be with the network connecting the business user's PC to the server, or it may be with the server itself. When accounting for the complexities of different types of hardware, software, and configuration differences, it is easy to understand why the help desk may not be able to solve a problem over the phone. The help desk must coordinate the efforts of other teams to correctly identify and eliminate the business user's problem as rapidly as possible, depending on the severity of the issue.

Optimizing the help desk is the primary role of the help-desk manager. This process begins by establishing a single help desk as the point of contact for the business user. Introducing multiple help desks almost always results in confusion for the business user about which help desk to call and the perception of finger pointing in the IT department. The costs of coordination of multiple help desks, even when organized by technology, geography, or problem type are quite high. An important characteristic of help desks is close geographic and physical proximity, to provide on-the-job training, the ability to quickly spot trends (e.g., several "down e-mail calls" coming in simultaneously helps in the diagnosis), and simple camaraderie on the help-desk team. The result of multiple points of contact is a frustrated business user and difficulty tracking problem trends and help-desk performance for the IT manager.

The help desk should strive to resolve as many questions or problems on the first contact with the customer as possible. This not only reduces the burden on the IT department but also results in dramatically increased end-user satisfaction. Simply taking problem information and forwarding it to another part of the organization for resolution creates numerous problems. The help desk must correctly diagnose the problem and send it to the appropriate group; after it is sent, there is an agency problem with no clear ownership for resolution of the end-user problem. Problem resolution statistics can be used to measure and improve first-contact resolution in addition to identifying the most common calls and developing a course of action to reduce the number of those calls.

Medium and large businesses normally elect to use an inbound call routing system (e.g., "Press 1 for a computing problem, press 2 for a telephone or voice-mail problem, press 3 for a new account"). In mid-size companies, this is typically a less-expensive, automated call distributor (ACD); in large companies, it may be a fully configured, full-featured phone switch (see the Telecommunications Services Group section discussion). Use of this type of system enables the business user to self-route to the person most likely to be able to help, and it provides call statistics, which can be analyzed for trends. The ACD can also be changed to update status messages and inform the business users who call the help desk during a major outage. While usage of these systems in larger companies can result in productivity gains for the help-desk team, the systems should be deployed intelligently, as they can also overinsulate the IT team from the end user and make the help desk too difficult to reach.

Management of help-desk activities is best facilitated through the use of full-featured help-desk application software that can manage customer calls, track progress on resolution, ensure that issues are closed, escalate urgent issues, automatically update end users on issue status, and provide reporting on help-desk performance. Whether a package-based or manual system is used, basic issue information must be captured to communicate with the business user experiencing the problem.

In addition, IT-specific categorizations are also necessary, such as the initial diagnosis of the problem, the scale of the business impact, user urgency, and the final problem resolution. The initial diagnosis of the problem identifies the tests performed to troubleshoot and narrow the possible causes and the group responsible for resolution if the help desk cannot resolve the problem. The scale of the business impact dictates the urgency and the resources that should be applied, with priority given to system or networkwide problems over most individual business user problems. The help-desk staff must identify when they are receiving multiple individual phone calls for what turns out to be a systemwide or networkwide problem. The final resolution should also be captured because it is critical for quantifying problems that are misdiagnosed initially, and it enables additional root cause analysis for future problem elimination or best practice documentation for resolving a particular problem.

A variety of help-desk applications are available that provide a wide range of functionality from simple to highly sophisticated. At the lower end of the scale, the pricing is quite reasonable and should not pose a significant hurdle for even small IT departments. The improved coordination, communication, user satisfaction, and root-cause analysis provided by more sophisticated packages usually makes the benefits far outweigh the implementation costs.

The help desk is often used as a training ground for new IT employees. These employees gain a broad exposure to all the systems and applications in use by the business, as well as the overall IT and corporate organization and the business of the company. However, the rapid transactional nature of a help-desk position does not enable the employee to learn the details of any one system or application. New IT staff can spend anywhere from one month to one year working on the help desk, depending on the business circumstances. The intensity of the daily experience on the help desk can quickly lead to staff burnout—properly setting goals, expectations, and a date to transfer into other parts of the IT organization can mitigate some of the burnout risk and provide a motivational goal for harried help-desk staff. Ultimately, the help-desk manager must monitor all of the staff and their performance levels with the business users.

While this experience can be very valuable in rapidly developing broad skill sets for new IT team members, it can be frustrating to the business users calling the help desk when they cannot get first-call resolution to their problems because of lack of knowledge or experience. Mixing experienced help-desk staff with new IT employees provides mentor resources that can be referenced by junior staff to accelerate learning and reduce the probability of business user frustration. To the extent practical, periodic rotations through different help-desk support areas for help-desk team members (or other staff, if possible) can ensure that the repetitive nature of the job does not become too onerous. The interaction with the more experienced staff is the key to rapid learning for the new help-desk employees.

When a help-desk employee cannot fix and close out a problem with the business user over the phone, he or she must hand off the issue to additional IT operations resources to assist in the problem diagnosis and resolution. These groups may include end-user support, network administration, system administration, application support, or telecommunications services. Chapter 9 provides detailed information on help-desk management and process.

End-User Support/Break-Fix Group

The end-user support/break-fix group is responsible for physical computer repair and field visits to customer (end-user) locations. This group is considered the second tier for problem management and resolution. Depending on the size of the group, number of employees, geographic footprint of the company, and complexity of calls and call volume, a manager typically organizes the staff into teams, which may be assigned to support a specific location, technology, application, or business group. These teams can be co-located with the business users to minimize the time required to get to users' desks, and to provide a better interface between users and the IT department. In large companies, each of the teams requires a team leader with responsibility for the performance of that team.

As with the help desk, a variety of technical skills, spanning all operations and applications areas, are necessary for the end-user support staff. The same type of problem-solving skills, methodology, and logical approach that systematically eliminates the possible causes of the problem is critical here as well. Exposure to the standard systems, applications, and networks is necessary to provide the insight required to execute the on-the-fly technical testing used to identify the cause of the business user's IT problem. The systems experience required is focused on the hardware and software on the business user's desk, as opposed to the server systems behind the scene. Ultimately, the end-user support group is responsible for all the equipment, client-side applications, and local software that operate on the business user's desktop computer. Responsibilities frequently include deployment of new equipment, maintenance of existing equipment, and upgrades to desktop equipment and software. As discussed in Chapter 7 (IT Standards), the level of standardization of hardware, systems software, and applications across the organization is one of the largest drivers of effort for both the help-desk and end-user support staffs. Highly heterogeneous environments are challenging to support and usually require much higher than average staffing levels to provide adequate service to the end user.

In addition to technical skills, associated with the systems supported, customer handling skills, and the ability to develop productive working relationships with the business users are as important as technical knowledge for ensuring a positive customer experience. End-user support staff may find that problems encountered result from lack of training for the business user; therefore, it is common for the end-user support staff to train the business user at his or her desk on various applications to reduce the likelihood of additional problem calls.

Furthermore, the demeanor and approach of the support staff is as important as their technical skills. Unfortunately, IT professionals often have a reputation for supercilious and arrogant treatment of end users. This not only damages the IT-business relationship, but also ultimately impairs the effective delivery of the IT service, as the staff members fail to help users learn to solve basic problems on their own. Operations managers should work to ensure that soft skills are a key screening criterion during the hiring process, are part of the ongoing appraisal process, are required for promotion within the department.

In weak IT organizations, it is common to find that business users circumvent the standard process of going through the help desk and consistently call the top team members in the end-user support group directly. This circumstance has obvious drawbacks and eventually erodes the morale and patience of the professionals that the IT team most needs to retain. This phenomenon highlights the importance of continually ensuring that reliable, customer-focused staff are on the break-fix team.

Occasionally, companies place their end-user support teams under the reporting umbrella of the business unit or department they support. The goal is to make IT more responsive to the needs of the business. While this can be an appropriate temporary fix, it is also usually indicative of serious problems within the IT department. As one client remarked, "The sales department is in the business of sales. I don't want to run my own IT shop, but I will if the IT department is incapable of providing the level of service required."

Establishment of this type of shadow IT support staff in business units or departments can create security and administration issues outside the control of IT. It also creates a new level of coordination and communication requirements for system changes. Not only must the business users be notified of an impending change, but also the shadow support staff must be briefed on the details and may be required to implement or test the changes. This promotes finger pointing and turf issues when modifications and system changes go awry. Further, the business loses out on any scale economies available in this area, as well as career track and training and development benefits for the team. In summary, the presence of shadow IT functions embedded in business units is a major indicator of IT department ineffectiveness and, when addressed, can usually provide major cost savings and service-level improvements. The benefits of such models are typically outweighed by negative impacts, including higher costs and lack of coordination and communication.

Typical staff progression in the IT organization transitions people with 12 to 24 months of experience at the help desk into the end-user support group. Normally, the end-user support staff then spends two to five more years developing detailed skills and knowledge about the systems, applications, and networks used by the company. After they have gained enough experience, staff members may be considered for team leadership or other lateral moves in the organization, typically after three to six years. The end-user support manager is normally promoted from the team leaders.

Network Administration Group

The network administration group manages all data network communication capabilities required by the business. Network responsibilities are typically separated into two broad categories—local area networks (LANs) and wide area networks (WANs). LANs are typically defined as network connections within a particular business location, and WANs are the network connections between business locations. For example, a LAN connects all of the PCs, servers, printers, and peripherals in the Dallas facility, while a WAN connects Dallas with Chicago. We use this terminology because it is the simplified, generally accepted view. Different technologies can be used to network a specific area; for instance, there are LANs connected with wires and cables and others that are wireless—both of which may be in use in the same location. Similarly, WANs can be created from frame relay connections, public Internet VPNs, point-to-point connections, and so on.

The network administrators are responsible for all wiring, hubs, and security for the LANs and the leased lines, routers, gateways, firewalls, and security for the WANs. They monitor network performance and upgrade capacity before the traffic on the network increases to the point that it begins to affect systems performance. To accomplish this requires a specialized skill set with knowledge of networking hardware, networking mediums (different types of cables with different capacities and performance characteristics), networking protocols (which define how messages are passed between computers), encryption techniques for secure messaging, and firewall security. The extensive hardware, application, and configuration knowledge required by a network administrator takes considerable time, experience, and training to build.

Networking hardware, software, and services costs can represent a large portion of the annual IT budget, particularly for companies with a large number of geographically disparate locations. Connecting remote sites via a WAN requires leasing a data line from a telecommunications company with enough capacity to handle all of the company's data traffic. A good senior network administrator thoroughly investigates all application, access, and data transfers that will occur over the WAN. Using this information, the network administrator determines the best medium and capacity for the situation and negotiates the contract with the telecommunication vendors. Proper needs assessment, capacity planning, and postimplementation traffic shaping can result in significant monthly savings in leased line costs.

Large numbers of vendors are often involved in networking infrastructure (e.g., local loop, local telco, frame-relay provider, and ISP), making it challenging to determine the exact costs and usage of the network. Compounding the issue is the complexity of the typical billing statements and the difficulty of tying the statements to the actual services provided. A recent analysis performed for one large client revealed that its network administrators could not identify the number of leased lines in use, the capacity of the leased lines, or the total monthly cost. It simply received monthly bills for its leased lines and paid them, without verifying any linkage to actual lines or services consumed.

Typical career paths begin with the junior network administrator who works at the LAN level. It takes several years to build the skills to master the many different types of technologies, mediums, and protocols. Progression to senior network administrator with responsibility for the WAN and teams of junior network administrators typically occurs after five to seven years of experience, and the completion of specialized network training.

In a small to mid-size corporate environment, the system administrator may also serve as the network administrator. As the computing environment grows in size and complexity, more specialized skill sets and additional capacity are needed to ensure reliable operation and system availability.

System Administration and Computer Operations Group

The system administration and computer operations group manages, monitors, tunes, and administers all of the IT servers and systems software that comprise the infrastructure on which the applications and data used to run the company reside. These systems include e-mail servers, file servers, web servers, print servers, and development, test, production, and failover application servers. Each of these servers may be based on different technologies depending on the requirements and standards established by the organization. For example, the e-mail server may use Microsoft technology, the web servers might be UNIX-based systems, the file and print servers might be Novell-based, and the production applications may reside on a mainframe server.

System administration encompasses all the efforts required to manage each of the business servers. Duties include deployment of new equipment, maintenance of existing equipment, upgrades to server equipment and operating systems or systems software, creation of regular backups of critical enterprise data, capacity planning, disaster recovery planning, user profile management, user changes, and system security. It takes highly detailed knowledge of how system software works to manage these tasks for the critical business infrastructure components. This is particularly true for diagnosing complex systems failures and to effectively close holes in security.

The best system administrators proactively manage their server systems to minimize the possibility of server problems during production hours and security breaches at any time via system monitoring tools and participation in Internet discussion groups and sites dedicated to the technologies that they support. Administrators also monitor system performance, track increases in server workload, and anticipate the need for additional capacity before performance shortfalls impact business performance. As a result, system administrator responsibilities require double duty—they must be on site during production hours to immediately address any server problems, and they must perform all maintenance work and upgrades after production hours and on weekends.

Few system administrators, in small or large companies, regularly install the software patches provided between major system upgrades that are necessary to close the system security holes. If an administrator postpones patches until a major upgrade is released, and these occur only once every 12 to 18 months, the environment has a considerable amount of exposure to hackers who attempt to enter systems for fun (control and bragging rights) or profit (data theft). These people know the security patches for each operating system and systematically search for machines where the patches have not been installed and configured properly so that they can gain access. Combined with the fact that it takes time to configure, test, and install a major operating system upgrade with the existing business applications, the exposure may last as long as two or three years.

Scheduled maintenance and upgrades must be carefully coordinated with the business units and other departments to ensure that production systems are available during critical times after normal business hours. For example, business users at a client company recently expressed frustration that the systems were unavailable when they had to work overtime one weekend. The business users had no idea whom to contact in the IT department and, therefore, IT received no notification of the business need. The IT department indicated that if it had known about the weekend work, it would have been able to reschedule its maintenance for another time.

This is a typical example of the lack of communication of process, roles, and responsibilities from IT to the business, and one of the most common complaints about IT departments that are struggling with communications issues. Because upgrades are complex and risky, and require significant advance planning and effort to complete, it can be easy to neglect informing the user community of the associated system impacts or outages. Each systems project that may cause downtime should be clearly communicated well in advance to business users.

The system administration and computer operations group also coordinates the introduction of new technology into the production environment. Senior system administrators are very cautious by both training and experience, and carefully plan tests to ensure that transitions to new technologies are performed in a controlled manner that does not adversely impact the operation of the production environment or disrupt the business. The ultimate goal is to ensure that all servers work 100 percent of the time so that their function is transparent to the business. The introduction of system changes into the production environment involves the process called change management discussed in Chapter 9. System administrators manage the process, ensuring that all changes have been tested and that rollback procedures (i.e., a method to restore the environment if necessary) are in place.

The support of server hardware and systems software is complex and, like many of the other third-tier IT operations functions, requires a specialized skill set to understand the details of the systems in use. It is not uncommon for an organization to require a specialist for each type of server used—for example, understanding the inner-workings of a UNIX-based system well enough to "tune a kernel" is very different from understanding how to "gen" a mainframe system; and it is a rare individual who has an extensive working knowledge of both. However, in smaller businesses it may not be cost effective to break responsibilities down to this level. We recommend including additional costs of skilled labor capacity in all purchasing decisions and minimizing the number of different computing platforms in the organization to minimize the different skill sets and staff required. The staff capacity issues can be further mitigated by cross training the system administrators or using contractors on an as-needed basis to minimize the costs.

In larger organizations, a group of operators may be included in the systems operations group. The operators are responsible for managing system operations functions such as printing, batch jobs, and user online sessions. Operators manage various jobs (print, batch, or online processes) on servers to ensure the correct processing power is available to the most critical resources and that the functions are executing and completing correctly. A critical component of the operators job is to ensure that processing capacity is available for applications. For example, if it is the Friday on the last day of a month and most orders come in that day, the operator can divert computer processing power to online sales sessions so that computer resources can quickly process the orders. Additionally, operators may prioritize application print jobs for critical reports such as invoices. Operators are necessary to maximize CPU usage and other computing resources and ensure a smoothly operating application. In smaller companies, the server typically auto-prioritizes various requests eliminating the need for full-time staff to perform this function.

Typical career paths for system administrators involve initial training to build a foundation of knowledge about the servers they will support. These junior system administrators typically work in an apprentice role under the close supervision of a senior team member to gradually shift responsibilities for the systems and build experience and confidence. Simply "turning over the keys" puts the organization at risk because the junior administrator needs time to understand the processes that minimize the risks of any system changes and the subtleties of the specific system configurations, which can vary from machine to machine at the server level.

Depending on the complexity of the server computing environment and the desired level of cross training, it typically requires four to seven years of experience as a junior system administrator before consideration for a senior administrator role is warranted. Senior system administrators manage a team of junior administrators, and in larger organizations, a manager may be required to coordinate the efforts of the senior system administrators across multiple locations.

Telecommunications Services Group

Many businesses find it cost effective to purchase and operate their own telephone systems. The telecommunications group manages all telephony and related services. Services include telephones, voice mail systems, fax machines, and video conferencing systems. The group must monitor system use, bandwidth consumption, and network security for the voice and video networks in a manner similar to the procedures used by the network administration group for the data network.

Telecommunications services require knowledge of telephony switch hardware (PBXs) and software configuration; wiring in buildings and demarcation facilities; trunk line capacities; call center configuration; voice mail system configuration and management; video conferencing equipment, and voice/video bandwidth requirements. Individuals without the appropriate knowledge can quickly interrupt telephone service.

The help desk normally handles inbound problem calls and requests for service to maintain the single point of contact for the business user. However, few help-desk staff members have the knowledge, experience, or authority to make changes to these systems, and the voice telecom requests are immediately routed to the telecommunications services group. In some larger companies, the telecommunications services group may assign one of its team members to rotate onto the help desk to address telecom requests and problems. In many cases, the skills required are highly specialized, and telecom support is fully or partially outsourced to a specialized provider. In these cases, the help desk may serve as the first line of defense for phone system questions but have the authority to schedule the contracted outside provider to rapidly fix the problems.

Telecom services analysts begin by supporting the wiring in buildings and develop expertise in the other areas over a period of several years. Specialized training from the PBX vendor is typically required to establish a basic understanding of the systems used by the business. On-the-job training with direct senior-level oversight is used to build on the foundation. Junior-level telecom analysts transition to senior-level telecom analysts after four to seven years.

Operations Manager

The operations manager is responsible for the performance of all the teams in the IT operations group. The operations manager must have a basic understanding of the technologies used in each of the areas managed, but the critical skills are the organization and management of the teams. Planning, setting reasonable service levels, managing staff, and actively participating as a "doer" are all part of the typical responsibilities of the operations manager.

The IT operations manager oversees the day-to-day performance of the IT systems to maximize availability and address user problems. Having a manager in this role enables the CIO to focus on the strategic direction that confronts an IT department, instead of worrying about "putting out the fires" on a daily basis. Because shortfalls in operations are highly noticeable to the entire organization (it affects everyone in the company when phones are out, e-mail is down, or the network printers are not working), the IT operations manager plays a critical role in ensuring that the utility functions provided by the department operate smoothly and do not negatively impact the business.

Very small organizations may have the system/network administrator also serve as the operations manager. As businesses grow, a dedicated management resource at this level is important to maintain the control and direction of the IT operations organization and reduce the number of managers and team leads reporting to the CIO. If the CIO has more than five direct reports, it is time to consider creating an IT operations manager position.

Process Responsibility in IT Operations

The IT Operations Group is responsible for all the processes described in Chapter 8 and 9. Some of the key operations processes overlap groups. A description of the process responsibility alignment follows:

1. IT operations manager is responsible for:
   - °a. Systems demand management process.
   - °b. Disaster recovery function.
   - c. All management processes.

2. Help-desk manager is responsible for:
   a. Help-desk function.
   b. Problem management process.
   c. Input to changes in standard operating procedure/problem diagnosis process.
3. End-user support manager is responsible for:
   a. Problem management process (break-fix portion).
   b. Fixed asset management process.
4. Senior network administrator is responsible for:
   a. Problem management process (Tier 3 network support portion).
   b. LAN/WAN management process.
   °c. Security management process (overall).
5. Senior system administrator is responsible for:
   a. Problem management process (Tier 3 system support portion).
   b. Systems administration process.
   c. E-mail administration process.
   d. Operators.
   e. Change control process.
   f. Asset management process (server equipment portion).
   g. Login management (add, change, delete).
   h. Security (server portion).
6. Telecom services manager is responsible for:
   a. Telecom administration.
   b. Problem management process (Tier 3 telecom support portion).
   c. Security (telecom portion).

Processes with an asterisk may actually be divided into a wholly separate group depending on the size of the company and the complexity of the systems. For example, many IT operations managers in large companies will have a single manager dedicated to security.

Key Drivers for IT Operations Structure and Staffing Levels

Five key drivers determine IT staffing levels:

1. Number of end users supported.
2. Number of systems supported.
3. Number of sites supported and geographic dispersion.

RESOURCE	COMPANY SIZE (NO. OF EMPLOYEES)				
	0–25	25–50	50–100	100–200	200–400
CIO/IT director	—	.25	.5	.75	1
Network/Systems engineer	—	.5	.75	1	1.5
Network/Systems administrator	.25	.5	.75	1	2
Helpdesk supervisor	—	—	.5	1	1
Jr. Network/Systems administrator	.5	1	1.5	2	3
Helpdesk/Desktop support	1	2	3	4	6

**Exhibit 5.2   Typical IT Operations Resources
Required for Small and Mid-Sized IT Departments**

4. Support requirements (e.g., 5 days a week, 8 hours a day, or 7 days a week, 24 hours a day).
5. Complexity of the computing environment—number of different types of applications, systems, and networks.

Exhibit 5.2, which is based on our experience with businesses across many industries, provides a rough estimate for staffing IT operations at small to mid-size companies and is based on the number of end users supported. These figures are estimates; investigate other industry research to better understand if the company is above or below peers and how staff signing impacts cost structure and long-term competitiveness. A more detailed method of calculating staffing levels for larger organizations is described in Chapter 8.

In smaller organizations, it is not cost effective to hire an individual for each position, and the complexity of the computing environment will usually not warrant doing so. As the business gets larger and the computing environment gets more complex, additional resources will be needed to properly manage and maintain the computing environment.

Application Development and Support

The application development and support group maintains all the critical business applications that are layered on top of the infrastructure provided by the operations group. The application group supports the production applications, gathers requirements for enhancements or additional functionality, develops specifications, programs the new system functions, tests the interaction of the old and new code, and integrates the changes into the production environment. The group is also in charge of managing, upgrading, configuring, trouble-shooting, and tuning all business applications. Because the majority of the large business-oriented projects are planned and delivered by this group, the management of the group requires a skillful balancing act of new development and baseline application support.

The IT application development and support group is typically organized into five to six major areas: application development, application support (may be combined with application development in some organizations), application testing, database administration, EDI/application interface specialists, and business analysts. Each of these groups focuses on an application, function, or a technology required by the business.

Application Development Teams

The application development team provides enhancements and support for business applications, based on the requirements gathered and documented by the business analyst team. In smaller organizations, the business analyst and application developer roles are often played by the same team members. The business applications may be custom developed in-house, or they may be packages purchased from third-party vendors and configured and customized for the specific business.

Application developers typically specialize in specific technologies and software development technologies such as object-based, web-oriented, client/server development, enterprise application configuration and customization (e.g., ERP, CRM), and electronic data interchange and application interface development (application integration).

The IT development group is typically organized around applications in three broad categories. Each category may use a variety of technologies to deliver all of the business functionality required. These categories are:

1. *Customer-facing applications*, which may include web-based customer access systems, order-entry and order-processing systems, and internal customer service systems.
2. *Production support*, the set of supply chain applications, such as procurement, manufacturing, warehousing, inventory, and logistics.
3. *Business support*, which typically incorporates systems completely internal to the business, such as human resources and accounting.

An application development team member typically joins the staff with skills in different technologies to manage and enhance the business applications in one of the three areas. This team is responsible for the creation of new capabilities within existing business applications, upgrading and patching third-party applications, testing existing and new application functionality before deployment in production, and support for the business application after it is in production. As the business system size and complexity increase, it may be necessary to dedicate staff to a particular application in one of the three categories and to have the team work together on cross-application interfaces.

Establishing a team for each business application enables cross training multiple staff members to support specific applications. The danger is a potential lack of ownership for the application; therefore, clear ownership and responsibility for delivery of the application enhancements and overall management of the applications must be established for each system deployed.

The IT development group must schedule and clearly communicate to the IT department, steering committee, and business users committed dates for deployment of new system capabilities. Communication must occur within the IT organization and the business organizations to ensure that everyone is aware of the timing and the functionality that will be provided. Major changes to applications should, in every case, be coordinated through the IT steering committee.

In addition, deployment of new system capabilities must show sensitivity to business cycles and should be timed to minimize disruption to the busiest business cycles. For example, one of our clients generates 70 percent of its business during the holiday season in the months of November and December. The IT application developers are required by the business to have system changes in place by the end of September to adequately prepare for the holiday rush. No additional system or application enhancements are allowed until after the end-of-year busy season.

We have witnessed a more recent trend among our clients of reducing or eliminating the business-specific customization of third-party software applications. The most notable areas are around enterprise resource planning (ERP) systems such as SAP, Oracle, or Lawson, and customer relationship management (CRM) systems such as Siebel. Businesses are increasingly finding that the costs of customization are very high for these packages because of significant investment in time and resources. More troubling is discovering that the expensive customizations do not work with the annual upgrades to these third-party products, and they face the choice of maintaining an older system after the vendor stops support or investing additional time and resources to remove the customizations, install the upgrade or patch, and recreate the customizations in the latest software release.

As a result, clients are installing new third-party software in as close to the standard, off-the-shelf form as possible. In some extreme cases, companies that have made investments to customize applications are backing out selected customizations and choosing to change the business processes to match the software instead. This has been to the mutual benefit of both software vendors and their customers.

Application Support Group

Mid-size organizations may have an application support group that is separate from the application development teams. The application support group is responsible for the day-to-day operation of critical business applications. The organization of the application support group typically parallels the structure of the development group to ensure ownership and accountability of production applications.

In large companies, separate groups may exist for the development and support of a particular application. In smaller organizations, the responsibility for supporting an application can reside with either the end-user support group or the application development group. As discussed previously, the operations help-desk and end-user support teams provide the first and second tiers of support. The third tier of support for business applications comes from the application support team.

The development group is responsible for identifying, developing, testing, and deploying new functionality to enhance the IT capabilities of the business through increased efficiency or creation of technologies and provide differentiation from the competition. While the development group focuses on new capabilities, the support group maintains the existing version and fields tier-three requests described previously. This separation of support and development has several positive effects for the organization. First, it eliminates distractions for the development staff so they can concentrate on new development. Otherwise, development is consistently being taken away from new duties to address the support requests. This inevitably leads to delays in the development cycle and pushes out the milestone and agreed on delivery dates. It also eliminates the lack of accountability that can occur when the two functions are integrated. It becomes easy to blame support requests for missed deadlines if a single group is performing both functions. It also becomes easy to provide poor service to users if personnel are dedicating too much time to new development activities and not enough time to support. By dividing the two functions into two groups, the accountability is clear and the groups typically work with better effectiveness. Having two groups also provides career paths from the support group to the development group for staff.

Application Testing

The application testing team is responsible for testing changes and upgrades to business application modules with the goal of eliminating problems and ensuring compatibility with other modules. Application testing occurs on multiple levels: Developers test the code in their modules as they are developing it, the application testing team combines groups of modules and tests for the interaction of their functionality, and, finally, the entire application is put together and tested in its entirety, along with its interfaces to other internal and external systems. These tests are typically called *unit, integration,* and *system testing,* respectively.

Few development organizations allow adequate time for full testing of business applications before deployment. Testing often begins in the week before the system goes live—resulting in a system that is not thoroughly tested, which makes it susceptible to problems when it is placed in production. Successful application development groups allocate as much as 30 percent of their development time to application testing. The groups that do this are rewarded with significantly fewer major problems after the application is put into production and easier ongoing management of the production systems in the post-implementation environment.

The application testing team should also incorporate business users to test the functionality of the applications. Business user participation in the testing ensures that the most commonly used functions are tested for system problems. In addition, providing business users with access to the new system before placing it in production creates familiarity and instills confidence and ownership in the new system.

Another critical aspect of testing the entire application is stress testing to identify system scalability, volume limitations, and catastrophic failure points. Knowledge of these stress points prior to production deployment will dramatically aide system performance monitoring and avert disastrous situations. Well-defined stress points enable system administrators and application developers to address the limitations before reaching them instead of after the thresholds have been crossed and have brought the business to a standstill.

In smaller application development groups, the application testing team may be a subset of the developers, database administrators, and system administrators. Larger businesses, or smaller companies engaged in a significant system rollout, may be able to afford a separate individual or team of individuals to perform the full testing of the application.

Database Administrator

Database administrators (DBAs) design the database architecture, install and configure the database software, participate in design and development activities with the development team, ensure data integrity, and monitor and optimize the database performance for the underlying database software used by the business applications. They are responsible for the databases in both the production environment and the development environment. Large-scale relational databases are highly sophisticated systems, and the DBA role is one of the highest technology skill positions on an IT team.

Because of the complexity of relational databases, specific skill sets are required, depending on the database technology used by the business. Like the system administrators on the operations side of the IT department,

DBAs are required to understand the most intimate details of their database to control, manage, and tune it effectively. Finding an expert in one database, such as an Oracle DBA, is not as difficult as finding an expert who is knowledgeable about Oracle, Informix, Sybase, and DB2. Performance tuning a database can have enormous impacts on systems performance and can often be the difference between viable systems and those that fail.

In larger organizations, the DBA role is often split between a development and a production DBA. In these cases, the development DBA is focused on the structural changes to existing databases required to support projects and enhancements, as well as the design of new database models for emerging applications. Production DBAs work to monitor and tune existing database performance and ensure that the integrity of the production database is maintained.

Electronic Data Interchange/Application Interface Specialist

The electronic data interchange (EDI) specialist is responsible for ensuring the accurate, timely, and speedy transport of data between applications inside the company and with strategic partners outside the company walls. Application integration is a critical component of streamlining system communication and databases across the business and across business partners. Each business system and application requires data in specific formats. Interapplication interfaces may be triggered by events and pass data on an as-needed basis (asynchronously) or on a given schedule, transferring a number of transactions (batch). The EDI specialist is a master at translating information so that it can be understood by the receiving system. In addition, he or she must maintain a schedule of data transfers to ensure that large data transfers do not all occur at the same time and cause slow performance or data transfer failures because of the load placed on a particular machine, database, or network. Application interface specialists are skilled in various tools that provide messaging management or systems connectivity. As the rate of business transactions increase and time pressures advance, more asynchronous, real-time communication between systems is necessary.

Multiple tools are now available that allow the construction of sophisticated cross-application, cross-platform asynchronous communications. These systems provide a common set of protocols, formats, and triggers for all applications to use for interfacing with each other. This enables the group to develop only one interface for each application (from the application to the messaging system) in a many-to-one relationship versus a many-to-many relationship. The messaging system then manages the timing and flow of all messages between applications.

Business Analyst Group

The business analysts work directly with the business users to understand how the systems are used and identify the enhancements that will provide the greatest benefit to the business. The responsibilities of a business analyst are divided equally between two major constituencies: the business users and the IT department application developers.

Business analysts develop relationships with the business users and maintain these relationships through regular meetings and requirements gathering sessions. They must understand the internal business processes and how IT applications are used in the process, including how the IT applications streamline or inhibit the process. The business analyst must proactively solicit, gather, and document information and requirements to drive high-value enhancements, customizations, and upgrades to the business systems. In addition, the business analysts must track and help prioritize all requests for application changes or enhancements. Integrating the business user into the prioritization of system changes as well as the testing before deployment ensures that the highest value items are addressed and the systems work as requested.

The most challenging aspect of the business analyst's job is understanding both business processes and the supporting applications and technology well enough to anticipate, identify, inventory, and articulate system changes that the business user may need but does not expressly request. For instance, a slight change in the system functionality, such as automatically populating customer information fields, may change the process the business users use and save them several minutes per order transaction. The business users may not know that this is possible; therefore, it is incumbent on the business analyst to identify the change and bring it up for discussion and evaluation.

The business analysts also work closely with the application development teams. Business analysts are responsible for authoring the high-level requirements documentation used by the programmers to create detailed programming specifications. The requirements documentation process is complex and requires a high degree of detailed documentation before any actual systems development activity occurs. Multiple iterations and refinements are required that include meetings with the business users and application developers to ensure the accuracy of the request and the documented systems specifications.

Manager of Applications Management

The manager of the applications management group is responsible for the performance of all the teams in the application development and support group. The application manager must have a complete understanding of the business systems used in each of the areas managed, but the most critical skills are the organization and management of the team. Setting priorities, managing the team, and completing project work are all part of the responsibilities of the application manager.

The application manager directs the applications teams according to the overall project priorities set by the IT steering committee. This manager oversees the delivery of the medium-term direction of the IT business systems to enhance capabilities, streamline processes, and successfully deliver priority projects to the business on time and on budget. Having a manager in this role enables the CIO to focus on IT governance and the strategic direction of IT in the entire business and address the funding issues that confront an IT department, instead of worrying about delivering the next round of functional enhancements in three months.

Very small organizations may have a lead developer/tester also serve as the application manager. As businesses grow, a dedicated management resource at this level is important to maintain the control and direction of the IT application organization and reduce the number of managers and team leaders reporting directly to the CIO. If the CIO has more than four direct reports, it is time to consider creating an application management position.

Key Drivers for IT Development Structure and Staffing Levels

There are five key drivers for determining the staffing levels for the IT application groups:

1. Number of applications.
2. Number of systems.
3. Number of different technologies used (e.g., databases, operating systems, interface tools).
4. Number and complexity of systems interfaces.
5. Number and complexity of systems changes requested or required.

In most environments, as the number and complexity of different applications, systems, and technologies grow, higher numbers of skilled people are required to maintain and enhance those business applications. This assumes that the systems are relatively stable. Often, complex systems are riddled with subtle, difficult-to-diagnose errors, increasing again the number of skilled staff to provide baseline support. The number of staff needed is based on several key drivers. For example, one developer may be able to support multiple applications if they are on similar systems, use the same underlying technologies, and are stable. However, because of the high number of cross-system interactions, the introduction of differing technologies may increase the number of staff required on both the old and new systems.

IT application development groups frequently claim that they need more staff. The real question to be decided by the CIO and the IT steering committee is the appropriate level of staff to provide cost-effective service to the business and to execute the priority projects required in the IT area.

As discussed throughout this book, the "right" level of staffing is dependent on a wide variety of factors: Are the application enhancements so critical to the business that an additional person is required? Are new technologies being introduced into the organization? Are the underlying systems and skill sets necessary in the IT organization changing?

If the answers are yes, the staffing levels and skill sets should be closely examined to determine if it is appropriate to add staff. Rapid growth in staffing levels and frequent requests by IT for additional headcount are the warning signs of an IT department in trouble. This is particularly true where the usual drivers of staff size, such as business growth or technology platform complexity, have not changed. In this instance, the IT steering committee should ensure that the CIO is not overwhelmed, which is often the case. Ultimately, the staffing level should be developed from the bottom up by estimating in hours the required time for the development projects approved and the hours required for system support based on the average number of support requests received.

Separation of Responsibilities between Operations and Applications Groups

We have uncovered a common practice among small and mid-size businesses of mixing the responsibilities of the IT application development group with those of the operations group in the IT department organization structure.

The effects of this lack of separation begins with confused priorities for the application developers. Should they work on the production problem of the day or focus their energies on the enhancements they are developing for the next major release? Major production problems must be addressed immediately, but business users are often persuasive in adding minor tasks to the immediate fix project plan. This inevitably leads to missed development deadlines because of reductions in the resources allocated to creation of the new capabilities because of the constant fire fighting. In addition, time is also lost because of switching costs associated with orienting a programmer to a particular problem and then reorienting him or her on the development assignment. Finally, it provides a convenient excuse for the development organization to miss the next release deadline or underdeliver on the functionality.

Avoid this scenario by adhering to the application development process and incorporating the most important requests into the regularly scheduled enhancement releases. Communicating the priority and availability of the enhancement requested is also critical to demonstrate that IT is responsive to the business user's needs and that he or she does not need to circumvent the IT process to get things done.

As we discuss in Chapter 11, while clearly defining the responsibilities of each group and keeping them from overlapping is the right policy, there are times when the application team may act as extra capacity in the operations area. The skill sets can overlap, and having built-in surge capacity available in the application area can allow the operations team to staff to its average level of demand instead of the peak demand, reducing overall IT costs. The cost of this approach may be some project slippage in instances where the application team is called on to assist the operations team, but the cost trade-off is usually favorable. This approach is particularly appropriate for smaller organizations where the cost impact of saving one or two full-time employees is most noticeable.

CIO and Administrative Support

The CIO is responsible for all aspects of the IT organization, from day-to-day operations to long-term strategies, the IT architecture, and customized development. The position requires a unique combination of technology understanding, leadership and managerial skills, and business knowledge. The critical nature of this position requires an in-depth discussion, which is provided in Chapter 6.

Administrative support is important in the IT department, just as in any other business department. While a secretary with limited technology skills may be acceptable in a small IT organization, as the organization becomes larger, an assistant with some interest in and knowledge of technology becomes very valuable to the CIO and his or her staff. One well-run organization we encountered provided a career path for administrative assistants into the end-user support groups after they had acquired the appropriate experience, training, and tenure.

Other IT Organizational Issues

Mix of Contract and Employee IT Personnel

Use of contract IT personnel is becoming more common because of the difficulty of hiring individuals with knowledge of new technologies. The topic is covered in more detail in Chapter 11. The decision to use contract staffing is usually based on one or both of two rationales: the provision of additional capacity so that priority projects can be completed or the provision of unique skill sets not found on the existing IT team.

In the first case, managers often find that high-priority projects mandated for completion by the IT steering committee cannot be completed without the addition of team capacity. In these cases, temporary capacity is added with outside contractors. In some cases, the outside contractors are used for specific roles in a project (e.g., testing, requirements gathering), or they may be deployed to provide baseline support for existing systems so that the full-time team members can spend the majority of their time completing the high-priority projects.

In the second case, managers often find that new projects involve technologies that are new to the market, or at least to the existing IT team. The temporary engagement of skilled professionals with experience in the new technology can provide both capacity and on-the-job training for the existing IT team.

In every case, the IT manager should work to ensure that he or she maintains control of the projects and technologies being deployed. This can be accomplished by selectively hiring contractors for short terms (i.e., 3 to 12 months), targeting skills unavailable in the current organization, ensuring cross training of employees to avoid dependency on a specific contractor or vendor, and establishing milestones to measure productivity and quality standards for performance. The manager should also establish clear reporting relationships between contractors and the full-time IT team members, and measure contractors by appropriate standards to ensure that the company is receiving full value for the services provided.

IT Accountability

The key drivers for accountability are different in the IT operations group and the IT application development group. The IT operations manager must:

1. Establish well-defined roles and responsibilities, a single point of end-user contact to prevent the end user from being forced to navigate the IT organization to obtain an answer or solution, clear ownership for end-user problems, problem status communication procedures (e.g., application outages, end-user problems, systems changes), clear problem hand off criteria and new ownership acceptance criteria, and problem closure and user acceptance parameters.
2. Measure help-desk response times, end-user problems (types and resolution times), end-user satisfaction via service ratings, and outages for systems, networks, and applications.
3. Recognize and reward rapid end-user problem resolution, identification and elimination of root causes of problems, and minimization of nonscheduled outages.

The IT application development manager must:

1. Establish well-defined roles and responsibilities, ownership for individual applications and new development initiatives, aggressive time lines and increases in application capabilities, deployment dates, testing time required, development time available (working backward from the deployment date to establish checkpoints and milestones), and ensure that the appropriate amount of time is allocated to testing.
2. Measure milestones and checkpoints met, functionality delivered, problems found in preproduction, and problems found in production.
3. Recognize and reward maintaining the time line commitments, meeting key milestones, minimizing problems with newly developed code.
4. Promote and ensure the use of an application development methodology to reduce risk, improve quality, and improve and ensure accuracy of workload estimates.
5. Ensure that IT demand management principles are adhered to in setting application development and enhancement priorities (see Chapter 17).

Large Company Considerations

While the organization structure and roles described in this chapter are relevant for any size of company, large companies dictate more division of labor because of the complexity and sheer size. Some of the more common additional considerations include:

1. *Architecture:* Information architecture, technology (infrastructure) architecture, and application architecture definition are the implied responsibilities of the CIO and his or her direct reports in small to mid-size companies. Large organizations typically separate this responsibility into another position usually called the chief technology officer (CTO). CTOs are focused on defining and developing the three- to five-year future architecture of internal systems. The architecture is then handed to various managers to "execute" and make reality over that time period. All systems built or implemented by the IT department attempt to adhere to the architecture road map. For companies in technology industries (e.g., software firms), the CTO may not reside in the IT department but may report directly to the CEO and be strategically focused on architecture for customer-facing technology or "products" that are actually sold to customers. Some CIOs may also have a similar role, but reporting to the CIO and with the title "Chief Architect" or "Systems Architect." This role may have

more day-to-day components to it such as approving new system designs. It is used to ensure that decisions made by different applications and infrastructure teams are consistent with the overall direction of IT. Chapter 6 discusses the role of the CTO in more depth.

2. *Security:* Security management may be a full-time position in some companies depending on the number of systems and access points into the company network and the industry the company operates within. Financial services companies, for example, should have a separate, full-time security position that may or may not reside in the IT department. Security personnel are responsible for implementing controls to limit the potential of unauthorized users from entering the company networks. This includes implementing firewall equipment, security monitoring software, encryption policies, access policies, password policies, physical access limitations, and detection and monitoring of fraud from internal staff.

3. *Audit/accounting control:* Large IT organizations must have additional command and control as a separate function from regular management to avoid agency issues. Companies that process financial transactions, such as banks, must also protect against fraud protection from internal employees. This group may report to the CIO or to the finance/audit department. This function reviews project approval requests, reviews project plans, and tracks project progress versus original project plans. It also serves as a risk management function to ensure that large projects are following the approved methodologies to reduce project risk and reviews security practices on projects that involve sensitive systems. Project audits are both scheduled and random to catch fraud.

4. *Project management office (PMO):* Very large IT departments will also usually have a large number of simultaneous initiatives. These initiatives need to be coordinated, tracked, and reported on centrally, which helps ensure that projects with interdependencies stay in sync, that projects do not drift off course, and inadvertent project competition does not arise. IT departments will usually create a PMO whose responsibility is tracking and course-correction for all IT projects. Studies have shown that PMOs improve IT project execution performance considerably in large organizations.

5. *Business analyst group:* In large IT departments, CIOs can consider creating a separate group for business analysts who are responsible for working with business end users in gathering requirements for projects, enhancement requests for existing systems, and ensuring satisfaction with systems and application performance. In companies with large business units, varying types of business units or differing customer bases, it can be advantageous to dedicate specific individuals to the analyst role for specific business units.

6. *Centralization versus decentralization:* There is a constant tension in large organizations between centralizing versus decentralizing IT operations. Centralizing results in increased control and lower costs for IT within the corporate IT entity while decentralizing results in more control at the business unit level and potentially at the user level. While the right balance requires careful analysis the two models are best used in specific situations. When business units require similar technologies, a high level of quality, coordination, standardization, and consistency in operation more centralization is preferred. Additionally, when the business wants to operate IT at its lowest possible operating cost and share capital intensive infrastructure and personnel, centralization works best. For companies that have dissimilar business units that require vastly different technologies and operate in an environment where time to market is the most critical component of delivering IT systems, decentralization is preferred. Decentralization works well when business units have a high level of independence, complex customers and products, and less leveragability of technology for other business units to share. In most organizations IT operations can be centralized without much argument while the IT application development organizations will be determined by the best fit option.

7. *Organization by business functions, application types, business units, departments, and/or geography:* With the application development and maintenance organization, the application team can be organized multiple ways. One way was presented in the previous discussion. The larger the company, the more possible permutations. Some companies organize the application team into its functional areas (e.g., finance applications, and supply chain applications). Others organize based on business units (e.g., online catalog, retail, and wholesale). Others organize by geography (e.g., East Coast, West Coast, Europe, South America). A combination of methods may also be used. The decision on the organization will hinge on cost, technology expertise required, level of industry knowledge required, level of functional knowledge required, size of the organization, and the needs and location of the end users.

Summary

The optimal organization of the IT department should at a minimum adhere to a split between applications support and operations support. CIOs should avoid any blurring of the lines between roles and responsibilities between and within groups. A disorganized IT department with competing roles and gaps in service coverage continually finds itself behind in project delivery and user satisfaction. The proper organization and clearly delineated roles in the IT department rank equally with proper IT leadership, IT demand management, technology standards, vendor management, risk management, and financial management as a crucial lever for creating the effective IT department. Large IT departments may want to consider the addition of certain specific roles and groups such as chief architect, project management office, IT audit group, and business analyst group. In every case, the CIO should ensure that the number of direct reports is five or fewer.

RESOURCES

Applegate, Lynda M., F. Warren McFarlan, and James L. McKenney. *Corporate Information Systems Management.* New York: McGraw-Hill/Irwin, 1999.

Kern, Harris, Stuart Galup, and Guy Nemiro, *IT Organization: Building a World-class Infrastructure.* Upper Saddle River, NJ: Prentice Hall, 2000.

NOTE

1. Attributed to John Kenneth Galbraith.

6

The Chief
Information Officer

This chapter highlights the importance of the chief information officer (CIO) in building and managing the effective IT department. Topics include scope of the role of the CIO, impact of the position on the productivity and capability of the IT department, skills and experience found in the most effective CIOs, and how those managers allocate their time. For IT department staff members, the chapter outlines the skills needed for promotion to CIO. The chapter also contains advice for senior managers seeking to hire or promote a new CIO, and explores how CIOs can go astray and become disconnected from the business imperatives, as well as how to use effectively the IT steering committee to substitute or augment the CIO.

Why This Topic Is Important

We have found that the quality of the individual in the role of CIO has the single largest impact on the overall effectiveness of the IT department. Whether that role is called the *CIO*, the *vice president of information systems*, or simply the *IT director*, this person is usually responsible for one of the largest operations in a corporation in terms of costs and the only operation that interacts with virtually every point in the organization. To be effective in this role, the person must have a wide range of management skills, communications skills, motivational ability, and political savvy. Leadership in this position is critical to the success of the IT department. As observed in Chapter 2, IT departments can, in best cases, be a source of competitive advantage and positively impact overall company productivity. In the worst cases, they can be endless sinkholes for corporate time and budgets. In the latter case, the ultimate cause of many of the problems plaguing troubled IT departments—failed projects, wasted dollars, and lost opportunities—is a lack of leadership from the top IT manager.

Because of the unique combination of technical and nontechnical skills required, the process of identifying the ideal candidate for the role is challenging and can be particularly vexing for the nontechnical senior management team members.

Internal promotion candidates are often technically skilled, but lacking in the requisite management expertise and communication skills. External candidates can be expensive and difficult to attract, particularly for smaller mid-market companies. Even after the right candidate is identified and hired, the position can often lead to conflicts of interest and agency problems that can be detrimental to the overall organization. The incentives and motivations of "star" IT managers are often incongruent with the incentives of the company overall. This chapter provides guidance for identifying, selecting, and motivating the right individual for this crucial role.

Critical Role of the CIO

As observed by David Foote, managing partner of Foote Partners, a technology research and management consultancy, "The pressure on CIOs today is just tremendous. In many ways it is the toughest executive job. IT cuts across the entire business and [the CIO has] to be responsive to a wide variety of business and business styles."[2] A study in the early 2000s found that humankind would generate more information over a three-year period than was produced over the previous 300,000 years combined.[3] Corporations are producing an ever-increasing amount of information that takes technology to sort, analyze, transact, and distribute. The vast amount of information will tax CIOs.

This rings true; next to the CEO, the CIO arguably has the most highly diverse and politically complicated position in most organizations. The responsibilities of the CIO cover a wide swath of territory—management of the utility functions that allow the business to conduct its basic operations (network, desktop computer support, e-mail) and to secure corporate data, the applications that are used to plan and manage the business (forecasting, manufacturing, finance systems), as well as applications used to grow the business and gain competitive advantage (customer-facing systems, customer relationship management applications). This far-ranging set of responsibilities also means that, while the role can be challenging, the CIO is uniquely positioned to add value to every business unit and function in the company and effect real change.

In spite of the inherent potential of the position, and because of the intense pressure and visibility, the CIO is one of the most maligned corporate professionals. The CIO position has only existed since the late 1960s and only became a widely accepted corporate position in the 1980s. Contrast that with the CFO position that has existed in some respects for thousands of years (albeit under different titles) dating back to ancient merchant trading companies and the like. The CFO and other corporate positions (e.g., VP Sales, VP Manufacturing) are well entrenched and have their respective power bases. Conversely, the CIO position has traditionally been thought of as a weak management position of a cost center making the CIO easy prey as the fall person. While a third of employed CIOs will lose their job in a year, almost 60 percent feel their job is at risk. Fortunately, historical perceptions of the position have been changing for the better, and the CIO position has been gaining respect on the corporate executive team. Recent data show that the tenure of CIOs is improving from the widely reported 18-month tenure statistics propagated throughout the 1990s. Although one survey shows CIO tenure as high as 5.6 years,[4] a number of others show considerably lower numbers. According to technology authorities at *Optimize Magazine*,[5] and at the Industry Advisory Council,[6] the average turnover rate for CIOs is better than previous measures but still a lofty 28 percent to 35 percent annually.

As outlined in Chapter 2, technology spending is the largest nondirect cost in most corporations, and it has driven many of the productivity gains in the U.S. economy over the past five years. In spite of this, IT departments in general, and IT projects specifically, have gained an often well-deserved reputation for being endless money pits associated with few real business results. While there are many proximate causes to this ineffectiveness, the ultimate cause is a lack of leadership and focus in the IT department.

Our most frequent consulting engagements have been focused on helping IT leadership improve, and they have provided volumes of empirical evidence for these assertions. Invariably, our clients' IT departments improve after the CIO is effectively coached or, failing that, replaced, and a solid strategic plan for IT is put in place.

In case after case, the only variable being changed in the newly improved IT department is the manager or top level of managers; the technology in place is the same, the staff is the same, the vendors are the same. Consistently the focus of the department improves, the processes and procedures improve, and the ultimate execution of the overall department is superior. This repeated "controlled experiment" has proven without a doubt that IT leadership is the principle determinant of the overall success of the department and that leadership falls squarely on the CIO.

The Talent Challenge

One of the most difficult challenges facing CIOs is that the traditional path to promotion has been from inside the IT department. Nearly 70 percent of CIOs have a career background primarily in the IT area.[7] The skills and disciplines that make a top performer in the IT operations or applications area are not the ones that best serve the CIO. In fact, although internal promotion candidates appear to be the most logical choice for CIO, they have been the type that we have seen fail most often, as they have had the most difficulty adapting to the new role and skills required.

The pre-promotion role for most CIO candidates consists of managing applications (i.e., director of applications or senior project manager) or operations (i.e., director of operations or senior network manager) where in-depth technology knowledge is required and where the individual reports to a manager with a similar technical background. Post-promotion skills are of an entirely different nature, with an emphasis on leadership, communication, planning, financial control, selling, and management. Exhibit 6.1 outlines several of the skills required or developed in the pre-promotion role, and Exhibit 6.2, the post-promotion role. Furthermore, the newly promoted CIO most often reports to a nontechnical executive, either the CFO, CEO, or

PRE-PROMOTION SKILLS
System requirements gathering and analysis.
Programming and systems development.
Application design and management.
System configuration.
Business process documentation.
Technology implementation.
Systems administration.
Systems performance management.
Technical, data, and applications architecture design and management.
Limited project management.
Upward reporting relationship with technical manager.

Exhibit 6.1   Skills Developed Pre-Promotion

POST-PROMOTION SKILLS
Management of both applications and operations portions of IT function.
Vendor selection, negotiation, and management.
Hiring, evaluating, managing, motivating, developing, promoting, and firing team members.
Decision making.
Cost containment.
Cost/benefit estimating; project economics estimation.
Budgeting.
Risk management.
Communications with business units and senior management.
Resource and project prioritization.
IT organizational design.
Standard setting and enforcement.
IT measurement and effectiveness.
Coordination of multiple, disparate projects, and initiatives across business units and internal functions.
Determining best use of scarce economic resources (staff, budget, time).
Maintenance of *steady-state* service levels for basic IT services.
Upward reporting relationship to nontechnical business manager, COO, or CFO.

Exhibit 6.2   Skills Required Post-Promotion

COO. Naturally, the combination of new required skills, new job pressures, a changed reporting relationship, and the inherent difficulty of the role lead to the high failure rates observed.

Based on these internal skill-set issues, many companies attempt to hire a CIO externally. This approach has difficulties as well. Large companies easily become victims of other companies' hiring mistakes while pursuing outside candidates. In some cases, poor candidates who may have been promoted past their level of competence leave their company and actually get a "promotion" by being hired to the next higher position at another firm. After a two-year tenure with lackluster results unbeknownst to external employers, they again embark on the job hunt for another unsuspecting company readily willing to hire and "promote." It may only be when they reach a position of high visibility such as the CIO rank, that the lacking skills are apparent. This is a major problem during periods of tight labor markets. Obviously, not all candidates lack the skills represented on their resume, however, qualifying an external candidate with brand name employers on the resume may not be as easy as it would appear.

Mid-market companies often have the most difficulty attracting the best talent. Their IT departments are smaller, and they have fewer dollars to invest in them. If a high-caliber business leader had all the experience and abilities listed in the exhibits, it is not likely he or she would want to come to work in a small to mid-size IT department—even as the director. Most small to mid-size companies simply cannot offer the level of responsibility and opportunities to attract the best professional from outside. A potential high-performance candidate may feel that he or she would not obtain enough visibility to make a difference in the organization.

Larger companies often have this difficulty as well, suffering from the poor reputation of IT and the perception that a career in the IT department offers little room for advancement to senior management. Only 7 percent of Fortune 500 companies placed CIOs in their group of five highest-paid officers.[8] Although the budgetary and staff responsibilities are significant enough to attract high-quality CIOs, they often lack upward mobility and a chance to be promoted to senior business roles (e.g., COO, CEO, SVP of unit).

We have dubbed this the *Groucho Marx* problem. Marx once famously quipped, "I don't want to belong to any club that would have me as a member." Applied to the CIO, it means that any individual willing to accept the job is, by definition, likely the wrong person, particularly in the instance of mid-market companies. An individual who would take a job with little corporate influence or with very little opportunity for upward advancement may be looking for a sinecure, or is simply not savvy enough to understand the implications of the position until its too late. A 2006 poll of CIOs by *CIO Insight* showed that nearly 41 percent of CIOs were looking or would begin to look for a new position in another company in the next 12 months.[9] To attract the best talent, senior management should ensure that the IT department is a "club" where an A player would want to belong. Further, the senior management team should be aware of the inherent transition difficulties for internal promotions, and they should work with the internally promoted CIOs to help them develop the skills they need to be successful in the role.

Another phenomenon we have observed in companies that have been successful in creating an attractive role for the CIO is the salary equation. After a company has attracted the right individual for the CIO role, it has trouble offering the right level of compensation to close the offer. For Fortune 500 companies, this means compensating the CIO at parity level with other executives at the same level in the corporation. For many small or mid-size companies, this ideal CIO, who can ensure the creation and management of a highly effective IT department, requires a higher compensation level than some members of the senior management team. Companies have worked around this issue by hiring relatively expensive "turnaround specialists" as temporary CIOs to improve or stabilize the department, then hiring a CIO to follow the temporary CIO in a caretaker role.

In every case, senior management must understand that in addition to providing an attractive environment, the salary structure must be competitive to ensure that the best candidates are available. A dollar invested in a high-quality CIO is returned to the company many times over from the effective management of IT.

Finally, companies should guard carefully against the agency problems implicit in the CIO role. Companies that successfully clear these hurdles, having attracted a top-flight CIO at a reasonable salary, often find themselves in a further dilemma. Aggressive, career-oriented CIOs are often *builders* who want to create new systems, build staff levels, and implement or enhance systems. In the worst case, we have seen CIOs who simply see their current position as a stepping-stone in their careers. In these cases, the CIOs made decisions that put their career interests over the best interests of the business. They worked hard spending corporate resources to expand their portfolio of experience in building systems and managing large-scale initiatives, regardless of the outcome for the business, in the hopes of departing for positions in other companies with even larger budgets and salary expectations. In other cases, we have seen the CEO or CFO restrict technology spending for business reasons and request a strategy of pure "system maintenance" in IT. In these cases, the companies had little chance of retaining or attracting A players to IT management.

As demonstrated throughout this book, ROI-focused growth of the IT department can create enormous value for the company. However, we have often seen out-of-control spending predicated on the *building* that improperly motivated CIOs feel is their mandate. Ensuring that the CIO's incentives are in line with those of the senior management team is critical in avoiding this trap. CIOs should be rewarded for providing the most appropriate level of service for the least cost to the organization, and ensuring that every effort of the IT department is focused on reducing costs, improving revenues, or affording more control over the business. It is up to the senior management team and the CIO to work together so that the *build* incentives are secondary to the priorities of the business or that the "maintain" strategy is readily accepted and understood by those in IT.

The skills required, difficulty of attracting the best candidates, salary constraints, and agency issues add up to a "talent challenge" that must be addressed by senior management. While this requires more than customary attention be paid to IT by senior management and a rethinking of the role of the CIO in many companies, it also provides the most important building block of the effective IT department: the right CIO.

Responsibilities and Skills Needed

The CIO is responsible for overall IT policy and the alignment of information systems across the business units. Gartner, Inc. has researched the CIO role extensively and created the following outline of responsibilities:

- *Business technology planning process:* Sponsor collaborative planning processes.
- *Applications development:* New and existing for enterprise initiatives and overall coordination for business unit/divisional initiatives.
- *IT infrastructure and architecture:* Running as well as ensuring that ongoing investments are made.
- *Sourcing:* Make-versus-buy decisions relative to outsourcing versus inhouse provisioning of IT services and skills.
- *Partnerships:* Establishing strategic relationships with key IT suppliers and consultants.
- *Technology transfer:* Provide enabling technologies that make it easier for customers and suppliers to do business with our enterprise as well as increase revenue and profitability.
- *Customer satisfaction:* Interact with internal and external clients to ensure continuous customer satisfaction.
- *Training:* Provide training for all IT users to ensure productive use of existing and new systems.[10]

Much of the complexity of the CIO role comes from the wide variety of business constituencies, outside suppliers, and staff that he or she must manage on an ongoing basis. The CIO needs to understand, communicate with, negotiate with, and influence a wide and diverse group, including:

- Senior management.
- Business unit general managers.
- Outside business partners/customers/suppliers.
- Functional vice presidents.
- Business process managers.
- Professional IT staff.
- End users.
- Vendors and service providers.

Each of these groups may have very different needs and conflicting agendas. In addition, each of these groups may require very different sets of communications skills to effectively manage interaction. The CIO must be able to reconcile differing agendas to properly align the role of technology throughout the corporation. This reconciliation requires experience in presentation, negotiation, conflict resolution, personnel management, and political conciliation.

A new CIO must be able to hit the ground running and immediately gain an understanding of the range of agendas presented by various stakeholder groups. Unfortunately, many CIOs are put into their positions because of their technical knowledge as opposed to their management savvy. Without prior management experience and expert communications skills, a new CIO is likely to encounter serious problems that cascade and grow exponentially over time. These problems can lead to many of the outward signs of IT distress discussed in Chapter 2. Eventually, these signs of distress can lead to true business failures and result in enough senior management dissatisfaction to lead to major IT restructuring, most often involving the departure of the CIO. As we noted earlier, it is no surprise that many IT professionals only half-jokingly claim that the *CIO* acronym stands for "Career Is Over."

A successful CIO typically has a unique combination of business strategy understanding, leadership skills, business/people management experience, financial planning/budgeting experience, communication and selling skills, and a broad understanding of business technology. Without this combination, there are bound to be holes in the CIO's skills that prevent him or her from being effective.

The CIO should have a strong understanding of the company's business strategy, competitive landscape and industry trends, business unit organization, business partners, major initiatives, and key corporate processes. This understanding usually comes after working in an organization for some time, but a new CIO needs to quickly grasp this information and become fluent in the organization's business context. Previous positions in business development in the industry, and strategy consulting experience can provide the bird's-eye view that helps facilitate the needed understanding.

The CIO must have extensive experience in project and people management. He or she should have significant experience in all the areas highlighted as skills required for the CIO in Exhibit 6.2. In addition, the CIO should have previously managed 5 to 10 significant technology-related projects from beginning to end, and proven that he or she can deliver expected results on time and within budget. At least some of those projects should have traversed multiple business units, functional groups, and outside partners.

Another key factor of success for a CIO is business line management and responsibility for profit and loss (P&L). Without experience managing P&L, many functional managers have trouble showing sensitivity to the effects of costs on the bottom line. The best way to gain this sensitivity and understanding is for a manager to spend some time in a role where he or she has direct responsibility for bringing in revenues and is accountable for delivering bottom line results. Having this experience also helps the CIO gain instant credibility with other business unit heads. Ideally, the CIO should also have an MBA that firmly focuses his or her thinking and skills on business imperatives. Although it is not a necessity for success in the position, the classical business concepts (e.g., negotiations, investment analysis) learned in an MBA program can be extremely useful.

Finally, the CIO should usually have a fairly deep understanding of a wide range of technologies in terms of their costs/benefits, pros/cons, and overall business value. While a CIO doesn't need to know how to write code or administer a database server, he or she should know the advantages and disadvantages of using particular platforms and how these will affect the business. The CIO should be able to quickly understand how any proposed technology solution will increase revenues, cut costs, or provide more management control over the business (and reduce risk). Ideally, the CIO should have previously been involved in a dozen or more projects involving technology evaluation, technology selection, build/buy decisions, system implementation, and ongoing operations management. Preferably, the CIO's experience should have spanned multiple business units, functions, and technology platforms.

Above all, the CIO should have impeccable communication and time management skills. The communications skills include a strong ability to listen to the needs of different groups, ability to make persuasive presentations, ability to inspire key potential employees, ability to effectively negotiate with a wide variety of stakeholders, ability to sell ideas, and general ability to develop amicable relations with a wide range of different personalities. Because of the immense pressures and changing responsibilities given to a CIO, he or she must also be able to effectively manage his or her time among various constituencies. Time management is a fundamental skill that must be carried out through efficient prioritization, meetings, delegation, and people management.

How Successful CIOs Allocate Their Time

Studies of the most successful CIOs have reached similar conclusions: Winning CIOs spend the majority of their time planning and communicating and the minority of their time "doing." Because the role can be challenging, particularly for the newly promoted, many CIOs retreat to managing and executing the tasks they find most comfortable, usually the tactical execution of projects or enhancements. While having the capability for hands-on execution is certainly a strength and part of the skill-set of the ideal CIO, it is often a refuge for the overwhelmed CIO.

CIOs should allocate the bulk of their time to communication with business unit managers, IT direction setting, and staff management. The best CIOs hire "A" players to lead their teams, avoiding the daily minutiae of managing the department by delegating the tasks that can be accomplished by a quality team. This frees up time for the CIO to develop the larger picture agenda and ensures that he or she develops the trusted relationship with the business required to accomplish that agenda.

A successful IT manager we know goes jogging at lunch every day with a group of business unit managers from his company. His close relationship with the business users, a natural result of half-an-hour per day spent with the management team, has resulted in a highly effective IT department that keeps the priorities of the business first.

New CIOs should spend the first 30 days in the position completing a full assessment of the department. The assessment should be fully documented and provide an unbiased review of all components (e.g., the organization, technical architecture, application architecture, projects, budget). The second 30 days can then be spent developing the three-year strategic plan. During this first 60-day period, a full schedule of interviews with each of the business unit and functional department leaders should occur. This develops a complete picture of the current satisfaction level throughout the business, as well as the technologies required by the business. Finally, the new CIO must sell the plan to the IT steering committee and the business, then develop an implementation plan to improve the department in critical gap areas to achieve targets in the strategic plan.

On an ongoing basis, the time allocation among competing activities differs depending on the size of the company and the IT organization. The CIO's time can be divided into five categories:

1. Administrative and financial.
2. Doing technical work or managing projects.
3. Cultivating relationships with senior management.
4. Communicating, marketing, and selling the IT department to the rest of the organization.
5. Leading and developing senior IT staff.

While all categories are important at one time or another, the CIO can gain the most leverage and make the largest difference by cultivating relationships with senior management and participating in the company's overall business management, while delegating many of the other activities to high-quality direct reports.

Financial and administrative matters can seem very important; however, they are never the catalyst of great success. If done badly, they can lead to very poor performance; however, successful CIOs learn to optimize and reduce time spent on such matters yet still execute well. No one should spend more than 10 percent of his time here if he is to excel.

Spending time doing technical work or managing projects depends greatly on the size of the company and organization. In a small company, a CIO may be forced to contribute in a hands-on role because of budgetary constraints. In such instances, the CIO should spend no more than 40 percent of his time "doing," otherwise he ceases being a CIO and becomes more of a glorified manager. Much of the strategic IT function will likely fall or reside in the CFO, or whoever is ultimately responsible for IT. The IT department in these cases will never perform well and the CIO will never be valued and, more importantly, will be blamed for the poor performance. In mid-sized IT organizations—staff greater than 15—the amount of time spent "doing" by the CIO should approach 0 percent and never be greater than 10 percent. Why 10 percent? CIOs must keep abreast of technology and close to those they lead. By keeping this edge they continue to earn the respect of those they wish to lead. While "doing" is not a highly leveraged use of time, it helps keep the CIO close to the work in his unit.

Cultivating relationships with senior management is important in order for the CIO to be involved with the business. If the CIO does not build respect with the business unit leaders, he or she cannot be a good leader. During this activity, the CIO can continue to learn the business as well as sell ideas to improve revenue or reduce costs in the business units. By doing this, the CIO becomes a valuable member of the company's senior leadership team. This time can also be used to continuously test the priorities of the business units to ensure that IT priorities are aligned and to perform quality assurance. In most cases, this activity takes 30 percent to 50 percent of the CIO's time.

Communicating, marketing, and selling the IT organization to the company is critical for the IT department to gain the respect of the entire organization. The CIO can also gain leverage by teaching others in the IT organization how to "sell" the department to the business. Promoting a culture of over-communication and relationship building will help the CIO accomplish this. Typically, this function can be well fulfilled spending 10 percent to 20 percent of time here.

Leading and developing senior IT staff is a high-value activity. The better the direct reports perform, the more leverage the CIO will gain from his or her staff. The performance of the IT department can be greatly increased by improving senior staff. Here the CIO sets direction for the staff, provides a vision, creates management frameworks, and helps the staff solve *their* problems. Finally, the CIO holds the staff accountable and either makes them better through coaching or counsels them out of the company when they are performing poorly. CIOs devote 20 percent to 30 percent of the work week to this activity depending on the size of the organization.

The percentages vary by company size and by individual skill; however, the CIO should review each of the five categories and determine what time allocation provides the best use of time on high-value and leveraged activities. Time spent outside the company (e.g., developing relationships with peers, within the industry, with clients, and with vendors) is also important and should not be neglected, but should not be a significant time sink either.

Recruiting and Retaining the Ideal Candidate

Recruiting and retaining the ideal CIO candidate can be difficult. The job must be constructed in a way that is attractive to the best candidates, and this often requires members of the senior management team to rethink the scope and influence of the role. Senior executives should ask themselves, "Would I take this job?" If the answer is no, there is no reason to believe that the best candidates would. Just because the job is technology-related doesn't mean that the candidates lack any of the career ambitions or interests of their counterparts on the senior management team. In fact, the reverse is true. The best candidates want to understand how their careers can advance, and they want to be in a position to influence decision making in their companies.

As outlined earlier, successful candidates have a solid base of technical skills, and they will have worked in an IT department, preferably with exposure to both applications management and IT operations. The best candidates have enhanced this basic experience with team management, staff development, business training, and a proven ability to deliver quantifiable results.

Many CIO recruitment processes fail because of an overemphasis on finding an exact match of technical skills required instead of the leadership, business, communication, and management background found in an ideal candidate. While specific knowledge of the operating systems, applications, and other pieces of the technical environment in a given company are helpful, such knowledge should always take a back seat to the candidate's proven ability to deliver results, prioritize work, communicate with the business, and manage people.

Another common failing in the recruiting process, particularly for growing companies, is to focus on candidates who have "built" an organization. One candidate we were interviewing had most recently held the role of CTO/CIO at a failed start-up. The company had been extraordinarily well funded and was highly reliant on technology for internal use, as well as for its main product line. The candidate had been responsible for all technology. When asked about his most important achievement while there, he proudly boasted, "I built an IT department of over 300 people inside of one year!" Too many CIO candidates are focused on what they "built" as opposed to how they use their budget, staff, and capabilities to drive revenues and reduce costs for their company. A good recruiting process identifies candidates who can generate these results for their companies, regardless of what they are asked to "build."

When interviewing potential candidates for a CIO position, a scorecard can be used to help drive the selection process and to ensure that the candidate has technology-specific knowledge. Subjective criteria covering all of the previously mentioned areas can be included on the scorecard along with weighting for each criterion based on the value necessary for the organization. Exhibit 6.3 is an example of a scorecard for evaluating potential CIO candidates.

Reference and background screening of candidates should not be overlooked. Often, when recruiting from the outside, in the rush to complete the sourcing, interviewing, and closing of offers, companies neglect to perform the most basic screening for the CIO position. Candidates should have their references and educational backgrounds verified, as well as the normal background screening that can encompass credit checks, criminal background screens, and so on. This process can usually be coordinated through the corporate human resources (HR) department, who most often have standard processes in place for completing background screening. Other highly valuable screening techniques include IQ testing (to determine raw

CRITERIA	SCORE
• IT operations management experience.	
• IT applications management experience.	
• Custom development (requirements gathering through deployment).	
• Project management/team leadership.	
• Profit and loss responsibility.	
• Departmental budgetary responsibility.	
• Non-IT business management responsibility.	
• Staff management (no. of staff managed).	
• Vendor management experience.	
• Vendor selection experience.	
• Business training (advanced degree, other).	
• Undergraduate and post-graduate degree training.	
• Verbal and written communication.	
• Senior management team participation.	

Exhibit 6.3   Example IT Director Evaluation Scorecard

intelligence capability), psychological and behavioral testing (to determine fit with senior management team), and situational interviews (to determine decision-making patterns). In all cases, the CEO, CFO, or manager of the CIO should spend time in a social setting (e.g., lunch, dinner, golf, or ball-game) with the finalists to make sure the person is likeable and a good cultural fit for the organization.

Other Factors Impacting the CIO's Role

The role of the CIO gradually changes over time with changes in the business. The role is primarily affected by the size of the company, scope of operations, and its geographic footprint. As the company grows and changes, so, too, does the role of the CIO and the skills he or she requires to be successful.

For smaller companies with a relatively small scope of operations, the IT department is usually smaller in size (10 to 50 people) and budget ($1 to $5 million). At this size, the CIO can be more focused on individual project management and can take greater ownership of specific initiatives as discussed earlier. An advantage of having a department of this size is that the CIO can generally have more personal relationships with all the heads of the business and functional units. When the steering committee is evaluating potential candidates for these positions, they can make trade-offs between experience levels and compensation. They can be less stringent on higher level requirements such as P&L experience and extensive program management. This can help expand the pool of candidates and lower the overall compensation costs.

As a company expands through either organic growth or acquisitions, the IT department will likely expand in size (50 to 200 people) and scope ($5 to $20 million). At this point, the CIO needs to gain key skills to remain effective, including:

- *Learning to get things done through people:* The CIO needs to modify his or her organizational structure to more effectively delegate responsibility to senior managers within the group. If the CIO cannot master this skill of delegation, he or she will likely fall into the trap of being cramped for time and not be able to focus on the more important high-level issues. In addition, he or she may not be able to stay in sync with senior management.
- *Learning to judge people and attract the best professionals:* As growth accelerates, the CIO will not have the time to get to know every candidate. He must spend less time with each potential new hire. For this reason, he or she must learn how to judge and evaluate people using objective measures and outside help from HR professionals.

- *Developing and managing people:* The CIO needs to become even more focused on the development needs of his or her staff. This includes ensuring that the best members are rewarded and that the poor performers are eliminated.

- *Focusing on the majors:* While the CIO could get into the details of specific projects with a small IT department, he or she needs to keep his or her head above the trees to avoid getting stuck in minute details as the department grows and larger issues surface.

- *Ensuring all projects are productive:* The CIO needs to continually ensure that all projects are focused on at least one of three objectives: (1) cost reduction, (2) revenue improvement, and/or (3) increased control of the business (risk reduction).

- *Developing partnerships with management:* Through diligent use of the IT steering committee and informal meetings, the CIO needs to build stronger relationships with the lines of business to stay on top of ever-changing and growing needs.

Eventually, the IT department may increase to over 200 people with a budget over $50 million per year. At this stage, the company is large in terms of geographic footprint, as well as diversity of operating divisions. As growth continues, the CIO should more closely reflect the image of the "ideal CIO." The focus of his or her work should shift from that of a large program administrator to that of a true business leader. The job will include less and less internal management, but more and more external coordination and bridge building within and outside the enterprise.

As the enterprise grows and changes, the role of the CIO must change. The IT steering committee should determine if the current CIO (1) wants to change his or her role and (2) has the requisite skills and experience needed to make the change. If the answer to either of these questions is no, time should not be wasted trying to "get by" until there is a serious problem. The steering committee should take a proactive position on finding a new CIO who is suitable for the role.

Other major factors influencing the type of CIO who is successful include industry and geographic footprint. The skills required of the successful CIO in education and government differ somewhat from the skills required for a private-sector CIO. The budgeting process for federal and state government and educational institutions is a different process than for private sector companies. The IT mission is also often different. Further, in federal or state agencies, the top official is often a political appointee with an agenda that may vary from the career professionals in the agency.

As observed in a General Accounting Office (GAO) study, "Implementing Effective CIO Organizations,"[11] "Agency . . . executives are political appointees who are often more focused on national policy issues than building capabilities essential for achieving the desired strategic and program outcomes," and "the federal budget process can create funding challenges for the federal CIO that are not found in the private sector," and, finally, "the relative inflexibility of federal pay scales makes it difficult to attract and retain the highly skilled IT professionals required to develop and support the systems being proposed." It is an understatement to say that the role of the federal IT executive is challenging. We recommend two GAO-created reports on the role of the CIO as reading for state or federal government CIOs—"Executive Guide: Maximizing the Success of Chief Information Officers" (GAO-01-376G) and "Chief Information Officers: Implementing Effective CIO Organizations" (T-AIMD-00-128).

In every case, the ideal CIOs for these organizations have exposure to, and understanding of, the budgetary and political factors that impact their jobs. Although the skills in the private sector tend not to vary from industry to industry, an understanding of the specific industry is always important for the CIO.

Getting Promoted

Because of the skills gap noted in this chapter, the promotion to CIO can be a traumatic, and often career-ending, experience for the new manager. The well-prepared new CIO can avoid being the victim of his or her new role by rapidly working to develop the core skills described. As we have too often observed, the newly promoted manager clings to his or her previous role as a "doer," and ignores the new skills needed to succeed in this role.

The first goal of the newly promoted CIO is to fill in the gaps in his or her knowledge of the business, senior management priorities, and the business itself. The CIO should work hard to establish understanding of the portions of the IT department where he or she has not had sufficient exposure, whether operations or applications. The CIO should next begin understanding the priorities of the senior management team. This can be done informally through lunch meetings and formally through the vehicle of the IT steering committee. Finally, the CIO should work to understand the components of the business and how they fit with the IT department goals. For example, the CIO in a manufacturing company should understand how forecasting, order management, manufacturing, shipping, and finance interact at a detailed level.

The Role of the IT Steering Committee

The role of the IT steering committee is described fully in Chapter 19. However, it is important to note that the committee is the most important vehicle for helping the CIO succeed and for ensuring that the priorities of the business are reflected in the IT department's projects, service levels, staffing, and budgets.

In companies where the CIO is weak or absent, the IT steering committee can be an effective prop in the interim until the right CIO can be found, serving as a virtual CIO. In many cases, the IT steering committee works in conjunction with an outside consultant who serves as a temporary CIO.

In every case, the presence of an IT steering committee helps potential CIO candidates feel assured that the proper management of the IT function is a top priority for senior management and is viewed as a business enabler rather than a cost pit. The potential candidate can feel confident that his or her views are respected in the organization by both senior management and the functional and business unit leaders.

Evaluating the CIO

To keep the CIO from overfocusing on systems growth and initiatives to the detriment of the overall business, incentives can be developed. Holding the CIO strictly accountable for value-increasing performance measures such as ROI helps keep the focus in the right areas; however, it may not be enough to prevent the CIO from crafting projects to justify unneeded expenditures. Incentive compensation should be tied directly to measures (e.g., reduction in company paper use, increase revenue per employee as productivity indicator, ROI achievement) that are collected independently through the ongoing IT performance measurement program. These incentives can help alleviate the agency problem by rewarding the CIO for increasing value and punishing them for destroying value. One CIO with a successful eight-year tenure at a Fortune 500 company says that his secret was "unswerving devotion to the dollar [budget], and [overcoming] resistance from the managers who [didn't share his] allegiance."[12] This is just another way of saying, hit your numbers, manage to the numbers, and provide return to the business and you can have some longevity as a CIO.

Examples of key performance measures (KPIs) are described in Chapter 18. These should be measured on an ongoing basis and used as inputs for an incentive compensation scheme developed in conjunction with an HR compensation specialist.

As the CIO gains tenure in the organization, he or she should be building relationships throughout the company to effectively and efficiently fulfill his or her mission. In addition to performing well against standard measurement indicators, the CIO should also be judged against the quantity and quality of relationships developed with major stakeholders. One of the themes of this book emphasizes the need for better alignment between IT and business/functional units. To achieve this end, personal relationships must be developed between the CIO and stakeholders. The organization meets the CIO halfway through the formation of the steering committee, but the CIO needs to make the effort to ensure that the relationships are forged and maintained.

One way the CIO can accomplish this is to perform a regular (quarterly) self-audit. Questions to be considered include:

- Have you read the latest company financial reports?
- Can you list key financial metrics (e.g., revenues, profits)?
- Can you list the company's top five customers?
- Do you understand the business strategy of the company's top five competitors?
- Can you list the top five key trends in the industry?
- Can you draw the top three layers of the company's organizational chart?
- Have you met or spoken with a customer in the past month?
- Do you know the secretaries/receptionists of stakeholders by name?
- Have you met in person, one-on-one, at least once with all of the business unit leaders in the past month?

If the CIO cannot answer all of these questions with a yes or an appropriate answer, he or she needs to start making additional concerted efforts to build relationships and enhance his or her strategic view of the organization.

The CTO

The chief technology officer (CTO) position became popular in the late 1990s especially with technology and Internet-based companies. There are several organizational models incorporating a CTO role. The two most prevalent are ones in which (1) the CTO does not report to the CIO, and is in fact a peer of the CIO reporting to the CEO or other top executive, and (2) the CTO reports to the CIO and is therefore a subordinate.

Model A is likely most prevalent in technology-oriented companies where the CTO is actually the head of research and development for the products facing the customer. In this model, the CTO is responsible for customer facing technology while the CIO is responsible for management of internal technology. The division of duties is fairly clear and the CTO in effect becomes the head technology strategist for any technologies that reach the customer. This model would also apply to customer facing

Internet applications. This model is most prevalent in software, hardware, and online businesses.

Model B is most prevalent in all other types of companies. In fact, model B, in traditional companies is likely the only choice. Having two top technology officers in a company whose products or services are traditional in nature is a recipe for disaster. The company must have one person who is ultimately accountable for IT in the company. Having two will reduce accountability of any one person and ensure that roles are ambiguous, overlapping, and conflicting. Model B ensures that the CIO is accountable for all spending and management of IT in the corporation. Under this model, the CIO is the senior executive technology officer of the company, strategic IT leader, and IT department manager. In this model, the CTO reports to the CIO and is the primary architecture specialist in the company. The CTO is held accountable to decisions and work product by the CIO ensuring better value and return for the expense of having a CTO. Most mid-size companies that are not technology companies will not have a CTO role at all. In large companies, the CTO role may be termed CTO and the responsibilities placed with one person, or the role will be divided among several senior managers and the responsibilities divided.

How can the CTO add value in a company? The CTO manages several important areas for the CIO/company. These skills and responsibilities include:

- Architecture strategy, design, and planning (e.g., SOA).
- Platform decisions and transition (e.g., Mainframe transitions to client/server, etc.).
- Innovative technology ideas (e.g., designing customer self-service technology).
- Evangelist for company technology (e.g., the promoter of internally developed technology).
- Long-term technology research (e.g., how should the company be storing internal documents for safeguard for the next 10 to 20 years).
- Architecture security (e.g., best methods for securing the systems for the next 5 to 10 years).
- Consistency of network, applications, and hardware packages (e.g., ensuring IT managers do not implement applications that are inconsistent with architecture strategy).

If the CTO role doesn't exist in the company then these responsibilities need to be assigned to other senior managers within the IT department. In technology companies, these responsibilities must be assigned to product managers within business units providing technology products to companies.

Organizations for CIOs

There are a number of high-quality national and local organizations for CIOs. The purpose of these organizations is to enable CIOs to network with peers, share ideas and best practices, and access senior level management training. A few of these organizations are:

- Association for Information Technology Professionals; (800) 224-9371; www.aitp.org AITP offer opportunities for Information Technology leadership, professional development, and personal growth.
- CIO Executive Council; www.cioexecutivecouncil.com A professional organization for CIOs enabling members to act as trusted, unbiased resources to one another while strengthening their businesses, impacting legislative groups, and collectively advancing the agenda of the CIO profession.
- IT Infrastructure Management Association (ITIM); www.itimassociation.com ATIM strives to be the IT industry's foremost member association for professionals responsible for the deployment, management, and effectiveness of IT infrastructure.
- Local Technology Organizations—These organizations typically sponsored by the Chamber of Commerce in your area or other local bodies. Good examples are the DFW Metroplex Technology Business Council (MTBC), the Technology Association of Georgia (TAG), and the Northern Virginia Technology Council. There is typically one to two strong technology associations or councils in each major metropolitan area.
- Society for Information Management; (312) 527-6734; SIM@simnet.org www.simnet.org SIM is one of the premier national associations for senior-level IT management providing both a strategic and tactical emphasis, learning opportunities, and peer networking.
- Women in Technology; (818) 788-9484; member-info@corp.witi.com www.witi.com WIT is one of the premier organizations empowering women in business and technology.

NOTES

1. Colin Powell, widely attributed to "18 Leadership Principles" lecture.
2. Mindy Blodgett, "The CIO Starter Kit," *CIO* magazine (May 15, 1999). Copyright © 2002 CXO Media, Inc. Reprinted with permission. http://www.cio.com /archive/051599/kit.html.
3. University of California, Berkeley, SIMS (October 27, 2003), http://www2.sims .berkeley.edu/research/projects/how-much-info-2003/execsum.htm (accessed December 13, 2006).

4. Allan E. Alter, "CIO Role Survey 2006: Achievement Is the Issue, Not Survival," *CIO Insight* (April 6, 2006), http://www.cioinsight.com/article2/0,1540,1963698,00.asp.

5. Arthur Langer, "Growing Tomorrow's CIOs" *Optimize Magazine*, Issue 22 (July 2006).

6. Industry Advisory Council, "IAC/CIO Task Force Report," (July 15, 1996).

7. Ted Smalley Bowen, "The Career Path of the Complete CIO", *CIO* (October 1, 2004), http://www.cio.com/archive/100104/hs_verdict.html.

8. Kim Nash, "How CIOs Reach the Top", *Baseline Magazine* (September 4, 2002), http://www.baselinemag.com/print_article2/0,1217,a=30663,00.asp.

9. See note 4.

10. CIO Executive Research Center, "The Mission of the CIO," Copyright © 2002 CXO Media, Inc. Reprinted with permission. (Stamford, CT: Gartner Measurement Services, April 23, 1999).

11. David L. McClure, "Chief Information Officers: Implementing Effective CIO Organizations," (p. 14), GAO/T-AIMD-00-128, (Washington, DC: U.S. General Accounting Office, March 24, 2000), www.gao.gov/cgi-bin/getrpt?GAO/T-AIMD-00-128.

12. Tom Steinert-Threlkeld, "What Matters More Than Your Staff?," *Baseline Magazine* (May 2005), http://www.baselinemag.com/article2/0,1540,1812014,00.asp.

7

IT Standards

"Would you tell me, please, which way I ought to go from here?" asked Alice.
"That depends a good deal on where you want to get to," said the Cat.
"I don't much care where—" said Alice.
"Then it doesn't matter which way you go," said the Cat.
"—so long as I get somewhere," Alice added.
"Oh, you're sure to do that," said the Cat, "if only you walk long enough."

—Lewis Carroll, *Alice in Wonderland*[1]

The nicest thing about standards is that there are so many of them to choose from.

—Ken Olsen, cofounder of Digital Equipment Corp.[2]

IT standard and direction setting includes the creation, documentation, propagation, and adherence to a set of standards for all elements of the technology platform in an organization—including hardware, software, peripherals, development languages, operating systems, desktop systems, network protocols, and telephony.

IT standard and direction setting often gets lost in the shuffle of myriad other decisions made in the day-to-day operation of the IT department, yet it is a decision area that has one of the largest impacts on the efficiency and overall productivity of the IT department—the flexibility of the department to handle changes in the business and new requirements. Furthermore, the IT standards model generally dictates a large part of the underlying cost model for the organization in terms of both labor and capital expense.

However, making choices around IT standards and setting overall technology direction can be challenging for IT leadership. A wide variety of factors and constraints impede the ability to see around corners. Technologies interact in different ways and are at different points in the technology life cycle, mastering the fundamentals of varying technologies that cover ground from hardware to development languages to network protocols is challenging, and it is difficult to discern real vendor products from "smoke and mirrors" and competing agendas from within and outside the IT department.

Compounding the issue of building a cohesive, standardized IT environment is the fact that most systems are built incrementally versus emerging as a fully articulated complete environment at once. The level of technical diversity is particularly high in companies that have had technology in place for a long time or have seen large changes to their business model. Therefore, the CIO's ability to control the existing footprint, as well as the timing of any future changes, adds to the already formidable challenge.

This means that technology direction and standard setting always falls short of the perfection, or even near perfection wished for by the IT manager; instead, IT managers are forced to "satisfice" in this area. Although the task is challenging, the manager must devise an approach that attempts to maximize the effectiveness of the IT department, but focuses on creating, documenting, promulgating, and adhering to an overall technology plan that includes standards for all technology departments.

Why This Topic Is Important

The decisions made around standards have a tremendous impact on the capabilities and productivity of the department. During an IT effectiveness engagement, we saw many of the typical complaints about the efficacy of the IT department from the client's senior management team; in particular, there was always a variety of excuses for being late with projects. When we interviewed the director of IT, he had this to say:

> Well, we try hard to get projects done but never seem to get any traction. We plan our projects well and follow all the normal project management disciplines. We have a dedicated staff, clear project goals, and the backing of the business. The number one thing getting in our way is the complexity of our environment. We have two accounting systems, two CRM systems—one for sales force automation, and one for help desk systems—as well as custom systems for production management and web sites written in both Java and ASP. We also have several operating systems—Solaris, Linux, Windows, and OS/2. All of the systems are interfaced with custom code and batch jobs. Every time we start a new project, despite our best planning, there are cases of unintended consequences resulting in system outages or errors, as well as unexpected delays because of the intricacies of the system interactions. This draws out even the simplest projects and makes complex projects nearly impossible. We spend so much of our time dealing with the project-related issues and downtime that we will never find a way to migrate to systems that we can manage.

We immediately understood why the IT department was having trouble getting its projects completed.

Although, as you would expect, this is a more commonplace occurrence with larger companies; we have seen this phenomenon nearly as often in smaller companies, with less complex requirements and technology environments. In this example, the client was a small company with less than $70 million in annual revenues. Ultimately, they found ways to reduce the chaos that had been created and get to a set of technology standards that was the right balance of capability, flexibility, and cost for their organization.

Although IT direction setting, via standards, is an important piece of the puzzle in an overall IT strategy and smoothly functioning IT department, it is not the only piece. Project prioritization and management, IT organization design, budgeting and cost analysis, vendor selection, and staffing are all equally important concepts for developing an overall technology strategy and are discussed in other chapters. These topics can all rightly be considered part of an overall IT direction; this chapter addresses the issues of establishing standard technology platforms to be used by the IT department, the migration of existing platforms, and the acquisition of new technology.

Standard Setting for Technology Areas

Standards should be set for any piece of technology deployed in the organization, particularly those for which the IT department is responsible.

Often, technology standards decisions are made based on grouping dependent and interrelated technologies. The choice of a certain operating system dictates the network protocol used; the choice of a certain CRM package narrows the field of hardware on which it will run. In these cases, it is important to recognize and make explicit the technology decisions that are being made in areas outside the area under consideration, so that the grouping of technology can be treated in its entirety.

Typically, the technologies involved fall into a few broad categories. A sample inventory is shown in Exhibit 7.1. This list varies widely by company, and the sample inventory here should be considered a starting point for the creation of a custom inventory plan for a specific organization.

Framework for Setting Technology Standards

We have developed a baseline framework for use by organizations in developing their own technology standards. Because each organization is different, this framework may require some customization for an improved fit, but it should provide a useful start for any technology manager. Exhibit 7.2 outlines the overall process.

The process begins by selecting the organizational scope and specific technology under consideration. The appropriate level of granularity for this

CATEGORY	TECHNOLOGIES
Computing hardware and servers	Desktops Laptops PDAs Network attached storage/SAN Servers
Application software	Package software (ERP, CRM, other point solutions) Custom developed software Application integration/middleware E-mail
Systems software	Operating system Virus detection/elimination System monitoring System performance management Configuration management Web services
Development	Development languages Databases Database design standards (normalization rules) Coding conventions
Infrastructure and facilities	Cabling Equipment storage (racks/shelves) Environmental controls
Network	Routers Hubs Firewall Patch panels
Peripherals	UPS Network printers Desktop printers Tape backup Media burner (CDRW/DVDRW)
Outside services	Consulting (by application/technology area) LAN/WAN cabling

Exhibit 7.1   Sample Technology Inventory

146

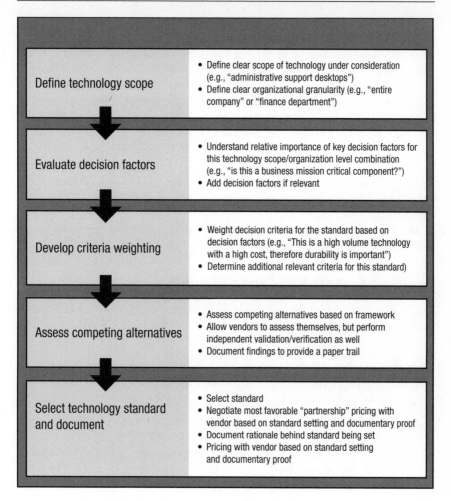

Exhibit 7.2   IT Standard Setting Process Overview

task varies but should be at a high enough level for the standard to have meaning (e.g., the *standard desktop* should be defined at the company level versus having a potentially differing standard for each department, while the standard set for servers may vary at the individual server level depending on what applications the server supports).

After the technology grouping is determined, the decision factors for the standard are evaluated. These factors are the key pieces of information that drive the criteria used in setting the technology standard. For instance, if the technology under consideration is the server for a companywide ERP system, the mission-critical nature of the deployment dictates that the standard set for such servers includes high reliability. However, if the technology being considered is a "dumb terminal" for use by dozens of data entry clerks, cost and durability become more heavily weighted than reliability. Exhibit 7.3 contains a detailed description of each of the potential decision factors.

The decision factor analysis determines which criteria are important for the standard. While the criteria should be kept the same for each assessment, their relative importance varies greatly according to the decision factors. Exhibit 7.4 outlines the criteria that may be considered in setting the standard, based on the relevant decision factors.

After the criteria weighting is complete, the analysis becomes a relatively simple comparison of competing alternatives, with a single choice emerging for the subgrouping of technology being considered. Exhibit 7.5 shows how the decision factors impact the importance and weighting of the technology standard criteria.

The remainder of this section outlines examples of technologies by factor and explains the weightings shown in Exhibit 7.5.

Decision Factor: Mission Criticality

Examples: Manufacturing planning and management system, warehouse picking and shipping systems, and hardware for running ERP system.

Primary Considerations

- *Reliability:* If the business cannot run when the system is down, reliability is of primary concern.
- *Labor availability:* A well-trained, fungible labor pool for the technology must be available to ensure continued operations.
- *Upgrade path:* A clear vendor path for continued upgrades/enhancements is necessary; if the system is of central importance for running the business, easy-to-implement, low-risk vendor upgrades supporting new hardware and business capabilities are important.
- *Current life-cycle position:* Technologies that are too early or late in their life cycles expose the organization's critical business operations to reliability issues or "dead-end" technologies.
- *Available support:* Existence of a vibrant third-party labor market ensures availability of productivity-enhancing tools and supplemental support, and prevents vendors from enjoying a support monopoly.

Secondary Considerations

- *Industry adoption:* Industry adoption by technologists and multiple businesses in your industry is important for mission-critical systems; the long-term reliability and viability of the system will be impacted by the adoption of the platform as an industry standard by technology

FACTOR	DESCRIPTION
Mission criticality	• Level on which the business depends on the system being up and functional. Mission critical systems are generally the application systems, which drive core parts of the business, such as order entry, manufacturing management, or customer service. Examples of other common nonapplication mission critical systems include telephony, LAN/WAN connectivity, and e-mail. • Systems that are considered "mission critical" vary from company to company. Determining the criticality of the systems requires a detailed understanding of both the business operations and the technology component.
Unit volume	• The number of units of the technology that will be acquired for the business and supported by IT. • Generally will be most applicable for hardware such as desktops, laptops, printers, PDAs, or other handheld computing platforms, as well as high-volume desktop-based software components (office automation, call center tools, etc.). • Low volumes imply that the factors such as unit cost or durability may not be important. • High volumes generally indicate that unit cost, ease-of-use, and industry adoption will be important decision criteria.
Stability of area supported	• Rate of change in the business unit or organization using the technology (e.g., core business unit with processes unchanged for years, vs. "startup" environment with undefined and rapidly changing requirements). • Drives level of importance of criteria such as industry adoption, consistency with existing systems, and upgrade path, which becomes less important if requirements change rapidly. • Drives higher level of importance for flexibility—system can react to changes in the business and can be adapted for other uses. *(continued)*

Exhibit 7.3   Decision Factors for Determining IT Standards

FACTOR	DESCRIPTION
Expected asset lifetime	• How long the asset is expected to last. • Payback period for system or low-lifetime estimates for assets that wear out over time, such as printers; rapid turnover for consumables such as printer paper or toner cartridges. • Implies ability to change standard over time for assets with shorter life spans and dictates level of effort spent on standard analysis. • If asset lifetime is low (consumables), cost and rapid availability become a primary consideration. • If asset lifetime is expected to be high, physical durability and manageability become primary considerations.
Level of customization	• Measure of the amount (cost) of additional labor effort required to deploy the system. • Examples: High: desktops that require large number of customizations to work in target environment or systems management software that requires ongoing configuration to operate properly; low: plug and play peripherals such as printers or mice.
Interfaces with other systems	• Number, frequency, complexity, and volume of interfaces between this technology component and other systems. • Applies particularly to application components, as well as interfaces outside the organization with suppliers or customers. • Examples: High-frequency, high-volume interfaces such as required EDI transactions to exchange inventory positions with suppliers for cooperative forecasting; low-volume/complexity/frequency: annual printout of depreciation schedule from fixed asset system for manual keying on monthly basis to general ledger system.

Exhibit 7.3 *Continued*

FACTOR	DESCRIPTION
Current and future transaction volume required	• Volume, frequency, and complexity of transactions to be carried out by system. • Current requirements as well as future estimated requirements. • Implications for scalability and reliability on high side and cost on low side. • Examples: High-volume: printers used for statement creation by a consumer-oriented company, such as a bank; low-volume: periodic ad-hoc MS Excel extracts of previous period sales data for marketing department analysis.
Organization growth plans	• Strategic plan for growth by the business. • Includes geographic expansion, acquisition of competing firms, vertical integration through the acquisition of suppliers or customers, or divestiture by selling off business units or entire company. • Implications for level of customization for systems to reduce integration costs in event of acquisition or sale. • Implications for level of cross-business-unit integration of systems in event of spinning off separate business units.
Size/type of user base	• Order-of-magnitude estimate of total volume of users. • Type of users (technically sophisticated "power users" or computer neophytes). • Usage profile: Business unit or business function. • Geographic profile: Wide range of geographies or international presence vs. small, concentrated user base. • Implications for technical support requirements, durability, ease of use, and cost.

Exhibit 7.3 *Continued*

FACTOR	DESCRIPTION
Cost	• Cost of technology component. • Includes costs of acquisition, installation, training, ongoing maintenance, changes to steady-state cost model, and effect of accelerated depreciation. • Cost details are included in the following section.
Industry adoption	• Level of adoption across the technology industry, or within the industry in which the organization or company competes. • Examples: MS Exchange as a technology-industry-wide standard e-mail platform; JD Edwards as an ERP system oriented to the mid-market manufacturing companies.
Consistency/interoperability	• Level of consistency or interoperability with current technology. • Examples: Selecting MS Internet Information Service (IIS) for Web services given enterprise MS Window 2000 deployment for both servers and desktops. Developing point solution applications in Lotus Notes/Domino based on corporate standard of Lotus Notes for Groupware/e-mail.
Labor availability	• Level of availability and cost of labor for the technology component nationally and in the local marketplace. • Examples: High availability of talented professionals for major ERP systems such as SAP or PeopleSoft; low availability of labor for systems regarded as "dead ends" or uninteresting to technology professionals.
Upgrade path	• Level of vendor and marketplace clarity on upgrade path for technology. • Generally, technologies backed by a major vendor with large number of customers and sophisticated third-party support market will have the most clear upgrade paths. • Upgrade path is often closely linked to the system life cycle; see following section on system life cycle for details. • Examples: Clear upgrade paths to major ERP and CRM systems from vendors such as Siebel, Computer Associates, and SAP; less clear upgrade paths for aging mainframe/legacy applications or for new offerings from unproven vendors.

Exhibit 7.4   Criteria for Setting Technology Standards

FACTOR	DESCRIPTION
Current life cycle	• Place in product life cycle of the technology product or service. • Implications for upgrade path, labor availability, cost, and industry adoption.
Reliability	• Number of failures across a variety of measures, depending on the technology component; can be tested as consistent output given a set of inputs, mean-time-between-failures, or other relevant statistics. • Often corresponds to complexity of technology component, particularly for applications that have a significant number of "moving parts." • Can be closely linked with product life cycle (the further into the product life cycle, the higher the reliability). • Examples: High reliability: high-availability, fault-tolerant servers with multiple redundant components (power supplies, disk arrays power supplies, processors, memory units, et al.), such as the Sun Enterprise Server 10000; low(er) reliability: desktop computer intended for general usage.
Scalability	• Ability for the technology component to handle additional volumes of work. • Examples: Consulting service organization having scope of experience and depth of staff to take on additional work in the organization; ability for on-line-transaction-processing system (OLTP) to handle increased volumes of transactions within a given time window.
Flexibility	• Technology components adaptability of different related or unrelated tasks. • Example: Server hardware that can become an e-mail server, a Web server, or an application server.
Timing/availability	• Current availability of technology component. • Lead time required when technology component is requested from vendor. • Highly available: Stock configuration PDAs available via retail or the Web within one-half day; low availability: high-end server requiring four-week manufacturing and configuration order lead time. *(continued)*

Exhibit 7.4 *Continued*

FACTOR	DESCRIPTION
Available support	• Presence of strong vendor-based capability or third-party marketplace for consulting and support services for technology component. • Example: Consulting firms dedicated to implementation and management of Great Plains accounting application.
Customer, supplier, and competitor use	• Extent to which the system/standard is used/adopted by customers, suppliers, and competitors. • Example: Similar forecasting and inventory management system used by supplier facilitates integration.
Ease of use	• Relative complexity of the technology component; end-user perception of difficulty of learning and using the system. • Implies level of technical support required for technology component. • High level of ease: Commercially available e-mail systems; low-level of ease: sophisticated order entry system for highly customized engineering product.
Durability	• Physical durability of the technology (generally hardware) component. • Important for harsh environments (manufacturing floor, marine usage), mobile/heavy travel users. • Example: "Hardened" machines with special casing and filtering to withstand the jostling and dust on a plant manufacturing floor.
Manageability	• Ease of managing the technology component. • Availability of remote management tools, similarity to system already in place to reduce training burden, management of incremental systems with existing tools/processes. • Example: Additional desktop systems that can be administered by existing remote management tools.

Exhibit 7.4 *Continued*

departments; a well-established user community for a given technology helps hold vendors accountable for producing reliable systems, forms an objective forum for sharing best practices on system usage, and provides large aggregate funding for additional functionality to the system via ongoing vendor maintenance fees.

• *Consistency/interoperability:* System should be able to interoperate with existing systems to ensure smooth running of overall technology

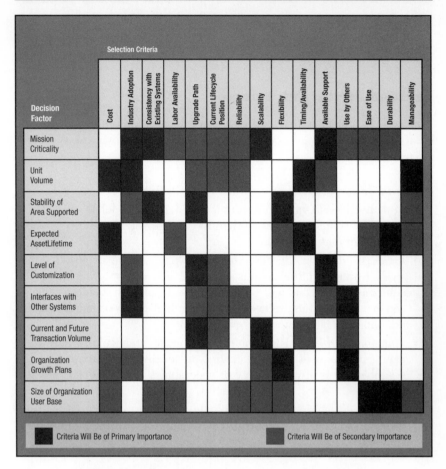

Exhibit 7.5   Decision Factor and Criteria Weighting Matrix

platform (consistent interface incompatibilities, particularly from systems that generate inbound transactions to a core system, spell trouble for a mission-critical system).

- *Scalability:* If changes to the business dictate increased volumes for a given technology component, business mission-critical components that scale appropriately lower the risk to the business by not requiring replacement.

- *Use by competitors:* Use of a given technology by the competition provides secondary validation to the standard under consideration.

- *Ease of use:* A business mission-critical system should have high ease of use to ensure that user community will more easily adopt the system and achieve the highest productivity gains from it.

- *Durability:* Mission-critical systems should be physically durable, particularly if used in mobile, manufacturing, or other harsh environments.

Systems that drive the business should either be durable or replacements immediately available and easily deployed with a minimum of configuration and additional labor effort.

Decision Factor: Unit Volume

Examples: Handheld computers for delivery drivers, laptops for consultants in large consulting organization, desktop-level antivirus software, and desktop printers.

Primary Considerations

- *Cost:* Even small variations in unit cost drive high dollar amounts for high unit volume purchases; therefore, achieving the lowest possible pricing per unit is crucial.
- *Industry adoption:* Because the technology will be deployed extensively throughout the organization, cost and effort of replacing the equipment over time will be prohibitive if industry standards change and new capabilities are needed; further, high levels of industry adoption should create, in theory, lower pricing.
- *Timing/availability:* High-volume equipment, particularly hardware, may need frequent replacement/repair; ideally, the units are readily available across a wide variety of geographies from vendor or reseller inventory.
- *Manageability:* The high unit volume magnifies any system management inefficiencies by orders of magnitude; the best high unit volume systems require little management or intervention by IT.

Secondary Considerations

- *Upgrade path:* Because a significant amount of capital is likely to be invested in a high-volume system, it is important that the vendor provide an upgrade path to ensure the highest longevity.
- *Current life-cycle position:* The inevitable changes to system standards, configurations, and costs as systems travel along their life cycles dictate that high unit volume systems are ideally in the "full adoption" or "steady state" segments of the technology life cycle.
- *Reliability:* Even small lapses in reliability create headaches for the IT department when multiplied by hundreds or thousands of individual units.
- *Available support:* Because high-volume units are often deployed across the organization and across disparate geographical areas, the systems should easily be supported remotely or with vendor staff or resellers in each geography; because high unit volume systems are generally a large

investment for the organization, the availability of support over the long term is an important consideration.

- *Ease of use:* Many high unit volume systems are end user oriented; in these cases, ease of use should be considered; small improvements in ease of use are multiplied across many users.
- *Durability:* If high unit volume systems are not durable, the IT team can be stuck with an endless supply of broken equipment; further, because purchases are often made in bulk, a lack of durability may show up simultaneously across many units, creating a tidal wave of work for the IT department.

Decision Factor: Stability of Area Supported

Examples: Spectrum of business activity from new business unit or start-up with actively evolving business model to stable, mature business with rarely changing business processes and technology requirements.

Primary Considerations
- *Consistency/interoperability with existing or planned systems:* If the business area supported by the technology is stable, the investment made in systems should be consistent with, or interface easily with, existing or planned technologies. The low turnover of requirements on stable business areas means that these systems will be deployed for the long term. Similarly, if the business area is rapidly changing, the IT department may take more latitude in making technology choices, given the likelihood that the business requirements change rapidly.
- *Flexibility:* If the business area supported is subject to considerable change, the flexibility of the systems to be upgraded, reconfigured, customized, or otherwise adapted to those changes is a primary consideration. This ensures that at least some of the technology investment made for the business will be salvageable as the business needs change.
- *Upgrade path:* Likewise, the upgrade path for technologies deployed in changing business areas should be clear. Often in these cases, other customers of a package, service, or product are experiencing the same changes, and the vendor will provide an upgrade based on these new needs.

Secondary Considerations
- *Industry adoption:* Industry adoption influences the long-term costs, upgrade path, related systems integration, and third-party support levels enjoyed by the technology. For stable business areas where the

technology is a long-term investment, level of industry adoption should be considered.

- *Manageability:* Manageability is a consideration for technologies deployed in business areas with low rates of change, because the technology will likely be supported for long periods of time in a static, unchanged configuration. This means that easy-to-manage systems pay dividends for IT over a long period.

Decision Factor: Expected Asset Lifetime

Examples: Heavy-duty high-volume printers, color printer cartridges, and handheld computers.

Primary Considerations
- *Cost:* If an asset has a short life span (particularly for consumables), it will likely be purchased repeatedly. In these cases, cost should be a primary consideration.
- *Timing/availability:* If the assets are short lived, the vendor should have short lead times for acquiring replacements and availability to provide them across a wide geographic area.
- *Durability:* If the asset is expected to have a lengthy time in service, it should be durable enough to last through the lifetime with a minimum of maintenance and wear and tear.

Secondary Considerations
- *Labor availability:* If the asset is a long-term asset, the availability of a skilled technical staff in the labor pool should be considered. If the technology is a short-term asset, labor availability is not an important factor.
- *Flexibility:* If the asset will be in service over a long period, it may be called on to adapt to changing business conditions or serve in different roles, making flexibility and adaptability higher considerations.
- *Ease of use:* High ease of use for assets in place for long periods ensures minimal aggregate user effort.
- *Manageability:* To reduce the support burden on IT, long-term assets should be easy to manage.

Decision Factor: Level of Customization

Examples: Highly customized order entry system for complex, highly engineered product versus "plain-vanilla" install of a general ledger package.

Primary Considerations

- *Labor availability:* If the system is highly customized, a large pool of skilled technical personnel to support and manage the system must be available.

- *Available support (vendor, third party):* Similarly, a large third-party support market ensures that the IT department will be able to bring supplemental resources to bear on a highly customized system.

Secondary Considerations

- *Industry adoption:* High levels of industry adoption ensure that the vendors or suppliers will be able to provide systems that are easier to configure and provide more options for customization.

- *Upgrade path:* For highly customized systems, a vendor upgrade path that supports the customizations with a minimum of new install effort is critical. Software maintenance spending generally entitles the organization to system upgrades; in these cases, the benefits are not available if the upgrade cannot be accomplished because of large amounts of system customization.

Decision Factor: Interfaces with Other Systems

Examples: Forecasting system which shares information with suppliers of ERP system via EDI; inventory system which feeds inventory positions and availability by SKU to customers; and CRM system that receives customer information from external order system.

Primary Considerations

- *Industry adoption:* Level of industry (technology or business) adoption often drives the number of interfaces to other systems created by the vendor of third parties. If a system becomes a standard in the industry, the vendor will have the resources to ensure that the system interfaces with related hardware or software. Industry adoption also drives suppliers of related systems or third parties to create interfaces or technologies that allow the systems to operate well together.

- *Use by customers, competitors, or suppliers:* If the interfaces with other systems touch outside entities, such as suppliers or customers (e.g., forecast or inventory position exchanges, or other EDI transactions), the systems chosen by those external parties may affect which technology should be chosen. Systems from the same vendor or systems with proven interfaces to the systems used by the external partners will be the front-runners.

Secondary Considerations
- *Upgrade path:* Because the system feeds or receives data from other systems, it should be able to "keep up" as those systems are upgraded or changed. Therefore, the vendor upgrade path for the system should be clear.
- *Current life-cycle position:* Because other downstream systems may rely on triggers or other information from the system being considered, it should be in the mainstream or steady-state portion of the life cycle with a proven ability to handle the transactions.
- *Reliability:* Likewise, to ensure overall platform reliability, the system must be able to hand off and receive data reliably to avoid impacting the other interfaced systems.
- *Available support:* Finally, because of the potential to impact related systems (and the potential for "domino effect" failures), vendor support for creating reliable interfaces should be readily available.

Decision Factor: Current and Future Transaction Volume Required

Examples: Florist with highly seasonal business and high transaction volumes during holidays or special events; nonseasonal producer of commodity product with long lead-time product and little variance in transaction processing volumes.

Primary Considerations
- *Upgrade path:* If the system is subject to high future transaction volume, a clear upgrade path from the vendor for adding additional capacity will allow the organization to purchase the amount of capacity needed currently, while maintaining the ability to bring on additional capacity for small amounts of incremental cost.
- *Scalability:* The system should be able to handle current required transaction volumes with ease, including transaction volume spikes because of seasonality or other factors. The system should also be able to handle long-term increases in the baseline number of transactions as well. Clear proof of scalability across all technology components (e.g., order processing software and the hardware it runs on: CPU, processor, memory, and network capacity) should be analyzed to avoid bottlenecking at low thresholds in one particular element of the technology.

Secondary Considerations
- *Current life-cycle position:* Products in the mature portion of the life cycle have higher field-proven ability to handle large transaction volumes.

- *Timing/availability:* Upgrades to the system or product should be easily available in the case of unexpected incremental volume or rapid changes in the baseline volume.
- *Use by customers, competitors, or suppliers:* Use of the product, service, or system by competitors with similar usage patterns or volumes is indicative of the technology's actual ability to scale appropriately.

Decision Factor: Organization Growth Plans

Examples: Acquisition of competing firms or suppliers with differing business-supporting technologies; geographic expansion of business; aggressive organic growth plans.

Primary Considerations
- *Flexibility:* If the organization plans include acquisition of competitors, geographic expansion, vertical integration, or other business model changes, the systems supporting the business should have the adaptability and flexibility to support the changes while minimizing impact to existing business and incremental investment to add new portions of the business.
- *Use by customers, competitors, or suppliers:* If likely acquisition targets (or buyers) use a particular set of technologies, the purchase of the same, or similar, technologies will facilitate future business integration or partnerships.

Secondary Considerations
- *Cost:* If business expansion plans involve adding incremental capacity to existing systems or rollout of additional systems (e.g., new laptop computers for salesforce of acquired competitor), the cost of incremental processing capacity or unit costs should be minimized or guaranteed in advance by the vendor.
- *Industry adoption:* Technologies with high levels of business-industry adoption indicate solutions that have the highest likelihood of being in place at suppliers or competitors or will be most attractive to acquirers, ensuring a minimum of retraining or conversion effort in the event of a business transaction.
- *Scalability:* Key business systems should have the additional transaction processing capacity to support strong expansion plans (geographic, acquisition, or organic growth).

Decision Factor: Size/Type of User Base

Examples: Scale of activity ranging from a large-scale base of heterogeneous users crossing a variety of business units and functions across wide geographies to a small office of a dozen users.

Primary Considerations

- *Ease of use:* Systems that will be deployed across a heterogeneous user base, across disparate geographies, or a large number of users (particularly technically unsophisticated users) should put a premium on ease of use to keep training (and retraining) costs to a minimum and provide the most efficient use of end-user time.

- *Durability:* Systems used by a large number of users, particularly in harsh environments (plant manufacturing floor, delivery trucks, traveling sales), should be durable enough to handle significant wear and tear without breakage or data loss.

Secondary Considerations

- *Cost:* Technologies that will be deployed across a large number of users should seek the least unit cost, particularly for consumables or high-turnover items. In the case of large-scale deployments across a wide variety of users, cost considerations should take a back seat to durability or reliability factors.

- *Consistency/interoperability with existing or planned systems:* Systems should interoperate effectively with existing or planned systems; large unit volume and widespread deployment magnifies any difficulties the system has with interfaces to other corporate systems.

- *Timing/availability:* For remote users or geographically spread users, new or replacement systems should be readily available for vendors or resellers.

- *Labor availability:* A large pool of available technical talent in each required geography should be available; this drives decision making toward well-known vendors and highly standardized technologies.

- *Reliability:* Systems for use in the field or by a large number of users should be highly reliable.

- *Scalability:* Systems should handle large changes in usage or usage spikes; systems deployed across a large number of users that cannot expand to handle additional capacity are difficult (and expensive) to replace rapidly; the initial and ongoing deployment of the technology should ensure that the appropriate processing capacity is in place for planned future business volumes.

- *Flexibility:* Because of the high replacement cost of widely deployed systems, ideal technologies have the flexibility to upgrade or reconfigure inexpensively in response to changes in the business.

- *Manageability:* Large unit-volume systems or widely dispersed systems should be easily managed from a support and configuration standpoint to avoid undue burdens on the IT staff.

The analysis described in this section cuts through the tremendous amount of data available for technology products and services and focuses the decision-making team on gathering and assessing only the relevant pieces of information. To further reduce the data gathering burden, after the decision framework has been established, the competing vendors (or other outside consultants) can be asked to assess themselves on the relevant criteria, subject to independent validation and verification by the team. The combination of a well-thought-out framework, a clearly scoped set of decision criteria, and a willing set of vendors makes for a crisp, rapid standard-setting process.

After the selection is complete, it should be documented as part of the standards manual, along with the decision factors and criteria weighting used in setting the standard. The documentation process is covered in detail in the following sections. Further, the team should commence negotiations with the vendor to achieve partnership pricing levels to keep costs under control. The documentation generated for the standard demonstrates to a vendor that the standard is taken seriously in the customer organization and that follow-on business will be a straightforward process. Vendors are generally willing to share some of their sales-process cost savings with customers based on their selection as a standard.

Technology managers should also concentrate their efforts for standard setting based on a commonsense assessment of the value of standards in each area. Applying the 80/20 rule to standard setting implies that standard-setting efforts should stay focused on the systems components that have the largest impact on the operations of the business, from the standpoint of cost, productivity, and IT effectiveness. A detailed standard around a passing or insignificant technology component is not time well spent.

An example standard-setting process is provided in the Summary section.

Cost as a Criterion

Cost is invariably an important factor in every round of standard setting and purchasing decision making. Often, technology component costing is done as part of an overall project estimation. See Chapters 17, 12, and 13, for detailed coverage of project costing and vendor selection and negotiation strategies. Only key considerations for technology component costing, an important part of the technology standard setting, are included here.

To understand the true cost of ownership of a technology component requires more than a superficial analysis of acquisition cost. Instead, a more detailed analysis of the full cost of acquisition and ongoing management should be undertaken. This is often called *total cost of ownership* (TCO). A complete analysis includes the following cost components:

- *Acquisition cost:* The total cost of original acquisition of all technology components.

- *Install cost:* Incremental labor (internal and external) required to configure, customize, integrate, implement, and deploy the technology component.

- *Vendor maintenance:* Annual fees because vendor is part of maintenance agreement entitling the end user to vendor technical support, upgrades, and input into the product development process, usually for application components.

- *Training cost:* Cost of training for IT staff and end users of technology component.

- *Labor cost:* Likely cost of internal labor (salaries of incremental staff needed) as well as external service providers; if the technology component is required to scale or needs additional support, the cost of incremental internal or external resources is relevant.

- *Steady-state cost model changes:* Any incremental costs (or savings) incurred in the organization, covering all portions of the IT budget. These costs are found across a variety of categories, including labor (additional staff), consumables (e.g., paper, power), facilities (additional space), and capacity (network, processor).

- *Accelerated depreciation:* Occasionally, the implementation of a given technology component makes obsolete an existing system or set of systems. In these cases, depreciation of amounts capitalized from the previous implementation is accelerated and taken as expense after the new system is deployed; the financial impact and accounting issues around this topic should be addressed in conjunction with the finance department and the chief financial officer.

Free and Open Source Software

In nearly any discussion of standards and software selection, the issue of when and if to use Free and Open Source Software (FOSS) can and should be raised. There are a large number of options for replacing and augmenting applications, operating systems, tools, and development platforms with FOSS options.

FOSS is a general term used to refer to application systems that are supported by a community of uncompensated developers. While there are a number of important differences between free software and open source software, what they have in common is no cost and a volunteer community for enhancements, upgrades, and support.

Clearly, quality software with no license costs and a wide support network is an intriguing option for organizations, particularly given the high costs of proprietary software provided by commercial enterprises. FOSS is readily available online to any end-user who cares to use it. The community development nature of FOSS means that its capability expands very quickly and it is able to rapidly react to opportunities and threats.

FOSS has a varied history of usage in corporate environments. At its best, FOSS is an ideal replacement for commercial software, and at its worst, it is the bad apple that spoils the bushel.

FOSS concepts have been around for over two decades. Its origins can be found in the GNU project initiated in 1983 by Richard Stallman. Although GNU began with a Unix-like operating system, the stated goal was to "develop a sufficient body of free software . . . to get along without any software that is not free."[3] Later in 1998, the Open Source Initiative was launched by Bruce Perens and Eric S. Raymond to promote the use of open source systems.

In 1997, Eric S. Raymond penned an essay on FOSS called "The Cathedral and the Bazaar." It was later published in book form in 1999. In his work, Raymond defines two models for software development. In the Cathedral model, a small, defined, and exclusive team is tasked with completing the project. The Bazaar model relies on a widespread, public team composed of dozens or more developers. Raymond asserts that complex bazaar-style development efforts can succeed because "many eyeballs tame complexity." Source code made public receives sufficient scrutiny to improve the speed at which the software can be developed and tested.

Early open source initiatives were focused on operating systems, which as a result, are some of the most mature FOSS options today. Early open source received a good reception in the hobbyist and academic community but struggled for footing in corporate environments for a variety of reasons, but primarily concerns over labor availability and a dearth of enterprise applications oriented to FOSS platforms.

Usage of FOSS in corporate enterprises has been increasing in the past few years. Today FOSS is poised to make significant inroads into the enterprise and should be part of the standards evaluation of any company.

There is a distinct cultural component to FOSS, and one of the defining characteristics of FOSS is the ardor of its proponents. This is unsurprising. FOSS efforts are community projects. They are operated by volunteers and require intense dedication and smarts. Naturally the developer community feels a strong sense of ownership toward their product. These feelings in turn can be accompanied by (and mixed with) other agendas such as political viewpoints that may be considered irrelevant by a private-sector evaluator.

The passion of the developer and end-user community is simultaneously one of the great strengths and weaknesses of FOSS. FOSS may be best characterized as a movement or a philosophy, and it therefore comes with the baggage, good and bad, that accompanies such things. FOSS adherents are often self-described as "revolutionaries" and cultivate an anti-establishment air. Proponents view the FOSS culture as idealistic, democratic, and egalitarian, and the realm of commercial software as inflexible, authoritarian, and stifling. The Wikipedia entry for *The Cathedral and the Bazaar* describes it as the "manifesto" of the open source movement. FOSS projects are often marshalled by iconic figures with larger-than-life reputations and sociopolitical agendas. The Free Software Foundation (FSF) web site describes it thusly: "the free software movement is a social movement, not a business, and the success it aims for is not a market success."[4] CIOs and corporate decision makers who are unaccustomed to the rough-and-tumble ideological nature of community software projects often find this offputting, which has slowed the adoption of quality FOSS options in the enterprise.

A further hindrance to FOSS adoption has been its traditional focus on function over form. However, the need for attractive and easy user interfaces to promote wider adoption has been recognized by the FOSS community. Mark Shuttleworth, founder of the Ubuntu Foundation and a noted FOSS advocate wrote "Pretty is a feature . . . if we want the world to embrace free software, we have to make it beautiful."[5]

Exhibit 7.6 is a good representation of FOSS taxonomy and ecosystem, showing the options in major application areas. In keeping with the anti-establishment tone of the FOSS movement, it shows Microsoft (the ultimate establishment presence in the view of many FOSS adherents) in the center, its product offerings beleaguered on all sides by competing FOSS options.

FOSS Benefits

- *Price:* FOSS generally has no charge for the software; in some cases, companies may charge a distribution or support fee.
- *Reliability:* Bazaar-model development implies fewer bugs in software due to increased numbers of developers and publicly available source code.
- *Innovation:* Likewise, bazaar-development is likely to be highly innovative because it draws on the creative talents of a larger pool of developers.
- *Licensing:* Most FOSS licensing provides broad rights to end-users of the product; proprietary systems generally have relatively restrictive licensing agreement terms; proprietary software may give the copyright owner permission to track usage or otherwise pry into the systems of the end-user; this is not the case with FOSS.
- *Compliance:* Because FOSS is gratis, there is no additional effort required by IT to ensure license compliance.

Exhibit 7.6   FOSS "Software Wars." (Courtesy of Stephen Hilton,
http://mshiltonj.com/software_wars. Reprinted with permission.)

- *Updates:* For actively supported FOSS projects, the large number of developers improves the rate of bug fixes and capabilities via new releases.
- *Interoperability:* Because FOSS systems are not commercial, they do not impose restrictions on access to information in the system and they will adhere to openly documented interfaces with other systems, making them easy to integrate into complex application architectures, reducing switching costs.
- *Modifiability:* All free and many open-source projects provide for the right to use and modify source code; this means that a FOSS project can be the starting point for custom development efforts and that FOSS can be easily customized to meet company-specific requirements.
- *Scalability:* As an organization grows, proprietary software requires additional license fees; FOSS does not. Organizations that implement FOSS early-on will reduce costs as they grow. This is particularly true for instances such as office automation applications that will have many users.

FOSS Options

There are FOSS equivalents to nearly any application deployed in the corporate environment. Exhibit 7.7 highlights a few of the categories of applications and major FOSS options. The most prominent uses of FOSS is in the operating systems area, where a large number of Unix variants have been developed over the years. FOSS has also dominated the web-server marketplace, with Apache.

The number of FOSS systems available spans the gamut of computer applications, from databases to software development languages to graphics packages and games. A directory of free software available from the FSF listed over 5,000 free packages available across over a dozen categories. Likewise, Sourceforge, a leading FOSS distribution site listed over 130,000 registered projects and 1.4 million users. Clearly, one of the challenges with FOSS is not availability of packages, but instead wading through the available options.

A number of Internet archives are the home to FOSS projects and provide downloadable code, documentation, and executables. Foremost among these is Sourceforge (www.sourceforge.net). The Free Software Foundation (www.fsf.org) provides an excellent list of free software projects as well.

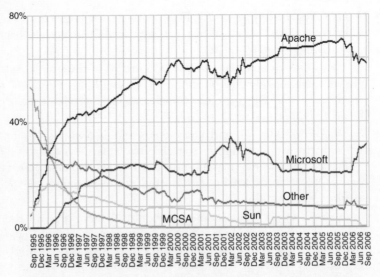

Exhibit 7.7   Market Share for Top Web Servers across All Domains, August 95–September 2006. (Courtesy of Netcraft, www.netcraft.com.)

The most prominent and popular FOSS initiatives at this writing are:

- *Linux* is a highly reliable server and desktop operating system that has seen robust growth and use in the corporate environment in the past few years. A mid-2006 report from eWeek speculated that "in the coming year, Linux is set to push Unix out of its traditional role as the Oracle operating system of choice."[6] IDC, a leading IT research house, showed that Linux had over 10 percent share of new server shipments worldwide in Q4 2005.[7]

- *Firefox* is an open source browser that has achieved an impressive 15 percent of the browser market share since its release in 2004.[8] The browser has been downloaded over 250 million times.[9] The *Apache* web server is the dominant server, with approximately 60 percent market share. Exhibit 7.7 shows Apache's share of web servers over a ten year period.

- *OpenOffice.org* (OOo) is a gratis desktop application system that includes word processing, spreadsheet, presentation software, and database application. In 2004, Computer Sciences Corp reported a Forrester estimate that OOo had achieved a 14 percent market share on the desktop,[10] and in 2005 the Yankee Group noted a 19 percent share for StarOffice, the OOo predecessor system, in small and mid-sized businesses.[11] OpenOffice.org reports that the software has been downloaded over 80 million times.[12] One of the most important features of OOo is the use of an nonproprietary open format for storing associated files, known as the Open Document Format (ODF). This feature provides portability across applications and allows the files to be manipulated by end-users as they see fit. OOo is available in an amazing number of languages.[13]

- *MySQL* is a robust multiuser relational free-software database, with a reported six million installations.[14] A late 2005 full version release (5.0) was hailed in *Intelligent Enterprise* magazine as a "serious contender for enterprise-level use" and that "MySQL can no longer be viewed as a limited, departmental database."[15] It is a key component of the common web-services LAMP (Linux/Apache/MySql/Php-Python-Perl) architecture, leading to wide usage and distribution.

There are well over 100,000 FOSS projects available, making the real challenge not finding FOSS, but finding relevant FOSS. Carnegie Mellon has established a service for evaluating FOSS projects' usability in the enterprise via the *Business Readiness Ratings* model available at www.openbrr.org.

We have also inventoried some of the most prominent FOSS offerings by category in Exhibit 7.8.

AREA	APPLICATION	NOTES
Operating system	BSD Unix	Berkeley Systems Distribution of Linux originally built at Berkeley in the 1970s; variants of it include OpenBSD (1995), Dragonfly BSD (2003), FreeBSD (1993), and NetBSD (1994).
	Linux	Unix-like OS originally developed by Linus Torvalds, originating in 1991; Linux is the most common FOSS operating system; variants include Slackware (1993), Debian GNU/Linux (1993), openSUSE, Red Hat/Fedora Core (1994), Gentoo (1999), and Ubuntu (2004). Ubuntu, a linux package oriented to desktop end-users has seen a recent surge in popularity.
Systems tools	Nagios	Systems monitoring.
	VNC	Remote desktop access.
	WINE	MS Windows Software emulation.
	Apache	Web server (most web servers use the "LAMP" platform an acronym for Linux/Apache/mySQL /PHP-PERL-PYTHON.
Desktop	OpenOffice .org	Open office is a replacement for typical desktop-level end-user applications; it includes word processing, spreadsheets, presentations/graphics and database utility; while the system began life as proprietary software, it was made open source by its then owner Sun Microsystems in 2000. It has seen numerous full and partial updates since.
	Firefox	Internet browser developed by the Mozilla Corporation; released in 2004, it had been downloaded over 200 million times by 2006.
	Democracy Player	Desktop video player; supports wide variety of video formats.
	KDE	K Desktop Environment; provides GUI and desktop applications on Unix and variant operating systems.
	GNOME	A free-software desktop system and development platform; for Unix and variants.
	GIMP	GNU Image Manipulation Program—photo and graphics editor and authoring tool
	Inkscape	Open source graphics editing application.

Exhibit 7.8 Selected FOSS Systems

AREA	APPLICATION	NOTES
	TeX/LaTeX	Typesetting and document preparation; system was originally created in 1984; numerous editing and add-on packages are available.
	GAIM	Instant messaging desktop tool.
Enterprise applications	SugarCRM	Customer relationship management system; comes in both open source and proprietary versions; started in 2004, built on PHP and MySQL.
	Openbravo ERP	Enterprise resource planning system with core financials, procurement, inventory management, manufacturing and sales; oriented to small and mid-sized businesses.
	phpBB	Forum/discussion management system.
	eGroupWare	Multi-user web-based groupware application: email, address book, calendar, task list and other capabilities.
Database	mySQL	Popular multi-threaded, multi-user open-source database system released in 1995.
	PostgreSQL	Open-source database system started in 1986.
Development languages	FOSS scripting, development environments and compilers	Perl, PHP, Python, Ruby, Tcl, GCC

Exhibit 7.8 *Continued*

FOSS Licensing

Within the FOSS community, there is some debate on nomenclature and what constitutes "free" software. Free software movement pioneers felt that it was important to make a distinction between the price of the software (gratis) and constraints on its usage (none). In the FOSS world, to truly qualify as free, users of the software should have completely unfettered rights to use and modify it in any way they see fit. The Free Software Foundation bifurcates the software world into "free" and "proprietary" and defines free software thus:

Free software is a matter of the users' freedom to run, copy, distribute, study, change, and improve the software. More precisely, it refers to four kinds of freedom, for the users of the software:

- The freedom to run the program, for any purpose (freedom 0).
- The freedom to study how the program works, and adapt it to your needs (freedom 1). Access to the source code is a precondition for this.

- The freedom to redistribute copies so you can help your neighbor (freedom 2).
- The freedom to improve the program, and release your improvements to the public, so that the whole community benefits (freedom 3). Access to the source code is a precondition for this.

A program is free software if users have all of these freedoms. Thus, you should be free to redistribute copies, either with or without modifications, either gratis or charging a fee for distribution, to anyone anywhere. Being free to do these things means (among other things) that you do not have to ask or pay for permission.[16]

This definition for free software is similar to, but different from open source software, which can have varying restrictions on distribution or adaptation. A large number of licensing schemes exist, such as the GNU Public License (GPL), GNU Lesser Public License (LGPL), and BSD license. There are dozens of variations of free software licenses. Understanding what rights you have, and how the system may be modified and adapted for your use and under what conditions it may be transferred are important steps in considering utilization of FOSS in the enterprise.

Justifying FOSS in the Enterprise IT Department

CIOs have traditionally faced challenges in advocating FOSS adoption in the corporate enterprise. Some of this is due to incongruent corporate and FOSS cultures, as outlined previously. Other issues have arisen because of support and completeness of solution. These issues have been solved with the ever-expanding library of complete open source offerings, as outlined previously. Another hindrance is the lack of polish evident in many open source applications. A speaker at the Linux World expo in early 2006 noted "Open source has an unprofessional appearance, and the community needs to be more business savvy in order to start to make inroads in areas traditionally dominated by commercial software vendors."[17]

DILBERT. (*Source:* Scott Adams/United Media. © by Scott Adams. Distributed by United Feature Syndicate, Inc. Reprinted with permission.)

Finally, in many cases, senior executive decision makers are simply unaware of FOSS options. This is not surprising, bearing in mind that a significant portion of proprietary software company budgets are spent on advertising and customer education. FOSS, however, typically grows through grassroots, word-of-mouth efforts and articles in the industry press.

We recommend the following tips for promoting FOSS to nontechnical senior management:

- *Explain why it is free.* Business people are naturally wary of free things, believing that either the product is inferior or that there is some "catch" that they are missing. Outline the motivations of FOSS developers—a strong ethic of social contribution, desire for recognition, community spirit, and the excitement of working on innovative systems of your own choosing are all things executives can understand.

- *Defend the support model.* Much of the lifetime investment in software is in the support and enhancement labor post implementation. Executives know this. For enterprise-critical applications, explain how support will be available and the advantages of the IT team having access to the source code. Be quantitative in comparing FOSS and proprietary software labor rates, or other measures such as the number of job board resumes or postings for FOSS versus commercial technology. Demonstrate that support will be available and will not be expensive.

- *Compete on merit, logic, and ROI not ideology.* Advocates are often passionate about their judgment of the superiority of FOSS options. While enthusiasm for any recommended system is important, zealous evangelism should be saved for venues outside the boardroom. Senior decision makers are best swayed with logical arguments and return on investment.

- *Avoid sounding like a hobbyist.* Choose terminology carefully and orient it toward business language. Assume that senior executives are not conversant with the latest version of your recommended Linux variant, and haven't been closely following the latest debate on the merits of an obscure open source system detail. Stick to clear themes and broad facts and be ready with details only if asked.

- *Provide historical context.* While FOSS has only recently made enterprise inroads, it has a venerable history of over two decades of development and research. Showing the consistent lineage and development path of your recommended system will improve executive comfort level.

- *Don't talk about it, show it.* Systems recommendation discussions can be abstract; people like seeing and experiencing things. A demonstration of the FOSS system can be the turning point in approval for adoption.

FOSS Resources

There are extensive resources for FOSS on the Internet. Some of the most prominent include:

- GNU: http://www.gnu.org
- Usenix: http://www.usenix.com
- Enterprise Open Systems Journal: http://www.eosj.com
- Open Source Initiative: http://www.opensource.org
- Free Software Foundation: http://www.fsf.org
- Cathedral and the Bazaar: http://www.catb.org
- SourceForge: http://www.sourceforge.net
- Slashdot: http://slashdot.org
- Freshmeat: http://freshmeat.net
- Open Software Business Readiness Ratings: http://www.openbrr.org
- Enterprise Open Source Magazine: http://opensource.sys-con.com

Product Life-Cycle Analysis and Implications for Technology Standard Setting

An important consideration while setting technology direction is the product life cycle for the technology under consideration.

The product life cycle for most technology products, and the life-cycle relationship to cost and reliability, is fairly well understood by most technology managers. The speed at which technology life cycles move varies by product, but is generally rapid. Exhibit 7.9 shows an overview of the typical adoption and retirement cycle for a product or service, and the relationship between adoption level and cost and reliability.

Exhibit 7.9 demonstrates several key dimensions of the typical product life cycle. Most important is the usage curve that shows the aggregate total users (or units deployed) of the technology. Successful technology products, like most other products, typically move from consumer awareness and trial to adoption acceptance and repeated acquisition over time. Users become aware of a new service or product, use or test it in a limited fashion, then push to full adoption as the product is proven. Thus, the primary determinant of where the product is in its life cycle is its level of adoption as measured by number of users or deployed units.

Overall level of adoption and life-cycle stage in turn drive two other key factors. Technology costs decrease as additional volume helps vendors achieve scale economies and generate experience curve effects, which com-

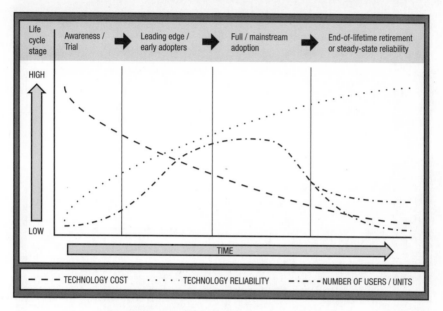

**Exhibit 7.9 Existing Technology Life Cycles and
Relationship to Cost and Reliability**

bine to lower overall costs. Costs are also driven down by the entrance of competing products and services. Likewise, reliability increases over time as the product improves with end-consumer feedback and the scale and experience efficiencies begin having a positive impact on manufacturing and delivery.

Most technology vendors are keenly aware of product life cycles and work hard to keep their customers at the appropriate portion of the curve. However, end consumers should satisfy themselves that the products or services are being purchased at the optimal point of reliability, cost, and adoption for their own purposes.

An understanding of these life-cycle fundamentals is useful when setting technology direction and standards. First, the IT manager must understand where on the life cycle all current technology resides so that appropriate investment and retirement decisions can be made for each technology component. Further, as new or replacement technology is added, it is essential to understand where in the life cycle the investment is being made to ensure the highest longevity, least cost, and best reliability and usability of the product or service.

From an internal standpoint, the technology manager (particularly a newly promoted or hired technology manager) should evaluate existing systems to understand where in the life cycle they are. Exhibit 7.10 outlines the framework for such an assessment.

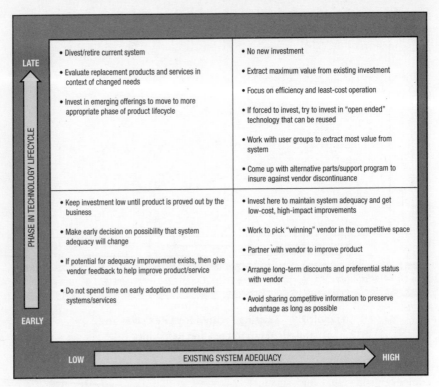

Exhibit 7.10 Existing Technology Life Cycle Assessment Framework

To determine a course of action for each piece of technology currently in place, in some cases, the manager must first group the pieces in chunks that make sense from a business standpoint (e.g., Should the CRM system be considered part of the ERP or as a separate evaluation? Should the hardware that the ERP runs on be grouped with the application or should it be considered separately?). This provides decision outcomes that make common sense and are actionable. For example, a decision that the finance system is at the end of its life cycle should be made in the context of the hardware it runs on and, potentially, the end-user hardware as well.

The appropriate grouping depends on factors such as age of the system, interdependency of systems, system functionality, level of customization, and number of instances of the system. Often, the grouping consists of a single technology, simplifying the analysis greatly. The grouping should be done on a case-by-case basis by the manager.

Next, each technology grouping should be evaluated along two key characteristics, which together suggest a course of action to take for each grouping. First, the technology grouping is evaluated for where it is in its technology life cycle. The previous exhibits and discussion on this topic should be used as a guide, but this analysis requires the exercise of some judgment on the part of the manager and may be augmented with outside information from vendors, consultants, user groups, research organizations, and industry publications. (See later section in this chapter for web sites and other sources of information for data gathering in this analysis.) The second characteristic is rating of existing adequacy. The four scenarios for grouping existing technology are:

1. *Early phase/low existing adequacy:* The IT group should minimize investment (training, support, incremental deployment) for these systems. If the system shows promise for improving, the IT group can provide input to the vendor to help the system improve in exchange for future discounting or early looks at beta versions.

2. *Late phase/low existing adequacy:* Systems in this quadrant should be targeted for priority replacement. Replacement services or products should be evaluated to enhance, upgrade, or replace the aging technology. Potential replacements should be at an earlier point in their life cycles to maximize the lifetime usefulness of the replacement system.

3. *Early phase/high existing adequacy:* Systems in this quadrant are at an ideal point for early investment and partnering with vendors. These systems have the longest "legs," and pushing these systems forward yields the highest business impact with the least cost. The IT department should bias investment dollars for existing systems toward the technologies in this quadrant and partner with the vendors to achieve preferential status, input to the product development process, and long-term discounting.

4. *Late phase/high existing adequacy:* High-adequacy, late-cycle technologies should be "farmed" by the IT department to extract best value, while minimizing new investment. The focus for these systems should be on high-efficiency, least-cost operation so that remaining budget dollars can be invested in high-impact, earlier-cycle products. In many cases, stable systems, which are at the extreme end of their life cycles, can continue to support the business indefinitely. In these instances, vendors may discontinue support for these "sunset" systems. The IT group should create alternate support plans by stocking up on parts, identifying additional sources of technology expertise, and teaming with other organizations to ensure the ability to support the technology through the extreme end of its life cycle.

Exhibit 7.11 shows real-world examples of each of the technology scenarios described and how the client company chose to approach technology and standard setting based on this framework.

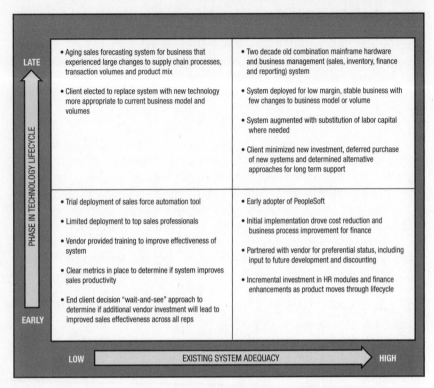

Exhibit 7.11   Client Examples of Existing Technology Assessments

The technology product or service life cycle should also be considered as technology managers make decisions about new investments or replacement of technology groups being retired. A framework similar to the existing technology approach is useful in evaluating these investments and their life-cycle position. Exhibit 7.12 shows the approach taken for new investments based on business criticality of the technology component and its relative expense.

This framework uses the level of expense and the impact on business operations to drive decision making on what point in the technology life cycle to invest. This analysis can be executed in a fashion similar to the existing technology life-cycle analysis in terms of technology groupings and data gathering.

New systems should be assessed on the left-hand axis according to impact to the business. In general, this should be measured as the systems' contribution to driving revenues, reducing costs, or achieving better control of the business. The bottom axis rates technology grouping options according to their cost, including all relevant cost elements (see costing discussion earlier in this chapter for coverage of technology group costs).

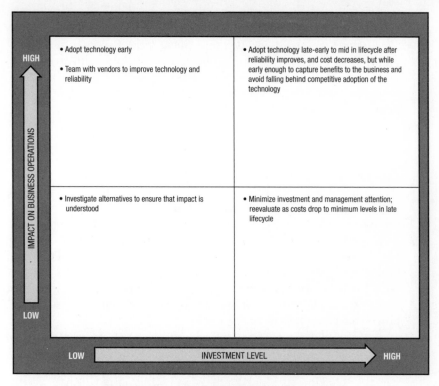

**Exhibit 7.12 New or Replacement Technology
Life Cycle Assessment Framework**

Business impact and investment level can be challenging to assess, particularly for early life-cycle products whose cost-of-ownership and business benefits may be difficult to ascertain. Again, enlisting the assistance of the business for the left-hand axis ensures the most complete analysis. As in the previous analysis, vendors, industry groups, peer companies, publications, and other related sources are useful in making the most complete estimate of cost. The company chief financial officer can also be helpful in understanding the full cost of ownership, as well as where the investment might rank compared to other alternatives for the company's capital. The scenarios for grouping new or replacement investments are:

- *Low impact on operations/low investment level:* The technology should be investigated further to ensure that business impact is properly understood. If the impact on the business operations is low and shows no potential of changing, the technology should not be adopted. Decisions to invest in this area have low risk of damage to the organization because of low costs, but can be distracting for the IT department and run the risk of large opportunity costs for IT.

- *Low impact on operations/high investment level:* Expensive technologies with little impact for the business should be avoided. As the technology moves through its life cycle, costs drop, reliability improves, and product capabilities change, the technology should be reevaluated periodically to determine if it has moved to a different quadrant.

- *High impact on operations/low investment level:* Systems, products, or services that are in the early phase of their life cycles and have no, or inadequate, counterparts in the existing system platform should be further investigated. If the new system shows promise, the IT group should invest time with the emerging system vendor. This can often mean helping the vendor further refine the product or service and serve as a testing ground for a trial implementation of the product. By helping promising vendors early, the gap in system adequacy can be filled sooner, and the organization will have stronger ties with the vendor, ensuring input to the ongoing product development as well as potential early adopter discounts. If the system indeed produces a high impact for the business with low investment, it should be adopted rapidly by the organization.

- *High impact on operations/high investment level:* Most technology choices that have a high impact for the business also require substantial investment to acquire, configure, implement, and deploy. These technologies should be investigated as they mature and followed closely by the IT department, so that adoption plans can mature as the product moves through its life cycle. Understanding the costs and business impact of the technology allow the IT department to determine the ideal inflection point that maximizes business impact and reliability while minimizing cost.

After new or replacement technologies are assessed, the mapping will suggest the appropriate point of entry in the product life cycle for the technology. Exhibit 7.13 provides specific client examples of new/replacement technology assessments.

Communicating IT Standards to the Business

After the IT standards have been determined through the previous analyses, they should be clearly documented as a preface to communicating them throughout the organization. The overall process for documenting and communicating the standards is shown in Exhibit 7.14.

HIGH

• Acquisition of wireless network cards for laptops for consultants with high travel/hoteling office arrangements

• Mobile/wireless e-mail capability for mobile sales force

• ERP, CRM system

• Finance system

• Laptop computers for traveling consultants

IMPACT ON BUSINESS OPERATIONS

• Upgrade to end user e-mail clients

• Point software solution automating manual process and supporting small portion of the business

• Large capacity redundant hardware for nonbusiness mission critical system

• High end desktop computers for data entry clerks

LOW

LOW — INVESTMENT LEVEL — **HIGH**

Exhibit 7.13   Client Examples of New or Replacement Technology Assessments

The first step after documenting the standards is to have them debated and validated internally by the IT department. This step ensures that the standards are refined, that any potential inconsistencies or surprises in the standards are identified by the team closest to the actual technology, and, most important, that the IT team feels ownership of the standards. This sense of ownership helps to ensure that every member of the IT department can explain and defend the rationale behind the standards internally and externally. The IT staff is also the first line of defense in ensuring that the overall organization adheres to the standards. The IT review process will likely be an iterative process, requiring several rounds of document refinement and review with the department or subteams.

After the IT department has signed off on the standards document, the next step is the ratification of the standards by the IT steering committee (for more on IT steering committees, see Chapter 19). This round of review ensures that the top business managers understand and support the standards. This step, review and sign-off by the senior managers, is important because it takes the standards from being something by and for IT to being a

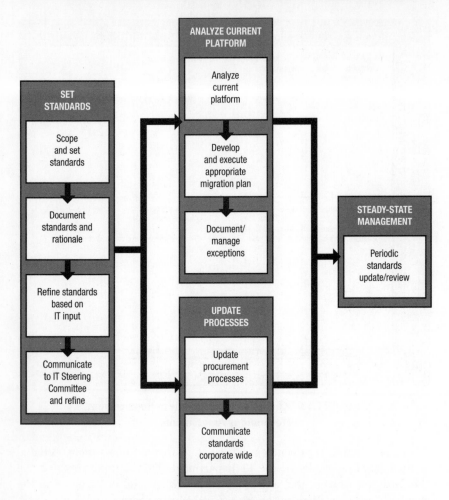

Exhibit 7.14 IT Standards Documentation, Communication, and Update Process

business decision owned by all departments. The agenda for the IT steering committee meeting should include a review of both the standards and the data gathering and analysis process used to generate the standards. Because adherence to IT standards can have such a tremendous impact on productivity of the department, the committee must understand the importance of the standard setting and the high level of due diligence that the IT department has invested in setting the standards.

As with the IT department review process, the standard setting with the IT steering committee follows an iterative process. The process may surface previously undiscovered pockets of nonstandard technology in the organization, or provoke a debate over direction. In every case, this level of engagement and review on the part of the business is healthy and results in standards that are owned by all parties.

The final step in the review should be a cover sheet approving the standards (or updates to the standards), signed by the members of the IT steering committee or members of the company senior management team. This step is more than a symbolic effort; a highly effective method for getting stakeholders to pay attention is to have documents signed by concerned parties. There is something important about the literal act of signing off on a decision that forces ambiguities and disagreements to the forefront so that they can be solved. We recommend this step for all critical IT documentation, including the standards document. After the document has been revised and approved by the steering committee, it should also be signed off by the IT department members.

Next, IT should work with all business areas dealing with procurement to ensure that IT standards are recognized and followed for all new equipment purchases or replacement purchases. In many small organizations, purchasing is handled by a small, centralized group or by the IT department itself. However, in larger organizations, finding all the points of procurement can be challenging. A critical component of migrating an organization to a homogeneous, standardized environment is finding each of these points and ensuring that the buyers understand the standards and the reasons behind them.

After the standards have been established, a migration plan for the existing technology platform should be evaluated. Technologies or platforms ending their life cycles, or at least their useful lives for the company, represent an opportunity to begin replacing the disparate technologies in a deliberate, consistent fashion. This analysis and process is covered in the Product Life-Cycle Analysis and Implications for Technology Standard Setting section in this chapter.

The final step is keeping standards "evergreen." Today's standards are not static; availability of new technologies, new business initiatives, changes in the competitive marketplace, customer and supplier demands, and technology cost changes all conspire to rapidly make obsolete any set of standards created by IT. The standards process should be revisited on a quarterly basis as part of the overall IT planning process and on an as-needed basis as well. The life-cycle analysis process discussed in this chapter can be a helpful way of prioritizing technology standards to be reviewed. In every case, keeping the IT steering committee and the business engaged and in partnership in the establishment and enforcement of the standards will create the best environment for a least-cost, high-productivity IT department.

Enforcing IT Standards

After standards have been documented and communicated with both IT and the business, the overall approach to standard enforcement should be based on creating an environment where the standards are followed because adhering to them is the easiest course of action. Making it easy for business and IT to follow standards means that the standards must have clearly documented rationale and reasoning, reasonable lead times from vendors, and clear linkages and reinforcement in the approval and procurement processes. Business users have little tolerance for IT standards that they do not understand, that appear arbitrary and capricious, or that get in their way. IT will achieve the benefits of the standards only if they work hard to create a path-of-least-resistance around the standard.

The approach to enforcement should be built on these key principles:

- Clear documentation of the standards distributed to business and IT.
- Clear documentation of the rationale/reasoning behind each standard.
- Purchase approval and procurement processes that support the standards.
- Support of the business senior management for the standards.
- Reinforcement of the standards by periodic recommunication.
- Ensuring that standards stay relevant and respond to changes in the business by frequent revisiting and updating.
- A commonsense approach to making exceptions to the standards.

Rigid enforcement of standards is generally counterproductive. Without good documentation and communication of the standards and no signoff by the business, the purchasing process can escalate into an organizational clash of wills that generally results in a double loss for the IT department: The business prevails in a nonstandard purchase, and IT tarnishes its relationship with a business unit management team. The IT department loses a chance to work with the business to solve a problem and, worse, winds up with the responsibility for supporting a chaotic, heterogeneous environment. In all cases, having the support of the CFO, the purchasing department, and the IT steering committee helps ensure much higher adherence to the standards.

When an exception is made to a standard that has been set, it should be documented, along with the rationale, presented to the IT steering committee and added to the standards document. This increases the perception in IT and with the business that the exception is truly "exceptional" and ensures that the reasons for the exception are preserved for future reference.

The same steps should be followed when IT discovers an exception after the fact. In these cases, any potential changes to cost of ownership or impacts to existing or planned projects should be documented for the IT steering committee as well. The important thing is for the IT department to remain engaged as part of the process and to work in conjunction with the business to achieve the cost-reduction and simplicity goals of the standards without the standards becoming a straitjacket.

Several categories of typical exceptions have emerged through our consulting work with clients. One type of exception is "leading-edge technology products" (read: toys) for senior executives and IT staff. These users are often the early adopters of new technologies and trial products that are interesting or have the potential for providing additional productivity. These tools can be hardware or software. In most cases, these are relatively harmless exceptions to the rule, unless they begin consuming significant amounts of IT attention for support.

Other instances of exceptions are for high-volume products where cost is a factor. For example, one of our clients had established a hardware standard of Dell desktops, laptops, and servers for his or her business units. However, one business unit (a call center) had a large number of employees performing low-intensity, repetitive computing tasks. The combination of low-intensity requirements and high volume led them to adopt a "buy cheapest" approach for their call center computers. To mitigate the support costs and overhead, broken computers were replaced with newer models and retired or repaired at leisure. The overall costs for the business were thus lowered, and a commonsense exception to the hardware standard made.

A final type of exception is one adopted because of customer requirements. For example, a large or important customer may require integration to his or her systems using a certain network protocol or type of software. In these cases, the benefits of pleasing an important customer or of conducting business transactions smoothly with a large number of customers almost always dictates an exception to the standard, or the creation of an additional standard to support the customer base over the long term.

What to Do When You Inherit a "Highly Heterogeneous Environment"

In many cases, the IT manager assuming the role at the same or a new company inherits a "highly heterogeneous environment," or "mess." It is critical for the manager to aggressively address the issues, or the chaos created by the environment will be a tar pit from which neither successful projects nor the manager's career will escape.

Changing a status-quo environment invariably also involves changing the culture in the IT department. This adds to the complexity and risk involved with what is certain to be a large challenge. Further, support from the business may be low, and a large amount of education for both the business and IT is in order. These challenges must be addressed rapidly, however, or the IT manager will die the "death of a thousand cuts." If the cultural and process hindrances cannot be overcome after significant effort, at least the manager will quickly understand that and be able to move on to greener pastures.

Throughout the process, the IT manager should work to enlist the aid of the business unit managers and the finance department/CFO. They can be helpful in understanding the history, constraints, and potential costs and benefits of standards migration. Further, having been part of the process, they will feel additional ownership of the results.

First, Understand "Why"

The first step is to develop a clear understanding of the history of the previous decisions that created the existing environment. An environment filled with exceptions generally emanates from a series of one-off decisions that, taken individually, made sense, but do not fit the overall context for the IT department. Interviewing IT staff, business users, purchasing agents, and finance team about the history behind the standards or purchasing decisions will reveal the "why" behind each of the previous technology decisions. Cases in which off-the-cuff decisions were made also become apparent. Understanding the full scope of the history helps the new manager understand where to tread lightly and where to move ahead with changes. The interviewing and data-gathering process also help the IT manager understand the potential competing agendas within and outside the IT department.

Document Everything

A technology platform covers a lot of territory (hardware, package applications, custom applications, system tools, networks, help desk); understanding the full scope requires writing. Often, the existing system documentation is at varying levels of detail, several years outdated, and available piecemeal. Building your own maps of server footprints, application inventory, and application functions will begin establishing context and ultimately serve as the overall guide for navigating out of the chaos.

Quantify the Implications

After the scope and diversity of the technology environment have been captured, the IT manager should quantify anywhere possible the operating or productivity costs of nonstandard technologies. This should be done by order of magnitude, so that the biggest impacts are identified and explored early. The IT manager should also be selective about the level of detail required; the analysis should be done top-down, sacrificing a few percentage points of accuracy for improved speed.

A typical analysis might be as simple as "having two separate financial systems supporting similar business units requires three extra full-time employees in the IT department for support. Consolidation of financial systems will generate approximately $200,000 annually in savings."

Build a Migration Plan

With the data in place and the costs of the environment quantified, the migration can be planned. The plan should be at an adequate level of detail to understand the timing, dependencies, resources, and costs involved. The plan, however, should not cover in unnecessary detail the migration of pieces that generate small benefit. Priority should be given to steps that produce the highest gain with the least risk and effort. For the top priority projects, a return-on-investment analysis based on costs and benefits should be attached. Chapter 17 discusses project planning and ROI analysis in detail.

Set Expectations

The next step is to set expectations about the IT department's ability to be effective in providing support and successfully completing projects. The discussion should be positioned as expectation setting and should be managed in a cooperative manner. It is easy (and perhaps typical) for communications of this nature to be perceived as "IT whining" by the business; therefore, the manager should have built a quantitative, data-based case for the impact of the environment before expectation setting. It is critical to build a reputation with the business users for being accountable and to avoid any sense of finger pointing, while at the same time driving home the effectiveness implications of the disparate environment.

The primary venue for setting expectations is the IT steering committee, and the environment assessment and plan should be on one of the early agendas.

Finally, the manager should communicate within the IT department the implications of technology chaos and what is being done to fix it. The team will appreciate knowing there is a plan with clear goals and that the migration will allow them to work on helping the business instead of focusing on the next workaround. The IT team should also understand that while the environment may hinder productivity, they should plan their work around it and not use the environment as an excuse for missed deadlines or reduced service levels.

Execute the Plan

After the migration plan has been completed and prioritized and expectations properly set, the migration should begin. There is often a host of constraints, including cost, time, resource capacity, business requirements, and others that prevent a rapid migration. The approach, therefore, should be gradual and opportunistic. The manager should reconcile himself or herself to a slower pace of change and a part-time migration.

In a heterogeneous environment, many times the cost of migration or requirements of the business may make a standards-driven migration impractical. In these cases, the manager should at a minimum conduct a life-cycle analysis and start the standardization efforts with retiring, end-of-life-cycle equipment.

The manager should work with vendors to get the costs down and get free resources to help with the migration. If the vendor believes that the company is serious about establishing its product or service as the standard, the vendor will work hard to help with the migration. If not, this vendor may not be the appropriate vendor.

Summary

Setting IT standards is an exhaustive process that requires significant effort on the part of the IT manager and a clear understanding of the long-term benefits on the part of both IT and the business. The result is a set of standards that allows the IT department to be managed at least cost and highest productivity, and ensures that the technology platform is maintained at the life-cycle point that generates the best return on investment for the business.

Exhibit 7.15 briefly recaps the overall process discussed in this chapter. It shows the main components of standard setting, analyzing the current platform, updating procurement processes, and keeping the standards current.

Sources of Information for Assessing Technology Standards

A variety of research and information sources on which the IT manager should rely to flesh out a set of IT standards can be used. These resources provide recent information to use in performing product life-cycle analysis and in evaluating competing IT standards according to the appropriate criteria:

- *Industry-focused groups:* These are industry groups focused on specific technology areas or on the industry segment in which the organization competes; for example, ERP users groups, manufacturing industry special interest groups.
- *Technology publications/industry publications:* There are dozens of credible, independent publications focused on the technology industry.

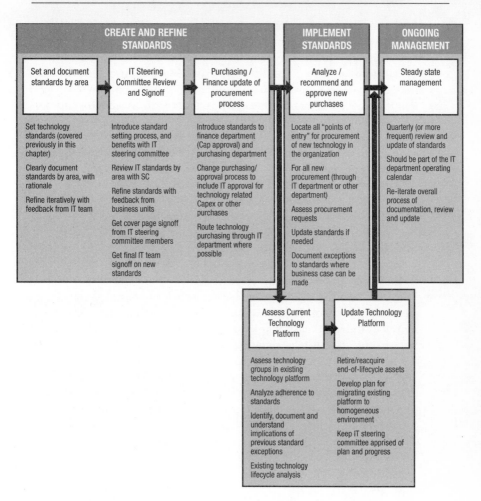

Exhibit 7.15   Start-to-Finish Overview of Standard Setting Process

InformationWeek and *CIO* magazine are among the leading publications that address enterprise-level technology management. Others include Baseline and Optimize. Publications focused on the industry in which the organization competes can also be a source of information related to technologies that apply specifically to the business; for example, mobile/handheld computing for direct-store-delivery companies.

- *Vendors:* Technology vendors are an obvious source of information on their own products, and they often will provide additional information on complementary and competing products and services. Although the content and delivery of data is naturally vendor-slanted, the data can still be valuable and help to find the blind spots of competing vendors.

- *Peer companies:* Technology managers from firms in the same industry, or firms with other organization similarity (size—revenues or employees, geography, technology platform), are an often-overlooked source of information and can be particularly valuable for their objectivity. Developing peer relationships with similar companies can provide insight into their decision-making processes and rationale, as well as jump start vendor data gathering.
- *Technology industry-focused web sites:* A search of web sites focused on enterprise-level issues in the technology business can turn up additional information. These include:

  —*CIO Magazine:* www.cio.com

  —*CMP Media:* www.techweb.com

  —*Computer Business Review:* www.cbronline.com

  —*E-Week:* www.eweek.com

  —*Tech Republic:* www.techrepublic.com

  —*Darwin* magazine: www.darwinmag.com

  —*Analyst Views:* www.analystviews.com
- *End-user web logs:* Consumer-driven web logs (blogs) dedicated to monitoring technology trends and technology companies are often a source of unbiased customer experience information, as well as insider information. It can take some effort to separate fact from opinion on the blogs, and the signal-to-noise ratio on a given topic can sometimes be low. Nevertheless, catching up on the undigested news available through these sources should be part of the IT manager's research. Particularly notable are the most popular technology-focused blogs:

  —Slashdot.org

  —Techdirt.com

  —news.com

  —techrepublic.com

  —hardocp.com

  —anandtech.com

  —zdnet.com

  Because they contain the unedited, unfiltered opinions of end users, these blogs are a highly instructive source of information.
- *Technology research firms:* There is a full-scale mature industry of research firms dedicated to assisting companies in setting technology direction and helping companies understand in which technology standard they should invest. While these sources provide high-quality analysis, their expense can often make them prohibitive, except for decisions involving large capital expenditures. Although this marketplace has dozens of players in it, some of the industry leaders include:

  —Aberdeen Group.

  —AMR Research.

  —Forrester Research.

  —Gartner Group.

—Giga Information Group.

—International Data Corp (IDC).

—META Group.

- *Financial analysts:* Most large investment banks have one or more full-time analysts covering the market in which a given vendor competes. The analysts can be an invaluable source of information about vendors and the overall marketplace, as well as a specific product. Analysts spend considerable time talking with end customers and can be an unbiased source of very up-to-date information. If the company has a banking relationship already, that can be a good place to start. If not, the analysts can often be found lurking in various forums for the product under consideration, soliciting user input.

NOTES

1. Lewis Carroll, *Alice in Wonderland*, Chapter 6, "Pig and Pepper." (New York: Penguin Putnam, 1865).
2. Attributed to Ken Olsen, http://www.quotationspage.com/quote/4679.html.
3. Wikipedia contributors, "GNU Project," *Wikipedia, The Free Encyclopedia*, http://en.wikipedia.org/wiki/GNU_project (accessed October 5, 2006).
4. The Free Software Foundation (FSF), http://www.gnu.org/philosophy/words-to-avoid.html.
5. Mark Shuttleworth, blog, http://www.markshuttleworth.com/archives/63 (accessed December, 2006).
6. Lisa Vaas, "Linux Muscling to Top," *eWeek* (April 10, 2006), p. 30.
7. IDC press release " Worldwide Server Market," (February 22, 2006), http://www.idc.com/getdoc.jsp?containerId=prUS20074406.
8. OneStat.com, "Global Usage Share" (July 9, 2006), http://www.onestat.com/html/aboutus_pressbox44-mozilla-firefox-has-slightly-increased.html.
9. Spread Firefox! http://www.spreadfirefox.com.
10. Computer Sciences Corporation, "Open Source: Open for Business" (September 2004), www.csc.com/features/2004/uploads/LEF_OPENSOURCE.pdf.
11. Jay Wrolstad, "OpenOffice.org 2.0 release delayed," *Top Tech News*, (October 13, 2005), http://www.toptechnews.com/news/OpenOffice-org-2-0-Release-Delayed/story.xhtml?story_id=03100339SMZN.
12. Open Office.org, *Market Share Analysis*, http://wiki.services.openoffice.org/wiki/Market_Share_Analysis (accessed November 2006).
13. "Openoffice.org Is Available in the Ten Most Spoken Languages in the World," (August 27, 2006), http://ooonewsletter.blogspot.com/2006/08/openofficeorg-is-available-in-ten-most.html.
14. Wikipedia contributors, "MySQL," *Wikipedia, The Free Encyclopedia*, http://en.wikipedia.org/wiki/Mysql (accessed December 18, 2006).
15. Jacques Surveyer, "MySQL Upgrade Targets Enterprise Deployments," *Intelligent Enterprise Magazine* (November 2005), p. 13.
16. The Free Software Foundation (FSF), Used with permission, http://www.gnu.org/philosophy/free-sw.html.
17. "Ponytails Hurt Open Source," Enterprise Open Source News Desk, (March 29, 2006), http://linuxworldexpo.com.au/press_detail.asp?PRID=1014.

8

IT Operations and Infrastructure

It ain't bragging if you can do it.

—Dizzy Dean[1]

You can't build a reputation on what you are going to do.

—Henry Ford[2]

IT operations refers to the *utility* services provided by the IT department and is used synonymously with the term *IT infrastructure.* IT operations cover management of hardware, network, enterprise security, communications, user administration, and e-mail systems.

This chapter outlines practices for effectively managing the IT operations department, along with key processes and responsibilities of the department. It details the measures of success and concentrates on the areas that drive user satisfaction and minimize business risk.

Approaches for effectively managing the operations area by implementing standard operating procedures (SOPs) for the most common, repetitive tasks are provided. This chapter also covers techniques for improving quality through process improvement and root cause analysis for diagnosing system problems. Additionally, it covers methods for calculating appropriate staffing levels for the operations areas.

Finally, this chapter outlines ways to raise the IT operations profile and call organizational attention to its successes. As a utility provider, the operations unit most often receives only negative attention when service outages occur, and rarely receives positive recognition. The techniques discussed in this chapter can help raise the visibility, service level, and positive feedback in the organization.

192

Why This Topic Is Important

The IT operations area is one of the two major areas that bifurcate the traditional IT department: operations and applications. The software development and applications area typically receives the predominant share of attention from users and leaders because of users' involvement in application projects and the business driving nature of e-commerce, web development, and packaged software. In addition, almost no business users are involved in IT infrastructure unless new or updated infrastructure is a prerequisite for a new application. In reality, IT operations have an equal, if not greater, impact on customer satisfaction than application development does. If e-mail or the phone system goes down for a day, the IT operations area receives considerable attention from users at all levels. If EDI or any other type of electronic commerce is suspended for even an hour during a peak business transaction period, the company could be crippled by its inability to process orders.

The IT operations group suffers from a "Cinderella" complex. When the services are running normally, no recognition is offered because satisfactory performance is the expected behavior. There are few events that can occur in the operations area in which a business unit employee would offer praise for the department because the group reaches the pinnacle goal (e.g., no disruptions, fast response time). Similar to Cinderella's stepsisters, the group is asked to "do this, do that"—a multitude of requests to fix everything from PDAs to large mainframe computer systems. A rain of criticism drowns the IT operations organization that is not customer service oriented. A service might be stable and running well for 355 days a year, but if it goes down for one day—especially during a critical period, for example, the last day of the quarter—the entire image and satisfaction of the operations group and IT department can be shattered.

Service failures can negatively and rapidly impact large numbers of customers, suppliers, and internal staff. Network outages, server failures, e-mail downtime, and broken desktop computers can significantly reduce the productivity of the entire company.

The nature of the activities managed by the operations function in IT dictates that when the operations team is executing effectively and achieving the most success, it is also invisible. This means that the IT department should engage in proactive public relations around successes in the IT operations area to generate positive recognition for a job well done and bank goodwill with business users. Outages will plague an operations group at some point, so building "goodwill" provides some buffer against the negative public relations impact an outage causes.

Besides system failures, possibly the next single largest driver of customer satisfaction is the IT help desk. The help desk interacts with business users on a constant basis. Response time, courtesy of the representative, level of follow-up and follow-through, and resolution speed are all factors that drive customer satisfaction on a daily basis. It takes only one botched request from a high-level officer in the company to tarnish the reputation of the entire IT department. Effective management of the help desk is a complex topic, and so, while clearly a part of IT operations, the topic has been reserved for Chapter 9.

Several other areas affect the user base, including user administration, capacity planning, disaster recovery, and security. Significant costs are at stake on a daily basis in the IT operations group, and it should be managed with as much rigor as the applications group typically receives.

Scope of Operations

Operations incorporates the processes and areas as shown in Exhibit 8.1. A brief description, key management practices, and critical success factors of each of these areas are provided in the following sections.

IT OPERATIONS SCOPE
• LAN/WAN infrastructure management.
• Systems management.
• Systems monitoring.
• Security management.
• Data center management.
• Messaging management (e-mail and other electronic communications).
• Telecom equipment and administration.
• Disaster recovery (business continuity and contingency planning, backup and restore procedures, test plans).
• IT asset management (configuration management, contract and software distribution management, inventory).
• Daily systems operations (cost recovery, facilities, job scheduling, output management performance, production control, quality assurance).
• Change control (change requests, analysis of impact of changes, test plans).
• Demand management (service level management, service request management, workload monitoring).
• Problem and request management (help desk; covered in the following chapter).

Exhibit 8.1   IT Operations Overview

LAN/WAN Network Infrastructure Management

LAN/WAN network infrastructure management incorporates the design, implementation, administration, and monitoring of a company's network infrastructure. Network management involves monitoring to ensure that all components of the network infrastructure (hubs, routers, switches, etc.), as well as any connections or interfaces to outside managed networks (ISPs, frame relay, etc.), are operating properly. Network monitoring can help alert the company's network administrator to any potential problems on the network and may be able to help him or her take proactive measures to avoid network downtime or outages.

LAN/WAN network infrastructure also involves management of any dial-up connections, remote access connections, or virtual private networks (VPNs) that a company may have. This helps increase company productivity and accessibility of critical information to those who may need it.

Two types of specialists are required—the local-area network specialist (LAN) and the wide-area network specialist (WAN). The LAN specialist has knowledge of network settings in the server and desktop operating systems such as Microsoft Windows XP, required networking protocols, routers, and other network equipment like switches and concentrators. They are responsible for designing and establishing the local network at the office, configuring the internal network addresses, setting up wireless routers and hubs, monitoring the network, and managing capacity.

The WAN specialist has responsibility for connecting networking hardware to frame relay, ISP/Internet, MPLS, and other telecommunications/data vendor networks. The WAN specialist should also have knowledge of network trouble-shooting devices and be adept at working with vendors. They will typically monitor the WAN using third-party tools and be in charge of connecting web servers and DNS servers to the Internet connection.

The following best practices have been found useful in managing the network:

- Standardize on a network platform. Avoid mixing multiple vendors, hardware, management systems, and protocols if possible; migrate inherited environments running on multiple platforms to a homogeneous environment over time. As outlined in Chapter 7, the benefits of standardizing will typically outweigh the cost of the transition. Running mixed technology complicates both the management of the network as well as increases the potential for hard-to-diagnose errors.

- Ensure that the network support staff employs network monitoring tools that proactively notify them in the event of a network failure or other problems. Not all data centers are staffed 24/7. The technical support personnel can be paged automatically in the event of network issues.

- Change management processes are critical in the network area. If a network configuration (e.g., domain name server, internal IP schema) is inadvertently changed, network chaos can rapidly erupt. Any changes to external IP addresses and DNS servers should be executed with the understanding that these changes take time to propagate through the Internet. Enforce policies that dictate that all changes to the network configuration are discussed and documented with appropriate roll-back procedures.

- Make sure that major changes to the network are made after hours and preferably on a Thursday or Friday evening. (Thursday night allows one business day to work with vendors to correct if there is a problem the network could be down for the entire day.)

- Beware of the streaming media usage from the Internet, as well as peer-to-peer file sharing systems. While nonbusiness usage of the Internet can be a benefit for staff, it can also monopolize the shared network bandwidth. If the usage becomes material, IT should set a policy to limit or block the use of streaming multimedia on the network. Consider configuring the firewall to selectively filter non-business protocols.

- Ensure that network personnel are not only getting the necessary training they need in the network area but are also achieving appropriate certifications. This helps you benchmark their skills and ensure that your internal resources are staying current with the latest advances in networking. Networking technology changes rapidly, and a well-planned training and development program ensures that the networking team can provide the best service for the company.

WAN specialists need a skill set similar to LAN specialists, but also need vendor management skills. Managing telecommunications vendors takes specific experience. Telecommunications vendors will often provide WAN monitoring services; these services can identify (and fix) network issues before internal monitoring. However, careful attention should be paid to service level agreements for vendor-supplied monitoring and uptime, particularly outage penalties. Further, even if the vendor is engaged to monitor uptime, the network team should perform at least rudimentary monitoring to audit vendor performance. It may be necessary to actively manage your telecommunications vendor during outages. If a connection is down, the vendor will open a trouble ticket and notify you when the problem is corrected. However, the network engineer can affect the timing of the fix and get the problem resolved earlier by calling and requesting faster turnaround time from escalating levels of management with the vendor. If the issue is severe, the team should involve a senior manager within the telecom company early on.

The network team should also revisit the telecommunications vendor selection at least every two years and create an RFP for the selection effort.

Telecommunication rates change frequently and the company can often save significant dollars through renegotiation. Additionally, revisiting the network architecture to take advantage of lower cost connectivity technologies is recommended at least once a year. Chapters 12 and 13 cover vendor selection and management extensively.

Systems Management

Systems management incorporates the monitoring and administration of a company's systems software and servers. System administrators are responsible for ensuring that systems are running at optimal levels, operating systems are continuously updated with the appropriate patches and releases, server capacity meets business needs, daily backups are performed, and servers do not have unplanned or unexpected outages. In smaller teams without a dedicated security staff, systems administrators will also be in charge of adding, changing, and deleting user information on corporate-wide systems, as well as keeping user profiles current. Systems management is important to the business because it ensures that the supporting systems are running efficiently. Proactive management and monitoring servers can help to avoid system downtime:

- To facilitate common processes, the administration team should create checklists and procedures for routine system administration processes (e.g., capacity planning, memory usage, CPU usage).
- To ensure that systems are managed consistently and that administrative procedures are adequately documented, the team should create routine procedures for as many systems administration processes as possible.
- In larger departments, system administration resources can be segmented by the technologies they support (e.g., mainframe, midrange, Windows NT, Unix, AS/400, Vax VMS, and others). Simplifying the environment and reducing the number of platforms greatly decreases support costs and simplifies the management of the unit.

PATCH MANAGEMENT. Nearly all systems software, operating systems, tools, and even embedded on-chip software needs periodic updates, or patches. These updates are used to:

- Add new capabilities.
- Provide improved performance.
- Add new interfaces with other systems.
- Fix flaws or bugs.

- Cover security holes that have emerged.
- Provide updates to data within the application that have changed (e.g., tax tables, postage rates).

Most systems vendors have a specific methodology for downloading and applying patches, usually over the Internet or through a built-in interface within the software.

The IT team must manage the application of patches to ensure that systems are running at top performance, have the maximum capabilities added and, most importantly, to prevent security threats. According to Gartner, Inc., approximately 90 percent of all security breaches are a result of patch management failures.[3] The IT team must be rigorous in evaluating and applying patches. In the worst case, a single missed patch or individual computer can compromise the entire network and create immense amounts of work for the IT department.

To perform this task, IT should consider the following practices depending on the criticality of the system being updated and the magnitude and importance of the changes in the update:

- Know when patches for all supported systems, especially business critical systems, are made available.
- Know where to obtain the patches and how to apply them.
- Understand fully the content of each patch before it is applied; conduct Internet searches or other appropriate research to determine if others have experienced problems with the patch.
- Evaluate the usefulness and applicability of the patch to the supported systems; make a determination on whether the patch should be applied.
- Evaluate any potential conflicts with customization, configurations, and interfaces that might be affected by the patch.
- When feasible, test the patch in a limited environment before launching into general production.
- Determine full inventory of machines and systems affected; implementation of a configuration management database (CMDB) will help immensely in this task.
- Apply patches in the correct sequence (often new patches will rely on previous patches).
- Adhere to normal production system change control processes when applying the patch (create backups prior to patching, apply patch during nonbusiness hours, have application vendor staff on stand-by in the event of problems).

- Have a roll-back plan for the patch to return systems to previous version if a problem emerges.

- Attempt to have all machines running a given type of software (OS, etc.) at the same patch level to keep standards in place and avoid any issues created by separate versions.

The most frequent patches will be for server and desktop operating systems. These are the most common (every computer has an OS) and complex pieces of software in the organization and are upgraded constantly. Large IT departments should evaluate investing in software that manages and executes the patch distribution process. Like monitoring and CMDB (discussed later), the software can use agents or be agentless with the same trade-offs.

CONFIGURATION MANAGEMENT. Configuration management is the process of documenting and tracking relevant information about the computing devices that are the responsibility of the IT department. This is usually done through a configuration management database (CMDB) system. Such systems automate the process of collecting, storing, reporting, and comparing IT systems configuration information.

Superficially this process seems simple. The IT department should know what sorts of equipment it has and what is running on it. In practice this is difficult. First, there is a large amount of ever-changing data to gather. Even a small organization can have dozens of servers and network devices, and hundreds of computers and peripherals. Each of these in turn has dozens of configuration items that must be tracked, which means the department is responsible for tracking thousands or even hundreds of thousands of individual data points. In addition, the configurations change periodically, meaning that the information must be updated and compared to previous configurations. This is especially challenging in large companies that have hundreds of applications, servers, and devices and tens of thousands of end-user computing devices scattered across multiple locations. Companies in flux, through turnover, business volume growth, addition of offices, or mergers-and-acquisition activity add to the complexity.

Second, in many organizations, IT does not fully control the addition of assets. Different parts of the organization may establish their own computing environments, including mobile devices, networks, servers, desktops, laptops, and production applications. This may be done outside of the officially sanctioned procurement process. While undesirable, in organizations of any real size, this is inevitable. Finding, documenting, and being part of the management of these assets is the job of the IT department. Regardless of how they were procured, IT will ultimately be held accountable for their effective and secure operation by senior management.

While the work is challenging, maintaining even a simple CMDB is important because of the large number of areas that it impacts and enables within IT management. The amount of information produced and utilized by a CMDB can be overwhelming. The IT department must make sure the linkages to impacted areas are understood and built in to the IT management process for each. The CMDB's primary purpose is to support and improve each of these activities:

- *Help desk:* Access to CMDB allows help desk to be more responsive by providing a complete blueprint of IT equipment during a problem or request call; reduces help desk call time because agent does not have to query the end-user for configuration information, and information is more accurate.

- *Problem troubleshooting and diagnosis:* Similarly, the Tier 2 and Tier 3 resources can be much more productive in diagnosing systems issues if they have detailed configuration information for the system causing trouble, as well as wider contextual information about the blueprint of the overall IT department infrastructure.

- *Security:* Providing a complete inventory of devices of all types allows comprehensive analysis and disposition of security risks posed by individual devices with open ports, unpatched security holes, open network connections, and so on; identifies rogue devices not previously known or controlled by IT that pose security risks.

- *Asset management:* Provides an actual inventory of equipment to compare with expected inventory based on purchase records and/or the finance department asset list; can feed back to finance and procurement departments for depreciation purposes as well as for updating, changing, or retiring assets.

- *Audit:* Identifies all equipment and associated configuration information for fast response to internal and external audit information requests.

- *Monitoring:* An inventory of all systems and the production processes running on them facilitates adding them to the enterprise monitoring tools that are a must for the effective IT department.

- *License compliance:* By identifying all assets, OSs and applications running, allows cross-checking versus software licenses purchased to determine compliance level.

- *Systems and network administration:* Identifies unapproved/rogue application servers on the network, determines which servers are not on latest security patch, OS, or application update; identifies proper parties affected by systems changes for notification and allows for more comprehensive change control during production updates.

- *Disaster recovery:* Only a comprehensive inventory of production systems and their configuration (particularly capacity) can allow for proper disaster recovery planning; this facilitates the creation of the properly sized and appropriately configured DR environment.
- *Insurance:* In the event of loss through damage or theft, the CMDB can provide precise information on the item in question for insurance purposes.

Key Features of an Effective CMBD. The CMDB, at a minimum, must provide a repository for storing information about each computer, device, and application. The information that must be recorded is diverse, and should include such items as disk capacity/usage/type/speed, CPU size, memory size and type, network interface hardware, peripherals, ports, network address, OS type, last reboot, up-time, patch level, application names, install dates, patch level, processes/threads/running programs, memory use (by process or application), CPU utilization (by process or application), network performance/throughput, OS-generated errors and alerts, access rights, and application interfaces.

The most effective CMDBs will automatically populate these fields from active devices on the network through an exhaustive scan that can create and update this information and more. There are two mechanisms for performing this auto-discovery process. The first utilizes a passive network scan, which examines network traffic and uses information from standard, built-in services available from the operating systems on each device. Simple Network Management Protocol (SNMP) and Windows Management Instrumentation (WMI) are the two most common passive protocols for devices reporting their configuration information.

The second method is to have small application running on each device. These software agents can provide detailed information about the system, and can be customized to report information not available via passive protocols.

Each of these methods has risks and benefits. Passive discovery tools do not require the systems administrators to know about the existence of each device in advance, and they do not require any additional effort at the individual machine level. Furthermore, they report information in a standardized format that is easy for CMDB tools to digest. Agent-based configuration discovery can give more detailed information and can do it in real-time by pushing updates to the CMDB server. However, they also use some server capacity, and introduce complexity risks (additional applications running on a machine) as well as security risks (an application that provides system information and access to an outside query). In general, passive discovery tools are an appropriate way to automatically map an unknown network and manage systems overall. Agent-based CMDB tools work best for specific business-critical application servers that need real-time, specific application information. In every case, the best CMDBs will have automatic templates for data to retrieve from devices by their role, such as database server, application server, mail server, and network management server (Exhibit 8.2).

The data discovered and managed by the CMDB should be easily searchable across device types and all fields. It should produce reports by major categories such as machine type, OS, device role. The most useful systems will store configuration information by device for given points in time, and provide reports showing any changes over time to a given device.

SERVER VIRTUALIZATION. The number of applications and functions, and therefore servers, supported by IT usually increases over time. Server virtualization, a method of running multiple, separate operating system environments on a single piece of hardware, is an effective means for combating server sprawl.

A large number of servers is undesirable. There is a large incremental (and rapidly depreciating) capital expense for each additional piece of hardware. Each additional piece of hardware introduces an additional failure point into the environment, and increases the overall complexity of the environment making problems harder to diagnose and fix. Additional servers also take up physical space in the data center, and require additional power to run, uninterruptible power availability and air conditioning to cool. Each server will also have its own CPU, memory, and storage resources that, because they are fragmented, may be underutilized.

Many applications work best when operating in their own operating system environment (and therefore not competing with other applications for operating system resources). IT departments have been willing to suffer the cost and complexity of additional hardware to gain the benefits of a simple application environment on each individual server. The result in many data centers is a large number of servers, all running at low capacities.

Server virtualization systems allow a given server to create multiple, stand-alone environments. Each application enjoys its own separate environment, the number of servers goes down dramatically, and the servers in use are better utilized. As most IT professionals with much tenure will remember, the server virtualization concept and benefits closely mirror those of mainframe OSs—server virtualization is therefore not a new concept, simply a new application of an old idea.

The typical server consolidation project will result in hundreds of servers drawing down to dozens (Exhibit 8.3).

The primary benefits of server virtualization are clear—fewer servers produce less heat, use less electricity, and take up less expensive data center space. Solving these problems in the data center has become increasingly important as hardware densities increase due to the deployment of smaller and smaller physical servers. The cooling and power needs of large numbers of

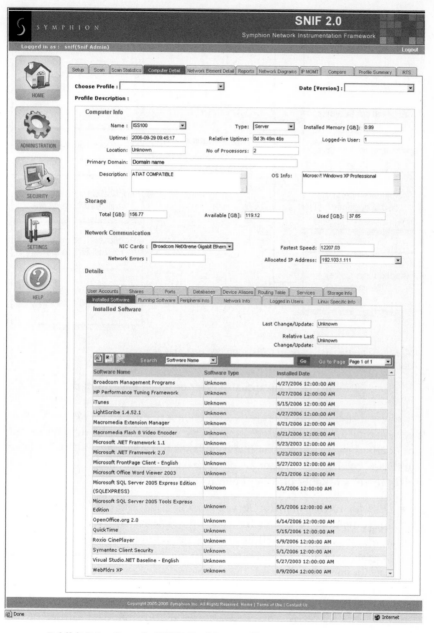

Exhibit 8.2 Sample CMDB Tool Screen (*Source:* CMDB Tool Screen courtesy of Symphion, www.symphion.com.)

Capacity = aggregate usage of CPU, memory, disk and network
Assumes all application servers above are of roughly equal configuration

Exhibit 8.3   Conceptual Server Consolidation Approach

densely packed servers are costly and complex. Further, fewer servers reduces overall IT infrastructure complexity and reduces the number of failure points. Finally, server consolidation takes full advantage of the hardware purchased by the organization by eliminating fractional usage.

There are a number of other benefits as well:

- *Disaster recovery:* After server consolidation, there will usually be an ample number of spares for creating a disaster recovery environment; in every case, there will be fewer servers (and therefore one-time and ongoing expense) required to create and manage a hot, warm, or cold backup environment.
- *Business continuity:* With the right hardware configuration (shared disk storage), most virtual OS management systems provide tools for swapping the virtual environment to another physical hardware box; this capability allows for rapid recovery in the event of primary server hardware failures.
- *Capacity management:* The ability to swap environments from physical server to physical server allows IT departments to easily provide additional memory or CPU capacity to specific environments.

- *Rapid deployment:* New applications can be deployed rapidly by eliminating the usual hardware order and setup lead time.
- *Portability:* In the event that hardware must be relocated, the server number reduction simplifies the task.

While the benefits of server consolidation are clear, there are some points of caution:

- The primary server must be sufficiently robust (and therefore expensive).
- Many of the environment management benefits (moving environments from server to server) are dependent on separate, shared disk storage to be accessed by all the servers.
- For environments running on a single physical server, there may be bottleneck contention of common physical resources (ports, specialized hardware devices, disk storage).
- Some applications are not good candidates for virtualization given their specific requirements (constant access to all hardware, high transaction volume, known code deficiencies, etc.).
- Many third-party vendors will not support their application running in a virtualized environment.
- Tier 1 to 3 troubleshooting more difficult because of higher potential for subtle problems; for example, diagnosing hardware problems that affect all environments, versus application problems that only affect a single environment.
- Multiple environment management tools are still immature; need ability to mass change multiple environments simultaneously versus logging in to each one.
- One physical hardware problem affects multiple environments and applications simultaneously.
- Production changes (mid-day reboots, maintenance windows) affect more applications and require wider communication and explanation.
- Introduces additional licensing complexity; application and OS license structures may not account for virtualized environments and will need to be renegotiated or restructured.
- Consolidation project may require additional one-time capital expenditure up front to capture future benefits and furthermore may accelerate depreciation on servers that are consolidated; this is an issue that should be coordinated with the CFO.

IT departments performing server virtualization at this writing will still be pioneers because only approximately 5 percent of firms have converted to this model.[4] There are a number of both commercial and FOSS options for creating and managing virtualized server environments that are easy to identify and apply to a variety of commercial and FOSS operating systems.

BRANCH OFFICE SUPPORT. One final sub-discipline of systems management is the responsibility for providing systems support to branch or remote offices. This is usually a difficult proposition because of the inability to physically access the systems in question. Remote offices in a significantly different time zone, or with challenging local requirements (access to power, network, technology, skilled labor) add to the burden.

The IT team must take care of a few basics to reduce this load. First, they should establish a reliable method of remote system login. As outlined in the help desk section, the ability to remotely access end-user systems and other remote hardware is critical; a number of highly reliable commercial and FOSS applications are available to solve this problem. Any application chosen should provide appropriate security for both login and the network communication between the controller and the controlled device.

Second, establish reliable local support. This will usually be an employee who has a primary role at the location, but also has interest, willingness, and ability to participate in limited IT support. The on-site employee can usually handle simple tasks that need to be completed (server reboot, equipment moves). For more sophisticated tasks that require on-site labor, identify a reliable consulting firm or contract with an agency that can supply skilled labor on short notice.

The remote office is a good place to substitute capital for labor. Minimize problems by investing in reliable infrastructure, particularly reliable power, data communication, and telecommunication services as well as quality networking equipment. Also work to minimize the total amount of equipment in the branch office.

Consolidate branch office vendors for data and telecommunications where possible, to reduce administrative friction, achieve volume discounts, and streamline the trouble-reporting process. Standardize process and technology as much as possible to minimize troubleshooting and break-fix effort. For desktop support in particular, it is usually easier to ship the desktop hard drive, or the desktop itself back and do a complete new install of the standard image software than attempt a remote fix. Recognize when data will be stored on local hard drives and make accommodations for backup (see the disaster recovery section in this chapter for a discussion of backup strategies).

Systems Monitoring

Systems monitoring is the continual evaluation of systems via systematic means to determine their operating status. Effective systems monitoring ensures that the IT department will have as much notice as possible to respond during a systems problem.

A wide variety of FOSS and commercial software is available that provide systems monitoring capabilities. These systems vary in effectiveness, features, and cost. Some important capabilities include:

- Basic "up or down" notification—shows when devices are visible to the network or not.
- Status on specific processes running on the system or on specific operational statistics such as number of users logged in, network throughput, or remaining disk capacity.
- Alerts based on thresholding for process or statistical monitors; thresholds set for green/yellow/red status; alerts should be configured to send via e-mail or text message.
- Trending and historical reporting information by device; this information is useful in establishing appropriate operating and alert thresholds as well as troubleshooting problems during outages.
- Custom defaults by server types and operating systems; production application servers, e-mail servers, database servers, telephone hardware, and networking equipment all have a variety of specific processes and statistics that should be monitored.

Exhibit 8.4 shows the output from an enterprise-class monitoring system. Ideally, monitoring takes place from outside the IT department server environment, such as from a separate co-location facility. This eliminates the possibility of a systemic failure that also affects the monitoring systems and their ability to generate alerts. A monitoring system that is part of the environment it monitors is of limited benefit.

After IT selects and implements a monitoring system, it should be integrated into the problem management system. System monitor alerts should be assigned severities as described in Chapter 9. Severe alerts for production systems problems that last over a certain threshold (minutes) should auto-generate a problem ticket on the help desk. The help desk, in turn, should have a clear escalation matrix for informing tier-2, tier-3, and IT management of issues. In this way, monitoring of systems translates into appropriate and rapid action by IT.

Systems monitoring trending information can detect anomalous network or CPU usage that indicates a security problem. It can also provide system usage trending information for disk, memory, CPU, and network capacity for effective capacity planning.

We strongly recommend the implementation of a process and statistics-level monitoring system for all production equipment. The enhanced information for troubleshooting, security management, capacity planning, advance notice

Exhibit 8.4 **Sample Systems Monitoring Tool** (*Source:* Monitoring Screen courtesy of Contego Solutions, www.contego.net.)

for problems and improvement in the perception and reality of proper control in IT make systems monitoring an essential capability for the well-run IT department.

The monitoring of employee usage of corporate technology is a separate issue addressed by policy in conjunction with corporate counsel.

Security Management

Security management includes all of the activities that protect the organizations IT assets from external and internal threats. These include user administration (adding, changing, and deleting system users), security/firewall installation support and monitoring, virus protection, intrusion detection, security policies and procedures, organization data protection, and protection of all organization systems from unauthorized use and abuse.

This function helps ensure that company assets and information are protected from unwanted intruders and unauthorized users. Security management encompasses all activities necessary to secure the network, servers, and applications. It assures computing security by authorizing and enforcing the appropriate level of access to applications and data for internal and external personnel. It is the primary user and administrator of an enterprisewide security policy. Three critical components of security management include the creation of an effective add, change, delete process for users, firewall implementation, and the rollout and management of virus protection. The primary goal is to provide easy access to systems and applications for authorized users and to allow authorized information to flow in and out of the network unimpeded, while preventing unauthorized activities and programs from taking place or running on internal systems.

The diversity of security threats, physical and electronic, and from inside and outside of the organization make security management a complex topic. The specifics of security for a given application, system, network, or device are beyond the scope of this book. Instead we cover the general principles that must be considered in establishing a security plan for the organization.

Systems security cannot be ignored; the costs of systems compromise far outweigh the investment required to implement reasonable measures. Paradoxically, the effort for small and mid-sized companies is usually the highest. While these companies may have fewer devices, locations, and employees, the equipment they do have is usually just as complex (and therefore vulnerable) as that found in a large company. An enterprise class firewall used by a small company may differ only in capacity or number from that used by a large company.

Nonstop Threats.   Both the IT environment and the nature of security threats are frequently changing. As a result, security management should be considered an ongoing process, and not something that can be definitively completed. A few factors that have made security management more challenging:

- Systems are faster, and network bandwidth usually has considerable extra capacity; as a result, system invasions may be less noticeable and the compromise can be completed more quickly.
- Easy availability of highly portable large-scale data storage (USB hard drives, flash-memory drives); this means that large amounts of data can be very easily transported physically in or out of facilities.

- More mobility of devices; end-users frequently use mobile phones, laptops, and home computers to access organization network and applications, meaning that IT security concerns must extend to those devices as well.
- Higher requirements for remote access; traveling and telecommuting end-users require remote access to systems, in turn requiring IT to provide secure options for this access.
- More interactions between internal systems and between separate companies; cross-organization interfaces between systems require architectures that facilitate the communication and limit vulnerability.

While much of the value derived from IT comes from these advances, each advance usually carries a corresponding security implication as well.

A dramatic illustration of this ever-changing security landscape comes from the CERT®, a center dedicated to Internet security at Carnegie Mellon University. The center is the first computer security incident response team. CERT® saw over a six-fold increase in reported incidents from 2000 through 2003 (Exhibit 8.5). In fact, incidents became so numerous after 2003 that CERT® began tracking other more meaningful statistics. Exhibit 8.6 shows the rapid increase in malicious programs targeted against desktops, laptops, and servers.

SECURITY BREACH CONSEQUENCES. The consequences of compromised systems can range from relatively benign to devastating. The results of an IT security problem fall into a few general areas:

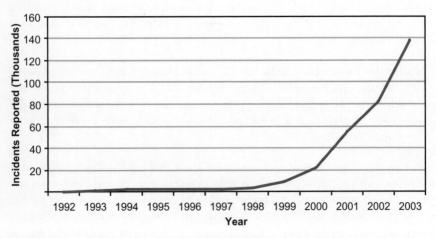

Exhibit 8.5   Security Incidents Reported to CERT®, 1992–2003 (*Source:* CERT®.)

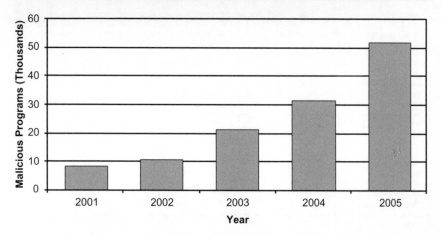

Exhibit 8.6   Number of Malicious Programs, 2001–2005
(*Source:* eWeek/Kapersky Labs.)

- Unauthorized use of resources.
- Loss of control of system.
- Loss of use of system.
- Destruction of data.
- Theft of data.
- Fraudulent use of trusted systems/masquerade.

In previous years, companies were primarily concerned with the loss of use of an asset or destruction of data. More recently, the exposure of customer information or other individual personal information has become an overwhelming concern (Exhibit 8.7). The Privacy Rights Clearinghouse estimates that over a recent 15-month period, security breaches exposed the personal information of over 55 million individuals.[5] The embarrassment, negative publicity, and legal liability that are part of the unintentional release of such data can be incredibly costly and disruptive to a firm. Examples of such events have made the headlines dozens of times; the CIO has no excuse for not protecting confidential customer data.

COMMON THREAT SOURCES.   There are a number of common IT-related security vulnerabilities in companies. Most of these are related to peripheral systems and human factors. Centralized servers are usually safe for obvious reasons: they are easy to identify, control, and protect. The security challenge comes from the constantly changing electronic perimeter, and the fact that periphery systems can support important production processes, have data that must be secured, and can compromise access to the centralized system.

Threat	Internal / External	Threat Consequences
E-mail with virus	External origination, internal use	Could infect system reading e-mail and subsequently spread thoughout entire organization.
Network virus	External	Could enter through unprotected ports, compromise whole network.
Web based virus	Internal browsing to external site	Could cause compromise on system doing browsing and subsequently affect other internal systems.
Web server attack	External to web servers	If web server is compromised hacker could gain access to other systems internal to network.
Denial of service attack	External	External services such as web, email and ftp could become unusable. If router is attacked, whole network could go down.
Network User Attack (internal employee)	Internal to anywhere	Traditional border firewalls do nothing for this attack. Internal segmentation firewalls can help contain damage.

Exhibit 8.7   Typical Threat Types (*Source:* Christopher Leidigh, Fundamental Principles of Network Security, © 2005 APC.)

Some of the most common vulnerabilities that the IT department should guard against include:

- *Attacks against end-user systems:* End-user desktops and laptops are inviting targets. They are plentiful, relative to other IT equipment, they contain considerable data and passwords, and they can provide a gateway to other corporate server-based applications and data. The sheer volume of computers with common operating platforms means that a common exploit can be launched against millions of machines before it is cured. Common threats against these targets include Trojan programs, viruses, keystroke loggers, browser redirection, spyware, malware, and rootkits. All of these types of threats are variations on a theme, in which the attacker attempts to subvert control of the system to its own ends. The challenge for IT is that the attacker only needs to compromise a single system; IT needs to provide 100 percent protection.

- *Periphery network devices:* Network attached devices such as printers, thin-client terminals, small switches, and hubs often fall under the radar for protection, and are therefore vulnerable to attacks. Any device connected to the network is a potential threat and should have a security plan.

- *Niche application exploits:* Niche applications, used by an individual department or a few users in the organization are often subject to security exploits. Organization attention is often biased toward securing enterprisewide applications (which usually have effective security to begin with). Applications from niche vendors may not have the stringent security standards of larger applications, but the application may have been granted a high level of administrative privilege on the corporate network. Compromising these systems can be easy, and may go undetected.

- *Social engineering:* Also known as pretexting, this is the attempt to compromise systems by manipulation of individuals. IT professionals have long been on guard against classic social engineering techniques such as calling end-users and pretending to be from IT to get them to reveal their password. Other classics include sifting through trash, and gaining physical access by masquerading as an employee. While these techniques are as dangerous as ever, new social engineering techniques are constantly emerging. A recent clever example involved a security audit company leaving small, inexpensive USB flash-storage devices scattered around a corporate facility. The hapless employees picked up these "gifts" and promptly plugged them into their desktop computers, launching a software exploit.

- *Unauthorized/unknown platforms:* In organizations of any significant size, invariably unauthorized applications will be deployed by various departments. Because they are not part of the overall IT architecture, these servers and systems are unpatched, unmonitored, and vulnerable to attack.

- *Data theft:* Customer personal and business data is an increasingly valuable commodity to thieves seeking to exploit identity theft. Business-to-consumer companies are at particular risk to be targeted. The business consequences for customer data theft are devastating. Over 20 U.S. states have legislation that requires notification of customers in a reasonable amount of time.[6] Companies doing business with residents of other states may be subject to the regulations of those state. For example, California SB1386 requires public disclosure of security breaches exposing information of CA residents.

- *Insider threats:* Most IT threat management is focused on eliminating outside threats; however, insiders (employees, vendors, other trusted parties) can pose an intentional or inadvertent threat. IT must take reasonable precautions against insider compromise of systems and data.

- *Fuzzy network perimeters:* Traditionally, networks could be controlled by ensuring physical control. Systems now have ready availability outside the physical boundaries of the company, via mobile devices and laptops with access to the corporate network. Further, the network can be extended inadvertently by end-users by simply adding a wireless network hub that broadcasts beyond the walls of the organization.

- *New technology:* New technologies deployed can create unanticipated security risks; for example, voice-over-IP (VOIP) requires special security considerations not previously needed.

COMMONSENSE IT SECURITY PRECAUTIONS. There are a number of commonsense and technical precautions that the IT department should take. While most IT departments regard the odds of a security beach as remote, the damage that can be done is enormous and all reasonable steps must be taken. There is little defense left to IT departments that suffer a breach while ignoring easy-to-implement actions, such as:

- *Implement full suite of standard protection:* The CIO should be educated regarding the standard threats facing IT departments and the common techniques to avoid them (antivirus, antispam, malware management, firewalls, systems threat monitoring, intrusion detection, etc.). Tools to manage these threats are commonly available in both commercial and FOSS licensing. The IT department should ensure that a security plan is in place for all devices—desktops, laptops, servers, network equipment, and mobile systems.
- *Build multiple layers of defense:* Building a hardened secure network perimeter is insufficient. Experts recommend building multiple defenses: for example, use of firewalls to protect the network from external threats, and additional server-level and application-level protection in the event the firewall is defeated.
- *Ensure physical security:* Secure IT physical environment appropriately, particularly the data center (if on-site) and all IT equipment rooms throughout the facility. Remote facilities should have adequate security as well; at a minimum, door locks on all IT equipment closets. The section on Data Center Management in this chapter has additional information on physical security for IT assets.
- *Shred printed information:* All potentially sensitive information on paper must be shredded; IT should contract with a shredding service and place locked disposal bins at convenient spots throughout the IT department.
- *Implement reasonable password management and policies:* End-users typically like easy-to-remember and therefore insecure passwords. Implement password policies that require reasonably secure passwords (e.g., mix of upper and lower case, some non-alphabetic characters required), and periodically expire passwords. Enlist end-users to aid in security through education of password sharing risks. Cultivate a culture of accountability/responsibility for passwords. Find ways to help users remember password; if end-users find password rules too onerous they will simply write their passwords down and stick the note to their display for anyone to see.
- *Build appropriate authentication methods:* Systems authentication rigor should correspond to risk. For users logging in from an internal network device, a secure password may suffice. For users logging in

from outside the network, additional verification may be needed. Identity verification methods range from passwords to physical tokens (swipe cards, RFID tags) to biometric identification. Use single sign-on technology when and where possible. This simplifies user administration, end-user experience, and reduces the potential for error in setting user security privileges.

- *Use automatic discovery tools:* Use network device interrogation tools to identify all devices on the network. Periodic auto-scans of the network should be compared to previous results to identify rogue (and potentially dangerous or insecure) servers, desktops, and devices. Of particular concern are unauthorized wireless network hubs. A good CMDB tool (discussed elsewhere in this chapter) will have an auto-discovery scanning tool.

- *Work with niche vendors:* For niche applications deployed in the organization, meet with vendors to understand their security model. They may have a list of known weaknesses and working together will usually identify unknown issues. Use network security to cordon off niche applications when necessary, which will avoid a single application compromising the entire network.

- *Manage patches and monitoring:* As outlined elsewhere in this chapter, rigorous patch management is essential to covering known exploits in systems. Monitoring systems and network usage help identify potentially compromised systems by spotting unusual trends.

- *Encrypt data, e-mail, and network traffic:* For added security, consider use of encryption for especially sensitive data, e-mail, and network traffic. A wide variety of consulting and third-party products exist for this purpose. These products provide varying levels of security at equally varying costs of computing capacity and complexity.

- *Evaluate theft protection services for mobile devices:* Mobile devices such as laptops or PDAs with network access and sensitive data are one of the most significant security risks. Services that can remotely remove the data (and potentially report the missing items whereabouts) should be evaluated and deployed where appropriate.

- *Appropriate detail logging of access and events on systems:* Ensure that systems are generating the appropriate level of detailed log files to perform forensics in the event of a system breakin. For instance, data center key card access logs, database access logs, system login date/time/username logs.

- *Define and implement appropriate user security privileges:* Applications and O&I systems must be architected to provide a compartmentalized security based on role. End-user (and IT user) system privileges should be established based on their role. This will limit the damage if an end-user or IT staff account is compromised, and will minimize the risk from insider malfeasance.

- *Change vendor-default passwords:* Most systems, applications, and devices come with default passwords set by the vendor. IT must change all of these passwords, even seemingly unimportant ones such as peripherals. Any device on the network that can be subverted represents a potential threat. Individuals have shown great ingenuity in exploiting even small security holes to cause mischief.

- *Eliminate nonessential services running on systems:* Operating systems often run network services and application processes that are nonessential to the core operations of the server. These add to environment complexity and add another point of risk. They should be turned off in every configuration.

- *Set a policy for compromised equipment:* When equipment is compromised, it should be completely rebuilt. Most often it is impossible to be certain that the equipment has been resecured, and the labor to accomplish a thorough cleaning is unjustified. This is particularly true for end-user desktops and laptops that are infested with malware or viruses.

- *Dispose of equipment properly:* Equipment thrown out will often have proprietary data or security configuration information. See the asset management section of this chapter for details.

- *Educate end-users:* End-user education is a critical line of defense because their actions are one of the most common sources of security breaches. They should be educated on e-mail security (do not open suspect attachments), good Internet browsing hygiene (use caution when downloading programs from the Internet), use of good passwords, why sharing logins/computers is a risk, how to avoid social engineering efforts. Above all they should be cautioned against adding devices to the network without clearance from IT.

- *Perform periodic audits:* IT should engage a reputable outside consulting firm specifically focused on security to perform periodic audits; this helps identify vulnerabilities, quantify the cost to cover those vulnerabilities, and provide evidence of proper governance regarding security issues.

- *Evaluate outside-party security risks:* Large IT departments have a variety of other constituencies involved—outsourced service providers (labor or applications), contractors, offshore workers, and consultants to name a few. The CIO must be sure that contracts and agreements with them appropriately cover firm security concerns and nondisclosure requirements. The CIO should ask tough questions before establishing a new relationship and do the same with existing vendors.

- *Accommodate visitors:* Be aware that visitors on-site in an organization can compromise security when they are allowed free use of the network. Vendors, customers, and friends of the organization may be on site every day. Open access to the network (wireless or wired) can result in serious inadvertent or intentional security breaches. IT should make arrangements in advance for visitor network access, printing, and Internet access that do not compromise internal security arrangements.

- *Escrow system passwords:* One to two corporate officers should have access to and knowledge of all IT asset passwords and keys. This prevents the potential of the CIO or systems administrator departing with all the knowledge and presenting a potential server lockout.

PLANNING FOR DATA THEFT. As part of the disaster recovery plan, the CIO should work with the ITSC and legal counsel to build some basic plans and policies for what to do in the event of data theft. This team can help identify what sorts of data theft may occur, and what response should be made in each instance (e.g., what to do if a laptop with sensitive data is missing versus what to do in the event of a known loss of data to a network attack).

The organization should identify a public relations (PR) firm in advance with experience in such matters, or identify individuals at the company retained PR firm who will be available during such an event. The organization should also determine who the proper spokesperson will be, and under what circumstances will a data breach be made public.

Circumstances under which law enforcement will be notified and involved should also be determined. A recent FBI study found that while 25 percent of organizations notified law enforcement in the event of a data security breach, 65 percent of organizations said it was likely that they would report future cybercrimes to the FBI.[7]

Finally, the steps taken to secure systems and data must be documented in an easy-to-understand form. The IT department should also keep a log of third-party security audits undertaken. During a public data breach, this demonstrates that reasonable precautions were taken.

As with any emergency, having even a broadly defined plan in place will be invaluable during a chaotic public relations and IT emergency.

OTHER CONSIDERATIONS. The CIO, legal counsel, and the ITSC should be aware of any regulations that apply to systems and data security for the organization. A number of common U.S. regulations include:[8]

- *Sarbanes-Oxley:* Defines corporate information retention duration and content.
- *Health Insurance Portability and Accountability Act of 1996 (HIPAA):* Regulates patient healthcare information access, retention, and format.

- *Family Educational Rights and Privacy Act (FERPA):* Regulates student records' privacy.
- *Gramm-Leach-Biley Act (GLBA):* Governs customer information of financial institutions.

A helpful resource for security management comes from the Computer Security Resource Center (CSRC), part of the National Institute of Standards and Technology (NIST) Information Technology Laboratory. The CSRC mission includes raising awareness of IT vulnerabilities, researching and advising on techniques for IT security and data privacy, and developing validation programs for IT security. The CSRC provides helpful information through its series of frequent special publications that cover emerging security problems. CIOs should also look to CERT at Carnegie Mellon University, mentioned earlier in this section. Finally, the ISO 17799 standard, covered in Chapter 4 provides compliance guidelines for IT security.

Data Center Management

Data center management includes establishing and maintaining a safe and reliable physical location for the centralized equipment managed by IT. It includes selecting facilities, determining appropriate physical deployment of servers, cabling, and the equipment racks that hold them. It also encompasses ensuring proper power availability and conditioning, providing effective cooling, ventilation and environmental controls, as well as physical security and fire prevention, detection, and suppression.

Data center management is an important component of providing reliable enterprise computing services. It requires a variety of non-IT oriented skills and knowledge and is therefore an often neglected area. The responsibility for establishing and managing the data center usually falls to the IT organization, which is much more comfortable with software and systems hardware than data center management (DCM). DCM terminology is usually unfamiliar and the knowledge required is different, particularly for designing cooling, ventilation, and power subsystems. There are also numerous local, state, and national building, fire, and environmental regulations that must be incorporated into the design. These can vary considerably from site to site.

Establishing a good data center is expensive, time consuming, and difficult. There are significant one-time capital and ongoing operating expenditures. For a data center of significant size (over 5 to 8 racks), we strongly recommend an outsourced hosting solution. The company benefits from engineers with specific expertise in cooling, ventilation, power distribution, environmental management, fire suppression, physical security, code compliance, and the other diverse requirements.

Furthermore, outsourcing avoids wasted data center space, and expansion space is generally readily available. Research shows that most data centers are over designed with regard to capacity, which has significant up-front and steady-state budget impacts. Over 70 percent of data centers are under 50 percent utilized compared to their ultimate capacity.[9] In an outsourced model, the IT department can add data center capacity as it is needed. Further, as IT equipment requirements change through growth or server consolidation, the IT department avoids the laborious process of re-calculating all of the associated data center design characteristics (see Exhibit 8.8).

In every case, the CIO must understand the critical components in data center design, whether building a small equipment room (where the knowledge will help identify and be aware of any appropriate shortcuts taken), building a full-scale data center, or selecting an outsourced hosting facility. We address the key elements for effective data center management in this section, covering physical site selection, power, cooling, and ventilation, and fire prevention, detection, and suppression.

In large organizations, data center design decisions are often the joint responsibility of both the IT department and the facilities group. If primary responsibility is borne by the facilities group or other department, IT should ensure that their unique requirements are reflected in facility engineering decisions that affect power availability and condition, cooling, ventilation, and physical and fire security.

For data center management and design issues in general, and power and cooling engineering issues specifically, we strongly recommend the excellent series of whitepapers from APC (www.apc.com) and available through APC's Data Center University (www.datacenteruniversity.com). The papers are written by expert engineers with a thorough grounding in theory and practice and cover the full spectrum of relevant topics in comprehensive detail.

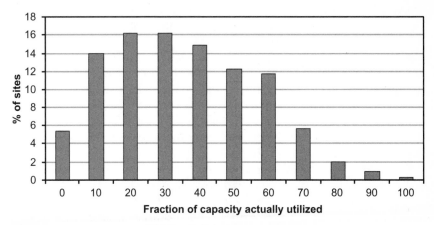

Exhibit 8.8   Ultimate Utilization Fraction of Typical Data Centers (*Source:* APC.)

PHYSICAL SITE. The first decision in establishing a data center is where it will be located. For in-house data centers, the location can be any of the corporate offices (although the best candidate is the office with the largest number of users, the best facilities, or the corporate office). If an outsourced data center is used, there are many potential geographic options.

The focus for a data center is continuity of operations. The site should be selected to minimize the impact of natural disasters such as hurricanes, tornadoes, earthquakes, floods, and severe weather. Also to be avoided are locations with likelihood of civil unrest or war. The biggest risk to data centers is from flooding; the location should be evaluated for flood risk. U.S. Federal Emergency Management Agency (FEMA) resources are helpful.

Once a geography is determined, the specific building to be used is selected. The age of the building has a major impact on its performance as a data center (ease of fire and flood protection, wiring for monitoring and security systems, availability of blueprints, ease of upgrading, etc.). Newer buildings are better, and will have the least degradation of internal plumbing, power, ventilation, and cooling infrastructure.

Prefer buildings with good proximity to transportation infrastructure and reliable power delivery. In the event of emergency evacuation of equipment or post-emergency deployment of staff, transportation is critical. Locations near emergency services (police, hospital, and especially fire) are also helpful for quick deployment. The building should also have lightning rods and appropriate electrical grounding to deal with severe weather. Finally, nearby businesses should be evaluated as both good and bad neighbors.

In addition to avoiding flood-prone areas, the building itself should be flood proofed, with walls and a roof that resist water penetration. The full evaluation of flood worthiness of a facility is beyond the scope of this book, but important. In every case, the CIO should understand the related building codes and be certain they are met or exceeded.

Within the building, the data center should be located in the core, preferably with no outside walls. If the room has an outside wall, it should not have windows. If windows are present, they should be sealed with storm shutters or otherwise secured against access and exposure to the outside. If the building is shared with other tenants, the data center should be located away from shared walls. The adjoining tenants should be evaluated for likelihood of fire or flood. The data center should also be located away from any walls containing plumbing. If should be placed away from any possible flooding from above (e.g., an upstairs kitchen or bathroom above or nearby).

The data center should be placed to provide for adequate future expansion with a minimum of equipment moves and room demolition.

Within the facility, items should be secured to withstand building shaking from seismic activity or severe weather. The team should secure everything, and avoid any loose items, top-heavy shelving, or heavy equipment that is not tied down. All equipment cabling and interconnects should have a small amount of slack to provide room for movement during seismic activity.

Physical security for the building is another consideration. The building design must support secure access policies. The IT department should determine who is allowed access, under what conditions, and to which pieces of equipment. The access control mechanism should have the appropriate balance between determining identity and cost (it is more costly to precisely determine identity). Options range from an open door (no determination), a keypad (need to know the number), to a key (limited distribution), a swipe card (theoretically identifies an individual), a password, to a biometric scan (fingerprint, etc. which provides total identity determination).

The building design should also avoid typical social engineering ruses such as piggybacking (waiting at the entrance for "help" with entry from an authorized user) or tailgating (following an authorized user closely to catch the door before it closes). A "mantrap" (vestibule between two doors with room for only one person) can avoid this. Finally, recording or motion-activated cameras should be deployed covering entrances and exits to the facility and the server room.

In the extreme case, the building may employ security guards. The International Foundation for Protection Officers (IFPO) *Security Supervisor Training Manual* is a good reference for the typical responsibilities of facilities security guards.

Additional security considerations that should be evaluated include:[10]

- Position the data center door in such a way that only traffic intended for the data center is near the door.
- Use steel doors and frames with solid doors instead of hollow-core doors. Make sure that hinges cannot be removed from the outside.
- Data center walls should use materials sturdier than the typical sheet rock used for interior walls. Sensors can be imbedded in the walls to detect tampering.
- The room used for the data center should not abut any outside walls.
- Allow long and clear lines of sight for any security stations or cameras within the data center.
- Make use of barriers to obstruct views of entrances and other areas of concern from the outside world. This prevents visual inspection by people who wish to study the building layout or its security measures.
- Be aware of the placement of ventilation ducts, service hatches, vents, service elevators, and other possible openings that could be used to gain access. Tamper-proof grills should be installed on all openings that exceed 12 inches in width, to prevent human entry.
- Avoid creating spaces that can be used to hide people or things. For example, the space beneath raised floors could be a hiding place. Make

sure that potential hiding places are secured and not easily noticed by someone walking through the facility.

- Install locks and door alarms to all roof access points so that security is notified immediately upon attempted access. Avoid points of entry on the roof whenever possible.

- Take note of all external plumbing, wiring, HVAC, etc. and provide appropriate protection. If left in plain sight or unprotected, these infrastructure components can be used to sabotage the facility without having to disable security measures.

- Eliminate access to internal runs of wire, plumbing, and ventilation ducts inside the facility. You may have a data center thoroughly secured, but if a person waking down a corridor can gain access to a run of power cabling or data cabling, the data center is compromised.

- Consider the placement of the data center within the building when retrofitting an existing facility or constructing a new data center within an existing structure. Avoid vulnerable locations or man-made risks. For example, avoid placing a data center underneath or adjacent to kitchen facilities, manufacturing areas with large machinery, parking lots, or any area with frequent traffic or vehicular access. Anything from kitchen fires to car bombs or traffic accidents can pose a threat.

- Protect the central security monitoring station by enclosing it with bulletproof glass.

- If the data center is housed in its own building, keep the exterior of the building plain. Do not use identifying marks such as company names or logos that would imply that a data center lies within.

- Use concrete bollards or other obstructions to prevent unwanted vehicles from getting any closer than a predetermined distance from the building.

ENVIRONMENTAL AND SECURITY MONITORING. Within the data center, the IT department may want to implement a monitoring regimen to provide security from inadvertent, accidental, and intentional physical threats. The basic threats in the data center include temperature, humidity, liquid leaks (water or coolant), personnel access, smoke or fire, and hazardous airborne contaminants.[11] There are commercially available sensors for monitoring, evaluating, and alerting staff to each of these types of threats. As with all security-oriented decisions, the design should be consistent with any governing regulations such as Sarbanes-Oxley or HIPAA.

Advanced monitoring can include rack-level sensors (rack door open, vibration sensors for equipment removal), motion sensors, glass break sensors, and video cameras with recording devices. As with systems monitoring, data center monitoring involves determining threat levels, implementing monitoring equipment, determining appropriate threshold levels for each threat monitored, and establishing alerting and escalation processes for each threat type.

EMERGENCY POWER OFF SWITCHES. An emergency power off (EPO) powers down all equipment in the data center with a single button push. EPOs can be required by a number of national regulations and local codes, most importantly National Fire Protection Association (NFPA) 70®. An EPO can be required for a facility if it qualifies as an IT space, which in turn gives other code leniency (e.g., installation of cabling under raised floors).[12] It is of particular use in an emergency because it allows firefighters to turn off all power to the room and avoid personal risk during firefighting operations. If an EPO is required or recommended in a given installation, then it brings about the obvious risks of sudden power outage for sensitive equipment and applications. If installed, it should be positioned by the door of the installation. It should be protected from accidental triggering by a cover, and carefully labeled. It can also be wired to the monitoring system to provide alerts and a date/time stamp in the event of a trigger. It is also helpful to have video camera coverage of the EPO to dissuade sabotage or unauthorized usage. EPOs should be periodically tested, preferably in a mode that does not actually impact production equipment.

POWER. The availability of adequate uninterrupted power is a clear prerequisite for data centers of any size or type. A study by the Electric Power Research Institute documented that U.S. industrial and digital firms lose over $45 billion per year due to power interruptions.[13] Nonetheless, commercial power is subject to disruptions from a large number of sources, including weather, equipment failure, traffic accidents, local construction, power consumptive neighboring firms, and even routine maintenance. After proper site selection, arranging for a highly available source of power is the next step in establishing a data center.

First, the CIO must have an understanding of the range of power consumed by the IT equipment. This is usually easy to calculate, as the power consumption for all IT equipment is specified by the manufacturer in watts. As shown in Exhibit 8.9, IT equipment accounts for about 44 percent of all power used in the data center. The sum total of all IT equipment power multiplied by 2.3 gives an approximation of total data center power consumption. The number can be reduced proportionately to account for nonessential equipment that would be powered down in the event of an emergency.

It is in the interest of IT to minimize total power consumed. A number of methods exist for reducing total data center power requirements. Old, disused systems can be retired, servers can be consolidated, and current production systems can be moved to newer energy efficient platforms. One of the most important ways to use less power is to ensure that cooling systems are not overengineered—a topic discussed later in this section. Reducing power

Power System, 15%

Lighting, 3%

IT Loads, 44%

Cooling, 38%

Exhibit 8.9   Electricity Consumption Sources in Typical Data Center (*Source:* APC.)

consumption also reduces ongoing costs directly, by lowering current power bill, and indirectly, by lowering cooling requirements for the data center. Power usage reduction has received more attention as the cost per kilowatt-hour has increased and environmental concerns have asserted themselves.

The ideal location for the data center will be in an area with ready access to reliable power. The mechanism for distributing power to the building should be evaluated. Above ground power distribution is more vulnerable to weather and other outages, but is also more quickly repaired. Below-ground power has the opposite characteristics.

To ensure power availability at all times, the facility should have available alternate sources of power. This is typically done via a combination of uninterruptible power supplies (UPS) that are usually battery based and standby generators that are natural gas, gasoline, or diesel fuel driven. UPSs are used for short-term outages (a few hours or less) while generators provide longer-term power. The economics of each option differ with the amount of run time required during an outage. UPSs require incremental batteries to provide additional time, while a generator system has a relatively high up-front fixed cost, with low incremental cost of fuel once in place.

In some cases, using a generator for standby alternate power may be infeasible. This can happen due to emissions or noise restrictions, local code compliance, ordinances, shared building infrastructure, or other local constraints. In these cases, alternative standby power options such as fuel cells or microturbines should be evaluated. These options are usually less cost-effective than generators, but can serve as reasonable stand-ins.

Depending on the total load of the data center, the economic cutover point can be as little as 15 minutes for a 12kW load or as long as 1:15 for a 2kW load.[14] The larger the total power load for the center, the more quickly an external generator becomes economical. In the extreme high load case, UPSs should simply be relied on to provide coverage for extremely short outages and generator start-up time, and the organization should rely on using generators almost immediately. For extremely small loads (less than 1kW), batteries may be adequate for as much as 7 to 12 hours.

When planning for outages, the primary decision to be made is when a cutover should be made from UPS power to generator power. Small data centers may forgo a standby generator in favor of a graceful shutdown in an extended power outage. If the center is in operation during a power outage then provision must also be made for adequate cooling as well. High-density equipment can shut down from overheat within five minutes, and even low density equipment can overheat in under one-half hour.[15]

The implementation of stand-by power subsystems can create a number of physical plant issues. For instance, UPSs use a variety of lead-acid battery types, depending on application. The battery type (vented vs. VRLA/MBC), building codes, and simple proper health and fire safety may require a specific kind of ventilation for gases given off. The IT department should consult with the material safety data sheets and facilities engineers to ensure that the proper environmental design is followed.[16]

Furthermore, in the United States, large UPS implementations may require reporting to the Environmental Protection Agency (EPA) and possibly OSHA as hazardous materials. Significant penalties (both civil and criminal) can result from failure to appropriately declare and comply with regulations relative to the hazardous materials (such as lead and sulfuric acid) that are contained in these batteries. The IT department should be aware of these regulations and make a determination of whether or not they should report. A good starting point is the white paper "Battery Technologies for Data Centers and Network Rooms: Environmental Regulations" by Stephen McCluer available from APC.

The selection and management of a stand-by generator must account for a number of factors as well. Each locale will have specific guidelines on allowable noise and vibration. Environmental agencies (the EPA in the United States) may also have regulations on the allowed emissions from the equipment. Once the equipment is selected and installed, its ongoing maintenance regimen will include engine cooling, lubrication, air and fuel filters, starter motor and battery checks.

Similarly, the appropriate stand-by generator selection will ensure that the generator is easy to use. The IT team must avoid learning generator operation fundamentals on the fly, and should have ready answers to seemingly mundane questions as:[17]

- Does the team have physical access to the generator?
- Does the staff know how to start it?
- Can the staff tell when it is on?
- Does it have indicator lights or readouts that show successful operation or the indicate the nature of any problems?
- Does it display fuel remaining or the more relevant measure, time remaining?
- Are the service logs easy to read and understand?
- Is the maintenance vendor easy to reach?
- Does the team know what kind of fuel the generator uses?
- Does the team know how to procure more fuel and refuel the generator?

Because the power generator is unlikely to see frequent use, it should be tested periodically to ensure that not only does it work, but also that the IT team understands how to operate it. The most common generator problems are related to start up. The IT team risks looking unprepared when it turns out that their costly generator is locked behind a fence to which only the facilities team has access, or when IT cannot procure additional generator fuel (or cannot find the gas tank fill lid when it does).

Conditioning the power to avoid equipment damage is another important consideration. There are a wide variety of power disturbances as defined by the IEEE such as transients, interruptions, sags, swells, waveform distortions, voltage fluctuations, and frequency variations. There are a number of UPS designs that incorporate both back-up power as well as power conditioning. These designs vary in cost, reliability, and amount of power supplied. The details of selecting the appropriate UPS and power conditioning system are outside the scope of this book. In every case, the data center must invest in both data center design and the proper equipment from a reputable vendor that will deal with all of these power problems.

The investment decision for power coverage and conditioning relative to the costs of system downtime and damage (cost benefit analysis) should be done on an ROI basis as described later in this chapter, and in Chapter 17. Every business will have a differing profile for its cost of downtime, which is the main determinant of the appropriate power availability design.

One method for quantifying the cost of outages is the revenue per employee per hour. Exhibit 8.10 has a chart detailing some of these rates, by industry.[18]

COOLING. Heat is detrimental to the operation of IT equipment. It reduces the lifespan of the computer, and those around it. It increases the odds

INDUSTRY SECTOR	REVENUE ($)/ EMPLOYEE/HOUR
Banking	130
Chemicals	194
Construction and engineering	216
Consumer products	127
Electronics	74
Energy	569
Financial institutions	1,079
Food/Beverage processing	153
Health care	142
Hospitality and travel	38
Information technology	184
Insurance	370
Manufacturing	134
Media	119
Metals/Natural resources	153
Pharmaceuticals	167
Professional services	99
Retail	244
Telecommunications	186
Transportation	107
Utilities	380
Average	205

Exhibit 8.10 Costs of Downtime by Industry (Data courtesy
APC, *Network Computing Magazine* and META Group.)

of hardware failure and can produce difficult-to-diagnose problems. Swings in temperature are also damaging to equipment; a steady temperature (and humidity) is as important as a low temperature. The need for steady, low temperatures in the DC drive specialized cooling and ventilation requirements.

Data center cooling needs have increased over time. High-powered servers and network equipment use more energy and therefore produce more heat. A trend toward server consolidation and blade servers has increased the density of equipment in the data center. Higher utilization of existing servers consumes more energy and also produces more heat.

In general, the maximum density of equipment that can be placed in a room or on a row of server racks is dictated by the available maximum cooling capacity and airflow. Low density data centers will find that hard floors and low-end air conditioning systems are adequate. However, medium-to-high-density data require sophisticated air-flow design such as perforated-tile raised floors, and server room specific air conditioning. At the high-end, there is considerable mathematical design that goes into something even as seemingly simple as the perforation style of the flooring.[19]

Cooling is not only important for keeping IT equipment functioning. Cooling consumes about 40 percent of data center power. Because of this consumption ratio, even small improvements in cooling efficiency can result in material reductions in both one-time and ongoing costs.[20]

When selecting a cooling system, IT must also evaluate future requirements and flexibility to change out pieces of the AC unit. IT equipment turnover (typically a 3 to 4 year lifespan) and low turnover in cooling equipment (a 5 to 10 year lifespan) means that cooling equipment should be modular and expandable.

One of the first tasks in sizing up cooling needs is to get to common definition of heat energy output; it is typically measured as joules, BTUs, calories, tons, or watts per unit time. One of the difficulties in determining heat loads and commensurate cooling power is this diversity of terminology. The most standard definition is a watt and most industry solutions are trending toward this usage.[21] A conversion table of common heat load measures is found in Exhibit 8.11.

GIVEN A VALUE IN	MULTIPLY BY	TO GET
BTU per hour	0.293	Watts
Watts	3.41	BTU per hour
Tons	3,530	Watts
Watts	0.000283	Tons

Exhibit 8.11 Conversions between Common Heat Load Measures (Courtesy of APC.)

The total data center heat output in watts dictates the cooling requirements for the data center, not including environmental sources such as windows, walls, and the roof, which may or may not be significant depending on the amount of sunlight or outside heat received.

IT equipment that requires 1 watt of power consumption will require 1 watt of cooling. Some nonserver items (UPS systems, power distribution systems, lighting, people) do not adhere to this rule. A helpful rule of thumb for estimating the total cooling requirements is that the overall IT heat load in watts accounts for about 70 percent of the overall cooling requirement (see Exhibit 8.12).[22] Multiplying the IT heat load by 1.3 yields the approximate required total cooling capacity. Additional cooling systems may be required to provide backup capacity.[23]

VENTILATION.   Raw cooling power is only one component of proper cooling design. Air flow within the data center has an equally important impact on cooling (Exhibit 8.13). Suboptimal ventilation will result in the purchase of expensive additional air conditioning capacity to solve overheating issues that can be easily addressed through improved air circulation. Use of this brute-force method of cooling needlessly adds to capital expenditures and ongoing power and maintenance costs. Proper air circulation makes existing cooling capacity effective.

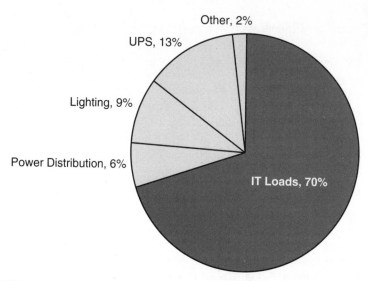

Exhibit 8.12   Data Center Thermal Output by Source (*Source:* Neil Rasmussen, "Calculating Total Coding Requirements for Data Centers," ©APC white paper rev. 2003-1 (2003), p. 6.)

Exhibit 8.13   Data Center Layout for Optimal Air Circulation

A few rules of thumb apply in properly ventilating equipment:

- Use rack configurations that promote proper air flow (blanking panels, server density): Good racks that facilitate proper airflow will require a small incremental upfront investment but provide a good return in reduced cooling capital and ongoing expense; blocked intakes, obviously constricted airflow; unused rack space (allows hot air to get back over to the intake side); if you don't have equipment, use blanking panels to cover all the unused spots in the rack.
- Organize equipment cabling; keep server cabling organized.
- Minimize dust; keep things clean, dust free (dust coats cooling devices, reduces effectiveness, and traps heat); put in air cleaner; if raised floor, check subfloor for excessive dirt/dust.
- Create hot and cold aisles: likewise, face racks/equipment the same way so that hot air coming off the back isn't blowing right into the intake of other equipment; construct overall room airflow to pull hot air away from the back of the properly oriented equipment, and blow cold air to its intakes; use additional equipment on racks to pull away hot exhaust air and move it to the return intake for the room cooling system.

- Properly position AC vents; position air conditioning supply and return vents to pull from hot aisles and supply cold aisles.
- Cables should be well organized and run to the side of the rack, rather than hanging down behind equipment where they can inhibit the flow of hot air away from the equipment; cut cables to appropriate length.
- Remove extraneous equipment from room and under floor; it also constricts airflow.
- Make sure existing airflow systems don't have gaps cracks—plenum, under floor, pipes, conduit, returns.

HUMIDITY. Data centers need carefully controlled humidity; too much moisture is damaging to equipment, too little moisture promotes dangerous static discharge. Most IT equipment has manufacturer recommended humidity requirements. The ideal level in the data center is between 35 percent and 50 percent relative humidity.

Data center humidity can be difficult to keep level because the cooling units will constantly work to remove humidity. Simply adding a separate humidifier will result in a constant balancing act between the cooling and humidifying equipment. Multiple AC units will have differing humidity levels and will work against each other.

The preferred solution for data centers is a precision cooling unit, which works differently with humidity than air conditioners designed for human comfort. Such systems are expensive, typically costing as much as 10 times more than a regular office air conditioner; however, they are designed to operate throughout the year under much higher loads and provide appropriate control over data center humidity.[24]

Finally, the data center should have a vapor barrier in its construction that prevents the exchange of water vapor from in or outside the room.

EQUIPMENT DISTRIBUTION. The average IT equipment rack consumes less than 2kW of power; high-density racks (propelled by ever-shrinking equipment sizes, blade servers, and server consolidation/virtualization) can consume 10kW or more.[25] This means special cooling needs and precise delivery of cooled air. In many cases, the power and cooling requirements for ultra-high density racks are simply more than can be fiscally or physically accommodated. In every case, the most inexpensive solution is to encourage IT to spread out the power load distribution throughout the server room to facilitate the efficient provision of proper power and cooling.

Conventional wisdom in data center management is that the primary driver of costs is square footage consumed, which in turn indicates that system consolidation reduces costs. However, due to the increasing costs of power delivery and cooling for high-density enclosures, there are diminishing marginal total-cost-of-ownership returns to equipment consolidation after a power density of 3kW per rack, and negative returns after 6 to 7kW per rack.[26] The bottom line is that server consolidation, decreasing the number of total servers used, delivers clear benefits; server compaction, co-locating multiple high-density servers within one rack within the data center, does not beyond a certain point.

For extremely high-density equipment loads, some manufacturers such as APC have a self-contained rack that incorporates all cooling, power, and fire suppression equipment.

The most up-to-date cooling strategies are geared to the individual rack and row of equipment, instead of the traditional approach of cooling the entire room. This pinpoint strategy, while requiring more up-front capital, has a lower cost of ownership and mitigates most of the airflow, cooling, power, and humidity problems with a whole-room approach. A rack or row-oriented approach requires specific equipment and design, but provides a significantly higher percentage of usable capacity from the total capacity of the air conditioning units (and commensurately lower one-time capital and ongoing electricity and maintenance costs).[27]

FIRE PREVENTION, DETECTION, AND SUPPRESSION.   A fire in the data center is catastrophic to the IT and the business, and can potentially be fatal to the organization. Fire loss statistics show that over 40 percent of businesses that are closed by a fire never reopen, and 29 percent of the businesses that do return are gone within three years.[28]

Data center fires usually start with power problems in concealed areas such as raised floors or in walls. They can also be the result of natural occurrences such as lightning, or intentional sabotage, or arson.[29]

In every case, the CIO must take a three-part approach to mitigating fire risks, through:

1. *Prevention:* Avoiding conditions conducive to fire or that create fire hazards.
2. *Detection:* Ensuring that when fires do happen they are detected rapidly before they can do material damage.
3. *Suppression:* Building the capability to minimize or stop fires once detected.

The National Fire Protection Association (NFPA, www.nfpa.org) has created a standard for data center fire protection, known as NFPA 75. The standard contains best practices for fire prevention, detection, and suppression and should be used in the data center fire mitigation design.

The CIO has a variety of fire detection mechanisms to choose from, including smoke detectors and heat and flame detectors. The most effective equipment is the smoke detector, particularly when properly placed for full coverage. A specific type of smoke detector, the Very Early Smoke Detection (VESD) device is highly sensitive and can distinguish dust particles from combustion particles.[30]

While a large number of fire suppression systems are available for general use in buildings, only a few of them are appropriate for the data center. The majority of them, while effective against fire, ruin the equipment they are intended to protect in the process. Data centers generally use total flooding fire extinguishing systems, which work by eliminating the oxygen required by fire. The system floods the room with a gaseous agent. Data centers are generally well sealed and self-contained and can hold the gas long enough to extinguish the fire. The gaseous agent has the additional advantage of infiltrating every niche and hard-to-access area in the data center. It can later be vented from the room with little long-term impact to the equipment.

In the past, various forms of Halon gas were used in these systems. With the advent of various environmental regulations, Halon is no longer used. A number of gaseous agents have replaced Halon, including carbon dioxide, Inergen (IG-541), HFC-23 (FE-13), and HFC-227ea (FM-200). Each of these agents has its own characteristics with regard to required space, effectiveness, hazard to personnel, and cost.

Finally, the data center should have an adequate supply of fire extinguishers. These are effective against fire by providing a means of stopping the blaze before it spreads. Further, the center should have ready access to pull stations as a means of triggering a facility-wide alert to any fire.

An abridged list of best practices for fire prevention, detection, and suppression, courtesy of the NFPA and APC follows:[31]

- The data center should be built far from other buildings that pose a fire threat.
- Emergency procedures should be posted on all fire alarm pull stations.
- A smoke purging system should be installed in the data center.
- All electrical panels should be free of obstruction.
- EPO buttons and fire alarm pull stations should be clearly and consistently labeled.
- Fire extinguisher locations should be clearly labeled with instructions about which type of fire the extinguisher will handle best.
- Openings in data center walls should be sealed with approved fireproof sealant.
- All data center exits should have a list of emergency phone numbers clearly posted.
- A strict no smoking policy should be implemented in the data center.
- EPO switches should not be activated by fire alarms.

- Fire dampers should be installed in all air ducts in the data center.
- Fire marshal approval should be obtained for operation of data center AC units when the fire system is alarmed. (IT equipment especially needs cooling to mitigate the heat during a fire.)
- Trash receptacles should be eliminated from the data center.
- All data center furniture should be constructed of metal (chairs may have seat cushions).
- On-site magnetic media should be stored in a fire vault with a rating of at least one hour.
- Essential supplies such as paper, disks, wire ties, and so on should be kept in completely enclosed metal cabinets.
- UL approved extension cords used to connect computer equipment should not exceed 15 feet in length.
- The use of acoustical materials such as foam, fabric, and so on for sound absorption should be eliminated.
- Do not run extension cords or other power cords under equipment, mats or other covering.
- All cables passing through the raised floor should be protected against chafing by installing edge trim around the floor opening.

Messaging Management

Messaging management includes all electronic systems used for interactive communication within the organization, not including telephones. This covers e-mail, instant messaging, and text messaging. The most important system is e-mail.

E-MAIL SYSTEM SUPPORT. E-mail system support is a unique operations area because of the heavy reliance most companies have on e-mail systems. In the past decade, e-mail has graduated from a utility application to a business mission-critical service. As such, e-mail should be managed as an enterprise application, even though responsibility typically falls to the O&I team. Keeping e-mail up and running is perceived by many organizations as a simple task; in reality, it is quite difficult.

A number of factors make e-mail management challenging, including:

- E-mail is open to receiving information from nearly anyone in the world with the ability to send an e-mail; nearly anyone can force the e-mail system to consume resources (network, CPU, storage, and memory) at will. This creates enormous security, volume, and management problems that other applications do not experience.

- E-mail is an easy target for unsolicited commercial e-mail (UCE) or spam; estimates are that nearly 60 percent to 80 percent of all e-mail communications are spam.[32]

- E-mail is an easy target for security threats such as malware, Trojans, and viruses.

- E-mail will usually have the maximum number of possible users in the organization. Most other applications only have a limited subset of organization users.

- E-mail is often used for file storage and other purposes not in its original design.

- E-mail is often the communication medium of record for disputes involving litigation, human resources, client contracts, insurance filing, and internal decisions.

- E-mail is easiest to operate centrally; yet the data must often be distributed for speed performance reasons, leading to complex architectures that attempt to solve for management and performance issues.

- In most organizations, e-mail is used 24 hours per day, 7 days per week, meaning that it must have the highest levels of availability.

- E-mail is important to traveling executives and business staff, meaning that it needs to be available remotely.

- E-mail must be accessible through any number of end-client software on a variety of devices—from mobile applications such as Blackberries to VPN connections, to web-based access from home or Internet-café computers.

- E-mail usage is difficult to govern and is subject to considerable non-business communication.

- Some industries, such as financials services, legal, or medical, have strict compliance guidelines regarding the usage, control, and retention of e-mail.

In sum, e-mail is one of the most difficult to manage enterprise applications yet its operation must be nearly perfect. Ensuring effective e-mail operations should be the top priority of the CIO and O&I team.

E-mail systems are often segregated and organized based on geography differences, so that users in a given geography can enjoy the maximum performance from the e-mail system. Each geographic location should have a support plan in place, even in a centralized IT department. The approach for e-mail support is similar to application support, which is discussed in Chapter 10. However, because of unique aspects of e-mail management—such as user administration, security, virus protection, a dedicated e-mail server, and a variety of other unique technical specifications—it is included as a major operations area in this chapter. A number of best practices have emerged in this area:

- Architect e-mail environment (server capacity, network capacity, power) to maximize reliability, availability, and security.
- Ensure that e-mail is covered in the disaster recovery plan.
- Standardize on a single e-mail application (server and client). Adopt new versions of the e-mail application on a trailing basis, to avoid any potential problems with new releases. Lagging the release of a new version by 6 to 12 months is a conservative approach to ensure most critical bugs have been addressed in maintenance releases.
- Establish systems monitoring specifically customized for e-mail systems; monitoring should cover message queues, length, number of users, storage capacity, CPU and memory usage, in and out-bound message rates; the best monitoring will periodically test the systems ability to go through the complete process of successfully sending and receiving e-mail to an external site.
- Set policies for organization of employee e-mail appropriate usage.
- Set policies for e-mail retention (how long can individuals retain e-mail, how long should the organization retain e-mail) consistent with external regulations or corporate policies; a number of industries (financial services, legal, health care) may have specific requirements on retention and content of corporate communications; if there are specific compliance issues regarding e-mail communication, ensure that the e-mail system is effectively capturing all communications; the CIO should work with legal counsel to ensure proper compliance. Considerable penalties have been levied against firms that do not follow these regulations.
- Set policies for individual e-mail box sizes (number of messages or total storage space consumed); evaluate setting limits on maximum size of individual e-mails that can be sent and/or received. Provide other easy-to-use methods for moving and storing large files—public folders, FTP access, or web-accessible file management systems for moving large files between users.
- Provide e-mail access over the Internet via a web client interface. This helps alleviate some of the remote computing issues and help desk support burdens within the company.
- For environments where secure communications are critical, consider e-mail encryption; a number of third-party systems provide this capability; e-mail traveling over public networks should not be considered secure.
- Ensure that a virus protection application is installed on the e-mail system, filtering attachments and detecting e-mail virus activity.

- Determine if e-mail tagline disclaimers are required or desirable for the firm (usually for law and financial services firms), and implement the automatic addition of these taglines to e-mail; consult with legal counsel to determine requirements and precise verbiage.

- Standardize the signature line and format for all e-mails and provide templates to end-users.

- Implement a system that will filter out unwanted e-mails (UCE or spam); the best filtering systems will produce relatively few false positives, let individual users allow e-mail from specific sites or users, provide periodic list of e-mails that have been filtered out to users so that they can ask for delivery, filter dangerous attachments, and constantly update their internal engine for scanning e-mail content; we do not recommend sender-verification systems that require users to register or need a response from the sender before delivering an e-mail message.

- Consider implementing a two-tier server architecture for e-mail—The first tier should have a dedicated hardware appliance or server that utilizes e-mail management software that accepts inbound e-mail connections and filters e-mail for virus, UCE, and other dangers as well as rejects repeated multiple connections from the same servers (denial-of-service attacks); the second tier is the e-mail server that accepts the now-clean stream of e-mail message from the first-tier system; the e-mail server on the second tier should not be accessible outside of the internal network for inbound e-mail.

- Build and periodically test rigorous back-up procedures; evaluate tools and systems for back up that allow the entire e-mail server to be restored, or a single users e-mail box.

- Perform periodic health and performance checks on the e-mail system by running diagnostic tools; a large and robust third-party marketplace exists for most major e-mail platforms.

- Periodically, reduce the e-mail storage required by evaluating the usage of the top 10 or 20 users and asking them to reduce their storage requirements.

OTHER MESSAGING.   Other messaging systems that are in use in companies should be governed by IT as well. In the past few years, instant messaging (IM) and text messaging (usually done from a mobile phone) have become popular alternatives to phone calls and e-mails. According to the Radicati Group, there are over 816 million consumer IM accounts world wide.[33]

IT must work to provide governance and support of these alternative messaging functions for two reasons. First, use of unsanctioned IM systems on the organization network can expose the organization to security risks from viruses and other attacks that come through an unguarded system. Second, many firms have policies or regulation that all internal communications be retained. Rogue systems that do not properly capture the information can expose the firm to liability.

Telecom Equipment and Administration

Telecom equipment and administration is a unique operations area because of its tight integration with outside service providers (local telcos, long-distance providers, and equipment suppliers) and its necessary geographic segregation. Each geographic location generally has its own phone system (key system, PBX, or other switch); thus, a local support plan should be in place to manage each location's telecom needs. The support and management for telecom equipment is based on size and employee footprint of each organization. In some cases, if support size is small, telecom equipment support could be handled by a network administrator or a help desk person. In a large company, or if turnover is high in an organization, more people or a separate unit of people may be needed to manage the telecom changes. Telecom support is needed in an organization to ensure that phone communication is up and available and that phone numbers in a system are accurate. For companies with large numbers of offices with small employee counts, a centralized internal support staff combined with an outside provider that can work in each local office on an as-needed basis works best:

- Telecom user administration should be tied to system user administration and to security. HR initiates a new hire and the request flows to telecom and IT security.
- Negotiate regularly with your telecom provider; often the telecom provider provides bundled services-frame relay, ISP, local telephony, and long distance, necessitating a combined team pricing and contract negotiation process.
- Understand clearly what volume commitments are being made to the telecom provider, and provide for the ability to renegotiate pricing in the event of material adverse changes to the business.
- Avoid multiple contracts with varying end dates; telecom providers will use noncontemporaneous end dates, combined with volume commitments to make canceling an agreement with them difficult. Having differing end dates for various contracts, but an overall organization commitment for dollar volume gives the telecom vendor significant negotiating power. For instance, take the simple example of a company with a single telecom vendor, providing voice and data services under two separate contracts, with differing end dates, but an overall agreement to spend a certain dollar volume with the vendor. When the voice contract expires, the data contract is still in place; unless the voice contract is renewed, the total dollar volume commitment goes down, and

the data contract pricing escalates; the only way to get back to adequate dollar volume, then, is to re-sign a telecom contract. When the data contract expires, in turn, the reverse pressure is applied. The result is an inability to ever change telecom vendors without paying a stiff cancellation fee.

VOICE OVER IP. An important new topic in this area is voice-over (VOIP). Estimates show VOIP usage rising significantly, from 16 million in 2005 to 55 million by 2009.[34] VOIP phones provide considerably improved manageability and options from traditional telecom equipment. VOIP systems integrate well with other IT systems and provide advanced features such as web conferencing, video conferencing, and teleconferencing. In fact, VOIP is seeing the highest usage in call centers, which usually lead the way in telecom innovation because they can achieve the most significant benefits from improvements. However, the technology also comes with additional network management considerations such as capacity management (it generates significant additional network traffic) and traffic prioritization (voice quality transmission over IP requires speedy and consistent delivery of network information). VOIP implementation also comes with new and emerging security vulnerabilities. While choosing and implementing a VOIP system is beyond the scope of this book, an immense amount of literature on the topic is widely available.

Disaster Recovery

Planning for disaster and subsequent recovery is widely recognized as critical to any company's technology operations. A disaster is generally described as an event that makes the continuation of normal system functions impossible. A *disaster recovery plan,* also known as a *business continuity plan,* should be in place to outline steps to take in the event of a disaster. A disaster recovery plan helps to minimize the negative effects and rapidly restore critical business functions. Businesses have a number of reasons for needing a good disaster recovery plan. The primary reason is to ensure the continuing operations of the business. Other factors include regulatory compliance, the need to protect the company's image with the public, and senior management's accountability for risk management.[35]

Nearly half of all U.S. businesses do not have a business continuity plan, while nearly 45 percent suffered an IT failure during the year.[36] An increasing percentage of companies are developing plans, but there is an even more significant relative decrease in business tolerance for downtime. Nearly 75 percent of respondents found that 24 hours was the maximum acceptable downtime, and 12 percent had zero tolerance.[37]

Disaster recovery plans are often neglected in organizations because creating a comprehensive plan is regarded as too complex. The result is a dangerous framing of disaster recovery plans as an all-or-nothing choice.

Medium and small businesses often believe that due to their size, they cannot afford a reasonable disaster recovery plan. A study by Infonetics Research found that mid-sized businesses (between 100 and 1,000 employees) suffering an IT downtime lost an average of $867,000 in revenue and experienced 140 hours of downtime.[38] A basic plan, along with measuring and monitoring tools described elsewhere in this chapter, can provide sufficient coverage to reduce such numbers dramatically.

We advocate a commonsense, practical approach to disaster recovery planning, which seeks to provide the maximum benefit for a minimized investment in capital, time, and operating expense. This means examining the systems that must be up for the business to function, and ensuring that they can be recovered in a matter of hours. A minimal disaster recovery plan should include:

- Server and necessary network hardware with duplicate configuration (does not have to be as powerful as production hardware, but OS and tools must be configured identically).
- Copies of most recent code base for all critical applications (should be installed on the back-up server and ready to go live).
- Backups of application data that can be loaded to the back-up servers.
- A plan for when and how the systems will be cut over.
- An alternative location for operating both the equipment and the business operations in the event of a disaster that renders the current location unusable.

In a poorly run IT department, the CIO will have elected to do nothing about disaster recovery, often claiming lack of budget or time. In the event of a disaster as simple as a broken pipe that floods the server room, not having purchased an inexpensive redundant server and made a good backup of application code and data is foolhardy and negligent.

The most effective means of disaster recovery is a well-designed redundant infrastructure that may help avoid or quickly recover from a disaster. With fail-safe hardware, backup network services, and redundancy of mission-critical infrastructure either on-site or in a different location, the chance of a seamless system recovery increases significantly. A disaster recovery plan, however, entails much more than redundant hardware and backup procedures. It encapsulates the steps and processes the staff will take to reinstate business functions. A good disaster recovery plan forces the IT department and the business users to think through the specific actions they would take in each anticipated event, so that during the event their focus can be on execution and recovery instead of planning and thinking.

CREATING A DISASTER RECOVERY PLAN. The disaster recovery planning process should start with anticipating the range of possible events that can cause service interruptions. These can be natural disasters such as hurricanes, earthquakes, tornadoes, or floods, or manmade such as civil unrest and terrorism, or simply electronic such as power outages, cooling system failures, system outages or external network attacks. The plan should contemplate all likely disaster scenarios and devise a specific response to each potential event. The plan should include the contingencies, as well as the cost for covering the contingency. The IT steering committee can help the team in assessing the likelihood of each event, and the cost/benefit analysis to determine how much risk the company can accept. This in turn dictates the investment the IT team makes to ensure proper recovery. Risk management and planning are detailed in Chapter 16.

The CIO and ITSC should decide which systems must have immediate availability, which can afford to be down for a limited period and which can wait indefinitely. The IT department will then design a disaster recovery architecture that provides systems availability according to priority—"hot"—immediate failure over to alternative hardware/software, "warm"—delayed failure (usually 4 to 24 hours) and cold (usually 24 to 100 hours). Each of these options has significantly differing investment implications. The CIO should also interview their applications and hardware vendors to understand possible additional options for systems recovery. Further, the CIO should evaluate the option of retaining a disaster recovery vendor. A number of vendors provide facilities, processing power, and other services on a subscription-fee or one-time basis.

The CIO and company senior management must also decide a number of nonsystem disaster recovery-related things including:

- Who has authority to declare a disaster of each type (recover systems on-site, recover systems off-site, etc.).
- How will internal communications take place (phone tree, faxes, externally hosted web site postings).
- Inventory of essential staff (business and IT) that will work in the event of a disaster.
- Identification of alternative work locations.
- Identification of telephone options for ongoing operations during the disaster.
- Notification policy and process for customers and vendors.

The IT portion of the disaster plan should focus on doing much of the anticipated work resulting from a disaster in advance. If the team knows they will need a properly configured Linux server with a certain application installed during a disaster, they should build it far ahead of time and ensure that it is easy to locate when needed. Every component of the required systems should be evaluated to determine how to minimize the amount of effort required to duplicate and recover them after the disaster strikes. This effort will likely highlight the benefits of locating the equipment in a third-party data center, which, as mentioned previously in this chapter, we strongly recommend.

For the disaster recovery plan to be truly effective it must be tested periodically. At a minimum, the test should be annual and preferably will take place every six months. There is no substitute for an actual test for fleshing out the details of the plan and identifying small but critical details that will hinder or even stall recovery. A real disaster is not the time to find that a missing patch cable, a recovery room with insufficient power, or some other trivial (or serious) issue is impeding progress. The team should furthermore conduct a post-action review, incorporate findings into the plan and report the review and changes to the IT steering committee.

The plan must be documented and copies kept both on and off site. It should also have the names and contact numbers of all organization officers and key IT department staff.

After the plan has been developed, a primary challenge for the IT team is keeping backup and production systems in sync. System configurations change, code bases are updated, applications are patched and transaction data is updated continuously. The team must take on the duty of ensuring that the backup systems are synchronized with these changes.

An IT department with good discipline in change management, asset management, configuration management, and planning will find disaster recovery planning a much easier task. Asset management and configuration management ensure that the team knows what is in place and how it operates. Change management helps ensure that production changes are mirrored to the backup systems. IT departments that are not effective in these areas will have a hard time with disaster recovery planning, and will have an even rougher time in an outage.

PERIODIC DISASTER RECOVERY PLAN REVIEW. The CIO should ensure that every six months they review and get IT steering committee approval on the following:

- Disaster recovery plan covering critical IT applications and services.
- Detailed plans, policies, and processes by disaster or event.
- Execution of testing plan to ensure that disaster recovery process is tested periodically.
- Audit of backup procedures to ensure that backup routines and processes are working correctly.

- Training plan to ensure IT and business employees are trained on the disaster recovery processes.

- Communication of the plan, costs, and associated risks to the IT steering committee, annually or twice per year.

DATA PROTECTION: IMPLEMENTING EFFECTIVE SYSTEM BACKUP SOLUTIONS. One of the most important elements of any disaster recovery plan is the ability to recover the systems, applications and data used by the organization. Having good backups is a basic discipline for IT.

For both disaster recovery and day-to-day data recovery needs, the IT department should have a method for backing up all the critical information. This includes:

- *Applications:* Code, executables, libraries, patch information, and configuration information necessary for each application to operate.

- *Data:* All data used by applications (entity, lookup, and transaction data) as well as end-user files such as spreadsheets, documents, and presentations.

- *Configurations:* For server and network hardware and operating systems; network hardware (routers, switches, firewalls).

- *Systems tools:* Information used by the IT department to execute, includes desktop images, performance tools, systems monitoring information.

All of these components should be evaluated. A separate method for each area may be required depending on the ease of access and the frequency the information changes. We refer to these in aggregate as *data* in this section.

BACKUP MEDIA. Traditionally, backups have been made to *magnetic tape.* Tape backups have the best ratio of cost to performance of any option. Because of its longevity as a backup option, tape has a very strong third-party vendor and support marketplace. While this media is cost effective, it has several drawbacks. First, information on the tape is accessed sequentially, so that any retrieval of partial information must usually scan the tape(s) in sequence until the right data is found. Tapes are significantly slower than disk (usually by a factor of 10 or more) for both read and write performance. Tape systems have more moving parts, and are therefore more prone to failure and, over time, the media can degrade due to physical wear. Simple tape systems also often require an operator to remember to change tapes daily or weekly, making them prone to human error. Usually tapes do not usually have enough capacity to hold an entire system backup; a backup will consist of a number of tape volumes that must be loaded in sequence to retrieve all data. In the event that a tape in the sequence is missing or damaged, often the entire backup can be compromised. Tapes are also easily physically portable. While this makes them easy to transport off-site for disaster recovery purposes, it also makes them vulnerable to theft and loss, exposing the company to serious data security problems. Notwithstanding these issues, tape is the prevalent means of backup for most IT departments.

Mirroring all data or keeping a compressed data backup on a second set of *disks* is another backup option. Keeping a real-time copy of data is an expensive proposition because it requires the purchase of duplicate storage but also sufficient server and network bandwidth to keep the data synchronized. Another disk-media option is to create backup volumes on disk in a compressed format, similar to tape-based backups, reducing the total amount of space required and moving processing to a nonpeak backup window. Disk backup is also appropriate for user-file data, which usually has simple backup requirements. Disk-based backups are faster and more reliable than tape-based backups, but also usually more expensive due to higher one-time media costs.

A *virtual tape library* (VTL) is a disk-based device that emulates a magnetic tape device. The emulation ensures that any existing backup processes and software can use the VTL without any changes. Because the VTL is composed of disk storage, it has all of the speed and reliability advantages of disk and avoids the many drawbacks of tape. It is a good choice in a large enterprise that currently relies on tape and wants to avoid the effort and expense of rearchitecting their entire backup regime to work with disk. The ever-decreasing cost of magnetic disk storage makes disk or VTL alternatives increasingly attractive.

Storage service providers (SSPs) have backup services that operate over the network. For a fee, usually based on storage space consumed, they provide storage space on their network that is guaranteed to be available and will be on enterprise-class systems with guaranteed reliability, performance, and availability. The services usually have the flexibility to add capacity at any time. These services can be expensive, but are a good option for small-to mid-sized businesses.

MEDIA ROTATION. Another consideration is the rotation of the media; whether a physical tape, a disk volume, or a VTL library, the team must decide how many backups to keep and how far back in time they would like to preserve. Ideally, the team can restore to any period, however this is cost-prohibitive regardless of media choice. The decision about what period of data to store should be determined by the CIO and ITSC. In low-change environments, a monthly backup, with daily backups for the past week may be sufficient. In a high-change environment, daily backups for the previous year, with weeklies going back for several years may be needed.

There are a variety of schemes for the proper rotation of tapes; one of the most common is the grandfather-father-son method. It uses three sets of tapes for daily, weekly, and monthly backups and requires 12 total sets of tapes. The first set is used for daily backups, four days per week (Monday through Thursday). The second set of tapes is used to make a weekly backup on Fridays (four times per month). The final set of tapes makes a full backup on the final day of the month, and is turned over on a periodic basis (usually three to four months of history).

Another scheme is the six-tape weekly backup This approach uses the same tape for each day of the week, and alternates a tape each Friday (which can then be taken offsite for archival). This schema minimizes the number of tape sets required, but increases tape wear and requires the IT department to remember to periodically pull Friday tapes from the rotation for a permanent archive.

INCREMENTAL AND FULL BACKUPS. Regardless of rotation, daily backups may either be incremental or full. Incrementals only backup data that has changed since the previous incremental or full backup. This approach minimizes the amount of time and capacity required for daily backups. A periodic (usually weekly) full backup ensures that the most incremental tapes required for a restore will be five or six. The disadvantage of incremental backups is that they require a sophisticated backup system for determining which data has actually changed. If the system is in error, then data will be missing. Further, a full restore takes longer because the last full backup must be restored, followed by every incremental backup versus simply restoring the last full backup.

A full backup is the most expensive in terms of media, time, and processing power. However, it ensures that all data is secure and up-to-date.

The most sophisticated backup systems take incremental backups a step further by implementing content awareness. These systems keep track of all files and data they have backed up and do not back up additional copies of the files, but instead create a pointer to the previous copy. This approach minimizes the backup time and space required. It is especially useful for end-user backups where many people may have duplicate copies of the same file (such as an operating system file, or a commonly used spreadsheet or memo). Only one copy of this is needed to serve as a backup for all users. If the file changes for an individual user, the backup system notes it, and backs up the now-customized file for the user.

COMPRESSION AND ENCRYPTION. The most sophisticated backup systems also compress data to minimize media consumption. A variety of algorithms are used for this. The effectiveness varies considerably depending on the type of data in question. These systems also provide encryption to protect against unauthorized access to the backup. Encryption and compression both come with the penalties of increased processing power required to backup the data. Further, encryption requires that the keys be available during a restore and so the disaster recovery procedure must account for availability of that information.

ARCHIVING DATA. The backup strategy may make a distinction between backup data and archival data. Backup data is operational in nature and will be used to perform partial or full restores of the system in the event of an emergency or simply a lost file. Archival data is intended to provide compliance with data retention regulations and is a static snapshot of a point in time (generally end-of-year or end-of-month). Because it is not needed for operational purposes, it may be put in slow-access, off-line storage such as a DVD or tapes. The ITSC should determine the requirements for archival.

OTHER DEVICES. While most IT backup policy is directed at centralized application and systems servers, most organization environments also consist of end-user data stored on laptops, desktops, and mobile devices. Although storage of master copies of organization information on these devices is suboptimal, it is also inevitable. Even architectures designed for information centralization have exceptions for senior executives, traveling sales staff, or legal or HR staff with high confidentiality requirements.

While it is tempting to disclaim responsibility for the data stored on these end-user devices, it is also an inevitability that IT will be given responsibility for preserving the information.

Backing up these devices is difficult because they have unpredictable network connectivity (traveling laptops) and they are usually numerous, requiring significant storage space.

Systems specifically directed at providing backup coverage for these devices are available and usually employ an agent on the computer (see the description of software agents in the CMDB section of this chapter). Intelligent agents will be sensitive to the quantity and quality of bandwidth available for backup to avoid annoying the end-user. They will perform both incremental and content-aware backups, which will minimize bandwidth and storage space usage. The nature of the end-user data in question means that such a system has a high return on investment; the loss of one senior executive's laptop can be devastating for the organization and create dozens of hours of work for IT.

IT Asset Management

IT Asset management is the tracking and inventorying of a company's hardware and software. It also includes procurement and configuration of those assets, as well as the integration of the tracking for the assets with the company's accounting systems, to ensure that the proper amount of depreciation of the original capital expenditure is being allocated to the operating budget.

There are a number of other reasons why the company needs a systematic process to keep track of IT assets, including:

- Proper stewardship of company assets means that they must be accounted for at all times.

- In the event of theft of items, a thorough record keeping system is essential to prove ownership.

- In environments with large numbers of assets (particularly mobile equipment such as laptops) a comprehensive inventory is the only way of determining if anything is missing.

- Many IT assets are leased; accurate inventory ensures that the items can be found when they are to be returned at the end of the lease.

- Reduces additional capital expenditures by identifying equipment that can be re-purposed instead of purchased new.

- Assists with software licensing compliance.

- Provides better pricing from third-party vendors whose pricing depends on number of assets in place.

- Helps ensure proper disposal of assets at their end of life.

Asset management, though tedious, is not difficult. Most important is a tight linkage to the equipment procurement process. The IT department must know whenever any equipment is added, changed, or retired. Usually asset inventories are fairly accurate for centralized equipment controlled by IT—servers, network equipment, systems software, and centralized applications. Less accurate are inventories for corporate desktop computers and the least accurate inventories are usually for field office equipment and for portable equipment such as laptop computers. The further away, the more portable and the cheaper the item, the less likely the IT inventory will be accurate.

As noted in Chapter 7, IT departments that attempt rigid control over the procurement process will often fail. The best cure for organizations that flout the process is to ensure that the process is responsive to the needs of the organization. Whether there is a procurement department that helps with process enforcement, or IT is accountable for new purchases, the process must be easy and fast for the end-user. If it is not, end-users will inevitably procure their own equipment and the asset management (and security and support) process will be compromised.

One emerging and special consideration for IT assets is in their disposal. Computer hardware, monitors, and peripherals, and laptop batteries and UPS systems in particular, often contain hazardous and/or toxic materials. In the United States, the Environmental Protection Agency has regulations and guidelines regarding the disposal of the toxic substances found in electronics. Other regulations that govern the disposal of these substances vary widely by locale. We recommend identifying and retaining a firm that specializes in disposing of equipment in an environmentally friendly and regulatory-compliant way. The CIO should also confirm through a site visit or other means that the vendor does indeed dispose of the equipment as advertised. Finally, the CIO should also consult with hardware vendors at the time of purchase on the availability of equipment that does not have special disposal requirement, or on programs the vendor may have to assist with disposal.

A second important disposal consideration is data and system security. Disposed equipment will often have unerased or easily recoverable media that will expose company data. Even network equipment may contain revealing configuration information that is useful to someone intent on a network break-in. The IT department must ensure that all user data and configuration information is irretrievably erased from any equipment before it leaves their custody. This may include the physical destruction of hard drives or other media.

A few other important considerations for IT asset management are:

- Asset management procedures are relatively simple and can be standardized easily. Any addition, change, or retirement of equipment should have a corresponding asset action. Main processes should be documented, standardized, and published and followed by the staff.

- Asset management tracking systems can be effective and streamline asset tracking. These are often a part of the overall financial system implementation, particularly in companies that have invested in large-scale ERP systems. However, an effective procurement and tracking process combined with a simple spreadsheet is a practical, low-cost alternative for small companies. Also, many help desk management systems have a built-in or optional IT asset tracking capability.

- Use bar-coded or otherwise easy-to-read asset tags to uniquely identify all equipment that belongs to the organization; the tags should also have contact information for IT.

- Create a central repository (preferably the asset management system) for storing original proof-of-purchase, date-of-purchase, and other vendor-support related materials for each asset; availability of this information will streamline help desk use of vendor support for break-fix and insurance claims for lost/damaged items.

- Create a closed loop process to ensure all assets enter and exit from one group/location. This entails centralizing the procurement of hardware and software. It also dictates that retired equipment or employee departures are handled by the same group. Periodic inventories can be executed through the use of CMDB systems and ensure that the logical recorded inventory matches with the physical inventory and location. Chapter 7 covers the integration of IT standards and corporate procurement in detail.

- Periodic reviews of the inventory with senior management level and audits of the physical inventory and the procurement process promote process adherence and identify improvement opportunities.

- Require users to sign an equipment responsibility form that states their agreement to take care of the equipment and make sure it is safely returned to the IT group, particularly for easy-to-transport equipment such as laptop computers.
- Consider implementation of systems that allow the remote erasure of end-user data for portable, easily stolen equipment such as laptops; a number of third-party vendors provide the ability to remotely erase and disable laptops when they connect to the network.
- There are clear linkages between asset management and the problem management process, configuration management, and systems monitoring.

Daily Systems Operations

Daily operations consist of functions such as batch scheduling and monitoring, managing print queues, physical print distribution, server and printer hardware maintenance, and IT facilities maintenance. Operators are generally responsible for managing all activities in the IT server room, including cabling, maintenance, uninterruptible power supply (UPS), environmental controls, fire prevention/suppression, and flooring. Operators also ensure that the daily reports and jobs are run and distribute reports to the appropriate personnel.

Change Control

Change control is the set of systematic and formalized policies and processes for introducing and implementing changes (hardware or applications) into a managed environment. Controlling any changes made to a business-mission critical production environment is essential to providing uninterrupted, quality service. Managing the process can be tricky, not only because of the inherent risk of rolling out specific technology changes, but also because of the interdependent nature of sophisticated corporate systems. For example, installing a new application on the network may affect other applications adversely. A good change control process incorporates standard tools and methodologies to introduce changes into an environment and involves a gatekeeper who controls what changes are introduced and what changes are not. Change control is important to the business because it helps to reduce the number of unwanted "bugs" or mistakes that get into a production environment. This, in turn, facilitates business continuity and reduction in system outages and downtime:

- Ensure that a change process is in place and has manager approval.
- Create change request forms that require management and end-user signoff, to ensure that senior management maintains control of the timing and content of production system changes.

- The IT team should perform an implication analysis for major application, network, hardware, operating system, or infrastructure changes, involving representation from all IT areas potentially impacted.
- Timing and implications of any changes made to systems should be widely communicated to the internal IT team, as well as the end-user community.
- Maintain a document change log that lists all changes in sequential order as well as a copy of each change request.
- Testing should occur in the testing environment not the production environment and be complete before production environment changes are authorized.
- A rollback plan should be in place for each major change made to production systems.
- Backups of application data and configurations, hardware configuration, and other critical information should be made prior to implementing any large-scale changes.
- Changes should be implemented in off hours (nights and weekends) to minimize disruption to end-user base, as well as provide additional time to roll back changes in the event of unforeseen problems.

Demand Management

Demand management consists of managing demands on operations staff capacity for projects and service from business users. The operations demand management process includes setting expectations for response times, taking action to minimize requests through continual improvements, and moving IT resources to the most highly demanded and mission-critical activities. In addition, IT management must be prepared to work with application managers to consider additional resources or capacity needed to complete a project or request.

Having a formal demand management process in place helps IT management to better account for needed resources and capacity, and ensures that capacity is flowing to the highest value activities. Understanding the metrics (e.g., number of trouble tickets per day, number of user change requests per day, and the current staff numbers) will aid in making decisions on staffing levels and setting appropriate service levels.

An important part of operations demand management is helping the business users understand the trade-off between service levels and cost. For instance, if end users are asking for faster response time from the help desk, the trade-offs for the business unit executive can be easily quantified (e.g., to reduce response time from four hours to two hours a doubling of the current staff would be required at double the annual cost). Executive management and business leaders can then decide whether they wish to increase investment in the group for the increase in response time. Setting appropriate service levels and managing risk are discussed in Chapter 16. Chapter 17 covers the demand management concept in detail, with a particular focus on application-oriented projects.

Performance Management and Service Level Agreements

Performance management of the operations area is important due to the business-critical nature of the services provided. Most companies have a high reliance on the operations infrastructures that they have created. Outage of telephones, e-mail, file, and print capabilities can cripple a company. This heavy reliance means that extremely high reliability is required of the assets managed by the operations group. To ensure that the services provided by the applications group are being properly met, the group must quantify metrics for measuring their performance. The process for establishing these metrics begins with setting objectives based on business requirements, determining targets, creating a service level agreement, and specifying the targets. Once each service level has been defined and quantified, have each operations area—the CIO and the business—sign-off on the agreed terms. After the service levels have been defined and approved, the operations team tracks and analyzes their performance and makes adjustments in each area depending on the analysis.

Each operations area should be managed on an ongoing basis according to the performance criteria summarized in the service level agreement (SLA). The SLA documents the expected tolerance levels that a particular process should operate within. For example, it may state that the help desk must respond to user requests within four hours of receiving a request. Another example is the WAN must be available and operating 99.8 percent of the time.

The SLA spells out processes, procedures, policies, and targets for each area. It dictates the metrics the IT groups will track (see Chapter 18 on IT Performance Measurement). The SLA is essentially the document that defines the acceptable ranges for each performance metric dictated by the business. Often IT managers implement a "dashboard" as a mechanism of reporting the actual performance results against those metrics in a simplified manner. The dashboard is created by selecting one to two key metrics from the SLA for each IT process. The CIO can also effectively manage each area by providing a one-page dashboard with appropriate SLA metrics.

For the SLA to be effective, it must be created in cooperation between the IT department and the business units. Operations departments that do not have an SLA established with their business users are missing a critical component to providing good service. The SLA has clear implications for problem management, monitoring, and staffing levels.

Techniques for Standardizing IT Operations

Many of the tasks in the IT operations area, while critical to the functioning of the business, are nevertheless routine and repetitive and thus can be standardized. The organization benefits from creation of standards for these tasks by improving staff productivity, work quality, and consistency, as well as reducing training costs and providing objective measurement standards for setting staffing levels and evaluating staff.

A large number of operations tasks are ideal candidates for standardization, including:

- Employee events: additions, moves, departures.
- Data backup process.
- System shutdown/start up.
- Password resets.
- Large volume print job management (invoices, payroll checks).
- Capacity management.
- System upgrades.
- Change management.
- New desktop rollout.
- First-round vendor invoice verification.

The operations manager can work with his or her team to identify the full suite of routine tasks that make ideal candidates for standardization. The team then creates standard operating procedures (SOPs) for each of the tasks inventoried. Typically, these tasks are either calendar-driven, periodic tasks (monthly closing process, nightly backup), or asynchronous, event-driven tasks (e.g., new employee administration, a security breach). As part of the operations documentation process, the key driver (period or business event) should be documented and overall volume estimated. Once an SOP for a task has been established, the team can estimate a standard amount of time for completion of the task. Then the combination of SOP labor standards, event volumes, and processing calendar can feed into the resource requirement estimating the process for the operations group. That process is covered later in this chapter.

A variety of benefits are associated with the implementation of SOPs for easily routinized tasks. These have been recognized for years in other task-oriented environments, such as manufacturing. The most significant of these include:

- *Training/staff skills:* Complete documentation of core procedures in the operations area provides a platform for rapidly and easily training new team members or team members moving between roles. Further, it facilitates easy coverage when team members are on vacation or otherwise unavailable.

- *Staff productivity:* When the subtasks needed to complete each work task are clearly understood and easily completed, overall staff productivity goes up. The amount of "scrap" time caused by each piece of work being approached on a one-off basis can be surprisingly large.

- *Work quality:* Because the SOPs are designed and tuned by "experts" who understand the tasks the best, the process and associated checklists produce the best results. By following the SOPs, less-experienced team members are able to achieve the same results as the more expert, experienced team members.

- *Measurement standards:* The idea of work standards for routine tasks has been around since the original time-and-motion studies conducted by Fredrick Taylor in the early 1900s. The same concepts have applicability to the tasks in the IT department. After SOPs have been established, the IT manager is able to set reasonable standards of effort for each task. This gives the manager another useful tool for measuring the performance of team members in the operations area, as well as tools for setting resources.

- *Operations consistency:* The implementation of standards and checklists for task completion ensures that each task is completed to the same level of detail and in a similar fashion. This improves the consistency of the results from the team member and results in improved customer satisfaction by reducing variability in service.

Exhibit 8.14 outlines the approach for identifying, documenting, and implementing standard procedures in the IT operations area. The following sections describe the processes.

Create Inventory of Routine Tasks

The first step in creating a solid set of SOPs is to identify the full inventory of potential tasks. These tasks should have the following characteristics: clearly defined scope, no large variances in work steps based on decisions that must be made by the operator, reasonable number of subtasks to complete (fewer than 20), and clearly defined inputs and outputs. Defining the inventory of potential task candidates is a relatively straightforward process that can be completed in a brainstorming session with the IT operations team. After the inventory has been identified, it should be prioritized by determining which of the task candidates is generating the highest volume of work and/or producing the highest amount of variability in work quality or performance.

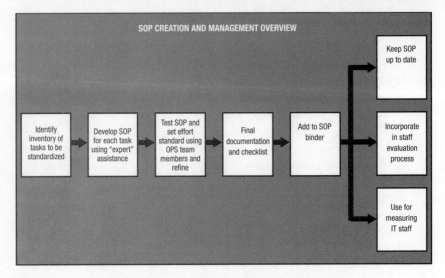

Exhibit 8.14 Standard Operating Procedure Creation and Management Overview

Develop Standard Operating Procedure for Task

For each task identified in the previous step (in priority order), the team should thoroughly document the procedure for completing the task. Each task should be broken into a reasonable number of clearly defined work steps. Each work step should have an easily understood set of inputs and outputs, and the staff member performing the task should be able to easily assess if the work step has been completed correctly before proceeding to the next work step. The ideal way to develop the standard operating procedure is to use a systems expert from the team—most often the operations manager or senior systems administrator.

Test the Standard Operating Procedure

After the preliminary process for the task has been defined, it should be tested under actual operating conditions. Ideally, the testing is done by the staff members who are ultimately responsible for completing the tasks. The testing should be supervised by the creator of the process, who is responsible for gathering feedback and refining the process until the work steps can be completed quickly and easily by the junior team members.

Set Labor Standard for Task

After the process has been tested and refined, a set of labor standards should be created. This standard should document the level of effort (time or other relevant measure) that the task should require. In some cases, the task might have several levels of effort associated with it, depending on the skill of the analyst performing the task.

Create Final Documentation and Checklist

After the process has been defined and labor standards set, the team should create the final SOP documentation. This should include at least two sections: (1) an *abstract* description of the task, which should provide context, show what inputs and outputs are expected from the overall task, and describe not only the *how* or *what* is to be done, but also explain the reasons or *whys* behind the procedure; and (2) a *checklist* to be completed by the analyst as each task is performed. The checklist items should be a sequential subtask list that can be checked off and documented.

Add to SOP Master List and Train

When the SOP is completed, it can be added to the master list of SOPs (most often, a binder organized by IT operations specialty area). The team members responsible for the task area should be trained in the final process and begin using the checklists to manage their work.

Incorporate into Staff Evaluation Processes

To help team members adhere to the SOP and to signal that the SOP is to be taken seriously and used by the team, the appraisal and review process for operations team members should be updated to reflect SOP usage as a key metric for success.

Use for Managing and Measuring Staff

After labor standards have been established, the adherence to SOPs and the team execution of the SOPs within reasonable variance of labor standards can be used as a measure for staff performance. This can be an effective tool for the operations manager and CIO to rapidly identify staff performance issues, as well as help staff members who are struggling.

Update/Refresh SOP

As with any business process, the SOPs should be periodically reviewed to ensure that they are still accurate and relevant. The SOPs should be reviewed annually at a minimum and adjusted based on new information, and the affected staff retrained.

Even more sophisticated tasks such as troubleshooting end-user service requests can be optimized. Basic troubleshooting across all IT support areas

STEP	DESCRIPTION	COMPLETED			
		1st Q	2nd Q	3rd Q	4th Q
1	Initiate SMS software discovery				
2	Prepare software inventory database and configure				
3	Hardware inventory process has been completed previous to this step (confirm)				
4	Validate servers and PCs are logged into network				
5	Examine record and mark complete				
6	Complete for each record				
7	Summarize software asset data				
8	Map actual software inventory to purchased software licenses				
9	Summarize software license gap information				
	Date Performed:				
	Performed by:				
	Signature/Initials:				

Exhibit 8.15   Example Procedure Chart

can be flowcharted to help guide the Tier 1 support team in diagnosing problems by providing a flowchart or scripted standard set of questions to follow in troubleshooting, along with solutions to the most common problems. For example, the following troubleshooting regimen might apply:

- Is the equipment on? (if no, check power).
- Is the network light lit? (if no, check network connectivity).
- Is the network light green? (if no, check cable or outlet).

This kind of troubleshooting methodology assists the Tier 1 team in making a preliminary diagnosis and even solves some of the easy-to-fix problems. Finally, the SOP can improve the productivity of the next tier support team by requiring the Tier 1 team to gather additional information (computer type, operating system configuration, etc.) before handing off the service request.

Exhibit 8.15 shows an example procedure chart.

Setting Staffing Resource Levels

Setting staffing resource levels correctly within the IT organization operations area is an important part of managing costs and achieving the committed SLAs for the end-user community. Having the appropriate resource levels means having the capacity to support both business and IT needs in a cost-effective manner.

One method for estimating the appropriate staffing levels in the operations area is based on the key driver of capacity in the function (e.g., average help desk trouble-ticket volume drives number of staff required for the help desk area). Standard staffing ratios, expressed as the number of IT staff necessary to support the area per some driver, can be determined in each area. Because the driver of activity within each operations area (e.g., systems administration, LAN/WAN support, help desk) is different, each area will have its own staffing ratio. The driver is often the number of end users, but could be other factors that drive the amount of work, such as the number of servers.

For the help desk, this ratio is typically the number of support personnel required per number of end users. A ratio of 1:100 means that one IT support staffer is required for every 100 users. If there were 1,000 users, the company would require 10 IT help desk resources. Developing a staffing ratio for each area assists in determining ongoing staffing levels as the business changes (e.g., number of computer users increases or decreases because of merger and acquisition activity or the number of systems increases because of complexity in the business). The ratio helps determine and justify increases or decreases in IT support personnel.

One way to ensure that the right resource levels are set in the department is to first gather information about past, current, and projected workloads, and then compare the information to a recommended ratio of support personnel to workload from a research specialist such as Gartner Group (Exhibit 8.16). However, the number of help desk personnel needed varies based on business

TYPE OF COMPANY	RECOMMENDED RATIO
Companies competing at the cutting edge of innovation	25:1 or 50:1
Companies who compete on full service and overall value	60:1 or 100:1
Companies competing on a thin cost margin and scalability	125:1 or 200:1
Low	12:1

Exhibit 8.16 Help Desk Support Ratios Based on Business/IT Goals

and IT goals. The ratio is influenced by use of different technologies such as remote access and end-user self-support tools and policies enforced by the IT department. Remote systems management software, for example, can increase the staff leverage within the operations support area.

The ratios include staff for all three levels of help desk support. Since the needs of each organization are different, specific company factors influence the appropriate ratio. A general guide to calculating ratios is described below. The formula considers variables in the working environment to help develop a possible ratio of end users to support staff. To use this formula, start with a base value and add or subtract numbers to come up with a specific ratio tailored to the environment:

- To compute the beginning number, the base value:
  - —If there are a variety of operating systems and no standards for hardware, the base support ratio is about 45:1.
  - —If there is a single operating system and established standards for hardware purchases, the base support ratio is about 75:1.
- Subtractions:
  - —If IT is decentralized and users are allowed to control and adjust their setting, software, and peripherals, then subtract 30:1.
  - —If support personnel must drive or fly to users, divide the support ratio by the ratio of remote users (e.g., if 500 of 1,000 users are remote, reduce the support ratio by 50%).
- Additions:
  - —If IT is centralized and user desktops are locked to eliminate user control of system settings and loading software, add 15:1.
  - —If remote control tools are used to support desktops and install software, add 20:1.
  - —If disk images and configurations are standardized, add 15:1.
  - —If a centralized help desk exists, add 15:1.

This formula provides a general guideline for determining the number of support staff needed. Additional factors affecting staffing ratios include staff attrition levels, standardization, complexity of environment, backlog of work, and required service levels.

Importance of Process Improvement and Root Cause Analysis

The *root cause* of a problem is the fundamental issue that, if corrected, prevents recurrence of the problem. In most IT operations departments, solving problems is not a point of weakness since the team is charged with problem fixes every day. However, most teams do not pursue the root cause of the recurring problems, which, if identified, can be fixed, thereby eliminating the recurring issue.

The operations area of an IT department is the most fertile ground for identifying problem root causes and solving them to reduce overall help desk staff burden. The implementation of a problem tracking system helps identify problem trends. For example, the system might identify a repetitive problem with a given brand and model of desktop computer, helping diagnose a root cause of a manufacturing defect. Often, however, IT departments are caught up in day-to-day problem resolution and do not find time to reduce their overall burden by assessing root causes and taking remedial action.

There are several reasons the root causes of systems problems are not solved:

- When problems arrive at the help desk, the issues are urgent, requiring quick thinking and action.
- The high stress of solving help desk issues can further cloud staff thinking and response.
- IT systems analysts and support personnel are well trained on the technical aspects of systems but not on problem solving and root cause analysis.

One of our clients with a struggling operations department experienced an episode highlighting the issues caused by poor root cause analysis. The client's e-mail service had ceased to work. The IT team rapidly jumped to the conclusion that the WAN link to the Internet was down. The IT department decided that the outage was the "fault" of the outside vendor providing the WAN connection. The telecom vendor providing the link opened a ticket in its system. By the time the ticket traveled through the vendor trouble-ticket system and the vendor service representative called the IT department, 90 critical minutes had passed. In the meantime, the operations staff had not performed additional diagnostics or testing while waiting for the vendor response. The vendor service representative notified the internal operations staff that the T-1 Internet link was running fine, and said that the problem must be with another component of the e-mail system. Time was wasted by a quick jump to an erroneous conclusion. The staff then hurriedly deduced that an internal router table had been modified, causing a link error. Compounding the issue, the company had no change management process in place. Critical questions such as how the table was modified, who modified it, and how the same issue could be prevented in the future were never discussed.

The operations manager can take two actions to improve the capability of the team to correct problems and minimize potential for recurrence, thereby lowering overall IT support costs in the future. First, develop a framework by which system problems must be analyzed, corrected, and documented to minimize recurrence and generate key insights. Second, train systems administrators and operators in hypothesis-driven root cause analysis.

For the purposes of diagnosis and problem solving in the infrastructure and operations area, we advocate adoption of classical root cause analysis, entailing:

- Identification of the problem associated with a particular unwanted situation.
- Identification of the elements that describe what happened in the situation (what barrier or control problems existed).
- For each barrier or control problem, identification of the management elements that permitted the problem and why they existed.
- Description of each of the problems and some brief conclusions on findings and recommendations of how to fix the problem so it does not recur.

To develop a root cause analysis framework:

- Determine the situations that are candidates for root cause analysis. Naturally, removal of the cause must save more than continuing to deal with the symptom.
- Have the operations staff create fishbone diagrams (Exhibit 8.17) to explain the root cause of issues to IT management. This ensures that staff are thinking critically about the problems.
- Long term, adopt a root cause framework for problem resolution and use it to make adjustments to the operating checklists and management procedures described earlier in the chapter.
- Have root cause analysis training as part of the ongoing education in the operations department.

In the long run, improving the root cause analysis capabilities of the operations team greatly improves the reliability, efficiency, and cost of the support provided to the organization.

Communicating Success

Customer satisfaction with IT operations can be greatly improved by communicating appropriately to the business end users. As observed earlier, the operations area provides an "invisible" service to the business; when the operations team is executing well, they go unnoticed by the business. When op-

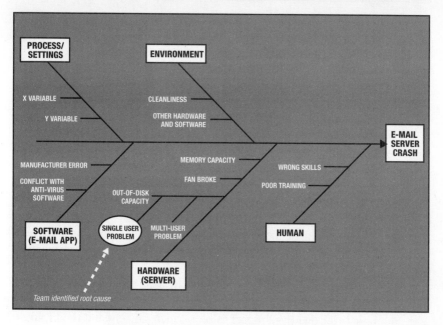

Exhibit 8.17   Conceptual Fish Bone Diagram

erations break down, the team receives negative scrutiny. This phenomenon, combined with the fact that the operations area has an enormous impact on user satisfaction, means that the IT department must proactively engage in public relations efforts to ensure that their operations efforts are properly acknowledged and appreciated by the business team. IT management should ensure that the successes of the IT department are celebrated. In cases where success is measured as service availability, the operations team can point to uptime, systems availability, or other statistics such as speed of service or overachievement of SLAs. In every case, the operations team can select factors that are of material interest to the business and publicize their performance.

There are other ways to ensure that the business users maintain an awareness (and positive perception) of IT successes. First, any major type of application or hardware rollout should have a communication plan. Users should be told when it will commence, when it will be completed, and any potential risks that could disrupt their work. Furthermore, the help desk should set users' expectations for when calls will be responded to, the target time for resolution, when the problem is fixed, and a request of acknowledgment from users.

The communication effort should be an ongoing process for the operations team. Simple efforts such as e-mail communications to the business when milestones have been achieved, or posters and signs highlighting the number of days without unplanned outages can make a difference in the business unit perception of the IT department. Communication devices that can be employed include:

- Periodic IT newsletters detailing service levels, major accomplishments, and upcoming projects relevant to users. The team should keep the newsletter concise.
- Notification of system maintenance at least 5 to 10 days in advance of maintenance. This includes network maintenance, web site maintenance, e-mail upgrades, operating system upgrades, computer hardware rollouts, and so on. Notifications should be sent out in advance of the maintenance.
- Report major project successes, infrastructure upgrades, and what benefits these will deliver to the users. Claim victory when it is achieved and communicate success regularly.
- Publish frequently asked-question lists covering the top 10 IT help desk questions regularly.
- Submit a brief one-page report to senior management and the IT steering committee on the state of infrastructure once a month (again keep it short).
- Ensure the communication between help desk personnel and users is effective. The help desk should be communicating all of the following: receipt of the trouble ticket, the commencement of work on the ticket, and an estimated time to completion. Communicate to the user every 24 hours until the problem is solved.

Communication within the business is perhaps the single most important task the IT operations group can do to affect the perception of performance. By ensuring that IT successes are highlighted, the team can have a major impact on the perception of IT within the organization. In addition to the companywide communication efforts, the IT steering committee provides an excellent venue for IT management to communicate key operations successes. Chapter 14 covers additional ideas for ensuring that the IT department properly communicates successes to the business.

Evaluating Infrastructure Investments

Infrastructure investments are capital expenditures made for division-wide or corporate-wide technologies to support activities in the IT operations area. These investments are usually made in support of a new project to replace existing technology or to enhance technology. Examples of these kinds of investments include:

- Replacing printers for a division.
- Migrating from one e-mail server and client to another companywide.
- Purchasing a new PBX for a branch office.
- Upgrading the communications hardware or speed of the network linkage between offices.
- Replacing employee laptops or desktops with new equipment.
- Implementing new application servers to provide additional processing capacity in support of increased business volume.
- Implementing an enterprise backup storage solution.

Infrastructure investments are notoriously difficult to evaluate because they exhibit several of the following properties:

- High initial investment costs relative to ongoing costs.
- High level of intangible benefits.
- Indistinct linkage to the actual revenue or cost reduction benefits the investment supports.
- Often a stand-alone project without dependencies on other investments.
- Benefits accrue to multiple groups or divisions within the company (e.g., a shared resource such as a new corporate firewall).
- Benefits accrue over long periods.

These properties make infrastructure investment evaluations distinct from the evaluation that is conducted for investment in software or application development projects discussed in Chapters 12 and 17. Infrastructure investments also tend to be more tactical and require more effort to identify, quantify, and calculate benefits and costs. However, in every case, the infrastructure investments must match closely with a strategic technical architecture plan and set of corporate standards as outlined in Chapter 7. These investments are typically identified as part of the annual planning, IT strategy, or IT architecture efforts.

These investments should go through a rigorous investment evaluation process that aims to make the best use of the firm's capital. Fortunately, much of the evaluation process should be similar to that of projects, as discussed in Chapter 17, including:

- Assessing strategic value.
- Determining the financial value.

- Assessing risk impact on priorities.
- Assessing adequacy of existing infrastructure.
- Determining investment priorities.
- Prioritizing and sequencing of investments.

A major difference between application and infrastructure projects is that many infrastructure investments can be considered in relative isolation, resulting in fewer dependencies and complications. Another major difference is that it may be difficult to readily assess the benefits of a particular initiative because they may accrue to the entire organization. Additionally, there are often many intangible benefits that are difficult to quantify and include in a regular analysis.

In any case, the investment decision can be broken into multiple subdecisions, allowing more time to elapse prior to investment, providing additional information for making the subdecisions. For example, rather than purchase 10,000 new desktop computers for all employees in the company, the IT team purchases them in lots of 500 on an as-needed basis throughout the rollout, providing for pricing negotiation and configuration changes.

Popular Methodologies

There are many popular methods in practice today to evaluate IT investments, along with new methods developed virtually every month by both academics and practitioners. Many of these methods are subsets of traditional capital investment evaluation models, while others are specific to information technology investments. This chapter does not comprehensively evaluate every method but briefly describes the characteristics of the more popular methods to illustrate the wide range of methods used today.

Some of the most common methods are financial approaches that are used in evaluating not just IT investments, but any capital investment made by a firm. At a fundamental level, these are based on the commonly understood concept of weighing costs and benefits. Costs and benefits are quantified over the investment's life cycle using various methods. These are generally combined into a single figure called the net present value (NPV) using an appropriate discount rate over the investment life cycle. The NPV, along with the time period and payback period, is used to calculate the project's return on investment (ROI).

We recommend using an evaluation method that combines speed, ease of use, and communication with various stakeholders while maintaining a firm grounding in analysis and quantitative methods. This method is effective because it can be implemented quickly and provides immediate credibility to the IT organization.

Keep in mind the purpose and goals of investment evaluation when developing an investment evaluation process:

- Prevent investments with high risk of a negative return from being funded.
- Ensure that the best projects receive funding.
- Ensure that the organization understands and follows the evaluation procedure.
- Ensure that the costs and benefits of projects that are funded can be measured to assess the value and effectiveness of the screening process.

An Investment Evaluation Framework

The framework in Exhibit 8.18 outlines the process for identifying, evaluating, screening, approving, managing, and measuring infrastructure investments for the IT operations area:

- *Identification of potential infrastructure investments:* This process can take place through formal requests submitted by business/functional

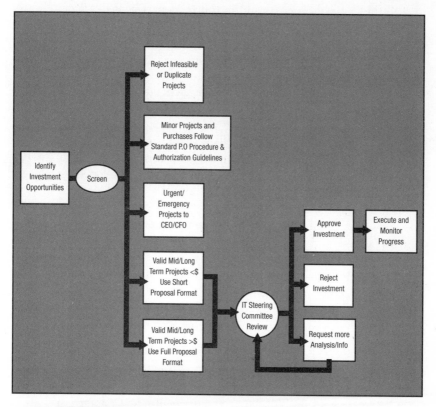

Exhibit 8.18   IT Infrastructure Investment Analysis Framework

units, deficiencies identified in IT evaluation studies, proposals from the IT department, developed and identified in an approved IT strategy document or in an IT architecture plan. When ready to begin the evaluation process, these potential investments should be presented in a simple single-page summary with a description, estimated costs, proposed benefits, and a "preliminary" financial value calculation.

- *Screening of potential ideas:* Before a full proposal is created, a simple screening process should eliminate ideas that are already being considered, are irrelevant to the organization, violate company policies, are not part of the approved IT standards, or do not otherwise stand up to scrutiny.
- *Prioritization of ideas:* The proposals should be prioritized based on their urgency and potential value to the organization.
- *Undersized:* If the idea is sufficiently small, it should be redirected to the appropriate sourcing channel in the organization (e.g., central purchasing).
- *Full proposal:* If the proposal is of material cost, it should be sent to the original proposer and/or the IT department to generate a full proposal.
- *Partial proposal:* If the idea falls between an insignificant expenditure and a major expenditure, a partial proposal should be completed. This should follow the same format as a full proposal but without a detailed financial value assessment, and it needs only one alternative to the recommended solution.
- *Urgent approval:* If the investment is especially urgent and critical (e.g., data center replacement because of a catastrophe), it should be sent to the CFO or COO for immediate approval of at least an interim solution. If necessary, a later proposal should be developed for a longer term solution.
- *Review by the steering committee:* Just as project proposals are reviewed by the steering committee, so too, should infrastructure proposals be reviewed.
- *Investment management:* If the project is approved, it should be managed and tracked throughout its life cycle to ensure that all the proposed benefits are realized.
- *Ongoing measurement:* Any lost benefits or extra benefits should be recorded and reported to the IT steering committee. This will help to verify that the investment evaluation process is working correctly.

For financial value assessment, a model should be created that calculates the financial value of the proposed project. The inputs to the model should include the project's benefits, costs, and discount rate. Chapter 17 discusses methods for calculating financial value of a given investment.

The benefits of a particular project should include any value produced by a particular investment. In their book *Smart Business,* David Chapman and Barry Sheehy provide an exhaustive list of potential benefits that should be identified and quantified. The following is adapted from their list:

- Improvement in revenue, gross margin, time to profitability, and profit margin.
- Improved quality of customer products and services.
- Improvement in overall customer costs.
- Improved implementation of products and services.
- Reduction in overhead costs and cost to serve.
- Avoidance of costs.
- Displacement of costs.
- Increase in cash flow.
- Reduction in cost of information technology.
- Reduction in skill requirements.
- Improvement in new product cycle time.
- Acceleration of new knowledge, experience, and opportunity to improve performance.
- Provides new knowledge that gives a competitive advantage.
- Reduces overall capital expense.[39]

Estimates should be made for any identified benefit as both an initial (one-time) benefit and an ongoing benefit over time. For each benefit, a point estimate should be provided *plus* either a probability distribution or a range that can be used to determine the risk of the project. In addition, for each benefit, references should be included in the proposal that explain the source of the data and methods used to estimate the range or probability distribution. The proposer should also ensure that potential benefits are not duplicated in the model.

If there is significant strategic value embedded in the project that cannot be captured through standard benefit discovery, real options analysis (ROA) should be considered to identify and value the flexibility that is provided to the organization. Real options analysis provides a way to identify and properly value strategic features that can be included with the benefits of the investment.

Costs of the investment should be just as carefully estimated as the benefits. These costs should include every cost that would be considered in a total cost of ownership (TCO) analysis:

- Capital equipment investment (e.g., hardware).
- Software.

- Management and planning.
- Installation and testing.
- Training.
- Connectivity.
- Technical support.
- Maintenance.
- Required upgrades.
- Increased overhead.
- Increased cost to serve.
- Negative effect on any operating variables (e.g., gross margin, profit margin).
- Negative effect on any capabilities (e.g., ability/speed of customer service).

All of these variables should be considered for both the initial cost and ongoing cost in the future. Just as for benefits, for each cost, a point estimate should be provided *plus* either a probability distribution or a range that can be used to determine the risk of the project. In addition, for each cost, references should be included in the proposal that explain the source of the data and methods used to estimate the range or probability distribution. The proposer should ensure that potential costs are not duplicated in the model.

The cost of capital should be developed coordinating with an analyst from the company's finance group based on the firm's weighted average cost of capital and the discount rate of a company that shares risks that are similar to the proposed investment.

In addition to the financial assessment, the proposal should include a strategic assessment that qualitatively addresses the value and position of the project within the strategic framework of the company. Items to be addressed in the strategic assessment include:

- *Strategic match:* How well does the investment support the strategic plans in the company?
- *Competitive advantage:* If the investment will provide some competitive advantage to the company, how significant will it be?
- *Management information:* How will the investment provide more control over the organization?
- *Competitive response:* How long can the investment be delayed without a significant reduction in the company's competitive strengths?
- *Strategic architecture:* How well does the investment fit in with the company's IT standards, policies, and enterprise architecture?

These items should be judged qualitatively and have a short text description that backs up the qualitative assessment. If desired, they can be weighted and scored for ranking purposes.

Finally, a high-level risk assessment should be included. The financial assessment should already implicitly include a risk assessment by having a range or distribution for the input variables, and thus a range or distribution for the output variables, including financial value. This section should address a qualitative risk assessment that includes:

- *Project and organization risk:* How capable is the organization of carrying out the investment?
- *Definitional risk:* How much uncertainty is there regarding all the costs and benefits associated with the investment?
- *Technology risk:* How technically prepared is the company to implement and use the IT investment?

Summary

The IT operations area typically receives less attention than the applications portion of the IT department. Yet, it often accounts for more than half of the spending in the department, and provides the tools and infrastructure that users see most often. The help desk is the only interaction and communication with the IT department for many corporate users. Therefore, an effective operations department is critical to good customer service, the perception of a well-run IT department, and a high level of customer satisfaction. By implementing standard operating procedures, service level agreements, process control, root cause analysis, and infrastructure investment assessment methodologies, IT managers can greatly improve the performance of the operation team and the infrastructure they manage.

RESOURCES

Operations:

IT Infrastructure Library (ITIL). www.itil.co.uk. Provides best practices for IT infrastructure management.

Investment financial value calculation:

Bodie, Zvi, Alex Kane, and Alan J. Marcus. *Investments.* New York: McGraw-Hill/Irwin, 1993.

Brealey, Richard A., and Stewart C. Myers. *Principles of Corporate Finance.* New York: McGraw-Hill, 2002.

Gardner, Christopher. *The Valuation of Information Technology: A Guide for Strategy Development, Valuation and Financial Planning.* New York: John Wiley & Sons, 2000.

Moskowitz, K., and H. Kern. *Managing IT as an Investment: Partnering for Success.* Upper Saddle River, NJ: Prentice Hall, 2002.

Remenyi, Dan. "IT Investment: Making a Business Case," *Digital Equipment* (December 1999).

Remenyi, Dan, Arthur Money, Michael Sherwood-Smith, Zahir Irani, and Alan Twite. *The Effective Measurement and Management of IT Costs and Benefits.* Boston: Butterworth-Heinemann, Computer Weekly Professional Series, 2002.

Van Grembergen, Wim. *Information Technology Evaluation Methods and Management.* Hershey, PA: Idea Group Publishing, March 2001.

NOTES

1. Jay H. "Dizzy" Dean, "Biography—Dizzy Dean," http://www .hickoksports .com/biograph/deandizz.shtml (December 19, 2002).

2. Henry Ford, "Henry Ford Quotes," http://www.quotationspage.com/quotes /Henry_Ford (December 19, 2002).

3. David F. Carr, "Patch Management," quoting Gartner Group research, *Baseline Magazine* (May 2005), p. 75.

4. Network World, August 21, 2006, p. 46.

5. Beth Schultz, "The Hacker Resistant Database," *Network World* (May 22, 2006).

6. Ephraim Schwartz, "Budgeting for Break-Ins," *Infoworld* (April 10, 2006), p. 14.

7. Amy Schurr, "When It's Time to Bring in the Feds," *Network World* (August 14, 2006), p. 8; source: 2005 FBI Computer Crime Survey.

8. CMP Media, *IT Security Consultant*, p. A14, www.itsecurityconsultant.org.

9. "Avoiding Costs from Oversizing Data Center and Network Room Infrastructure," APC white paper rev. 2002-4 (2003), p. 7. ©APC.

10. Suzanne Niles, "Physical Security in Mission Critical Facilities," APC white paper 82, rev. 2004-1 (2004), p. 13. ©APC.

11. Christian Cowan and Chris Gaskins, "Monitoring Physical Threats in the Data Center," APC white paper, rev. 2006-0 (2006), p. 6. ©APC.

12. Ashok Kulkarni and Stephen McCluer, "Understanding EPO and Its Downtime Risks," APC white paper rev. 2005-2 (2005), p. 4. ©APC.

13. Electric Power Research Institute "The Cost of Power Disturbances to Industrial and Digital Economy Companies" (2001), www.epri.com.

14. Wendy Torell and Victor Avelar, "Four Steps to Determine When a Standby Generator is Needed for Small Data Centers and Network Rooms," APC white paper 52, p. 11. ©APC.

15. See note 14, p. 8.

16. Stephen McCleur, "Battery Technology for Data Centers and Network Rooms: Ventilation," APC white paper 34, rev. 2002-2 (2002), p. 11. ©APC.

17. Kai Johnstand and Matt LePard, "Essential Standby Generator System Requirements for Next Generation Data Centers," APC white paper rev. 2005-0 (2005), pp. 4–8. ©APC.

18. See note 14, p. 6.

19. James Vangilder and Roger Schmidt, "Airflow Uniformity through Perforated Tiles in a Raised-Floor Data Center," APC white paper 121. ©APC.

20. Neil Rasmussen, "Avoidable Mistakes that Compromise Cooling Performance in Data Centers and Network Rooms," APC white paper 49 (2003), p. 3. ©APC.

21. Neil Rasmussen, "Calculating Total Cooling Requirements for Data Centers," APC white paper 25, p. 3. ©APC.

22. See note 21, p. 6.

23. See note 21, p. 6.

24. "How and Why Mission-Critical Cooling Systems Differ from Common Air Conditioners," APC white paper 56, rev. 2003-2, p. 12. ©APC.

25. Neil Rasmussen, "Cooling Strategies for Ultra-High Density Racks and Blade Servers," APC white paper 46, rev. 2005-4 (2005), p. 3. ©APC.

26. See note 25, p. 18–19.

27. Kevin Dunlap and Neil Rasmussen, "The Advantages of Row and Rock-Oriented Cooling Architectures for Data Centers," APC white paper 130, rev. 2006-0 (2006), pp. 2, 15. ©APC.

28. Avelar, "Mitigating Fire Risks in Mission Critical Facilities," rev. 2003-0 (2003), p. 3.

29. See note 28, p. 3.

30. See note 28, p. 6.

31. See note 28, p. 15–16.

32. Postini, "Managing Business Messaging: The Executive Guide to Integrated Message Management; Security, Availability, Compliance and Visibility," (December 2, 2005), www.postini.com/whitepapers/?WPJD=34.

33. Elena Malykhina, "A Culture of No" (sidebar), *Information Week* (June 26, 2006), p. 26; The Radicati Group.

34. "In-stat January 2006 study," *Baseline Magazine* (March 2006), p. 26.

35. CPM Group and Deloitte & Touche, "Continuing the Journey: 2005 Business Continuity Survey," (p. 8), http://www.deliotte.com/dtt/cda/doc/content/us_assur_2005%20BCM%20SURVEY%20REPORT.pdf.

36. KPI's, *Intelligent Enterprise Magazine* (May 2006), p. 13, Opensky Research. www.intelligententerprise.com.

37. See note 35, p. 9.

38. Infonetics Research (www.infonetics.com), quoted in *Var Business Magazine* (www.varbusiness.com).

39. Dave L. Chapman and Barry Sheehy, *Smart Business* (Provo, UT: Executive Excellence, May 1, 2002). pp. 53–56.

9

IT Problem Management

Each problem that I solved became a rule which served afterwards to solve other problems.
—Rene Descartes[1]

A problem well-stated is a problem half-solved.[2]
—Charles Kettering

This chapter outlines the best ways to manage the IT help desk function, also known as problem management or request management.

Why This Topic Is Important

As outlined in Chapter 4, problem management is one of the major scope areas of the effective IT department. The help desk is important for a number of reasons. First, when properly implemented, it is the single point of capture for nearly all baseline support issues. As a result, it provides the best leverage for senior level resources, by triaging problems—solving easy issues rapidly and escalating difficult problems quickly. Second, because information on problem volumes and how they are handled yields so much data, it is the IT sub-area with the easiest to monitor and quantify performance. Finally, as noted in the previous chapter, outside of complete system failures, it is the area that has the largest impact on overall customer satisfaction.

Problem and Request Management

Problem and request management is the overall support infrastructure, tools, processes, procedures, policies, and organization focused on reacting to and resolving end-user problems or issues and requests. These types of problems range widely in terms of type, complexity, and urgency, and include everything from a password reset request to printer problems. In our overall map of the IT department, problem management is handled in the help desk, O&I baseline support, and application support areas (Exhibit 9.1).

The process for problem management is optimally organized into three distinct tiers, as shown in Exhibit 9.1. Each tier has very specific tools, processes, and procedures. The first is tier 1 support, usually made up of help desk personnel taking requests from end users. Tier 1 support personnel log calls into trouble-ticket tracking software, attempt to resolve common issues on the spot, triage calls to determine who in the IT organization should fix the problem, and provide overall customer support such as status updates for existing requests.

Tier 2 support is made up of more technically specialized personnel, including programmers (for application problems), network administrators (for network problems), or system administrators (for systems or server related problems). Tier 2 support in most organizations is also responsible for desktop and laptop support and deskside equipment break/fix support. If tier 1 is unable to resolve issues, usually within a given time frame or service level agreement (SLA), the issue is escalated to tier 2 support.

Tier 3 support is comprised of the most highly skilled technology specialists and may include outside vendor experts and vendor support personnel. Tier 2 personnel are senior analysts with a diversity of technical skills, while tier 3 personnel are generally at the highest skill level in a given technology

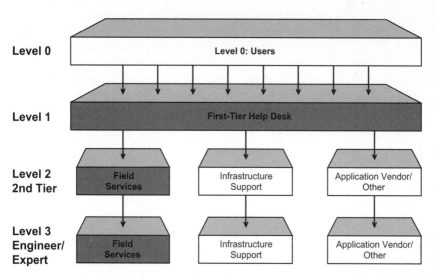

**Exhibit 9.1   Typical Escalation Process for IT
Problems and Requests**

discipline, such as network management, systems administration, security, application management.

The most effective method for managing the issue reporting process is the use of a packaged help desk management application. This application provides for the issuance of tickets associated with each end-user issue, which allows status tracking of the issue for its lifetime. The system also allows prioritization of issues according to urgency and ensures that issues get properly closed. End-users can even be granted read access to the ticket system for status updates.

In addition to providing a consistent, reliable interface for end-users, a ticket tracking system confers a number of important internal IT management benefits. First, the system provides an immense amount of objective data about the volume of business requests handled by IT; this information in turn feeds the process for determining staffing levels in IT. Second, the system can provide a wide variety of objective IT performance metrics (discussed later) that allow the CIO to improve service as well as clearly demonstrate high service levels. Finally, systems facilitate spotting recurring end-user issues that can lead to root cause analysis (eliminating the problem) or, in some cases, automation (eliminating the labor associated with the problem).

Implementation of a request ticketing system provides basic control of all baseline support activities in IT, and therefore is critical to the overall effective management of the IT department. Management of the tier 1, 2, and 3 support activities can account for as much as 70 percent of the activity within IT. Without the ability to take inbound user requests, record them, prioritize them, and ensure that they are handled properly, the IT department will race from problem to problem leaving a trail of dissatisfied end-users, IT staff, and senior management.

A wide variety of ticket-tracking and management software is available in the commercial marketplace, and can help an organization ensure that the help desk operates smoothly, and that problems do not go unaddressed. A few of the help desk management systems with the highest market penetration include:

Help Desk Management System	*Company*
ARS	Remedy
c.Support	GWI Software
HEAT	FrontRange Solutions
HelpSTAR	Help Desk Technology International Corp.
Magic	Remedy
Peregrine	
Track-It	Intuit

The ticket tracking system will be operated by the IT department, and will be accessed and updated by all three tiers of support staff.

Managing an Effective Help Desk

The management of the process and systems for tier 1 (help desk) support provide the fundamentals for overall effective problem management. The help desk is important for a number of reasons, including:

- It is the first point of contact for user requests.
- It is responsible for attempting first-contact resolution.
- It sets priority for problems through triage.
- It determines proper escalation for problems it cannot solve.
- It is the coordinating organization for ensuring ultimate ticket resolution, regardless of which tier ultimately works on the ticket.
- It is counted on to reliably enter all of the information regarding end-user problems and requests.
- It is the focal point for most end-user interactions; therefore, it has a disproportionate impact on overall perception of the IT function.

The help desk plays a unique and important role in IT effectiveness. Several aspects of management of the help desk are covered in this section, including staffing, escalation, metrics, and technology.

Help Desk Staffing

Staffing of the help desk is a complex proposition requiring the right balance of staff technical skills and personality, as well as the right number of staff to appropriately cover the inbound user requests.

The nature of help desk work ensures that the staff are primarily dealing with unhappy end-users with systems problems. The profile of the best help desk agents is a mix of technical expertise, troubleshooting skills, a winning personality, and above all patience.

The most important traits of the successful help desk agent are nontechnical. Agents can be trained in specific technologies (and because every IT department generally has a unique application footprint, this is a necessity). However, the most important skills are soft skills, which are more difficult to quantify and train. Important soft skills include clear diction, patience, effective listening, problem-solving expertise, a sense of humor, the ability to stay calm under pressure, and a genuine interest in helping people. These skills are so important that over 98 percent of the respondents to the Helpdesk

Institute's 2005 *Practices and Salary Survey* rated soft skills as "very important." The next highest rated category was technical skills, with only 66 percent of respondents rating it as very important.[3] Further, the survey also found that "Customer Service Skills" were the number one factor used to determine salary increases for help desk staff, compared to specific technical knowledge for tier 2 and tier 3 staff.[4]

Screening new staff for these skills can be difficult. We recommend an interview process for help desk staff that includes behavioral testing. The help desk manager can recommend the best existing staff for behavioral assessment, and thereby create an ideal personality profile. New staff can be assessed and compared to the ideal profile. Furthermore, new staff should be interviewed by top help desk performers in an informal environment (e.g., out of office lunch meeting) to evaluate soft skills.

The help desk staff generally separate into two groups based on overall career goals. Some staff consider help desk work as a stepping-stone to future work. They know that their help desk experience serves as a proving ground and training regimen for other jobs in the IT department. In fact, these staffers often make the best tier 2 and tier 3 resources because their technical skills increase over time. They know how to work well with the help desk team, and have the ever-important soft skills that can often be missing from direct-hire tier 2 and tier 3 staff.

Other staffers are interested in their position as a permanent role. They value the predictability of the job, and the fact that the help desk role rarely involves any "take-home" work. They are most comfortable when they feel that they have a broad enough knowledge to answer most help desk questions, and therefore seek to become a broad expert in the overall operations of the company. Their presence reduces staff turnover and can provide a steady influence over the entire team due to their experience, historical perspective, and positive long-term relationships with end-user staff.

The help desk leadership should understand that the management needs of these two groups differ slightly. The former type will be most interested in technical training, certification, and development, as well as evidence that the help desk role can eventually lead to other IT jobs. The latter is more interested in culture, work environment, and incentives that liven up the work from month to month.

In every case, we recommend that staff receive certification and training specific to the help desk function. The most important industry group for help desk training, knowledge, and certification is the Help Desk Institute (www.thinkhdi.com). HDI certification covers the breadth of skills needed for staff, including technology, process, and soft skills. Sponsoring help desk staff for HDI certification is a worthwhile investment in their productivity, and sends a clear message to the team about the importance of their role in the IT department.

Staff Training: Specialists versus Generalists

Another decision to be made in managing the help desk function is the organization of the staff. The main trade-off is breadth versus expertise. Specializing staff in specific applications or technologies improves productivity on specific call types. Calls can be routed to the help desk expert on a given topic. The drawback of this specialization approach is the exposure created when the experts are on the phone or absent.

The alternative is a staff of generalists who have a breadth of knowledge that covers most applications and technologies supported by the department. The drawback is that these jacks-of-all-trade may be master of none and result in unnecessary escalation of issues to tier 2.

We recommend the following approach for staffing and cross-training help desks by size of staff:

- 1 to 5 help desk staff—Generalists with good rules for tier 2 escalation.
- 6 to 15 help desk staff—Specialists, with cross-trained "minor" in multiple other specialties.
- 16 to 25 help desk staff—Specialists, with generalist "minor."
- 25 staff and above—Specialists, with 10 percent floating generalists.

DETERMINING REQUIRED AGENTS. The CIO must determine business hours for the help desk, which in turn will dictate how many shifts should operate. At a minimum, the help desk should operate during normal business hours (Monday through Friday, during the workday), with possible increments of additional nighttime and morning hours, 24 hours per day, Monday through Friday, and weekend support. The requirements of the business should dictate the help desk coverage hours. International operations, or offices spread through multiple time zones may dictate additional minimum hours of coverage (Exhibit 9.2).

The minimum staffing for noncore hours for a 24/7 help desk are three additional full-time staff. This will cover 16 additional hours per day for 5 days and 48 additional weekend hours, a total of 128 hours.

The optimal number of agents required for a given help desk is based on call volume and average length of call. The industry standard for determining the number of agents as well as expected wait times is the Erlang C model that utilizes a proven mathematical model (Exhibit 9.3). There are a number of free or inexpensive systems that use hours-of-coverage and average-call-time to determine the required number of help desk agents to provide coverage.

The Erlang C models are very effective but not perfect. Some of the limitations include the assumption that callers wait in queue (vs. abandoning calls) and that calls are randomly distributed (underlying call causes

**Exhibit 9.2   Sample Output from Erlang C
Modeling Tool** (*Source:* KoolToolz.com.)

such as a key system outage mean that call volume distribution is less random). More sophisticated call centers, which use skill-based routing (calls are routed to the appropriate specialist as outlined earlier in this chapter) also diminish the effectiveness of the Erlang C model. Erlang C tools that provide additional input parameters can account for these factors. The industry has also seen the emergence of systems that go one step further and simulate call volumes and staffing levels based on actual help desk data.

Regardless of estimating model used, the help desk manager should balance the appropriate service level versus cost to determine the optimal staffing level. These opposing tensions make determining the optimal staffing model a formidable challenge.

An additional difficulty in staffing help desks is due to the natural peaks and valleys found in call volume (Exhibit 9.4). Not surprisingly, the help desk call volumes correspond to patterns in day-to-day business activity—an initial burst in the morning, a lull during lunch, and additional bursts after lunch and prior to the end of the business day.

Again unsurprisingly, the highest call volumes are start-up problems on Mondays, and a final push to resolve any open issues prior to leaving on Fridays (which is often offset by staff vacations or early departures on Fridays). Certain businesses with high seasonality may find additional call variances by month or quarter as well (Exhibit 9.5 on page 280).

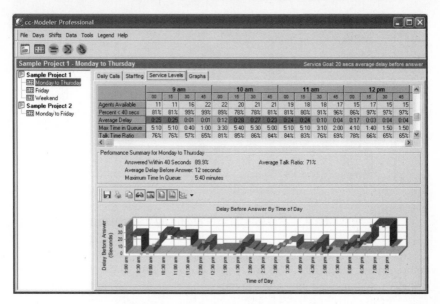

Exhibit 9.3 Sample Output from Erlang C Modeling Tool (*Source:* KoolToolz.com.)

The CIO must determine the trade-off between the cost of providing full coverage for peak call times versus containing help desk staffing costs. Fortunately, the call patterns are very consistent across most IT support organizations. Knowing that Monday mornings will always produce the highest call volumes allows the IT department to prepare appropriately. We recommend staffing that covers average call volumes, while deferring noncritical problems

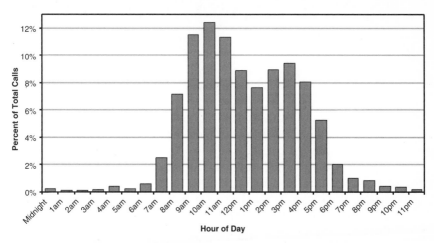

Exhibit 9.4 Typical Ticket Volume by Hour of Day

Exhibit 9.5   Sample Ticket Volume by Day of Week

from peak hours to nonpeak hours. Agents should simply take a ticket for non-priority problems that are called in during nonpeak hours, and then revisit the ticket during lulls in inbound calls.

Staff Incentives

The repetitive nature of help desk work and the high-pressure environment present a challenge in staff motivation. We recommend initiating periodic special incentives based on both individual and team performance. These will keep the staff energized and interested and pay for themselves several times over in improved performance and the corresponding end-user satisfaction.

Some sample incentives that can be used include restaurant gift certificates, MP3 players, handheld video game, movie and sporting event tickets, compensated time off, electronics store gift certificate, and gas cards. For a spontaneous reward, coupons for any of these items can be put into a grab bag from which agents can draw after achieving a performance goal. Examples of these goals are number of resolved incidents, calls taken, and customer service feedback.

Other meaningful incentives include a trophy that is displayed at the work station of the top agent each month and monthly team outings based on achieving performance metrics.

Finally, the help desk manager should recognize that one of the tools at his or her disposal is implementation of more casual appearance standards. The majority of end-user interaction takes place over the phone; as a result, the help desk manager may elect to eliminate some of the typical appearance standards that apply to the department overall. For some, this minor freedom can be an important incentive.

Help Desk Escalation

Help desk escalation consists of determining the severity of problems and routing problems to the appropriate support tier for resolution. In many cases, the problem will be solved by the initial contact—first tier resolution.

For problems that are not solvable by the first tier, there must be a predictable escalation to other tiers based on the problems difficulty and severity. Help desk agents must be trained to triage problem's by quickly diagnosing severity and difficulty and determining how quickly to involve other tiers. This requires IT management to predefine severity conditions and their corresponding escalation. There is a material difference between a workgroup printer running low on toner and a production server outage that is preventing a payroll check run. A matrix of severity conditions ensures that big problems are quickly escalated and communicated to effect the most rapid resolution, and, equally importantly, to facilitate rapid communication of major problems to senior management.

In most cases, the help desk agent taking the initial call will involve the end-user in determining the appropriate severity assignment for the problem. Severity one issues will generally be self-evident (and will most often generate multiple calls) and are therefore easy to assign. See Exhibit 9.6 for a sample severity matrix.

To ensure proper communication of issues, the help desk agent should be provided with a matrix of IT and business staff to be informed in the event of issues of varying severity (Exhibit 9.7 on page 283). This will reduce the chance of undercommunicating or an uncontrolled communication. The list of people to be informed will vary by problem severity.

IT management must also create an agreed-on time-to-resolution for tickets based on severity. These targets are important because they form the backbone of the service level agreement with the business and impact staffing levels, capital investment, and system availability. The target resolution time should therefore be sensitive to both the business disruption caused by the magnitude of the outage, as well as the IT expense required to support the commitment.

The IT department and help desk team need a tool that dictates how often status should be communicated for a given ticket. This ensures that for emergency and nonemergency tickets alike that the status updates are taking place at predictable and reasonable intervals. Preplanning the communications regime for each severity level reduces the number of panicked calls from business users requesting status updates. For high-severity situations (levels 1 and 2), the IT department should also utilize businesswide communications mechanisms for the periodic status updates, such as system login messages or overhead speaker announcements. One of the least expensive and most effective methods is a simple phone tree that includes the administrative team for each office, group, or location.

SEVERITY	DEFINITION	EXAMPLE
1	Causes complete loss of critical business function	• System is inaccessible by all users • Unable to perform year-end close on time
2	Causes significant loss of critical business function or revenue	• System is inaccessible by some users • Unable to produce business critical reports in a timely manner • Unable to produce billings to Accounts Receivable
	Creates financial risk	• Unable to produce accurate financial reports, invoices, or checks
3	Causes immaterial loss of critical business function or revenue	• Process fails but can be restarted successfully
	Creates the possibility for financial risk	• Payments to vendors are past due and cannot be fulfilled in a timely manner • Invoices to customers are delayed • Management or statistical reports are incorrect or will not run
	Impacts IT's individual productivity	• Takes an individual significantly more effort to do same job • Takes an individual significantly more elapsed time to do same job
4	Causes partial loss of noncritical business function and revenue	• Minor tasks that should be automated must be done manually • Inquiry panels need corrections
	Has some impact on individual productivity	• Individual takes more effort to complete same task • Individual takes more time to compete the same task • Individual must do something unusual to make the system work correctly
	Increases costs	• Costs more to do the same function • Query needed to speed verification by user, therefore reducing time spent on a task
	Reduces revenues	• Supply of data to customer • Turnaround time on system setup risks client relationship

Exhibit 9.6   Sample Severity Matrix

SEVERITY	DEFINITION	EXAMPLE
	Offers "Nice to Have" additions	• Any form of customization or development that will make individuals job slightly less complicated or faster
5	Severity has not yet been determined, or problem is to be worked on a time available basis and not included in the metrics	• Default when a problem is first logged

Exhibit 9.6 *Continued*

The ticket management system should facilitate this process by providing automatic escalation of open tickets based on severity and time open (Exhibit 9.8). Most systems provide this configurable feature. The CIO and IT Steering Committee should be involved in creating and provide final approval for all of these lists.

The CIO should ensure that escalation procedures are clearly documented and updated every six months, and conduct regular training and refresher courses in the escalation process for tiers 1, 2, and 3 staff. This helps ensure

PROBLEM SEVERITY	PEOPLE TO CONTACT
Severity 1	Call Originator Customer Functional Manager Information Technology Group
Severity 2	Call Originator Business Functional Manager IT Functional Support Team IT Applications Development Manager IT Operations Manager IT Help Desk Manager
Severity 3-4	Call Originator IT Applications Development Manager IT Help Desk Manager
Other (unable to determine)	Call Originator IT Help Desk Manager

Exhibit 9.7   Sample Severity—Contact Matrix

SEVERITY	CALL ACKNOWLEDGED	PRODUCTION SUPPORT TEAM RESPONSE TIME	TARGET RESOLUTION	STATUS UPDATE FREQUENCY
Severity 1	5 minutes	15 minutes / 15 minutes	12 hours	Every hour
Severity 2	15 minutes	15 minutes/ 60 minutes	1–2 business days	Every 3 hours
Severity 3	4 hours	4 hours/next business day	5–10 business days	One time every 2 business days
Severity 4	24 hours	1 day/next business day	Per agreed-to plan	Upon closure
Basic (non-priority) service request	24 hours	1 day/next business day	2–5 business days	Upon closure

Exhibit 9.8   Sample Severity—Communication/Resolution Matrix

that problems are addressed and solved by the appropriate skilled personnel, and that problems are escalated at the appropriate rate within the operations group. Additionally, it ensures that appropriate business and IT executives are notified in case of emergency situations or when problems are not being addressed in a sufficient time frame. Escalation procedures tend to become outdated over time because of staff turnover, business reorganizations, and business process changes. The processes should be revisited and revised on a regular schedule.

TICKET STATUS.   To facilitate communication of status (and to provide status by any agent that an end-user happens to reach) the help desk must establish a standard for ticket status. There should be a sufficient number of status to provide better than simple open or closed information, but fewer than a dozen status codes to keep matters simple for the help desk and end-users. A suggested set of status codes for help desk tickets is shown in Exhibit 9.9.

One useful help desk evaluation technique is to have the ticketing system automatically send an e-mail to the end-user for some reasonable interval of closed tickets (say, every 10 or 20 tickets). The e-mail asks for customer service feedback on agent helpfulness, speed-to-close, and overall satisfaction. This can be facilitated with a web-based tool or a simple e-mail reply.

TICKET ACQUISITION.   The most common method of ticket acquisition is a phone call from an end-user to the help desk. Other methods include e-mail, web-based forms, walk-ups, voice mails, online chat rooms, and faxes.

STATUS CODE	DEFINITION
Open	The IT team has received the service request but has not started working on the request yet.
In process	The IT team has received the service request and/or the service request has been removed from either a wait or hold status and returned to the IT team for further action.
Waiting	The individual assigned to complete this service request is actively working on it and is in need of a specific action by someone outside that individual's control. When a service request is in a wait state, work on that request is suspended until reason for the wait is resolved.
Hold	Indicates that the service request has been temporarily removed from the active work queue.
Resolved	A solution has been developed, proposed, and tested for the request and it may be waiting for either migration (promotion to production) or authorized business user acceptance.
Closed	The service request does not need any further activity.
Enhancement	This status is reserved for issues that are considered to be a change to system functionality and will be assigned as a small project as part of the IT demand management process.

Exhibit 9.9 Sample Ticket Status Definition

Over 60 percent of all ticket communications were via phone call, followed by e-mail at 20 percent. The remaining 20 percent was composed of other methods.[5] The technology subsection that follows discusses the use of technology for ticket acquisition.

There are two important help desk ticketing linkages to other O&I areas. The first is systems monitoring. By virtue of its ready availability (often 24/7), the help desk is an ideal point of escalation for systems monitoring issues. When the tools that perform the system monitoring notice an outage over a predefined threshold, they can automatically create a ticket in the system to be evaluated by the on-call help desk staff. The help desk in turn can escalate the issue appropriately. This linkage of systems monitoring tools and the human intelligence of the help desk creates a powerful tool for ensuring that IT is ahead of systems outages and improves the value of the monitoring tools immensely.

The second linkage is to the asset management tools and/or CMDB (configuration management database). Because help desk tickets are often assigned to both a user and/or a piece of equipment, the help desk is the natural benefici-ary of up-to-date detailed information on the desktop, server, and network equipment associated with the ticket. Easy access to CMDB information from the help desk system facilitates more rapid ticket resolution and reduces on-the-phone time because the help desk agent will not be forced to quiz the end-user about system configuration information.

The most important consideration in ticket acquisition is to ensure that end-users experience a simple and fast process. End-users will inevitably cir-cumvent the help desk and direct-call tier 2 and 3 resources if the help desk process is not effective. This will, in turn, negate most of the benefits of a structured problem management process and reduce overall staff effective-ness. While it is possible to instruct tier 2 and 3 resources to ignore such calls, the preferred mechanism for enforcement is to create a path of least resistance by having an absolutely reliable and responsive help desk organi-zation and process.

TICKET ASSIGNMENT. Regardless of severity level, each ticket should be assigned to a help desk agent. The ticketing system should allow for assign-ment of multiple responsibility (one person in each tier). A single person should be responsible, however, for the life of the ticket—ensuring that the agreed-on escalation and communication is taking place. This should usually be the help desk agent initially assigned to the ticket.

Ticket assignment at each level depends on how the help desk (and IT de-partment) has structured responsibilities for applications and infrastructure. As discussed earlier, help desk agents may be organized as specialists or gen-eralists, or a mix of both.

One of the difficult decisions help desk agents face is knowing when to pass on a ticket. Naturally, the most effective means of disposing of a ticket is on the first call, or in the first tier. This is also most satisfying for the end-user. However, more difficult problems that require specialized skills to re-solve should be escalated rapidly to tier 2 or 3 which will reduce overall time-to-resolve. The decision to escalate tickets requires good judgment; im-proper escalation decisions will result in lengthy time-to-resolve (agents not escalating tickets quickly enough) or an aggravated and overwhelmed tier 2 and 3 group (agents escalating tickets too quickly).

The majority of the tickets fall on a simple continuum of difficulty-to-solve and time-to-solve—simply, the more difficult the problem, the longer it takes to solve. The escalation of these tickets is fairly routine—if the prob-lem resolution goes over a certain threshold (say, 15 minutes) then the agent should automatically escalate to tier 2.

A variety of problems fall outside the normal correspondence of difficulty and time. We characterize these outliers as "Type I"—difficult-to-solve but quickly resolved and "Type II"—easy-to-solve, but time consuming. Type I problems are typically very difficult to diagnose by anyone but the most expert resource in a given area. However, once diagnosed, they can be resolved in moments by that expert. For instance, a misconfigured router or a miscoded system path for an application module. In these cases, the help desk agent can spend nearly infinite time on the issue, but never reach resolution. Identifying Type I problems quickly and escalating them almost immediately is important. Otherwise, help desk agents will burn valuable IT and end-user time on issues that they cannot solve.

Type II problems are simple, but time consuming. An example of a Type II problem might be the installation of new software on a desktop that requires multiple reboots. In these cases, the issue does not require any sort of tier 2 or 3 expertise, but does tie up the IT resource for the lengthy duration. When help desk resources are given a simple mandate to escalate issues that take longer than a certain time frame to resolve, Type II problems will inappropriately be escalated to tier 2 and 3 resources (Exhibit 9.10).

In both cases, the help desk team should be trained to recognize both types of outlier problems and have a procedure for rapidly escalating Type I and deferring Type II to a time when there is extra help desk capacity to solve, during one of the lulls in calling.

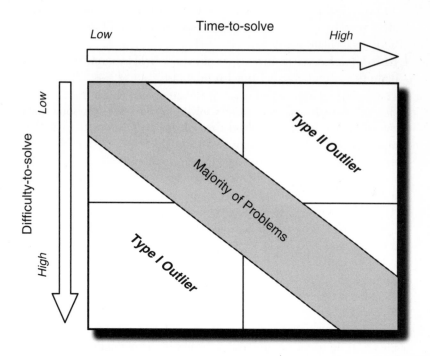

Exhibit 9.10   Help Desk Ticket Distribution by Type

Help Desk Metrics

There are a number of performance metrics that can be measured and evaluated on an ongoing basis to identify improvement opportunities as well as changes in the required support profile for the business, including:

- *Call volume:* Total calls inbound to the help desk over a specific period of time; usually measured daily, weekly, and monthly.
- *Average wait time:* Average amount of time spent by help desk callers waiting for an agent to answer; one of the most important predictors of end-user satisfaction with the help desk.
- *Average talk time:* Amount of time spent on the phone per inbound call by help desk agents.
- *Ticket volume:* Total tickets taken by the help desk, regardless of source (call volumes ignore the 20 to 40 percent of tickets that come from other sources such as e-mail or walk-up service).
- *Ticket type:* Ticket volume by category of service, such as application, desktop issue, e-mail, and so on; should be evaluated for trends over time and used for root-cause analysis.
- *Ticket severity:* Ticket volume by severity; used to determine appropriate thresholding for severity as well as assess overall IT department systems performance.
- *Pass-through percent:* Percentage of overall ticket volume that is passed on to tier 1 (reciprocal of tier 1 resolution).
- *First call resolution:* Percentage of tickets solved on the first call; note that this is different from tickets solved in tier 1 because some tickets solved in tier 1 may be solved through multiple interactions with the end-user (and difference from pass-through).
- *Average time to resolve:* Average time to resolve all tickets; usually most informative if organized by ticket type and/or ticket severity and evaluated weekly or monthly.
- *Abandonment rate:* Percentage of calls that are disconnected before being answered by a help desk agent; this can be because the end-user feels the wait is too long, runs out of time to wait, decides the problem is not important, or resolves the problem without help.
- *Time-to-abandon rate:* Average amount of time callers wait before abandoning the calls; if this time is excessive, it may indicate excessive wait times.
- *Staff utilization:* Amount of time help desk team is working on the phone (time spent on inbound calls and outbound calls combined as a percentage of total time available).

As discussed previously, the CIO and help desk manager must work with the IT steering committee to determine what is the appropriate balance of cost and responsiveness for the help desk.

The statistics should be reviewed periodically by the CIO and the help desk manager. These reports are also appropriate for inclusion in the appendix material for each IT steering committee meeting (Exhibits 9.11 and 9.12).

Some helpful guidelines in setting thresholds for some of these measures are available from the Help Desk Institute (www.thinkhdi.com) Exhibits 9.13 through 9.18. The help desk manager may find that reviewing the metrics by agent helps to identify outstanding performers and those who need further development. Further, the manager may consider breaking down statistics by

(continued)

Exhibit 9.11   Help Desk Telephone System Metrics

Average Speed of Answer

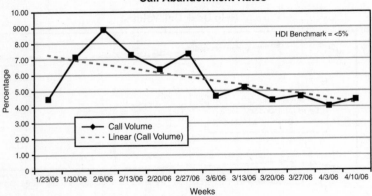

Call Abandonment Rates

Exhibit 9.11 *Continued*

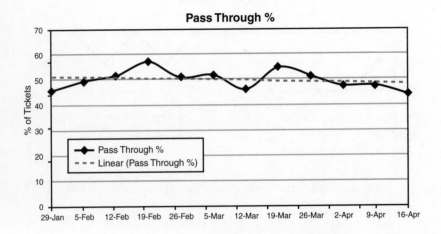

Pass Through %

Exhibit 9.12 **Help Desk Ticket System Metrics**

290

Exhibit 9.12 *Continued*

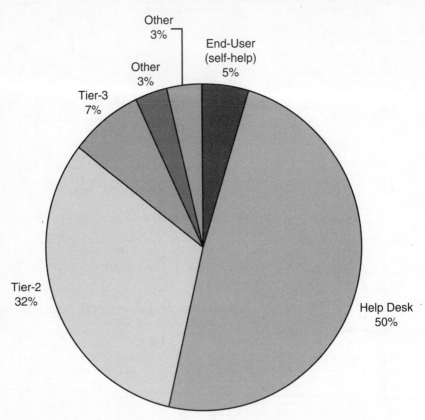

Exhibit 9.13   Percentage of Incidents Resolved by Tier (*Source:* HDI.)

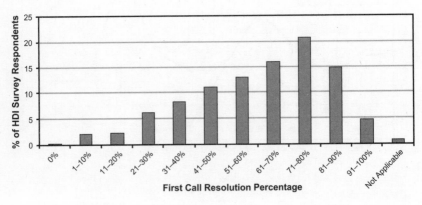

Exhibit 9.14   First Call Resolution Rates (*Source:* HDI.)

Exhibit 9.15   Average Speed to Answer Calls (*Source:* HDI.)

office, geography, line of business, department, or other meaningful category to determine if there are other specific areas for improvement.

Finally, we have found that displaying real-time call statistics on a large monitor in the help desk area (and in the CIO's office and the help desk manager's office) has a meaningful impact on team performance. A visual scoreboard provides instant feedback on how the team is doing and provides motivation and interest (Exhibit 9.19 on page 295).

While having aggregate statistics can improve the help desk, the specific data points can help as well. Calls or tickets that are statistical outliers (exceptionally long hold time, long time to resolve a ticket) can be clues to performance failures. Furthermore, the help desk manager can focus on outliers and give those specific end-users additional attention in solving their problems. Finally, having access to average statistics and outlying data points, the CIO and help desk manager can avoid overreacting to anecdotal data. The team can avoid judging on a single problem phone call if they know that 99 percent of the calls are handled appropriately.

Finally, having metrics in place and available allows the manager to link annual bonuses or other staff incentive compensation to help desk or operations performance. Because help desk ticket statistics are easy to

TALK TIME (MINUTES)	
MEAN	MEDIAN
5.4	4

Exhibit 9.16   Help Desk Talk Time Statistics (Data courtesy HDI, www. thinkhdi.com.)

ABANDONMENT RATE (%)	
MEAN	MEDIAN
5.2	4.0

Exhibit 9.17   Help Desk Call Abandonment Rates (Data courtesy HDI, www.thinkhdi.com.)

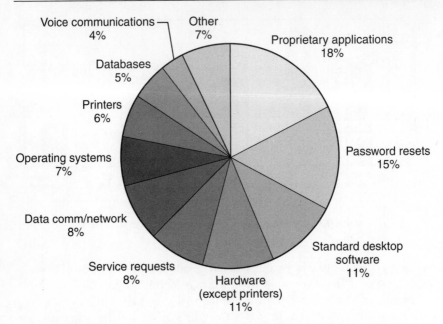

Exhibit 9.18   Ticket Distribution by Type of Request (*Source:* HDI.)

quantify and track, the operations manager can establish compensation or other incentives based on target numbers for the team.

Help Desk Technology

The help desk uses a number of technology platforms in its work. There are five important technology categories:

1. Telephony.
2. Ticket management.
3. Alternative ticket acquisition.
4. Self-service.
5. Remote login.

TELEPHONY.   Because the majority of end-users will contact the help desk via the phone, the quality of the telephone system used by the help desk agents is critical. At a minimum, the phone system should be able to support hunt groups, which allow incoming calls to be routed to the first available agent or to the next agent in the queue. These automatic-call-distribution (ACD) systems are a standard for help desks.

Exhibit 9.19 Sample Help Desk Agent Monitoring Tool (*Source:* Image provided courtesy of Inter-Tel (Delaware), Inc. Image is the copyrighted material of Inter-Tel and Inter-Tel reserves all rights in the image.).

More advanced features include integrated voice response (IVR), which requires user interaction to route calls to the appropriate agent, and the whisper feature, which announces to on-hold callers their current position in the queue and estimated wait time. Integration with the ticket management system can provide automatic recognition of callers based on their phone number and open up existing tickets and/or start the ticket entry process for the help desk agent.

Finally, the phone system may record each individual call. This is invaluable for training purposes, evaluating individual agent performance and resolving the occasional end-user dispute about a sequence of events on a ticket.

TICKET MANAGEMENT.   As outlined earlier in this section, a systematic way of recording, assigning, tracking, and resolving tickets is essential. Other considerations for ticket management systems include integration with the ACD, the asset management system, and will often provide alternative ticket acquisition capabilities.

ALTERNATIVE TICKET ACQUISITION.   While the phone is the primary mechanism for ticket acquisition, other methods can be more productive for the help desk team. A one-on-one interaction on the phone is the most expensive and time consuming method. Other possible methods include e-mails (most ticket management systems can automatically create a ticket based on an e-mail sent to the help desk), live chat (using an enterprise of freeware instant messaging system), or end-user entry of ticket information into a web-based portal. Web portals have a small advantage over email systems in that they allow the end-user to provide some preliminary information in the proper format (e.g., ticket severity, ticket category).

SELF-SERVICE. The IT department can provide access to an online knowledge management system that allows end-users to search a knowledge base for potential solutions to their problem. This arrangement has a number of benefits. End-users can find solutions at any time of the night or day, and do not have to wait for an available agent. The IT department can avoid some calls altogether, saving time and resources. A well-organized online knowledge base can be used by the help desk agents as well.

The best knowledge bases are created by experts and kept up to date to reflect systems changes. The IT department will have the option of purchasing a third-party system with prebuilt answers for common systems. These systems can be customized with specific information and are a helpful tool in creating a cost-effective help desk.

REMOTE LOGIN. A final technology component that improves IT help desk performance is remote login tools. Often end-user issues can be quickly resolved by having the help desk agent take control of the end-user computer and work through the solution. This saves considerable talk time because the agent can see what is happening on their screen instead of the end-user having to explain it. Further, the agent can take control and drive the process. There are a large number of remote desktop control software packages available, including some free and OS built-in options. There are clear security implications of such an arrangement that should be worked through by the systems and network administration team (event logs/audit trail).

Help Desk Outsourcing

It is clear that the help desk is a complex operation, requiring sophisticated processes, a skilled and motivated staff, rigorous metrics, and a significant technology investment. The ongoing capital investment and recruiting requirements, combined with the discrete process (clear inputs and outputs) make the help desk an ideal candidate for outsourcing. In an outsourcing arrangement, the IT department can be the beneficiary of the major investment required for proper telecom, ticket management, and staff development systems. Large scale outsourcers will have the scale economics to manage the help desk in the most cost-effective manner.

The process for selecting a vendor partner is covered in Chapter 12 and the overall outsourcing decision process is covered in Chapter 13.

NOTES

1. http://www.quotationspage.com/quote/26952.html (accessed December 3, 2006).
2. http://www.quotationspage.com/quote/34282.html (accessed December 3, 2006).
3. The Helpdesk Institute, "2005 Practices and Salary Survey," p. 82.
4. See note 3, p. 122.
5. See note 3, p. 54.

10

Application Management

We sometimes get all the information, but we refuse to get the message.

—Cullen Hightower[1]

This chapter outlines major processes, key decisions, and approaches for managing business applications in the enterprise. It further covers best practices for organizing and managing applications, including support, enhancements and upgrades, direction setting, and portfolio analysis. Additionally, we discuss the importance of working with the business to set and manage service-level expectations and soliciting business input on direction setting. Understanding the evolution of applications over their lifetimes and the implications for application strategy and overall architecture is also covered.

This chapter is organized around the major components of application management: *Application architecture* covers the methodology for documenting the current landscape of your company applications, as well as the process to create the targeted optimal application architecture that will provide the company better integration, functional coverage, and lower cost of support. *Application strategy* covers determining when to retire current applications and the best replacement—based on custom development, best-of-breed package implementation, or an integrated package implementation. *Maintenance of existing applications* outlines the responsibilities of the applications maintenance group in managing the day-to-day operations of the application. Finally, the chapter covers *custom applications* and the *implementation of package systems*.

Why This Topic Is Important

The CIO and applications team are faced with a difficult balancing act, akin to trying to make progress in a leaky canoe. They must split their time between bailing (application help desk, bug-fixes), rowing (application enhancement and upgrades), and steering (high-level application strategy setting).

Of particular importance is *application strategy setting*. The IT department must understand how to best support the business, deciding between implementing new systems versus upgrading existing ones, selecting packages versus creating custom systems, picking comprehensive enterprise resource planning (ERP) systems versus cobbling together best-of-breed packages by area, and a host of other decisions. To make effective application strategy decisions, IT must not only engage the business, but also develop a deep understanding of the company's business.

Complicating matters further is the fact that even at a steady state, applications require significant effort to maintain. Continual changes to the environment in which the applications operate (interfaces to other applications that change; changes to hardware, software, and operating system environments; new data from users or imports) mean that even in a steady environment, a dedicated team of applications developers and specialists are required. The more typical environment involves user enhancement requests, required application software upgrades, customer- and supplier-driven changes, business acquisition integration, new system interface requirements, and other events that increase the complexity of managing the application environment.

Architecture

The whole intent of developing an application architecture is to define a "habitable" set of applications that support the company now and into the foreseeable future. The architecture includes the manner in which the components of an application set are organized and integrated.

Exhibit 10.1 highlights four major components of IT architecture: business, information, application, and technical architecture. This chapter is focused on application architecture and its implications for application management. Brief descriptions of the four components follow:

1. *Business architecture:* Major business activities, functions, and their supporting processes. It further translates the business processes into enterprise business requirements that can be organized into functional groupings. These requirements are supported by information flows and package and custom applications.
2. *Information architecture:* Information flows, data entity relationships, and enabling tools that are dictated by the business processes and activities from the business architecture.

Exhibit 10.1   Enterprise Architecture Framework

3. *Application architecture:* Software programs that automate and support business processes; the functions of the applications; articulates the platform where the applications reside; details the set of applications that will support the business in the future; and displays the linkages between both internal applications and the company's applications and those of its vendors, suppliers, and customers.
4. *Technical architecture:* The computing infrastructure (i.e., systems software, hardware, network) that supports the information and application architectures.

The first step in managing business applications and determining application architecture strategy is to understand the current systems deployed.

Application Architecture

Application architecture is the description of all software applications and how they interface with each other. There will generally be two architecture models in an organization: the current deployment and one that represents the portfolio of applications that the company will migrate to over time (called the *target*). We use the name *target application architecture* synonymously with *application portfolio strategy*—or the optimal application portfolio for the company over some period of time in the future (typically two to five years).

Defining and documenting the application architecture is important because:

- It allows the application support team to organize applications on a companywide basis; without a well-defined application architecture and target, application enhancements and new applications will be completed without adhering to an overall plan for information sharing and coordination. The result is a hodgepodge of systems unable to share information and with duplicative functionality.
- It promotes information sharing across the organization by providing a road map to the information being captured in each application.
- It promotes information sharing and real-time data exchange with customers and suppliers by facilitating conversations with those partners on interapplication interface opportunities.
- It helps guide corporate information technology investment priorities and allows the assessment trade-offs quickly by more easily identifying capability gaps in the existing set of systems.
- It allows the application support team to serve customer needs better, faster, and more cost effectively by helping identify the implications of any system change throughout a complex set of interdependent applications.
- It reduces systems development, applications generation, modernization time frames, and resource requirements by providing a clear view of application functions, interfaces, dependencies, and capabilities from which system management, enhancement, and replacement plans can be drawn.

The need for application strategy increases with the size of the business being supported by IT (e.g., the more complex the business or application portfolio, the greater the need for an application strategy). For example, in a medium-sized services company, the application environment may be fairly simple: an accounting package, one application dedicated to the major business activity (e.g., loan processing), a customer database, a business transaction web site, and an electronic data exchange with suppliers. A simple architecture such as this does not take much effort to document.

In contrast, a Fortune 500 company can easily have hundreds of stand-alone and integrated applications managed on multiple platforms by a variety of support groups. In both cases, it is important to document what is in place currently, understand any capability gaps in the existing application portfolio, develop a consistent set of standards (as outlined in Chapter 7), and build a plan for delivering day-to-day service and additional application

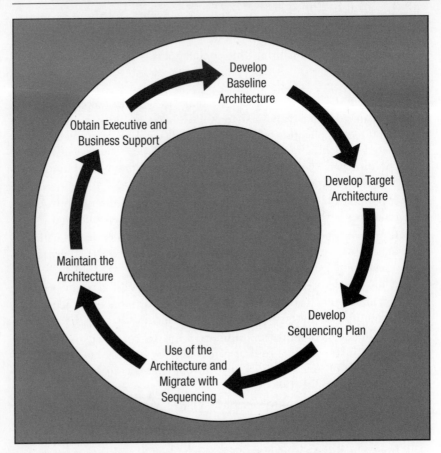

Exhibit 10.2 Application Architecture Definition Process

capabilities. It is easy to see both the value and complexity of an overall application architecture in the latter case.

Exhibit 10.2 outlines the application architecture definition process. It is important to note that the process is an ongoing effort; when the team has successfully migrated to the target architecture, changing business requirements and newly available technologies will most often dictate that a new target architecture be defined and the migration begin again.

Application Architecture—Baseline

Creating a strategy for application architecture begins with establishing a baseline documentation of the existing architecture. This baseline should depict the set of software applications in the current enterprise application landscape. The baseline should contain three key elements (1) an inventory of the applications by functional area that the applications support, (2) a view of how these applications communicate with other internal and external systems, and (3) a description of each application and its purpose. This is the "as-is" state of applications in the company.

To create the baseline, the team should first catalog and categorize all applications by functional area. This application inventory provides a comprehensive view of the suite of applications currently used and supported by the enterprise.

Exhibit 10.3 shows an application architecture diagram for a representative company. In this case, the company has dozens of applications supporting the business. The applications have been categorized along two axes. The first is by major functional area, such as finance, manufacturing, and marketing. For most companies, the applications should be categorized into fewer than a dozen business-unit or functional categories. The second axis segments the systems by the three primary functions that the applications might provide:

1. *Planning and control:* Systems that aid in operational planning, configuration of business systems, and general control of the business.

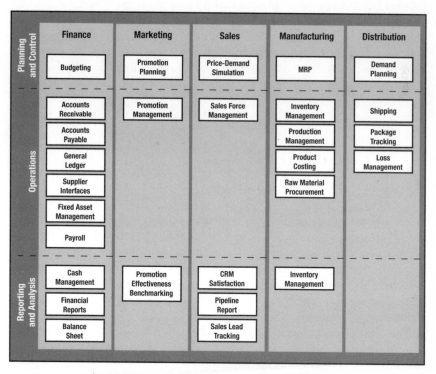

Exhibit 10.3   Example Application Portfolio

2. *Operations:* Transaction-driven business applications; for example, accounting, order entry, manufacturing planning, inventory control, warehouse management.

3. *Reporting and analysis:* Applications that primarily aggregate data from the planning and operations systems to produce reports and analysis, which are used to operate the business.

Segmentation is important because each application requires different types of maintenance and support, as well as a defined level of investment. Furthermore, this portfolio analysis of existing (or target) application architecture may point out areas of weakness in the overall suite of applications (e.g., insufficient planning and control applications for marketing, overburden of reporting applications for HR).

In many cases, the corporate applications were designed and implemented without consideration for the overall application portfolio, but instead to optimize a specific function in the organization, such as order entry or inventory management. Unless the company has implemented an ERP application, there is likely an accumulation of individual applications that support the organization on multiple computing platforms for a diverse user base.

After the full inventory of applications is categorized, the team analyzes how the applications interface with each other and with external applications. This analysis includes understanding the business event or calendar that drives application interfaces, as well as the communication content, method, and protocol. An application architecture diagram that illustrates the current interfaces between the applications discovered in the application portfolio process is shown in Exhibit 10.4. Several key items are depicted, including:

- The application or application submodule and its primary functions.
- Interfaces between the applications or modules.
- Notation of the platform/third-party software that runs the application.

An interesting outcome of this assessment is the identification of applications that run in a "silo" with little or no interface to other applications, and the identification of areas of duplicate data maintenance or opportunities to avoid manual data entry by implementing additional application interfaces. The assessment also shows the level of complication in the environment; that is, number of platforms being supported and complexity of the cross-application interfaces.

The final piece to the application architecture is a system inventory that describes the applications depicted in the application architecture diagram (Exhibit 10.5). The key information that should be collected for each application includes:

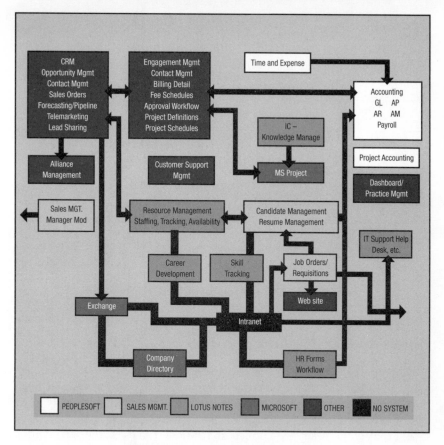

Exhibit 10.4   Application Architecture

- *System:* The system name.
- *Name:* A description-based name for the application.
- *Functions:* The primary functions of the application.
- *Platform:* A description of the platform that runs the application, the level at which it runs (e.g., department, corporate, plant, warehouse).

After the application support team has finished the existing application architecture inventory, they should have a clear picture of the current environment supporting the business. The analysis should be presented to the IT steering committee, along with any findings from the assessment (e.g., missing planning, operations, or reporting capabilities, additional application interface opportunities).

SYSTEM	NAME	FUNCTIONS	PLATFORM
XYZ-360	Management Reporting	• Maintain product characteristic information • Maintain corporate product master files • Load inbound sales data • Print quarterly sales reports	Corporate VM/XA Mainframe
LL-720	End Customer	• Enter, maintain, and transmit inventory position files	Customer System
RPR-328	Product Management	• Sales clerk keys all transactions into system (invoices, orders, receiving, inventory, etc.	Sales Register at Local Store
PA-PM	Local Sales	• Processes local sales transactions • Generates forecast for local store • Communicates information to corporate forecasting system	In-Store Application

Key column information in the table is as follows:
• *System:* The system name
• *Name:* A description-based name for the application
• *Functions:* The primary function of the application
• *Platform:* The technical platform for the application and the level at which it runs (e.g., department, corporate, plant, warehouse, branch)

Exhibit 10.5   Example Application Description Table

Target Application Architecture

The *target architecture* is the set of applications that the organization implements over time, that are planned to improve IT support for business functions. The target architecture is often referred to as the "to-be" architecture.

To begin defining the target application architecture, the application team should review the prioritized project list to understand what business initiatives will have an impact on the application portfolio—what new applications will be needed, what additional capabilities will be added to existing applications, what changes or enhancements to existing application interfaces will be required, and what additional application capacity will be demanded. The process for creating, defining, and prioritizing the list of projects is covered in detail in Chapter 17. Reviewing this set of projects will, in turn, dictate the application architecture over the mid-term (2- to 4-year time frame).

Further, the team should review the existing application architecture to determine the "sunset" on existing systems. This can include systems that will be decommissioned because they are no longer needed by the business; applications that will no longer be supported by the vendor and will be replaced; or applications that have been superceded by newer, more effective technology. The target architecture can then be defined based on the changes emanating from the project list and the systems life cycle for the application.

A critical variable in the target architecture is deciding the time frame the target will cover (i.e., what period of time must the plan cover, by what date must the target architecture be implemented). Typically, a two-year window in smaller companies is appropriate, while a three- to five-year window in larger organizations is more useful.

Document the desired end-state architecture (the three diagrams described earlier), the benefits, and the anticipated costs. The documentation can be done by defining differences from the current model or as a completely new set of diagrams.

Building the Target Application Architecture Migration Plan

The *path to target* or *sequencing plan* is a document that defines the strategy for migrating the enterprise from the current baseline to the target architecture. It defines and schedules the activities that evolve the architecture to the target. The plan should include required company resources, budgets, work tasks, sequencing, dependencies, and time constraints. In some cases, the migration plan may call for several intermediate steps before the target application architecture can be achieved.

In any case, the plans, costs, and benefits of the migration projects should be documented and then serve as input to the IT demand management process outlined in Chapter 17. The IT demand management process will ensure that architecture migration projects are prioritized along with the full suite of other possible IT projects.

Service-Oriented Architecture

Service-oriented architecture (SOA) is an arrangement that utilizes the network as a hub and publishing system. Software services are "published" on the network and made available to all other systems that have security rights to access those services. A "service" can perform a number of functions. It may "publish" or provide information to a requesting application (e.g., status of a shipment). It may "transact" business with another service (e.g., accept an electronic payment for an invoice). Services can be diverse and useful. The benefit of SOA is that services can be accessed internally or with business partners fairly transparently. Software services act independently from each so eliminating the bottlenecks and strict interface procedures typical with older systems. However, there are established industry protocols, security, and other requirements that maintain the integrity of work flow and security. The architecture environment utilizes services and resources on the network that are available as independent entities that can be accessed by other applications, devices, or services independent of the actual technical platform implementation. The "network" in terms of SOA includes the company's internal network (both LAN and WAN) as well as any other network the company's network communicates with including the Internet.

This architecture is in contrast to traditional large custom-developed legacy systems and ERP applications utilizing strict interface procedures and protocols that are proprietary to each company or package. Legacy applications may have been monolithic and performed all company functions and were difficult for external applications to communicate with. Adding the ability for a third party to interface with a legacy application required massive reengineering of the application as well as development of a proprietary interface. Integrating data required fairly onerous development and data integration on a one-to-one basis. SOA allows one-to-many and many-to-many relationships and makes implementation of new capabilities much faster. That is not to say that legacy and ERP applications are bad. ERP application vendors are transforming their applications to support SOA.

In primitive terms, an information-based service is akin to a telephone request. For example, let's say you work in the customer service department for a catalog company. A customer calls you to determine the status of an order. You look up the order and determine it was shipped UPS. So, you call UPS, provide the tracking number, and the UPS representative provides a shipping status of the package. You call the customer back and provide the status. This entire interaction is similar to a "service" in the SOA model. The customer called and requested information. You requested the customer to provide an order number for identification. You then looked up status and needed to call another provider to get all the information to satisfy the customer's request. It didn't matter what type of telephone the customer called on and there was a lot of information that didn't really matter for the request. If you were to build a "service" on the network to handle these requests, it might be called the "sales order status request" and you would make it available for your customers. In technical terms, there are a host of protocols that would make this service possible and some of those are listed at the end of this section.

Wikipedia defines SOA as follows: "In the context of Architecture design the term Service refers to a discretely defined set of contiguous and autonomous business or technical functionality. This is not to be confused with web Services which is just one way of implementing the automated aspects of a given business or technical service."[2] An example would be the decomposition of the business function "Manage Orders" into services such as "Create Order," "Fulfill Order," "Ship Order," "Invoice Order," "Cancel/Update Order."

SOA provides a way to develop a flexible technical architecture that allows companies to implement systems in a more compartmental way while at the same time integrating critical business processes better than traditional large applications. Additionally, the architecture components are less technically dependent, which means that companies have more flexibility and choices on the technical side of the equation (e.g., using different languages or hardware). With the speed at which businesses change, enhancing or modifying a service is much faster than customizing large monolithic computer programs.

Finally, with SOA services can deliver information faster and to more systems. In the previous example, the customer service department could establish routines for requesting the "shipping status request." The manufacturing or sales department can also use the same routines for requesting the same information. In traditional systems, specific interfaces would need to be developed (one for each unit to and from UPS). Now, each unit can utilize the same service and UPS only needs to setup a protocol and message format that everyone can use.

In the past, an organization could develop hundreds of disparate interfaces between systems and these were typically poorly documented. Moving to SOA does not alleviate an organization of the responsibility to document data exchanges and if anything requires additional documentation to alert users, which Service area is available and how to communicate with the service, initiate a call, what information to send, and what to expect back in return. There also needs to be a linkage to the organization's information model showing what information the "Service" owns (creates, updates, and deletes) and which information the service references and is owned by other "Services" and a list of downstream services it utilizes.

The base level of web services standards relevant to SOA includes the following:[3]

- *XML:* A markup language for describing data in message payloads in a document format.
- *HTTP (or HTTPS):* Request/response protocol between clients and servers used to transfer or convey information.
- *SOAP:* A protocol for exchanging XML-based messages over a computer network, normally using HTTP.
- *Web Services Description Language (WSDL):* XML-based service description that describes the public interface, protocol bindings, and message formats required to interact with a web service.
- *Universal Description, Discovery, and Integration (UDDI):* An XML-based registry to publish service descriptions (WSDL) and allow their discovery.

Note, however, that a system does not necessarily need to use any or all of these standards to be "service oriented." For example, some service-oriented systems have been implemented using Corba and Jini.[4]

If you are not already implementing SOA, you will want to start slowly because the task can be daunting and perplexing. One method that seems to work effectively is picking one process or business function and targeting them for the new architecture. You can easily define the services provided by this function or process and its users and consumers, then work with the business to develop a project to implement these services. One successful implementation will encourage the addition of more services.

Application Strategy

After the target application architecture has been defined, one of the most critical decisions required of the CIO is what strategy the company will undertake for delivering the capabilities required in each area. Exhibit 10.6 contains the basic decision tree required from the IT manager for each application. The remainder of this section outlines each of the critical decisions and what factors should influence the CIO in making those decisions.

Application Priority Assessment

Determining when to retire an application is an important, yet often neglected, analysis in the IT department. Companies can generate consider-

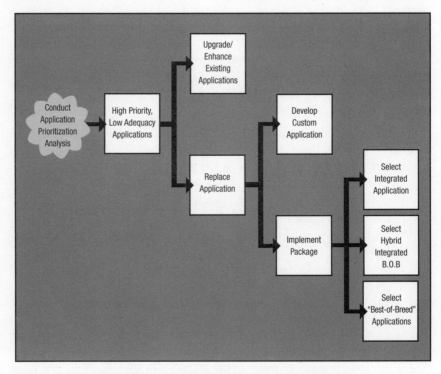

Exhibit 10.6 Application Assessment Decision Tree

able operational efficiencies and cost savings by rationalizing their application portfolio and retiring applications of little value, particularly those that use uncommon technologies and require excessive support and maintenance. The analysis that should be performed to make this determination is similar to the project prioritization analysis presented in Chapter 17. First, the team must assess the current system's adequacy. If no major modifications are made to the current application, how long can the business continue to use it? Develop a scale to assess system adequacy (e.g., 1 to 10) based on criteria set by the business community (e.g., Low = Next 3 to 6 months, Medium = Next 6 to 24 months, High = Next 2 to 4 years).

The second piece of the analysis is to determine the relative value of the application to the business. Chapter 17 outlines several methods for determining the business value of a project or application and highlights the variables that the team may want to consider. After the current system adequacy and potential business value of the system have been determined, the options can be plotted as depicted in Exhibit 10.7.

If the business importance of the application is low, then the application should receive little or no new funding or attention. All applications with low

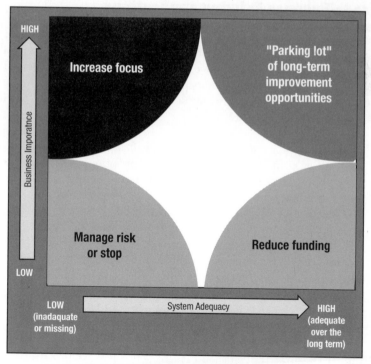

Exhibit 10.7   Application Prioritization Framework

business importance are candidates for retirement. In the case where the system adequacy is low, the team should add projects to the project inventory that show the cost savings or other value generated by decommissioning the system. For low-value, high-system adequacy systems, the team should adjust service levels and resource focus to minimize new investment or effort in the system.

If the business value is high, then the course of action will be determined by current system adequacy. If the current system is adequate, a decision on new investment in the application can be deferred for 6 to 12 months. In the meantime, the team should ensure that adequate resources are maintaining the system.

If the business importance is high and the system adequacy is low, the application should be upgraded. You must then determine whether enhancing the current application or replacing it is more cost effective and better fulfills business needs.

Most of the information needed for this analysis is provided during the *package selection* phase discussed in Chapter 12. Enhancement to the application needs to be treated in the analysis similarly to purchasing a new application.

Upgrade/Enhance Existing Applications versus Replacement

For each application that falls into the "increase focus" quadrant of the application priority analysis, the team should determine an application strategy. For each application, the team may choose to upgrade/enhance the existing application or replace the application entirely. This decision will be divided between two key criteria:

1. *Total cost of ownership (total costs over the life or remaining life of an application):* Analyze the total cost of each option over the life span of the application. For example, if one option is to upgrade the current order configuration custom application, then the total costs to code the enhancements, roll out the changes, train the users, and maintain the application must be estimated. A similar analysis needs to be done for the other alternative, which may be (1) developing a totally new application or (2) implementing a third-party packaged application.

2. *Functional fit:* As Chapter 12 details, the applications team should document the requirements of the system and assess the package alternatives that can fulfill the requirements. Add additional factors into the analysis as described in Chapter 12.

Exhibit 10.8 shows the decision between enhancing the existing application versus replacement. After completing this analysis, the team will be able

	EXISTING APPLICATION	REPLACEMENT APPLICATION
	DIRECT COSTS	
ONE-TIME COSTS	• Software—Total cost of developed or purchased enhancements to application. • Cost of additional support software. • Implementation costs for redeployment or conversion. • Training—Cost of training (personnel), expenses, capital. • Hardware—Cost of additional hardware required (include: expensed and depreciated, lease fees, upgrades, spares, supplies).	• Software—Total cost of selection, new application license, development. • Implementation costs for redeployment or conversion. • Training—Cost of Training (personnel), expenses, capital. • Hardware—Cost of additional hardware required (include: expensed and depreciated, lease fees, upgrades, spares, supplies).
ON-GOING COSTS	• Operations—Cost of continuing support and maintenance (include technical services, performance tuning, Tier 2 problem resolution, maintenance labor, operating system support, user administration, capacity planning, backup, service desk [Tier 1], DBA's, functional and technical application support, process and planning management, and maintenance contracts). • Administration—Cost of supervisory management, administrative assistance, asset management, auditing, purchasing, vendor management, IT course development and training, End user course development and training.	• Same as "Existing Application" plus:— Software maintenance fees.
	INDIRECT COSTS	
INDIRECT COST	• End-user operations—Cost of peer support, casual and formal learning, file or data management. • Downtime (end user or IT).	• Same as "Existing Application."
	FUNCTIONAL ANALYSIS	
FUNCTIONAL COSTS	• Assessment of functional fit across key business requirements (see vendor selection chapter).	• Assessment of functional fit across key business requirements (see vendor selection chapter).

Exhibit 10.8 Analysis Framework: Replace Existing Application versus Replaced with Package or Custom-Developed Application

to quantify cost trade-offs for each alternative and be able to judge whether the additional cost for one option is worth the additional functionality and ease, or whether that option poses more costs for less functionality.

Developing Custom Applications versus Implementing Package Applications

Once the decision has been made to replace an application, the next question is whether the company should purchase a package or custom develop software internally. Chapter 12 presents a detailed methodology for the assessment of package applications that provides a road map for determining the costs, benefits, and fit of the package.

In general, the team should work to determine if any package option exists. The benefits of packaged applications usually outweigh the potential functional give-ups. The significant development costs and high-support burden of custom-developed applications make them an unattractive option for most companies. In previous decades, building business applications from scratch was the only option available due to lack of software for particular business areas. However, a host of application companies emerged to provide business applications to fill increasing demands to automate almost every business process. Today, there are few application areas or business models with no offerings from third-party software companies. Exhibit 10.9 outlines the major advantages of package applications.

Exhibit 10.9   Package Application Approach Advantages

The final decision of whether to buy or build can be driven by the answers to the questions in Exhibit 10.10 that provide a clear indicator of whether a package is viable. As mentioned, the burden of proof should rest with the custom-development option. In only a few unusual cases will the custom-development option be the appropriate approach for an application replacement.

DIMENSION	DESCRIPTION
Time to market	• How fast can solutions be deployed to operations?
System capabilities	• Robustness—How complete and rich is the functionality? • Quality—How free of problems/bugs the solution is likely to be? • Flexibility—How easy is it to adapt code to meet requirements?
Cost/Investment levels	• Development—Initial investment in building the solution. • Buying—Costs of purchasing the solution. • Deployment/Implementation—Costs related to rolling out the solution to the different operations. • On-going support/maintenance—Costs involved with troubleshooting/solving solutions technical problems. • Research and development—Investment required to keep the solution technically and functionally advanced. • Testing—Costs related to ensuring technical and functional quality. • Training—One-time and ongoing end-user and technical training.
Continuous improvement	• Best practices—Including industry best practices put into the solution. • Advantaged capabilities—Incorporating leading edge functionality into the solution. • Technology renovation/update—Maintaining the solution in the most advantageous/economically sound technology platform.
Risks	• How prone is the solution to fall short of expectations (e.g., time, costs, functionality, technical soundness)? • What are the costs of failure? • How new are the technologies both provided by packaged vendors as well as the development environment if developed internally?

Exhibit 10.10   Key Decision Criteria for Buy versus Build Decisions

Software as a Service

Software as a Service (SAAS) is a way to purchase software through a service model that has become increasingly popular over the past few years. SAAS is a model of software delivery where the software provider hosts the application, maintains the hardware, provides technical administration of the system, backs up the data, and provides the user a remote interface (via the Web or remote desktop) to the application. One of the best known SAAS providers is Salesforce.com which provides CRM software through the Internet.

SAAS can provide applications via this delivery method for small and large organizations alike. Some organizations with 500 or more salespeople are using online CRM systems. SAAS providers are able to interface with existing and disparate corporate databases, and make data integration much more viable than in the past. The model provides value to the company via the delivery of the software as well as providing no maintenance hardware and hosting behind the scenes.

SAAS is differentiated from application service providers (ASPs) in a few ways. ASPs are typically hosting hardware and applications dedicated to the client and are closer to a data center or hosting arrangement than SAAS, which is providing the software rather than acting as a high-end hosting provider.

SAAS providers and applications affect the decision to buy versus build software. SAAS is another application to consider and a software delivery mechanism to consider when analyzing all the potential options. When selecting software, it is possible to look at both a SAAS option and a non-SAAS option. How well each option meets the business requirements will likely be a major determinant of the direction you decide to take. Additionally, the costing model of SAAS and non-SAAS software options will look different but can be compared. For example, SAAS software typically has an upfront deposit or initiation fee and potential setup fees along with a recurring monthly charge per user. The other option, purchasing a software package entails paying a license fee, acquiring hardware, expending labor for the setup, installation, and configuration of the application and hosting/ongoing maintenance. The costs for each option can be compared on a one-time and monthly basis to see which option costs the least over the life of the project.

In many cases, SAAS may be a better functional fit and less expensive option than alternatives and should be seriously considered. It may not be the answer for every application.

Key providers include @Road, 24SevenOffice, 37signals, Apptix, Ariba, Backbone Systems, BritishTelecom, Citrix Online, CollabNet, CSC, eMeta Corporation, Google, Intuit, Journyx, Microsoft, NetSuite, Oracle, Replicon, RightNow Technologies, Salesforce.com, Serials Solutions, Snap Technologies, SPS Commerce, Sun Microsystems, Twinfield, WebEx.[5]

Integrated Applications versus "Best of Breed"

If the replacement decision has been made in favor of a package system, the team is now faced with a final choice: Whether to implement a best-of-breed package or an integrated ERP suite.

Best of breed is the process of selecting the best package or set of packages available that provide a narrow set of capabilities, but which are highly specialized and configurable for the specific function they cover (e.g., forecasting system for industries with highly variable demand, product design system for highly engineered product, or manufacturing planning system for custom garments). Best of breed is the process of selecting the solutions that provide the most robust feature sets in vertical functional needs, yet provide the openness to integrate as an enterprise solution with other best-of-breed packages or with an integrated ERP system horizontally across the enterprise.

Under this definition, a best-of-breed financial management solution provides a win-win solution with depth of financial management capabilities in the vertical functional domain and with the ability to scale and integrate with other best-of-breed vertical systems across the enterprise.

Enterprise resource planning (ERP) applications are an amalgamation of a company's application systems designed to bind more closely a variety of company functions and operations. These systems usually provide support for the entire internal company supply chain (forecasting, manufacturing planning, procurement, manufacturing management, shipping, distribution), as well as functional areas such as human resources, finance, and marketing. ERP software applications were initially created in the 1980s as a response to demand for more enterprise integration. Today, these packages incorporate internal integration across business operations and functions, as well as to external entities such as suppliers and customers. ERP software companies, such as SAP, Oracle, Microsoft, Lawson, and many others, offer integrated ERP applications. Additionally, many of these vendors have specific configurations and package modules that are geared toward specific industries.

The best-of-breed approach generally delivers the closest fit to a company-specific business process by providing the richest functionality, the greatest flexibility, and the fastest time to market for new initiatives. The argument for a single, integrated approach is that it is much simpler, has cross application integration built-in, carries less vendor and implementation risk, and will likely have lower implementation and support cost.

Best-of-breed applications, on the other hand, pose a challenge to the integration front. Because of the complexity associated with integrating multiple applications in a best-of-breed scenario, many companies have chosen a hybrid approach that implements a core ERP system for basic functional areas and business areas that do not have unusual requirements. They then use a best-of-breed application in the one or two areas that have strategic advantages or are critical to the company.

Business and functional areas with strong best-of-breed applications include:

- Supply chain management.
- Product pricing and promotions.
- Inventory management.
- Forecasting and demand management.
- Warehousing and logistics.
- Delivery/route planning.
- Order management.
- Order configuration (for highly engineered products).
- Professional services management (client/hours tracking).
- Human resources/employee recruiting systems.
- E-business applications (e.g., content management, web commerce).
- Customer relationship management (CRM) software.

Analysis of the three package-based options is required to determine if the trade-off of less integration makes sense given the functional fit, the objectives, the costs, and the overall application architecture plan. Exhibit 10.11 lists specific characteristics between best-of-breed and ERP. Exhibit 10.12 on page 320 further compares and contrasts the focus of the two approaches. The final three sections of this chapter cover the application maintenance, development of custom systems, and the implementation of package systems in further detail.

Maintaining Existing Applications

The Application Help Desk Concept

As outlined in Chapter 9, nearly all IT departments have a help desk function which manages inbound calls from end users. The application help desk is a similar function, but it is charged with supporting the application and resolving application-related issues. It is typically organized into teams dedicated to specific applications.

In support of the help desk, it is important to ensure that responsibilities in the IT organization are clearly divided between developing/enhancing applications and fixing applications as seen in Exhibit 4.1. Too often, the development team is asked to meet critical deadlines for a new release of an application while, at the same time, being barraged with urgent calls from

BEST-OF-BREED CHARACTERISTICS

Best of Breed

- Built for optimization of a key business process.
- Must itegrate with other applications (poses challenge).
- Can better leverage a legacy environment.
- May deliver competitive advantage (assuming superior functionality—this is not always the case).
- Flexibility (provides options on future direction).
- Quicker implementation timeframe (assuming less modules).
- Greater dependency on internal staff for knowledge of application and integration with other applications.
- Must build complex interfaces to other application.
- Dependency on multiple, smaller vendors.

INTEGRATED ERP CHARACTERISTICS

Enterprise Application

- Core modules delivered for most functional areas.
- Uses best-of-breed applications or custom development for weak areas.
- Implementation could include full breadth of functionality.
- May have industry specific solutions.
- Leverages vendors scale, user base, and expertise in industry and building software.
- More standardization in environment (user interface, security, user administration, platform, database).
- High level of integration (data flows are built-in).
- Dependency on a single vendor.

Exhibit 10.11   Characteristics of Best of Breed versus ERP

end users for day-to-day maintenance issues. Because the team is faced with handling ongoing application support, while simultaneously attempting to add new application features, development falls behind, and the new release comes in late and over budget. When possible, the development team should be separated from the application support team.

Exhibit 10.13 depicts how the development process can be significantly longer if the application support and development teams are mixed. In this example, the team in the top row is responsible for both development and support expends 40 hours on the development effort and 24 hours on support. When separated into two teams, the development team still expends 40

ISSUES	BEST OF BREED	INTEGRATED ERP
Time to implement	6 to 12 months	18 to 48 months
Value	Focused on business process.	Company-wide
ROI	12-month payback	2 to 5 year payback
Integration with other applications	Build interfaces to other applications.	Built-in except for outlier applications.
Functional fit	High in business process area.	Depends on area and vendor.
Quality	Similar	Heavy spending by vendor in R&D.
Vendor risk	Many smaller vendors.	Few larger vendors.
Users	Small functional group.	Company-wide
Training	Focused	Focused for function but company-wide.

Exhibit 10.12   General Guidelines for Best of Breed versus ERP

hours, but the support takes only 16 hours. Two phenomena are occurring. First, when split into two teams, the development schedule is completed 37 percent earlier because the development team does not need to split its focus. The support is completed in fewer hours because the support team focuses strictly on support issues to which they are able to respond quickly, not having to wait for users, and where they can optimize the knowledge base.

**Exhibit 10.13   Separation of Application Development and
Support Responsibilities**

To effectively manage the application help desk process, two processes should be put in place. First is the support process for trouble-ticket tracking and break/fix calls, as described in the Chapter 9.

The second process to put into place is the enhancement request process. *Enhancements* are generally defined as features/functions that were not designed in the original system specification. If the application is still in a developmental stage, the enhancement team may be the original development team. Enhancements should be prioritized with other development efforts and projects. Enhancement requests are usually delivered several ways:

- User requested fixes or changes.
- Through the business owner—usually in a monthly or quarterly meeting.
- Through the IT department—the help desk or enhancement team categorizes some set of recurring issues with the application and recommends a long-term enhancement solution.
- Through the IT steering committee.

Any type of enhancement should fall under the same scrutiny as development projects. A group of enhancements should be approved and batched into an interim "release" of the application. General communication flow should be as follows:

1. An electronic or paper form should be completed documenting the enhancement request.
2. The system designer and business users should meet to review the request, or a batch of requests, to understand the context, the business processes affected, and the objective of the request.
3. The technical team should estimate the effort required to complete the request, by detailing the requirement and designing the fix.
4. Final sign-off should be given to the business user after they review the "cost" of the enhancement to ensure it is worth the effort.

Setting Service Level Agreements

Just as with the operations support area, application service level parameters should be set for all key business applications. Doing so helps manage the support team, determine roles and responsibilities, establish resource requirements, as well as set mutual expectations between the IT group and the business users. Key parameters to consider include:

- Roles and responsibilities (between the application support team, technical support team, help desk, and business users).
- Support hours of operation.

- System request process (a process diagram showing how system requests are routed).
- Problem resolution procedures (how calls are handled, tracked, and closed).
- Severity levels (assign level of importance to each request; it is not the user's responsibility to assign severity; it is a joint determination).
- Priority levels (priority denotes a level of importance in a group of service requests of the same severity).
- Status codes (detail whether the tickets are open, closed, in-process, waiting for information from user, waiting for information from vendor).
- Escalation process (details the process by which calls are escalated up the organization in level of importance).
- Key metrics to track all application support performance:
  —Mean time to resolve tickets on first call.
  —Percent of tickets resolved on first call.
  —Mean time to resolve calls.
  —Time to complete enhancements as percent of total time.
  —Percent of tickets resolved correctly.
  —Average satisfaction score (1 to 5 scale) from customers with tickets.

Key Roles in Application Management

Roles that need to be fulfilled by members of the application management team include:

- Batch job scheduling.
- Application print management.
- Application start-up/shutdown.
- Application data integrity.
- Application production status monitoring.
- Review of software patches, upgrades, bug fixes, and service packs (packaged software).
- Implementation of software changes, upgrades, and service packs.
- Configuration and customization management and documentation (packaged software).
- Coding modifications, unit and integration testing.
- Conduct user acceptance testing for enhancements and fixes.
- Application performance tuning.
- Application security management (if not responsibility of operations security group).
- Application service request management.
- Application change control.

- Application administrative functions (user ID requests, group changes, user-level configuration/profiles—if not handled by operations group).

Application Environments Management

To provide the application development/management team with the ability to develop and test changes prior to deployment into production, they should create several systems environments outside the production area in which the applications can run. These environments can be logical partitions on one server or, ideally, separate servers entirely. Optimally, the team will maintain three environments, one each for development, testing, and production. In some cases, teams will establish additional environments for specialized purposes, such as end-user or volume testing. The purpose of three environments is to:

- Keep the production environment stable and minimize production changes to fully-tested application enhancement installs.
- Develop enhancements in a separate development environment, which is free from production capacity issues or scheduling constraints.
- After code set is ready for testing, it can be frozen and moved into the testing environment. This reduces the number of moving parts (testing team won't think code is changing daily). Additionally, it allows the development team to continue work while the testing team is testing.

Application Performance Management

Maintaining application functionality is critical to the life cycle of an application system. Equally important is managing the performance of the application. Application performance management (APM) is the discipline of monitoring and maintaining the performance of an application over time. Performance can be characterized in terms of availability of the application, speed of transactions processed, and the amount of transactions processed over a particular period. The business should specifically state the performance expectations for various business processes and applications so that the IT department can guarantee those metrics. APM is critical to tracking the reliability and performance of applications over time and pertains to both custom and package software implementations.

Basic best practices include:

1. Install monitoring software on servers running applications to ensure real-time notification of hardware performance.
2. Configure monitoring software to include application processes (e.g., is the application running or not; is the application processing transactions properly).

3. Monitor hardware capacity and processing usage over time (e.g., trend the data so you know if performance is degrading over time).

4. Perform periodic (e.g., weekly, monthly, or quarterly) and standard maintenance on applications, including installing patches, and performing application data updates.

5. Track an issue list of the top five processes and any maintenance performed on these processes.

6. Make sure the most critical business applications receive the majority of APM attention.

Application Release Management

When managing custom developed and customized package software, application release management is a critical function. It includes planning, tracking, and organizing changes to the application. In many cases with less formal rollouts, the development or implementation team will implement a new application. Immediately, they begin fielding calls from users regarding functionality questions and bug reports. In short order, these calls and the resulting work orders begin to consume more and more time from the team. What looked like the end of a project and a declining workload will result in more work and a never-ending project. The best way to alleviate or eliminate this issue is to define a hard date when new applications will go into a state called production or steady state. Once an application changes status from implementation to steady state, a new support structure is required. Instead of users calling the implementation team directly, calls should start routing through the normal help desk and be subject to escalation procedures. All issues and questions should be tracked so the team can look at trend lines and eliminate root causes. Bugs and application enhancement requests should be the responsibility of the development team, but a release management strategy should be implemented.

Release management entails queuing up the list of bugs and enhancements and looking at all the work in total and determining how items should be prioritized. Next, resources are assigned to the prioritized list. Release schedules can then be set. Some organizations release patches and maintenance updates weekly, some monthly, and some annually. The release schedule and frequency will be dictated by the labor available, the application, and the severity of the issues.

An individual needs to be assigned the responsibility for conducting release management. In larger organizations or those with complex applications, a full-time manager could be required. This person is typically referred to as the release manager or the product manager. The responsibilities of this function include managing the enhancement and bug list, developing the prioritization criteria, overseeing development and testing, and determining release schedule.

The benefit of formalizing this process is that organization priorities can be managed more effectively. Rather than one or two users dominating the implementation team's time with requests that might be important to an individual but not the entire organization, the team can work on a prioritized list of items that accounts for a wider input of organization priorities.

Web Management

Website development, management and maintenance is a specialized area of application development for several reasons:

- A large number of unique skill sets are required for successful creation and ongoing management of a site.
- Sites are often oriented to a diverse audience which may include customers, internal staff, shareholders, regulators, customer prospects and even competitors.
- Sites are externally accessible, and therefore are subject to the security risks and challenges discussed in Chapter 8.
- Sites can receive varying, unpredictable user loads creating a capacity management challenge.
- The techniques, tools, and technology for web development have traditionally evolved rapidly.
- Sites can be an important source of information for customers (e.g., downloadable product information) and consequently reduce the customer service burden in a company.
- Sites can provide an alternate venue for end-customer purchase of products, alleviating order entry burden (for non e-commerce companies).
- Sites can be a helpful source of information for companies based on source, type, and volume of web traffic.

Because of the specialized requirements, one of the largest challenges in managing organization websites is the diverse skill sets required on the team. (See table on p. 326.) Determining responsibility for these roles within an organization can be confusing. This is also an area where outside consultants are often used, due to the specialized nature of the tasks (e.g., search engine optimization).

While a web site can be viewed as just another application in the IT department and managed as such, web site management has some distinct characteristics that may warrant unique approaches to maintenance and administration. No one will argue that the web site hardware, network, and

Area	Role	Sample Project Responsibilities
Management	• Project manager	• Responsible for overall project delivery and client accountability • Create and manage work plans, business integration, and overall team leadership
Technical	• Developer	• Develop application logic and code • Typical technologies include Java, .NET
	• DBA / data architect	• Database design/architecture • DB implementation, tuning, data conversion
	• Systems engineer	• Technical setup (load balancing, network equipment, web server, OS, DB installs) • Technical configuration of all systems
Design	• Designer	• Create visual design, images, and HTML for site • Focus on combining appropriate and consistent visual impression with usability and simplicity for end-users • Sometimes may split duties between designer and end-user interface specialist
	• Information architect	• Design structure/hierarchy of information to be presented based on content and business priorities • Focus on site navigation and content presentation
Steady-state	• Webmaster	• Administrative responsibility for logins, content, traffic reporting, issue tracking, and resolution • Main point of contact for internal and external constituencies
	• Optimization/ SEO	• Ensure that site content and external linkage bring site to top ranking in major search engines • Ongoing process
	• Content management specialist	• Responsible for ongoing management of content on the site (addition, removal, enhancement of content) • Usually non-IT role (department end-user, content owner)

data should be managed by the IT department or a vendor managed by the IT department due to the technical complexity of these pieces, however, many will debate who should manage the web site application itself and there are a number of options. These options include the IT web development function, the marketing department, the sales department, or an outside vendor.

The IT department should manage the technical aspects of a web application including the development and enhancement of the supporting code base. All technical maintenance should be performed by the IT department or a vendor managed by the department. The application code itself should be managed by IT or a vendor managed by IT as well. One reason why these technical items are not managed by IT in some organizations is when IT is not getting the job done and there may be various reasons for that. In those cases, the other departments are more than justified in taking over the function. If, however, the IT department is managing the function competently, there is no justification for change.

Regarding the content of the web site, this function must be delegated to other parts of the company and should not be an IT function. Web applications should allow the users to update their own content and publish to the web site on their own time frame. If the application does not have a function that allows users to upload or change content themselves, then it is best for IT to train a user in another department on how to update the content where there are more technical challenges. In general, the largest concern between IT and other departments in this area, is when another department wishes to update site content and provides that content to IT, but then IT drops the ball or takes too long to implement the content changes. This issue can be alleviated by giving the appropriate users the ability to change the content themselves.

Application Life Cycle

Applications have a life cycle just as any other technology component. Although significant attention is usually given to the initial development effort, that effort tends to be a very minor portion of the overall corporate investment in the application over time—usually coming to 10 percent to 20 percent of the total investment. Although many "legacy" applications have seen decades of use, technology and business priority changes usually dictate a three- to five-year lifespan for the typical application. Exhibit 10.14 outlines a typical application life cycle.

Application Management Best Practices

A variety of best practices have emerged for documenting current architecture and are noted here:

- To minimize new investment and system disruption, new application strategy should be chosen according to the following order of priorities: re-use, buy, build (custom develop).
- In general, business process redesign should precede system development, particularly in the case of new capabilities being supported by

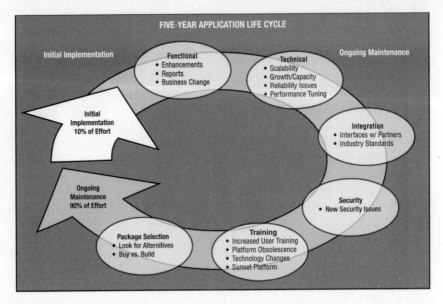

Exhibit 10.14 Application Life Cycle

the application. The application requirements should emerge from the business process redesign effort.

- Third-party package software should comprise the majority of newly implemented systems.

- The application support team must aggressively limit package customizations to reduce the threat of an unsupported package that is highly customized and eliminates the upgrade path. Heavy (and undocumented) customizations eliminate the benefit of a packaged application and drive overly high maintenance costs.

- When implementing packaged software for noncritical business processes, attempt to modify the business process to match the package application where feasible to avoid excessive application customization and configuration efforts.

- If business process modification is not feasible, an alternative is limited use of bolt-on packages or self-contained, tightly-scoped, custom-developed applications for package gap areas.

- When selecting application platforms, select those that can operate on low-cost infrastructure and technologies that are less costly to support over the long term (labor and support costs).

- Integrate applications using a middleware messaging tool (enterprise application integration [EAI] tools). This allows replacement of systems as needed into a messaging subsystem rather than modifying intersystem interfaces each time an application is changed in the portfolio.

Developing New Applications

Entire books are available that cover in great detail the process for building custom-developed applications, from scoping and requirements gathering, through technical design and development to quality assurance and user acceptance testing, data conversion, and implementation. The body of knowledge available for this particular topic is extensive, well-explored territory and is readily available for any systems professional, therefore, we briefly address only a few key management considerations in developing applications.

The major work steps that comprise an application development effort include:

- Planning and estimating.
- Requirements definition.
- System design.
- Detailed design.
- Testing.
- Implementation.
- Ongoing support.

Each of these steps should be planned in detail; the plans should be revised at the completion of each major step, particularly the requirements definition and system design tasks that may result in changed assumptions about the project timing, benefits, and costs.

The application team should give special consideration to estimating custom-development projects. Although there are multiple estimating methodologies, many times the estimating effort is neglected or ignored altogether. Often project estimating, when it is attempted at all, is done on a top-down basis, resulting in overly optimistic predictions for resources, timing, and completion dates. A preferable method determines the key drivers of effort for the project, such as number of functions, interfaces, tables, and screens in the application. Based on these, or other appropriate predictors of overall work effort, the team can build a credible estimate of the likely effort to complete the project.

Structuring Projects

For large development projects, the team requires resources for the following roles: graphical and user interface design, functional expertise and configuration, database design and management, data conversion, code development, and quality assurance testing and infrastructure configuration and engineering. Additionally, the team should have representation from at least one business user who will take ownership of the business requirements and help with application design. Exhibit 10.15 lists and describes the minimum deliverables that should be expected from the team.

PHASE	DELIVERABLES	DESCRIPTION
Planning and estimating	• Client business overview	• Overview of company—lines of business, operations profile/footprint, organization, key statistics on business.
	• Business situation/problem assessment	• Description of business issues that project should address.
	• Cost estimating	• Cost estimating.
	• Project goals and priorities	• Concise goals and priorities of project.
	• Key success factors	• Specific challenges or hurdles that exist for the project.
Requirements definition	• Audience analysis	• Overview of potential audiences for system (users, operators, administrators, etc.).
	• Comparable site application analysis	• Inventory of comparable sites. • Select for similarity of underlying business model, process, navigation, or design. • Critique of process or design elements. • Inventory of elements to be incorporated.
	• UI Site design	• Site colors, typefaces, look-and-feel. • Rationale for design, incorporating information from audience and comparable site analysis.
	• Screen templates	• Inventory of key user/administrator system interface screens. • Preliminary user interface designs. • Highlights key user selections, screen design elements (pick boxes, lists, radio buttons, etc.). • Data required to populate screens. • Triggers and data resulting from screens.
	• Information architecture	• "Road map" inventory of all pages on application with short description of content. • Parent-child relationships and preliminary navigation links.
	• Navigation design	• One-page template showing primary top-tab and side-link navigation approach.

Exhibit 10.15 Overview of Project Phases, Key Worksteps, and Deliverables

PHASE	DELIVERABLES	DESCRIPTION
System design phase	• Business process diagrams	• Inventory of key business events and their impact. • Organized to show people, processes, systems, and information used by the process. • With accompanying specifications sheets.
	• Context diagram	• Overview of key business components and their interactions. • Used to set context and terminology for the remainder of the visioning and systems designs documents. • All components should be linked back to the overall context diagram.
	• Functional requirements	• What the applications must "do."
	• Application architecture	• Inventory of applications. • Cut by business process and application type to show coverage of important areas. • Shown by function, interface, and platform to demonstrate key elements of application, communication, and functionality.
	• Data architecture	• Overview of tables, fields, data types, unique keys, foreign keys, and so on. • Organized by master files, lookup files, and transaction files. • Referential integrity requirements and approach.
	• Technical architecture	• Overview of technical platform to support deployment of the application. • Key elements include servers, clients, OS, system software, network, cross-application interfaces.
	• Workplans for construction phase	• Detailed workplan for entire construction phase. • Workplan elements should include: –Key project phases. –Tasks/subtasks, timeline. –Resource assignments. –Key milestones. –Deliverables/description of deliverables. *(continued)*

Exhibit 10.15 *Continued*

PHASE	DELIVERABLES	DESCRIPTION
Design phase	• Report design	• Inventory of all reports to be produced by system: operational reports, system management reports. • By report: format, data required, trigger (on-line, batch), frequency.
	• Testing plan	• Overview of testing approach—should exercise every functional element of systems as well as cross-module interfaces and referential integrity. • Inventory of test cases.
	• Migration plan	• Migration workplan; timing requirements, data availability, and so on. • Should cover conversion of old systems (when shut off), approach to converting to new systems (by geography, division, etc.). • Workplans and checklists at the server, client, and application configuration levels.
	• User documentation	• User-level documentation: FAQs, training, and instruction manuals.
	• Technical documentation	• Technical documentation oriented toward technical systems support and application developers.

Exhibit 10.15 *Continued*

Managing the Software Development Effort

Finally, application managers should become familiar with several control and quality issues associated with large systems development efforts, for example:

- *Software version control:* There are multiple tools available to help the team manage software versions and manage the code, objects, and executables during development.
- *Documentation:* Documentation covers business process, requirements, database schema, and software code. There are tools available that cover these categories as well. For smaller projects, the documentation effort can easily be accomplished with word-processing and spreadsheet programs.
- *Productivity measures:* There are a variety of methodologies for assessing and measuring both the quantity and quality of development resources. The development manager should become familiar with these and implement them where appropriate.

- *Milestones:*
  —Estimating and work steps to drive a project plan.
  —Adhering to the project plan and the major milestones is critical to instilling discipline in the team environment. Ignoring missed deadlines sends the message that deadlines do not matter. Even if a deadline is not critical to the project, a missed milestone should be treated seriously. Missed deadlines can often help highlight potential project issues, or identify poor productivity in individual team members.
- *Testing:* Testing serves to simulate real-world environments to make sure the software performs as designed and as needed. Developers and users should be involved with testing. In large projects, a dedicated quality assurance testing team may be necessary. There are generally four steps to the testing phase:
  —Create test plan.
  —Create unit and system test scripts.
  —Create performance test scripts.
  —Create user acceptance test criteria.
- *Maintenance:* The development team will likely move into the maintenance team when the software goes live.

Development Methodologies

There are numerous viable development methodologies used to bring structure to the software development and implementation projects. Here we summarize some of the most popular methodologies. However, be aware that there is a tremendous amount of in-depth information published specifically on each methodology. For usage, we recommend reading one of the other texts listed in the resources section, as well as easy-to-find on-line resources.

Popular development methodologies include Waterfall, RAD, Agile Development, and Extreme Programming.

Each methodology has pros and cons as well as derivative works. There are multiple variations on these methodologies. In fact, methodologies combine concepts and derive from already existing methods. Like most technical topics, the "right" methodology is a topic of hot debate in IT communities.

While the methodologies vary priority and emphasis placed on various processes and deliverables during software development, they usually share elements of the software development lifecycle (SDLC) in common. The overall components of the SDLC are generally acknowledged to include analysis (determining requirements, i.e., what the software must do), specification (specifying requirements), software architecture (designing the system), implementation/coding, testing, documentation, training and support, and finally, maintenance.[6]

Waterfall.   The waterfall methodology or traditional approach to software development consists of the following steps in sequence:

- *Requirements definition:* The process of documenting the users functional requirements for the application. This is typically accomplished by functional area or by business process.
- *Technical design:* The process of taking the functional requirements and translating them to the technical aspects of the system.
- *Development:* Synonomous with terms like construction, build, or code. In this step the computer programmers take the designs and begin developing the system to meet requirements.
- *Testing:* Typically consists of a unit test where the developers test the application they are working on. The development team tests all the applications that make up the system in a cohesive integrated manner as if it were in production. And user testing is where the users test the functional requirements and accept or sign off that the piece they are testing works according to their requirements.
- *Integration or implementation:* Implementation is the process of installing, training, and rolling out the application to the users in a production mode.
- *Maintenance:* The steps where the application switches over from the development team to the maintenance team.

All of these steps are important, but perhaps the most critical (because all the other steps are downstream) is requirements definition. If requirements aren't captured and documented sufficiently, it becomes very difficult to get anything else right. Additionally, with this methodology, documentation is critically important especially as the project gets larger or the timelines are long. In large formal projects typically the users are asked to sign a document stating that they have reviewed the requirements and agree that the requirements are sufficient and comprehensive.

EXAMPLE WATERFALL METHODOLOGIES. Each step is completed sequentially (Exhibit 10.16). However, project failures in large-scale application development have caused derivative methodologies to be more iterative in nature. They use the same steps, but breakdown the work into smaller pieces and execute multiple times (Exhibit 10.17). The benefits of the waterfall approach is that it is well understood and does incorporate all the necessary steps to develop an application. The largest drawback is the belief that the application must be perfected by going through these steps in lock step. The problems occur when the project is scoped to large and the time frame between the steps is so large that work in a previous box may be out of date by the time two or three steps have gone by. This increases the risk of a development project by orders of magnitude. Typically, large projects should be broken up into small manageable phases to increase the probability of success. The waterfall approach has been in existence since at

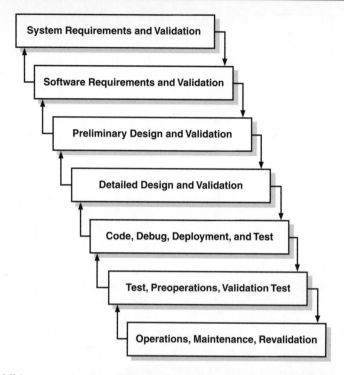

Exhibit 10.16   Version of Waterfall Development Methodology (*Source:* Wikipedia contributors, "Waterfall," *Wikipedia: The Free Encyclopedia,* http://en.wikipedia.org/wiki/Waterfall_model.)

least 1970 and is one of the most commonly used methodologies. If you decide to use it, make sure the project size and project timeline is between three to six months.

RAPID APPLICATION DEVELOPMENT.   Rapid Application Development (RAD) is another methodology that incorporates full life cycle application development from design through implementation. It was developed in response to the problems inherent with the waterfall approach. James Martin developed the RAD approach during the 1980s at IBM and published a book about it in 1991.[7]

RAD consists of:

- Prototyping.
- Iterative development.
- Time boxing.
- Team members.
- Management approach.

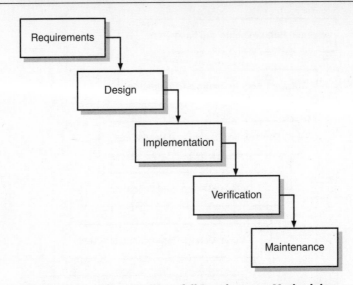

Exhibit 10.17   Alternate Waterfall Development Methodology
(*Source:* Paul A. Hoadley, "Waterfall," http://en.wikipedia.org/wiki/Waterfall_model.)

With RAD, the goal is to build the application in an iterative approach. At the start, the team is just trying to build a working prototype. A short time frame is assigned to the project as well as fewer team members. Senior management must be involved with the project. Once the initial prototype version is complete, subsequent rounds of programming are accomplished while adding increasing functionality over time.

RAD allows teams to build applications faster and additional has some built-in/defined quality targets. However, the applications are typically not the final end product but a product with limited functionality. It is difficult to use RAD with large scale applications as it does not lend itself to large teams of developers.

AGILE. Agile development methodology is a lightweight methodology whose motto could be "less is more." The methodology was developed in a response to the heavy waterfall methodology that requires strict documentation and planning. Agile is an alternative for developers who dislike heavy methodologies but want to use some methodology rather than no methodology. Agile incorporates minimal processes but processes nonetheless. It favors face-to-face communication, short time-boxed development cycles, and efficient testing of applications. An in-depth description of the methodology can be found on Wikipedia at http://en.wikipedia.org/wiki/Agile_software_development. For many reasons, we don't advocate Agile in corporate environments except for skunk work projects or where the team is especially small (fewer than three people) and the deadline is unrealistic with a traditional methodology.

Extreme Programming. Extreme Programming (XP) is another methodology born of the distaste for heavy methodologies like the traditional waterfall. Extreme programming is typically utilized on small teams (fewer than five developers). The developer takes accountability for the design and coding and will have one other developer check their code. Developers essentially swap code. There are multiple variations of XP but our recommendation here is the same as in Agile: there is a place for XP but only on very small and tight timeline projects. A full definition of XP is available on Wikipedia at http://en.wikipedia.org/wiki/Extreme_programming.

There are a variety of other popular methodologies and variants that may be considered. These include:[8]

- Cleanroom Software Engineering.
- V-Model.
- Rational Unified Process (RUP).
- Spiral.
- Iterative.
- Feature-driven development.
- Adaptive Software Development.
- Dynamic Systems Development Method (DSDM).

All of these models have extensive entries in Wikipedia, with accompanying examples and external links.

There are a number of factors that might cause you to choose one methodology over another. We'll explore a few of those factors here:

- *Criticality:* How important is the application?
- *Development team experience:* How experienced is the development team?
- *Requirement stability:* How well defined and stable are the user requirements?
- *Development team size:* How large is the development team?
- *Project planning culture:* How experienced is the company at planning projects?
- *Application size:* How large is the potential application?

These factors help dictate which methodology is best suited. Don't embark on an application development project without defining the methodology first. It is a well-documented fact that project teams that define a methodology and process for development are more likely to achieve success.

Typically, for large scale projects, with high criticality, more junior developers, and well-defined requirements, the waterfall methodology will fit better.

For smaller projects, shorter time frames, less critical applications, a few senior developers, and people that don't mind working with a lot of change, one of the iterative lightweight methodologies is going to work better.

SEI, CMU, CMM for Software

For any company or IT department that has significant in-house development responsibilities, Capability Maturity Model (CMM) or the Capability Maturity Model Integrated (CMMI) should be evaluated. CMMi was developed by the Software Engineering Institute (SEI) at Carnegie Mellon University. CMMi is a set of instructions an organization "can follow for the purposes of gaining better control over its software development process."[9]

The Software Engineering Institute is a federally funded research and development center sponsored by the U.S. Department of Defense and operated by Carnegie Mellon University founded in 1984 with offices in the United States and Germany.

As outlined in Chapter 8, SEI is also the home of CERT®, an organization dedicated to researching, diagnosing, and reporting computer secuity incidents. Additional information on CERT® is found in that chapter.

Statistics analyzed by SEI using data of companies that adopted CMMI show positive pay back for adopters in terms of productivity of developers, higher quality, lower costs, and improved project delivery times.

CMMI describes the characteristics of effective processes and is predominantly used for software development environments. The CMMI framework is the structure that organizes the components used in generating models, training materials, and appraisal methods.[10]

CMMI consists of five levels that are used when a company refers to itself as CMMI certified. These five levels correspond to the maturity of an organizations development team in following a controlled process and their ability to repeat those processes. There are a number of subject areas on which the organization is evaluated. Level 1 maturity essentially implies that there is no standard process while Level 5 is the highest level achievable and implies a standard and repeatable process.

Before considering CMMI, evaluate the payback for implementing it. There is significant data available at http://www.sei.cmu.edu/cmmi/adoption/adoption.html that will aid in the analysis.

Factors to consider are:

- How large is your development group (the larger the group the higher the probability of savings)?
- What type of applications do you build (the larger the applications and the larger the team, the higher the probability of savings)?

- What is your current defect rate (the higher the defect rate the higher the probability of savings)?
- Do your customers care (does development quality affect your customers)?

The process to become CMMI certified entails assigning someone internally to champion the project. Anyone in the quality assurance department or with a process background would be a good candidate. This person needs training on CMMI. Next the organization must decide which development team to certify. You can either tackle the training and implementation yourself or hire a consulting firm to help. At the end of the process, you will have to engage an authorized firm to come in and certify the team. The process typically takes one year per level. The cost of the initiative can be high but companies who implement CMMI report earning back $4 to $5 for every dollar expended on the certification.[11]

Implementing Packaged Applications

Work steps for package implementation are similar to development projects except the development phase is generally replaced with application configuration). Common work steps for package implementation include:

- Package selection (covered in Chapter 12).
- Planning, estimating, and definition.
- Design.
- Configuration and customization.
- Testing.
- Deployment/implementation.

Estimating

As noted, there are many methods for estimating the total work effort and costs for implementing an application; most major vendors have their own method that is tailored to their application. While vendor-based estimating tools are useful, the application team should perform their own estimate as well.

The estimating process should identify the key drivers of effort for the customization, configuration, testing, implementation, conversion, and roll-out of the system. Typical drivers of effort in application package implementations include:

- Number of business events that trigger financial changes from inside or outside the company (e.g., purchase orders or invoices).

- Number of system functions—number of options that would appear on a main menu for the application.
- Level of customization required to provide the capability—usually a mix of configuration and customization.
- Number, size, and complexity of database tables.
- Number, size, and complexity of files.
- Number of user interfaces to be developed.
- Number of major inputs to the system and outputs generated by the system.
- Number of minor inputs to the system and outputs generated by the system (screens and reports).
- Number of sites to be rolled out.
- Number of people on the project.
- Number of technical alternatives (how many infrastructure alternatives are to be considered).
- Number of systems/modules being replaced.
- Number of test cycles to be completed.
- Number of user system tests.
- Number of new modules to be implemented.
- Number of training sessions to be completed.
- Average length of training sessions.
- Number of geographies/offices required for rollout.

With some thinking, the package implementation team can build a comprehensive list of the key drivers of effort for their specific effort, using the sample list as a starting point.

Managing Milestones

As with application development, milestone management is critical to the success of the package implementation effort. The implementation manager must request and receive proof of completion for each major task. If project schedule slippage forces the team to modify the due dates and push the milestones back, the manager should document the root causes and take any actions required to ensure that the team is productive.

Typical milestones for package implementations include the following:

- Requirements complete.
- Business process documents complete.

- Project plan complete.
- Gap analysis complete.
- Installation of hardware/software complete.
- Conference room pilot.
- Configuration/customization of software complete.
- Development of gaps and interfaces complete.
- Unit testing complete.
- Integration testing complete.
- Volume testing complete.
- Parallel testing complete.
- Go live—rollout and final data conversion.

To ensure that the application vendor's interests are aligned with the implementation team's, the manager can tie vendor compensation or payment to the timely achievement of the key project milestones.

Conference Room Pilot

An often-overlooked critical step in the package implementation is performing a conference room pilot (CRP). This step allows the team and end-users to preview the system or selected subfunction of the system with company-specific data, executing a company-specific business process. Many applications vendors try to dissuade the CIO from completing this step because of the time commitments required from both parties. However, there is no better assurance that the system meets the business requirements than by viewing it in a more realistic environment than the canned demonstrations the vendors normally perform. The pilot should be conducted on the company site with a business process (end-to-end) tested for critical functions. Company data should be converted so that the software is processing easily recognizable information, and should involve business users for the specific functions tested. The success or failure of the conference room pilot is highly predictive of the overall success of the project.

Business Process Definition

Another often overlooked task is the definition of company business processes. Implementing a package is almost impossible without good documentation of business processes. Detailed documentation of existing business processes provides for detailed gap analyses that highlight areas where the application will require additional customization. Chapter 12 outlines the business process definition and gap analysis process in detail. This process should be an integral part of any package implementation.

Other key points that should be observed by the application team when implementing a package include:

- Keep data clean in the package. Do not assume the package will maintain data integrity appropriately. For mission-critical applications, the team should schedule periodic data checkups to make sure that data integrity is being maintained.
- Minimize package modifications. A highly customized package solution reduces the major benefits of package software.
- If modifications must be done to the package, ensure that they are well-documented and are constrained to as few package modules as possible. This will facilitate the later implementation of package upgrades and patches, which can be challenging to install in highly customized package environments.
- Ensure that the applications team, and not the vendor, is driving the agenda during and after the implementation. Chapter 13 addresses vendor management concepts.
- Find ways to influence the development and enhancement priorities of the application vendor so that new releases of the application will provide incremental features with value to the company.
- Do not assume that one major training program at the end of the implementation will suffice for the end user. There should also be retraining sessions every three to six months to ensure consistent usage of the application and to help achieve the planned benefits from the system.

Quality Assurance Testing

Quality assurance (QA) testing in software development is a critical step to ensure the code matches design documents and operates as designed. QA teams or QA testers are tasked with auditing the application to make sure it will meet or exceed the design requirements of users. If the software fails, it is up to the QA tester to document the failure and notify the development team of the failure.

The technical team can lose sight that the application is being built for end-users and that the end-users are the arbiters of whether the application matches specifications. The development team may develop the code exactly to the design documents however the design documents might not accurately reflect the requirements. Or, the development team may take privilege in unilaterally modifying a requirement to simplify the coding; however, it is typically the end-user who will decide whether that was a good change. Testing is designed to determine:

- Does the application meet the functional requirements?
- Does the application meet the technical requirements?
- Does the application satisfy customer needs (explicit and implicit)?

The more complex the application, the higher the probability of problems. Therefore, as the application and project size increases, QA testing importance increases.

Complex software projects can be accomplished with minimal rework and high customer satisfaction, however, formal policies, procedures, and guidelines must be defined upfront for success.

Quality assurance gives users confidence that their requirements are going to be met. In smaller environments, having a QA step and process will ease the end-users concerns that the application project will be completed to their expectations. In larger environments, it is almost impossible to complete a large-scale effort without formal methodologies and a QA process and team.

The benefit of implementing sound QA processes into the application team are the savings and productivity improvements that typically is generated from QA. The savings or "cost avoidance" is staggering when reviewing the national statistics:

- It takes 5 to 17 hours to fix bugs in released code, as compared to 1 to 1.5 hours during code reviews and inspections.[12]
- Software defects cost the U.S. economy some $59.5 billion a year (2002).[13]
- On average, developers make 100 to 150 errors in every thousand lines of code. These statistics are different developer to developer and project to project and language to language.[14]
- Software defects cost the U.S. economy almost $60 billion annually. Eighty percent of the total development costs are consumed by developers identifying and correcting defects.[15]
- Cancelled projects due to quality issues in the United States, cost $55 billion.[16]

There is significant data proving the benefit of QA testing and the positive return on investment that can stem from the correct investments in testing. To be effective, testing must be implemented correctly. There are multiple types of testing that need consideration in any testing program, including:

- *Functional testing:* Testing the functionality of the application (e.g., Is the save button located on the screen? Does the application add to formulas correctly?). Usually tested by the QA testing group with the participation from end-users and driven from requirements.

- *Unit testing:* A test completed by a programmer after completing a discrete piece of code (a "unit" of code) (e.g., Does this piece of code once written perform to the technical design?).

- *Integration testing:* A test completed by the QA testing group with the participation of the development team and end-users. Do all the applications completed by multiple programmers perform to the specification documents (e.g., Are the five programs that work together to produce a payroll check sending the right data back and forth and producing a payroll check?)?

- *Regression testing:* A test completed that verifies all functions are still working correctly after a change is made to an application (e.g., a data element is modified to support a data entry screen change. All other applications that depend on that data element must be regression tested to ensure they still work even though their code may not have been modified.).

- *Platform testing:* Testing the application on multiple computer platforms if necessary (e.g., Does the application work across MS Windows, UNIX, and the AS400?).

- *Multiple session testing:* A test that simulates multiple users for the purposes of testing online screen speed and scalability (e.g., Can the application support more than 50 users simultaneously?).

- *Stress/performance testing:* A test that simulates large transaction volumes to determine the peak transaction bandwidth of an application (e.g., Can the application support 10,000 transactions a day?).

Testing involves numerous activities, but we will focus on a few best practices:

- Good requirements definition is the key to a good QA plan. Ensure that end-user requirements are gathered to sufficient detail and receive final approval from end-users.

- Write the test script scenarios right after the requirements are gathered while the technical design is being completed. Developing the test scripts right after the design requirements are documented will provide the most accurate test scripts.

- Ensure a member of the IT team (or a QA test manager) has the responsibility to communication timelines and plans to the end-user team well in advance. With good planning, end-users will be available for the testing dates if they have enough advance notice. Routine updates on project status are also critically important.

- Test reviews should always include end-users.

- Make sure the testing schedule, test scripts, and test results are organized and well managed. There are numerous tools available for organization of these items for larger projects.

- Keep statistics on test performance (e.g., number of test scripts, number failed, number succeeded, average defect per program or lines of code). This ensures that testing progress is visible and highlights any problems in advance. If possible, set goals for each statistic and reward team for achieving goals.

- Once the application is moved into production and is running in a live environment, set up a release schedule so that groups of bugs and functionality are delivered on a set calendar rather than real time. This will make sure that issues are prioritized and a regular testing schedule can be developed (e.g., tests take place in the third week of every month).

- Ensure that the QA process is part of each step in the system development life cycle. Are the requirements documents reviewed and signed off by end-users? Are the technical designs reviewed prior to development?

During larger application development projects, test automation should be evaluated. Significant productivity in testing can be accomplished by using an automation tool to automate some of the testing. This allows for organization of testing scripts, faster execution of tests, automatic tracking of results, and simplified volume and stress testing.

Scenarios where test automation makes sense include large projects, repetitive testing tasks, significant data loading, multiple platform testing (test tools can run the same test on multiple platforms), and scenarios involving ongoing development cycles. Any environment where the organization is running testing scripts repetitively should be good candidates for test automation and a positive return on investment.

Integrating quality assurance into any development project is critical. The testing process begins at the beginning of the project and continues long after the application is released and in use. As with any project requiring a predictable outcome, rigor in setting up the process and being able to repeat that process on an ongoing basis takes some investment, but testing has been shown to have positive returns on this investment. Never forget the end goal, which is to deliver a quality application that meets or exceeds the business users expectations and design requirements. After all, if you can't meet the design requirements or the funding of the project has been cut to the point where design requirements can't be met, there is no point in moving forward with the effort.

Summary

Managing application decisions in a company is complex and requires significant forethought and planning. Applications should fit into an overall strategy and be tightly integrated where appropriate. The application portfolio should be analyzed periodically by the application management team to spot weaknesses where inadequate planning, operations, or reporting capabilities exist in a given business area. Periodically, all applications should be assessed based on business value and current adequacy. In cases where the applications should receive more focus (high business value, low adequacy), an additional assessment to determine enhancement or replacement strategy should be conducted. If the application is to be replaced, the application management team must develop a strategy based on custom development, best-of-breed package, ERP package implementation, or a hybrid approach.

In a steady state, the application management team will split their time between application support and development of enhancements and customizations to the existing systems. Ideally, these duties are split between individuals to facilitate the most rapid completion of the scheduled enhancements. The development portion of the application team may be responsible for the creation of new custom systems, as well as the implementation, configuration, and customization of package systems. In each case, the standard disciplines for effective project management apply and help the team to be successful in planning, building, and managing the application portfolio.

Notes

1. Cullen Hightower, "Selections from Cullen Hightower," http://www .conservativeforum.org.
2. Wikipedia contributors, "Service Oriented Architecture", *Wikipedia, The Free Encyclopedia*, http://en.wikipedia.org/wiki/Service-oriented_architecture.
3. See note 2.
4. See note 2.
5. Wikipedia contributors, "Software as a Service", *Wikipedia, The Free Encyclopedia*, http://en.wikipedia.org/wiki/Software_as_a_Service#SaaS_providers.
6. Wikipedia contributors, "Software Development Lifecycle", *Wikipedia, The Free Encyclopedia*, http://en.wikipedia.org/wiki/Software_development_life _cycle (accessed December 31, 2006).
7. Wikipedia contributors, "Rapid Application Development", *Wikipedia, The Free Encyclopedia*, http://en.wikipedia.org/wiki/Rapid_application_development (accessed December 31, 2006).

8. See note 6.

9. Software Engineering Institute: http://www.sei.cmu.edu/about/index.html.

10. See note 9.

11. Gibson, Goldenson, and Kost, "Performance Results of CMMI", CMU/SEI-2006-TR-004, ESC-TR-2006-004, Copyright Carnegie Mellon University.

12. US National Institute for Standards and Technology, "Economic Impact of Inadequate Infrastructure of Software Testing," (May 2002) http://www.nist.gov/public_affairs/releases/n02-10.htm Why Test?

13. See note 11.

14. See note 12.

15. The Standish Group. CHAOS Chronicles v3.0 (March 2003).

16. See note 11.

11

IT Human Resources

If you don't want to play in championship games and you don't want to achieve at the highest level, then I don't want you here, because that's what I'm trying to do. I am not trying to finish fourth.

I'm convinced that if you get people onto your team who share the same goals and the same passion, and if you push them to achieve at the highest level, you're going to come out on top.

—Bill Parcells, NFL Coach[1]

This chapter introduces the IT human resources (HR) life cycle for management of the IT-specific staff employment issues. The HR and employment issues that must be managed by the CIO can be unfamiliar territory for corporate HR departments; thus, the IT department must work in conjunction with HR to effectively manage the IT staffing process. The IT HR *life cycle* covers major processes that are the responsibility of the CIO and managers, including resource planning, candidate sourcing, interviewing, hiring, and managing.

This chapter is organized around the IT HR life cycle that has five key steps:

Step 1: *Determine personnel needs:* Determining what type and quantity of human resources are required to deliver projects and maintain service levels.

Step 2: *Candidate sourcing strategy:* Determining best sources for candidates to hire, deciding if the position should be contract or permanent, and processes for prescreening candidates to reduce the interviewing workload.

Step 3: *Effective interviewing:* Best practices for interviewing and identifying star performers.

Step 4: *Effective hiring:* Management of the process after the offer is made and before the team member comes on board.

Step 5: *Managing the workforce:* Ongoing management of the IT team, including distinguishing performers, training and career development, staff retention strategies, and handling staff departures.

This chapter provides an overview of HR issues as they relate to information technology and IT departments. Most often, the staffing focus of the IT department is on interviewing candidates for open positions and on management of specific projects. This results in a lack of focus on other HR practices that are critical for the group, such as appropriate use of contract staff, training and development, and performance improvement. This chapter outlines the full life cycle of HR management issues faced by the CIO and emphasizes the balance needed to run an effective IT unit.

Why This Topic Is Important

Labor costs range from 30 percent to as much as 60 percent of the IT budget. Labor can be more than 50 percent of costs if outside contractors and consultants are included. Clearly, IT labor is a significant expense for companies and their IT departments. Furthermore, the quality of the personnel within the IT department has an enormous impact on the effectiveness of the IT function, end-user satisfaction, extraction of full value from the IT investment, and proactive use of technology. The right IT team can be a significant competitive advantage for a company; a poorly performing team can be devastating. Given the size of staff-related expenditures and the criticality of IT to corporate success, appropriate staff management is essential for IT success.

Regardless of the state of the overall economy, the market for highly proficient IT resources, skilled in the latest technologies, is competitive. Talented technologists who keep their skills updated and can deliver on their promises are seldom without plentiful employment opportunities. Most research predicts that the supply of the best technical talent will likely be constrained for the next decade; hiring and retaining the best resources will continue to be a critical success factor for the CIO and the department.

Adding to the complexity of IT HR management is that, relative to the general pool of labor, IT professionals are most often highly skilled, well-educated individuals who have held a variety of positions in several companies. They typically have a diverse set of career aspirations, often putting factors such as interesting projects, access to training, and working on new technologies ahead of more typical career desires such as compensation, status, and advancement. This factor poses an additional management consideration for IT leadership.

Most often CIOs and IT managers are not particularly well trained, by experience or education, in managing human resources. Furthermore, they (rightly) see their main responsibilities as implementing systems, executing projects, monitoring networks and other technology-related efforts; therefore, those tasks get the bulk of their attention.

Adhering to the processes in this chapter can generate large benefits for the organization. Turnover costs are enormous and can be as much as one to two times the departing employee's salary. For example, in a mid-size IT department with 50 employees, if the attrition rate is 10 percent, five employees leave during the year at an average salary of $60,000. This firm may spend $250,000 to $600,000 in recruiting costs, lost team productivity, reset project deadlines, and other turnover costs. In large companies with hundreds of IT workers, the costs can be overwhelming. An effective IT HR life cycle can reduce and control turnover and the associated expense.

Understanding how to optimize the department HR assets is critical to being successful and running a productive and cost-effective operation. This chapter discusses how IT managers and consultants can more effectively hire and manage their workforce to build a high performance team.

Introduction to IT Human Resources

Managing the human resources in an IT department is a complex task consisting of finding, hiring, managing, evaluating, coaching, promoting, training, developing, and releasing staff. While these processes are similar in other departments in the organization, IT poses an especially difficult challenge because of the dynamics of the technology industry. Technology life spans are short; thus, the skills of workers can quickly become obsolete as technology platform changes and they have difficulty transitioning to newly required technologies and platforms. Evidence of this phenomenon was visible in the early 2000s, as demand for COBOL programmers dropped off rapidly after most year 2000 remediation work was completed. Many COBOL programmers had difficulty retooling in new technologies such as Java and found themselves out of work. This meant that hordes of COBOL programmers on staff would have similar difficulty being retrained in e-commerce applications, which was a focus of corporate IT spending and initiatives at that point. A similar trend occurred as the dot-com era ended and Java programmers became the next victims of a weak demand cycle. Companies are constantly having to balance and match in-house skills with new technologies being implemented in response to changing business imperatives. Compared to other functional departments such as finance, marketing, or HR, the pace of change for the base skill sets required is much more rapid. The skills required by any employee in a given company evolve over time, but most often at a much slower pace than within IT.

Many IT managers and CIOs have pursued career tracks that have given them little chance to build staff development and management skills. IT managers receive little training and less experience in HR policies, staff hiring, management, retention, and development. The IT management team rarely has exposure to the nontechnical aspects of their jobs prior to promotion, leaving them weak in the very skills that will provide the most value to the department.

Likewise, HR departments in companies often have little experience with the unique development, training, and mentoring needs of the IT professional. The scarcity of IT professionals in emerging technologies, coupled with the training demands of the existing workforce and the rate of technology obsolescence, has created a training and career development challenge for IT managers and HR practitioners alike.

Finally, many large companies have implemented centralized procurement of contract and permanent staff in order to enjoy the discounts attendant with high-volume purchasing agreements. Unfortunately, this arrangement can insulate the hiring manager in IT from the vendor providing the contract technical professionals or the permanent employment candidates. The importance of IT department specific knowledge and high cost of recruiting and attrition makes IT involvement in the recruiting and candidate sourcing process even more critical.

This chapter examines policies, procedures, and tools for identifying, interviewing, recruiting, and retaining the best IT professionals and effectively managing this staff. We accomplish this by reviewing each step in the IT HR life cycle.

IT HR Life Cycle

The IT HR life cycle is the continuous loop of key HR processes in the IT department. It follows a logical progression of HR activity, beginning with identifying staffing needs, then hiring, training, and retaining the staff. The first step is determining the actual people/labor needs of the IT department. There are a variety of approaches for determining the answer, and we provide some examples in this chapter. After the full breadth of resource needs is understood, the second step is to put together a candidate sourcing strategy and begin identifying potential new employees. The third step is interviewing candidates for the positions that have been identified. The next step, the hiring process, has multiple substeps and is the area we have found to be most often undermanaged. We have highlighted the best practices in this step. The last and longest step in the process is actually managing resources. We focus on management as it specifically relates to HR issues. The IT HR life cycle process is repeated in scheduled intervals to make sure that the health of the IT organization is well protected. Exhibit 11.1 shows the steps in the IT HR life cycle.

Step 1: Determine Personnel Needs

USE THE ORGANIZATION CHART. It is the responsibility of the CIO to assemble the team that will give the company the best chance of succeeding in achieving the goals established for the IT department in conjunction with

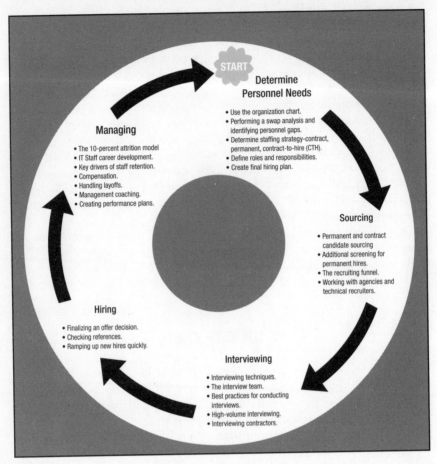

Exhibit 11.1   IT HR Life Cycle

the IT steering committee. The current organization chart is the right place to begin determining the configuration of the required team. Creating a clear organization chart prior to hiring is essential and Chapter 5 outlines in detail the most effective organization structures as well as organizational roles and responsibilities. The required roles and responsibilities, as well as the organization chart that will best support the IT department's goals, should be compared to the existing team and organization to identify gaps or overlaps that will drive the hiring process.

Completing the exercises in Chapter 17 will help the IT manager determine the right resource levels. Because labor demand in IT departments is driven heavily by project work, the inventory of prioritized projects will dictate much of the overall hiring and staff capacity plans.

Finally, the committed service level areas (SLAs) in the operations and applications support areas will drive required staffing levels for those functions.

PERFORM A SWAP ANALYSIS AND IDENTIFY PERSONNEL GAPS. A swap analysis is a review of the existing resources, including their skills, and a mapping of this information against the skills needed to execute the current work in the department identified in the previous step (support, projects, service levels). If there is a mismatch between the capacity and technical skills available and what will be needed, the CIO must "swap" overlapping or no longer required resources for replacement resources with the skill set to achieve the desired end work product. The existing resource must be released from his or her current duties to open the spot for a new person to take over. In some cases, the existing resource may be released from the company, but the team member can sometimes be retrained for the new requirement, or moved to another area within IT or within the overall company.

The intent of the swap analysis is for the IT manager to objectively assess the organization needs versus the capabilities of the existing staff. As new business demands are made on the IT department and new technology capabilities become available, a mismatch between current staff skills and required skills emerges. The swap analysis highlights the mismatches and ensures that team members with skills that are no longer required can be identified rapidly so that their disposition can be determined. Swap analysis can be executed for a small group or for the entire department. We recommend that the swap analysis be completed quarterly or, for rapidly changing departments, even monthly. Creating a swap analysis the first time can be time consuming because of the detailed nature of the task; however, on an ongoing basis, the job is much smaller.

In a typical swap analysis, the IT manager might have a small application development group consisting of two individuals—one with a background in Cold Fusion and the other a Microsoft.net programmer. The IT manager will list their full suite of skills and review the upcoming six-month project schedule. In addition, the CIO has determined that the company will suspend any development on the Cold Fusion platform. Meanwhile, all development is scheduled to be Microsoft-based. The project plans call for two full-time employees (FTEs) for the next six months of application development. After executing the swap analysis, the manager determines that the Cold Fusion programmer needs to be transferred to either another development group in the company, sent to training to update skills, or released to another company that uses Cold Fusion, and the team needs to add another Microsoft developer. Although this example is simple, it can become complicated as the number of resources increases. The well-organized IT manager will, however, have the service level definitions, project plans, application, and technical architecture definitions built in advance, making the resource determination effort considerably easier.

Often the CIO is asked to execute cost-cutting measures in the department. For instance, the senior executive team may have requested a 20 percent reduction in IT staff costs. The CIO then executes the swap analysis, determines the team members that possess skill overlaps, selects the best resources and then plans to release the others.

Exhibit 11.2 depicts each step of the swap analysis process, for example:

- *Analyze required skills needed to support IT.* Exhibit 11.3 shows a form that can be used to inventory all key skills required to support IT operations and projects, along with the relative skill level of each IT professional in the department. Use information on current platforms and upcoming projects to develop this list.
- *Determine required number of FTEs by position.* This information should be calculated based on the SLAs and project schedule. If executing a cost-cutting initiative, this should be the minimum FTEs that could hold that position and still keep basic service.
- *Determine whether positions should be permanent, contract-to-hire, or contractors.* Choosing between contract and permanent staff is covered later in the chapter.
- *Analyze skills of current IT team members.* Map each current employee's skills versus the required skills for the upcoming year. Exhibit 11.3 shows a sample analysis. Employees' names are listed across the top row; skills required are listed vertically. For every technology required, the staff member should be assigned a rating: Blank = Not ap-

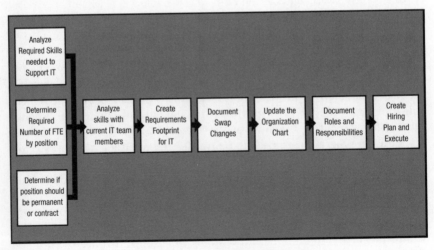

Exhibit 11.2   Swap Analysis Process

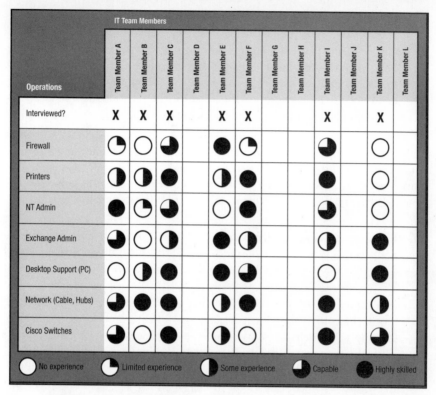

Exhibit 11.3   Skill Mapping and Assessment of Current Employees

plicable, 0 = None or poor skills, 1 = Entry-level skills, 2 = Average skills, 3 = Above average skills, and 4 = excellent skills.

- *Create requirements footprint for IT.* Determine the positions and skills required for optimal staffing. This is the inventory of skills and the resource capacity required, by skill.

- *Document swap changes.* Document staff movement within the IT department, and staff being released from the IT department (anyone who does not fill a required spot in the new organization). When planning to release any staff from the company entirely, work with the HR and legal departments to ensure that the process is handled according to company policy.

- *Update the organization chart.* Reflect the swap changes created from previous analysis.

- *Document roles and responsibilities.* To support the IT department, roles and responsibilities should be listed for each position on the new organization chart. Chapter 5 outlines the typical roles and responsibilities within the IT department.

- *Create hiring plan.* Summarize new positions in a document that can be handed to the responsible managers and to HR and corporate recruiting. Each position should have a profile detailing the skills, experience and educational background required for the position, as well as an inventory of likely sources for ideal candidates.

When the swap analysis is complete, the CIO will have a new organization model and a finalized disposition determined for each staff member. The four possible dispositions include: keep in same role, move to new role, release to other company department, release from the company.

DETERMINE STAFFING STRATEGY. The CIO must next determine whether a position calls for contract, contract-to-hire, or permanent staff. There are four ways to satisfy IT demand and execute work:

1. *Permanent staff:* Hired as full-time employees of the company and form the core of the IT department staff. Best suited for positions that last with little change; for example, management positions, analyst positions, programming positions for applications that likely won't change, basic infrastructure positions, and in areas where the technologies are part of the long-term plan for the corporate technology architecture. Additional permanent staff is well suited for areas of competitive advantage or information sensitivity to the business. The benefits of using permanent staff are:
   - Permanent staff salaries and benefits combined can be 10 percent to 30 percent less expensive than using outside contractors.
   - Maintain knowledge of systems in the company.
   - Have industry and company specific idiosyncratic knowledge of systems and interfaces.
   - Focused on their careers within the company and will be long-term participants in the team, driving decision making focused on the company's best interests.

2. *Contractors:* Temporary workers engaged for their specific skill set for a short period of time are *contractors.* Contractors are best used for areas that require a surge of work over a three- to nine-month period, after which the contractors depart the organization. Retaining contractors for this period eliminates the need to hire full-time resources and dismiss them immediately after the work is completed if no additional work emerges. Contractors are also appropriate for use in areas that need highly specialized skills that may not be available internally. The benefits of using contract staff include:

- Help keep resource costs variable because contractors can come and go in very short time frames, with no HR implications.
- Pay for only the amount of work that is needed.
- No training is necessary.
- Hire the exact skill needed.

3. *Contract-to-hire:* The process of hiring a resource on contract for one to three months and then hiring that person full time if their performance is good and the resource need turns out to be permanent. This "try-before-you-buy" approach minimizes the risk usually associated with permanent hires that do not perform to expectations, as well as provides time to determine if the demand for the staff member's skills will continue in the long term. The company enters into a contract with the candidate that states that he or she will be evaluated at the end of the contract period for a full-time position. If the candidate was contracted through an agency or recruiting company, there will usually be a conversion fee at the end of the contract. For long-term contracts (greater than 6 to 9 months), the conversion fee may be waived by the contracting company.

   One disadvantage of the contract-to-hire approach is that top candidates may prefer an immediate offer of full-time employment. If a bidding war erupts for their services, or if another company makes them a permanent offer during the contract term, the IT team runs the risk of losing them.

4. *Consultants:* Consultants are resources hired by firms who take responsibility for the delivery of an entire project or operation area. They are responsible for delivering to you an end product or service based on expected service levels. Consulting firms are best used for discrete projects for a period of three to six months with well-defined requirements, work plans, and deliverables. Additionally, they can be used to outsource infrastructure or application areas. The benefits of hiring a consulting firm are greatest when the expertise to complete the project is not in-house and is difficult to find, or the company is trying to reduce costs by outsourcing. If a project is particularly risky or of critical business importance, hiring a consulting firm with experience in similar endeavors can help mitigate the risk and increase the likelihood of success.

Contract and consulting staff can make up from 10 percent to 50 percent of the IT staff in a company, depending on the rate of change, the variability of demand on the IT department, and the current project priorities within the company. As a rule of thumb, target about 25 percent contract staff and vary the ratio, depending on what works best for the IT department and company at a given time. If the company runs into economic difficulties, contract labor costs can be shed rapidly.

Typically, managers and analysts should be permanent staff, especially key leadership positions unless the function is outsourced. The CIO should annotate the organization chart showing which positions must be permanent and which positions may use permanent or contract resources.

The overall goal of a staffing mix is to maximize productivity of permanent staff, reduce turnover, increase throughput of the group, provide rapid access to specific skill sets, allow costs to be easily varied, and boost morale by allowing permanent staff to avoid some of the less desirable work in the department. Exhibit 11.4 outlines a framework for determining the staffing strategy by application type and employee risk.

Steps for analysis in this framework include:

- *Build an inventory of systems and applications:* This step involves pulling together the inventory of systems to be supported. The activities completed in Chapter 10 will have resulted in the application portfolio being readily available for this exercise. This inventory can be used to understand skill requirements, systems complexity, and risk.

Exhibit 11.4 Staffing Strategy Overview

- *Determine systems complexity/business risk by technology area:* For each system or area supported, measure the risk on a scale of 1 to 5 (least risk to most risk). Risk categories include system size and complexity, business value (e.g., Is the application revenue driving?), business criticality (e.g., Can the application sustain downtime?), number of system interfaces to other systems (complexity), and level of customization (complexity). The sum of these scores generates a system complexity/business risk score for each system or area supported.

- *Determine employee risk and skill level required by area:* For each system, measure the employee turnover risk level and skill level required to manage and maintain the system. Low ratings should be assigned to systems with easy-to-find skills in the general IT labor pool and low likelihood of employee departures. High ratings should be given to areas in which employees will have highly demanded skills that command a premium in the market or high-pressure areas that result in increased staff burnout and turnover.

- *Creating the permanent versus contract staff matrix:* Each system should be plotted on the grid in Exhibit 11.5, according to the application and employee risks determined in the previous step.

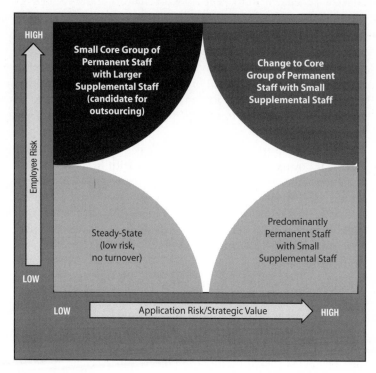

Exhibit 11.5   Permanent versus Contract Staffing Strategy

The resulting mapping dictates a specific strategy for mitigating business and downtime risk as well as properly staffing the area:

- The northwest quadrant suggests a small core group of permanent staff to manage and direct these systems supplemented with a larger contract staff. The business risk with these systems is low, therefore there is a low likelihood of trouble caused by system outages; however, the skills are in high demand, making a contract staffing model more appealing. An application or function in the northwest quadrant can also be a good candidate to test the outsourcing waters. At minimum, receiving bids from outside firms to maintain this system could provide benchmark data as to how current costs compare to the costs and benefits of outsourcing.

- The northeast quadrant also suggests a small core group of permanent staff with some supplementation through contract staff. The situation is similar to the northwest quadrant, except that the systems in this quadrant are of high strategic value to the company, meaning that a reliable core set of permanent employees should be overseeing these systems. The team should be supplemented with outside contractors or consultants who bring in the most recent, in-demand skills for these areas to help the permanent staff keep up with changes to the technology.

- The southeast quadrant suggests mostly permanent staff. For systems that are strategic in nature, where the internal skill set matches well to the skills required, and where, in general, employees like the work and are not likely to be enticed by outside opportunities, there is very little reason for the organization to use temporary staff in this area. A small number of contractors can be used to supplement the team on an as-needed basis and to manage peaks and valleys of project or seasonal demand.

- The southwest quadrant suggests no changes to the current staffing situation. It covers applications and systems with lower strategic importance to the business and where the existing permanent employee skill set is a good match. Systems in this category may also be scrutinized to determine if they are good candidates for outsourcing, which may lower overall support costs for the area and allow permanent employees to focus on the higher value systems.

DEFINE ROLES AND RESPONSIBILITIES. Whether new or existing, each position in the IT department should have a clearly documented skills, experience, and education profile, as well as a detailed job duties description, completed and filed in IT and HR. This provides the IT team with very clear instructions on the CIO's expectations and their responsibilities. Additionally, the documents should outline the objective performance measures on which the position is evaluated. The following need to be known for each position:

- Position title.
- Role within the organization (position on the organization chart).
- Reporting relationships (direct reports supervised by this position, where does this position report).
- Job requirements: technology skills, educational background, work experience, company tenure.
- Documentation of day-to-day ongoing responsibilities.
- Priorities for responsibilities.
- Objective and subjective measurements of success in the role.
- Promotion criteria.
- Success criteria or objectives.

This information can also be used by internal or external recruiters as hiring specifications, as well as for evaluation criteria during the annual employee review process.

CREATE FINAL HIRING PLAN. At this point in the life cycle, the CIO will have a list of key personnel actions, a list of new open-to-hire positions, and a determination of whether those hires are contract or permanent positions. The final stage of Step 1 is producing a hiring plan. A sample hiring plan worksheet is shown in Exhibit 11.6.

Position Title	# of Positions	Permanent or Contract	Manager	Recruiter	Position Description	Skills	Target Offer Date	Target Start Date
Consultant – Peoplesoft	2	Contract	JD	TL	Y-Attached	Psft functional, Financials – AR/AP/GL.V8.0	1-Jul	15-Jul
Network Systems Engineer	6	Permanent	JM	TL	Y-Attached	Senior network, CCNA	1-Jul	15-Jul
Programmer Analyst	2	Permanent	JD	TL	Y-Attached	Visual C++, SQL Server	15-Jul	1-Aug
Technical Analyst	1	Contract	SG	TL	N-TBD	3 years technical support, NT, Windows 2000, MSCE	15-Jul	1-Aug

Exhibit 11.6   Example Hiring Plan Worksheet

The hiring plan details the following information:

- Position title.
- Number of positions to be filled.
- Type of resource (permanent or contract).
- IT department manager responsible for hiring this position.
- Recruiter responsible for managing the recruiting process for this position.
- Yes/no flag indicating if a position description has been written up and is available.
- High-level summary of skills required for the position.
- Target offer and start dates for position.

The CIO should also work with the HR department to determine target salary rates for each position. This should be based on a combination of corporate standards for the role, market rates, and current compensation levels within the IT department.

The hiring plan neatly summarizes the current hiring needs of the organization. It is also a useful tool for facilitating communication between IT, the steering committee, HR, and internal and external recruiters.

Step 2: Candidate Sourcing Strategy

After the hiring plan is complete, determining approaches for identifying candidates from the at-large labor pool is called *sourcing*. The process will vary, depending on the urgency of the search, the position type (permanent, contract), the rarity of the skills required. The sourcing process is made up of the following steps:

- *Develop candidate profile:* Detailed job specification that shows the full requirements for the position. The internal or external recruiters use this information to screen candidates. This profile can be easily derived from the roles and responsibility document created for the position in the previous step.
- *Prescreen strategy:* Necessary to ensure eliminating low-potential candidates with a minimum of effort. Implement several filters for eliminating candidates. For example, one common filter is years of experience: "If candidate does not have three years of Oracle functional experience, eliminate from consideration." Other typical prescreens include degree requirements, geographic location (local candidates only), and industry-specific experience (e.g., financial services, energy, telecommunications).

- *Importance of timing:* While the CIO should interview a sufficient number of candidates, they should also work to minimize the search time. The more rapidly they can carry candidates through the screening, interview, and offer process, the more likely the manager is to get an acceptance from the desired candidate. Candidates who move slowly through the pipeline are at great risk of either receiving another job offer during that time or being forgotten about, particularly in high-volume hiring situations. If more than three weeks elapse between the candidate's first interview and the decision to make an offer, then the process is moving too slowly and is likely to lose appropriate candidates.

- *Technical testing:* Another useful screening (or prescreening) tool. Technical testing through one of the many online providers such as Brainbench or ProveIt provides third-party verification of the candidate's technical skill level. For management positions, the team should include other testing, such as cognitive tests, behavioral profiles, or tests of other nontechnical required skills.

PERMANENT AND CONTRACT CANDIDATE SOURCING.   There is a substantial difference between recruiting a permanent hire and a contractor because of the hiring cycle and nature of the individuals who are looking for the opportunities. Contractors are comfortable working on a temporary basis under highly uncertain conditions. Contractors are willing to accept and manage the risk of not working for some time until their next engagement comes through.

The hiring cycle is normally about five days for a contractor (the time between an interview and an offer). The hiring cycle for a permanent job position ranges from 20 to 30 days, because both the company and the candidate require additional time to gather information and perform a mutual assessment given the permanent nature of the hiring decision. Different strategies are appropriate for sourcing permanent hires. The best sources for hiring permanent technical candidates include:

- Other companies that use the same technologies or skill sets.
- Previous employers of current IT employees.
- Referrals from existing employees (this is the most productive source for most companies).
- Staffing agencies and recruiters that cater to permanent IT professionals. The Yellow Pages of your local phone directory lists pertinent companies under Permanent Placement Services, Computers—Technical Recruiting, or Recruiting and Placement Services.
- Internet job boards are a source for hires, but unfortunately, they cater to candidates who are actively looking for jobs and who may be frequent

job hoppers. For permanent hires, many companies prefer the "passive candidates" that are best identified by using staffing agencies or internal recruiters. Some of the most prominent and well-trafficked sites are www.monster.com, www.hotjobs.com, and www.careerbuilder.com. With tens of millions of resumes on the Internet and similar numbers of job postings, the Internet is an important factor in technical recruiting.

- Universities, colleges, junior colleges, and technical training centers provide candidates through their placement offices.
- Technical associations and industry associations can be very helpful in finding technical candidates. The National Association of Computer Consulting Business (NACCB) and the Information Technology Association of America (ITAA) both cater to the technical market.

The following is a list of resources available to assist in hiring temporary technical candidates:

- Staffing agencies that cater to contract IT professionals. Your local phone directory Yellow Pages lists pertinent companies under Technology Consulting, Computers—Information Technology Consulting Services, Computers—Temporary Placement Services, or Computers—Technical Recruiting.
- The magazine *Electronic Recruiting News* (www.interbiznet.com/ern) tracks Internet sites for contract and permanent recruiting resources.
- The *Airs Directory* is a premier directory of recruiting resources located at www.airsdirectory.com.
- Contract staffing-focused web sites such as Dice (www.dice.com) cater specifically to the contract-oriented candidate.
- Project managers and peers can provide referrals. Ask your project managers and other peers for a list of the firms they use to help hire contract resources.
- Technical associations and industry associations, such as NACCB and ITAA, can help with temporary resources.

The other difference in sourcing the two types of candidates is the specificity of information. With contract resources, the position must be very specific, the pay rate set to a certain range, and the time frame for the project clearly communicated. This allows contract recruiters to cut through a huge candidate pool quickly.

ADDITIONAL SCREENING FOR PERMANENT HIRES. For permanent hires, the IT manager may choose to do additional screening. Some additional things to look for when reviewing resumes include a consistent history, a proven ability to stay employed for a material length of time (e.g., longer than 18 months), and a clear, consistent track record of logical career progression. There are a number of quality assurance checks you can add to the recruiting process to help diminish the likelihood of hiring a candidate who is a poor fit, including background testing and behavioral screening. Depending on corporate-level policy, a permanent hire may require the ability to gain a U.S. government security clearance or to pass a drug test. In any case, the IT team should work closely with the HR department in developing the appropriate set of screening criteria for permanent candidates.

THE RECRUITING FUNNEL. The recruiting funnel refers to the reduced number of candidates that are carried through each step of the recruiting process (i.e., out of 100 potential candidates, fewer make it through each successive screen, all the way through to the job being offered). For a given position, the manager should interview a minimum of three candidates in person, after they have been passed through all the prescreening and preliminary phone interviews. A high interview-to-job-offer ratio may indicate that the recruiters do not understand the specification, that the manager is being overly selective, that the requirements are too narrow or possibly all three.

Exhibit 11.7 shows one method for tracking the recruiting funnel. The exhibit shows activity against each of the key steps in the process (candidate identification, interview, offers, acceptances) by open position. The team should maintain an activity summary chart to provide tracking and status of progress against open positions.

Position	Recruiter	Open Positions	Candidate Interviewed	Candidate Deselected	Sent to Mgr	Offers	Offer Declined	Offer Accepted
1	JP	7	58	35	14	9	3	6
2	JB	6	44	21	21	11	2	9
3	SW	1	52	28	7	17	8	9
4	JK	7	42	24	14	8	3	5
5	WQ	4	15	8	3	0	0	0
6	FD	0	0	0	0	0	0	0
Total		25	211	116	59	45	16	29

Exhibit 11.7 Recruiting Activity Summary

Additionally, by position, someone (usually the recruiting department) tracks each candidate in the pipeline. The CIO should request a periodic report that shows status similar to the example in Exhibit 11.8.

Understanding the recruiting funnel helps the team monitor how well the hiring process is proceeding. Typical rules to follow:

- Recruiters searching for passive candidates make 75 to 100 calls to get one qualified resume.
- Referrals can greatly enhance the productivity of recruiters.
- Ten resumes screened result in one interview.
- Three to five interviews produce one hire.

WORKING WITH AGENCIES AND TECHNICAL RECRUITERS. Working with technical recruiting companies can be a productive way to find candidates for open positions. Agencies can reduce the time and cost of identifying quality resources as well as locate candidates who may not have been found by the IT department or the internal recruiting department. Agencies have highly efficient recruiting and sourcing processes that are hard to match within a given company.

The interface between the hiring firm and the agency is the agency salesperson. Referrals from other CIOs are a good way to identify potential agency sales professionals. If referrals do not produce good results, the CIO should call the agency and speak to the general manager of the office. The general manager should provide a referral to the agencies top salesperson; this person should have at least five years of experience. It should be made clear to the agency that they must provide an experienced account manager, preferably with knowledge of the industry.

Other agency screening questions include:

- *Size:* Work with a firm that has a large database of candidates. An indicator of size is the number of full-time employees (sales, recruiting, and technical). A firm with 10 or more sales and recruiting personnel in the local market is the appropriate size. Other size metrics include annual revenues and number of consultants or placements the firm makes annually. Because of the low barriers to entry in the staffing business, the industry is filled with small, undercapitalized players.
- *Fee arrangement:* For permanent hires, the placement fee will range from a low of 10 percent of the candidates starting salary to as much as 35 percent. When the agency is working on multiple positions, and particularly if the agency has exclusive rights to filling the position, it is easy to negotiate lower fees. On the other hand, a difficult-to-find, one-position specification generally commands 25 percent to 30 percent. Agencies will usually charge the end client the placement fee on the candidate start date. The agency will also usually provide a replacement

Candidate Name	Position	Source	Recruiter	Manager	Screen	Presented	1st Int.	2nd Int.	Offer	Accept	Start	Follow-up
Jones, Cheryl	Network Systems Eng	Referral	JM	JD	1/20/2007	1/20/2007	1/21/2007	1/22/2007	1/23/2007	1/24/2007	2/15/2007	
Smith, Chris	Programmer Analyst	Dice	JM	JD	1/20/2007	1/20/2007	1/22/2007	1/23/2007	1/24/2007			
Floyd, Terry	Consultant	Advert	JM	JD	1/20/2007	1/20/2007	1/24/2007					
Jones, Mary	Lead Technical Analyst	Referral	JM	JD	1/20/2007	1/20/2007						

Exhibit 11.8 Candidate Tracking Summary

guarantee for a certain period of time. The guarantee is that the agency will replace the candidate free of charge if the hired candidate does not work out or resigns during the guarantee period.

Fees for contract consultants are handled differently. There are no separate fees associated with contract consultants. Instead, the agency will be quoted an hourly bill rate for each candidate presented. Bill rates are very negotiable and are driven by market demands for the skill and resource the team is attempting to hire, as well as committed contract length, geographic location, and type of work. The agency applies a markup to the cost of the consultant that covers employment taxes, benefits, and a profit for the agency. The markup is usually between 20 percent and 50 percent, depending on skill set, demand, contract length, and geography.

- *Retainer fees:* Firms should generally avoid paying retainer fees for agency recruiting, except for searches targeting the most senior executives. Another arrangement, similar to retainer-based recruiting is on-site recruiting. In this case, the firm strikes an agreement with the agency to have recruiters work on-site and recruit exclusively on the company open positions. This is economical if there are a substantial number of positions to hire and internal recruiting support is inadequate.

- *Years in business:* Ask how long the company has been in business. Staffing agencies operate in a very competitive environment and longevity of more than 5 to 10 years indicates an ability to please clients and adapt to changing markets.

- *Top five clients:* Ask the general manager who are the agency's top five customers. This provides an indication of the market the company caters to as well as the relative success of the company. Companies that have good relationships with blue-chip clients, particularly over long periods of time, usually have the best recruiting capabilities.

- *Size of database:* Ask how many technical candidate resumes are on file or in an online database. The larger the database, the faster the recruiting process will be and the stronger the agency's ability to provide the best-fit resource.

- *Number and location of recruiters:* The number of recruiters is an indication of agency size and ability to rapidly work on new requirements. The location of the recruiters is important as well. Recruiting is fundamentally a local process and recruiters in the geographies in which the search is taking place will have much more success identifying the right candidates. Also, the agency recruiting team should be dedicated to recruiting and not mix sales and recruiting responsibilities.

- *Top skills hired:* Understand the skills sets that comprise the firm's core competencies. For example, do not hire a firm for programming job openings if the firm specializes in recruiting network professionals. Determine competency by asking for a list of the skills placed over the past 6 to 12 months.

- *References:* Ask for recent references from the company and call at least one of them to determine if the agency is successful at producing positive client references.

- *Screening process:* The agency should provide its candidate prescreening methodology. The agency can also prescreen candidates using technology tests, background checks, reference checks, education verification, or other checks. The agency should provide a list of screens that it can complete as part of the recruiting process.

- *Candidate sourcing approach:* The agency should provide their candidate sourcing methodology as well as their primary source for candidate resumes. The best agencies are effective at using their internal proprietary database, finding passive candidates through aggressive phone calling, and through referrals from existing contractors or candidates. Weaker agencies simply search job boards for candidates without expending the extra effort to delve into other sources.

While this list is helpful for identifying one or two agencies to work with, for high-volume, long-term hiring needs, the team may want to select vendors via the competitive bidding process outlined in Chapter 12. The previous list provides a starter set of requirements for the full-scale vendor selection process.

If the company has a central HR or procurement function, they will often have a vendor list of recruiters and temporary staffing firms that are approved to work with and are proven resources.

After signing up staffing agencies to assist with open positions, the company should also be sure to add an off-limits clause that states the recruiting company cannot recruit employees from the company. Usually these clauses are in effect for a full year after the start date of the last permanent or contract candidate hired from the agency.

Agencies can be particularly useful for positions that are difficult to fill. For lower end positions that are easy to fill or for positions that internal recruiters are successful at filling, agencies are not necessary.

Step 3: Effective Interviewing

In this section, we discuss best practices in interviewing. The interview process should be focused on understanding how well the candidate fits the profile, as well as the corporate and IT team culture. The process should also provide some information to the candidates on the company, department, and position, although the primary focus is on identifying candidates that will receive offers. Once an offer has been made, the IT team can focus on providing information to the candidate. Specific approaches for successful interviewing include:

- *Compose an interview team for the position:* The manager responsible for the position, his or her direct superior, and one or two people from the team the new hire will be working with should provide the right balance between ensuring top quality and team dynamics. Each interviewer brings a slightly different focus to the interview (e.g., technical skills assessment, culture fit assessment, or understanding management experience).

- *Create a candidate scorecard:* The interviewing team should agree on and create a scorecard for assessing each candidate interviewed. This scorecard should be based on the candidate profile that has been created in Step 1 of the IT HR life cycle.

- *Prepare ahead of time:* One of the most common mistakes made by interviewers is failing to prepare for the interview. Managers and IT teams are busy and often have schedules booked right up to the interview time. Many times the interviewer is taking his first look at the candidate's resume after the candidate arrives and the interview starts. Instead of listening to the candidate, the interviewer is scrambling to think about what questions he will ask. A more effective interview preparation approach is to read the resume at least 15 minutes prior, circling each items of interest and making notations of specific questions to ask. Second, plan the interview and develop an interview script if you interview for this position repeatedly.

- *Conduct the interview in 10- to 15-minute time increments:* The interview should be 30 to 60 minutes and the time should be allocated into three equal components. First, have the candidate walk through his or her background. The candidate should be able to show a clear history of logical career progression and an explanation of why each successive career move was made. The interviewer should also ask the candidate why he left his previous job, or is considering changing positions. Next, the interviewer should give a brief overview of the objectives for the position, give the candidate an opportunity to show that he understand the position and can map these objectives to something in his past experience. Finally, the interviewer should see how well the candidate thinks on his feet by giving the candidate a short business case (see below), or asking appropriate technical questions. Allow the last 5 to 10 minutes to answer the candidate's questions and discuss next steps. To save time in the in-person interview, an advance phone screen is sometimes useful for getting resume background conversations out of the way. If the team is hiring for multiple positions or needs to talk to many candidates, the phone interview can help screen out some of the candidates without having to conduct a full-scale interview.

- *Allow the candidate do the talking:* The candidate should be talking 80 percent to 90 percent of the time. The interviewer should not make the mistake of consuming excessive time by talking about how great the position, group, or company is. There will be time for that conversation after the candidate has been made an offer.

- *Check off key criteria during the interview:* Culture fit, energy, leadership, technical skills required, history of achievement, or performance.

- *Focus candidate on individual accomplishments:* Interviewees often spend too much time discussing group accomplishments in an interview, without addressing their specific contributions to the accomplishment. Allowing the conversation to focus on group or team accomplishments can disguise shortcomings in the individual candidate's abilities. The interviewee should focus on his or her specific contributions to the team and prior company.

- *Write the interview assessment on a scorecard:* Develop a scorecard with important criteria. Give a scorecard to everyone in the interviewing process. Ask them to return the scorecard immediately after each interview so they can write what they think, versus listening to everyone else first and then developing their opinion biased by others' feedback. Writing down the assessment also helps document the interview in case the person reappears in the future.

- *Candidate testing:* Can provide some objective feedback on candidates, particularly for technical positions. The test results can also show how candidates for a position score relative to each other. Tests may include technical testing, cognitive testing, or business knowledge testing.

- *Behavioral testing:* Psychological behavioral tests have also been effective in determining the personal behavior traits of successful candidates. Behavioral tests work best when a pre-existing profile of successful candidates has been completed and new candidates are compared to that profile.

- *Business case interview:* Case interviewing provides another chance to test the thinking skills of the applicant. Cases are business problems that are presented to the candidate verbally, or in writing, to analyze. The candidate provides a recommendation on what actions they would take to solve the case issue. A typical case will pose a business problem to the interviewee, such as "how would you evaluate competing application vendors given a certain set of facts?" While for most case questions, there is no specific correct answer, the candidates response will provide insight into how well they can logically dissect a problem, ask for additional information, and construct an argument and set of recommendations.

- *Perform additional screening:* A variety of background screens can be helpful in determining candidates likelihood of success and distinguishing between candidates in a close race for the same position. The internal HR department, the recruiting agency, or other third-party services can conduct drug tests, criminal background checks, reference checking, and education/degree verifications. The IT department should coordinate with the HR department before conducting any of these screens, to ensure compliance with company HR policy.

- *Assess candidates in an informal setting:* Spending time with candidates in more informal settings, such as lunch, dinner, or a sporting event, can help in further assessing their fit. This can be particularly helpful for differentiating between closely matched prospects. Characteristics revealed away from the office setting may be just as important as work skills.

HIGH-VOLUME INTERVIEWING. If the hiring needs analysis determined that the department needs to hire a large number of candidates (more than four or five at a time), the process differs from filling only one position. The short-cycle scheduling effort consumes considerable time, let alone conducting the interviews themselves. The best process is to set aside a block of hours and a conference room on the same days of each week to concentrate on interviewing. Recruiting companies also have space for interviews and they can arrange for the interview team to see candidates at the agency office, which will minimize the distractions that are a natural part of on-site interviewing. This process will facilitate making rapid hiring decisions based on the entire candidate pool; without setting aside time for structured interviews the complicated scheduling logistics and the passage of time will be an irritant to both interviewers and candidates. By handling all interviews for a specific position over a short period, the decision can be made immediately and the candidates informed of the decision.

INTERVIEWING CONTRACTORS. Interviewing contract staff entails a different process than permanent hire interviews. The time cycle, content, assessment, and the negotiations are different from permanent hires. Questions and tips for contractor interviews include:

- *Assess contractor technical skills:* Usually companies will be willing to accept less exact fit for permanent employees, provided cultural fit and other experience is appropriate. For contractors, the technical fit should be exact, since they are usually being brought in to provide a specific set of expertise. The contractor should complete technical testing, as well as a technical interview with experienced team members to ensure proper knowledge.

- *Assure contractor reliability and quality:* Often contractors are brought in to provide a short-term surge of effort to push through a major project. In this case, if the contractor is unreliable or cannot provide quality service, the company incurs a high cost and loses crucial time. Referrals from the agency or previous contracts can be helpful in determining the contractor's ability to deliver quality work on time.

- *Establish a contractor day rate:* Unscrupulous contractors will occasionally charge excessive hours for unnecessary work, recognizing that the project is short-term and that they will soon move on to another project. Ask the contractor if they will provide a cap to their daily billings (8 to 10 hours) and require manager sign-off on additional hours is a way to help avoid this issue.

- *Understand contractor employment status:* Contractors may not be incorporated as a business and will have to be considered W-2 or 1099 contractors for tax and benefit purposes. These statuses each have specific implications for the company hiring the contractor and may imply certain benefit and tax liabilities. While contractors provided through an agency may be slightly more expensive than those hired direct, the agency deals with W-2, 1099, and contractor incorporation issues, providing a seamless interface and mitigating liabilities for their client. If contractors are hired directly by the IT department, the CIO or hiring manager should consult with the HR and legal departments to ensure that the contractor status is in line with corporate hiring policies.

- *Make clear final hiring intentions:* If the position has the potential to convert to a permanent position and the contractor will be considered for that role, he or she should know up front. This will prevent the contractor from prematurely looking for a new position when the contract is close to ending.

- *Make a rapid decision:* Once the interview is complete, the team should make a decision within one to three days. Contractors are accustomed to rapid turnaround in the decision-making process. Often the contractor will have several simultaneous opportunities and will generally take the first forthcoming offer. Once the interviewing team has identified the appropriate contract resource, they should move to rapidly make an offer.

Agency recruiters who are presenting a candidate can help with the assessment. If the contractor has been on previous engagements through the agency, the agency can provide references and feedback from the contractor's previous work.

Permanent hire interviews follow a more traditional process and time frame. Typically the process of determining the candidate profile, sourcing candidates, interviewing, offering, and closing the position can take up to 30 days. Permanent hires are making a major career decision, whereas contractors are simply making a commitment for the next two to six months. The permanent candidates require a more detailed scrutiny and need more information from the team on their career path, job stability, strategic direction of the company, training, culture, and team fit.

Step 4: Effective Hiring

The next step in the IT HR cycle, effective hiring, is often overlooked. The bulk of the attention is paid to sourcing, recruiting, and interviewing. After the hiring decision is made, the team's focus and activity level drops off. The recommendations in this section can help ensure that offers are accepted and can help make the difference between a successful hire and an unsuccessful one.

FINALIZING AN OFFER. After receiving feedback from the other interviewers and everyone agrees that the candidate is a hire, make the decision without procrastinating. Procrastination only increases the chance that the candidate will go elsewhere. One of the critical hiring errors interviewers make is the search for the mythical perfect candidate. After all the interviews and background checks, there is little likelihood of new information emerging that will change the decision. Once the decision is made, the offer should be extended to the candidate as soon as possible and followed up with a formal offer letter.

When the candidate is offered the job, the manager should be frank as to the expectations for the job—roles, responsibility, work hours, career mobility, and any policies or other issues that may affect his or her decision. The offer letter should be specific, spelling out the expectations that have been communicated verbally. In addition to describing the roles and responsibilities, the offer should also establish specific performance objectives and time frames for the role. For example, the offer might specify the following objectives: Candidate must complete five modules for the new billing system by the end of the third month after the start date. Candidate must complete requirement gathering for the asset-tracking database in the first 90 days of employment. Candidate must attend the following training classes in the first year of employment. This part of the offer is often included in an addendum to the formal offer letter. This approach helps both the new hire and the manager in ensuring the expectations have been clearly set and provide an objective, pre-agreed measure for assessing performance, allowing the manager to detect hiring errors as early as possible.

The first 45 days should be an evaluation period with a formal review cycle. The CIO or manager should schedule a meeting with the candidate 45 days after the start date to review performance to date against the preset performance metrics and objectives.

The candidate should sign the offer letter and the job expectations and performance metrics addendum, accepting the offer and acknowledging that he clearly understands the expectations; make sure a signature line is on the offer letter. This letter goes into the candidate's personnel file in HR as well as into the IT manager's files.

CHECKING REFERENCES.   Rarely does a reference not check out well, especially when checking the candidate provided references. A few rules of thumb to improve the quality of reference checking are:

- Check three references for each candidate and document the conversations and feedback.
- Check at least one reference that is not given by the candidate (e.g., a previous project manager) and ask that person for names of others who worked with the candidate who can be called as well.
- Ask pointed questions on reference calls. Would you work with this person again? What are his or her weaknesses? What does this person do well?
- Use care when interpreting the references. Seldom are references negative; generally they are either positive or neutral. Therefore, for a quality candidate, expect all the references to be highly favorable. If they are not, it may indicate that the manager has not had a good experience with the candidate, but is bound by company policy or other considerations to avoid revealing this.

RAMPING UP NEW HIRES QUICKLY.   The faster a new hire can become a successful part of the team, the more productive the IT department is going to be. Typically, people expect the first week on a new job to include background reading, meeting their coworkers, and learning more about the company. Many new hires expect to take several weeks to get to the actual work they were hired to accomplish. The IT team can avoid this expensive ramp-up period by laying the groundwork for a successful first week for the new team member:

- Have administrative staff establish workspace before the start date; for example, office, cubicle, computer/laptop, voice mail, business cards, payroll and benefits setup, and other administrative details.
- Have the employee meet with HR to take care of signing up for payroll and benefits prior to the first day on the job.
- Arrange a team breakfast or lunch the first day to have new hires meet team members.
- Give the new hire or contractor IT department and company background information to read prior to the start date.

- Have the first week of employment scripted in advance, with specific goals.
- After the first week, have the new hire detail and document his or her work plan for the next 30 days and review it in person.
- If the new hire's main job or project is not ready to kick off immediately on the start date, have a secondary project lined up and ready to go or delay his start date until the main task can be started.

Step 5: Managing the Workforce

Managing the professionals in the IT department can be challenging. There are scores of management books and leadership books available, oriented toward both general management as well as specific approaches for leading IT teams. In this section, we cover some of the specific models we have employed in successfully managing IT staff.

THE 10-PERCENT ATTRITION MODEL. The *10-percent attrition model* means that every year the CIO should release the bottom 10 percent of the workforce. This process ensures that the department is constantly upgrading the team. It also helps the workers falling in the bottom 10 percent. This model is applicable to most IT departments; after a few cycles, the IT team will be a stable, high-quality group and the attrition model may no longer apply. However, we have found this situation to be the exception. Also, although we have emphasized the high costs of turnover in the introduction to this chapter, the costs of an ineffective team far outweigh the impact of losing the poor performers.

To accomplish this attrition, during each review cycle, the CIO should rank IT staff according to relative performance. One useful method is to adopt the A, B, C, D model, which equates A to the top 10 percent of performers, B to the middle 60 percent, C to next 20 percent, and D to the bottom 10 percent. Adhering to a 10-percent attrition model works, at least for a struggling IT department, because the cost of D players is significant. The obvious costs include the cost of compensating employees who are not producing value for the organization. However, this is only a small portion of the cost to the department. D players traditionally command too much management attention either because of personal issues or performance problems. Management's attention could be focused on driving projects forward and otherwise ensuring the department success. Further, management or teammates have to cover for the nonperformance of the D-ranked staff members. Finally, and most corrosive, D performers tend to drive away the A and B players, who ask "Why am I getting paid the same for producing twice as much work?" Management's attention should be spent on caring for and developing A and B players and on reducing their attrition to zero. The forced-attrition model and the swap analysis are powerful tools for building a world-class IT team.

IT STAFF CAREER DEVELOPMENT. Training and career development are the two most important aspects of a job for technical professionals. Besides having a good relationship with their direct supervisors, training and career development are top reasons technology professionals keep or change jobs.

The hallmarks of a good training program are:

- *Relevance:* The training should provide skills directly useful to the professionals in the execution of the major portion of their responsibilities (e.g., systems administration training for tier 2 staff; requirements analysis training for developers).
- *Timeliness:* The best training is timely as well as relevant, and delivered to staff at the point in their career where they have enough experience for the training to be relevant, but early enough that they can reap the benefits of it.
- *Linkage to promotion objectives:* Training will often take a back-seat to other objectives and unavoidable business emergencies. However, because training is an effective and important way of improving staff performance, the CIO must find ways to promote and enforce objectives. One way to ensure that this happens is by tying standard training classes to promotion objectives.

Training is the number one benefit desired by technology employees. Technology employees value training because they enjoy the challenge of learning new skills and recognize that keeping current with rapidly changing technology ensures interesting future assignments and helps guarantee job security. To facilitate the delivery of this benefit, each position identified for the organization (Step 1 of the IT HR life cycle) should have a specific training regimen. This should include both recommended and required training for each level. Promotion should be made contingent, in part, on completing the required training. The HR department can work with IT in establishing a training program and can help with conducting training, tracking completion and certification, as well as identifying outside providers for delivery of the training. This should be done in conjunction with the IT staff, who can identify the training that would be both interesting and useful for the role. For example, network support employees who have achieved their Microsoft Certified Systems Engineer (MCSE) certification might want to follow up with Cisco training and achieve additional networking certification.

Because training invariably involves significant time and expense for the company, the IT manager should ensure that employees make a reciprocal commitment to the organization. In exchange for the training, staff should sign a training certificate. This certificate outlines the training program and the cost for each piece. The employee should sign an agreement stating that he will reimburse the company for training costs if he leaves the company voluntarily within 12 months after completing the course. This acknowledgement accomplishes two things: First, it shows the employee the actual dollar amounts invested by the department in his training. Second, it reduces the risk of investing in employees who depart the company as soon as he receives the training, lowering attrition in the IT department.

As employees receive training, their market value increases and they will likely graduate from one job to the next. To keep the staff interested and engaged, they must be provided opportunities to move ahead, use the new skills they have learned, and continue to learn new technology skills. If the company does not provide employees with these opportunities, the best employees will find an employer who will. Providing training, development, and a chance to use new skills generates loyalty and goodwill.

In some cases, the team member may be trained outside of the company. After completing a training regimen and improving his technology skills, the employee's value continues to increase. At some point, the organization may not be able to provide him the on-the-job responsibility that he would command in the open market, and he may elect to move on. This is a natural outcome of having qualified employees, and, while employee retention is critical, should not be cause for alarm. We have heard good IT managers characterize it thus: "The department should be more like a college than a prison. We miss our best team members when they elect to move on, but if we cannot provide them opportunities to grow, then they must seek them on the open market." Allowing employees to leave on good terms will also mean that they may return eventually.

Providing rigorous training and development opportunities entails some short-term expense for the IT department, but will be a crucial factor in the department's ability to retain the A players. IT organizations that fail to train, develop, and challenge their staff will only retain those who cannot find employment elsewhere.

KEY DRIVERS OF STAFF RETENTION. A variety of studies have unearthed key drivers of retention and attrition in IT departments. Based on analysis of these studies, as well as first-hand experience, we list the following key drivers of retention in priority order:

- *Satisfaction with immediate supervisor:* Because of day-to-day contact, employees identify with the company through their immediate supervisors. If an employee does not have a good relationship with his or her immediate supervisor, that employee is at risk of leaving. Conversely, if that employee has a productive working relationship with his supervisor, risk of the employee's departure drops precipitously. To reduce the likelihood of uncontrolled attrition, CIOs must ensure that their managers are top performers whom people respect. HR can help the CIO track attrition by manager to determine if there are problems with a particular manager.

- *Opportunities for training:* As outlined, investment in training is a major driver of IT employee satisfaction.
- *Satisfaction with team and coworkers:* Dysfunctional teams and coworkers drive out employees quickly. Additionally, when best practices of a particularly good team emerge, find out what these are and pollinate them across the other teams.
- *Opportunities for career growth and ability to move to different projects:* The CIO must create opportunities for staff to move through the organization. This can be accomplished through regular staff rotations, through promotion or lateral responsibility changes, and through project work. This provides the technical staff with challenges to satisfy their demand for learning.
- *Compensation:* While the most obvious variable, compensation is not the number one factor in the career decisions of technical workers, as long as the compensation is within 10 percent of the market rate. If an employee's compensation is far below market they will, of course, seek alternative employment (or possibly reduce their efforts). To avoid under-compensating staff, the CIO should benchmark department salaries against the market every three to six months. An annual schedule for compensation reviews, tied to performance appraisals, is usually sufficient. For certain high-demand skills, a six-month incremental evaluation is necessary to make sure the market has not changed significantly. Salary adjustments can work both ways (i.e., down as well as up). If the market has come down significantly, downward salary adjustments may be in order.
- *Opportunities for promotion:* Not all technical employees care about titles or moving up in the organization because of responsibilities that are concomitant with such positions. For the staff who have advancement ambitions, the CIO should be sure that there is a clear promotion ladder. The department should also ask individuals to perform at the level of skills the promotion requires before actually promoting the person. This ensures that employees do not fail because they could not handle the increased skill level.

The retention program should incorporate these variables. Macro-economic trends will influence an organization's ability to find and keep IT professionals. However, in both good times and bad, there are still ample opportunities for top-echelon technical talent and when the economy starts to grow, the market will shift. An effective retention program now will avoid trouble later.

COMPENSATION. As outlined in the previous section, compensation is an important element of overall employee satisfaction. Research has shown that as long as compensation is within reasonable (plus or minus 10 percent) range of employees marketplace expectations, then other factors are more important determinants of overall career and job satisfaction. However, when compensation strays outside those ranges, it becomes the number one predictor. Inattention to compensation can quickly ruin an IT department through mass exodus of key staff.

Compensation setting can be challenging for IT departments. Salaries and benefits are usually the largest direct cost for IT, and therefore controlling compensation expenses has the largest impact cost control. On the other hand, the CIO's effort to recruit the "best and brightest" and deliver good service can be severely hindered by an uncompetitive overall compensation package.

Good compensation practices for IT departments include:

- *Clearly defined compensation programs:* Establish base salary, bonus, and other compensation expectations for each role. While you may not elect to have an exact salary for each level, ranges of compensation are appropriate.

- *Total compensation concept:* Employee base salary and other cash compensation is only a portion of the total employee expense for professional services firms. Benefits, training, and other forms of compensation can range from 10 to 30 percent of the total cost of an employee. Because employees often only consider direct cash compensation when benchmarking themselves against peers in other organizations, the company should establish the concept of total compensation for employees, and report the total package of compensation and benefits costs incurred.

- *Periodic staff compensation reviews:* Annual review of compensation for each staff member. These should usually be tied to the staff annual appraisal. Periodically the IT department may perform market-adjustment compensation reviews that are not linked to the appraisal cycle.

- *Periodic compensation benchmarking:* To avoid under-compensating staff, the firm should benchmark professional and administrative salaries against the market every four to six months. An annual schedule for compensation reviews, usually tied to performance appraisals, is sufficient. For certain high-demand skills, a six-month incremental check is necessary to make sure the market has not changed significantly. Salary adjustments can work both ways (i.e., down as well as up). If the market has come down significantly, downward salary adjustments (or re-acquisition of staff) may be in order. Downward salary adjustments can be incredibly de-motivating for staff and should be avoided if possible.

- *Publication of salary and benefit benchmarking data:* Because IT staff will inevitably conduct their own benchmarking research, the firm can mitigate any negative impacts by proactively researching total compensation appropriate for the department employees. Benchmarks will vary by level, industry, geography, and macroeconomic conditions. This benchmarking should be used to set total compensation levels competitively, as well as ensure that staff are satisfied that objective criteria are used in assessing market levels.

HANDLING LAYOFFS. Layoffs or reductions in force (RIFs) are unavoidable at times and the CIO may not have a choice if business conditions dictate cost reductions that are mandated by the board and senior management. If the workforce must be reduced because of budget cuts, these procedures can minimize the impact of the process. As with our previous recommendations, policies and process dictated by the corporate human resources or legal department should always take precedence:

1. Evaluate employees as described earlier in this chapter (A, B, C, and D ratings).

2. Build a preliminary list of potential staff members to lay off from the ranking, from the bottom up.

3. Prior to making a final determination, ensure that critical projects can be covered by the remaining staff. If cutting resources jeopardizes projects, the low priority projects may be deferred or eliminated. This can be determined in conjunction with the IT steering committee.

4. Provide the list to the HR department and review with senior management to ensure that the cuts provide the anticipated cost reduction benefit.

5. Decide on severance by employee level. Generally, this is set by the executive team or HR; however, if no rules are in place, the CIO must determine the severance level. This is generally set by title level in the organization or years of service.

6. Develop separation letters for each individual. The separation letter should include anything the employee is to do in return for accepting severance; for example, noncompetition and nonsolicitation of employees and nondisclosure of company information. Most severance letters ask for a general release of liability from the employee in exchange for the severance amount. There are a variety of legal restrictions that impact companies conducting a layoff and the legal

department or external counsel should advise every company con-
templating large numbers of layoffs.

7. Determine a time, place to meet, and communicate the separation
clearly and simply to the individuals affected. Give them the separation letters and ask them to sign and return by a specified date to receive their severance.

8. Keep communication short. Because the decision is final and is usually based on factors beyond the employees' control, there is little to
be gained from a lengthy discussion.

9. Conduct the meeting quickly and professionally. Allowing staff to
leave with dignity helps the company preserve a good reputation in
the market even in the aftermath of layoffs.

10. Do not leave staff with the impression that there may be a reprieve
from the decision. Inexperienced managers sometimes say, "We really
want you to stay; however, my hands are tied and I'm being asked to
let people go. I will talk to senior management to see if there is any
other potential for you to stay. Let me get back to you." This creates a
variety of problems and will improperly raise false hopes for the staff
being laid off.

MANAGEMENT COACHING.   Much of the day-to-day professional development for IT staff comes from work experience and direct feedback from
end-users and IT management. This informal, real-time feedback is an important kind of training for staff, and therefore managers should be aware of
the best ways to work with their teams in providing feedback.

Robert S. Bailey of the Center for Creative Leadership has developed a
framework for guiding manager feedback styles for employees based on their
current performance. The framework highlights that the management style
most appropriate for under-performing employees is different for moderate-
performing employees and again different for high-performing employees.

The distribution of employee performance falls roughly on a normal
curve, placing them in one of four quadrants (Exhibit 11.9). The most appropriate management style for each employee type is outlined in each
quadrant.[2]

A final management coaching issue for IT staff to be aware of is the challenges created for staff as they transition from individual producer roles to
roles which incorporate management responsibilities. This can be a difficult
transition, particularly in IT departments, which tend to value high levels of
output and technology expertise for entry-level and early-career professionals. These staff tend to fall back on individual producer habits, even after
promotion to manager. Eventually the amount of work required cannot be
completed by an individual, making leverage and management expertise
critical. Training and monitoring new managers to learn how to effectively

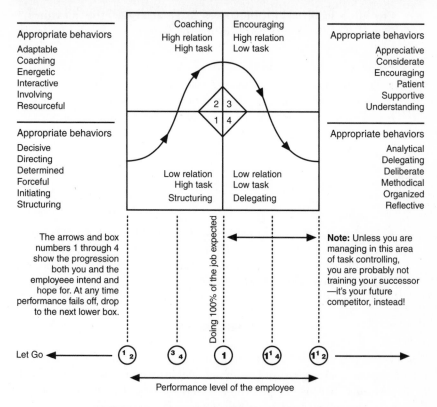

Exhibit 11.9 Manager Feedback Approach Matrix

achieve results from their teams is a critical part of helping the new manager to succeed and avoid burnout.

CREATING PERFORMANCE PLANS. While a host of management books with advice and guidance on effectively managing the workforce are available, the management of employees can often be overcomplicated by the pundits. The CIO should pick a management philosophy that matches her personality and capabilities. In most cases creating a high-performance team boils down to four things:

1. Setting (and documenting) clear objectives and expectations of superior performance.
2. Developing a joint plan that lays out execution of those objectives and expectations over a period (usually quarterly or annually).
3. Measuring progress against those objectives and expectations monthly or quarterly and at annual review time.

4. Providing feedback to employees after analyzing the measures in Step 3. Feedback can occur in one of four ways, depending on the situation:

- *Positive feedback:* Give positive reinforcing feedback to individual.
- *Negative feedback, but employee has potential:* The CIO must assist the individual who has potential to get back on track. This may entail weekly meetings to help mentor the individual.
- *Repeated negative feedback:* After repeated attempts to help the person or after concluding the person is not capable, make the employee take responsibility by putting him or her on a performance improvement plan where he or she is accountable to achieve some short-term objectives in a short time (e.g., 45 days) or risk being terminated.
- *Negative feedback and employee has failed his or her performance improvement plan:* It is the CIO's responsibility to the company and the IT team to terminate the employee or move him into a position that requires fewer skills.

Summary

The IT HR life cycle is a continuum of management processes focused on hiring, training, managing, and retaining the best workforce available for the IT department. Because IT practitioners have a natural preference for technology management, these issues are often undermanaged by the CIO, leading to poor overall performance of the department. The bottom line is that the IT department's success is contingent on identifying and retaining an effective IT workforce. Implementing the strategies in this chapter helps build that high-performance team and should be approached with as much rigor as the other disciplines outlined here, such as IT demand management or vendor selection.

By implementing the recommendations in this chapter effectively, the CIO improves odds of success in:

- Determining how to staff the organization and how many people are needed to accomplish the objectives set out in the strategic plan.
- Eliminating C and D players from the team and raising the overall performance of the entire team, resulting in more successful projects, lower budget variance, and a lower defect rate in implementations and applications.
- Hiring new employees with greater speed and success.
- Optimizing the mix of permanent employees and contract workers in the IT department.

RESOURCES

Following is a list of web sites that may be useful in determining the best way to hire and manage the IT workforce:

Recruiting-related information
- www.techrepublic.com
- www.airsdirectory.com
- www.recruitersonline.com

Online job boards
- www.monster.com
- hotjobs.yahoo.com
- www.headhunter.net
- www.dice.com (specializes in contingent workforce)
- www.flipdog.com

Technology professional salary information
- www.salary.com
- www.payscale.com
- www.itworld.com
- www.salaryexpert.com

NOTES

1. Bill Parcells, "The Tough Work of Turning around a Team," *Harvard Business Review* (November/December 2000).
2. Joseph A. Demkin and The American Institute of Architects, *The Architects Handbook of Professional Practice* (New York: John Wiley & Sons, 2001).

12

Vendor Selection

Thinking is the hardest work there is, which is probably why so few people engage in it.

—Henry Ford[1]

This chapter outlines the process for selection of major outside service and product providers and the subsequent management of the vendors. The list of external vendors used by even a small IT shop is often lengthy. Vendors provide products and services across a wide variety of categories—telecom, networking, consulting, software, and hardware. In a given category, often multiple vendors are used by the department.

This chapter is organized around the first of two major vendor-related tasks facing the IT manager: selecting vendor partners and products. The next chapter covers the management of the vendor relationship "after the sale." It provides a comprehensive methodology and approach for vendor selection. Most often, the major vendor selection activities of an IT manager are focused on the selection of software to support the business, with decisions on vendors for hardware, services, and supplementary systems emerging from the primary package decision; therefore, this chapter is primarily focused on the selection of package application software and accompanying products and services.

The selection approach defined here is intended to be a full-fledged, comprehensive methodology that results in the most rigorous, thorough (and painstaking) process for determining the "best" vendor. The steps described can, and should, be skipped or otherwise de-emphasized, depending on the specific situation facing the IT manager. As with all other frameworks described in this book, common sense should prevail and the applicable portions of the methodology applied to the specific situation at hand.

Why This Topic Is Important

The successful selection and management of vendors plays a large part in determining the overall success of the IT department and, as importantly, the ease with which the department achieves that success. Successful selections are also most often complex and lengthy processes that require the collection and analysis of large amounts of information. Vendor-supplied technologies are often the largest pieces of the IT picture that are most visible to the business and have the largest impact on end-user satisfaction. Well-thought-out vendor choices and solid vendors who behave as partners can ease the work of the IT manager considerably. Conversely, poor vendor selection can hamstring the organization with constant fire fighting, failed projects, and angry users.

Because the operations and applications in most IT departments rely heavily on outside vendors, the IT budget generally has a significant component allocated for third-party vendor spending (i.e., 30 to 60 percent of the operating and even more of the capital budget). Because vendors are necessary suppliers of products and services, as well as significant sources of expenditure, the CIO cannot afford to ignore their proper selection and management.

Vendor interests and incentives, unfortunately, are not always precisely aligned with those of the CIO. While client satisfaction is part of the equation for vendors, so are other factors such as profitability, sales commission, quarterly revenue, and market penetration. A vendor salesperson's natural role is as an advocate for his or her product or service. This means that to be most productive for the IT department, the director must supervise and actively manage the delivery of services and products on an ongoing basis to ensure that the delivery and execution are consistent with the expectations and goals of the organization.

Picking the vendors on which to rely is a high-risk proposition. The selection and subsequent implementation of software or hardware can go awry, wasting millions of dollars, disrupting the business, and ending careers for IT staff. As outlined in Part I of this book, the IT landscape is littered with failed implementations. The fact that many of the failed projects were conducted inside successful companies and supervised by smart IT managers highlights the inherent risk of the process, even in the best of circumstances.

In spite of the criticality and risk associated with vendors, experience has shown that IT managers are at a significant disadvantage in the vendor process, particularly vendor selection. A technology professional may manage a vendor selection for package software a handful of times in his or her career, whereas his or her counterparts on the vendor side are generally senior-level sales professionals who close multiple deals each year. This puts the IT manager at a distinct disadvantage to the vendor, from an experience standpoint alone.

Compounding the issue is the fact that once a vendor selection is complete, it is generally difficult to undo. If it turns out that better, more appropriate vendors are available, often the sunk-cost and previously committed contractual obligations prevent them from being used. Because of the high investment in hardware, software, and services to deploy a vendor product, the opportunity to replace a vendor may appear only once every few years, at best. This means that vendor selection can be a one-way street with very few turning off points and that vendor selection and management are a critical part of the successful IT manager's toolkit.

Application Vendor Economics

The software selection process most often drives the vendor selection process for hardware and software. The economic rationale for the acquisition of package software applications, therefore, is important for IT teams to understand.

In general, companies purchase package software in the hopes that the combined pool of research and development (R&D) dollars from a large number of customers will produce greater aggregate benefit than the drawbacks created by the implementation of an off-the-shelf system. Software vendors plow a significant portion of new license and maintenance revenue back into their applications, providing enhanced features and a clear upgrade path for their customers. To compensate for the standard approach required by package applications, vendors have worked hard over time to provide configuration options and customization points of entry to allow the most commonly varying features of the package to be most easily changed.

A package software customer also benefits from the scale benefits attendant with a large marketplace presence. Software packages with a large following create a set of standards that allows the emergence of a robust set of third-party options for add-on software and consulting. Standards created by packages for a variety of application characteristics—application interfaces, technical and data architectures, user interfaces, and so on—mean that follow-on customization and system integration become much easier and cost effective to execute.

Last, packages provide a level of standardization in the labor marketplace. A company running SAP can rely on recruiting additional SAP resources that can get up to speed in a reasonable time.

The marketplace has proven over time that the combined benefits of pooled R&D, sophisticated third-party service, and a ready pool of skilled labor more than outweigh the compromises created from the implementation of noncustom systems for supporting critical business functions.

Vendor Selection Methodology

Overview of Methodology

Exhibit 12.1 shows an overview of the vendor selection methodology covered in this section. The methodology is intended to provide a comprehensive, thorough approach to the vendor selection process.

Exhibit 12.1   Vendor Selection Process Overview

The process begins with the definition of scope for the product (or service) being acquired and proceeds through the identification of a team to support the selection process, the identification of potential vendors, the issuance of an request for proposal (RFP), the selection of vendor finalists, due diligence on the finalists, selection of supplemental vendors (if needed), project planning, and final vendor pricing negotiations. Each of these steps is further detailed in the following section with a diagram highlighting the subtasks, required information, and outcome for each subtask.

Of critical importance throughout the selection process is to ensure that at all times the effort is being managed, organized, and driven by the IT manager in charge. Top vendor sales professionals did not reach that status through passivity. Vendors are well practiced at the art of seducing the hapless IT manager and will take on as much of the work, and own or drive as much of the effort as the manager lets them, to remain in control of the process.

A second critical component to vendor selection is the evaluation team's discipline in creating, updating, and maintaining the documentation for the analysis. Organizing a large amount of information being gathered from a variety of disparate sources is difficult for the most diligent team. Keeping clear documentation on the raw data, analysis, and outcome of each step covered in this chapter helps explain to outside observers how the decision was reached, serves as organizational memory, and, most importantly, ensures that no steps are skipped and that the analysis is completed in a rigorous, thorough fashion.

The third key to success is the detailed requirements analysis done by the team in preparation for the vendor analysis process. This step should be completed long before the first vendor is contacted. Vendors long ago perfected the courtship required to manage clients through the sales process, and if IT managers have not done their homework in the form of the up-front analysis and scope work, they will be at the mercy of a sales process they neither control nor fully understand. The necessary objective analysis becomes lost in the feel-good haze of endless vendor dinner outings, rounds of golf, and vendor-led conference calls and demos. The result is, at best, a distorted, suboptimal outcome. We have observed dozens of software selections and have rarely seen success emerge from a vendor-driven process.

Scope and Requirements Definition

SET SCOPE FOR BUSINESS AREAS SUPPORTED. The IT manager should first seek to clearly understand the full range of business activities to be supported by the systems in question. The business, vendor, and technical requirements for the system flow entirely from this scope, making this a critical step in the overall analysis. The efforts during this step provide dividends later as vendor due diligence is executed. The evaluation team will be able to ask clear, concise questions of the vendors and understand the priorities for the business, based on scope.

To accomplish this, the manager must understand the business reasons for the system's initiative. Common reasons include:

- Replacement or renewal of end-of-life cycle or otherwise obsolete systems.
- Changes to business model (new lines of business, acquisitions, divestitures, increased volumes).
- Cost recapture (through productivity improvement, substitution of capital for labor, etc.).
- Benefit capture (increased sales, market presence).
- Response to other systems changes (supplier or customer demands).
- Competitive parity (response to business initiatives or technology capability-based offerings from competitors).

The outcome of a vendor selection, like any other systems initiative, should help the company drive revenue, reduce costs, or gain control over the business. The scope of the system effort should be based on the business imperative, and the systems should have the capabilities required to support them. The scope covered should be wide enough to justify the selection of a vendor for support but constrained enough to be achievable within a single implementation.

The application scope is generally focused on a specific business function with clearly defined boundaries and interfaces to other business processes. Examples include purchasing, materials requirements planning (MRP), warehouse logistics, fixed assets, customer service, or purchasing.

The scope definition can also be achieved by defining what is not in the scope. For example, the scope might be defined as "all purchasing activities, not including receiving, payables, and forecasting" or "all purchasing of products, not including office supplies." The scope definition should also draw clear distinctions between business processes or systems that are replaced or supported versus affected but not changed as part of the project.

A useful tool for understanding the scope is a context diagram that shows the business process area in relation to other areas that interact with it, demonstrating both what is in and out of scope (Exhibit 12.2).

In every case, a detailed document that defines the specific scope under consideration is the first step in the vendor selection process. The document should define the scope in as detailed a manner as necessary, with appropriate illustrative charts and diagrams.

The final scoping step is to get sign-off from the IT steering committee. Any final ambiguities or inconsistencies in the scoping should be clarified under the scrutiny of the committee. Getting final scope sign-off may take

Exhibit 12.2 Example Context Diagram

several iterations of presentations and questions and answers before the committee.

ESTABLISH EVALUATION TEAM. After the scope has been defined, the next task is to establish an evaluation team to provide expertise and effort to complete the selection process. The scope definition helps identify business and technical knowledge required for a successful assessment. Vendor selections, particularly if covering a large scope, are labor intensive and require a team of dedicated resources.

The team should include members from outside the IT department and have some representation from each business area affected (e.g., accounting, marketing, manufacturing). This ensures that both the technical expertise and the business unit- or business function-specific knowledge are incorporated into the requirements and evaluation process from the start. Further, early participation from business users facilitates the most rapid acceptance of the vendor selection outcome by the business. Finally, business users tend to catch potential issues that may be missed by IT or that IT is unaware of; for example, the length of time required to replace and train customer service representatives in a high turnover environment.

The overall team size varies by company size, scope of business functions under consideration, and the size of the investment being made. A small vendor selection team might consist of one full-time team member from IT, one from the business unit or function affected, and one part-time manager to drive the effort, along with ad hoc participation from IT and the business. A large-scale selection team, assessing, for example, a full-scale ERP implementation for a large organization might contain 15 to 25 full-time team members and as many as a dozen part-time members. The mix would likely be 50 percent to 70 percent IT team members and the balance from the business.

The most effective way of building team membership is through nominations from the IT steering committee. The list of potential team members should be interviewed by the IT manager and/or the committee to determine if they have the requisite skills, knowledge, interest, and ability. Exhibit 12.3 shows an example selection team structure.

Ideally, the team is co-located with dedicated office space to facilitate communication and maintain focus. Part-time team members should also have dedicated workspace in the team area, so that they can easily pick up their work where they left off and easily join the team on their own schedules.

Achieving the right skill mix, participation level, and environment for the team will have a strong impact on the overall effectiveness and results of the selection process. Even small-scope vendor selection efforts are large undertakings and require considerable sustained effort on the part of the team.

INVENTORY BUSINESS REQUIREMENTS/SET PRIORITY/WEIGHTING.
One of the toughest realities of vendor selection is that the only way to truly understand if a package (or other vendor product or service) is a good match (and where its weak points are) is to first understand the in-scope business processes at a painstaking level of detail. A complete understanding of the business processes, events, calendars, volumes, and policies governing the area under consideration allows the team to rapidly and accurately assess the

FULL-TIME TEAM MEMBERS	PART-TIME TEAM MEMBERS
• Team lead—Director IT • Applications manager—IT • Developer—IT	• DBA-IT department • Developer • EDI specialist—IT department • Systems engineer—IT department
• Business analyst—Purchasing • Business analyst—Manufacturing • Business analyst—Distribution	• Business analyst—Finance • Corporate controller (payables) • Business analyst—Fixed asset management • Director—HR
IT STEERING—VENDOR SELECTION SUBCOMMITTEE	
• Chief operating officer • Chief financial officer	• SVP—Manufacturing • VP—Sales and Marketing

Exhibit 12.3   Example Selection Team Structure

systems being considered and determine the optimal approach for covering the gaps in the system.

Unfortunately, the work of blueprinting business processes and documenting requirements is unavoidably difficult and tedious. However, it is an *absolute prerequisite* of a successful vendor selection, and it forms the bedrock foundation of a successful implementation. Without understanding the business processes supported, the team cannot possibly judge the level of software fit, what the shortcomings are, how they are dealt with, the level of change required by the business, and the expense of configuration and customization to make the system work well. Superficial, weak understanding of business requirements and the inevitable weak analysis that follows are primary reasons for the failure of large systems implementation projects. Requirements gathering for vendor screening is similar to that for custom systems; the team should not neglect this effort simply because a product or package is being considered.

Because starting the "courtship" process with vendors is infinitely more enjoyable than nonstop internal team meetings where business processes are white-boarded at excruciating levels of detail, this step is also the most commonly skipped. The smart CIO waits until the proper amount of homework has been done before making the first vendor contact.

There are literally dozens of methodologies for capturing business system requirements, and most are good. The important factor in capturing system requirements is ensuring that the appropriate level of detail has been substantially documented. The most common failing of any of the methodologies is a tendency by the team to gloss over the details by neglecting to document its efforts. The only true way to demonstrate a complete, satisfactory, and comprehensive understanding of a business process is to map and document it clearly. One of our favorite catch phrases during the business requirements definition process is "writing is thinking." The effective IT manager ensures that his or her team has done its homework by both understanding and documenting areas of responsibility. Exhibit 12.4 shows a sample business process flow diagram.

Most of the common system requirements gathering methodologies are focused on custom development but serve very well for software selection projects, as the information needed for package requirements is similar. The resources for this chapter identifies several books covering this topic.

Documentation should start at a high level of detail for setting scope and context and proceed through one or two descending levels of business process detail. The requirements should capture business events and the processes that handle them. The documentation should also capture not just what the systems do, but also what the people operating the systems are responsible for, what business policies or practices affect the process, and the information required and produced by each step. The documentation should also draw a distinction between the current business process and the planned or "to-be"

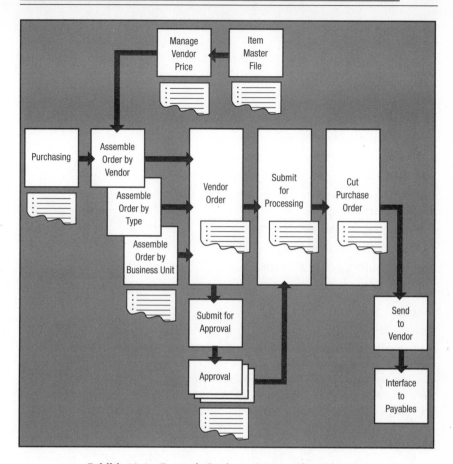

Exhibit 12.4   Example Business Process Flow Diagram

processes. Iterative interviews with business managers and end users are an effective way to flesh out the document.

If the vendor under consideration replaces an existing product or service, the existing requirements, training material, process flows, or other documentation can serve as a baseline for the new requirement's definition. This is particularly true in the case of package software selection. The working, existing systems are the most complete articulation of the business requirements, and the things the existing system does right make a great starting place for what the new system should do as well. In this case, if the existing system does not have documentation, the team should conduct baseline requirements gathering and documentation based on the current system capabilities. Further benefits of an existing system baseline include a clear understanding of interfaces or other systems being affected, a clear definition of the overall technical environment, and an early start on rollout, data conversion, and cutover planning.

Typical deliverables emerging from the requirement phase for a package selection may include:

- Business process flows.
- Process descriptions showing required inputs, outputs, procedures, calculations, interfaces, and human intervention.
- Business event triggers (synchronous, asynchronous).
- Data content (entity, lookup, transaction) and format requirements.
- Processing calendar—daily, weekly, and monthly transactions; volumes, events, and reports.
- Processing volumes.
- Reporting requirements.
- User interface requirements.
- Security requirements.

When choosing a methodology, simpler is better—if the team spends time wrestling with a tool, it winds up with a second-rate analysis. Our favorite systems design tools are a whiteboard, a graphics package, a spreadsheet, and a word processor.

Once defined, the business requirements should be assigned a preliminary importance or criticality weighting so that as the vendor alternatives are assessed, the assessment team can understand early on the significance of potential give-ups in the system. Simplicity is again the rule, particularly for this preliminary rating. We suggest a high, medium, or low rating for each requirement, with a goal of 25 percent or fewer "high" priority requirements and 30 percent or more "low" priority ratings. Any weighting system can be used, but more than 10 grades of priority begins to lose meaning.

An example requirement prioritization might be: "Fill rate for Customer A must always be above 98.5 percent because of contractual obligations; system should warn for potential stock-outs in products ordered by Customer A—priority HIGH" or "Statistical forecast calculation should compensate for seasonality based on manually maintained adjusting factors for items flagged as *seasonal*—priority MEDIUM."

As with any requirements definition, the temptation is for all requirements to have a high priority; if they weren't requirements, they wouldn't be in the document, after all. The team should understand that every requirement will be assessed, and the priority ratings are for ranking the requirements relative to each other. The high priority requirements have a large impact on the selection process (vendors that can meet the requirements most easily, with least configuration rise to the top) and drive much of the focus work during the vendor due diligence. Therefore, it is important to take a hard line on which requirements are allowed a high priority stamp. Selections with a large number of "must-have" functional requirements often run into trouble later in the process during vendor due diligence. The team should also understand that at this point, only functional requirements are being prioritized—the technical and vendor requirements are prioritized as part of a later process.

Depending on project size, the team may want to engage outside help in completing the business process mapping and requirements definition. The primary reasons for this are the provision of extra capacity and the addition of knowledgeable resources that have conducted such an exercise previously. The IT manager should use outside help judiciously. Third parties involved in the selection can have agendas and motivations that are at variance with the organization, creating an agency problem. Also, by sidestepping the difficult work of the analysis, the vendor selection team loses the benefits of developing a complete mastery of the content and process. The best use of third parties is in an advisory role, helping guide the process and provide coaching for the vendor selection team. The best third parties for this role have extensive experience in vendor or package selection and are not necessarily candidates for an implementation partner.

Finally, invariably during a rigorous review of business processes such as this, business process improvement or reengineering opportunities are identified. Ideally, the team should document and inventory these and put them in a "parking lot" for later analysis by the business. The temptation to achieve business process improvements as part of the analysis (or later implementation) can be difficult to resist, but the team should not confuse knowing about an improvement opportunity with an obligation to implement it. Trying to achieve major business process change as an integral part of a system implementation has been the downfall of many projects and should be approached with great caution.

GENERATE PRELIMINARY COST/BENEFITS MODEL. With a business case created, clear scope defined, combined business/IT team built, and the systems requirements defined and prioritized, the final step in this phase is to generate a preliminary cost-benefit model and estimated project time line. Although this may seem premature given that a system has not been picked, it is important to create at least order-of-magnitude estimates of project costs and benefits at this point in the project. This accomplishes several things for the team. First, it starts a paper trail of estimating models that can be revised as new information is added and provides a common set of assumptions that can be confirmed or disproved during the further process.

Second, having an early forecast of the potential costs and benefits gives the selection team (and company senior management team) numbers that provide context for the rest of the project. It also provides at least preliminary validation for moving forward with the project based on best estimates of return on investment (ROI). The process also gives the team a head start on finding ways to quantify some of the softer, more-difficult-to-estimate benefits of the project. Finally, it ensures that the team is focused early on the most important aspect of the effort: creation of benefits that outweigh the costs for the business. The chapters on project estimating, IT budgeting, and return on investment (Chapters 15 and 17) cover the topic of cost-benefit estimating in more detail.

We have observed on many occasions a hesitance on the part of the IT team to complete a forecast of costs and benefits at this point in the project. The numbers, however difficult to determine, must be *something*. There is little harm in at least creating a starting point for costs and benefits, so that all the subsequent conversations can be around revisions of these baseline numbers. IT must overcome its reservations to "commit" to a number and, instead, be willing to put a stake in the ground. In the eyes of most corporate senior management teams, it is more acceptable to be wrong, with an explanation of what new information changed the estimate, than to obstinately refuse to generate even order-of-magnitude estimates around costs and benefits. Exhibit 12.5 is an example of a cost-benefit summary.

The final step in this phase is to present the results to the IT steering committee. This is an opportunity to show the committee the results of the requirements gathering, get final agreement on scope, and show preliminary results of the cost-benefit analysis. This is also a good time to present the

PROJECT COSTS		ONE-TIME BENEFITS	
Hardware	$50K	Inventory carrying	
Software	150K	Cost reduction	$450K
External resources	225K		
Internal resources	75K		
	$500K		$450K
Net one-time cost	$50K		
CHANGES TO STEADY STATE COSTS		**ONGOING BENEFITS**	
Additional IT FTE	$60K/yr	Reduce whse rent	$120K/yr
Additional processor usage	TBD	Improve fill rate	TBD
Ongoing SW maintenance fee	15K/yr	Reduce spoilage	25K/yr
	$75K/yr		$145K/yr
Net on-going benefits	$70K/yr		
Payback: Approximately nine months after successful implementation for on-going benefits to cover gap between one-time costs and one-time benefits.			

Exhibit 12.5 Cost Benefit Analysis for Project Alpha

parking lot of potential business process improvement opportunities for possible further action by the committee. In addition, it is also the right time to begin enlisting the aid of the senior management team in helping drive the benefits. In some cases, the committee may want to refine the scope or pose follow-up questions on the project economics; the selection team should plan two or three iterations in front of the committee before final sign-off.

As reiterated throughout this book, we are strong believers in a literal sign-off at major project milestones, and this process is no exception. The important psychological step of document signing forces ambiguities and disagreements to the forefront where they can be resolved. We highly recommend this step for *all* critical IT documentation. After the document has been revised and approved by the steering committee, it should also be signed off on by the selection team for the same reasons.

Preliminary Vendor Screening

The goal of the vendor-screening step is to quickly build a comprehensive list of potential vendors. These vendors form the pool from which to make the final choice. A successful preliminary screening lets the team quickly review a comprehensive set of vendors to ensure all options have been considered but then rapidly narrow the list down to a handful of vendors for full due diligence. Exhibit 12.6 shows an overview of this process, from data gathering through due-diligence vendor selection. The following sections cover the process in detail.

PRELIMINARY VENDOR IDENTIFICATION AND SCREENING. The first step of vendor screening is to identify a full set of potential vendors. The approach for this step is to conduct a sweep of the marketplace for vendors whose offering fits the scope of business processes defined in the previous step. If the scoping step was completed well, the vendor marketplace participants should be relatively easy to identify.

The team should employ a variety of sources for its vendor search:

- *Consultants:* Large-scale technology consulting firms often have entire practice areas specializing in the selection, implementation, and management of the technology in question; in these cases, they are often willing to provide free, up-front advice in exchange for an opportunity to be involved in the bidding for a later customization and deployment.

- *Technology and industry publications:* There are dozens of credible, independent publications focused on the technology industry that can provide vendor lists. *InformationWeek* and *CIO* magazine are among the many publications that address enterprise-level technology management. Publications focused on the industry in which the organization

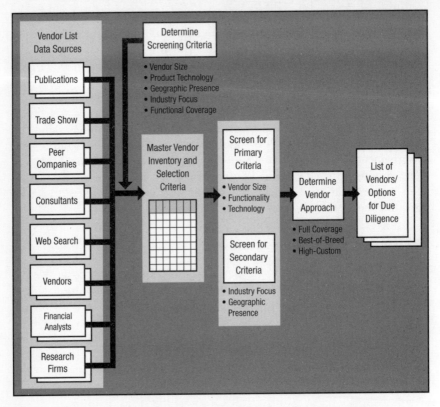

Exhibit 12.6   Preliminary Vendor Screening Process Overview

competes can also be a source of information related to technologies that apply specifically to the business. These are most useful for vendors that supply technology very specific to a particular type of business (e.g., insurance, financial services, manufacturing).

- *Industry and technology trade shows:* Many of the larger players in a particular technology field have a presence at technology trade shows. Vendors with industry-specific technology solutions also exhibit at industry-focused trade shows.
- *Peer companies:* Technology managers from firms in the same industry are an often-overlooked source of information, and they can be particularly valuable for their objectivity. Developing peer relationships with similar companies can provide insight into their decision-making processes and rationale as well as jump-start vendor data gathering. Peer managers who have recently been through a similar vendor selection exercise can be particularly helpful.

- *Focused web search:* A web search can turn up candidate vendors as well. The search should be focused on technology-specific web sites, as opposed to generalized search engines; for example:
  —*CIO* magazine: www.cio.com.
  —*CMP Media:* www.techweb.com.
  —*Computer Business Review:* www.cbronline.com.
  —*E-Week:* www.eweek.com.
  —*Tech Republic:* www.techrepublic.com.
  —*IT Manager's Journal:* www.itmanagersjournal.com.
  —*Analyst Views:* www.analystviews.com.
- *Vendors:* Although reading between the marketing obfuscation found in many vendor brochures and web sites can be difficult, vendor-supplied information can be useful once a specific set of vendors has been identified.
- *Technology research firms:* There is a full-scale, mature industry of research firms dedicated to assisting companies in setting technology direction and helping companies understand in which technology standard they should invest. While these sources provide high-quality analysis, their expense can often make them prohibitive except for decisions involving large capital expenditures. Although this marketplace has dozens of players in it, some of the industry leaders include:
  —Aberdeen Group.
  —AMR Research.
  —Forrester Research.
  —Gartner, Inc.
  —The Standish Group.
  —IDC.
  —Burton Group.
- *Financial analysts:* Most large investment banks have one or more full-time analysts covering the market in which a given vendor competes. The analysts can be an invaluable source of information about the vendor and overall marketplace, as well as a specific product. Analysts spend considerable time talking with end customers and can be an unbiased source of up-to-date information. If the company has a banking relationship already, that can be a good place to start. If not, the analysts can often be found lurking in various Internet forums for the vendor under consideration, soliciting user input.

The evaluation team should manage its search using each of these sources to ensure that a comprehensive list is built. The team should start with technology publications, reports from research companies, and trade show information and proceed to detailed data gathering from consultants, peer companies, and vendors. This research order provides early results for the team and context during later data gathering after a preliminary set of vendors has been identified. The team will be able to ask specific, targeted questions of consultants or managers based on their earlier research.

As the team reviews a variety of sources of data, the right list of vendors should emerge. Except for the most unique searches, the team should avoid feeling that it needs to "scour the earth" to identify the suite of potential vendors—vendors that are difficult to find after multiple searches across a variety of sources are not likely to be viable vendors. Good vendors should not be needles in a haystack—the location of an obscure vendor is not necessarily the harbinger of success. The best vendor names emerge repeatedly from the research.

The result of this step should be a list of vendors ranging from as few as four to as many as several dozen entries in length. Although vendors may be added as additional information is uncovered, this is probably the vendor list from which the winning candidate is drawn.

BUILD FIRST-SCREEN EVALUATION FRAMEWORK AND WEIGHTING. As vendors are added to the list, screening data should be gathered in a template to facilitate analysis. The specific information gathered depends on the vendor selection being completed, but it generally falls into a few categories. These categories are outlined next, along with potential information to gather in each category and how much weighting each category might be given.

Vendor Size
To consider: Vendor should be of adequate size to continue to invest in the product and continue to attract additional customers. Exception may be niche-product vendors providing highly specific products or services.

Potential information to gather:
- Vendor revenues.
- Vendor profitability.
- Acquisition history.
- Number of employees, developers, product specialists.
- Number of customers.
- Number of end users.

Product Technology
To consider: Does the selection of the vendor limit technology platform choices in a way that matters to the business or IT? Is the product compatible or consistent with existing or planned technical architecture?

Potential information to gather:

- Server technologies supported.
- Database technologies supported.
- Development technology.
- Technology supported under original product.
- Percent of user base on a particular server or database platform.

Geographic Presence

To consider: Does the vendor have the appropriate geographic focus and availability? Is the vendor sufficiently focused on the geographies that matter for the company (United States versus Europe versus Asia versus other geographies that impact how the technology works or support is delivered)?

Potential information to gather:
- Corporate headquarters location.
- Nearest branch office.
- Number of branch offices.
- Proximity of branch offices to company branch offices.
- Primary location of development team.

Industry Focus

To consider: Does the vendor have sufficient expertise in the specific industry to ensure development of the best solution? Does the vendor have a product or service line dedicated to the company industry? Is industry-specific expertise relevant for this evaluation?

Potential information to gather:
- Industry-specific additions/modifications to product.
- Industry implementations of product (number of implementations/ users).
- Presence of leading industry customers.

Functional Coverage

To consider: Does package or product provide this broad functionality?

Potential information to gather:
- Proven ability for package or product to support business function in question.
- Presence of function-specific modules.

This type of information is relatively easy to gather and can be used to narrow the vendor list down rapidly. As the information is gathered, the team should begin building a spreadsheet to capture the information.

This process is the most rapid, least-effort method to review the largest number of vendors and quickly screen out the vendors that are not viable contenders for carrying through to due diligence. The preliminary screening forces out undercapitalized, unfocused, or otherwise inappropriate vendors, as well as allows the remaining vendors to be preliminarily ranked. The team should constantly ask the commonsense question: "Can you envision a scenario in which we would actually choose, implement, and rely on this vendor?"

The result is a comprehensive list of vendors participating in the marketplace, along with a clear, consistent rationale for the inclusion or discharge of each one. Exhibit 12.7 shows a sample rating sheet.

DETERMINE PRELIMINARY VENDOR APPROACH. The full vendor list review helps the team understand what marketplace components need to come together to provide a solution that covers the full scope in question. Generally, one of three vendor approaches emerges (particularly for package application searches):

- *Full coverage:* Functions covered by a single vendor with minimum customization.
- *Best-of-breed:* Majority of coverage by a single vendor, with one or more complementary vendors providing applications for specific, clearly defined functions (e.g., pricing) or functional areas (e.g., accounting).
- *High custom:* Most functions covered by a single vendor with some specific custom-coded modules and product customizations.

The potential solution set may include one or more solutions in each of these categories. The team should go beyond a superficial analysis to be sure all of the possible combinations and potential solution platforms have been identified. Generally, full-coverage solutions are the most desirable because the system requires no integration, requires a single vendor, and has been proven to work in practice. However, in some cases, the specific functionality advantages created by the other two options are enough to overcome the inherent disadvantage and increased cost and risk of integration and multiple vendors. For the remainder of this chapter, the term *vendor* refers to a single vendor, or a best-of-breed combination of vendors.

Exhibit 12.8 on page 406 shows an example set of "finalist" vendor solutions for a package selection. The result of the vendor screening process should be a list of as few as two but no more than six vendor approaches. A list of three or four vendors is ideal. More than six vendors makes the RFP effort too onerous,

Vendor	Package/System Name	Vendor Revenue ($ millions)	Corp. Headquarters	Nearest branch office	Total Vendor Staff	Developers on Staff	Product Age (months)	Notable Customers	Industries Served	Installed Base - customers	Databases Supported	Server Platform	Installed Base - users	Function A	Function B	Notes
Vendor A	System A	325	UK	local	599	150	72	ITT Cannon, Dunlop, Bic	All	250	Oracle/SQL Serv	NT	25k+	X		
Vendor B	System B	722	CA	local	1397	350	32	AMD, Boeing, Mercedes	Mfg.	400	Informix/Oracle/IBM	UNIX	45k+		X	
Vendor C	System C	125	OH	none	217	52	9	Alcatel, Ericsson, Siemens	Dist.	75+	SQL Serv Supra	NT	10k+	X		
Vendor D	System D	425	IL	local	922	190	49	Nike	All	550+	Oracle	NT	100k+	X	X	
...dor D							24	Seiko			...Serv	UNIX	5k+	X	X	

Exhibit 12.7   Example Vendor Data Gathering Sheet

405

Exhibit 12.8   Example Vendor Approach Options

and only one vendor provides limited options and makes relative comparison impossible. A one-vendor approach also lowers the team's negotiating power with the single vendor during the pricing phase of the process.

As with each of the major process steps for vendor selection, the IT steering committee should sign off on the results from this phase.

WHAT IF NO VENDOR OR SET OF VENDORS EMERGES FROM THE ANALYSIS?   Occasionally, at the end of a preliminary vendor screening process, no viable vendor or combination of vendors emerges, or a vendor emerges but it feels like a tremendous stretch in terms of customization. In these cases, the team should go back through the analysis and look for these common missteps in the process described previously:

- *Scope set incorrectly:* Too narrow or too broad for a vendor solution to emerge.
- *Scope indistinct:* Difficult to assess vendor capabilities because of lack of clarity on scope.
- *Not enough vendors identified:* Not enough data sources searched to yield proper number of vendors; search of data sources too superficial.

- *Vendor data incorrect or missing:* Team did not gather enough vendor data, or vendor data is incorrect leading to vendors screened out improperly.

- *Primary or secondary screening criteria set too tight:* Criteria for vendor screen set too tight, forcing out viable vendors.

- *Additional criteria needed:* Team adds additional relevant criteria with higher weighting, allowing viable vendors to pass primary and secondary screening.

The team should analyze the process for these common mistakes, as well as other holes in the overall analysis. If the team concludes that the analysis has been completed correctly, the marketplace for the scope in question has no vendor participation. In this case, the team needs to pursue one of two paths. A close-finish vendor may be interested in developing the required functionality or enhancements to its package or product. The team can approach the vendor and work with its product management group to investigate the potential for adding the capabilities. Second, the team may have to consider a custom-built solution based on the requirements. The economics, benefits, planning, creation, implementation, and management of custom-built solutions are separate topics treated elsewhere in this book. In both cases, the IT steering committee is also a valuable sounding board for how to proceed.

Manage RFP Process

A *request for proposal* (RFP) is a time-honored method for choosing vendors, in which the company gives a group of vendors the opportunity to show their capabilities by responding to a specific set of requirements and information requests. These typically request a broad swath of information—product data, technical architecture, vendor company financials and structure, customer references, qualifications with similar work, training and support capabilities, and more.

Requiring interested vendors to respond to a well-thought-out RFP can be a highly effective approach for both gathering additional data without imposing incremental workload on the team and screening vendors for ability to produce quality work. There are a variety of good reasons to conduct an RFP:

- Distributes immense data gathering to multiple vendors instead of internal team.

- Allows vendors to withdraw if the RFP focus indicates they are not a good match.

- Introduces an element of natural selection to the process—vendors that cannot manage their way through an RFP process are not likely to be viable long-term partners.

- Gives a view of the vendor's capability for producing a "finished product" early on with little risk; if vendors cannot produce quality RFP responses (typos, clarity, answering the questions asked, organization), there may be similar issues with their products or service.
- Allows vendors to "self-team," working and proposing in concert on areas where a multivendor solution makes sense.
- Creates a level playing field for the vendors; all vendors see the same RFP request and provide the same response information; this has the double benefit of encouraging vendors to participate if they perceive a fair selection process and of forcing the internal evaluation team to consider each vendor equally, mitigating any potential biases.
- Multiple analyses of the requirements and information in the RFP by highly skilled vendor sales and delivery staff may point out shortcomings or inconsistencies in the previous analysis by the internal team.

Not every vendor selection is a good candidate for a full RFP. The team may elect to not conduct a full RFP for a variety of reasons. In these cases, the team may proceed straight to the vendor due-diligence process. Some examples include:

- The number of vendors identified during the previous screening is small enough to justify proceeding directly to due diligence.
- In a seller's market, the RFP may be considered too onerous by target vendors and discourage participation; they will opt to go after easier-to-win business.
- The preliminary vendor selection conducted in the previous step unearths enough information to satisfy the selection team.
- The final decision needs to be made rapidly and not enough additional time is available for a full RFP-response-analysis cycle.
- Vendor(s) being selected is minor or level of investment is minor enough and does not justify the effort of a full RFP.
- There is such a large separation between first- and second-place vendor, so first-place vendor takes the decision by default.

Creation of a high-quality RFP requires the team to have an in-depth, unambiguous command of the vendor and functional and technical requirements. If creating a good RFP is difficult for the team, it is likely that the scope and requirements were not clearly defined in the previous section or that the team has not fully delineated the priorities and weighting by which it will judge the target vendors. A good RFP not only reduces the effort for the team, but also ensures enthusiastic and full participation by target vendors.

Exhibit 12.9 provides an overview of the RFP process. The remainder of this section covers this process in detail.

Exhibit 12.9   Vendor Request for Proposal Process Overview

CREATE RFP.   A well-constructed RFP contains two primary sections: an overview of the project, which gives the responding vendor information on the company and project to help in its response; and a section for vendors to provide a detailed response to specific questions on company, capabilities, functionality, and other relevant considerations.

This section outlines how to lead the evaluation team through the creation of an effective RFP. In larger corporations, the team should also consult the corporate purchasing or procurement department to ensure compliance with corporate policies regarding vendor selection, as well as for advice and help in creating the RFP. The purchasing department can be particularly helpful with legal or process questions.

The project overview portion of the RFP should be detailed enough to answer most potential vendor questions and provide a full orientation. An effective project overview section minimizes the follow-on questions from vendors and ultimately saves considerable time for the evaluation team, particularly for selections involving a large number of vendors. The overview portion also helps create a level playing field for vendors by showing all the vendors the same information in the same format at the same time. It also encourages vendors to participate by demonstrating that the company intends to undertake a credible, serious approach to the selection process and that the lead is a quality opportunity with a reasonable probability of closing.

The project overview portion of the RFP contains three subsections—information on the company, the process, and decision-making criteria. Typically, each of the sections contains all or some of the following details:

Company Information

- History of company.
- Size of business—three- to five-year revenue history, number of employees.
- Geographies covered—headquarters, branch offices, and plant locations.
- Product or service line overview.
- Key customers or markets served.
- Current technical architecture.
- Key points that differentiate the company business operations (e.g., large number of geographically separate customers, highly engineered product, hard-to-forecast "fashion" product).
- Single point-of-contact e-mail address for all questions and responses.

Project Information

- Business rationale for project and anticipated results.
- Budget approval (Is a budget approved for the project, and if not, when will one be approved?).

Process Information

- RFP distribution method.
- Response required (number of copies, format).
- Who (decision makers) is on the evaluation team?
- Vendors invited to participate.
- Time line for response and review of RFP.
- Anticipated time line for project start and completion.
- Project scope.
- Criteria for selection and relative weighting (e.g., vendor size, functionality match, pricing, references).

The focus of the document should be on providing information helpful to the vendors, as well as answering the qualifying questions that most smart vendors ask before pursuing a lead:

- Is the scope under consideration a good match with my product or service?
- Is the playing field level?
- Is there a budget approved?
- Who will make the decision?
- How long will the evaluation take?

- Which of my competitors will take part?
- Does the client have a clear understanding of what they are doing and a good process for getting there?

Although clearly the buyer of products or services is in the driver's seat during an evaluation, going to the trouble of providing the right kind of information to the candidate vendors in this section ensures that the opportunity is attractive to successful, smart vendors—the exact kind that will be ideal partners.

Because the vendor orientation section of the RFP often contains company proprietary information, the team may want to consider having the vendor recipients sign nondisclosure agreements (NDA). The corporate legal team or retained counsel can put together a simple NDA to be completed by all participants prior to receipt of the RFP.

The second major section of the RFP should be focused on gathering the detailed data from the vendors; this helps determine which vendors should be carried forward through vendor due diligence. This information is similar to the data gathered for the preliminary vendor screening, but goes into considerable depth. Achieving this level of detail is possible because the individual vendors alone have the expertise to fully answer the questions and because the work is distributed across multiple vendors instead of the selection team.

The typical categories of information to be gathered in this section include:

- *Vendor:* Information concerning the vendor company—size, stability, and resources.
- *Functional coverage:* Coverage of the full scope of required functions or capabilities by the vendor application, product, or service.
- *Technical:* Information impacting the technical deployment of the product, including available hardware, operating system, and database platforms.
- *Customer qualifications:* Positive references from existing customers with similar requirements.
- *Project/implementation approach:* Preliminary information from vendor as to its approach for implementation and time lines.
- *Economics:* Vendor list pricing schedules; drivers for pricing (seats, servers, units, etc.).

Generating the full list of questions for this section is, after the scope and requirements definition, one of the most challenging tasks in the vendor selection. If the scope and requirements definition has been done properly, the functional coverage assessment should be fairly straightforward. However, to help vendors understand how they are evaluated (and to provide a guideline for the team after the RFPs have been returned), the team must weight each category appropriately, at the levels described previously, and within the levels.

This question generation and weighting process can be difficult because it requires the team to go beyond a superficial vendor selection based on functional fit and consider broader issues such as vendor strength, customer qualifications, and technical platform implications. Because the work must be completed eventually, however, the team should wrestle with this issue now to inform the participating vendors how the RFP will be evaluated.

The easiest approach for category weighting is to distribute 100 points among the five categories. Usually, the category receiving the bulk of the points is the functional coverage category. After all, if the product or service in question cannot provide the required capabilities, the other categories have little relevance. This primary weighting for the functional coverage category puts added pressure on the team to understand the relative importance of the functional requirements in the category. This prioritization of requirements (high, medium, and low) was completed in the previous step, and the RFP should provide the priority ratings along with the functionality requirement description to the vendors for response.

The remaining categories are weighted differently in each vendor selection, depending on what is important to the selection team. Vendor stability and customer qualifications are good candidates for second-place priority behind functional coverage. A stable vendor with a large customer base and the financial strength to provide support and improvements for a product over the long haul is a good choice for a partner in a critical role. Likewise, a vendor's ability to produce solid clients who can provide a reference for the client and who have solved similar business problems in similar environments provides empirical evidence of the vendor's ability to successfully achieve the results again.

Technical architecture and project/implementation approach tend to be the lowest-weighted categories. Most large vendors are at competitive parity concerning technologies supported—major vendors are able to support nearly any technology platform that might matter to the end client—therefore, this category offers little opportunity for them to differentiate themselves. Project implementation approach is also usually similar across vendors and may not offer a chance for differentiation. Occasionally, a vendor has a unique or proprietary approach in this category and should receive correspondingly high points relative to the competition.

Examples of the type of information that an RFP might include in each category, with a slant toward RFP questions for applications vendors follow:

Vendor

- Company overview, including history, services, core capabilities, office locations, management team, and organization structure.
- Contact information for this RFP—account manager, technical sales representative, senior manager in charge.
- Financials—three- to five-year revenue and profitability history for vendor.
- Financials—three- to five-year revenue and profitability history for the product or service in question.
- Overview of vendor product lines and revenue distribution among product lines.
- Total company employees.
- Number of developers or engineers working in product development and location.
- Account management approach (account representative organizational structure; are accounts managed by region, by industry, or other?).
- Customer input method—how it works (along with reference to client who has provided input to development process).
- Service levels—how does the vendor measure its delivery or product or services—measures might be quality, user satisfaction, support calls, or other; how does the information get reported internally, and how often; how does information get reported to the customer?
- Timing and results of last user satisfaction survey conducted by vendor or third party.
- Service levels available for the product under consideration and what they mean (usually gold, silver, platinum, or other tiered support structure).
- Training—number of professionals, class schedule (administrator, end user, etc.).
- What does vendor regard as its competitive advantage(s)?
- Is vendor qualified for disadvantaged business minority/women-owned-business preferences?

Functional Coverage

The RFP should contain an indexed list of each functional requirement identified early on in the vendor selection process:

- Vendor should provide a mapping of system modules or capabilities to functional requirements with particular emphasis on high-priority areas.
- Each requirement should be rated by the vendor as "works with no customization," "works with customization," or "not present."

- For each "works with . . ." rating, vendor should provide a brief explanation of where the functionality exists (screen or submodule reference).
- Brief overview of how configuration is accomplished in the product.
- Brief overview of how customization is accomplished in the product (usually associated programming-language based).

Technical

- Overview of technical architecture of the product—application, data, network, hardware, or other technology component.
- How does required or recommended technology work with current or planned technology platform in the client company?
- Technologies supported by product (operating systems, hardware, databases)—along with number of seats/customers/implementations in that architecture combination.
- Release and patch history for product (dates, summary of incremental functionality, and bug fixes/enhancements in each release and patch).
- Third-party products required to operate; inventory of the products and their roles.
- Demonstrated product scalability—volumes for key areas (in the lab and on real clients).
- Interface method—how interproduct interfaces are accomplished; variances between batch and asynchronous interfaces.
- Security—how it is managed at the user level; what levels of management it can handle; does it integrate with other security packages?

Customer Qualifications

Vendor should show customers with closest possible match to target environment across a variety of aspects; although it is difficult to find an exact match to the target, the vendor should be able to produce a variety of clients with at least a few similarities:

- Customers competing in the same industry or with the same business model.
- Customers using this specific product or service (and latest version).
- Customers with same technical platform (existing or planned).
- Customers with similar size (measured in revenues, number of users, totals staff, or other proxy).
- Customers with corresponding geographic footprint (number of locations, same states, countries, language requirements).
- Customers with similar business volumes or patterns (seasonality affect, orders, invoices, stock keeping units [SKUs], etc.).

- Customers who have interfaced same systems as the target environment requires (if applicable).
- Customers whose implementation of the product was similar in size/scope.

An ideal way to get relevant references from a vendor is to provide a matrix for marking which implementations have functional, industry, technical, or other relevance for the RFP. Exhibit 12.10 shows such a sample matrix as it would be completed by the RFP respondent.

The vendor should also include any relevant awards and third-party recognition for excellence, as well as any relevant industry certifications (ISO, SEI CMM, etc.).

Finally, the RFP should make clear that the vendor response is completely optional and in no way obligates the company to engage any vendor or to carry the project forward past the RFP process. This avoids any possible misunderstanding on the part of the vendors and creates an exit path should the RFP results prove unsatisfactory or the business mandate change during the process.

	Same industry or same business model	Specific product or service	Same technical platform	Similar size	Corresponding geographic footprint	Similar business volumes or patterns	Interfaced same systems as target	Similar size/scope of product implementation	TOTAL
Customer A	X				X		X	X	4
Customer B				X			X		2
Customer C	X		X		X	X	X		5
Customer D		X		X	X	X	X		5
Customer E		X	X		X	X			4

Exhibit 12.10 Vendor Reference Matrix

Project/Implementation Approach

- Implementation approach—outline of any specific or proprietary approach that will be required, how long the implementation is likely to take, and any unusual requirements for implementation.
- Does current or target technology and product platform (or other factors such as office locations, number of users, volume) dictate a certain implementation approach?
- Approximate effort to implement—hours, cost, or other.

Economics

- What are the main drivers of product acquisition pricing (number of seats, number of servers, number of units, or other driver)?
- List price or approximate total for installation.
- Maintenance pricing terms (percent of license fees or other basis).
- Other associated product license pricing (third-party software or other licenses required).
- Pricing and terms for training.
- Other professional services pricing and terms (hourly bill rates).

To facilitate later comparison and analysis, the RFP should provide a clear format and organization for responding to questions. The RFP should also specify the number of hard copies that the vendor must provide, as well as desired electronic formats. The responses should be standardized as much as possible; reading through a large number of responses inconsistent in format and organization adds considerable work to an already labor-intensive process.

ISSUE RFP. After the RFP has been created, it should be distributed to the target vendors. The best way to manage the issuance process is to send paper and electronic copies to the sales professionals who have been identified at each vendor. A team member should be designed to make a follow-up call to each vendor to ensure that the package has been received.

To gauge interest in the RFP and provide an equal-footing forum for vendor questions and answers, the evaluation team should conduct a bidders' preconference one to two weeks after the RFP is issued. This timing ensures that the vendors have had enough time to review the information and show up with good questions. The invitation should limit the number of attendees per vendor to three or fewer. Otherwise, vendors sometimes send a small army of sales and technical people, particularly for large proposals. More than one bidders' conference we have attended has been so oversubscribed that it had to be postponed or moved to a new location. Rare is the bidders' conference that is not standing room only. The conference is also an ideal time to distribute additional technical information to interested vendors in electronic or paper form.

The team should require each attendee to sign an attendance roster and enforce the sign-ups by allowing RFP responses only from vendors who send at least one representative to the conference. This list can then be published to all vendors. Vendors should be allowed to partner where appropriate (particularly for best-of-breed solution approaches), but they should make clear in their joint RFP response which capabilities are provided by each party.

The agenda for the conference should be simple. The team lead should introduce the selection team members and give a brief overview of the material in the vendor orientation portion of the RFP, with a particular focus on expected business benefits and evaluation process. A brief explanation of how the vendor invite list was created may be appropriate here as well. The bulk of the conference should be an open-ended question-and-answer session for the vendor representatives. A scribe should document the questions asked (and answers given). If vendors ask questions for which the team does not have a ready answer, the question should be documented and a response sent later. In some cases, the team may simply choose not to answer the question. The entire process should take between 60 and 90 minutes, depending on the RFP complexity and the number of vendors in attendance.

After the conference, the team will have some new information to process. First, the vendor attendance should indicate the level of overall interest that the RFP has generated. If a number of vendors do not attend, there may be several reasons, including a mismatch between the project scope and vendors' capabilities, a misread of the RFP by the vendor, or even a simple mistake. In any case, the team should contact the vendors who have opted out to solicit their feedback and possibly revise the scope, RFP, or process based on the information.

Second, based on the questions asked by the vendors, the team may find holes in the project scope, requirements gathering, RFP questions, or RFP process. In this case, the team should decide if any of the previous work should be revisited or refined and the corrective action, if any, to take. Unless the fault is particularly egregious, there should not be any disappointment in a few mistakes. Vendors are highly experienced in scouring and picking apart RFPs and have undoubtedly invested many hours in analysis before the conference.

Within a few days of the conference, the full transcript of questions answered during the session, as well as follow-up questions, should be e-mailed to all vendor representatives. As incremental questions are asked by vendors, they should be documented and the questions and answers should be sent to all vendors.

Often a host of uninvited firms show up at bidders' conferences. Interestingly, these firms are generally there to meet the sales and technical teams from the potential bidders, in hopes of forming a relationship and potentially subcontracting on a given bid. Depending on how open the team members are keeping the RFP process, they may choose to have attendees bring business cards or other proof of vendor association to gain entry to the conference.

Other possible forums for vendor data gathering that the team may want to provide during the RFP vendor analysis period include individual vendor site visits, allowing vendors to come on site and interview evaluation team members or other business or IT staff. If a large amount of information on technology infrastructure, application architecture, or other IT components is easily available, nonproprietary, and useful for the analysis, the team may elect to create a "data room" that vendors may visit to do additional research or data gathering. Access to the room should be strictly controlled, and the room should be available equally to all vendors.

During the RFP analysis process and the following vendor due diligence, the team should resist the urge to hold information too closely. While some information should not be revealed (e.g., target project budget), most information should be shared as widely as possible. A common misconception is that keeping information concealed or responses ambiguous and nonspecific somehow improves the team's negotiating position or otherwise compromises the process. Quite the opposite is true—most vendors want to put their best foot forward and win a deal by having the superior product or solution for the client's needs. Sharing as much information as possible with the vendors facilitates the process and ensures a quality selection. Often, a selection team's hesitance to share information with the vendor is indicative of a lack of confidence on the part of the team.

Finally, during the RFP analysis period, the team may want to contact a few vendors to see if the amount of time allowed for the RFP response is adequate. While, invariably, every vendor wants more time, some probing questions can ascertain if the response period set by the team is inadequate. In these cases, the team should not hesitate to provide additional time for a quality vendor response.

RFP Response Assessment.　The process should allow between one and four weeks for the vendors to formulate a response, depending on the complexity of product, level of investment in question, and depth of the RFP questions. Vendors should provide the requested hard copies and electronic versions of their responses by the date and time established in the RFP.

Vendors should also be asked to refrain from additional contact with the evaluation team during the evaluation period, with disqualification as a possible penalty. Without this threat, the most resourceful (or aggressive) vendors will pester the team (and anyone else in the company that may have influence) endlessly with follow-up questions, status checks, and offers to "provide additional information." By communicating clearly the evaluation process and setting hard deadlines for the decision, the team can satisfy the vendors' need for understanding the timing of the next steps.

In some cases, the team may have determined additional questions or data points to gather during the RFP response period or after reading the responses. In these cases, supplemental questions should be aggregated and distributed to the vendors via e-mail with a reasonable, but rapid, time frame for response.

The actual evaluation process should have the team reading each RFP in no particular order and scoring the vendor response based on the requirements and weighting determined before the RFP distribution. In some cases, the team may break out its evaluation by specific functional expertise (the representative from manufacturing scores manufacturing capabilities and the representative from finance scores finance capabilities). To the extent possible, the team members should conduct individual reviews of the RFP responses to avoid biasing one another. Team members can debate the merits of each RFP after all the individual scoring is complete.

After the RFP reviews are complete, the scores should be summarized, with a final score by vendor and category created from the mean of the team scores. Exhibit 12.11 outlines this process.

REFINE VENDOR LIST. After the vendors have been scored across each category and the mean score from the team members has been assigned by vendor, it is a straightforward exercise to force rank the vendor options by total score (Exhibit 12.12).

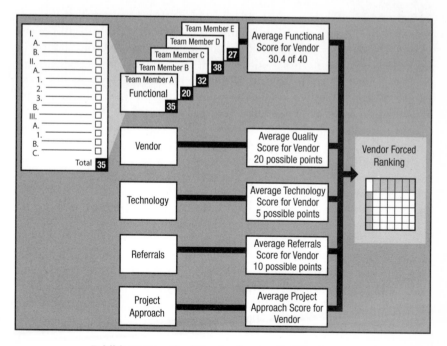

Exhibit 12.11   Final Vendor Scoring Roll Up Process

	Functional	Quality	Technology	Referrals	Project Approach	TOTAL
Vendor A	30.4	20	4	8.9	14.3	**77.6**
Vendor B	35	17.6	4	10	13	**79.6**
Vendor C	32.6	15	3.5	7	14.2	**72.3**
Vendor D	28.9	13.4	5	8.5	12	**67.8**
Vendor E	37.7	19	2	7.2	12.5	**78.4**

Exhibit 12.12   Vendor Forced Ranking

The team should conduct a final round of debates to ensure that the outcome passes a "sanity check" and that everyone agrees with the results of the quantitative analysis. After any alterations to the score have been made and a final force-rank vendor list is complete, the team should decide which vendors to carry through to the due-diligence process. The team should make the cut at the first point in the force ranking where there is a significant drop-off in score. This should usually be between two and four vendors, although a thorough due diligence on more than two vendors can be a challenging effort.

As with all previous major end-of-phase work products, the evaluation team should walk the IT steering committee through a summary of the process and outcome and get a sign-off from the committee and the evaluation team so that the evaluation can proceed to vendor due diligence.

After the results have been finalized, the team should inform each of the vendor participants of the outcome in writing. The notification should thank them for their participation and provide a contact if the vendor would like follow-up information. It is not necessary to inform the losing vendors of the scoring or disclose which vendors will be carried forward through due diligence. A courteous, professional notification ensures the future participation of the vendors and provides a backup set of vendors if the due-diligence process produces unsatisfactory results. If time permits, the team should provide feedback to the losing parties. Most good sales professionals are interested in understanding how they can compete successfully in the future; they appreciate the feedback and will incorporate it into their next sales pursuit.

Vendor Due Diligence

The focus of this piece of the work is to prove to the satisfaction of the team the assertions made by the vendors in their RFP responses. The particular focus is on understanding the details of how the functional requirements are covered, how the system will operate from a technology standpoint, and talking with other vendor customers to understand how well the vendor has served them, as well as beginning to build relationships with them for future information exchange. The team accomplishes this primarily by working with the vendor sales team and taking the actual product through its paces.

Exhibit 12.13 shows an overview of the vendor due-diligence process. The remainder of this section covers each of the steps in detail.

UPDATE DUE-DILIGENCE EVALUATION FRAMEWORK. Because the RFP evaluation contains a detailed list of the required functions, technical capabilities, and vendor references, the framework for the due diligence simply mirrors the criteria from the previous phase—the *what* to assess has been created and refined by the team in the previous two phases. Focus of this portion of the work is on the proof of the vendor claims made in the RFP. Scoring sheets used by the team should be the same as those used in the RFP evaluation, with the same weightings and priority. A few minor

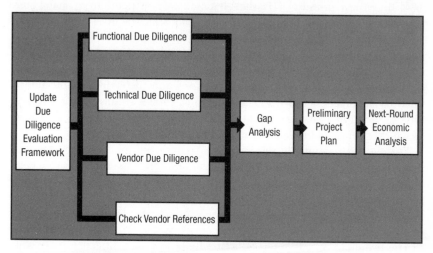

Exhibit 12.13   Vendor Due-Diligence Process Overview

adjustments emanating from the work in the RFP exercise may need to be made to the framework and assessment questions.

As the team proceeds through the due-diligence exercise, it should focus the majority of its attention on points of differentiation between the vendors, as it is on those points that the ultimate vendor decision is made. For example, if order entry is a required function and both vendors handle the order-entry process similarly and to the proven satisfaction of the team, the team should not spend time attempting to differentiate the vendors based on capabilities in this area. Similarly, if both vendors demonstrably support the latest release of Microsoft's SQL Server database with dozens of end-client installs, ability to support SQL Server is not a potential point of differentiation. Because vendors are often at competitive parity on many of the functions provided, adherence to this approach dramatically cuts down the breadth of analysis required for due diligence, as well as ensures that the ultimate selection is based on the factors that provide real differentiation between the competing alternatives. The focus on the key business areas helps the implementation team later avoid most surprises that so often plague a large project.

In vendor selections where investment is low, functionality is well understood, or a single vendor is the clear winner, the team may elect to deemphasize certain portions of the due diligence. In these cases, minimum research by the team should include a focused vendor demo and a set of good reference checks.

CONDUCT FUNCTIONAL DUE DILIGENCE. The focus of the functional due diligence is to prove, to the satisfaction of the selection team, that the product or package can perform the required business functions in a way that is acceptable to the business. This portion of the due diligence is the most important because it is the element most difficult to evaluate and, therefore, the area with the potential for concealing the most surprises to be discovered during implementation.

The depth of business process knowledge required and level of detailed examination of the system can be daunting. The functional due-diligence process can be tedious, particularly if the vendor is having trouble understanding the business process. The team must steel its resolve to plow its way through multiple demos and to keep asking questions until it gets an answer that makes sense and is consistent with what it sees the system doing.

During one memorable selection we participated in, a vendor remarked that our selection team "was just too detail oriented." We took this as a compliment of the highest order. If the vendors participating in due diligence are not complaining about the level of detail orientation, the team is not chasing out the ambiguities. Vendor discomfort with detailed analysis is a sign that the effort is going well.

The principle vehicle for conducting functional due diligence is the vendor product demonstration. This is a familiar venue for vendors and customers alike, and it is one of the best ways for vendors to put their products through the appropriate paces.

We recommend that each vendor participating in the due-diligence process conduct two separate demonstrations. The first should be an unscripted, open demo in which vendors can demonstrate the product with any agenda they care to put together. The second demonstration is a highly scripted walk through of the top priority requirements using data and procedures assembled by the evaluation team.

Incredibly, vendor demos are the point at which we have observed many companies beginning the vendor selection process. Naturally, these superficial, vendor-driven, ill-fated projects were profitable for the vendors fortunate enough to be invited and ultimately led to failed implementations and massive budget overruns for the companies in question. In one particularly egregious example, we were asked by the senior management team of the company in question to help think through possible solutions after a three-year failed implementation resulted in an unusable system. When asked about their original selection and implementation process almost every worst case scenario we have described occurred including a poorly documented and vendor-led selection effort. In another example, a company spent two years evaluating two vendors, negotiating pricing, interviewing implementation partners yet could not get the final purchase approval from the board of directors because of the superficiality of analysis and a lack of understanding of the business requirements on the part of the selection team that let the vendors dictate the process and refused to document business processes and requirements.

The order of these demonstrations is important—all vendors, correctly or not, feel that they know the best way to show their products. Providing them with an open, anything-goes forum for doing so is the only way to satisfy them that they have had every chance necessary to show what they can do. It can be difficult for a team to let the vendor take the driver's seat during these demonstrations, but it is important to let vendors "get it out of their system." The second demonstration provides ample opportunity for the team to drive the agenda. The team provides a detailed list of the desired functions, along with sample data and outcomes they would like to see in the second demonstration, to the vendor at the conclusion of the first demo.

The content of the second demonstration is crucial. The team must understand not only how the product accomplishes each of the key requirements, but also how the function is configured and what level of customization is required to make it work. The answers to these questions can be difficult to pry out of the vendor, and many clients have been dazzled by a highly customized "smoke and mirrors" demo from the vendor. A running joke in most vendor demos is the repeated "It can do that," which, of course, is always true. The real question is how much has to change from the default installation to get there. Bearing in mind that heavy configuration and customization drives considerable labor cost in the end implementation, the team should keep track of the approximate level required to meet each of the requirements being evaluated. The vendor should be asked for as many additional demos as it takes to satisfy the team members that they understand in detail how each of the functions will be accomplished.

In addition to the key functional requirements, the team may want to review some of the nontransaction-oriented portions of the system. This can include workflow, configuration tools, customization language, third-party integration tools, application programming interfaces, data extract tools, event scheduling, and reporting capabilities. Many of these are typically covered by the vendor in the first demonstration, but they can be areas to investigate further in the scripted demo if questions are still outstanding.

To best facilitate the rounds of vendor demonstrations, as well as the technical due diligence and customer review sessions, the team should establish a due-diligence calendar to be distributed to all participants—team and vendors alike. The team should set the first demos for each vendor during the first week and the second demos during the following week. Each demonstration session should be planned for an entire day. The one to two weeks afterward should be dedicated to customer references and additional vendor research. The team should have adequate time between demos to recover and document its findings, but the events should be scheduled close enough together to ensure a good comparison between vendors. A break of one day between demonstrations is a nice interval. Exhibit 12.14 shows a typical vendor calendar for a due diligence involving three vendors.

Key tips for having the best possible outcomes from a vendor demonstration include:

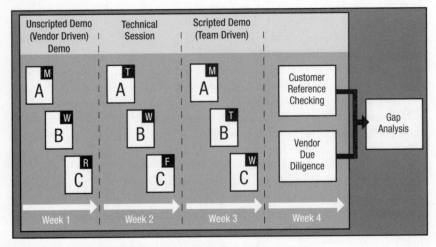

Exhibit 12.14   Due-Diligence Vendor Calendar

- Set vendor expectations clearly on the meeting agenda for the scripted and unscripted demos.
- Make sure all attendees are on time and pay attention; selection team members should take the demonstration seriously.
- Ensure that the evaluation team asks questions and stays engaged for the full session.
- Conduct the demonstrations on the vendor site—the vendor can give the best show there and won't have any excuse for not having the right technical pieces in place.
- Have the evaluation team set aside the entire day so that no other commitments interfere with attendance.

CONDUCT TECHNICAL DUE DILIGENCE. The technical due diligence is focused on ensuring that the full suite of required technical components are understood by the team and that any implications for the current or planned technical architecture are surfaced and dealt with. The technical due-diligence sessions are usually conducted with one or more technical sales staff from the vendor, evaluation team members, as well as select technical managers from the IT department. The agenda for the technical due diligence should concentrate on a few key areas, which are discussed in the following sections.

Technical Platform—Options and Requirements. The technical team should cover the technical options that are available for deployment of the system. For applications vendors, this should include operating systems supported, hardware supported, and databases. Large applications vendors support nearly all major platforms but may have more installs on certain platforms.

The team should ask for details on the target platform. If an application vendor selection has as a target technical platform Sun Solaris on Sun Servers with EMC DASD and an Oracle backend, the vendor should demonstrate that the product has worked in the target environment for a specific client. The client reference process, described in the following section, contains more details on how to conduct a technical reference check. The team should also examine the evolution of the product; if it was originally deployed on a specific technical platform, then migrated to others, it may operate more effectively on the original platform. If this is possibly the case, the team can look for vendor proof that the product has been completely migrated.

The team should also unearth the minimum standards, recommended standards, and probable requirements for all technical components. To minimize cost implications, application vendors sometimes focus attention on the minimum requirements. Probable requirements are the most important, as they are the primary driver of cost if new hardware, software, networking, or other equipment is required as part of the deployment.

The team may choose to investigate a variety of other technology areas during the due diligence. The most important outcome is a complete understanding of the likely cost picture from a technology standpoint so that the team can begin creating project budgets at the end of this phase. The potential questions are selection-specific—the technical staff and the evaluation team should decide in advance which technology questions will impact the overall decision and which have implications for overall cost. Examples of areas to investigate include:

- Preferred technical architecture: OS, servers, clients, DASD, network, database.
- Number and type of required servers.
- Integration tools and approaches (middleware, batch, API, object level, or other).
- Third-party applications required to run the application (middleware, reporting, database applications).
- DASD requirements for application and operating system.
- Minimum client-side requirements (browser based or other).
- Bandwidth/network capacity required between servers and clients.
- Load-sharing capabilities (clustering, balancing).
- Backup requirements and approach.
- Failover and recovery capabilities.
- Start-up and shutdown procedures.
- Recommended and probable requirements for failover, development, and test environments.
- Systems security and audit—user setup and administration; systems security capabilities.

An additional option that may be considered by an application selection team is hosting. Many application vendors and hardware vendors have teamed to offer hosting and data center services as part of a comprehensive package of offerings. Many vendors have also developed application service provider (ASP) options, which provide for offsite hosting of the entire application.

Outsourcing of hosting is a topic beyond the scope of this text. Like most other IT decisions, it should be investigated with a clear understanding of the costs and benefits involved, and it should generate a clear ROI for the company. The benefits and long-term implications of ASP/SAAS relationships are still uncertain. However, as discussed in Chapter 10, ASP/SAAS services can be valuable for noncore applications (e.g., salesforce contact management, HR/recruiting). The data-gathering section of this document points to web resources where the latest thinking on the topics from industry leaders can be found.

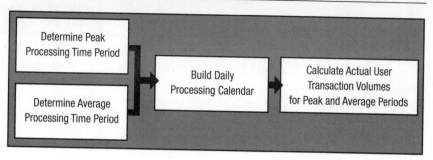

Exhibit 12.15   Process for Required Volume Support Calculation

Transaction Volume Support and Scalability.   The second key area of inquiry for the test team is to validate the system's ability to support peak transaction volumes and handle changes to future business. Scalability considerations for new hardware and software acquisitions are covered in detail in Chapter 8.

The technology due-diligence team should first ascertain the current peak batch transaction and online user volumes. This is a three-step process, which first determines the current peak processing day and time, then takes actual transaction volumes and user count from the point of peak processing. Exhibit 12.15 outlines the process.

As Exhibit 12.16 shows, the peak annual/monthly/weekly usage period should be determined first. This accounts for seasonality factors (for businesses with lumpy annual transaction volumes), as well as any monthly (e.g., month-end statement and financial processing) and weekly (e.g., end-of-

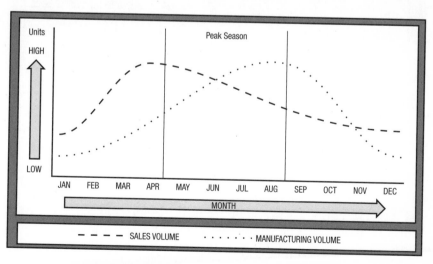

Exhibit 12.16   Company X Peak Period Analysis

week order surges) effects. A variety of factors can be used as a proxy for volume, depending on the company. Exhibit 12.16 shows sales and manufacturing unit volume. The actual drivers, which need to be determined by the team, vary by industry, company type, customer concentration, business seasonality, and other factors.

After the highest volume day, week, month, and year are determined, the technical team should build a detailed daily processing calendar to determine which online and batch processes are running at a given hour of the day. Exhibit 12.17 shows a sample daily processing calendar, with the peak online usage and batch processing periods identified. Because designing the system for peak volumes can be cost prohibitive, the team should also identify an average, or typical, processing day.

With the peak day and interdaily processing hours identified, the team can estimate (or pull from system logs and transaction history) the number of online users and transaction volumes for the peak and average periods. This

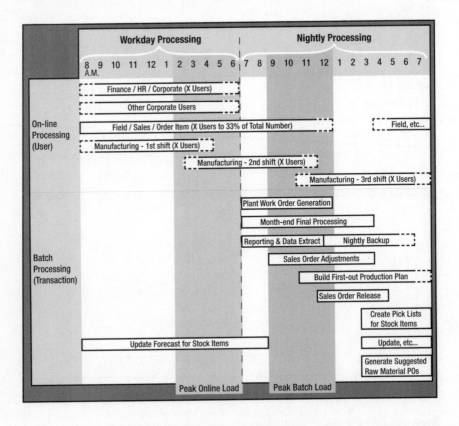

Exhibit 12.17 Company X Daily Processing Schedule

information should be summarized as input to the volume validation process. Exhibit 12.18 shows the volume summary from Exhibit 12.17.

Now that the peak and average volume requirements for users and transactions are documented, the team can compare them to the proven volumes supported by the systems under consideration.

Vendors usually have two types of proven volume capabilities. The first is created from lab-based stress tests, which show the maximum system capabilities under a variety of technical environments and conditions. The second is empirical evidence created in actual customer implementations of the product. These can be particularly useful for the team, especially if the benchmark implementation is similar in terms of business processes and volume.

If the vendor supplies the benchmark information for clients, the team should follow up with a call to the client to validate the numbers and get the client's feedback on performance management and the system's handling of peak volumes. A detailed conversation with the end-client often produces relevant details not volunteered (or understood) by the vendor. The solicitation of this feedback can be incorporated into the customer reference calls described later in this chapter.

A host of possible benchmarks can be assessed, but the bottom line assessment should answer at least these two questions:

BATCH/TRANSACTIONS	PEAK	AVERAGE
Invoice processing	50	35
Order release	45	25
Sales to work order conversion	100	50
Shipping label print	20	5
Production plan generation	125	100

ONLINE/USERS	PEAK	AVERAGE
Order entry	250	90
Manufacturing—Heavy usage	75	25
Manufacturing—Light usage	150	110
Corporate	25	20
Finance/accounting	100	80
Other	50	20
Total user estimate	650	345

Exhibit 12.18   Company X Peak and Average Period Transaction Volume and User Estimates

1. Will online users have reasonable response times from the system during peak usage?
2. Will the system be able to process all the work required within a reasonable period of time (ability to handle a day's work in a day's time)?

Development Environment/Approach. The technical due diligence should also allocate some time to understanding the development methodology and technologies used by the vendor for its system or product. These two factors have implications for the overall cost structure of the vendors. Vendors that have made an investment in implementing highly structured development methodologies (SDLC, CMM) for managing their development process or vendors with quality certifications such as ISO may have lower long-term cost structures. The technology due-diligence team can validate the actual adoption level of certifications and methodologies within the vendor by interviewing the team lead from the certification process, internal developers or researchers who use the methodology, or verifying the certification from the third party that grants it.

Similarly, vendors who use standardized development tools and technologies may ultimately have lower cost structures. The more common the toolset, the higher the availability of the skills in the workforce, and the lower the labor costs. By virtue of their widespread use and, therefore, constant refinement, common toolsets and technologies can also lower vendor costs by improving the productivity of the development team. The team can investigate the technologies and standards used by the vendor, as well as talk to the head of development or research to gather details. Again, the evaluation team can do some basic validation with the vendor; for example, ask the vendor to produce its development standards manual.

The technology due diligence is rarely an area in which vendors are able to separate themselves from the pack. Most application vendors are at competitive parity: They support the same technologies, use the same development tools, provide the same interfaces, and have support for volumes far in excess of expected or anticipated peaks.

With this in mind, the technical due diligence should be focused on understanding the potential costs involved with the system deployment from a hardware and infrastructure standpoint, as well as any surprises (particularly on scalability or platforms supported) that emerge from the analysis. The exercise also sheds light on the vendor's likely internal cost structures, which influence pricing, competitiveness, and viability over the long run. Further, the effort in understanding peak and average volumes will be used in the sizing exercise if the system deployment requires new or upgraded hardware.

CONDUCT COMPANY DUE DILIGENCE. The focus of the company due diligence is the verification of the RFP data provided by the vendor. Because most of this information is factual, this portion of the due diligence should be a fairly rapid "check the box" exercise. Information verifying the vendor's locations, revenue history, and relevant product lines should be readily available from a variety of sources on the Internet.

In addition to verifying the information supplied in the RFP, the team should do an analysis on the vendor-supplied revision and release history for the product in question. A product history with multiple service packs or bug fixes may indicate a product that was prematurely released with a large number of flaws. In these cases, the vendor should provide a detailed explanation behind the large number of service pack and patch releases.

Typically, applications vendors have a major release every 12 to 18 months. Vendors without a major release in more than 18 months, or who have unusually long release cycles, may be having issues pushing forward their product. Because software maintenance fees usually entitle the licensee to the benefits of product upgrades and patches, the customer may not receive full value of the maintenance fees paid to a vendor with difficulties in this area. In these cases, the team should get the committed vendor release plans for future releases, with highly specific details on planned functions and upgrades. Vendors should not be able to avoid this issue—after all, if the systems development team is working on it, there must be a set of requirements that can be shared. This also mitigates against another common strategy that application vendors employ—charging clients for a new product when the functionality and enhancements should have been included in a new release of the already-purchased application as part of normal maintenance and upgrades.

The vendor should also be able to give examples of how customer input is gathered for new release requirements and show an example of how the requirements were carried through into a new release. The client who participated in the process should be contacted by the evaluation team to get another perspective on how well the vendor listens and incorporates input from clients to the development prioritization process.

Finally, to gauge the level of support the vendor can provide, the team may want to conduct a few mystery shopper calls to the vendor's technical support line to see how quickly the phone is answered and how convoluted the integrated-voice-response menu system is. Additionally, the team may request access to the online product knowledge base and run a few scans for typical application questions.

CHECK VENDOR REFERENCES. Vendor reference checking provides two important benefits. First, it provides independent verification and validation of a vendor's claims. Although the odds of discovering adverse information about the vendor are low, the effort expended is moderate, and the value of any adverse information is very high. The search, therefore, must focus on uncovering adverse or disconfirming evidence—any good management scientist knows that the value of information is inversely proportional to its probability. The evaluation team would appear foolish and shortsighted indeed if a few phone calls would have turned up such critical information. Our consulting practice was helping a client salvage a particularly rocky implementation, where a few reference checks might have changed the outcome of the vendor selection. The client CEO remarked to the evaluation team: "So, this was important enough to spend two million of my dollars on but not important enough to call a couple of people on the phone?"

Second, calling vendor references establishes a relationship with other IT departments, which can later facilitate best practices sharing, vendor information sharing, and other mutually beneficial exchanges. This can be particularly valuable as the project proceeds with a particular vendor—other customers can often help the implementation team avoid many of the missteps that they made. Over the long haul, having a relationship with other customers increases the company's ability to influence the vendor as well as provides additional information for negotiations.

Exhibit 12.19 provides an overview of the vendor reference process. There are two sources of customer references for a given vendor. First, as part of the RFP process, the vendor should have provided a list of clients according to similarity. The preceding section of this chapter on RFPs covers the list in detail. The client references should be ranked according to similarity to the company, size, technical platform, planned product, business volumes, or geographic footprint. The evaluation team should call on the references that have the most similarities to the project underway.

The second source of references is those customers of the vendor identified by the evaluation team without assistance from the vendor. This is an important step because by going off the pre-planned program devised by the vendor, the team improves considerably the odds of unearthing any adverse information. There are a variety of ways of identifying target vendor clients. Although vendor web sites and technology trade-focused magazines can be helpful, we have found other methods to be the most effective:

- *Internet job board postings:* A scan of the top job boards reveals which companies are advertising for positions with a specific skill set; presumably, companies advertising technology positions for vendor skill sets have that technology in-house. The best boards for this purpose include TMP's Monster Board (www.monster.com), DICE (www.dice.com), ComputerJobs.com (www.computerjobs.com), Careerbuilder (www.careerbuilder.com), and Hot Jobs (www.hotjobs.com).
- *Internet job board resume search:* If the team has access to the searching capabilities on any of these boards, it can do a resume scan for the vendor in question. Individual resumes generally have the technology used listed, along with the employer. This rapidly identifies companies

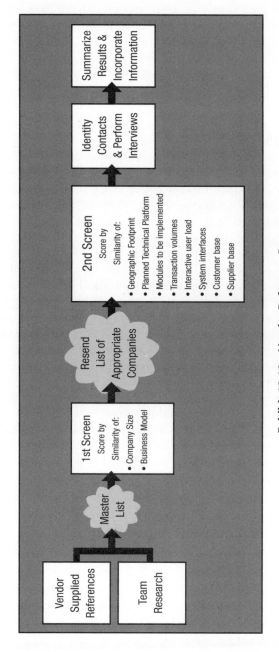

Exhibit 12.19   Vendor Reference Process

with the technology and has the added benefit of identifying their geography and type of business and size of the implementation.

- *Technology staff augmentation companies:* If the team does not have access to job board resume searching, it can turn to a local contract staffing company that specializes in technology resources. These firms are generally happy to conduct these searches for a small fee and, further, can usually easily identify every company in their service area that uses a specific vendor.

As with the vendor-supplied references, these potential references should be scored according to similarity for prioritization.

The vendor-supplied list and the team-constructed list form a master list of references to call. Depending on the size of investment being considered and the depth of the due-diligence effort, the team should plan to call between two and eight vendors from each of the lists. The vendor-supplied list provides contact information, and the vendor will likely prepare its customer contact for the call. In the case of the team-generated list, the team should identify the CIO or director of IT at each potential reference and send a letter or fax in advance of the call, outlining the reason for the call and providing a list of questions in advance. The team should then follow up with a phone call to perform the interview or determine whom the CIO would designate from his or her team to take the call. If possible, the team should conduct the interviews in person and make a site visit as part of the interview.

The list of questions that the team asks varies from project to project. The team should have a specific list of questions prepared in advance but should also leave time for open-ended responses from the reference. Many of the most interesting findings come from the unscripted portion of the interview. Focus is on determining how the vendor has performed for the client both before and after the sale, as well as getting a preview of any key lessons learned during the implementation.

Some of the questions that we have found effective in a vendor reference interview include:

- What products did you consider as part of your evaluation?
- What were your key decision criteria when making this decision?
- How did you complete the functional assessment, and what business functions were the most important?
- How did you weight the criteria (what was important to you)?
- How will you achieve a payback or return on investment from the system?
- What period did (will) it take to achieve a payback on the system?
- What were the benefits to the system (cost reduction, revenue enhancement)?

- When did you make your decision?
- How long did you take to complete your vendor evaluation?
- What modules or products did you purchase and implement?
- Did the technical architecture work as planned?
- How was the vendor service after the sale?
- Did you use an implementation partner to accomplish the implementation?
- Have you had input to the product development process?
- Have you had any technical/user support issues? How did the vendor respond? What was the escalation level required for resolution?
- How have the system and technical architecture scaled with volume changes?
- What were the surprises (good and bad)?
- What are the key lessons learned from the selection process and the subsequent implementation?
- Would you do it again?

CONDUCT GAP ANALYSIS. The gap analysis effort is intended to accomplish two objectives. First, the analysis should confirm that there is a satisfactory approach for handling each of the requirements, particularly the high-priority areas. Second, given the approach for each priority requirement, the team can estimate the effort required to cover the gap, which is usually one of the biggest components of the implementation costs.

Each requirement that the team has identified in the previous exercise may qualify as a gap, depending on how the system handles the function. A way of prioritizing the requirements for gap analysis is to assess each requirement according to its importance to the business and the level of fit the application has "out of the box." Exhibit 12.20 outlines the methodology for prioritizing requirements for the gap analysis.

After the requirements have been assessed along the two axes and mapped to the two-by-two framework in Exhibit 12.20, the gap analysis should be conducted on the requirements appearing in the northwest corner. The requirements in the other quadrants either have lower importance to the business (therefore, the business will accept cost-effective methods to cover the gap) or can be handled by the application with a minimum of change and are, therefore, adequately covered.

The next task in the gap analysis is to complete a detailed assessment of the method for covering each northwest quadrant requirement. For each one, the approach will be some mix of two options—reconfiguring or customizing the product or changing the associated business process and requirement. In most cases, the answer will be some mix of the two. For highest priority requirements for the most critical business processes, coverage may involve a solution that has no impact on the business process.

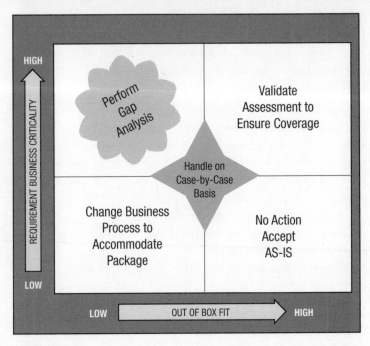

Exhibit 12.20   Requirement Prioritization Matrix for Gap Analysis

Exhibit 12.21 shows a typical gap analysis spreadsheet. The key elements to be captured include priority; a description of the method to cover; estimated effort to cover; and a checklist for configuration, customization, or business process change for gap coverage.

This analysis can and should be done in concert with the vendor, and it should be a principle outcome of the scripted demonstration, follow-up demos, and question-and-answer sessions. This is another main source of surprises during implementation and an area that drives much of the labor cost of implementation. Therefore, it is important for the evaluation team to put a thorough, exhaustive effort into the work—"measuring twice before cutting once." The team must also adhere to strict discipline in documenting the gaps and approach to cover. These documents facilitate later negotiations (and help resolve disputes) with the vendor. These sources of disputes in the implementation often center on the product's ability to cover the gaps as represented in the due diligence. Vendors are aware of this and sometimes resist the gap analysis. The evaluation team must keep asking tough questions until it is completely satisfied with the approach for key functions.

When the gap analysis is complete, it should be reviewed to understand what overall level of configuration and customization is required to make the system work well and satisfactorily cover all requirements. If the level of

Gap #	Requirement	Req #	Gap Description	Method to Cover	Consultation	Customization	Price Change	Estimated Effort
2.09	Forecasting	7.32	• System must hold forecast for final market intelligence adjustment by territory managers	• Add consensus FC system and workflow step for manual incorporation and release		X		2 FTE days
2.10	Fixed Asset Management	5.09	• Cannot calculate dep for general ledger in weekly increments • Supports monthly only	• System will be configured and customized to work in weekly increments for GL drop	X	X		10 FTE days
2.11	Inventory Management	8.21	• System does not allow tracking of product variations by color below SKU level	• Will have to add custom code and make database changes to accommodate • Biz process change to support entry/maintenance of product color schemes		X	X	57 FTE days

Exhibit 12.21   Example Package Gap Prioritization Assessment Sheet

customization is particularly high (more than one-third of the modules have customizations or several modules have major customizations), the application begins to lose its appeal as a package. Because customization drives large costs in both implementation and steady-state maintenance, makes vendor upgrades and enhancements difficult to install, and defeats the purpose of a packaged product, the team should take a step back and revisit the process for vendors who require heavy customization.

Supplemental Vendor Selection

In the case of a packaged application vendor selection or other product requiring additional hardware or professional services for implementation, the team may be faced with a subselection process to determine which supplemental vendors to use.

This subselection process should be managed as a subset of the activities covered in this chapter. The key sequence of scope definition, requirements gathering, vendor identification, vendor demonstrations, and reference checking can usually be completed rapidly. The front-runners for the primary vendor will have emerged, narrowing the scope for the supplemental selection considerably. In most cases, it is not necessary to go through the effort of a complete RFP process. Furthermore, the scope and requirements for the supplemental vendor selection should easily emerge from the previously completed work—for example, the volume processing calendars and technology footprint driving hardware selection, preliminary project plan, and resource estimates driving professional services vendor selection.

A starting point for the supplemental vendor selection list can come from the vendor reference calls completed as part of the due diligence. The managers will usually divulge which supplemental vendors they used for hardware, additional software, and professional services. After several references, the team usually sees the same names of supplemental vendors begin to turn up.

After supplemental vendors have been selected, the project plan and economic analysis can be updated based on new information.

HARDWARE VENDORS. If a supplemental selection is required for a hardware vendor, the selection team may want to evaluate the following hardware vendor specific considerations:

- *References:* Look for references with similar configuration and processing profiles (peak and average volumes); for hardware, the processing and configuration similarity matters more than business model similarities.
- *Versions:* Hardware vendors have rapid product cycles; reference accounts are usually on hardware a generation or two behind the hard-

ware under consideration; in these cases, the vendor should provide a clear inventory of changes in the platform.

- *Reliability/service:* If the application being deployed is mission critical, the hardware should provide the appropriate reliability, including failover and subsystem redundancy; the vendor should have four-hour or faster component replacement as an available service.

- *Pricing:* The vendor should provide pricing for varying levels of capacity; often professional services and applications vendors have entered into agreements with hardware vendors as resellers and, therefore, have access to discount pricing that is not available to the one-time purchaser. In these cases, the application or services vendor will work with the hardware provider to provide pricing.

- *Upgrade path:* If the application scalability requirements entail ability to expand capacity at a later date, the hardware vendor should propose systems that have a clearly defined upgrade path that minimizes incremental cost and implementation disruption.

- *Existing environment:* If the hardware must fit into a pre-existing environment, it should be proven to interface with the existing equipment and systems; customer references can help surface any potential integration issues.

- *Sales model:* Hardware vendors often use an indirect sales channel; in this case, the hardware vendor can help identify a value-added reseller (VAR) that can provide pricing and service. Generally, the hardware vendor co-sells in conjunction with the VAR to ensure that all questions are answered to the prospect's satisfaction.

Chapter 7 provides a detailed model for ensuring that technology-purchasing decisions are made in a consistent, cost-effective fashion.

PROFESSIONAL SERVICES PROVIDERS. If a supplemental selection is required for a professional services vendor, the selection team may want to evaluate the following vendor-specific considerations:

- *Pricing:* Is the provider willing to enter into a fixed-pricing contract? If the evaluation team has completed the scoping and requirements definition phase at the appropriate level of detail, the vendor should be willing to fix-bid the project, as most of the details and gaps have already been documented and understood.

- *Performance guarantee:* Will the vendor tie its compensation to completion of specific project milestones and/or the achievement of the anticipated project benefits? Will the vendor enter into a "gain-sharing" agreement with bonuses and penalties tied to performance during the implementation?

- *Bench discounts:* Will the vendor provide discount rates for consultants on its bench who have a solid skill set but do not have experience with this specific type of implementation?
- *References and experience:* Has the vendor seen the full implementation of this project previously with a similar client (company size, industry, modules implemented, project budget, business model)?
- *Staffing:* Have the specific team members proposed for this engagement participated in a similar engagement with the vendor? Will the vendor provide proposed team member resumes in advance and allow client veto or approval power for team members? Will the vendor provide the hire dates of the proposed team? Will any of the team members be provided to the vendor from third parties?
- *Approach:* Does the vendor have a proprietary, client-proven approach for this type of engagement? Does it reduce risk or cost or otherwise improve the outcome? Has the vendor submitted a potential work plan that demonstrates a detailed understanding of the key challenges for the project? Has the vendor performed an implementation with a conversion from the system being replaced?
- *Location:* Will the proposed team work on-site? Where are the home offices of the team members? What is the vendor policy on travel costs and per-diems?

The team should be inclined to sharing information (e.g., requirements documentation, gap analysis) with vendors during all parts of the process, and the supplemental vendors are no exception. Often, vendor selection teams are hesitant to provide information to vendors. This reluctance usually slows down the process and results in a lack of clarity in communication with the vendors. Obviously, the team should not compromise proprietary information that might hurt the company, but reputable vendors are always willing to sign nondisclosure agreements in exchange for a clearer understanding of the process.

Finally, the evaluation team should investigate both a consulting and staff-augmentation approach to outside professional services help. Consultants are generally willing to assume responsibility for the project and will provide both doers and leaders. A staff-augmentation approach provides the implementation team with contractors for specific skill sets, but the responsibility for project delivery rests completely with the internal team. Both approaches have been proven successful, and the team should decide the appropriate use of outside resources based on cost, availability, references, level of internal expertise, project risk, and estimated return on investment.

Project Planning and Approval

BUILD PRELIMINARY PROJECT PLAN.   The next task for the team is to create a preliminary project plan and revise the previous first-cut economic analysis. Labor effort to cover the gaps, particularly when provided by outside professional services firms, is one of the largest drivers of cost in an implementation. Therefore, after the gap analysis has been completed, much of the information that produces variability in the project economics is known, and a re-estimate can be completed.

As with requirements gathering and analysis, the creation of a quality project plan is a topic that justifies a separate book (or three). There are a wide variety of project planning methodologies available. Books covering a few approaches are listed at the end of the chapter. Chapter 17 of this book discusses the topic in more detail. A few key principles are outlined here. The project plan should include these elements:

- *Work tasks:* This inventory of tasks and subtasks required to complete the project should have 5 to 10 major tasks at the top level and each level of detail breaks down into an additional 5 to 10 subtasks for as many levels of detail as required.
- *Sequencing and dependencies:* Plan should account for the order in which tasks should be completed; the plan must highlight which tasks are required predecessors of following tasks and which provide a deliverable that feeds a following task.
- *Deliverables:* The plan should identify the document, function, submodule, or other clearly defined outcome of each task.
- *Milestones:* Identification and inventory of major points of completion and way-points in the plan facilitates later measurement of progress against the plan.
- *Task timing and duration:* The calendar date for the commencement of each major phase of the project should be identified, along with the duration of the tasks and subtasks.
- *Resources:* Includes level, skill set, and amount of resources required to complete the task (e.g., "Senior-level SQL Server DBA for four weeks"); the resource should be identified as an internal or external resource. These requirements will drive the overall labor cost for the project.
- *Rollout and cutover:* The rollout and cutover portion of the plan shows how the system will be deployed to the user base; the rollout plan may be organized around department, geographic region, plant location, or other bundling of users that facilitates training and minimizes business disruption.

- *Training:* The plan should show the number and type of end users that require training, along with an estimate of training hours required per user, and a plan for executing and managing the training process (vendor supplied, internal training, classroom based, etc.).

- *Lead times:* The plan should factor in vendor lead times required for shipping, receiving, installing, and configuring hardware, software, or other vendor-supplied components. The team should perform a "right-to-left" analysis so that the order date can be calculated based on the lead-time and date required.

- *Business calendar:* The development, implementation, and deployment schedule should be audited to ensure that no key events conflict with important events on the business calendar; this is particularly true for highly seasonal businesses (e.g., grocery stores at Thanksgiving, florists on Valentine's Day).

Because this plan is merely the first-cut, preliminary effort, the team should produce the plan in a top-down fashion and avoid overcomplicating the plan with excessive detail. For example, tasks measured in hours or even days are probably too much detail at this point. The plan should instead lay out in broad strokes what comprises the overall effort, at the level of major pieces of work measured in weeks.

Similarly, the team should avoid overcomplicating the preliminary plan with excessive use of project planning tools. A host of applications is available for project organization and management. Particularly for first-round plans, these tools complicate matters. The IT manager should be cautious of a desire from the team to delve into project planning tools (and the concomitant distraction of installing, training, and tweaking). The first draft is best done in a spreadsheet or word processing document. Over reliance on a tool can often mask a lack of content. A good plan stands on its own, regardless of format.

PERFORM NEXT-ROUND ECONOMIC ANALYSIS. After the preliminary plan is complete, the team can update the costs portion of the costs-benefit model. The new information to be incorporated comes from three fronts:

1. Preliminary project plan supplies updated estimate of internal and externally supplied labor, along with resource type, quantity, and estimated hourly cost.

2. Updated application or product costs—at a minimum, the vendor will have supplied list (or pre-negotiation) pricing for the product being selected, along with an understanding of the key drivers of pricing (servers, seats, processors, or other).

3. Preliminary estimate of hardware, supplemental software. The processing calendar and sizing performed as part of the technical due dili-

gence will provide enough information to attain a preliminary estimate of any additional hardware or software required; as with software costs, these numbers will also be order-of-magnitude pre-negotiation estimates based on vendor input.

The team should produce the following components of a complete project economic analysis:

- *Project cost:* The total cost of original acquisition of all technology components and their complete configuration, customization, integration, implementation, training, and deployment, based on the preliminary project plan.
- *Vendor maintenance:* Estimated annual fees due to vendor as part of maintenance agreement for all technology components—hardware and software.
- *Steady-state cost model changes:* Any incremental costs (or savings) incurred in the organization, covering all portions of the IT budget. These costs are found across a variety of categories, including labor (additional staff, different salaries based on new technology), consumables, facilities, and capacity.
- *Accelerated depreciation:* Some projects will obsolete an existing system or set of systems. In these cases, depreciation of amounts capitalized from the previous implementation may be accelerated and taken as expense after the new system is deployed; the amounts and accounting issues around this topic should be addressed in conjunction with the finance department and the CFO.

As with the project plan, economic analysis should be simplified by taking a top-down approach and making assumptions and documenting them where information is missing or incomplete. The economic analysis should also be a spreadsheet-based exercise, which rolls project costs up into the traditional "hardware, software, people" categories and takes a stance on probable postimplementation changes to steady-state IT costs.

Often, evaluation teams (and very often vendors) are uncomfortable with beginning to assign numbers to the project. Each round of economic analysis should be positioned as a preliminary estimate only. At some point, the team will have to put a stake in the ground and begin talking about what the numbers are. Completing this exercise early allows key assumptions to be surfaced and examined and provides context for all of the cost-benefits discussions with senior management.

After the project and steady-state costs have been re-evaluated, the team can re-calculate the project return on investment, payback period, or other relevant cost-benefit measures. Any additional benefits identified during the RFP or due-diligence processes should be added to the model as well.

Finally, based on this analysis, the team may begin to see some separation between the vendors at this point because project economics are always a major factor in any vendor selection process. If a particular vendor is at a major cost advantage (or disadvantage), the team may elect to shift its focus to the front-runner.

PROJECT PRESENTATION/APPROVAL.   At this point, the evaluation team should present the results of the vendor due diligence, preliminary project plan, and economic analysis to the IT steering committee. Based on the vendor due diligence, vendor scoring, and economic analysis, the team should have identified the vendor of choice, as well as supplemental vendors. The package presented to the committee should have every element of the planned project identified, except the final pricing negotiations with the vendors.

This provides the committee a last chance for input to the process before final selection of a vendor and before the team invests significant effort in negotiations with the vendor. Because a thorough vendor selection can take several months, the committee will often have new information regarding business benefits and refined requirements.

As with all previous steps, the members of the evaluation team and the IT steering committee should sign off on the recommendation before proceeding to the next step.

Vendor Negotiation

After the IT steering committee has approved the project and vendor selection, the final vendor pricing negotiations can commence. It is important to wait until this point to maximize negotiating influence with the vendors. If vendors know the project and budget have been approved by senior management, they will know that the deal is imminent and will be prepared to rapidly get to their best pricing.

Vendor negotiation is a complex topic; IT managers generally find themselves at a disadvantage in negotiations. Vendor sales professionals participate in pricing negotiations every single week. The IT manager does not have the advantage of either practice or complete information. Because of this, IT managers often bring in consultants who are experienced in conducting vendor pricing negotiations. The best consultants are objective and not associated with a firm that implements or resells any vendor's products. They will also have conducted a negotiation with the specific vendor in question during the prior twelve months. The high cost of a large-scale vendor investment allows the client to recoup the negotiation specialist's consulting fees many times over.

Often, IT managers have an inherent hesitance to ask for discounting before closing a deal with a vendor. There are a variety of reasons for this, including inexperience negotiating pricing, not understanding vendor pricing drivers, or unwillingness to push back on the vendor sales reps. Unfortunately, this can be costly for the company and earn the IT manager a reputation for being a patsy. IT managers lose nothing by at least asking the question of vendors. We were asked to review a ready-to-be-signed contract for a new client as a "formality." We called the sales manager and asked if this was the best pricing available. The manager remarked that no one had asked for a discount, but that he would provide a 10 percent discount for an immediate execution of the contract. One phone call, five minutes, $20,000 in savings generated.

Because of the large number of different factors involved in a large technology purchase—licensing, maintenance, training, professional services, terms and conditions, and more—the IT manager must proceed cautiously. Often, vendors will turn a loss on one portion of the negotiation into a major win on another piece. Therefore, the IT manager must understand and negotiate each variable (license, support, financing, peripherals, etc.) with a specific strategy and lock down agreed upon items in the process. In buying a car, if you negotiate a trade-in on your used car, the price of the new car, and the financing separately you are much more likely to receive the best possible deal on each versus negotiating all together to get to a desired monthly payment. The same is true for vendor negotiations in technology. Negotiations can be lengthy, but time is on the side of the buyer. The manager should tightly control both the agenda and, most importantly, the pace of the negotiation. This allows the manager to keep the upper hand and achieve the best pricing and terms.

We have collected a few practices from participating in a host of software, hardware, and services vendors' negotiations. Key points are provided in the following listing. However, we highly recommend the engagement of a negotiation expert for large-expenditure items, or at a minimum, self-study with the negotiation texts mentioned in the bibliography for this chapter:

- *Negotiate each point separately:* Vendors are experienced in achieving a higher total price by bundling and shifting prices of individual components throughout the negotiation process. The opportunity of vendors to obfuscate the true pricing is high if licenses, maintenance, hardware, financing, professional services, training, future discounts, and a dozen other terms are negotiated simultaneously. Instead, the buyer should carefully and separately negotiate each point, starting with the points that drive the largest amount of cost first. Often, the vendors will give up ground on this piece, hoping to gain back lost ground on the subsequent pieces.

- *Keep at least two vendors in the mix:* Keep a second option open until there is ink on the final contract; if the vendor senses that it is the only option, the manager's negotiating power declines significantly. As soon as a vendor thinks a final selection has been made—whether the winner or not—negotiating will become more rigid. Further, it is possible that the negotiations would produce pricing concessions from the second-place vendor that would move it into first place.

- *Don't single-source the negotiation:* Because many vendors offer a full suite of services in addition to their application, they often have a natural advantage in proposing consulting or training portions of a project. The team should still consider competing services to ascertain which vendor can deliver a better price or better service. The outcome of the negotiations may very well be a single-source approach for implementation, but driving to this solution early lowers the client negotiating power.

- *Timing is everything:* Like any other company, software, hardware, and professional services vendors are under pressure to achieve monthly, quarterly, and annual goals. A little research should reveal the fiscal calendar for the vendor in question. The maximum negotiating power is at a quarter or fiscal year end, as the vendor works to achieve its financial targets.

- *Keep talking to current and prospective customers:* Current data from other prospective customers as well as the installed base can give you insight into areas where the vendor might be more willing to offer concessions. With the right relationship built, IT managers from peer companies will be willing to share costing and negotiation information about a specific vendor.

- *Don't compare apples to oranges:* Because of the large number of pieces involved in a complex negotiation, it can often be difficult to compare individual elements of the pricing to adequately compare vendors. The team should continue to ask questions and deconstruct vendor-pricing proposals until they can be compared side-by-side on an element-by-element basis.

- *Nominate a "bad cop" for your team in advance:* The team may occasionally need someone to take a tough line with the vendor. If a "bad cop" is needed during the negotiations, the company CFO is often happy to fill that role.

- *Ensure that the vendor must close the deal:* Ensure that throughout the process, vendor invests considerable amount of time in the deal; the vendor sales team then often engages in "sunk cost fallacy" and believes that it must complete the deal because of the high level of investment so far. This has the effect of swinging the balance of power considerably.

- *Employ "bogeys" to force reciprocal concessions:* This is a common negotiating tactic to put forward points that are not actually material considerations ("bogeys"), then quickly capitulate on the point to force reciprocal concessions from the vendor on other points. This can be an effective strategy, but should be used with caution; they can quickly produce the reverse effect in the event that the vendor agrees to the nonmaterial concession early.

- *Check the contract for liability limitations:* Vendors generally try to contractually limit their liabilities to the total of their fees or to the limits of their insurance coverage. These liability limits often do not begin to approach the actual damages experienced by a business if an implementation goes wrong (see Chapter 1). The team should push for liability limitations that acknowledge the risk for the customer, not the vendor. For high profile, large-investment projects, the vendor should also carry "malpractice" or errors and omissions (E&O) insurance from an insurance carrier with a rating of A or better.

- *Never prepay maintenance:* Occasionally, vendors offer discounts for prepaid maintenance or other items. The IT manager gives up significant future influence over the vendor's behavior by prepaying these charges. We have seen clients with several years of prepaid maintenance credit that is worthless because the vendor has gone out of business. However sharp the discount, the risk associated with prepaying is too high.

- *Know when to disappear:* If the sides are at an impasse, the IT manager can "go dark" and avoid responding to vendor e-mail and voice mail; time is on the side of the buyer and the dearth of information will put increased pressure on the vendor if the vendor's negotiators perceive that the deal is slipping away.

- *Know when to say when:* When the negotiation is close to complete on all pricing, terms, and conditions, the manager should have at least one final concession at the ready; the vendor usually gives this final concession on the promise that the manager will sign the contract immediately.

- *Watch the licensing terms:* The team should carefully examine the licensing assignment rights in the contract. Often, applications vendors do not allow reassignment of the license. This can become a problem in the event the manager decides to outsource some or all of the application maintenance to a third party. The vendor may charge any third parties that the manager brings in to work on the system or even refuse to allow the third party to work on the system. Often, vendor contracts provide provisions revoking the license if maintenance fees are not paid. In those cases, the manager loses the ability to withhold maintenance dollars if he or she feels the dollars are not being allocated properly to development or if the vendor is not being responsive.

A variety of the key negotiating points that should be addressed in the vendor pricing conversations for application software is provided in Exhibit 12.22.

NEGOTIATION POINT	COMMENTS	TERMS
License (server, seats)	• In addition to getting the overall price as low as possible, the timing of payment should be delayed as long as possible. • Typical discount should range from 10% to 30%. • Influencing factors include maintenance load, how close it is to quarter end, and whether purchase is done direct with the vendor or through a VAR.	• Typical to pay 50% of cost at signing. • Attempt to delay payment of remaining balance as long as possible—at least 90 days after satisfactory installation, to be defined by customer.
Future license discounts	• The time of the initial purchase is when the buyer has the most leverage. • Therefore, discount rates on potential future purchases should be negotiated at that time. • Being "optimistic" when estimating future needs gives the vendor more incentive to be generous.	• Rate—the current license discount or better should apply. • Duration—the negotiated rate should be in effect for at least one year after initial purchase. • Payment timing—agree to longer terms on future purchases.
Service level/Help desk support	• Usually hierarchy of "silver," "gold," "platinum." • Depending on internal support plan, often not a high priority.	• Try to get free upgrade to next highest service level.
Consulting/ Professional services	• Vendor typically pushes for some professional services to be included to ensure "proper installation." • Depending on the implementation partner, professional services may not be needed. • Keep commitment low in first agreement—it can always be increased later.	• Typical fees range from $150/hour to $300/hour with an average of $225–$250/hour. • Need to prearrange costs while negotiating power is high; the price should be documented in the contract.

Exhibit 12.22 Key Negotiating Points for Package Application Pricing

NEGOTIATION POINT	COMMENTS	TERMS
Training	• Vendor typically has a price per person, not including travel and expenses. • Vendors try to link training discounts to the number of participants. • "Training the trainer" is an effective way to manage costs.	• As part of bundled negotiation, training prices can sometimes be reduced to zero. • If it is not feasible to get training for free, vendor should be able to discount by at least 10%. • Achieve volume discount by applying leverage as number of trainees increases.
Future training	• Negotiate the discount rate for any future training at the time of initial purchase.	• Rate—the current discount or better should apply. • Duration—the negotiated rate should be in effect for at least one year after the initial purchase.
Maintenance fees—First year	• Because of its recurring nature, this component can have a significant impact on ownership costs. • Pay an annual fee to receive upgrades until a specified future release. • Usually a hierarchy ("gold," "platinum," etc.).	• Usually 8–30% of price. • Negotiate to have price based on discounted pricing—not list pricing. • Can also negotiate payment timing—try for date after last license payment.
On-going maintenance fees	• The key is determining if the basis for annual maintenance fees after the first year is software net price or list.	• Rate—the original discount or better should apply. • Duration—the negotiated rate should be in effect for as long as you are eligible for maintenance. • Payment Timing—agree to longer terms for future annual payments.
Additional required software	• Depending on package, this can include database, integration tools (SDK), or third-party bolt-on packages.	• Negotiate same as points for licensing. • High costs for these additional items may give a buyer more leverage on the license price.

Exhibit 12.22 *Continued*

Vendor negotiations can be a daunting, difficult, and exhausting experience. However, it is also an unavoidable part of a system selection process and has to be managed carefully to ensure the best pricing and terms. As a CIO acquaintance of ours once remarked, "Every customer gets the system they deserve."

RESOURCES

Requirements methodologies:

Hatley, Derek J., Peter Hruschka, and Imtiaz A. Pirbhai. *Process for System Architecture and Requirements Engineering.* New York: Dorset House, 2000.

Hay, David C., and Barbara Von Halle. *Requirements Analysis: From Business Views to Architecture.* Upper Saddle River, NJ: Prentice Hall, 2002.

Sommerville, Ian, Pete Sawyer (Contributor), and Aan Sommerville. *Requirements Engineering: A Good Practice Guide.* New York: John Wiley & Sons, 2000.

Project management:

Charvat, Jason. *Project Management Nation: Goals for the New and Practicing IT Project Manager—Guidance, Tools, Templates, and Techniques That Work!* New York: John Wiley & Sons, 2002.

Murch, Richard, *Project Management: Best Practices for IT Professionals.* Upper Saddle River, NJ: Prentice Hall, 2000.

Phillips, Joseph. *IT Project Management: On Track from Start to Finish.* New York: McGraw-Hill Osborne Media, 2002.

The Project Management Institute. www.pmi.org.

Negotiating:

Cialdini, Robert B. *Influence: The Psychology of Persuasion.* New York: William Morrow/Quill, 1993.

Fisher, Roger, and William Ury. *Getting to Yes.* New York: Penguin, 1991.

Russo, J. Edward, and Paul J. H. Schoemaker. *Decision Traps: Ten Barriers to Brilliant Decision-Making and How to Overcome Them.* New York: Fireside, 1990.

NOTE

1. Henry Ford, attributed.

13

Vendor Management and Outsourcing

People who work together will win, whether it be against complex football defenses, or the problems of modern society.

—Vince Lombardi[1]

If, after the first 20 minutes, you don't know who the sucker at the table is, it's you.

—Unknown

This chapter outlines management practices for ensuring that the IT department manages outside vendors in a manner that delivers the most value to the company in exchange for considerations paid to the vendors, all the while working in a partnership with the vendor to further the aims of both the company and the vendor. The chapter emphasizes the importance of properly managing vendors and provides techniques for monitoring and assessing vendors' performance. The chapter also covers the vendor management role within the IT department, how to take control of vendor relationships, especially those inherited, how and when to recompete vendor contracts, and provides guidance to the CIO on managing vendors in turmoil or financial trouble. This chapter is a companion to Chapter 12, which also contains a variety of critical vendor management concepts.

Why This Topic Is Important

Almost without exception, IT departments are highly reliant on a wide variety of vendors. Outside vendors provide the hardware, system software, application systems, networks, and peripherals that power most of the

451

IT functions. Because IT managers get little training in managing outside partners, including measuring service levels, selecting service providers, and negotiating pricing and terms, many IT departments fall short in vendor management. This can be highly damaging to any IT department not only because of the reliance on vendors to provide mission-critical hardware, software, and services but also because of the high expenditures on outside vendors. Outside providers generally comprise between 20 percent and 40 percent of the typical IT budget. Failure to manage this expenditure suitably can be devastating.

A cooperative and amicable relationship is necessary to extract the most value out of vendor relationships, while applying good management practices that ensure that the vendor is performing up to expectations and meeting committed service levels. This can be challenging. A wide variety of vendors must be managed. Often, IT departments cover shortfalls in vendor performance by adding staff or other expenditures rather than confronting nonperforming vendors and instituting standard vendor management processes and procedures. CIOs and staff must work to hold nonperformers accountable.

Vendors, like most companies, also pay the most attention to the customers who provide their largest revenue stream or the customers who are most vocal. This means that smaller companies must learn to aggressively communicate their needs to vendors and to band with other small customers to influence vendor policies and priorities. It also means that larger companies with significant vendor spending should ensure that the vendor is reflecting their needs appropriately in product or service development priorities, rather than submitting to a vocal minority.

Vendors as Partners

The most effective vendor relationships are the ones in which the vendor and customer build a close partnership. However, this relationship can be difficult to achieve. Vendors have a different set of incentives and priorities than the IT manager, and finding ways to work to mutual benefit takes effort and willingness on both sides to accomplish. Although we do not repeat them in this chapter, many of the techniques and approaches outlined in Chapter 12 on vendor selection are relevant to the ongoing management of vendors.

There are a host of ways for IT departments and vendors to work in partnership to mutual benefit. To illustrate the value and effect of a partnership, we take the example of a partnership with a packaged software provider. In a partnership, the vendor can provide a wide range of benefits to the customer, including:

- New features customized for the customer by the development team and included in the next release.
- Free minor application updates in advance of release.
- Access to alpha and beta tests for new applications or new functions in existing applications.
- Telegraphing major company announcements in advance of official notification.
- Concessions on license pricing for future purchases.
- Discounts on maintenance packages.
- Dedicated 24/7 emergency technical support representatives.
- Information on undocumented application features and application programming interfaces (APIs).
- Access to source code for customization or deeper understanding of application architecture.
- Introductions to other clients with similar technology platforms.

In return, the customer might provide:

- Acceptance of minor service level agreement (SLA) violations by the vendor.
- Continued business without any unnecessary recompetes.
- Detailed bug reports and product functionality and enhancement feedback.
- Press releases and references for vendor sales prospects.
- Specific letters of recommendation for vendor's sales calls.
- Contacts for vendors with companies in same industry or contacts from other professional relationships.

Most of these items are provided to the opposite party on a best-efforts basis. As shown in the previous list, items proffered in a partnership are of relatively low cost to either party, but they can be of tremendous value. This relationship could significantly increase the value of the contract without requiring arm's-length contract addendums whose cost and difficulty of enforcement may destroy much of the potential value.

The longer the relationship exists, the higher the potential benefits for both parties. For the vendor, sales costs are virtually eliminated and over time the cost-to-serve generally declines which results in long-term gross margin improvement. For the customer, the vendor's cost reductions are typically shared with the customer via pricing discounts. The customer's cost to manage the vendor also declines and "learning curve" costs from new vendor entrants are eliminated. Finally, the customer benefits from a vendor whose staff understands the business in intimate detail and can provide customer-specific solutions.

One of the most significant benefits of participating in a close relationship with a vendor is the opportunity to influence the vendor's product development process. This is particularly true for package applications but can apply to hardware and services vendors as well. Successful vendors have immense resources at their disposal for investment in current and future products. Software vendors have an income stream emanating from maintenance contracts to invest in enhancements and new system features. By partnering closely with vendors and providing input to the prioritization process for new feature or capability development, the client company can leverage vendor R&D investment amounts far in excess of the amounts it could dedicate to internal development. The client steers the product direction to its ultimate benefit.

One software vendor invited its top 25 customers to its corporate headquarters twice a year for product development and demonstration sessions. The product manager created a log of all enhancement requests, interface suggestions, and functionality recommendations from the biannual two-day affair and worked with the development staff to incorporate as many of the ideas as possible and appropriate. Although the software vendor had thousands of clients and an annual users' conference, these 25 clients drove a disproportionate amount of software enhancements and greatly benefited from partnering with the vendor.

An important fact to consider in building a partnership is that some vendors may wish to partner initially; however, the partnership can rapidly turn negative if problems arise. A variety of events can cause the partnership to go awry with the vendor, including turnover of key personnel, a merger/acquisition for the vendor or client, a strategic focus change for the vendor or client, financial difficulties for either party, or even another customer who is providing much greater benefits and monopolizing the vendor's attention and resources. In these cases, it is best to reevaluate the value of the partnership to ensure that the client organization continues to receive the expected partnership benefits.

In the final analysis, the customer is paying for the product and/or services. This should naturally put the customer in the position of most influence and provide final control of the terms of the relationship. When money has changed hands, vendors have a fiduciary obligation to discharge their contractual responsibilities. Vendors may try to take advantage of the relationship if the customer is unaware, too busy, or inexperienced in dealing with vendors. Savvy customers know that they are, ultimately, the "boss" in any vendor relationship. Given a choice between a partnership and an adversarial relationship, all parties prefer the former. However, if a partnership is difficult to achieve, the CIO should be certain that his or her company's needs are met by the vendor even if aggressive, confrontational action is required.

Vendor Management Role

The vendor management function in the IT department is vital to capture the benefits of vendor partnerships as discussed in the chapter. The CIO and direct reports should be intimately involved in building relationships with vendors. Other functions of the vendor management role should be delegated to an administrative resource. Tasks performed by the vendor management function include:

- Maintenance of all contracts.
- Assistance to IT managers in processing new contracts.
- Provide reports on vendor performance and contract status to management.
- Coordinate activities between internal IT teams and vendors.
- Define and enforce processes and procedures for vendor management.
- Assist with RFP and vendor selection administrative process.
- Develop standard approach to deal with each type of vendor.
- Summarize service level requirements by vendor.
- Execute vendor quality surveys.
- Track and report upcoming vendor milestone dates.
- Maintain deliverable sign-off records.
- Report progress on fixed bid contracts (e.g., qualitative progress, percent complete versus percent billed).
- Analyze vendor pricing compared to industry average.
- Collect and distribute service level reports from vendors.

The tendency in most IT departments is to ignore the vendor management function and by default decentralize all vendor activities. However, the organization can benefit through reduced costs, reduced risk, and more effective communication between the company and its vendors by centralizing the function. The vendor management role helps ensure the company drives the relationship versus being driven.

Taking Control of Vendor Management

A defined process exists for taking control of vendor management. Most CIOs at some point will likely inherit a variety of disparate vendor relationships in various stages of health and efficacy. Without gaining control of these relationships, service problems can quickly arise from vendors in poor partnerships who are looking to take advantage of the chaos or changes in IT management at customer organizations or from benign vendors who are simply paying attention to the customers working hardest to manage their relationship. Without careful management, inattentive vendors can wreak havoc on IT departments; an IT management transition period or weak management of the function is a time when the vendor and client agendas can diverge, and the relationships deserve special attention and tight performance management during these times. Exhibit 13.1 depicts the vendor audit/cleanup process.

The first task is to assign the vendor management role to someone on the staff. This person will be responsible for the tasks previously described. This person will also be integral to the audit/cleanup process. The second task is to identify all current vendor relationships. These may exist in various sections of the IT department, business unit, functional units, and geographies. For every vendor relationship identified, all related legal, financial, and operational documentation should be collected in a single repository. The CIO should read each contract and make notes about service level commitments, prices, maintenance contracts, and evaluation/reporting procedures.

It can be difficult to locate the actual contracts for all service vendors in an IT shop. Particularly for long-standing relationships, the contracts may have been signed by an IT manager who has long departed and the original documentation lost. A contract may be filed in the purchasing department, legal department, or human resources department; it can be copied for use by the IT department. Failing the location of an internal copy, the CIO can request a contract copy from the vendor. As a last resort, the IT director and vendor can renegotiate a contract to govern the ongoing relationship without

Exhibit 13.1 Vendor Audit/Cleanup Process

necessarily changing the original terms. Often, long-standing contracts will have expired without renewal, while continuing use of the service or product. These situations create an ideal opportunity for the CIO to renegotiate the terms of the agreement.

As a next step, the CIO should meet individually with each vendor (if possible, depending on the number of vendors; otherwise select a vendor audit team) to gain a deeper understanding about the vendor, its organization, products and services, history of the vendor-client relationship, contractual obligations, recent events, and any outstanding issues. This vendor checkup provides a clear view on which vendors are true partners with the IT department and which vendors simply have arms-length relationships for specified products/services.

Finally, the CIO should rapidly install vendor performance management to supervise the vendor relationships based on the self-reporting and audit cycles described in this chapter. This drives out underperforming vendors and ensures that money paid to vendors is providing the company the maximum possible return.

Beginning New Vendor Relationships

Getting off to a positive start with new vendors is critical to the success of projects and to the overall productivity of the IT department. Put processes in place to ensure that the organization is ready to work with the vendor on the agreed to install/start date. One process we have seen work well is a "readiness" check performed by the vendor manager. The "readiness" checklist is performed one week prior to the vendor coming onsite and is signed off by all involved internal parties. It ensures that the internal team is free and ready to begin work with the vendor on the agreed date, the dependent hardware and software is ready to go, the work space is ready, the contract is signed and filed, and the vendor has reconfirmed the start date. If any of the items are not checked, the date is postponed. This process will ensure that no vendor shows up before the company is "ready." This saves critical down time for both internal teams and vendor teams. It helps to keep vendor costs down—in the spirit of the partnership hopefully benefiting the company in the long-term.

Vendor Contracts

A solid legal agreement should always form the foundation of any vendor relationship. While contract negotiations can be painful, contracts can often outlive the tenure of the individuals negotiating the terms on either side. We have seen many contract negotiations fall short of the proper due diligence because the individuals involved had personal relationships or ample reason to trust one another. After these individuals left their respective firms, their successors are left to interpret what may have been agreed on but not documented.

In every case, the contract should explicitly set forth the terms that govern the relationship and define each party's responsibilities to the other in unambiguous detail. Further, the contracts for many vendor relationships, such as application software, are most often turgid, impenetrable, and complex. For purchases of any material significance, we recommend engaging attorneys or company legal counsel with experience negotiating contractual terms for technology assets or services. These professionals have seen the outcomes from poorly negotiated contracts and know which terms matter long-term, and they can identify the sometimes hidden, but significant, clauses in a contract.

The outcome of poor contract negotiations is often detrimental to the client company, who is generally the loser in interpreting ambiguities in the contract. In one case, an applications vendor found enough room for interpretation to ensure that the new functionality in its product be considered a "new product" and required new licenses to be purchased by the end clients. The functionality should have been included in a standard upgrade release and, therefore, provided free to all clients paying maintenance fees.

Negotiating the best terms for a vendor contract requires understanding the potential organization requirements not only today, but also in the future. In one case, we assisted a mid-size manufacturing company in the spin-off of a subsidiary unit. Fortunately, some forward-thinking person had negotiated terms that allowed the licenses for the ERP system used to run the business to be split between entities and reassigned in the case of such a transaction. This point was at variance to the standard vendor contract and would have likely resulted in significant new license cost from the vendor had it not been negotiated in advance.

In another case, a client decided to outsource its technology operations to a third party. The primary application vendor, also in the business of outsourcing, protested vigorously against a third party operating its system, arguing an invasion of their intellectual capital rights and asserting that their licenses could not be reassigned to third parties. Again, a prescient negotiator for the client had included the irrevocable perpetual right to assign the application license to any third-party vendor chosen as an outsourcing partner. Certainly, there was no consideration of outsourcing the technology department at the time of the contract signing, but the negotiation team made sure that all options were covered.

Next we define several important contract negotiating terms for services, software, and hardware contracts:

- *Insurance:* In many cases, clients taking on significant business risk require the vendor to maintain malpractice insurance (often called errors and omissions coverage [E&O]). In any case, critical vendors should be required to provide proof of general and professional liability coverage. Additionally, the client should be specifically named as an additional insured under the vendor policy.

- *Acceptance testing and deliverable sign-off:* Acceptance of services or delivery of software or hardware is probably the most important negotiating point. This is typically the point where payment is required. The risk is that the product does not perform as promised or the services are not completed as promised. To reduce the risk that the company will be obligated to pay regardless of performance, specific acceptance criteria should be constructed. For services, detail the specific deliverables required for satisfactory performance of the contract, the requirements for the deliverable, quality metrics for acceptance, and required delivery dates and milestones.

- *Assignment rights:* Software and hardware vendors generally like to restrict the assignment privileges of the customer. However, this is not in the customer's best interest. To allow for company reorganizations and potential merger and acquisition activity, the customer should include a provision to assign rights and transfer the contract in the event of ownership changes, reorganizations, and to subsidiaries and minority interest affiliates.

- *License and maintenance fees:* The best case in purchasing licenses is to obtain a perpetual, fully paid-up license that requires no annual license or maintenance fee. However, most software companies charge maintenance fees and aren't willing to support or provide upgrades unless an annual maintenance fee is paid. Set the future maintenance fees in advance otherwise the vendor will gain tremendous leverage during future negotiations of fees. Fees should begin only when the product passes the acceptance tests not when actually delivered.

- *Nonsolicitaton clauses:* It is in the interest of both the client and the vendor to specify that neither party may solicit to hire each other's employees or solicit each other's customers both during the contract and for some period, usually 24 months after the termination of the contract. This avoids both staff poaching, as well as potential agency problems.

- *Description of products or services:* Ensure that the description of the product or service to be provided is unambiguous. In the case of software, specify the current version number of the application, include future versions, and potential major upgrades as "inclusive" of the definition of the product. This helps reduce the risk that the vendor will rename the product at the next major upgrade cycle and require additional license fees from customers in order to upgrade.

- *Right to withhold payment:* Ensure the right to withhold fees if vendor services are not properly delivered or product upgrades are not delivered as promised.

- *Disaster recovery:* Occasionally, software provider licenses restrict the number of CPUs software may run on. Ensure that the contract provides the company the ability for mirroring, hot swapping, dual processing, and backup/recovery. With services, indicate who is responsible for backup/recovery of the development environment and the production application.

- *Dispute resolution:* Consider required mediation and arbitration alternatives that can reduce the cost of disputes and require negotiation prior to legal action. Also require notification in advance in writing for potential disputes.

- *Future pricing:* The vendor obtains significant leverage in the future if future pricing for products and services are not detailed in the contract. At a minimum, specify that future product pricing will be no more than the then current list less the current customer discount percentage. Ideally, the prices are specifically fixed.

- *Indemnification:* Vendors attempt to limit liability to the total sum of fees paid.

- *Liability:* Liability should be mutual with fair allocation of risk.

- *Outsourcing:* Provide the right for customer to transfer license to outsourcing partner without licensors consent and without fees. This enables the company to outsource a function without approval from the vendor.

- *Payment terms:* Payment terms specify the cash payments to be paid. Net 30 days is typical for service vendors. Allow for suspension of payments if vendor is not performing as agreed. Negotiate discounts for early payment.

- *Source code/working documents:* Most software contracts should allow for escrowing the source code of the application with a third-party escrow provider. This protects the company should the vendor fail; the escrow can be activated and the customer would receive the source code to the application. The fees for escrowing are very reasonable.

- *Warranty:* Require the vendor to warrant that the vendor has the right to license the software or provide the services. Warrant for Year 2000 compliance. Require disclosure of trojan horses or disabling devices built into software.

- *Training:* Negotiate free training with software products and specify in the contract.

- *Services discounts:* Pre-arrange volume discounts and specify in the pricing section of the contract.

The number of high-profile lawsuits involving hardware manufacturers, application providers, and professional services firms confirms that contract negotiation and tight management of the vendor relationship is crucial to avoid business disruption and litigation, which can follow. In a study of technology vendor litigation, Cutter Consortium found that the top three causes for litigation include missing functionality or performance in the product, missed delivery or promise dates, and defects in the product, yielding it unusable.[2] Exhibit 13.2 shows the percentage of grounds claimed in the technology lawsuits researched by Cutter. A solid contract helps build a strong relationship by clearly articulating key provisions and avoiding ambiguous and off-the-record statements that lead to future disputes.

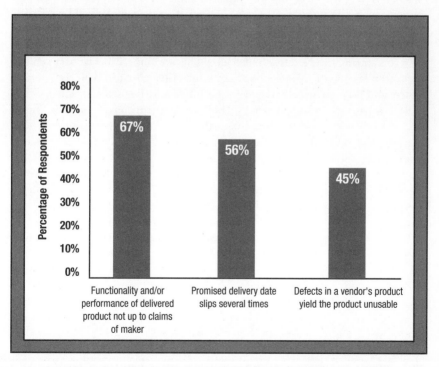

Exhibit 13.2 Primary Causes for Litigation in Technology Lawsuits

Managing Vendor Performance

A key piece of managing vendor relationships is mutually understanding expectations of the partnership and ensuring that the vendor fulfills those expectations. Often, the success or failure of the vendor in the IT department hinges on clearly setting performance metrics to be achieved and following through on those metrics. Ineffective IT departments rarely get past the first step of setting the metrics, and when they do, they do not follow up with periodic measurement of the vendor's performance.

The process is basic. For each vendor, define expected performance (may or may not be explicit in contract), track and monitor the performance, periodically report performance, take action to improve performance, or remove poor performing vendors. The designated vendor manager works in close connection with the CIO to manage vendor performance.

Because of the large number of vendors found in even small IT shops, determining measures and monitoring them can be a resource-intensive and, therefore, cost-prohibitive process. The most effective way to determine how to measure and evaluate vendors where the contract does not have specific deliverables (e.g., contract staffing vendors) is to ask them to provide metrics they believe are the most important determinants of their success with clients. Vendors know the most about their particular services and should be able to quickly articulate the top three to five metrics on which they should be evaluated. If they cannot identify how they should be evaluated, they are probably not a vendor that the IT department should be working with. The best vendors most often have internal benchmarks by which they measure their own performance, and they are usually happy to share those with customers who ask.

By having some vendors design their own performance metrics, incorporating them into contractual guarantees, and then having vendors self-monitor, the bulk of the effort to monitor and measure performance is absorbed by the vendor. To ensure that vendors are behaving honestly,the vendor manager should periodically and randomly audit one or two of the vendor-supplied, vendor-reported measures. If the vendor falls short, the potential of a random audit, coupled with contractual penalties, is generally enough to eliminate or at least minimize any dishonesty.

For the most mission-critical vendors, in addition to the vendor-driven approach outlined previously, the vendor manager and IT team should generate their own set of two to three key measures and perform the vendor assessments on a regular schedule. The CIO cannot afford to find out that a key vendor is falling short of agreed-on goals too late to mitigate the failure. The vendor manager should combine the key measures provided by the vendor with any other desired performance metrics to create a performance report card. This should be regularly completed and reviewed with the vendor to monitor ongoing performance and adherence to contractually established service level agreements (SLAs). If any SLAs have been violated, the customer can demand remediation in accordance with the contract specifications. Alternatively, in the spirit of partnership, the customer could make concessions in exchange for other benefits that could be provided without a monetary exchange, as illustrated in the previous section. In every case, the client should be rigorous in establishing and adhering to the regular reviews. Without these reviews, vendor relationships can go unmonitored for long periods, and significant problems can go unnoticed and unresolved.

In addition to vendor performance reviews, the vendor manager should periodically review all vendor contracts. This ensures that all service levels promised in the contract are being enforced or at least that goodwill is being built by not enforcing an agreed-on standard. Further, a review of the contract will ensure that any changes to terms or conditions based on changing business imperatives can be managed early on. We recommend re-examining every vendor contract annually at a minimum. For vendors on which the company has significant reliance, these reviews should be done on a quarterly basis.

Often, this periodic contract review is neglected by IT departments. A Cutter Consortium survey estimates that 7 percent of IT departments never review contracts, and fewer than half review contracts at greater intervals than annually.[3] Exhibit 13.3 shows research results in this area.

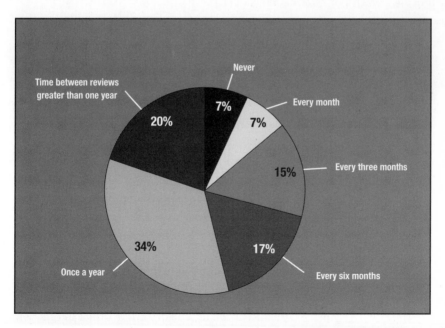

Exhibit 13.3   Contract Review Frequency in Surveyed IT Departments

In all cases, the client should ensure that it can withhold any fees (maintenance or otherwise) because of the vendor in the case of contract breaches on the part of the vendor. One of the most rapid methods for getting the attention of a vendor experiencing performance problems is to withhold approval on accounts payable.

The speed with which vendors respond from the highest levels once a steady flow of receivables dries up can be remarkable. While this approach should be a last resort, it is generally successful. When it is not successful, the IT department has at least avoided continuing to fund a vendor that will not be part of the long-term picture and has saved money to invest in a relationship with a replacement vendor.

Working with Vendors' Other Customers

One of the most important resources in managing vendors is information sharing with their other customers. There are usually well-established user groups for almost every product on the market with a reasonably sized client base. These groups typically communicate in online forums and web sites. For some of the major products, regional or national user group meetings or conferences can help facilitate communication among users. These groups provide a wealth of information, such as:

- Latest news about the vendors and their affiliated service or product provider partner networks.
- Features, functions, and enhancements planned for future patches and releases.
- Best practices for using current software versions.
- Bug fixes and workarounds for common (or obscure) problems.
- Common maintenance contract terms and SLAs.
- Useful add-ins, bolt-ons, or third-party services.
- Informal answers to common questions.
- Direct response and ideas for addressing specific problems.
- General pricing and contract terms information.
- Shared metrics for vendor performance measurement.

While most IT departments usually pay attention to the "official" vendor-sponsored special interest groups, an often-overlooked and powerful tool for influencing vendors and driving pricing discounts is informal work with other customers in the same geographic region or industry. More direct interaction with other customers can provide deeper and more candid insights than are likely to be shared in a vendor-sponsored, public forum. Coordination with other vendor customers may reveal specific pricing information, specific service level agreements or vendor metrics, legal problems or issues with the vendor, and other information useful in negotiating with and managing the vendor. The best customer partners are those using the same vendor, located in the same locale, but in a different industry. While working with other vendor customers in the same industry can provide highly valuable information on specific applications of the vendor's products or services, the competitive dynamic usually minimizes the information that each party is willing to share. The CIO may want to consider coordinating informal periodic meetings between managers and directors to get together and exchange information as a small group. The information exchanged, particularly on pricing or input to product development, can be used to win some concessions from a vendor or to significantly influence the research and development process. This is particularly true for smaller customers of a given vendor. As noted in the opening to this chapter, small customers often find it difficult to manipulate vendor agendas. By banding together with several other small customers, they multiply their leverage considerably. Small customers should take the advice of Ben Franklin in working with other small customers: "Yes, we must, indeed, all hang together, or most assuredly we shall all hang separately."[4]

Other sources of information can include analysts, consultants, publications, and even the vendor's competitors. A detailed list of these information sources is included in Chapters 7 and 12, which cover information gathering as part of the initial vendor selection or standardization process. These information sources (research analysts, Internet sites, consultants, and others) continue to be highly valuable sources of information on the vendor.

A frequently underused source of information for CIOs is technology industry analysts working in investment banks. These professionals are typically charged with having a complete understanding of how the company is expected to perform in the future. One of the most important ingredients for their research is the current opinions and experiences of customers. For this reason, analysts are usually enormously interested in talking with a vendor's customers about their experiences, and they may even collect informal surveys to quantify user opinions. These analysts can become a nerve center of information about particular vendors, providing insight into the health of the vendor, marketplace changes, and competitive outlook. In exchange for customer viewpoints and opinions, they are usually willing to share not only their objective third-party opinions concerning vendor direction and performance, but also their published periodic research reports. Further, the analysts are often willing to facilitate the introduction of the CIO to other customers for the formation of the informal information-sharing groups discussed previously.

In summary, the wide variety of information available on vendors with a minimum of research and effort should not be overlooked as a critical component of managing vendors, setting metrics, and ensuring best pricing.

Vendor Recompetes

If the vendor selection process is done correctly and the vendor relationship is properly managed as a mutually beneficial partnership, the need to recompete business should be infrequent. However, it is important to periodically retest the market for enhanced products, services, and pricing. A recompete may not result in a new vendor choice, but it can be the springboard to introducing new thinking to an existing vendor relationship or to an IT department. As a long-term client once remarked to a services provider, "We like you a lot and value the partnership; you just don't necessarily have the market cornered on good ideas." Times to consider a recompete include:

- The end of a lengthy (5+ years) contract. Products and services will have evolved considerably over the duration of a contract; retesting the market for pricing, product, and service changes is appropriate at the culmination of a long-term contract.
- Major changes in the marketplace in terms of pricing or service quality. Newer technologies or technologies in rapidly changing markets often improve in reliability and diminish in cost rapidly as the marketplace matures.
- Emergence of additional service providers offering better and/or more cost-effective products and services.
- Discontinuous changes in the technology, necessitating a new product or service.
- Any severe performance problems with the vendor resulting in damage or potential damage to the customer's business.
- Significant structural changes at the vendor or client (e.g., merger, acquisition, divestiture).
- Material financial problems at the vendor or client.
- Mandate from the IT steering committee to investigate additional vendor options.
- Overreliance on a single vendor, resulting in business continuity exposure.

When any of these events occur, a recompete should be considered, but a full vendor selection as outlined in Chapter 12 should not necessarily be completed. Exhibit 13.4 shows a decision tree for deciding whether or not to recompete. The first step should be an economic analysis to determine the expected value to be created by recompeting the contract. The benefits to be gained should include:

- The difference between the present value of all the expected expenditures from a new vendor and the present value of all the expected expenditures from the current vendor.

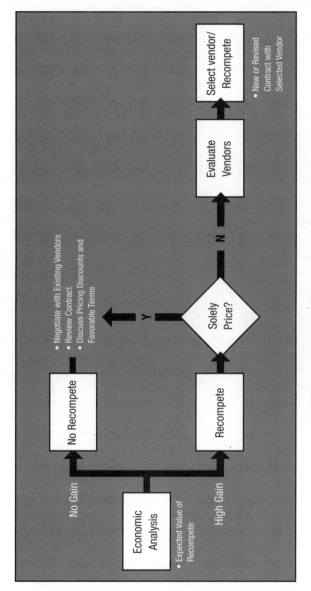

Exhibit 13.4   Vendor Recompete Decision Tree

- Other decreased internal costs (e.g., maintenance, management, training).
- Increased revenue.
- Improved control over the business (reduced risk).

In many cases, there are significant switching costs associated with changing a vendor. The costs should include all costs involved with switching between the original vendor and a new vendor. Examples of these costs should include, but are not limited to:

- Time and resources to be expended in a new vendor selection process.
- Any mandatory close-out costs dictated in the current contract.
- Initial upfront costs that must be incurred with the new vendor, such as additional hardware, software, documentation, training, and maintenance contracts.
- Internal resources lost to managing and implementing the transition.
- Any potential system downtime during the transition.
- Accelerated depreciation on assets whose lifetime is reduced by the vendor switch.
- Additional operating costs that must be incurred while learning the new system (e.g., management time, training).

Even with significant gains from switching vendors, the costs can often heavily outweigh the benefits. Vendors are very aware of these switching costs, and these costs are precisely the reason they are often able to increase prices for current customers while offering "great deals" to new customers. This switching cost only further emphasizes contractual obligations and vendor measurement issues, as discussed previously in this chapter. The CIO should understand vendor decisions that entail high switching costs (e.g., ERP systems, high-dollar hardware) and those relatively easy to switch (e.g., telecommunications services, contract staffing providers) and aggressively manage the inclusion of tight performance metrics in the contracts of the vendors with the highest switching costs.

If the economic analysis shows that the benefits still greatly outweigh the costs, a recompete should proceed to the next step. If the reason for the recompete is purely price, a simplified form of the analysis shown to the vendor usually results in a price concession. If the reason for the analysis is more than price or the current vendor will not budge on price, the recompete should proceed using the standard rigorous vendor selection process detailed in Chapter 12, which has been organized to facilitate limited-effort vendor selection processes where necessary.

The length of the contract up for recompete should be based on the potential discounts available from vendors in exchange for a guaranteed term. For technologies that are rapidly changing and are rapidly coming down the cost curve (e.g., telecommunications services), the contracts should be no longer than a year. The savings of a new contract usually more than compensate for the lost term discounts on the original contract. For vendors that are difficult or unlikely to be changed out often by the department (e.g., ERP package), longer term contracts with heavy discounting are more appropriate.

Offshoring and Outsourcing

Outsourcing and offshoring are increasingly popular options for improving service and managing costs in IT departments. Offshoring takes advantage of labor cost variances between countries to provide services by an outside firm at a lower rate. Outsourcing takes advantage of labor cost, scale economic, expertise, or other variances that produce a cost or capability advantage. Outsourcing and offshoring often get used synonymously but they are different. Offshoring is usually outsourcing; however outsourcing is not necessarily offshoring. The advantage for a large number of outsourced functions is not predicated simply on labor cost arbitrage.

All but the largest companies use an outside vendor to perform offshore work. Typical thresholds for creating a captive offshore presence are at least 300 to 500 staff.

Offshoring

IT has been a good candidate for offshoring because answered help desk calls, password resets, functioning source code, and project plans are easily transported from place to place electronically. Offshoring can be an effective solution for either repetitive tasks (such as the help desk) or large-scale projects (custom code development, ERP customization).

The economic benefit of offshoring is obvious: If the average cost per output is cheaper, the overall IT costs go down. However, there are a number of important considerations that should be factored into the decision to offshore work, including:

- *Friction:* Geographic distance, language and translation barriers, communication mishaps, and methodology differences create additional friction in accomplishing tasks offshore. The solution to this is the addition of management overhead offshore and onshore. This necessary step decreases the total value of the labor arbitrage.
- *Documentation:* Offshore projects, especially development efforts, are most effective when considerable clear requirements and process documentation is available. This usually means that smaller projects and rapid-development projects are not likely good candidates for offshore.

CIOs should work with offshore vendors to determine where the reasonable size and documentation thresholds are met.

- *Security:* Allowing third parties in foreign countries access to sensitive customer or financial data entails additional risk. A number of incidents in which customer information was compromised by an offshore outsourced service provider in the past few years has highlighted this issue. CIOs should evaluate contracts to ensure proper treatment and ownership of sensitive data, as well as assess offshore vendors' employee screening, monitoring, and controls. The IT steering committee should be informed of potential data security risks.

- *Hours:* Depending on time-zone offsets and work habits of the teams, the offshore group may not be working at the same time as the onshore IT staff. This has pros and cons. The offshore team may have completed a full day of work each morning when the IT team arrives to evaluate it. However, for rapid-response emergency items, one team or the other will need to be on the phone or working at unusual hours.

- *Access:* Offshoring is usually done with a vendor located thousands of miles away. If there are significant problems that require in-person visits, there will be considerable expense and time consumed.

- *Political environment:* Depending on the country and locale used for offshoring, there may be governmental corruption to deal with. In countries with high levels of corruption, it can be difficult to obtain permitting and licensing inside official channels. U.S. companies can face severe penalties for bribery of foreign government officials. Companies doing business in countries with high corruption also face the risk of competitive bribing resulting in compromise of information or service. Transparency International rates corruption by country via their corruption index at http://www.transparency.org.[5]

- *Legal:* Engaging in cross-country business can increase the complication and cost of contracts. Dealing with contract issues, breached agreements, or any other legal issues will have dramatically increased complexity due to unfamiliar laws, governing bodies, and legal processes. Contracts should be reviewed with legal counsel experienced in offshoring agreements with the specific country in question. In one recent case, an offshore vendor employee stole the source code under development and attempted to sell it to a competitor. The FBI agent assigned to the case said that the nondisclosure agreements in place "weren't worth the paper they were written on."[6]

- *Image:* Offshoring suffers from image issues. In a recent Opinion Research poll of 1,000 Americans, 72 percent strongly agreed that "the outsourcing of U.S. jobs is really all about corporate greed."[7] This should be part of the consideration of offshoring.

Outsourcing

Outsourcing is a good option for IT departments with insufficient scale or internal expertise in certain areas. Outside firms can provide certain services more efficiently, and with higher quality for the same or lower cost. Outsourcing firms also often conduct the work offshore, as discussed earlier, further lowering the costs.

Outsourcing is distinguished from consulting by its repetitive nature. Outsourcing engagements are characterized by long-term contracts whose pricing is fixed or non-time-and-materials fee structures. Consulting projects are one-time efforts with a specific end result.

A recent survey of over 400 companies revealed that while cost savings was the primary driver of outsourcing arrangements (65%) other factors were also at work including capacity flexibility, reliability, fixed cost reduction, operational expertise, improved support, lack of available personnel, speed to market, and improved IT performance.[8] That same study showed that 50% of respondents considered their outsourcing experience as successful, 33% neutral and 17% "disastrous."[9] Most contracts were over three years in duration (42%), with the remaining bulk one to three years (38%).[10]

The best candidate functions for outsourcing are commodity functions that are repetitive, can be measured, and have easily established labor standards. These are the functions that also see the biggest cost reduction from scale economies. The most prominent example in the IT department is the help desk, which is covered extensively in Chapter 9. Other functions that lend themselves to outsourcing include desktop support, remote office support, systems administration, patch management, purchasing, systems monitoring, and hosting. Often outsourcing will be accomplished with a mix of product and service (e.g., hosting and managed firewall) provided by a single vendor.

As can be seen, many of these activities are Operations and Infrastructure oriented, and covered in Chapter 8. These functions are often routine and are governed industry-accepted methodologies such as ITIL. This facilitates defining and managing the outsourcing agreement. The agreement should include specific, measurable metrics that are defined in advance and reported on at set periods. This ensures that all parties have set expectations properly and helps ease the burden of managing the outsourcing relationship.

Traditionally outsourcing arrangements have been through a single provider. Recent trends have seen the use of multisourcing, in which several vendors each provide a single discrete outsourced function. The benefits of avoiding single reliance and finding the best vendor for a certain function should be weighed against the increased multiple-vendor management overhead.

While outsourcing agreements generally work out to the benefit of all parties, companies should recognize that they may incur additional costs up front during the transition phase and budget accordingly. Work with the outsourcer to plan a schedule for realizing the long-term cost and service improvement benefits from outsourcing.

A final consideration when engaging in outsourcing a portion of the IT function is the effect on morale of IT staff. IT staffers who are worried about their job security are not be as productive as possible. Clear and direct communication about which functions are outsourcing candidates and how the decision is to be made will alleviate these concerns.

Managing Troubled Vendors

Because of the wide variety of vendors used by a given IT department, inevitably, one or more of the vendors will experience financial difficulties. The forward-looking CIO usually has ample warning of these troubles, particularly if he or she is participating in the informal forums and alternative information gathering discussed in this chapter. In these cases, it is crucial for the IT manager to aggressively protect the company's interests by ensuring that adequate coverage for the vendor product or service is available and that the company's financial exposure to the vendor is minimized.

For well-established, competitive vendor marketplaces, ensuring adequate coverage in the case of vendor failure should be a relatively straightforward process of assessing competitive offerings and estimating switching costs. For vendors providing highly specialized niche products or services, the IT manager may have to conduct additional research to find alternative products, approaches, or workarounds. Often, the effort of conducting this research can be shared among several customers who coordinate through the informal information-sharing groups.

The financial exposure to a vendor can come from a variety of sources. Prepaid or partially paid orders for equipment, prepaid or currently due maintenance fees, or other contractually obligated sums are common instances. We have seen many companies victimized by vendors that file bankruptcy while significant receivables have been paid by customers in advance of product delivery. Not only is delivery of the product delayed, but the monies spent to acquire the product are usually lost forever. The CIO should work with the CFO or finance department to minimize the risks of lost capital and work with the vendor to ensure that contractually obligated amounts due result in actual services received by the client. In extreme cases, the company must halt payment to the vendor and file a law suit to line-up for restitution when the vendor refuses to refund for services not performed. Many times the filing of the law suit will provide leverage—the vendor cannot usually raise money until the suit is settled, which provides motivation for the vendor to come to the negotiating table.

In one client situation, a worried CIO consulted us about the quarterly maintenance fee requested by a software vendor. While not concerned with the stability of the package, which was installed and operating properly, the director was worried that additional money invested in maintenance fees would be lost if the vendor continued to struggle. Careful research indicated that the vendor was indeed in serious trouble, and the client delayed the $100,000 maintenance payment based on various vendor contract breaches. One month later, the vendor filed Chapter 7 bankruptcy, leaving no hope of additional software development or application support. The impact of $100,000 spent for services that would never be delivered would have been devastating for the IT budget of this client.

In every case, the CIO should ensure that the IT steering committee is fully informed of the company's operational risk and financial exposure because of troubled vendors. The IT steering committee can be instrumental in helping reduce the risk and can help the director manage the advance planning and alternative brainstorming needed to minimize the potential risks.

Ethics in Purchasing and Vendor Management

Because IT purchases often involves large transactions and the vendor selection and ongoing management process involves often arbitrary-seeming judgment calls, it is critical that those involved in purchasing adhere to the highest standards of ethics. This ensures the avoidance of both impropriety and the appearance of impropriety, as well as ensuring that the organization receives the best value for its investment in IT spending.

Each IT department should establish and publish policies for transactions with outside entities. To avoid any later confusion, these policies should be acknowledged and signed by all individuals involved in the purchasing decision-making process. While each individual firm may set its own specific principles or standards, the National Association of Purchasing Management/Institute for Supply Chain Management (NAPM/ISM) has created a good baseline from which to begin (Exhibit 13.5).

An additional resource is the Illinois Institute of Technology's Center for the Study of Ethics in the Professions (CSEP), which has aggregated a tremendous number of codes of ethics—more than 850 at current count—available on its public web site (see the resources section at the end of the chapter). The CSEP library also includes guidelines and processes for establishing codes of ethics, resources links throughout the Web, and information on permissions. This searchable and comprehensive web site is the first stop

NAPM PRINCIPLES AND STANDARDS OF PURCHASING PRACTICE
1. Avoid the intent and appearance of unethical or compromising practice in relationships, actions, and communications.
2. Demonstrate loyalty, to the employer by diligently following the lawful instructions of the employer, using reasonable care and only authority granted.
3. Refrain from any private business or professional activity that would create a conflict between personal interests and the interests of the employer.
4. Refrain from soliciting or accepting money, loans, credits, or prejudicial discounts, and the acceptance of gifts, entertainment, favors, or services from present or potential suppliers which might influence, or appear to influence purchasing decisions.
5. Handle information of a confidential or proprietary nature to employers and/or suppliers with due care and proper consideration of ethical and legal ramifications and governmental regulations.
6. Promote positive supplier relationships through courtesy and impartiality in all phases of the purchasing cycle.
7. Refrain from reciprocal agreements that restrain competition.
8. Know and obey the letter and spirit of laws governing the purchasing function and remain alert to the legal ramifications of purchasing decisions.
9. Encourage that all segments of society have the opportunity to participate by demonstrating support for small, disadvantaged and minority-owned businesses.
10. Discourage purchasing's involvement in employer sponsored programs of personal purchases that are not business related.
11. Enhance the proficiency and stature of the purchasing profession by acquiring and maintaining current technical knowledge and the highest standards of ethical behavior.

Exhibit 13.5   National Association of Purchasing Management Code of Ethics (*Source:* NAPM.)

on the Internet for those interested in establishing a code of purchasing ethics or for a broader, organizationwide code of ethical behavior.

Summary

As emphasized throughout this chapter, well-executed vendor management is one of the keys to success for the CIO. Because the expense outlays are so large and the dependence on outside vendors so high, vendor management is an area that the CIO cannot afford to ignore. The most experienced CIOs find ways to share the burden of vendor management by instituting self-monitoring programs, which force vendors to report their own metrics and results and agree to be subject to periodic random audits of the scoring and performance. Further, they carefully allocate their attention in proportion to the vendor's overall importance to the business. These CIOs approach vendor relationships with a keen appreciation of the value of a partnership but also ensure that the vendors are delivering the value promised. Finally, the directors ensure that they receive a steady supply of information concerning critical vendors from objective third-party sources, including other customers and industry research analysts.

RESOURCES

Many of the resources and courses for purchasing are geared to manufacturing companies that purchase raw materials and finished goods from outside suppliers in large quantities, or for federal, state, or local governmental agencies that must adhere to strict policies in purchasing process. However, the same vendor management principles apply to the lower-volume purchasing experienced by professional services firms. Some resources are:

- *American Management Association*, http://www.amanet.org, provides seminars, best practices, and information on a wide array of management topics, including purchasing management.
- *American Purchasing Society* (APS), http://www.american-purchasing .com, is a professional association of buyers and purchasing agents. Requires membership and provides subscription to *Professional Purchasing* monthly magazine. APS confers two certifications for purchasing professionals, the Certified Purchasing Professional (CPP) and the Certified Professional Purchasing Manager (CPPM).
- *Chartered Institute of Purchasing and Supply* (CIPS), http://www .cips.org, is an international organization serving the purchasing and supply profession. CIPS is based in the United Kingdom and offers a variety of best-practice information, seminars, and other services to the purchasing manager.
- *National Association of Governmental Purchasing*, http://www.nigp .org/index.htm, provides public sector purchasing agents with training, education, research, and technical assistance.
- *National Association of Purchasing Managers*, http://www.napm.org, now renamed the Institute for Supply Chain Management, www .ism.org, offers a wide variety of resources for purchasing managers, including seminars, books, negotiation advice, an online knowledge center, and self-paced classes. The NAPM (ISM) confers two certifications

for purchasing professionals, the Accredited Purchasing Practitioner (APP) and the Certified Purchasing Manager (CPM).

- *Purchasing Management Association of Canada,* http://www.pmac.ca, is a Canadian-based organization providing resources and information for purchasing and procurement managers.

- *Templates and processes:* Many government purchasing agencies (federal, state, and municipal) post on-line their purchasing policies and processes. These can be valuable sources of information for the new purchasing manager or purchasing group. They are easily identifiable using keywords such as "purchasing," "procurement," "agency," or "office" in any Internet search engine.

- *Training and certification:* Many universities, colleges, and other educational institutions offer courses and certifications in Procurement or Purchasing management. The University of Alabama Huntsville is one, http://www.coned.uah.edu/procman.cfm, as well at the California Institute of Technology, http://www.irc.caltech.edu/courses/Strategic_Supplier_Management.htm. These are easily identifiable with a quick Internet search.

- *Vendor negotiation:* There are a variety of good books and courses on this topic. A few of our favorites include:

  Bazerman, Max H., and Margaret A. Neale. *Negotiating Rationally.* New York: Free Press, 1992.

  Cialdini, Robert B. *Influence: The Psychology of Persuasion.* New York: Quill, 1993.

  Fisher, Roger, and William Ury. *Getting to Yes.* New York: Penguin, 1991.

  Russo, J. Edward , and Paul J. H. Schoemaker, *Decision Traps* (New York: Fireside, 1989).

  Thaler, Richard H. *The Winner's Curse.* Princeton, NJ: Princeton University Press, 1994.

Notes

1. Vince Lombardi, "Vince Lombardi's Quotes about Teamwork," http://www.vincelombardi.com/quotes/teamwork.html (December 19, 2002).

2. "78% of IT Organizations Have Litigated," *The Cutter Edge* (Cutter Consortium, April 9, 2002).

3. See note 2.

4. Benjamin Franklin at the signing of the Declaration of Independence (July 4, 1776), *Bartlett's Familiar Quotations,* 17th ed. (New York: Little, Brown, 2002).

5. Wikipedia contributors, "Offshoring," *Wickipedia, The Free Encyclopedia,* http://en.wikipedia.org/wiki/offshoring#corruption.

6. Bob Brown, "FBI Special Agent Recounts Outsourcing Horror Story," *Network World* (May 16, 2006).

7. Stephanie Overby, "Outsourcing's Image Problem," *CIO Magazine* (November 1, 2005); data from Opinion Research.

8. Paul McDougall, "Outsourcing Report: Cost Conscious, but Demanding," *Information Week* (June 19, 2006), p. 49.

9. See note 8, p. 38.

10. See note 8, p. 40.

PART III

Senior Executive
IT Management

14

Business Communications

The play was a great success, but the audience was a disaster.

—Oscar Wilde[1]

They said come skating;
They said it's so nice.
They said come skating;
I'd done it twice.
They said come skating;
It sounded nice. . . .
I wore roller—
They meant ice.

—Shel Silverstein[2]

This chapter addresses the frequent failures in the day-to-day working relationship between the IT department and business users. This failure to work well together occurs at all levels of organizations—from IT management to IT staffers and from senior business managers to systems users.

Why This Topic Is Important

A key cause of IT ineffectiveness is the inability of IT personnel to work well with the business side of the organization. Sometimes IT leadership and staff fail to communicate clearly (or at all) with the business leaders and users and make little or no attempt to understand what is important to the business. The business leaders begin to ignore the IT department and make key decisions impacting IT without input from the IT department.

Failure to resolve these issues results in a variety of negative outcomes for both the IT department and the business units. The IT organization usually becomes more insular and internally focused, withdrawing even further from an effective relationship with the business. The business and other functional units, in the meantime, reduce their reliance on IT by hiring their own IT personnel and creating their own internal IT departments to compensate for the shortfall in service.

This is usually the beginning of a downward spiral in the relationship between IT and the business. IT staff complain that they are often brought in after the fact on key business decisions and are bypassed by the business on new projects, which are then later turned over to IT to support or, worse, save. Applications and hardware that do not adhere to standards or architecture cause major irritation and skyrocket support costs. The business maintains that IT neither understands nor attempts to understand business priorities and uses failings in IT to further distance itself from any attempts at reconciliation. The result is an IT department struggling to remain relevant, and business units making one-off suboptimal decisions on IT matters that do not fall within their knowledge or specialty area. This scenario is one of the main ways that companies wind up with the heterogeneous environments described in Chapter 7, and the symptoms described in Chapter 2.

Benefits of Improving the IT/Business Relationship

A solid relationship between the IT department and the rest of the corporation is critical for both IT personnel and IT unit success. It is also imperative in order to transform IT from an underused, unappreciated cost center to a proactive, highly regarded business enabler. The most notable benefits include:

- Ability to engage at the senior management level on both IT and business issues.
- Improved ability for department to endure difficult times.
- Ability to sell technology initiatives to the business.
- Greater IT employee satisfaction, alignment, and productivity.
- Increased ability to attract and retain talented IT people.
- Increased success of technology initiatives.
- Increased use of corporate IT department.

A good relationship enables most of the abilities that are required to run a successful IT department, thus, improving and managing the IT/business relationship is a necessary condition for success.

The relationship can be measured using specific factors that influence the strength/weakness of the relationship. These factors include:

- *Reliability:* The degree to which the business believes that products and services are delivered with reliability (activities and services run when they are supposed to).
- *Quality:* The degree to which the business believes that the products and services are delivered with quality (requirements met, professionally engineered, etc.).
- *Appeal:* IT personnel are generally liked from a cultural and intelligence standpoint.
- *Leadership:* Degree to which the IT leadership provides vision, business value, and builds a high-performance team.
- *Management:* Level to which people respect the IT management team and their ability to manage processes, procedures, and personnel.
- *Customer focus:* IT cares about users and results, not technology; strong commitment to deadlines.
- *Employee quality:* The level of overall talent of the IT employees, their fit culturally with the rest of the company, and communication skills and performance.
- *Financial performance:* Ability to manage budget, limit or eliminate project cost overruns, and deliver IT's portion of ROI promises.
- *Satisfaction:* The overall level of satisfaction with IT performance experienced by the business.

Without acknowledging that these factors influence the overall relationship between the IT department and the business units, it is difficult to develop specific improvement initiatives. The first step in improving the relationship is an audit of these factors. Grade each factor and set the baseline. Then develop goals to improve the weak factors. We discuss specific items that can dramatically improve the relationship by driving these factors.

How to Improve the Relationship between IT and the Business

In a March 2002 article titled "IT's Rodney Dangerfield Complex," Tischelle George highlighted the difficulties that many IT departments experience in working with the business. The author quotes the recently promoted CIO of a major corporation, who perceives as one of his biggest challenges overcoming the fact that the IT department "gets no respect" from the business. In fact, the article continues, "IT was left out of business-process or technology-related discussions."[3]

Set Goals for Each Level of the IT Organization

For each level of the IT organization, set goals and activities required for the next performance cycle. Divide the organization into levels appropriate for the unit. For example, one might segment the unit into four levels as follows: (1) the CIO; (2) the direct reports/senior managers; (3) the project managers; and, finally, (4) the analyst, operator, programmer, and DBA level. For each of the four levels, specific "business relationship" goals would be set. Taking the CIO as the first level, set goals around the factors that the CIO can affect. These include leadership, management, customer focus, and financial management. The CIO has the greatest influence in improving these factors, so specific targets should be determined. Additionally, activities that strengthen the IT/business ties should be detailed. Some examples include: The CIO will meet every two weeks with each business unit leader individually; meet every month with the IT steering committee; will tour one plant, five customers, two suppliers, and one functional department each quarter; will sponsor the IT newsletter; and so on. The CIO's direct reports have the most influence over management, quality of employees hired, and project reviews—goals around these factors are appropriate. Example goals for this group might include: executing the customer (end-user) satisfaction survey in January and June, meeting monthly with at least one business unit leader, ensuring 100 percent of project reviews are completed at project completion, and so on. Other levels in the organization should have business communication and activity goals as well.

Improve Social Interaction with the Business

One of the major causes of communication disconnects between the business and IT is a lack of personal relationships between IT team members and business users. When the personal relationships are absent, the number of interactions and flow of communication is much lower. A lack of personal relationships makes IT an easy target when business users become frustrated. This is particularly true when the IT department is geographically distant, or otherwise physically separated, from the rest of the business.

A highly effective way of promoting relationships between the parties is to facilitate informal interactions. A typical way that we have seen work includes the implementation of lunch-and-learn sessions led by IT or the business. In these informal lunches, a member of the business or IT team presents a topic of mutual interest, usually related to his or her job function.

Another very effective method for improving communication is starting an IT business "seat rotation" where IT team members, particularly those team members from the applications development and support areas, spend one to two days per week sitting with the business users. Although the team must sometimes solve a few technical issues to make this happen (e.g., acquiring laptops for team members or otherwise enabling them to work outside their normal seating area), the benefits of improved communication and personal relationships at the staff level far outweigh the costs.

The relationships must be improved at the management level as well. The CIO must work to create and improve his or her personal relationships with the senior management team in particular. The IT steering committee is the ideal vehicle for accomplishing this and provides a formal venue for frequent get-togethers with the senior management team. The CIO should seek informal get-togethers with the senior management team as well.

One of our clients had a particularly unproductive IT business relationship. We asked the CIO to set a personal quota of at least two lunches with business managers per week and one dinner per month. Gradually, over a period of a few weeks, some of the seemingly intractable tensions between IT and the business began to relax as the flow of communication and relationships improved.

The CIO should keep a mental count of the frequency of informal interactions between IT and the business, particularly for geographically distant groups of users. Time can pass more rapidly than the manager realizes, and the users can become increasingly disaffected. In one instance, our client had a manufacturing plant located several hours drive from the corporate headquarters, which housed the IT department. During a plant visit, we asked the senior managers when someone from IT last visited. The business team couldn't remember, but was certain it had been more than a year. They had hired their own IT support staff in the meantime. If necessary, a monthly calendar with joint business-IT events can facilitate the process.

Improve Verbal and Written Communication Skills

IT staffers often suffer from a reputation—deserved or not—for an inability to engage in effective verbal communication. Whether this is true or not, it is certainly an area in which almost anyone can benefit from an improvement in skills. Furthermore, a crucial part of the IT staff role is to negotiate with vendors, persuade business managers, and interview business users, all of which require better-than-average verbal communication abilities.

Richard Shell, a professor of legal studies and management at the Wharton School of the University of Pennsylvania, made a study of the communications skills of technical executives. In an article in *CIO* magazine, he provides feedback on how technical managers should approach communication with business users:

I have done work with more technically oriented people and they have this problem . . . they think the goal is to sit down and craft out the right answer. They don't give any thought to the fact that it matters who makes the proposal. Or that there's going to need to be a compromise because the other person needs to feel like he or she has had a hand in the solution. Even if the compromise is less optimal than the technically oriented person would like, it's better to have a nonoptimal decision that the other guy really implements than it is to have an optimal decision that everybody resists. This notion of being persuasive and getting a commitment—not just being right—is really hard to learn.[4]

We have observed on numerous occasions that technical professionals, while having a great appreciation for good content are often not as interested in format of presentation. While good content is critical, format and presentation are nearly as important. The best insights need to also be packaged so that the audience can comprehend them. The best CIOs understand this and combine content and format in ways that allow them to easily accomplish their agendas.

The best CIOs also spend much of their time communicating both internally and externally. IT departments are notoriously bad at written communications. While generally very structured thinkers, IT team members are often too rushed or harried to construct appropriately clear, well-written e-mails or memorandums.

One of the best examples of this phenomenon is an e-mail received from a manager in the IT department in response to a relatively straightforward request from a business unit manager. This e-mail, while a particularly egregious example, is not necessarily a major departure from the norm for e-mail communications emanating from the IT department.

In the copy of the e-mail that follows, the names have been disguised to protect the guilty, but the formatting, grammar, spelling, punctuation, and content remain unaltered.

Original Message

From: SVP>
Sent: Thursday, June 20, 2002 10:47 A.M.
To: IT manager>
Subject: Need help; please explain priorities

John—

The Accounting conversion team is telling me that you did not get the desktops in Colorado converted on Friday per your previous commitment and that some of the Utah desktops are still not converted. What happened?

Response

Yes the part that the machines did not get converted on Friday is correct. The original commitment I made was that when the machines from the 4 people in accounting where done being used on Friday or early Monday they would then bring there machines into IT and we would convert them. I spoke with Jane and they we not using it that day. On Tuesday at 12:05 I began the conversation of all 4 machine and they were all up on the new version by 12:35 P.M. (TUESDAY). I understand that there are problems with the software in Utah that Jill is aware of and Chicago was receiving the same error they were receiving in Utah. I just spoke to Jill about 10 minutes ago and she said she has a call into Jane for a different problem with a candidate that says he is assigned on a project and she removed him but it still says he is on a project (or something to that affect) as I am unfamiliar with how they use the accounting system and so forth. Since we only have 4 staff in Colorado what machines am I missing? Jane's desktop is up and running and she turned in her laptop to be rebuilt? Is that what the complaint is? As of what day is this information that you were given? I realize today is Thursday but I am unaware of any more machines that need to be converted. If there are more that need the software on them please have someone contact the IT helpdesk and let us know who's machines still need to be converted updated or installed on. We will gladly install the software as needed. I showed a few other people in IT how it installed and we are ready to install it whenever and wherever it needs to be put. Also to let you know the T1 sprint cloud in New York was upgraded on Friday from a 256k to 768k and the feedback I am getting back from Stan is the speed increase since that is great.

A relatively straightforward question was asked, and the response is literally impossible to decipher. Not only is the content impossible to understand, but also, the author has avoided even the slightest attempt at formatting or punctuation that might have at least improved the readability of the response. Sadly, this type of written communication often emanates from an IT department. Because the original request came from a member of the senior management team, we can also reasonably assume that this represents the highest standard that the respondent can achieve.

Because IT team members must often send global e-mails or e-mails to large numbers of corporate users simultaneously, they should be trained in how to construct the ideal communication. E-mail communications should provide a bottom-line message as the very first item in the communication. This ensures that those who tend to ignore communications with IT will get the most important part of the message and avoids the common complaint that IT is not clear in its communication. The e-mail should also include some additional information to avoid the common complaint that IT is too abrupt in its communications. An example of a better e-mail follows:

To: All corporate users
Subject: E-mail access will be down tomorrow, June 25, for 2 hours from 9 to 11
P.M.

Corporate users—

The e-mail system will be upgraded tomorrow, June 25, from 9 P.M. until 11 P.M. Users
will be unable to access or send e-mail during that time.

Questions may be directed to the IT team.

Why are we doing this? The e-mail system is being upgraded to a new operating
system and server. This should noticeably improve performance for all users and
provide more reliable access. The upgrade tasks will include the installation of a
new server, the archiving of old e-mail data, and the migration of e-mail accounts
to the new machines. We will be taking a full backup of the system in advance to
guard against any loss of e-mail. No special preparation on the part of the user is
required. We will send a global voice mail to all corporate users as soon as the
procedure is complete.

Finally, the IT team should not just improve the content of its communication, but also the frequency and reason. IT is often accused of not informing users of status frequently enough during emergencies or of not providing
ample warning of system maintenance or planned outages. An improved
awareness within IT of how its actions may affect business users and a commitment to communicate those actions clearly, in advance where possible,
will vastly improve the IT-business relationship.

The IT team should also work to determine the best medium—verbal or
written—for a given communication. The choice of channel can dramatically
affect how well the communication is received. "Written communications are
lousy at changing people's minds," says Steven Kerr, a vice president at General Electric. "Writing is such a seductive medium . . . it's cheap, you can get
the message to everyone at the same time, and you go home thinking you've
done your job. But you have no way of knowing whether your audience gets it
until it's too late."[5]

The IT team should pre-communicate sensitive issues or items requiring
persuasion verbally and in person. Kerr continues, "[In person] you can immediately gauge whether your message is confusing people or causing more
controversy than you expected because you can see their faces as they are receiving your message." Written communications documenting the previous
meetings can then follow.[6]

Hold the Business Units Accountable

As counterintuitive as it might seem, holding the business unit personnel
accountable for their responsibilities, both on projects and in relationship
building with IT personnel, will actually improve and strengthen the IT-

business relationship and respect for IT. Clear responsibilities for business unit personnel should be detailed in project charters and plans. Business unit employees must be held accountable for the activities and deliverables they are responsible for. In many cases, IT cannot get the help from a business unit it needs to complete a project. Yet, when the project deadline slips, the failure is typically blamed on the IT project team.

Since business unit personnel don't report to the CIO, grievance and issues with business personnel typically follow the appropriate chain of command. Ultimately, the CIO can discuss problems with the head of the business unit in extreme cases. Regardless of the discussion, it is important for IT to let the business unit know when they are failing to provide the necessary resources. These discussions should be documented and discussed in front of the IT steering committee. Projects with insufficient business unit resources should either be postponed or re-prioritized in the scheme of activities the business unit is involved in, so business unit personnel can reprioritize their time to the necessary level and correct projects. In the case of performance problems with a business unit resource, that resource should be replaced as soon as possible to eliminate project risk.

Ultimately, most people like to be held accountable for their commitments. It reinforces the fact that their work is important and valued. In the long run, holding business unit resources accountable will enable IT to successfully complete more projects in less time. Ultimately, the business unit will be pleased with the quality, rigor, and timeliness of projects executed under this management philosophy. IT customer satisfaction levels and respect will increase. From time to time, the approach causes discomfort and conflict, but in the long run, it ensures the success of the relationship.

Build Communication and Relationship Attributes into Personnel Reviews

What gets measured gets managed as the popular saying goes. This is true of relationship building and communication. The personnel review forms for each level of the IT organization should include a section for assessing both relationship building with the business as well as the communication (written and verbal) skills of the individual. First, this has the benefit of assessing individual team members on a very important success criteria. Second, it reaffirms the importance in the mind of the individual employee that those are two skills necessary for excellent performance in their job. Further, if those two attributes are missing from review forms, it has the double negative effect of reinforcing their unimportance.

Recruit Staff from the Business Side

One way to cross fertilize IT and business units is to hire business unit staff for appropriate IT roles. This is a double win for the IT department. First, they get a known quantity based on prior working relationships. Second, they get a person who has already built strong relationships in the business unit and can use those to further the mission of the IT department. Before looking for outside candidates, attempt to "recruit" star performers from the business units when there is skill fit. The most likely position to be filled by a business unit employee is the business analyst role, which can typically be filled by business unit analysts and super users. Additionally, administrative assistants, testers, functional experts (e.g., accounting), and managers are good positions to fill via business unit employees. Obviously, IT shouldn't "steal" employees from business units, so clear and proper communication and reciprocal agreements with business unit leaders are required.

Promote IT

Promoting the accomplishments, objectives, and priorities of the IT department is critical to improving communication among the various stakeholders in the company. Do not assume that everyone in the company knows the IT department's priorities or its promised service levels and performance against those. Most corporate employees outside IT probably don't even know what service levels mean or the rationale for setting them.

Communicate to the business via multiple methods including marketing material, e-mail, newsletters, and the intranet. These should be targeted to the distinct "customers" of the IT department. First, define the customers, then determine effective mediums for communicating to them and, finally, execute and deliver appropriate content using the determined mediums. Many IT departments we work with publish newsletters to the entire company. The most common mistake is to make the newsletters technology focused and not customer or business focused. Explain how IT is helping the company accomplish its goals (e.g., building revenue or reducing costs). Report on the performance of IT and its track record of delivering business-critical projects and SLAs. Make sure to periodically explain the rationale for the SLA metrics.

Communicating mandates and priorities determined by the IT steering committee is also important. Employees may not understand why the IT department is implementing a financial accounting software package instead of a warehouse management system, for example. Disgruntled workers on the warehouse floor might be saying, "Why do they keep tinkering with the accounting software when we can't even ship out multiple orders in one shipment. It makes no sense." Reporting in a newsletter that the corporate strategy entails tightening up financial accounting processes and thus IT is implementing new account software can bridge the unknown and raise the perception of IT accomplishments. Finally, relentlessly self-promote IT accomplishments like third-party industry awards received by the department. These will go a long way in positively shaping outside perception.

Build Online Communication Mechanisms

A corporate intranet is a great medium to both deliver news and provide service to internal customers. IT can be the lead department if the company does not already have an intranet. Building an IT page with features such as news, announcements, personnel directory, project statuses, and team work spaces can serve as both a communication and a productivity enhancement. One goal of the CIO is to make doing business with the IT department as easy and simple as possible. Developing a one-stop location to request office moves, phone extension changes, service requests, new employee notifications, project request forms, methodologies, online training, and so on will greatly help the effort, drive customer satisfaction, and improve IT's relationship with the business.

Make the Changes Permanent

It can be difficult to change the communication skills of the IT department and even harder to begin to build personal relationships where none previously existed. The best way to ensure that the IT team members adopt an open, communicative approach with the business is for the CIO to lead by example. An CIO whose verbal and written communications are clear and concise and who maintains close professional and personal relationships with corporate managers outside the IT department serves as a compelling example to his or her team.

The CIO should also implement formal and informal nontechnical training and development programs that help the staff learn and practice the requisite communications skills.

Informal methods, such as books and self-study courses in communication, are an easily executed approach. More formal training can be provided by a wide variety of vendors, such as noncredit courses at local colleges. Further, the CIO should encourage the team's participation in outside, nontechnical speaking groups, such as Toastmasters.

Achieving major cultural change in the IT department can be challenging. To encourage compliance, as well as to send a clear signal to the organization that these are important issues, the CIO should make improving verbal and written communications an integral part of the staff appraisal process. Excellent communications skills should be a prerequisite for promotion within the department.

NOTES

1. Oscar Wilde, "Humorous Quotes of Oscar Wilde," http://www .workinghumor .com/quotes/oscar_wilde.shtml (December 20, 2002).
2. Shel Silverstein, "Come Skating," *Light in the Attic* (New York: Harper & Row, 1981).

3. "IT's Rodney Dangerfield Complex," *Information Week* (March 28, 2002). All Rights Reserved. Reprinted with permission.

4. Danielle Dunne, "Q&A with Richard Shell, How to Communicate What's on Your Mind," *CIO* magazine (March 1, 2002). Copyright © 2002 CXO Media, Inc. Reprinted with permission.

5. Christopher Koch, "The Way You Say It," *CIO* magazine (November 15, 1996). Copyright © 2002 CXO Media, Inc. Reprinted with permission.

6. See note 5.

15

IT Budgeting and Cost Management

Economy does not lie in sparing money, but in spending it wisely.
> —Thomas Henry Huxley (1825–1895), British biologist and educator[1]

I will veto again and again until spending is brought under control.
> —Ronald Reagan, 40th U.S. President, on vetoing a bill that would have extended $2 billion in federal loan guarantees to farmers.[2]

This chapter presents a practical overview of IT budgeting and cost containment practices for the CIO. In creating the department budget, the CIO must analyze a large number of variables and balance multiple competing priorities, while devising the most cost-effective approach for delivering mission critical services. Because of the impact the budget has on the IT manager's ability to run an effective department, budget creation is one of the most important jobs an IT manager has.

The chapter is organized in four key sections:

1. *Budget components:* Key components of the IT budget and the typical ratios of spending in each component.
2. *Budget process:* Two processes for completing the annual budgets.
3. *IT cost drivers:* An overview of key cost drivers in the budget and strategies for reducing costs.
4. *Additional IT budget considerations:* Managing capital expenditures, cost audit practices, contingencies planning, managing the budget, chargeback mechanisms, lease/buy decisions, and handling out-of-budget business unit requests.

The first section describes key components of the IT budget, such as software, hardware, labor, and what ratios between the components the CIO

493

should expect to see. The process section presents two methods for creating the budget and compares their merits. The cost drivers section covers key items that drive IT costs that affect the year-to-year change in the operating and capital budgets. Next, the chapter presents a number of strategies for minimizing IT costs, especially infrastructure and capital expenditures. Finally, the chapter presents a number of key management considerations for the IT manager to contemplate, such as lease versus buy decisions, audits, chargeback mechanisms, and so on.

Why This Topic Is Important

At a basic level, the CIO is judged on the department's output versus operating and capital input required. The lower the capital input required for the same high output, the better the ratio, and the actual effectiveness of the IT manager is judged to have increased. Effective management of capital is of prime concern to both senior executives and the IT manager; thus, it is a topic of high importance.

Successful management of the IT department depends on the CIO's ability to operate a fiscally sound unit. It also entails the CIO making good decisions about spending priorities and ensuring that these spending priorities are aligned with the direction of the business. A good CIO also ensures that the bulk of discretionary spending is focused on fulfilling the demands of business units and in support of projects and initiatives focused on revenue-generating activities.

CIOs may not have formal training or education in the business and budget management processes, and thus learn via on-the-job training. This makes the responsibility a challenge, especially in difficult economic environments or when the company is in cost-cutting mode.

Compounding the issue, CIOs face unabated requests for technology, a rapidly shifting technology environment, and constantly changing vendor landscape, which all combine to confuse the IT economic analysis and spending decisions.

Chapter 3 addresses how to develop a benchmark range for IT spending. The CIO should use this as a general guide to double-check the IT budget.

A failed budget process, budget decisions, or poor management of fiscal responsibilities during the year, resulting in high budget variances has serious implications for the CIO's career. The corporate senior management team, CEO, CFO, lenders, and shareholders expect companies to plan well and accomplish their tasks within the plan. Because the company projected income, cash flow requirements, and capital requirements are based on budgets, the need for precise budget forecasting and aggressive ongoing management of the budget is critical. Going back to the CFO to ask for an additional unplanned budget to complete an ERP implementation when it wasn't in the original plan is often a career-ending move. The IT department is not in a position to ask to be trusted to wisely spend additional scarce capital when the original budgeted amounts have been poorly forecast and mismanaged. When the amount of budget or capital expense variance begins to attract the attention of shareholders or lenders, the IT department should prepare for unpleasant scrutiny.

Introduction to the Budgeting Process

For an IT manager, particularly the newly promoted manager, the budgeting process can be a harrowing experience. IT managers are expected to forecast events, projects, and emergencies up to 12 months in advance, often with minimal guidance from the business about priorities or initiatives impacting the IT budget.

This chapter provides guidance for the IT manager to help with successfully navigating the IT budgeting process. We introduce key drivers of cost in an IT department, such as required service levels, booked projects, hiring/attrition targets, equipment turnover, as well as expected budget components such as people, hardware, software, and outside services. The chapter also outlines ways to work with the business in creating the budget to avoid surprises and budget overruns during the year.

The Corporate Budgeting Process

Budgets are created to promote fiscal management and generate clarity around expected spending so that financial targets can be communicated to shareholders, lenders, and other stakeholders. The budget is part of the annual business planning cycle. A corporate budget, produced by the CFO, is a projection of the organization's income statement for the next fiscal year. The IT budget is a subset of the overall corporate budget, and the CFO and other officers are relying on the CIO to contribute his or her part. The IT budget includes estimates of operating and capital expenditures for IT. Other information is frequently included as part of the budget, such as key assumptions (e.g., no major acquisitions, business volume remains the same, headcount growth or decline).

Corporate and department budgets are necessary for a variety of reasons:

- Budgets provide the overall company and each manager of a department, function, or business unit with a target and a basis for decision making on competing spending demands. The alternative is fiscal anarchy.
- Budgets provide control over expenses during the course of the year. Management compares actual results with budgeted forecasts and then accounts for any significant variances. Large budget variances may indicate the presence of problems in the operations or with management,

or simply that the assumptions made in creating the budgets have changed. In any case, budget variances are cause for investigation.

- Budgets provide contingency plans for potential problems that may develop during the budget year.
- The budget process requires coordination throughout the organization. Each department or unit in the organization is responsible for preparing its part of the budget, which is then coordinated with the overall company budget. The units must also coordinate in cases where projects or initiatives they have planned will affect the budget in other areas.
- Responsibility is assigned to management in each organizational unit. Management is responsible for the development of the budget and its department's subsequent performance against its budget.
- Budgeting is an integral part of the planning process. Successful companies plan for their futures through the discipline of preparing an annual business plan, stipulating their financial and qualitative goals and strategies. The budget is an integral part of that plan.
- Budgeting is used by the corporate finance and senior management to put together a companywide forecast:
  —To communicate to investors.
  —To understand how much cash/capital the company needs over the period.
  —To manage expenses in support of a given revenue target that is committed to by the sales groups.

The corporate office uses the budget to create the corporate pro-forma income statement for the next fiscal year and to project cash flow. Separate from the budget for operating expenses is the capital expenditure budget that contains expenditures for fixed assets or projects whose costs will be depreciated over time. In sum, many corporate decisions and planning are based on projections in a budget. Further, the compensation of the senior management team, as well as business unit and functional managers, is often tied to budget performance. Budgeting is, therefore, a serious topic even in small companies.

Understanding the Difference between Enterprise IT Spending and the IT Department Budget

Enterprise IT spending includes:

- *Operational expenses:* Amounts spent on day-to-day IT operations within any corporate budget.
- *Capital expenses:* Costs for acquisition of new fixed assets and long-term projects.

- *IT services and outsourcing:* Expenses for external technology services (IT consulting, research services, hosting, etc.).
- *R&D:* Technology-creation functions (new product incubation, experimentation).
- *New products and technology:* Post-R&D costs for the implementation of new products and technology.
- *Salaries and benefits:* For IT staff.
- *Applications:* Cost of implementing and enhancing application systems that support existing business systems.
- *Maintenance and administration:* Cost of IT staff functions plus baseline costs of running and maintaining systems.

By contrast, the IT department operational budget includes:

- IT operational expenses *including* depreciation that falls within the IT budget. It does not include IT spending funded by the other business units (e.g., the sales team hires a Visual Basic and Access database programmer to develop a customer database application to track sales leads).
- Implementation costs for new applications and technology (as long as they are being implemented by the IT department).
- IT department expenses (e.g., personnel salaries and benefits, packaged software, outside services).
- Application support such as the cost of enhancing application systems and supporting them.
- Maintenance and administration costs of IT staff functions plus baseline costs of running and maintaining infrastructure systems.

The IT department capital expenditure budget (subject to the rules and regulations set forth by the accounting department) includes:

- R&D costs.
- Application software development and purchases of large-scale packaged software.
- Costs related to projects whose benefits will be realized over a long period of time.
- Hardware purchases.

The main difference between enterprise IT spending and the IT budget is total enterprise IT spending comprises all IT spending in the company whether managed or the responsibility of the IT department, and the IT budget comprises only the operational and capital budgets managed directly by the CIO.

Key Components of the IT Budget

The IT budget is composed of six key components, as outlined in Exhibit 15.1. The following sections describe each component.

Hardware

Purchases of computers and systems hardware are generally considered a capital expenditure (cap-ex) and affect the cap-ex budget. These assets are typically depreciated over three to five years, depending on the accounting principles and procedures adopted by the finance and accounting department allowing the appropriate portion of the cost of the item to be part of the subsequent annual operating expenses. In some cases, minor hardware purchases will not be capitalized. Assets with short life spans or low costs may not be eligible for capitalization, or may not be worth the effort to cap-

BUDGET COMPONENT	DESCRIPTION
Hardware	• Category includes all noncapital spending on hardware. • Includes depreciation of hardware capital assets. • Examples: Cables, peripherals, network cards.
Software	• Category includes all noncapital spending on software. • Includes depreciation of software capital assets. • Examples: Utility software, off-the-shelf packaged application software for one-off use.
Labor (internal personnel)	• Includes salaries and benefits of all IT department personnel not included in capital budget (e.g., capitalized software development efforts).
External service providers	• Includes all costs for outside service providers. • Examples: Consulting fees, security audit fees, contractors.
Data and communications	• Includes cost for network infrastructure services, WAN connections, LAN management, T-1 access, MPLS connections, cell phones, and pagers for IT staff, and so on. • Depending on company, this may or may not include the cost of voice communications.
Other	• All other miscellaneous spending is included in this category. • Examples: Training, recruiting fees, legal services, corporate allocations for space, and so on.

Exhibit 15.1   IT Budget Components

italize. A discussion with the company CFO can provide instructions for capital expenditures and the associated depreciation schedule to use.

The operational budget includes depreciation expense for prior hardware purchases in previous years. The expense line item for depreciation of hardware is calculated by the accounting department based on actual prior years' spending on capital assets. This will be a nonnegotiable amount, as the actual decisions that impact the depreciation expense will have been made in previous years. In some cases, accounting rules may accelerate the depreciation of an asset, or extend it, depending on new knowledge of the asset's likely life span. An important calculation to be made when assessing project costs is accelerated depreciation by obsoleting current systems or hardware because of implementation of the new project. Failing to perform this analysis can result in a "surprise" depreciation amount on the IT budget.

Items that go on the hardware expense budget include hardware upgrades, repairs and maintenance, short-life equipment, lease/rental expenses, and miscellaneous peripherals when not packaged with a computer system (e.g., one-off purchase of mouse, keyboards, disk drives, and other small hardware items).

Software

Investments in significant software development and applications packages go on the cap-ex budget and depreciate over three to five years, depending on the accounting principles and procedures adopted by the finance and accounting department. As noted earlier, the CFO can provide specific company policies.

The operational budget includes depreciation expense for previously capitalized software. The expense line item for depreciation of software is calculated by the accounting department based on actual prior years' spending on capital software assets.

Items that go on the expense budget include new software, such as utilities (e.g., backup utility), noncapitalized off-the-shelf packaged applications (e.g., development tools), software upgrades, software maintenance and support fees, noncapitalized upgrades to new versions of software, and one-year license renewal fees.

Labor

All internal personnel costs are part of this category. Examples of these costs are salaries, benefits (e.g., health, vacation), bonuses, and overtime. Some companies include recruiting and training costs in this category, while some put those costs into the "other" category.

External Service Providers

This category includes all costs for outside consultants and contractors. Their services are typically billed on a time-and-materials basis; therefore, when the invoice is received, the expense is allocated to this category. There may be some cases where outside consulting company fees can be capitalized as part of a large project (e.g., ERP system implementation); the accounting department can provide specific circumstances and company policies.

Other services such as backup and recovery, off-site storage, and shredding and disposal services from third parties will also be included here.

Data Communications

The data communications category includes costs for items such as:

- Dial-up lines.
- Leased data lines.
- ISP/WAN services.
- Wide area network.
- Remote dial-in support.

Generally, this category does not include voice communications.

Other

This category is the catch-all for expenses that do not fit in the previous categories. These expenses include items such as:

- Travel and entertainment.
- Supplies.
- Physical plant (data center, furniture).
- Legal fees.
- Allocations for other corporate overhead expenses, such as rent, utilities, and corporate functional budgets. These are usually outside the control of the CIO and are therefore amounts provided from the finance department that will be included in the IT budget.

The template the IT manager receives from the finance department contains a multitude of line items, which may not be bucketed into these components. However, it is useful to create a summary sheet and map the line items back to these component categories. This facilitates comparison of spending to industry and peer groups, which in turn helps identify any budget components that require further investigation.

Estimating Hardware Requirements

As part of the budgeting process, the IT manager will be asked to estimate hardware purchasing requirements for the next fiscal year. These estimates should include servers, desktops, laptops, and peripherals (e.g., printers). This area is often over- or underbudgeted because of poor planning and assumptions.

One of our clients had acquired a new subsidiary. Six months after the transaction closed, the CIO of the subsidiary submitted a cap-ex form for 300 new desktop computers and application software for nearly $500,000. The CFO of the acquirer was stunned to receive the capital expenditure request for 300 computers. During the purchase due-diligence process, he had assumed that the investment would be over 18 months away and, furthermore, could be phased in over time. The CFO discovered that the existing computers had insufficient processing power (they were about five years old at the time). Additionally, the subsidiary was out of compliance on software licenses and thus had to purchase a significant number of desktop operating system licenses increasing the price tag on each computer additionally. Clearly, this outcome was unpleasant for everyone involved (save the hardware vendor), and could have been avoided by better capital expenditure planning (and due diligence on the IT platform).

A recommended approach to estimating hardware requirements to minimize the potential of surprises follows:

1. Review the inventory of total assets deployed today. Most automated help desk packages will maintain a list of all deployed desktop assets, which are the hardest to inventory (corporate server assets are easier to locate and inventory). If a good inventory listing is not available, a variety of utilities can be used to prowl the network and automatically inventory hardware assets. If the company has an effective fixed asset system, or a centralized procurement department, then the finance or purchasing departments may be able to provide an inventory of all assets. In any case, the work should concentrate on desktops, printers, and laptops, as they will comprise the bulk of the assets.

2. Determine information about the current inventory:
   - How old are the assets?
   - Are the assets purchased or leased?
   - If leased, obtain the lease information—for example, payments and lease end date, terms, and conditions for return.
   - Where is the equipment located?
   - Who is using the equipment?

3. Determine the hardware refresh life cycle. Develop a standard time frame to keep IT assets (especially desktops/laptops) to be proactive

about replacing them. If an anticipated cycle is not adopted, the computer assets will begin to deteriorate as they age (either physically breaking down, or logically by becoming underpowered for running new applications). Support costs increase dramatically as the age of the assets increases. Depending on the business and IT strategy, a few rules of thumb may apply here:

- *Minimize IT/utility strategy:* If the company is in cash conservation mode, make the refresh cycle as long as possible. Adopting a five-year replacement cycle is the outer limit of reasonable life expectation of a desktop, laptop, or printer.

- *Late adopter/low calculation intensive environment:* Companies that have low-processing requirements and a late adopter philosophy should adopt a three-to-five-year replacement cycle if sufficient.

- *Average IT spender with significant numbers of knowledge workers:* Adopt a three-year replacement cycle.

- *Professional services with professionals that rely on laptops:* Adopt a two-year or greater replacement cycle.

4. Obtain the corporate assumptions on net employee growth or decline for the coming year. The employee growth assumptions are available from the finance department and should be an outcome of the other departments' budgeting process. Use this number to determine the net addition or subtraction of employees who require computers and the timing of those additions or subtractions.

5. Calculate equipment turnover:

- Calculate the number of new computers for net employee growth. For example, if the employment base (for employees who need computers) grows by 50 headcount next year, 50 new computers are needed to support that growth. Conversely, if the employee base is expected to decline, no net new PCs are needed for new employees.

- Calculate the number of computers that need to be refreshed in the coming fiscal year. Take the current age of computers and map that to the adopted refresh cycle. For example, if adopted refresh cycle is three years, any computer that will be over three years old next year should be replaced. This should also account for net employee declines. If the company employment base is expected to decline next year, the department may not need to refresh any computers. For example, if the calculation determines that 25 desktops should be retired and purchased next year, but the corporation is expecting a net decline of employment by 25, existing computers can be retired and there is no need to repurchase.

- While desktops, laptops, and printers make up the bulk of the hardware to be purchased, the team should also estimate the end-of-life on servers, workgroup printers, network hardware, and all other centrally maintained equipment. This exercise should be relatively easy compared to the desktop equipment analysis.

- The numbers obtained in this step are used for the hardware capital budget. Take the computer count and calculate the replacement cost. The total is used for the capital budget.

6. Review maintenance contracts as a final step.

- Catalog hardware maintenance contracts.
- How much is maintenance spending, for what assets? Is the asset still being used?
- Can any of the maintenance contracts be eliminated or renegotiated?
- What is the risk of self-insuring and not renewing the maintenance contract? Provide senior management with options on self-insuring and avoiding the maintenance contract expenditure.

These steps should also be taken for all hardware that can be identified by the team as a result of support records, fixed asset systems, purchasing records, and network scans, which combine to build a reasonably accurate picture of the total corporate hardware in place.

Estimating Software Requirements

As part of the budgeting process, the IT manager will be asked to estimate software purchasing requirements for the next fiscal year. These estimates should include packaged applications, software development projects, utility software, business application software licenses, and miscellaneous software used by the business.

There are two difficult areas to analyze in the software budgeting process. The first is software licensing. Depending on how computers are purchased (with or without operating system licenses and office productivity software), the company may or may not need to purchase software licenses for major operating systems and applications during the coming year. However, if IT does not maintain good control over business unit software usage, they will find tens, if not hundreds, of users who are running non-licensed software. Loading a single copy of an application on multiple computers is, unfortunately, a common corporate practice. In recent years, vendors have become more aggressive in policing software license usage by corporations. We recommend staying current with software license purchases and using automated desktop scanning applications to periodically inventory applications that business users are loading on their computers.

The other difficult area to estimate is software development and system implementation work effort. The CIO of one of our clients, a mid-sized manufacturing company, submitted a budget request of $500,000 to develop a new order entry application. Three months later, the CIO submitted a second unexpected request for another $500,000 to complete the same application. Although the project was eventually completed, clearly the misestimation of the costs caused enormous budget chaos in the short term. Unfortunately, this is a fairly common occurrence.

A recommended approach to estimating software requirements to minimize the potential of surprises follows:

- Look at total software licenses deployed today for company standard software.
  - Get accurate number of current licenses by software product.
  - Get accurate number of current users.
  - Use the recommendations under the Hardware section to determine the number of new employees and new software licenses that should be purchased.
- Answer these questions about software upgrading:
  - What software applications may need to be upgraded during the next year?
  - What are the business benefits of upgrading (e.g., lowers support costs, eliminates a project, new functionality that will lower processing costs, new revenue opportunities)?
  - What are the consequences of not upgrading (e.g., will the vendor still provide emergency support, or will the IT team provide it)?
  - What is the cost to upgrade?
  - What will the cost be next year if the upgrade is deferred (i.e., does the cost change next year; will it be more expensive next year)?
  - Can we lower the cost of the upgrade by buying from a new vendor or negotiating the current discount?
- Review the top software maintenance contracts:
  - Catalog software maintenance contracts—especially the top two or three.
  - How much is software maintenance costing?
  - What software is covered?
  - When is the renewal date?
  - Can any contracts be eliminated or renegotiated?
  - What is the risk of self-insuring and not renewing the maintenance contract? Give senior management and the IT steering committee options on self-insuring.

Finally, determine if business unit software requests will be charged directly to the unit's budget or hit the IT department's budget. If they will be on the IT department P&L, schedule specific discussions to forecast business unit software requirements and review the current approved projects. Make sure the software requirements and capital requests are added to the capital budget. If the initiatives are approved already, the finance department may have included them in the cap-ex budget forecast. Chapters 12 and 17 have additional information on estimating project costs and project impacts on IT budgets.

Estimating Internal and External Labor Costs

To estimate labor requirements, start with a baseline of whom it will take to run the basic infrastructure, operations, systems administration, and help desk. This becomes the *baseline* labor.

To analyze your current baseline labor critically, answer the following questions:

- Can the department be run at the same service levels with less labor?
- Are there any staff redundancies?
- What will change during the year that might affect the current staff configuration?
  —Changes to operating environment (e.g., new operating system).
  —Growth or decline in employees in the company. Set a support ratio that the business is comfortable with, and use this metric against employee headcount to determine needs. For example, a low-cost, minimal service level might be one IT support person per 250 employees. Average would be one IT support staff per 120 employees. High cost, high service would be one IT support staff per 75 employees. What is the difference in service and cost? Present these options to senior management.
- After a support ratio is set, use employee headcount to determine IT staffing requirements for the next year. The same exercise can be done for application support areas.

Estimating development and project resources is driven by project backlog. This is covered in depth in Chapter 17. Complete the steps in Chapter 17 to understand the resource requirements from your projects. Chapter 11 contains details on assessing staffing resource needs through the completion of a swap analysis. These resources can then either be transcribed to the IT budget for software if expensed or to the capital budget if the project is to be capitalized.

Typical Breakout of Spending

After the first draft budget is complete, the CIO can use some benchmarks to understand if the spending matches industry practices. Exhibits 15.2 and 15.3 list sample spending ratios by category and by industry that are useful for guidance. There may be valid reasons that anticipated spending by category does not match the industry averages. However, compare and then

CATEGORY	TYPICAL DISTRIBUTION OF EXPENSE (%)
Hardware	13
Software	15
Internal personnel	40
External services providers	19
Data communications	7
Other	6
IS budget	100

Note: For voice communication, add 10 percent to 15 percent to the IS budget.

Exhibit 15.2   Typical IS Budget Distribution

analyze any differences to make sure any obvious errors in the budgeting process have been avoided, and that major variances to industry standards can be explained.

Assumptions

Assumptions are necessary to detail the rationale behind a particular line item estimation in the budget. For example, if the IT department assumes

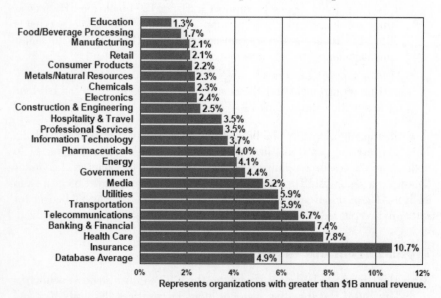

Represents organizations with greater than $1B annual revenue.

Exhibit 15.3   IT Employees in Organization as a Percent of Total Employee Population
(*Source:* Howard Rubin, Jed Rubin, "Worldwide IT Benchmark Service Trends and Findings for 2006," Gartner, Inc. www.gartner.com/teleconferences/attributes/attr_140228 _115.pdf. The data contained in this exhibit may not represent Gartner's current view.)

that company staff growth will result in a net addition of 250 employees in the coming year, it should be documented so that the CFO, controller, and IT steering committee understand the assumption. In many cases, the senior management team can help validate (or invalidate) the assumptions and refine the resulting budgets. The benefits of documenting assumptions include:

- Provides open disclosure and facilitates refinement of the budget.
- Sets expectations and communicates the basis for projections.
- Forms the basis of any explanations for variances later in the fiscal year.

If, during the year, support costs are not tracking to the budget, one issue could be that the underlying assumptions were incorrect, and the resulting discrepancies in the budget can be explained. If the assumptions are not documented, the CIO may be over budget and have trouble explaining the variance.

How to Budget

The Basics

To prepare for budgeting, collect in advance the following types of information to help streamline and improve accuracy of the budget:

- Actual operating, capital, and budget variance figures from the previous year.
- Initial statistics on employment growth or decline at the company.
- Initial statistics on profit and sales expectations for the company for the coming fiscal year.
- Any changes to company operating policies.
- Any changes to major applications in the past 12 months affecting support or development.
- Current approved IT project inventory and prioritization.
- Estimation of current peer spending (see Chapter 3).
- Payroll statistics for the IT department.

Following is an overview of the process:

- The budgeting effort is typically kicked off by the finance department in preparation for the next fiscal year.
- Most often the IT manager will be given the following information to get started:

—Detailed accounting reports of the prior 12-month IT spending.

—Template spreadsheet with budget categories already included and calculation complete.

—Estimation of overhead line items to be allocated to the IT department.

- Complete a first draft—there are two different approaches to building the budget:

—Zero-based budgeting (recommended, but more difficult).

—Run-rate budgeting.

These methods are outlined later in this chapter. The first draft should incorporate all known information on service level agreements and anticipated projects (see Chapters 9 and 17):

- Review draft with CFO or other direct reporting relationship.
- Produce and present second draft.
- Incorporate input and produce final draft.
- Final draft goes through approval with IT steering committee and senior management.
- Once approved, final draft is sent to the accounting department as the "final new fiscal year" budget for IT.
- All actions for the subsequent 12 months will be judged against this final budget.
- At times there will be a quarterly and/or mid-year budget review sessions to adjust the budget to account for new known information.

Timing

The budget cycle usually kicks off between September and November, or one to four months before the end of the company fiscal year. The budget, in most cases, needs to be finalized in the last month of the fiscal year.

Budget Creation Methods

ZERO-BASED BUDGETING. Zero-based budgeting is the method used to prepare a budget that starts with a "clean sheet" and builds from the ground up based on assumptions, required service levels, and projects. In a zero-based budget, each activity or line item to be funded must be justified each year on the current merits for spending money on it. This method, while time consuming, ensures that the annual budgets do not carry forward any poor assumptions from the previous budget, and that the underlying assumptions are reconsidered each year. Zero-based budgeting works particularly well in companies that are experiencing rapid rates of change (business growth, major initiatives, acquisitions or divestitures). The steps in zero-based budgeting are:

1. Determine components of the budget that are fixed (e.g., facilities, infrastructure, application maintenance, data communications) and those that are variable (e.g., hardware purchases, staff labor, training, software upgrades, enhancements).

2. Justify each fixed expense in the department. Is the expense reasonable given current market conditions? Can, and should, the expense be altered? Document assumptions and any actions that would contribute to cost reduction. Because these are fixed expenses, some creativity is necessary. For example, if IT leases its own office space, can the director go back to the realtor and negotiate a longer lease for a discount today? Does the expense change for any reason (step-up in vendor contract, annual increase in rate in contract, automatic fees tied to maintenance contracts)?

3. Total all fixed items. This total of fixed costs is called the *baseline* budget.

4. Document any potential cost reductions, and the associated reduction in service levels or project capabilities, and keep for presentation during the final budget review with the IT steering committee.

5. Build up the budget for variable cost line items (e.g., outside contractors, new software licenses) by performing an item-by-item analysis. Understand the key drivers of cost in the variability (e.g., number of projects, employees, and transactions). Make assumptions for each line item and calculate the variable budget. Once again, document assumptions, as you will use them in the budget presentation and need them to answer budget questions.

6. Clean up and prepare first draft.

RUN-RATE BUDGETING. Run-rate budgeting is used to prepare a budget based on the current year and current time frame expenditures. For example, if rent is currently $25,000 per month, it is likely to run $25,000 next month. Run-rate budgeting starts from the current average monthly rate of expenditure (the run rate) and is then refined from that baseline based on new assumptions (e.g., new project assumptions, new usage assumptions, service level changes). Each budget line item starts at its current level of spending and is adjusted upward or downward based on new or current information. Run-rate budgeting can be completed relatively rapidly, because the list of current line items is readily available. The process also incorporates the best thinking on what the budget will be, as it is based on actual current amounts. Run-rate budgeting works best in environments where there is relatively little business change expected year to year.

Steps for run-rate budgeting:

1. Populate budget template with current run-rate spending or the last 12-month actual spending. Accounting can provide this information.
2. Review each line item in the budget and document assumptions for why the spending should be at or near the current run rate, or will change. Modify the subsequent months based on assumptions. Add any new budget line items for known new categories of expense, along with amounts and assumptions.
3. Prepare first draft budgets based on the current run rate and assumptions on any changes.

A final note about the budgeting process: Give the senior management team (CFO, CEO) options for key budget decisions. For example, produce two budgets—one based on current level of service and one based on a reduced level of service. This allows senior management to assess the price of any cost cutting they would like to execute (e.g., lower level of service means one-day turnaround on help desk trouble tickets versus four hours). Another variable that can be adjusted is the number of projects that can be executed, providing options for executing the top 10 projects versus executing only the top 5 projects. Management can then make trade-offs of spending versus service. Even if management elects not to take advantage of these potential cost reductions, the IT team will enhance their reputation for thriftiness with the senior management team and IT steering committee.

Key Cost Drivers

Chapter 3 outlines a comprehensive list of IT cost drivers. This section lists some key factors that may affect the budget from year to year and some that are key considerations during the budgeting process (see Exhibit 15.4).

Efficiency and high productivity are important goals for the IT department. Every CIO should attempt to build the most efficient infrastructure, application deployment, and IT organization possible. Recommendations for keeping costs low and attempting to run an efficient operation include:

- *Develop baseline infrastructure costs as outlined previously.* Attempt to reduce this baseline on a continual basis. For each baseline budget line item ask, "Will reducing this number cause any change to business service?" If the answer is no, the cost should probably be cut. A large driver of cost reduction is standardization of the environment. Chapter 7 lays out a framework for standardizing the environment. Standardization can reduce IT baseline spending considerably. Every effort should be made to attain it. The average company spends 70 percent of IT dollars on

DRIVER	DESCRIPTION
• Complexity of infrastructure environment	• Infrastructure complexity increases support costs dramatically; it also drives unexpected costs due to the difficulty in controlling the environment. • Characteristics include multiple disparate platforms (e.g., AS/400, Unix, NT, Mainframe). • Build a risk factor into your budget and dollars to rationalize the environment.
• Revenue growth	• Revenue growth drives increased costs to support the business including additional capacity in servers, added support costs for end users, new applications to support customer and sales initiatives. • The higher the revenue growth the greater the demands on IT. Companies growing by 10 percent or more will see 10 plus percent increase in IT spending proportionate to the growth.
• Growth or decline in employee base (e.g., professional, clerical, users of PCs)	• Growth or decline in the number of end-users will have a tremendous affect on the IT budget. • Employee growth drives demand for capital expenditure in PC hardware as well as corresponding capacity on file and print servers and potentially end-user software licenses. • Employee attrition will reduce demand by a corresponding amount.
• Downturn in business economic climate	• Depending on the sector in which the company competes, the organization will likely feel the affect of a recession in lower sales growth or even sales decline. • In a recession, CIOs should be prepared for budget and spending cuts. Preparing ahead of time by prioritizing discretionary spending and being proactive in making adjustments is recommended.
• Acquisitions	• Acquisitions drive a tremendous amount of IT integration if the acquisition will be integrated into the main business. • Acquisitions are likely to drive integration costs of IT systems, end-user licenses, and standardization of operating platforms.

Exhibit 15.4   Key Cost Drivers

511

baseline and maintenance, creating significant opportunity for identifying potential reductions.

- *Work only on the projects that the department can complete on time.* Working on more projects than the department has capacity to execute causes whipsawing and makes the entire department less productive. Make sure no projects are started without proper business justification and ownership from one of the business units (except infrastructure projects). Chapter 17 contains an approach for ensuring that IT projects can be successfully concluded.

- *Develop a review process to critically assess current projects.* Each project should receive a status flag of green (going well), yellow (warning signs), or red (behind schedule or over budget). See Chapter 18 on IT metrics for a discussion on the project dashboard. The review will ensure that overbudget projects are dealt with before they greatly impact the budget.

- *Periodically renegotiate vendor contracts to obtain savings from company size.* If the company is growing, the department can often save IT dollars by aggregating spending into fewer vendors and demanding volume discounts in return. Chapters 12 and 13 cover vendor negotiation and management.

- *Reexamine service levels.* Make sure the service levels that the department is delivering to the business are actually what the business wants. Often service levels are actually overspecified—meaning the business could actually do with lower service levels, which would allow lower costs to deliver.

- *Tighten asset management.* Implement a sound process for managing IT assets, including their inventory and physical tracking. Critically assess requests for assets, and make sure that the assets are actually being used for high priority activities. Redeploy assets from low-return areas to highest return projects.

Managing Capital Expenditures

The capital budget is used for financing long-term outlays for assets that will be used by the company over a long period of time, such as hardware and large-scale software applications. Accounting rules provide for these assets to be expensed over their lifetime so that an appropriate portion of the expense for the item occurs in each year that the asset is in use. Capital budget items affect cash and the balance sheet, as the actual cash outlay for the item occurs in a short time period relative to the asset lifetime. Over time, the capital items are depreciated, and affect the income statement (and operating budget). A *capital expenditure* is any expenditure contributing value to the property and equipment of a business—expenditure toward capital assets rather than to cover operating expenses or purchase investments unrelated to the business. Accounting rules provide for the total cost (including labor) of some long-term projects to be treated as a capital asset. In many cases, accounting rules also provide guidance on the expected lifetime of the asset that will dictate how much of the asset's value will be expensed in each year's budget.

Capital budgeting is the process by which a company selects alternative capital asset investments. In making decisions on which capital investments to make, companies usually use a combination of formal financial criteria, including net present value (NPV), internal rate of return (IRR), return on investment (ROI), and payback period. Potential investments are also evaluated with respect to strategic consistency and risk. The capital budgeting process is designed to maximize company value by undertaking investments whose returns are equal to or greater than the average cost of capital.

An entity's capital budget and budgeting process are usually distinct from its operating budget and budgeting process. The two kinds of budgets represent different expenditures, are planned through different processes, use different criteria, and may even involve different managers. For a specific expenditure to be funded from a capital budget, its sponsors may have to justify it with a formal business case analysis, including estimates of NPV, IRR, ROI, payback period, and other financial criteria. If the company has limited funds for capital spending, moreover, the potential capital expenditure may have to enter a competitive capital review process, where all requested expenditures are compared on the same financial criteria and only the most favorable receive funding.

Computer and system asset components are generally capitalized as one unit (e.g., CPU, monitor, mouse, keyboard, software); however, if small components (e.g., a mouse or keyboard) are purchased separately from the system, they are expensed. Generally, assets above a few thousand dollars are capitalized. Hardware assets are generally capitalized over a three- to five-year period, while software and select application development initiatives are capitalized over three years. However, each company's accounting department has its own policies based on generally accepted accounting principles (GAAP); the finance or accounting department will dictate appropriate usage.

Minimizing Capital Expenditures

Suggestions for minimizing capital expenditures include:

- Make sure all computer and software capital expenditures follow the company standard capital expenditure process, including approval by the CIO and steering committee. This process ensures that only legitimate capital expenditures take place, those that have significant business value for the company.

- Require that all capital requests have a related business case justification completed and signed off by either the CIO (for infrastructure requests) or by both the CIO and the business unit general manager for other requests.
- Hold all requests in a batch and present them to the IT steering committee periodically to discuss in aggregate.
- When completing the cost side of the capital request, ensure that personnel have used standard vendors and previously negotiated discounts.
- Have requestors provide one or two alternative options to the recommended request. For example, if the department is requesting 25 computers, the options are simply to approve or decline the request. However, if the team presents two options, purchase 25 computers as plan A or purchase 15 computers and reuse 10 older computers with pros and cons of each, management can make a better decision by weighing the trade offs.
- Ensure that the IT department is finding the root cause of problems before requesting capital for hardware such as storage, CPUs, memory, and so on. Chapter 9 contains details on operations root cause analysis. Capital requests that appear legitimate are often rejected after analysis. For example, a capital request for a new backup system resulted instead in new policies for e-mail storage quotas, resulting in avoidance of the expenditure.

Lease versus Buy Decisions

Lease versus buy decisions should be made principally by the finance department. The CFO and the finance team will have an overall capital strategy for the company. This analysis affects every large capital purchase that can be either purchased with cash or leased from the vendor or through a third-party leasing company. The CFO will make the decision based on the company's balance sheet, lender covenants, current cash on hand, budget forecasts, and financial performance. The IT team should work closely with the finance department prior to committing the company to any large capital expenditure or long-term lease.

Buying Equipment

When purchasing equipment, the buyer can usually negotiate the lowest overall price for the asset. Additionally, the purchase approach may provide access to a greater variety of vendors since not all of them offer lease options. Buying assets that can be capitalized will consume the capital budget and the asset will be fully owned by the company and can be used for any purpose intended. Disposing of the asset will also be at the discretion of the company.

Leasing Equipment

Most major hardware (and, recently, software) purchases can also be leased from the vendor or third party; this is a common industry practice and large vendors have well-articulated finance and leasing programs. Leases usually have the same affect on the expense budget as a purchase, but very different impact on company cash and balance sheets. Additionally, vendors will usually offer capital leases, which affect the capital budget instead of the operating budget.

In leasing, the company is essentially renting the asset from a third party. As such, a number of rules come attached to the equipment, which may limit the flexibility in using and disposing of it. For example, by contract, the company may not return the asset prematurely without paying an early termination penalty. Furthermore, financing instruments such as leasing come with financing costs. The CIO and finance department must evaluate the total picture of asset cost, asset life, financing cost, and other variables to determine which option (lease versus buy) is a better financial decision for the company. The CIO should focus on developing the potential options and let the accounting department determine the better value and make the lease or purchase decision.

Auditing the IT Department

An important part of IT cost containment is close management of the details. Thousands of small expenditures add up to big dollar expenditures for the IT department. A typical example of this buildup is data communication lines. Each data line may be only $40 per month; however, if the department maintains 100 data lines and potential long distance dial-in charges, the amount can reach hundreds of thousands of dollars on an annual basis. Computer purchases are another example. Even though each desktop computer may cost only a few thousand dollars, the aggregate spending at the end of the year can be enormous.

The CIO has responsibility for ensuring that vendor invoices and staff expense receipts are audited. One or more designated managers perform this function; the designees should recommend to the IT manager ways to reduce either the expenses or vendor billing errors. Some common areas of billing errors and overspending include:

- *Data communications:* Line and long distance connections: As a company expands or contracts, adjustments to the original service are required. Otherwise, the department's monthly invoice will contain charges for items not being used. If a company is growing, the team should ensure that they are receiving proper volume discounts.

- *Cell phones:* Cell phone plans, cell phones, pagers, and wireless handhelds for personnel in the IT department—any regular recurring billing should be reviewed periodically to rationalize disposed of assets and unused telecom plans. Volume purchasing discounts should be considered here as well.
- *Software and hardware maintenance contracts:* Many companies are paying maintenance on applications that are no longer in use. Inventory all maintenance contracts and make sure all the software is still in production, and that it justifies a maintenance contract.

Perform an audit once a year. Have an auditor from the accounting department review all spending, contracts, and services to ensure they are still justified and are applicable to supporting the current business.

Contingency Planning

Risk is inherent in any assumption-driven analysis. The over- and underrisk of the budget and plan should be assessed accordingly. Understanding how the key assumptions will affect the budget, which assumption changes will have the highest impact, and the likelihood of the assumptions changing can be combined to perform a budget sensitivity analysis. This helps identify the key risk areas, which have the highest chance of causing budget variance.

Budget planners sometimes try to pad their budgets with extra costs, anticipating budget reductions during negotiations. While tempting, this is an inadvisable practice that sows distrust between the IT department and finance and senior management. One CIO we worked with needed to have capital approval for 25 new laptop computers. The CIO was overheard remarking: "Let's submit the request for an extra 7 laptops for 32 total. We need to add a little accountant bait in here, so they can feel that they have accomplished something when they talk us down to 25." Clearly, this manager had trouble establishing a trusted working relationship with the CFO and the IT steering committee.

Managing the Budget

The company, its officers, its employees, and its shareholders are relying on the IT manager to meet the budget. If the department overspends the budget, both the company and its employees may be adversely affected. The corporate budgeting process and its subsequent success is dependent on all budget managers managing their share of the overall corporate budget and performing according to plan.

There are a variety of approaches the IT manager can take to help manage the budget on an ongoing basis:

- Schedule a regular monthly meeting with the CFO, controller, or finance analyst to review actual versus budget numbers. During this session, variances should be investigated, and the CIO should develop a list of key actions to improve any negative variance. After the meeting, the director should delegate the action items and get them completed quickly to experience the benefits in the subsequent month.

- Give senior direct reports (usually operations and applications managers) budget responsibility for their areas and hold them accountable for hitting the numbers.

- When large variances occur, take fast action, as it takes time for changes to be reflected in the numbers. For example, if a vendor agreement is modified, it may take 30 days to finalize the agreement and another 30 days for the changes to take effect.

- Dithering and delaying decisions and ignoring high variances is a recipe for disaster. The CIO has a fiduciary responsibility for the department and must make the necessary corrections to perform as promised to the rest of the management team. Delay may lead to senior management or the IT steering committee making unilateral decisions without the involvement of IT.

- When anticipating a large negative variance in the budget, enlist the CFO as soon as possible to work to help correct the situation and explain it to senior management and the IT steering committee.

Handling Out-of-Budget Business Unit Requests

After the operating budget is set, business unit requests that might impact the operating budget need to be discussed in the face of other investment decisions the company is trying to make. While meeting the committed budget is important, over the course of the year, budget assumptions may change and some common sense and flexibility are necessary.

Business units often request projects that were not on their agendas when the budget was completed. As outlined in Chapter 17, projects should be evaluated on a business case basis and, if approved, executed. Large projects will likely hit the capital budget if approved and not affect the operating budget. Business unit project requests should be documented, along with a business case, and sent to the IT steering committee for review and approval.

Every new request must be considered in relation to the current operating budget and the capital budget. Possible outcomes include:

- Project is covered by the current capital budget and approved.
- Project is not covered by the current capital budget but is higher priority than another project. Downgrade the priority of the second project on the list of backlog projects and replace with the newly approved project.
- Project is not covered by the current capital budget. It is a high priority. There are no other projects to displace. New funding for the IT group is needed. The business case is sound, so additional funds are approved to complete the project, and the ongoing negative capital budget variance is approved (i.e., the capital budget is increased or some other nontechnology investment is displaced).
- Project is not a priority and has a substandard business case; therefore, it is not funded and further consideration is not necessary.

Chargebacks

Chargebacks are budget methods that charge the business units and functional departments for their use of IT by allocating IT costs to each unit. IT chargebacks are often considered when the business units would like more direct accountability from IT, and the senior management team wants to ensure that IT costs are being justified by the business.

In general, we do not advocate elaborate IT budget chargebacks for several reasons. First, they divert attention from the primary focus of the business, which is generating revenue and satisfying customers. Second, they take substantial effort from accounting. Third, companies with IT chargebacks often under-invest in common infrastructure projects; each business unit will only be interested in and approve projects that are of direct benefit. Finally, chargebacks effectively force the CIO to report to multiple department heads and business unit managers. This can create management chaos and an ineffective IT department.

In cases where IT chargebacks are appropriate, there are two options for infrastructure costs:

1. *Unallocated infrastructure:* Costs for the baseline IT budget are considered a corporate expense and are not allocated to the business units.
2. *Allocated cost center:* Costs for the baseline IT budget are allocated to business units based on some factor as a proxy for usage. Usage proxies can include the business unit's percent of revenue, number of employ-

ees, percent of profits, computer CPU cycles used, disk storage used, and so on.

Large companies with multiple divisions and a central IT department may be forced to use allocated cost center concepts.

In addition to infrastructure cost allocations, the company will need a mechanism for charging out IT systems development, package implementation and integration, and application maintenance different from those of the IT infrastructure. Several options exist:

1. Business units contract with the IT department on each project, agreeing to a cost including software licenses, time and material estimates, deadlines, and scope of project. Business units also contract with IT department on maintenance and support. Actual hours for supporting the business unit are tracked in a time reporting system and actual hours are billed. Service levels are defined and the IT department is responsible for achieving service levels guaranteed.
2. In this case, the business units actually own the budgets for IT projects and the IT department is used to support and execute the projects in those budgets.

Chargeback mechanisms are successful only if the chargeback drivers are fair and easily tracked, and the business has the ability to influence their usage of IT in order to contain costs. Otherwise, the chargebacks can cause underinvestment in critical infrastructure components, as well as cause significant internal dysfunctional behavior, putting significant burden on the accounting department.

Summary

IT budgeting and cost containment practices are critical skills for the IT manager to master. Developing a sound budget, which provides a road map for managing the department, and which can withstand business changes and economic changes, is a challenge. Additionally, anticipating, understanding, and forecasting the known variables about the business distinguish an average CIO from a star performer. The average performer is reactive to the environment while the top performer has assessed the reliability of key assumptions and the associated risks, and planned contingencies accordingly.

Concepts presented in the chapter, such as prioritizing discretionary spending areas and keeping this prioritized list handy, encourage the IT manager to act quickly and decisively to negative budget variances. Finally, ensuring that IT assets are deployed against revenue generating and customer-facing activities help ensure that budget dollars are flowing to the highest value activities. Companies whose IT managers routinely ensure this, as well as the business value of IT investments, see much higher productivity and profitability from IT investments.

RESOURCE

Strassmann, Paul *The Squandered Computer*. New Canaan, CT: Information Economics Press, 1997.

NOTES

1. Thomas Henry Huxley, *Aphorisms and Reflections,* ed. Henrietta A. Huxley (London: Macmillan, 1907).
2. Amy Wilentz, "I Will Veto Again and Again," *Time* (March 18, 1985).

16

Effective Decision Making and Risk Management

You want a valve that doesn't leak and you try everything possible to develop one. But the real world provides you with a leaky valve. You have to determine how much leaking you can tolerate.

—Arthur Rudolph, manager of the Marshall Space Flight Center
Saturn V program office[1]

A foolish consistency is the hobgoblin of little minds.

—Ralph Waldo Emerson[2]

Quit building me a space shuttle, when all I want is a trip to the grocery store.

—Client CEO to IT department managers

This chapter outlines and illustrates the pitfalls of incentives inherent for IT managers that lower the priority on cost containment and increase the priority for minimizing risk, often at great expense. Many IT decision makers view risk as a binary decision—accept the risk or mitigate the risk. In the effort to eliminate risk, these same decision makers often show little understanding or appreciation for the high incremental cost required to mitigate all risk.

We examine key areas in which IT managers consistently over-mitigate risks with excess spending or resource allocation. IT managers too often submit additional capital and labor requests without investigation into other alternatives. In addition, these requests demonstrate the limited knowledge most IT organizations have about the underlying business and its economics. We illustrate the phenomenon with multiple examples from client engagements.

The chapter is intended to raise awareness of the key failure points in IT-related decision making. Responsibilities exist for both the IT manager and the senior executive participating in the IT steering committee or approving

IT budgets and expenditures. IT managers must help the steering committee understand the spectrum of options, including costs and risks. While the steering committee must ask questions that ensure that due diligence has been performed and that the business impact, whether for growth or risk mitigation, justifies the expenditure.

This chapter does not address other risk management-related topics such as redundancy planning, uptime management, disaster recovery, failover methodologies, systems recovery, systems security, and privacy issues. The technologies and approaches for these topics are covered in detail in a host of books, magazine articles, and online publications. The key theme in this chapter is that effective decision making and intelligent assessment of cost versus risk should be applied to all of these areas.

Why This Topic Is Important

Poor decision making concerning risk is one of the primary drivers of IT ineffectiveness and, more specifically, IT overspending. The responsibility for this decision making is shared equally by IT managers and the senior management team. IT managers typically fail to present any but the most costly (and risk-free) options for a given decision to senior management. Senior management, in turn, fails to ask the penetrating questions, which may reveal creative options for accomplishing the dual objectives of risk and cost minimization. Instead, one of two undesirable results occurs; either the senior management approves the request at high cost or rejects the request. Rejecting the request results in nothing being done to mitigate the potential risk, and the company is exposed indefinitely. The IT manager then holds leverage if the potential failure occurs by blaming the senior management for declining the capital expenditure request.

IT managers experience difficulty in helping the business understand the cost trade-offs they are making in setting service levels and expectations inside IT. If business management thinks of the cost of a failover server in terms of incremental sales, would they be just as happy to save the cost of the server and endure a potential four-hour downtime while tapes are restored? These risk-management questions often go unasked and unexamined in the IT decision-making process. This chapter introduces the key areas of decision making often affected and covers specific examples from IT departments in a variety of industries.

IT departments are paid to serve the business units and often have trouble quantifying and explaining to the business the actual costs of the service. Many IT departments tend to overinsure by overspending on both labor and capital, which provides higher levels of service to the business but is often not the best deployment of resources for the company overall.

Furthermore, IT is commonly a nonallocated cost, which results in two undesirable effects: agency issues and the "tragedy of the commons." Agency issues manifest in IT as unlimited service requests pour in from all segments of the business, and the "tragedy of the commons" effect occurs because there is no incentive for the individual business departments to help IT save money or effort, yet the entire company suffers from overspending.

Risk Management: A Balancing Act

Risk management is challenging because it requires judgment in the face of uncertainty. A simplified model of risk management (see Exhibit 16.1) shows the effect of too little or too much risk in a professional services firm.

Too little risk results in the cessation of all IT activity. In the world of complete risk elimination, contracts and projects become too cumbersome, and decision making and client pursuits take too long. Too much risk can be equally debilitating; the firm is in constant firefighting mode and is torn apart by bad reputation and even litigation that ensues post poorly sold and executed work. Each firm must find the appropriate balance of risk and return, which will vary from decision to decision and project to project. This balancing act is challenging, and the decisions made ultimately depend on a host of variables. We have found that too much or too little risk have one thing in common: low business satisfaction with IT department performance.

Because each firm situation and each individual decision is unique, it is useful instead to develop the general skills needed to effectively balance risk and return in each case. The principle skill needed is high-quality decision making.

Not enough risk	Too much risk
• Over-engineered O&I • High IT budgets • Overstaffing • Stifled innovation • Rogue departmental IT initiatives • Slow project delivery • Low business satisfaction	• Frequent system failures • Artificially low IT spending • IT security compromises • Insufficient staffing to accomplish initiatives and support • Chronic software and package QA problems • Low business satisfaction

Good decision-making processes
balance risk and return

Decision-making process revisions are based on
analysis of the process and not the outcomes

Exhibit 16.1   The Role of Good Decision Making in IT Risk Management

The Critical Role of Decision Making in Risk Management

Good risk management ultimately depends on good decision making. Good decision making, in turn, is based on the rapid acquisition of the proper amount and kind of data, building a framework for deciding, moving forward, and incorporating feedback from past decisions as the feedback becomes available.

The field of decision science has been well researched, particularly in the past two decades, and a considerable amount of information on how to improve organizational decisions is available in the related academic and popular literature. The University of Chicago and the Wharton School at The University of Pennsylvania in particular have strong decision science specialties.

In *Winning Decisions,* J. Edward Russo and Paul J. H. Schoemaker outline the fundamentals to a good decision-making process:

- *Framing:* Determines the viewpoint from which decision makers look at the issue and set parameters for which aspects of the situation they consider important and which they do not. It determines in a preliminary way what criteria would cause them to prefer one option to the other.

- *Gathering intelligence:* Intelligence gatherers must seek the knowable facts and options and produce reasonable evaluations of unknowables to enable decision making in the face of uncertainty. It's important that they avoid pitfalls such as overconfidence in what they currently believe and the tendency to seek only information that confirms their beliefs.

- *Coming to conclusions:* Sound framing and good intelligence do not guarantee a wise decision. People cannot consistently make good decisions using seat-of-the-pants judgment alone, even with excellent data in front of them. A systematic approach will lead to more accurate choices—and it usually does far more efficiently than hours spent in unorganized thinking, particularly in group settings.

- *Learning from experience:* Only by systematically learning from results of past decisions can decision makers continually improve their skills. Further, if learning begins when a decision is first implemented, early refinements to the decision or implementation plan can be made that could mean the difference between success and failure.[3]

Russo and Schoemaker point out that one of the biggest faults of the decision-making process is that the quality of decisions is often judged on outcome rather than the process that was used to generate the decision. "Many people believe that good outcomes necessarily imply that a good process was used. And they assume the converse to be true as well: that a poor outcome necessarily signals a poor or incompetent process."[4]

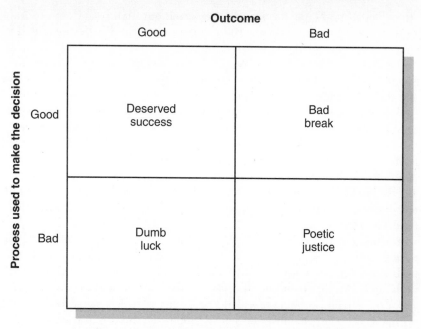

Exhibit 16.2   Relationship between Decision Making and Outcomes (*Source: Winning Decisions,* Russo and Schoemaker.)

Clearly, this is not true, particularly for decisions that are close (55 percent chance of a good decision and 45 percent chance of a bad decision) or in situations involving a significant amount of outside chance or luck. In fact, a good decision-making process often produces a failure but, on average, succeeds more often than it fails (Exhibit 16.2).

The way decisions are evaluated affects the way decisions are made in the future. Thus, in addition to a good decision-making process, the evaluation of decisions is a critical skill. This has serious implications for improving decision making in organizations, particularly for difficult-to-make decisions, such as those related to risk management.

A good conceptual model for the risk management decision-making balancing act is shown in Exhibit 16.1.

Relationship between Risk and Cost

In one of our most memorable client engagements, we were asked to fix a particularly distressed IT department. One of the first decisions implemented was to hold all capital and vendor expenditures until the larger issues impeding IT performance were sorted out. After six weeks of hard work, we were ready to review the requests from the IT department. The first request was for the renewal of a maintenance contract for three-year-old corporate file-and-print servers. The request was for more than $50,000 for annual maintenance. Given what we knew about server prices and the low number of users on this particular system, we asked what justified such a large expenditure relative to the replacement cost of the servers. "Well, if they go down, we can't print or access network files in the sales department" came back the answer. "But, given the configuration of fairly old equipment, couldn't the machines be replaced for less than one-third of the annual maintenance contract?" we argued. "That may be true, and we could even create a backup machine to be deployed in case of failure, but that would mean the possibility of as much as four hours of downtime," was the reply.

Fortunately, this debate took place in the context of an IT steering committee, and, at this juncture, one of the business unit managers weighed in with some common sense. "To save $50,000, I am willing to put up with a little bit of potential downtime. It costs me $500,000 in sales to cover a gap of $50,000." Further probing revealed a few other pertinent facts: The existing servers had never gone down in the past and had a three-year track record of flawless performance. Backup servers were actually already available and could be configured and deployed in less than eight hours after a failure of one of the main servers.

This anecdote illustrates several of the decision-making and agency problems that assert themselves in IT decision making. First, there is a fundamental agency problem with decision making in many IT departments, and it is the responsibility of both IT management and the senior management team. The incentives of IT managers are usually not oriented toward the most cost-effective management of risk, and the senior management team fails to ask the right questions to understand how much risk reduction they are purchasing with their IT dollars.

Second, many IT managers do not seem to understand the relationship between risk and cost, instead assessing risk as a binary outcome. For example, IT managers view a given hardware decision or IT staffing level as either risky or safe with no gradations between. By seeing only two possible alternatives, the IT decision-making process becomes one sided—either implement the safe solution or put the business at risk. IT departments are notoriously bad at explaining consequences and alternatives. They frame requests as all or nothing, with only one option presented to the business, instead of a variety of options with varying costs and risks. IT requests and decisions are often made without soliciting input from the business and helping them understand the trade-offs for optimal decision making. The request is typically presented in a way that leads IT steering committees and senior executives to choose the safe solution, despite a high cost, to avoid appearing irresponsible by putting the business at risk.

Frank conversations on these topics often yield surprises on both sides. IT managers are surprised at how much risk the business is willing to absorb to achieve cost savings, and senior management is surprised at the high cost of the reduced risk and high service levels they are purchasing. The primary cause of these issues is a lack of clear communication between the IT department and the business on issues of risk and service levels.

A fundamental agency problem is present in IT decision making as well. IT departments achieve by pleasing the business. The primary incentive for IT managers is to ensure that systems are operational and performing well. A common saying in IT departments is "You know you are doing a good job when everything runs so smoothly that no one from the business knows you are there." IT operations managers receive the most vociferously negative feedback when key systems, such as e-mail, experience outages. If they overengineer a solution to ensure e-mail uptime, they are triply rewarded—the e-mail system stays up reducing their support work, they avoid negative feedback from the business, and, furthermore, by consuming budget dollars, they are assured a similar budget for next year's expenditures. The normal cost-saving motivation that applies to a business unit manager in charge of a P&L statement are not present. When IT departments spend more money, in general, their lives get easier; therefore, the normal incentives do not apply.

This agency problem, while troubling, is overshadowed by the inability of IT managers to effectively trade risk and cost to achieve an optimal mix. Exhibit 16.3 shows the well-understood normal relationship between risk and

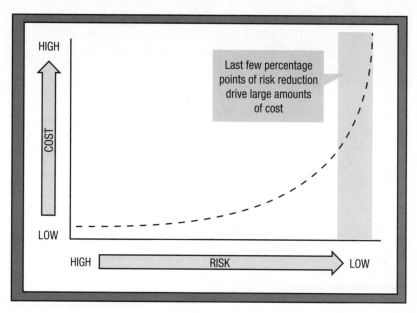

Exhibit 16.3   Typical Relationship between Risk and Cost

cost. This general relationship between risk and cost is applicable to IT decisions concerning investment and capacity. The exhibit highlights an enormously high level of incremental cost required to achieve the last few percentage points of risk reduction.

IT managers often do not acknowledge this relationship between risk and cost in their decision making. Instead, they see the decision as a binary choice between *no risk* and *risk*. This most often leads to high levels of service, low levels of risk, and, most troubling, high levels of cost in IT departments. Exhibit 16.4 outlines the decision-making behavior of many IT managers.

As shown in the exhibit, instead of viewing risk as a continuum, with ever-increasing marginal costs associated with marginal reductions in risk, IT managers tend to assess decisions more simplistically, with two outcomes: risky or not risky and costly or not costly. This mode of framing decisions, naturally, tends to favor outcomes that produce the minimum risk and the maximum cost.

While IT management deserves its share of the responsibility for such poor and uninventive decision making, the senior management team and the business are equally culpable for not asking the hard questions. When presented with requests from IT, the business fails to delve down to a meaning-

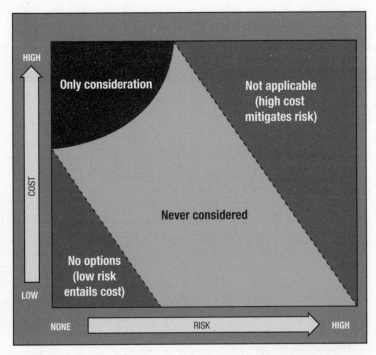

Exhibit 16.4   IT Approach to Risk Analysis and Decision Making

ful level of questioning that would expose other potential options. Push back is limited to a one-level deep question of "Why?" Only through Socratic, multiple-level questioning with adequate technical intelligence and push back do other possible options emerge from the brainstorming that ensues. When business management takes IT recommendations at face value, without signaling the level of risk tolerance they are willing to accept, they usually get a solution that minimizes risk and maximizes cost. As decision making improves, senior management must also work with IT to improve confidence that IT will not be solely liable for downtime or outages that were preventable, but not avoided, to achieve cost savings. The decisions about acceptable risks should be made and owned by both IT and senior management.

We have observed this tendency to over-insure and over-mitigate risk manifest itself in four specific areas of IT decision making:

- Capital expenditure or other spending requests.
- IT emergencies/disaster recovery.
- Setting and maintaining service levels.
- Setting staff and technology capacity levels.

We cover these scenarios in turn, illuminating each with specific client examples.

Capital Expenditures and IT Spending

IT spending and, in particular, IT capital expenditures are common areas where poor decisions are made. In their zeal to substitute capital for labor, IT teams have a particularly poor reputation because of the frequent over-purchasing of "toys." While it is true that part of the attraction of a career in technology for many people is the opportunity to work with an ever-changing variety of new technology, it has also led to a suspicion on the part of business managers that the IT team is purchasing more or better than is necessary. Compounding the issue is the fact that business managers are often rated on revenue, gross margin, expenses, or earnings before interest, taxes, depreciation and amortization (EBITDA); therefore, additional capital expenditure will have less effect on their incentives.

Recognition of these shortcomings enables IT departments and IT steering committees to analyze scenarios and ask questions, which either validate the business need for the IT expenditure or uncover other alternatives. With one of our clients, we were able to produce significant savings while at the same time keeping risk at very acceptable levels by participating in the IT budgeting and capital expenditure approval process. The IT team made an unplanned, mid-year request for virus-scanning software to be deployed to every single corporate desktop. The catalyst was a recent unexplained virus attack. This unanticipated expense would not only cause a significant budget variance for IT in the coming month, but also entail a significant software rollout project for the operations department and require additional ongoing support to monitor virus file updates. The position of the IT team was "either purchase this software, or we will be constantly at risk of viruses." Although senior management was sufficiently alarmed by the notion of viruses running rampant through the company to sign off on the request immediately, we asked to extend the debate. After much discussion, it was determined that viruses could only enter the corporate systems from one of three sources: inbound e-mail, diskettes brought from outside the company, or files downloaded from the Internet. Inbound e-mail was cleaned of viruses by a highly robust system, which was installed and operating on the corporate mail server and, therefore, could be discounted as a source. We asked the IT team to perform a quick analysis on the source of virus attacks for the past year. Their analysis concluded that less than 5 percent of the virus attacks had come from diskettes, and none of the attacks had come from downloaded files. Given this low level of probability, we suggested the alternate approach of disconnecting the floppy drives of most desktop computers, which were rarely used for business purposes anyway. The result was a highly acceptable level of risk and a response that was cheap, easy to implement, and commensurate with the actual threat posed.

A subsequent request from the team was for a highly sophisticated and expensive server, which would serve as failover capacity for an existing financial systems server. We first asked the IT team for more research: How often had the existing financial systems computer failed in the past year, and where a failover machine would be necessitated? The answer was, interestingly, zero. In fact, the machine had failed only once in three years. On that occasion, it was quickly fixed with the installation of a new memory module. However, we were certainly willing to contemplate the notion that a complete, difficult-to-fix failure was possible. What was in question, however, was the best response to the failure. Working with the CFO, we ascertained that the four-hour downtime required to restore the server from tape in the event of a failure was an acceptable price to pay in the unlikely event of a failure, particularly given the high cost of ensuring 100 percent uptime and reliability.

In another purchasing audit, we were asked to analyze a request for an automated, high-speed, high-capacity tape backup system for the corporate systems. The business rationale for the purchase was that a complete backup of the system could not be completed within a 24-hour window, and corporate standards mandated that a full backup be taken of corporate data each day. Before signing off on this request, we asked the operations manager what seemed to be causing the trouble. "Most of the data is from our e-mail server," he replied. After conducting a detailed analysis of the e-mail system, we found that more than 70 percent of the backup data volume was from the e-mail system, and more than 50 percent of that data volume was associated with 20 percent of the users. Those 20 percent were storing enormous music, video, and other large files in their network e-mail folders. The CFO said it best: "You mean we are buying a tape jukebox so these people can watch movies over the network while they are at work?" Needless to say, the jukebox purchase was declined and e-mail storage policies and procedures were implemented.

Our favorite example of creative thinking that produced simple, cheap approaches is from a client working on its disaster recovery plan. The client had established a well-thought-out plan for ensuring availability of backup tapes and servers, as well as alternate (nonwater-based) fire suppression. The only remaining issue was the presence of water-based fire suppression equipment in the machine room. They were concerned that sustained flooding in the room would ruin the expensive hardware located there. For a variety of technical reasons, the disabling and removal of this equipment was going to be difficult, disruptive, and expensive. Elaborate plans were hatched, including architects, building contractors, and blueprint redesigns for the machine room. At one of the final sign-off meetings, a junior analyst from the IT department finally piped up: "Well, I hate to try to stop a moving train, but I noticed on the blueprints a water cutoff valve for the pipes that feed the machine room is located in the plant closet. The closet happens to be right behind the security post, which is staffed 24 hours a day, year around. Could we just create a procedure for the security guards that, if there is a fire, the first thing they do is turn the valve off?"

Occasionally, the decisions take a turn down a trail that is at best deceitful and, at worst, outright fraudulent. In a client engagement, we were assessing a particularly disorganized and ill-managed IT department. We found ourselves reviewing the training and development records for the IT team for the past year. We noticed that several members of the IT team had attended lengthy and expensive Oracle database training during the past year. What struck us as peculiar was the fact that at no time had the company employed Oracle database technology nor was it currently under consideration. When we quizzed the managers and team members who had attended the training on the rationale behind the training, they were frank enough to admit the truth: "We went to the training so we could build the skills for our resumes."

IT Outages and Recovery

A peculiar blind spot we have often observed in IT departments is found in their reaction to emergencies. The disconnect seems to be both in the order of actions taken and in the level of urgency exhibited by the IT department when outages of key systems occur. First, the occurrence of an emergency in most departments does not invoke standard procedures as would be the case in companies with robust business continuity plans. Instead, a set of random acts result in random outcomes based on the on-call team. Second, we have seen particular insensitivity to what drives revenues and profits in the business. Few staff members in IT departments understand the impact when a key system is unavailable to business users. Unfortunately, we have witnessed this lack of IT understanding regularly demonstrated across many businesses. We provide three examples of actual client situations.

We happened to be on-site with a client in the inbound call center support business when the phone system, supported by IT, crashed. This idled hundreds of agents and sent the managers into a panicked search for the IT operations support team. After half an hour of downtime, we finally asked the IT team for the estimated fix time. The response from the team was, "We can restore service any time. Right now, we are trying to see if we can investigate what happened for our records." The IT team had little understanding of the thousands of dollars per minute costs of a phone system outage in the call center.

We witnessed a similar insensitivity to business mission criticality in work we were managing for a company that is highly reliant on its on-line presence. The particular company web site supported about three million unique customer transactions a month. In one instance when the web site went down, the technical professionals in charge attacked the problem with vigor, spending sleepless 24-hour shifts diagnosing the source of database trouble. When asked for an update and ETA, the team lead replied, "We could bring the site up in about 4 hours by restoring a backup, but I'd prefer to continue diagnosing the cause which could take 24 to 48 hours." Again, an IT manager was having difficulty comprehending the business urgency behind the system's outage. If they truly understood the business impact, the team would have quickly eliminated the second option, immediately restored the backup, then attempted to diagnose the root cause. Better yet, the IT team and senior business leaders would have already had the discussion months ago to agree on specific procedures to take in the event of this particular disaster.

A final anecdote occurred with a client where we were providing temporary IT leadership. A virus had managed to make its way into the corporate e-mail system, causing IT to pull the plug on the system. Like most businesses, this client was highly reliant on access to e-mail for communications with suppliers and customers. Like the thorough, deliberate professionals they were, the IT operations team began an exhaustive virus scan and removal on the entire e-mail database. "Should be up in just about six hours," came the diagnosis. In this case, the virus propagated only if a recipient *opened* the affected e-mail. "Couldn't we bring the system back up and notify everyone via e-mail and public address system not to open the particular e-mail?" we proposed. "After all, in the worst case, if someone opens the virus-laden e-mail again, we can simply shut the system down again. Best case, everyone can continue using e-mail while you can continue to scan and remove in the background. This way we don't lose an entire day of productivity." The IT team resisted, but ultimately the logic prevailed, and the system ran without further incident for the remainder of the day, while the virus scan and removal process worked diligently in the background.

Explaining the costs of system outages to the IT team and ensuring that the team behaves with sensitivity to those costs is the dual responsibility of IT management and the senior management team. There should be no ambiguity about the priorities for returning the systems to service as quickly as possible. This priority is rarely completely conveyed throughout the IT organization, resulting in slow-to-return service and fiddling with problems by IT before the system is placed back in operation.

Setting Service Levels

Another common failing in the decision-making area is related to setting service levels to the business. Most IT departments have been repeatedly informed that the business is their "customer." However, the level of customer service has been left to IT to determine, often without the normal cost and profitability constraints that dictate the setting of service levels in a normal company-customer relationship. In these cases, the service levels across a variety of business support areas are often treated as a single unit, without acknowledging potential differences in service level that may be appropriate (e.g., level of response to a desktop computer outage is treated the same as for a major server outage). Service levels are not only treated monolithically but also often set artificially high.

One of our clients was experiencing out-of-control IT costs. We were asked to investigate opportunities to reduce costs. In our interview with the IT operations professionals, they proudly claimed: "We can move any phone extension in the company from one desktop to another inside an hour." While this level of customer service was certainly appreciated by the business, it was not clear that the business benefits of rapid office moves supported the associated cost of service.

One of the difficulties with setting service levels in IT departments that most companies struggle with is the phenomenon of the "tragedy of the commons." Because inordinately high service levels in the IT department do not carry any associated *cost*, business users are perfectly content to keep the service levels artificially high. The incremental cost is absorbed by the company overall as part of its general and administrative (G&A) budget, but no business unit manager is forced to make good economic choices on his or her own budget. This phenomenon, combined with the natural instinct to please the business customer on the part of IT, leads to insupportably high and expensive service levels across the board.

Often, companies attempt to circumvent this problem by allocating IT costs to the business units they support. Doing this accurately can be exceedingly difficult and can force the IT team and the business to spend countless hours devising the perfect allocation mechanism, all the while pushing neither IT nor business initiatives forward. In clients where we have seen allocation methodologies implemented, individual business units naturally want to take control to manage their IT costs. The result is effectively the creation of an IT company within the parent company. The cost of IT may actually increase in the mid-term because of additional overhead required to negotiate service level agreements (SLAs), measure performance against the negotiated levels, prepare detailed explanations of the costs being allocated, and report to the individual business units. As P&L managers demand cost reductions in IT, IT costs may decline in the long term.

Although we do not recommend business-unit allocation of IT costs, the threat of allocation can serve a useful purpose. In the client mentioned, many of the cost savings we proposed were predicated on selective lowering of service levels on specific nonbusiness-critical items. This was, naturally, met with considerable resistance on the part of the business. Because IT costs were so high, we offered two options: Keep service levels the same and allocate IT costs to business units proportional to their revenue, or lower service levels and continue to incorporate IT costs into G&A. The business unit managers were unanimous in their vote to lower service levels to reasonable levels.

Setting Capacity Levels

The final area in which we have observed decision-making difficulties is in setting capacity levels. In making decisions about staff and computing capacity, again the incentives of IT to ensure complete, failure-proof coverage without the associated cost pressures asserts itself.

IT teams tend to allocate capacity at the maximum level of potential demand instead of the overall average demand for a given function. This is particularly true in the operations area where shortfalls in capacity are rapidly noticeable to the business users; e-mail outages, downed application servers, and desktop computers or phones not working get the immediate attention of the business. Exhibit 16.5 shows the variability of demand in a typical operations support department. While systems are running smoothly, demand is relatively low. An emergency, a transient business problem, or a periodic surge because of business cycles increases demand on the staff temporarily.

Because of the incentive issues noted throughout the chapter, the IT department tends to create capacity at the maximum requirement, rather than find creative ways to staff at the average levels and still provide adequate service. In the exhibit, it is easy to see the cost of staffing to the *surge* compared to staffing to the *average* capacity requirement.

There are a variety of ways to combat these staffing surge issues. Typically, IT departments are organized along two main lines—applications and

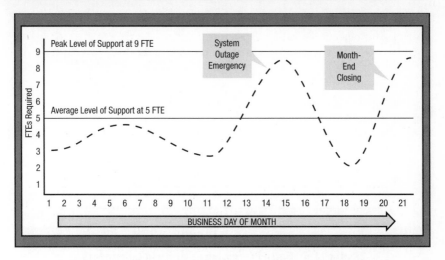

Exhibit 16.5   Monthly Demand for Operations Staffing Capacity

operations (see Chapter 5). One strategy for handling surges in capacity needed in the operations area, without resorting to overstaffing, is to cross-train developers in the required skills to provide surge capacity to the operations team. While this might not be a wildly popular strategy with the development team, generally, developers have the requisite technical skills to substitute in an emergency, thereby allowing companies to staff at the 60 percent to 75 percent of surge level, instead of 100 percent. Further, the IT department can find creative ways to selectively lower service levels by delaying baseline support tasks during emergency surges in demand.

Another creative way of ensuring that emergency capacity is available is to provide reciprocal tech-support capacity in nearby companies with similar technical environments. Locating these companies and having the operations teams spend an afternoon together once a month is a low-cost way of ensuring that a friendly army of extra technical consultants is available inexpensively and fast.

This setting of capacity to the maximum required level and, therefore, the maximum possible cost, is not limited to staffing. It is often found in the specification and purchasing of corporate systems as well. From the IT perspective, the desire is to provide the customer with the best possible service because the customer *sees* the service level and *feels* none of the cost directly. Therefore, it is easy to eliminate the risk of slow system complaints from business users by purchasing capacity equal to the maximum required level. Exhibit 16.6 shows a typical batch-processing calendar with system demand mapped against time of day.

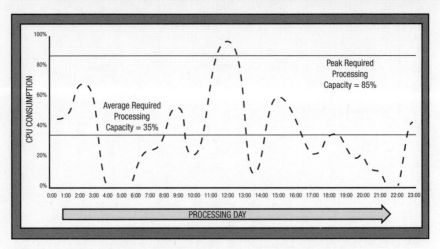

Exhibit 16.6   Batch Processing Capacity Requirements

Although the superficial answer is to request additional processing capacity or an entirely new system, again, the team can likely find creative ways to address the issues. In this specific case, an analysis of the batch job streams revealed nonurgent, noncritical path batch jobs that were competing with batch jobs submitted by online users during peak processing times. The team found ways to ensure that nonurgent batches are deferred automatically by the system until processing capacity becomes available.

IT steering committees must carefully weigh the costs of additional capacity decisions against other alternatives. When additional capacity is required, good IT organizations make every effort to design scalable solutions to provide a spectrum of options that enable the business to initially purchase the minimum requirement instead of the maximum. Scalability allows the business to expand capacity as needed, resulting in a step function of costs instead of a binary cost function.

Risk Management Methodology

Exhibit 16.7 shows a methodology for the risk management process for use by the CIO and IT Steering Committee in evaluating potential IT risks.

The first step in generating a risk management program is to (within reason) identify the possible undesirable outcomes. Each IT department must determine its specific potential risks. The most typical risks are the O&I business continuity risks outlined in Chapter 8.

After the possible risks have been identified and inventoried, the CIO must determine the expected value of the risk—the likelihood of occur-

Exhibit 16.7   Methodology for Risk Management

rence (probability) and the cost of a bad outcome. This is a difficult step and the most open to interpretation.

Probabilities of events are notoriously difficult to estimate, as are costs of outcomes. In fact, research shows that low-probability events are even more difficult to estimate—the very kind of disaster scenarios that the CIO must guard against. Individuals have the best chance of estimating expected value when a variety of low-probability events are aggregated to generate a probability (e.g., "estimate the probability that there will be either an earthquake, flood, or hurricane" versus estimating the likelihood of each event individually).[5]

These studies also indicate that individuals are more effective when assessing possible outcomes relative to low-probability events they are familiar with (e.g., "estimate the risk of a data center power outage versus the risk of having a traffic accident").[6] Making matters worse, similar studies found that decision makers regarding low-probability, high impact events tended to either over-insure, assuming that recurrence of a low-probability event was inevitable, or ignore the event entirely, thinking "that can't happen to me."[7] We conclude that the probability portion of the exercise is best done with an experienced CIO or consultant and should attempt to aggregate the probabilities of disastrous events.

Once the expected value has been determined, the risks can be prioritized for management. In some cases, the probability will be very low, but the cost very high (i.e., "Pascal's Wager"). In these cases, a commonsense approach to prioritization and mitigation should prevail.

The mitigation for a given risk will likely be a combination of actions, policies, or decisions as opposed to a single approach. Some of the typical options are changing behavior ("no more sodas in the server room"), changing decision processes ("let's implement better screening for new IT employee hires"), instituting policies or processes ("two signatures required on every vendor check over $10,000"), training ("all staff will attend help desk escalation skills seminars"), or other process/policy changes.

Incident Postmortems

Good decision making can be enhanced through implementing postmortem reviews for key events in IT: the conclusion of a large project, the acquisition (or firing) of a key vendor, the completion of a disaster recovery plan test. Significant events represent a chance to review what went well and what should change going forward, as well as understand better what went right (and determining if it was "dumb luck" or "deserved success"). While this practice entails extra effort, the improvement benefits will pay a more than adequate return to the investment. The concept of incident and project post-mortems is covered in more detail in Chapter 19.

Finally, one of the most effective risk-mitigation approaches employed by firms is simple, but well documented and reasonably enforced, policy and procedure. The larger the IT department, the more important it is to put risk mitigation on autopilot through these methods. IT policies are also covered in greater detail in Chapter 19.

Responsibility for Risk Management and Quality Assurance in the Organization

Ultimately, responsibility for appropriate risk management falls on the shoulders of the senior managers of the firm, and in particular the CIO and the IT steering committee. These are the individuals with the experience, background, and judgment to determine the best course of action in most cases. However, the information most needed to make the right decisions, as well as new ideas, usually comes from the internal IT staff. IT departments that effectively manage risk establish a culture that holds the entire team responsible for mitigating risks. Success depends on the involvement of all—the risks and troubles that assail the IT department daily are too numerous and varied to be mitigated by anything less than total involvement.

Some IT organizations may choose to appoint an individual to take charge of risk management. Decision science research shows that certain personality types may be more effective than others in this role. Schade and Kunreuther hypothesize that "a greater tendency to worry would intuitively be expected to lead to a higher level of [willingness to pay] for any protection."[8] In fact, their research demonstrated that the reverse may be true—that worriers may make more cost-effective decisions than nonworriers. The researchers contrast anxiety ("an emotion") with worry ("a cognitive phenomenon"). Worry leads to thinking, analysis, data gathering, and effective decision framing. Prior research by Tallis, Davey, and Capuzzo[9] found that worrying:

- Acts as a stimulant.
- Clarifies thoughts and concentration.

- Gives the opportunity to analyze situations and work out the pros and cons.
- Adds to the problems and, as such, leads to exploration of different possibilities.

The research concludes that "low-worriers are likely not to care much about the risk, and hence may not calculate values of objects, losses and prices for protection."[10] The implications of this for firms attempting to improve decision making, quality assurance, and risk management are clear: Contrary to intuition, an effective worrier, not prone to anxiety—the emotional component of worry—may be their best asset.

Summary

As shown in the previous examples, even IT departments with the best of intentions can spin wildly out of budgetary control. Indeed, it is the IT departments with the highest commitment to service that so often exhibit this behavior. As shown in the previous anecdotes, asking probing questions, assessing the *real* risk, and using common sense and creative thinking can help the IT department and senior management work together to minimize both risk and cost.

Intelligent risk management should be an exercise in common sense for the IT team and the senior management team. We do not suggest a "band-aid-and-bubblegum" approach to the maintenance of corporate systems. The mammoth cost of being wrong in this area almost always dwarfs the cost of insurance. What we are suggesting is that a monolithic approach to risk without even the most cursory investigation of potential options is a primary driver of overspending in an IT department.

A tremendous amount of value can be created by senior management by ensuring that the incentives for IT are geared toward intelligent risk management and decision making. Most IT departments have the philosophy "Systems should work at all costs." Senior management should lead a change in that philosophy to "Systems should work at reasonable costs, and here is where we are willing to accept some shortcomings to ensure that those costs stay reasonable."

One practical approach to facilitating the decision-making process is the implementation of standard operating procedures and checklists. The Operations area is not the only area where standard operating procedures can improve decision-making and process standardization. Other areas here include capital expenditure approval, operating expense approval, hiring, and capacity decisions. The specific items on the checklists vary from company to company and by decision type. However, the tool can be useful to ensure that the proper questions have been asked and that the risk has been set at the appropriate level. See Chapter 8 for an example and instructions to develop standard operating procedures.

By working cooperatively with IT and setting reasonable expectations on service levels, the organization can reap the benefits of getting capacity, service levels, emergency response, and spending "just right." An illustration of this comes from a recent client engagement. The senior management team of a manufacturing company asked us to validate its IT capital budgets for the coming year. The previous material might lead you to believe that the focus of the engagement was the minimization of capital expenditures. In fact, the engagement mandate was to understand the real requirements for technology capital expenditure, regardless of outcome. Whether this meant spending more or less mattered less to the senior management team than ensuring that they were spending the right amount on IT, minimizing risk, and not overinsuring. The theme of the engagement was finding the *truth* as opposed to any particular cost target.

RESOURCES

Decision-making science is a complex and well-researched topic of study. A variety of leading thinkers on the topic have produced highly approachable, practical guides to improving the decision-making process. A few books we recommend for IT and senior management decision makers are listed here:

Augustine, Norman, et al. *Harvard Business Review on Crisis Management.* Boston: Harvard Business School Press, 2000.

Barton, Thomas L., William G. Shenkir, and Paul L. Walker. *Making Enterprise Risk Management Pay Off: How Leading Companies Implement Risk Management.* Upper Saddle River, NJ: Financial Times/Prentice Hall PTR, 2002.

Bazerman, Max H. *Judgment in Managerial Decision Making.* New York: John Wiley & Sons, 1994.

Fink, Steven *Crisis Management: Planning for the Inevitable.* Backinprint.com, 2001.

Hammond, John S., Ralph L. Keeney, and Howard Raiffa. *Smart Choices: A Practical Guide to Making Better Decisions.* Boston: Harvard Business School Press, 1998.

Hassett, Matthew J., and Donald Stewart. *Probability for Risk Management.* Winstead, CT: ACTEX Publications, 1999.

Kleindorfer, Paul R., and Howard Kunreuther (Co-chairs). The Risk Management and Decision Processes Center, University of Pennsylvania, Wharton School. See http://opim.wharton.upenn.edu/risk.

Lam, James. *Enterprise Risk Management: From Incentives to Controls.* New York: John Wiley & Sons, 2003.

March, James G., and Chip Heath. *A Primer on Decision Making: How Decisions Happen.* New York: Free Press, May 1994.

Marrison, Christopher. *The Fundamentals of Risk Measurement.* New York: McGraw-Hill, 2002.

Pfeffer, Jeffrey, and Robert I. Sutton. *The Knowing-Doing Gap: How Smart Companies Turn Knowledge into Action.* Boston: Harvard Business School Press, 2000.

Roberts, Harry V., and Bernard F. Sergesketter. *Quality Is Personal.* New York: Free Press, 1993.

Russo, J. Edward, and Paul J. H. Schoemaker. *Decision Traps.* New York: Fireside Books, 1989.

Russo, J. Edward, Paul J. H. Schoemaker, and Margo Hittleman. *Winning Decisions: Getting It Right the First Time.* New York: Currency/Doubleday, 2001.

Thaler, Richard H. *The Winner's Curse: Paradoxes and Anomalies of Economic Life.* Princeton, NJ: Princeton University Press, 1992.

Wideman, R. Max, ed. *Project and Program Risk Management: A Guide to Managing Project Risks and Opportunities.* Newtown Square, PA: Project Management Institute, 1998.

NOTES

1. "Obituary of Arthur Rudolph," *New York Times* (January 3, 1996).

2. Ralph Waldo Emerson, *Self-Reliance and Other Essays* (Mineola, NY: Dover Publications, 1993).

3. J. Edward Russo and Paul J. H. Schoemaker, *Winning Decisions: Getting it Right the First Time* (New York: Doubleday, 2002), p. 6.

4. See note 3, p. 3.

5. Howard Kunreuther and Mark Pauly, "Ignoring Disaster: Don't Sweat the Big Stuff," working paper collection from the University of Pennsylvania, Wharton School, Risk Management and Decision Processes Center, October 11, 2001.

6. Howard Kunreuther, Nathan Novemsky, and Daniel Kahneman, "Making Low Probabilities Useful," working paper collection from the University of Pennsylvania, Wharton School, Risk Management and Decision Processes Center, December 2000.

7. Howard Kunreuther, "Protective Decisions: Fear or Prudence?" in *Wharton on Making Decisions* (New York: John Wiley & Sons, 2001), Chapter 15.

8. Christian Schade and Howard Kunreuther, "Worry and Mental Accounting with Protective Measures," working paper collection from the University of Pennsylvania, Wharton School, Risk Management and Decision Processes Center, February 20, 2001.

9. F. Tallis, G.C.L. Davey, and N. Capuzzo, "The Phenomenology of Non-Pathlogical Worry: A Preliminary Investigation," in *Worrying: Perspectives on Theory, Assessment, and Treatment,* ed. G. C. L. Davey and F. Tallis (Chichester, England: John Wiley & Sons, 1994), pp. 77.

10. See note 8, p. 6.

17

Demand Management and Project Prioritization

The heavens themselves, the planets, and this center
Observe degree, priority, and place,
Insisture, course, proportion, season, form,
Office, and custom, in all line of order.

—William Shakespeare[1]

This chapter identifies and outlines an approach for managing the demand for projects of all types in the IT department. We define *IT demand management* as a metaproject that determines which IT projects should be commissioned and executed by the IT department by calculating their financial value and prioritizing the projects based on that value and other factors, particularly IT department capacity and overall organization capacity. IT demand management includes the process of identifying and inventorying all ongoing and planned projects, estimating effort to complete, determining costs and benefits, other project dependencies, ease of completion, risks, technical implications, and adequacy of current systems. The result is a properly prioritized inventory of projects and a corporate decision on how many simultaneous projects are feasible.

Demand management is a distinct and separate consideration from project management and is often a neglected topic in IT. IT project management concerns itself with clearly defining project scope, requirements, tasks, time lines, milestones, internal and external resources, costs, technical, application and data architectures, and business impacts for a given project. This discipline usually begins after a project or set of projects has been commissioned. IT demand management is concerned with which projects are commissioned before any projects begin. There is a comprehensive body of work on the topic of IT project management, and the tenets of successful project management have been documented in dozens of books and articles, making it well-understood territory. Given this in-depth previous coverage, we do not attempt to address project management in detail but instead focus on overall IT project prioritization.

In spite of a host of well-defined, proven approaches for managing projects, as observed in Chapter 1, IT projects often fail, many times spectacularly. Our experience has shown that this often results as much from poor demand management and prioritization as much as from badly executed project management. Companies that do not allocate project demand on the IT department based on sound prioritization methodologies are plagued with dozens of competing projects with hazy objectives and often conflicting goals. The resulting project gridlock can often be perplexing to the hapless project managers, who find themselves failing in spite of their best efforts to adhere to accepted project management methodologies. Companies' inability to properly throttle project demand in the IT department is one of the top contributing factors in inefficient IT departments. Certainly, poorly prioritized and poorly run projects never stand a chance, but improper IT demand management is a common cause for the failure of otherwise well-run projects. Correctly managing the project demand on the IT department ensures that only "good" projects are commissioned and that only the appropriate number of projects are allowed to run simultaneously, giving well-managed projects a fighting chance.

Although the primary focus of this chapter is IT demand management, at the chapter conclusion, we offer some of the key success factors we have observed in the field of project management.

This chapter describes the concept of demand management and the issues associated with poor demand management. The prescriptive portion of the chapter is organized around a multistep process for project prioritization based on proven IT demand management principles.

As with the other chapters in this book, the ideas described are general best practices, and all or some of the concepts and ideas described may be applicable to each unique situation. In every case, commonsense application of the prioritization frameworks should always prevail.

Why This Topic Is Important

A most visible, and often cited, measure of the success of the IT department is the business success of the projects undertaken and the completion of those projects in a timely, cost-effective manner. Therefore, the successful selection, prioritization, and execution of IT projects play a large part in determining the overall success of the IT department. Selecting which, and how many projects are allowed on the IT department schedule is a critical determinant of the overall success of those projects.

Project prioritization is a complex process that involves identification of the different projects and assessment of the projects based on factors such as strategic value, financial value, risk, existing system adequacy, time to completion, as well as organizational capacity and technical complexity. These assessments are made to differentiate the *high-priority* projects on a project list based on relevant factors, particularly financial value. They are used to accurately reflect the priority of IT projects in supporting the business unit priorities—not IT's self-mandated priorities. The chapter outlines our methodology for this process.

The Impact of IT Demand Management on Project Performance

The success rate of IT projects is abysmal. The Standish Group statistics quoted in Chapter 1 show that fewer than 16 percent of IT projects reach successful completion.[2]

A major contributor to corporate dissatisfaction with the IT department is IT's inability to complete projects on time, within budget, and to business users' satisfaction and expectations. Paradoxically, almost all IT departments are staffed with hard-working, technically skilled professionals who have the best intentions and want most of all to move their company forward and to be successful at their work. Nevertheless, the IT department is perpetually "staying incredibly busy," but no actual results are achieved, projects completed, or benefits realized.

Typically, a struggling IT department has dozens, even hundreds, of projects underway simultaneously. This is a common phenomenon that we have observed in organizations, regardless of size. The overall project inventory, if one exists, is littered with dozens of ill-defined, partially completed projects of indeterminate origin, benefits, goals, and status. Compounding the issue is that the projects are scoped at wildly varying levels of complexity, size, and business impact, producing absurd results such as "fix Martha's laptop" at the same level as "implement CRM." Further, the project list has multiple dependencies (some identified, some not), internal inconsistencies, conflicting time lines, and unclear ownership on the part of both the business and the IT department.

In most cases, each of these projects is partially completed and in a perpetual state of being slowly shepherded to a fuzzy, indistinct, and elusive finish line by the IT department, with little real hope of solid completion. Indeed, most IT departments have dozens, if not hundreds, of simultaneous projects, each being pushed forward infinitesimally each week. Because IT is attempting to work on multiple competing objectives, in many cases, the original rationale for the project has become obscured by the passage of time, personnel changes, and changes in the business, often rendering the project irrelevant. Xeno's paradox, which states that if you can achieve half the distance to the goal with each step, you will never arrive, comes to mind. The most troubling result of this common dilemma is the damage done to companies who fail to complete, or even identify, the high-value, high-priority technology projects.

The Price of Project Failure

Poor execution and noncompletion of IT projects are a material waste of corporate resources. The Standish Group research cited in Chapter 1 shows that the vast majority of technology projects have missed deadlines and overrun budgets. In addition to the direct costs of failed projects, companies suffer from missed opportunities to reduce costs, drive revenues, or improve operations that the failed projects were intended to deliver. IT project failure can be at best a hindrance and, at times, fatal to a company. In every case, working on the right projects ineffectively or working on the wrong projects is a drain on precious corporate resources. A co-worker's performance review once read, "You're working on the wrong things, and, worse, you're doing them poorly." Unfortunately, this is the case in many IT departments today.

A variety of other costs are associated with poor IT demand and project management that erode the IT department effectiveness as well:

- Resources are allocated equally to low- and high-priority projects, implying that high-priority projects may go understaffed or not be commissioned at all.
- IT department managers overhire to provide staffing levels that support low- and high-priority projects equally.
- The large number of simultaneous projects makes individual projects difficult to monitor; therefore, significant rework efforts, missed deadlines, and budget overruns may go unnoticed, and individual project accountability is difficult to track.
- Multiple disconnected projects create a heterogeneous IT environment, driving additional complexity and, therefore, cost into the baseline support required. Chapter 7 outlines the perils of nonstandard environments in detail.
- Superficial and costly answers are adopted prematurely because the resources that can provide a long-lasting solution are tied up (e.g., additional hardware is thrown at an application performance problem as a quick fix, increasing capital expenditures).
- Deadlines are missed for key customer-required new business capabilities (e.g., EDI-based inventory position exchanges, mandatory online catalog, and product order access).

- Business units spend their own budgets on decentralized IT projects (in larger corporations, business units may fund the creation of their own IT group) because the centralized IT department is unable to adequately execute on priority projects.

- Hiring process emphasizes skills required for low-priority projects instead of, or as well as, high-priority projects, resulting in an IT staff with the wrong or weak set of technical skills to address the top business issues. To remediate, the organization will be forced to lay off and rehire or invest in expensive, time-consuming training.

- Dearth of IT successes results in low morale and high turnover in IT staff, driving up training, recruiting, and turnover costs, compounding the issues by driving out the top performers in IT.

These hidden costs can show up across the board in corporate spending as increases in capital expenditures, IT wage dollars, business unit budgets, increased baseline support costs, and extra external vendor spend.

Why Good Project Management Is Not Enough

A host of reasons explain why organizations manage individual projects well but fare poorly in project completion overall. The previously described symptoms and costs are associated with a set of common causes, which we have cataloged here.

Too Many Projects

IT staff tend to be "pleasers" by nature; the managers and developers fundamentally want to help the business and are usually excited about the benefits and solutions technology can bring to a given business problem. Unfortunately, this tendency often leads IT departments to have trouble saying no (or at least "get in line") to new project requests when they should. In the absence of a clear methodology for managing a project backlog, prioritizing the backlog, and chartering new projects, the IT department invariably takes on more than it should. The outcome is usually a pleased business user today and an angry one three months later when the promised results cannot be delivered.

IT professionals spend effort worrying over scope creep in a project but not enough time worrying about project creep at a macro level. A secondary, related issue is spending time talking about projects instead of doing them. When the IT department has a full set of projects underway, with completion of any of them in the distance, little value is added by discussing the backlog of nonchartered projects. New project ideas should be duly noted and added to the backlog for consideration when project capacity becomes available through the completion of an existing project. Discussing projects not currently underway can be particularly seductive because it closely resembles actual work. This is not to say that high-value projects should not be considered, but it would be a high-value project indeed that could convince the IT department and business sponsors to halt an existing project or to take on more project capacity and, therefore, a project that obviously merits additional consideration. The methodology detailed later in this chapter calls for a reprioritization of the existing backlog at each project completion to ensure that the current chartered projects always consist of the highest value known projects.

No Project Gatekeepers

If projects are allowed to commence without a clear justification, soon the in-process and backlog project inventory become cluttered with a morass of ill-defined projects. A good IT demand management process implements stringent requirements for adding projects to the project inventory. The process for adding new projects is documented later in this chapter, but, in short, it should involve a detailed understanding of the costs, business benefits, and scope of the project, as well as a defined business owner and preliminary effort/time line estimate. The project gatekeeping duties should fall to the IT steering committee, which should be both approving projects for the backlog and prioritizing backlogged projects as capacity becomes available.

In many organizations where we have helped institute IT demand management disciplines, the issue of how difficult it is to get a project started comes up. Most often, the senior management team is worried that we have erected too many barriers to justify new projects. In these cases, we know the methodology is working. Indeed, one of the key ways of keeping a clean project inventory is ensuring that the process has the effect of killing weak projects that have little return and no one in the organization passionate enough about them to fight for their existence. Institution of this form of "project Darwinism" creates a natural selection process that ensures that only the highest value projects survive and that the prioritization process is performed only on good projects. In fact, truly great projects are impossible to keep down and, based on their obvious benefits, rapidly make their way through any approval process.

Too Many Simultaneous Projects

It is hard for anyone to disagree that there is an upper limit on the number of simultaneous projects. Even in large IT departments and corporations, there are a finite number of projects that should be allowed to coexist. As the number of simultaneous projects increases, so does the likelihood of unintended consequences, difficulties of system integration, introduction of heterogeneous technology, and simple distraction for the IT organization. Further, and most practically, a given business unit or function can absorb only so much change over a period. Depending on company size, IT department size, and overall project size, the number of simultaneous projects allowed can be as low as three or four or as high as a dozen. We have seen project success rates fall dramatically when IT departments try to sustain several large projects and multiple small projects.

Moving the Goalposts

Business users are well known for changing the goals of the projects that they are sponsoring. This is a primary contributor to the perception that IT cannot generate clear successes. The whipsawing that occurs from changing the project charter or goals midstream can be damaging to the project, IT morale, and business users' confidence. IT managers have equal culpability here because they are all too often willing accomplices in changing project goals and scope midstream, and they wind up paying the price in the end as the project careens off course. One method for ensuring that the IT department can generate a clear track record of success, while providing flexibility over time, is to commission short-cycle projects (less than three months) with near-term, less ambitious goals. This technique ensures that IT can succeed in short cycles, yet refine the longer term goals at each project completion interval.

Too Much Elapsed Time

Particularly lengthy projects often fail because too much time elapses during their completion. During this time, a host of factors such as changes in the business climate, technology advances, staff attrition, and corporate senior management changes may impact the viability and value of the project. Breaking projects into smaller subprojects helps ensure that if conditions do change, clearly defined pieces of the project will be complete, maximizing their potential salvage value.

Overambitious Goals

Ambitious, large-scale projects suffer naturally from several of the woes outlined here. The length of time, functional and technical complexity, labor complexities, and tough-to-quantify benefits of large projects make them particularly difficult for even the best IT teams to complete. Breaking larger projects into smaller distinct phases provides a better probability for a successful completion.

Indistinct Goals

Projects with unclear goals usually fail spectacularly. If neither the business nor IT defines in advance what success entails, there is little chance of achieving it. While this is one of the more obvious causes of project failure, it happens with surprising frequency. IT professionals tend to have a bias for action over planning that often results in murky project goal setting.

Unclear Benefits

A project can have clear goals and still suffer from indistinct or difficult-to-measure benefits. Key projects, if chartered correctly, generate clearly defined benefits once the goals have been achieved. These usually take the form of cost savings, additional revenue opportunities, or additional control over the business. Good IT demand management discipline ensures that both goals and benefits are well defined before a project is allowed on the approved list.

Heterogeneous Technology

As we have documented in previous chapters, a heterogeneous technology environment can drive up project costs and complexity by an order of magnitude. Existing (or planned) chaotic, difficult-to-interface technical, application, and data architectures can doom an otherwise well-run project.

Overconfidence Bias

New or inexperienced managers often plan overaggressive projects with grand goals and tight time lines. Because of overconfidence, they are not able to anticipate the pitfalls of improper demand management outlined here. The result can be many of the other causes outlined in this section— overambitious projects, hazy end goals, lengthy projects, too many simultaneous projects, and third-party interference.

Outsiders Drive the Agenda

While certainly the IT landscape is populated with a host of well-meaning hardware, software, and service providers, their agendas are not always perfectly aligned with those of the end client. Through simple misunderstanding, a narrow point of view, their own inexperience, or outright negligence, third parties can damage a project. The risk is highest when outside parties are allowed too much control over the project and are being allowed to drive the overall agenda. Allowing vendors to manage large pieces of the project and to make key decisions can be tempting for the IT manager, and most successful vendors aggressively work for as much power as the client allows. The successful IT manager finds productive ways to use vendor expertise while maintaining control of the overall program. The proper role of vendors of all types as partners in helping projects succeed is covered in the vendor selection and vendor management chapters of this book.

No Individual Accountability

Not surprisingly, clearly defined accountability for project results is often absent in ineffective IT departments. For example, one of our clients had particularly weak project completion, and nearly every in-process project had three project managers from IT, none of whom was held strictly accountable for the results. When each project was assigned a single responsible individual who was required to report weekly status to the IT steering committee, project completion rates skyrocketed. There is no substitute for individual accountability and frequent project progress scrutiny.

Project Size

The larger the project, the more difficult it is to ensure that it can be completed. As outlined here, smaller projects with short cycle times, easy-to-define goals, and minimized complexity always have a higher chance of success than do large, unwieldy, complex projects. While large projects are not always avoidable, breaking them down into smaller components and executing them serially can mitigate the costs of complexity.

Too Many Moving Parts

Even projects that do not appear to be overambitious can suffer from over-complexity. Systems projects are by their nature highly intricate endeavors with many subtleties. Even seemingly simple projects can become rapidly complicated and frequently produce multiple unintended consequences. If a given project spans too many vendors, technologies, business processes, interfaces, locations, or other "moving parts," its complexity goes up significantly, and odds of success go down proportionally. This phenomenon holds true for all types of systems projects—applications, databases, and infrastructure implementations. Again, the proper approach is to break projects into more palatable chunks, increasing the likelihood of near-term success and reducing the time to completion.

Poor Communication

Too often in challenged IT departments a project is tossed over the wall to IT, with little or no communication between the business sponsor and the IT department during the project. The project end product, naturally, is then inconsistent with the intent of the end user, whether through indistinct definition or translation problems at the outset or changes in the business during the course of the project. At a minimum, project managers should be in contact weekly with the sponsor and final consumers of the project.

While each of these causes implies its own solution, the common theme is ensuring that only the proper number and type of clearly defined, prioritized projects are ever chartered. Proper IT demand management can mitigate the impacts of these causes on IT department project performance by ensuring that only the right number of high-value, properly defined projects is allowed to go forward. Good project management, in turn, ensures that those projects are successfully completed and deliver the planned value.

A Methodology for IT Demand Management

Our work with IT departments of all sizes in a variety of industries has resulted in a field-proven methodology for avoiding the perils of poor IT demand management. The remainder of the chapter outlines the methodology and covers our prescription for optimizing demand management.

A multistep, analysis-intensive, complex process such as this that must be completed before a project can even commence can put off even the most disciplined of IT departments. However, the benefits of improved project execution and completion, which are the natural outcome of adhering to a rigorous, analytical process for IT demand management, far outweigh the upfront costs of documentation and planning that we suggest here. Exhibit 17.1 provides an overview of the process. The following sections describe each step in detail.

Inventory All Potential Projects

The first step in the demand management process is to create the inventory of all potential projects to be undertaken by the IT department. This is most

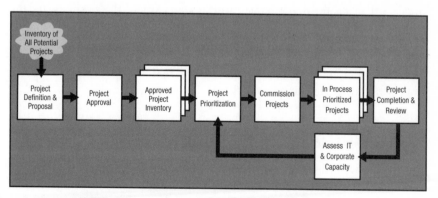

Exhibit 17.1   IT Demand Management Process Overview

often a lengthy list that requires considerable effort to assemble. Typically, the projects emanate from a wide variety of disparate sources scattered throughout the IT department and the company.

A good starting point in the search is the IT department project roster. Most IT departments have one or more lists of projects currently being worked or being considered. Interviews with business unit managers, functional department heads, senior managers, and business users will uncover other projects. Any current enhancement or upgrade lists from vendors or service providers should be obtained and consolidated into one overall project inventory.

After the full list of potential projects has been created, it should be rationalized by removing duplicate projects, as well as combining related small projects into a single effort, or breaking large projects into stand-alone components. This project rationalization (known more popularly as the "project rodeo") starts by creating a full inventory of all projects and then removing duplicates and overlaps, combining items to ensure that the work is defined at the same level. This work generally reduces the project list by 60 percent to 70 percent.

Most project inventory efforts also include projects that no longer have business sponsors or are no longer relevant for the company. These relics should be cut from the list. A key tenet of effective IT demand management is that good projects naturally assert themselves because of their self-evident return. It is common for IT departments, in an attempt to be conscientious and thorough, to keep projects on lists even if no one remembers how they got there. Managers should rest easy on this point—truly valuable projects find their way back onto the list, even if they are inadvertently removed. Bad projects that clutter the list, however, cannot usually sustain real scrutiny and do not survive this exercise.

The result of this process is an inventory of all potential projects, with a short description of each project. The team should avoid overcomplicating the exercise at this point with high-powered project management tools. A simple list of each project name, a brief description, the business and IT sponsor recorded in a spreadsheet or word processing document usually suffices. The content and comprehensiveness of the list are the focus, as opposed to fancy tools or excessive formatting. The projects will receive adequate attention in later steps to ensure that they are properly documented before being commissioned.

Project Definition and Proposal

The next step in the process is to clearly define the project's goals at a level that allows the IT steering committee to provide preliminary approval for the project to be considered for prioritization. This includes the objective of the project and preliminary estimates for the project effort, time line, costs, and benefits. These pieces of information quickly identify and help to provide a first-round estimate of the project's relative value.

Typically, the IT department creates a one-page form, which succinctly captures the critical information needed for the IT steering committee to understand and evaluate the project. The form should include:

- Project name.
- Brief project description.
- Requestor.
- Estimated duration.
- Estimated work effort.
- Current status or progress (if already underway).
- Estimated benefit to the business (reduced costs, increased revenues, better control of the business).
- Business unit sponsor.
- IT sponsor.
- Preliminary estimate of IT resource to be assigned.

Project Approval

Each of the projects, having been defined at the appropriate level of detail, should be presented by the business and IT sponsor to the IT steering committee for a disposition. The IT steering committee approves the project, rejects it, or sends it back for further clarification and definition. Project approval by the committee does not imply that the project will proceed immediately, merely that it is eligible for detailed analysis and participation in the project prioritization process that follows.

The approval is an important step in the process because each approved project will be part of the detailed project prioritization effort. The number of projects evaluated is a major driver of the effort in the prioritization process, so project approvals should be rigorous and serious enough to ensure that only legitimate projects make it through to the next steps. Any projects that are not clearly defined or are of questionable value can be reevaluated for approval at subsequent IT steering committee meetings.

The outcome of the process is an inventory of projects that have been reviewed by the IT steering committee and approved for prioritization. Again, sophisticated management tools are overkill for this process—a simple binder with one-page descriptions of the projects, the date of approval, and the sign off from the IT steering committee usually suffices.

As a point of process, it should be noted that the IT steering committee can at any time add projects to the approved list because new projects are not started until the prioritization process is executed. The prioritization process is triggered when new IT project capacity becomes available because a previous project has completed or because the IT department has added new team members.

Project Prioritization

Project prioritization is the process whereby the IT department determines, in conjunction with the business users and IT steering committee, which projects will generate the highest value for the company and how many can go on simultaneously, given the organization and capacity within IT.

The prioritization process generates four key benefits for the IT department and the overall organization:

- The IT department will always be spending effort on the highest value projects—resources naturally flow to their best use.
- The process ensures that IT and business consensus on project value and priority are built in advance of the project start.
- The IT department capacity analysis ensures that the number of simultaneous projects allowed will be manageable for both the capacity of the IT department and the organization's ability to absorb change.
- The process ensures that project goals and scope are clearly defined in advance and individual accountability for project success is assigned.

The project prioritization process is the heart of effective IT demand management, and it gives the IT department more than a fighting chance to avoid many of the pitfalls described earlier in the chapter. It is imperative that the business users have adequate representation on the steering committee because their input is critical to proper prioritization. Correctly assembling the steering committee and its membership can make or break the process. Chapter 19 covers this process in detail.

After a preliminary project prioritization is complete, the prioritization process takes place under three circumstances:

1. When an existing project is completed and IT project capacity becomes available.
2. When new IT capacity is added (or reduced), changing the total number of possible simultaneous projects.
3. The prioritization may be reassessed if high-priority projects that should be prioritized over existing efforts are identified. This instance is a rare occurrence because of the high cost of an IT project changeover, but it may happen in some instances (e.g., key customer demands new

Exhibit 17.2   Key Components to the Prioritization Process

capabilities, government regulation, or new technology that improves revenue or reduces costs).

Prioritization of approved projects is, therefore, not just a one-time effort but, instead, an ongoing process. While we outline here a quantitative approach for assessing the projects and prioritizing them, it is important to add a healthy dose of common sense to project prioritization. The methodology provides ample room for tilting the table for projects whose benefits it does not adequately incorporate. Exhibit 17.2 outlines the overall approach for project prioritization.

The prioritization process incorporates the best thinking of the IT and business leaders across the key project metrics that should drive project priorities: financial value, risk, strategic value, current system adequacy, and IT capacity. The analysis portion of the prioritization exercise should be completed by the IT department and business users and results presented to the IT steering committee for approval and sign off. In most cases, the process consumes several iterations of analysis after the first presentation to the IT steering committee, as additional information needs are uncovered through questions.

Key Components of the Prioritization Process

The analytic portion of the project prioritization process can be decomposed into seven discrete subtasks. The overall approach is shown in Exhibit 17.3 and is described in more detail in the following sections.

Determine Project Financial Value.   Generally, the single best measure of the value of the project is its financial value to the company. In simplest terms, the financial value is measured as the benefit stream that a

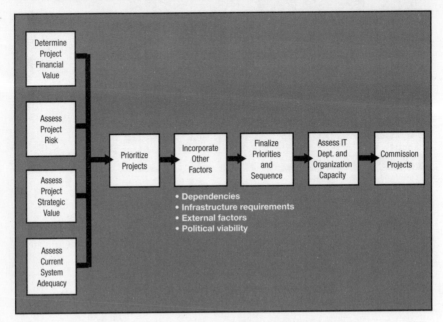

Exhibit 17.3   Overall Project Prioritization Process

project delivers compared to the cost to generate those benefits. Exhibit 17.4 shows an overall framework for evaluating project value based on the associated financial value.

There are many methods for calculating the financial value of a given project, including return on investment, value on investment, project payback period, net present value, and internal rate of return. All specific methods for measuring project return have in common the inputs needed to understand project value: costs and benefits. Project costs usually come in two forms: one-time project costs and steady-state cost changes (i.e., changes to the underlying operating model). Likewise, benefits have one-time and ongoing components. Usually, the majority of the costs occur in the one-time category, while benefits tend to come in the form of recurring savings or revenues.

Depending on the company requirements or IT steering committee's preferences, models of widely varying sophistication can be used to measure the financial value of the project. Our preference for project value measurement is a simple measure of the costs and benefits and clear documentation of the major cost drivers and assumptions for benefit generation. The analysis time saved by keeping the model simple can be spent on further validating the cost and benefit assumptions, thereby greatly improving the accuracy of the estimate. An estimate generated by a sophisticated calculation based on poor or incomplete assumptions is useless in helping guide investment decisions. Exhibit 17.5 presents our basic model for calculating project return. Because

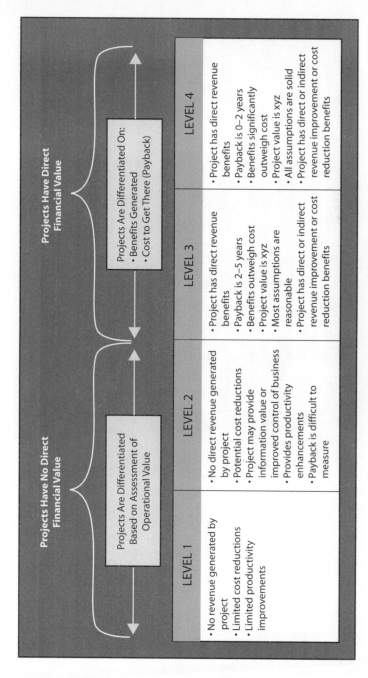

Projects Have No Direct Financial Value

Projects Have Direct Financial Value

Projects Are Differentiated Based on Assessment of Operational Value

Projects Are Differentiated On:
- Benefits Generated
- Cost to Get There (Payback)

LEVEL 1	LEVEL 2	LEVEL 3	LEVEL 4
• No revenue generated by project • Limited cost reductions • Limited productivity improvements	• No direct revenue generated by project • Potential cost reductions • Project may provide information value or improved control of business • Provides productivity enhancements • Payback is difficult to measure	• Project has direct revenue benefits • Payback is 2–5 years • Benefits outweigh cost • Project value is xyz • Most assumptions are reasonable • Project has direct or indirect revenue improvement or cost reduction benefits	• Project has direct revenue benefits • Payback is 0–2 years • Benefits significantly outweigh cost • Project value is xyz • All assumptions are solid • Project has direct or indirect revenue improvement or cost reduction benefits

Exhibit 17.4 Project Financial Value Scorecard

557

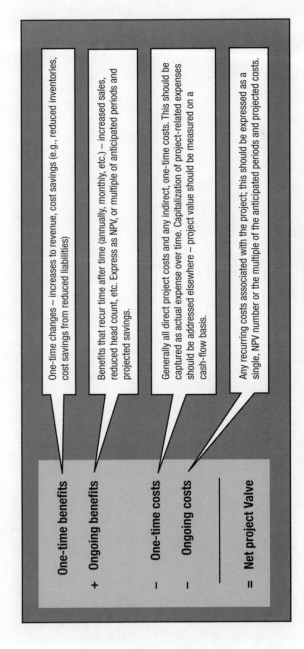

One-time benefits — One-time changes – increases to revenue, cost savings (e.g., reduced inventories, cost savings from reduced liabilities)

+ Ongoing benefits — Benefits that recur time after time (annually, monthly, etc.) – increased sales, reduced head count, etc. Express as NPV, or multiple of anticipated periods and projected savings.

- One-time costs — Generally all direct project costs and any indirect, one-time costs. This should be captured as actual expense over time. Capitalization of project-related expenses should be addressed elsewhere – project value should be measured on a cash-flow basis.

- Ongoing costs — Any recurring costs associated with the project; this should be expressed as a single, NPV number or the multiple of the anticipated periods and projected costs.

= Net project Valve

Exhibit 17.5   Project Business Value Calculation Approach

the model is simplified, particular attention should be paid to the timing of benefits. Speculative benefits in the distant future are of considerably lower value, especially when compared to real costs today. The assumptions behind the model should outline the stream of recurring benefits and their timing. Chapter 12 also addresses approaches for estimating project costs and benefits. An example of a simple project financial value calculation is shown in Exhibit 17.6.

It is also important to note that the financial value estimate should be done on a cash-flow basis. While accounting rules allow project, hardware, and software investments to be capitalized and the expense recognized over time, the project should demonstrate clear value on a cash flow basis, regardless of its final accounting treatment.

PROJECT VALUE FOR WEB SITE PROMOTION

	ASSUMPTION	CALCULATION
Estimated unique visitors per day	1,000	
Member points		
Visitors that become members (points)	15%	150
Members that earn coupons	75%	113
Number of Members earning coupons that visit store	50%	56
Revenue per day from Members earning coupons		$56
Contests and surveys		
Members that participate in contests	33%	50
Number of times visiting store for contest	20	
Store visits due to contests		990
Revenue per day from store contests		$2,267
Instant coupons		
Visitors that win instant discount coupons	5%	50
Number of people earning coupons that visit the store	65%	33
Revenue per day from instant coupons		$53
Incremental store visits		
Incremental visits per unique visitor per year	2	
Total participating visitors per day		183
Revenue per day from incremental store visits		$836
Total revenue per day		$3,213
Total revenue per year		$1,143,708
Gross margin on product revenue	90%	$1,029,337
Estimated cost of site		$245,000
Months to payback		2.86
Average price for product	$1.29	
Average price of uplift from product	$1.00	

Exhibit 17.6 Example Project Financial Value Calculation

The CFO and business unit owners also generally want to understand how the project will affect the current fiscal year budget, so they can prepare for any variances that develop as part of the project. In cases where the project costs can be capitalized, the impact on current year budgets should be minimal. The CFO also wants to understand the timing of cash outlays for the project to effectively manage corporate cash reserves. Understanding timing of project expenses ensures that cash is available when needed for the project external resources, hardware, and software.

Finally, the IT steering committee can be helpful guiding the IT team in evaluating the return on technology-related projects compared to other projects throughout the company. In most cases, the senior management team wants corporate investment dollars to be spent on the highest-return project corporatewide, and the IT steering committee can provide context for the IT department on competing nontechnology projects that have been proposed.

ASSESS PROJECT RISK. Assessing risk impact on company priorities is the next critical step in the prioritization process. The overall project delivery risk has a large impact on the organization's ability to realize the project benefits. Some categories of IT project risks include project complexity, user readiness, and technology to be used. The scorecard in Exhibit 17.7 shows other risk factors to evaluate when determining the value of a project. Depending on the specific project under consideration, other factors may be deemed appropriate by the evaluation team for evaluating project risk. In any case, the project should be assigned a risk rating relative to the other approved projects in the inventory, ranging from low to high.

ASSESS PROJECT STRATEGIC VALUE. *Project strategic value* is defined as the impact a project will have on external entities, particularly customers and suppliers. The strategic value of the project gives a better idea of how the project gives the company new capabilities that improve the company's ability to work with customers or suppliers of the project to the company and how easily competitors can duplicate the new capability. The strategic value should be estimated though business unit user input as well as the executive management viewpoints. Exhibit 17.8 on page 562 shows the scorecard used to evaluate the strategic value a project will have on a business. The result of the analysis should be a rating of the project's strategic value relative to competing projects, from low to high.

ASSESS CURRENT SYSTEM ADEQUACY. The adequacy of the current systems is also a critical factor to consider when determining the value of a project. In cases where systems already exist, they may provide adequate capabilities for the organization, minimizing, or at least reducing, the benefits from incremental investment and effort. We have observed a tendency in IT teams to look for incremental improvements in existing systems instead of tackling new initiatives, which may have higher value (and potentially higher

	Level 4	Level 3	Level 2	Level 1
Project Complexity	• Requirements well understood and documented • Scope well defined	• Good understanding of requirements • Limited potential impact of regional or customer differences	• Application supports new business practices not well understood • Limited experience with business function	• Major functionality blocks not clearly defined • Unclear understanding of IT requirements • Many outstanding issues
User Readiness	• Key resources have availability and capacity • Clear ownership and accountability • Specific and measurable targets	• Resources available • Shared ownership and accountability • Key issues tracked with impact understood	• Unclear or limited ownership • Broad accountability across several areas • Issues not tracked – no understanding of impact	• Key resources spread across many projects • No ownership of project or benefits • Limited accountability • Many outstanding issues
Technology	• Application built on stable platform in which IT has significant experience • Limited impact on operations	• Adequate time to test changes to technical environment and train appropriate staff • Release strategy easily understood and controlled	• Significant restructuring of technical environment with limited time for testing or training • Release strategy results in two or more versions of production code	• Application one of first delivered on new technical platform • Spans multiple technical platforms • Technology has unproven performance

Exhibit 17.7 Project Risk Assessment Scorecard

	STRATEGIC VALUE		
LEVEL 1	**LEVEL 2**	**LEVEL 3**	**LEVEL 4**

• Little or no strategic impact
• No external impact on customers or suppliers
• Competitors will easily duplicate capabilities
	• Supports keeping up with the market or provides competitive response
	• Sustains marketplace credibility
	• Provides better information
	  – Drives sales growth
	  – Supports better customer service
	• Reduces costs
	• Competitors duplicate capabilities in less than one year
		• Significantly improves customer and/or supplier relationships by creating measurable value
		• Creates temporary competitive advantage or positioning
		• Competitive parity will lag by one to two years
			• Establishes industry leadership position/delivers sustainable increases in market share
			• Helps solidify long term relationships with customers or suppliers
			• Creates sustainable, hard-to-copy competitive position
			• Competitive parity is difficult to match

LOW → HIGH

Exhibit 17.8 Project Strategic Value Scorecard

risk or effort). The adequacy of the current system is, therefore, an appropriate metric for understanding overall project priorities. Overall capabilities can be measured in two categories—from both a systems technology standpoint and because of the process and procedures that are in place to support the system.

Exhibit 17.9 shows a system/process scorecard for varying levels of adequacy, which can be used to judge the level of coverage from the current systems capabilities.

PRIORITIZE PROJECTS. Now that the four key project assessments—financial value, risk, strategic value, and system adequacy—for the project values have been made, an overall project prioritization based on those evaluations can be done by plotting the approved projects on two-by-two grids according to the values assigned in the previous exercise.

The first evaluation is a comparison based on strategic and financial value of a project. Strategic versus financial value comparisons showcase the "worthy" projects, namely projects that provide the most benefit to the organization. Exhibit 17.10 on page 565 shows the various classifications of projects, based on their strategic and financial values. The projects with lowest relative financial and strategic value are in the lower left-hand corner of the quadrant. These projects will probably not be considered for the highest-priority project list, and possibly their addition to the approved projects list will be revisited.

After screening out all the low-financial/low-strategic value (lower left-hand quadrant projects), the remaining projects should be evaluated based on current system adequacy. Exhibit 17.11 on page 566 shows the two-by-two matrix for assessing projects based on financial value and system adequacy. In each case, the quadrants into which the projects fall suggest a course of action for the project. Projects that fall into the upper left-hand quadrant are high-value projects that have inadequate supporting systems capabilities. These projects become the high-priority projects that will receive organizational focus. Exhibit 17.11 also shows a typical sampling of actual projects and how they may fall on the prioritization grid.

Finally, projects from the upper left-hand quadrant, *increase focus* projects, should be further evaluated and ranked based on "doability" (cost, speed, risk) versus financial value. Exhibit 17.12 on page 567 shows this analysis. The purpose of this ranking is to ensure that the projects that combine high value and ease of completion receive the highest ranking. This ensures that the benefits of the projects can be enjoyed by the company as rapidly as possible. Projects that fall into the upper right-hand quadrant are *gems*, which are easy to do and provide high financial value. This quadrant is where the top projects fall and is composed of the projects that the IT department should make first priority. Most of the projects that have made it to

	Level 1	Level 2	Level 3	Level 4
System	• No system currently handling the function proposed by the project • Current system handling function is unstable or not delivering necessary functionality	• System handling current function is adequate for next 0–6 months	• System handling current function is adequate for next 7–12 months	• System handling current function is adequate for next 1–2 years
Process	• No process currently handling the function proposed by the project • Current process handling function is unstable or not delivering necessary functionality	• Process handling current function is adequate for next 0–6 months	• Process handling current function is adequate for next 7–12 months	• Process handling current function is adequate for next 1–2 years

SYSTEM ADEQUACY

LOW ⟶ HIGH

Exhibit 17.9   Current System Adequacy Scorecard

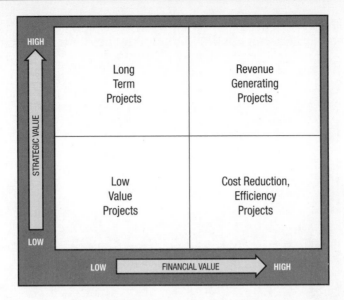

Exhibit 17.10   Project Strategic Value versus Financial Value Assessment

this phase of the analysis are likely to be valuable projects; this final prioritization simply helps force rank the projects.

In every instance, the outcome of the prioritization should pass a "sanity" check. If the analysis produces skewed, or nonsensical results, and a careful check of the assumptions yields no changes in outcome, common sense should always prevail over methodology-generated priorities.

After each of the projects has been evaluated based on strategic, financial, risk, and system adequacy values, the scores for each variable should be recorded on the project prioritization analysis shown in Exhibit 17.13 on page 567. Based on the scorecards discussed, a numerical score can be recorded (typically 1 to 4) for each variable, depending on the project evaluation. The approved project inventory should be updated with the results of each piece of analysis. An example of the project prioritization is shown in Exhibit 17.13. The total score for each project can then be calculated and sorted in priority order from highest scores to lowest. The list and the priority rankings are periodically added to and reevaluated as new projects are added or projects are completed.

INCORPORATE OTHER FACTORS.   Assessment of other factors is the next step in the project prioritization process. A variety of factors may be considered by the team that may change the overall project priorities, including:

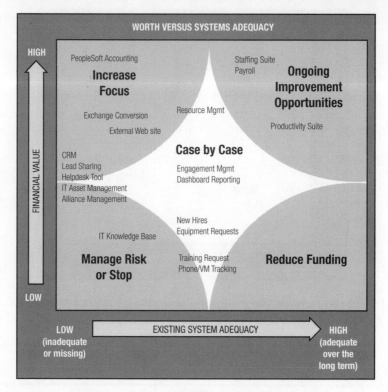

Exhibit 17.11   Example Project System Adequacy versus Financial Value Assessment

- *Dependencies that the project has on other projects or that other projects have on the identified project:* In these cases, the project dependencies may force serial sequencing of equally high-priority projects.
- *Infrastructure investment needed to complete the project:* Some projects may depend on infrastructure or facilities capacity that is not currently available and, therefore, must be deferred.
- *Project timing:* External factors may dictate when a project is appropriate to begin or complete. For instance, implementing a new order system is a poor idea during the peak season in a highly seasonal business. Likewise, going live with new financial systems during year-end close is similarly poor timing. These externalities should be taken into account as part of the final prioritization.
- *Political viability:* End-users and business decision makers must have a full understanding of the purpose of the project and the quantified benefits that can be achieved because of the project. Projects, regardless of high value, sometimes must be sold to the organization

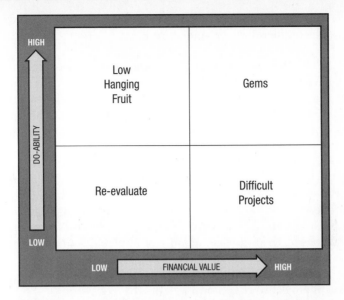

Exhibit 17.12   Do-ability versus Financial Value Assessment

over time and, therefore, must be deferred until they are politically viable.

- *Technical or systems dependencies:* System upgrades such as file expansion, code standardization, or software patches may need to be executed before new software can be implemented. These dependencies should be taken into account.

FINALIZE PRIORITIES AND SEQUENCE PROJECTS.   After all of these factors have been taken into account, the projects can be force ranked, producing an inventory of the projects in the order that they are to be worked.

Exhibit 17.13   Sample Project Prioritization Data Gathering Template

The next step determines how many of these projects can be worked simultaneously and will, therefore, be commissioned.

Assess IT Department and Organization Capacity. After the projects have been prioritized, the team must determine how many of the projects can be worked simultaneously. This number is dependent on two factors: the resource capacity within the IT department (or external capacity justified by the project benefits) and the overall capacity of the company to absorb new projects.

The capacity of the IT department depends on a variety of factors, including the number of project managers available, the allocation of staff time between baseline support and project capacity, and the specific technical and functional skill sets required for the project. Each project must have a project manager and a team with the requisite skill sets. The project schedule is dictated by the aggregate number of available hours for project work from the team.

An example of a capacity chart for determining how many hours can be dedicated to project work is shown in Exhibit 17.14.

Reviewing the number of hours required to complete projects, categorized into various functional areas, is also helpful. Exhibit 17.15 shows number of hours of project work needed versus number of resources available.

Project management capacity, in addition to IT capacity, must be taken into consideration when developing project schedules. Overall, on average, project managers can handle only a handful of projects at a time. The size and complexity of the projects need to be considered. Larger projects should be broken down into smaller projects, with three-month phases. On average, a project manager can complete four three-month phase projects over one year. In addition, if the project manager handles two projects simultane-

	IT Programmer	Network Support Personnel
Total Hours/Week	40	40
Emergency Work/Week	5	5
Project Work/Week	30	30
Operations/Base Support/Week	5	5

Exhibit 17.14   IT Organization Capacity Chart

DEPLOYMENT				
Project Functional Area	Remaining Development Effort (FTE Hours)	Remaining Roll out Effort (FTE Hours)5020	Total Remaining Effort (FTE Hours)	Current BU and IT Resources Available (FTE Hours)
Sales	300	50	350	200 BU, 100 IT
Marketing	50	20	70	10 BU, 30 IT

Exhibit 17.15   Functional Organization Capacity Chart

ously, he or she can complete eight smaller projects. Project manager capacity and capability relative to the project importance should be carefully weighed when trying to determine how many projects can be completed, as well as size of each project. Exhibit 17.16 shows an assessment between the adequacy of current project manager versus project business value.

Finally, the overall organization or company ability to sustain multiple, simultaneous projects should be evaluated. This number varies from company to company, based on factors such as company size, culture, geographic distribution, and business cycle. While the number varies, no company can absorb the change and disruption associated with large-scale projects. For our mid-size clients ($100 million to $500 million revenues), we recommend no more than two major projects and no more than four to seven simultaneous projects in total. For our Fortune 1000 clients, we recommend no more than

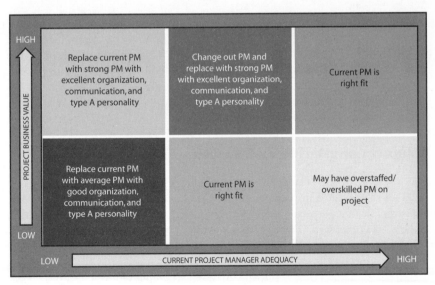

Exhibit 17.16   Current Project Manager Adequacy versus Project Business Value

one major program and five major projects. The subprojects underneath these majors vary widely but typically range from one to five.

The result of this step is a determination of how far down the project prioritization list the team can go and a decision on which projects are allowed to start.

Commission Projects

After the projects have been prioritized and IT capacity estimated, it is possible to commission a specific set of projects. The total project work estimates can be compared to the available resource estimates, and the process of working down the project inventory begins. A threshold is set at the point where available project resources are exhausted. No additional projects can be commissioned past this threshold until (1) a project is completed, (2) a project is cancelled, or (3) the budget is increased to add IT internal or external resources.

The majority of the work of IT demand management is complete at this point, and the standard, well-documented disciplines of IT project management, including scope definition, requirements gathering, work planning, and final estimating begin. For the top identified projects, each sponsor should sign off on a project initiation form to kick off the requirements, design, and development of the project. Most important, the business owner and the IT team should ensure that they have a clear definition of how project success and completion will be measured.

In-Process Projects

When projects are underway, the normal project management disciplines aimed at ensuring the proper planning, execution, reporting, and management of the effort apply. From an IT demand management standpoint, it is important that changes in the assumptions that led to the project's taking priority be rapidly communicated. Material changes in anticipated costs or benefits, risk, strategic value, or other prioritization factors may result in a reevaluation of the project priority.

Project Completion and Review

As projects are completed, the event should be confirmed by both the business users and the IT steering committee through a formal sign-off. A final analysis of the project costs and a renewed look at the project benefits should be completed. This is also a good time to record lessons learned and conduct team personnel reviews.

After a project has been completed, the next project on the priority list can be commissioned by the IT department. If, since the previous prioritization, new projects have been added to the approved list, they must be added to the prioritization analysis so that they can be considered for commissioning. Further, if any assumptions concerning financial value, strategic value, existing system adequacy, and risk for previously prioritized projects have changed, those changes should be taken into account.

Key Success Factors for Project Management

Having outlined our methodology for IT demand management, the remainder of the chapter briefly covers a few helpful practices for IT project management. As we have observed, there are a wide variety of well-defined, highly effective methodologies for IT project management. While a comprehensive look at the components of good project management cannot be covered in this chapter, we highlight a few of the critical components for successful project management.

Good project management is a necessary complement to effective IT demand management; the overall management of the project dictates the success or failure of the project, even if it has been properly prioritized.

Two key components of these key tools to managing a project are the project initiation document and the project plan. The project initiation document identifies the project sponsor, a business user sponsor, a project manager from IT, internal and external resources, scope, goals, financial returns expected, anticipated resource, hardware and software costs, and executive level sign-off on the project.

The project plan should incorporate the following:

- Defining 5 to 10 high-level tasks to complete the project (e.g., assess functionality, analyze economics/ROI, check references).
- Identifying dependencies between tasks so that task priorities, timing, and sequencing can be optimized and opportunities for concurrent execution of tasks can be leveraged.
- Defining specific outcomes/deliverables that must be achieved for a task to be deemed complete.
- Defining tasks at a high level of detail to make clear the actions that must be taken and the effort that the work step requires.
- Identifying a single owner who is responsible for completion of each task. Other members of the team who will participate in the task can then be defined.
- Promoting project discipline by diligently achieving key milestones and updating the plan to reflect current status.
- Using the deadlines as leverage to get vendors to perform according to the project timetable.
- Having formal discussions with business sponsors and the IT steering committee when deadlines are missed so that reasons for shortfall are clearly communicated and new expectations can be set.

Managing Resources Effectively

One of the key project management success factors is to be able to manage project resources effectively.

When starting a project, one of the first things is to set the tone of the project. This involves reviewing the project objectives and putting aside other agendas for the duration of the project. Setting the tone also involves ensuring that reporting relationships and accountability within the teams are clearly defined. The project manager has responsibility for delivering the project and, therefore, must be the ultimate decision maker.

When starting a project, milestone review dates should be announced and clearly documented. All team members should be aware of the key milestones, schedule, and criticality of meeting the dates. The project manager should delegate tasks and subprojects to team members and make sure that they understand what they are responsible for.

Over the life of the project, project managers should take care to reward and recognize deserving personnel when milestones are achieved and celebrate significant team accomplishments. On the other hand, if time lines and milestones are not being met or performance issues arise, the project manager should move to rapidly address the deficiencies with the team. Many project managers have a tendency in these situations to ignore the underperformers and hope that the issues will resolve on their own. This type of approach is detrimental to not only the person with the issue but also the whole team, sending a signal that poor performance and missed deadlines will be tolerated.

In this situation, the project manager should work with the team member to remediate the problems with specific, actionable recommendations for changes in behavior. The manager should also make clear the consequences of further failures. The conversation with the team member should be documented in a letter with specific milestones and dates, and both project manager and team member should sign the document to ensure complete clarity. A subsequent performance evaluation with the team member should be made at a short interval, usually 30 days. Standard periodic reviews scheduled with each individual team member are an easy way to catch these issues early and provide a venue for ensuring that they are addressed.

RESOURCES

Project financial value calculation:

Bodie, Zvi Alex Kane, and Alan J. Marcus. *Investments.* New York: McGraw-Hill/Irwin.

Brealey, Richard A., and Stewart C. Myers. *Principles of Corporate Finance.* New York: McGraw-Hill.

Gardner, Christopher. *The Valuation of Information Technology: A Guide for Strategy Development, Valuation and Financial Planning.* New York: John Wiley & Sons, 2000.

Remenyi, D., Arthur Money, Michael Sherwood-Smith, Zahir Irani, and Alan Twite. *The Effective Measurement and Management of IT Costs and Benefits.* Boston: Butterworth-Heinemann, Computer Weekly Professional Series, 2000.

Project planning:

Brooks, Frederick P. *The Mythical Man-Month.* Boston: Addison-Wesley, 1995.

Cassidy, Anita, *A Practical Guide to Information Systems Strategic Planning.* Boca Raton, FL: CRC Press, 1998.

Project management:

Charvat, Jason. *Project Management Nation: Goals for the New and Practicing IT Project Manager—Guidance, Tools, Templates and Techniques That Work!* New York: John Wiley & Sons, 2002.

Murch, Richard. *Project Management: Best Practices for IT Professionals.* Englewood Cliffs, NJ: Prentice Hall, 2000.

Phillips, Joseph, *IT Project Management: On Track from Start to Finish.* New York: McGraw-Hill Osborne Media, 2004.

Project Management Institute. www.pmi.org.

Team leadership:

Parcells, Bill, "The Tough Work of Turning around a Team." *Harvard Business Review* (November/December 2000).

NOTES

1. William Shakespeare, "Troilus and Cressida," Act I, Scene iii, p. 1602.
2. The Standish Group. *The Chaos Report* (West Yarmouth, MA: The Standish Group International, 1994), http://www.standishgroup.com/sample_research /chaos_1994_1.php.

18

IT Performance Measurement

If you can't measure it, you can't manage it.

—Tom Peters[1]

This chapter outlines a method of measuring overall IT performance. It distills the most practical measures of performance and discusses approaches for implementing an IT performance measurement program in the organization. The chapter covers the following key topics:

- The value of performance measurement.
- Developing and managing an IT measurement program.
  —Defining the IT dashboard.
  —Conducting a baseline survey.
  —Developing management, analysis, and reporting processes.
  —Managing the measurement program.
  —Reassessing the program.
- IT metrics.
- Commissioning and managing a corporate IT health check.

This chapter presents a pragmatic viewpoint to implementing an IT performance-reporting program.

Why This Topic Is Important

Today's CIO is confronted with an unending growth of new responsibilities. This book discusses many of them: strategic planning, infrastructure planning, operations management, personnel, and many others. In addition, managers are regularly confronted with urgent and critical situations that must receive focused attention immediately. Unfortunately, at the bottom of the priority list is a performance management program. As the daily urgent matters monopolize the available time, the need to perform is much greater than the need to track performance; thus, this tracking gets perpetually delayed. Implementing performance management and process control can increase the performance and productivity of the unit dramatically. However, suspending some activities temporarily to establish a program is challenging.

Measurement, if executed well, can help the IT organization align work to key business objectives and help the organization gain credibility with business unit leaders through performance improvement and objective measurement reporting. To communicate effectively to the rest of senior management, the CIO must implement objective measures defining a common language that explains excellent versus poor performance. Without this language, business leaders have difficulty establishing performance targets and understanding actual IT performance levels. They also have a high degree of distrust for any subjective measures that then must be used to describe performance. Almost all other business units and functions in a company have defined targets and measures that must be achieved (e.g., inventory levels, sales quotas, day sales outstanding). Why IT organizations are not often held to this level of rigorous measurement is perplexing. This is especially confounding because the CFO, the typical owner of the IT function, is generally the strictest proponent of measurement systems in a company. Usually CFOs and other senior management don't have the training, experience, or technical education to construct meaningful measurements of IT performance and generally accepted metrics are not readily available for reference. Furthermore, as outlined elsewhere in this book, if the CIO wants to establish a peer-level relationship with senior management, he or she must measure their performance just like any other business unit.

Implementing a standard, repeatable system for measuring and tracking performance enables the CIO to establish a common framework to use in his or her communications with the lines of business. Consistent use of this system allows the CIO to build trust and gain credibility across the organization. A performance management and reporting system can help the CEO and CFO track the return on technology-invested capital. Understanding and disclosure replaces ambiguity and unanswered questions.

Many IT/senior management communication programs are a result of the lack of standard measures. While executives would not ask a factory manager to cut costs or increase productivity without asking for common ratios such as units produced per day, they frequently ask IT to do the same without any knowledge of internal IT processes or operations. While most manufacturing and financial functions are controlled and measured by time-tested metrics,

IT has relatively few measures that are useful for tying its operations to the business. IT measurement helps address this problem by providing a consistent framework that directly links IT to business unit objectives.

The benefits of implementing process control and performance measurement can be dramatic. The Software Engineering Institute's Capability Maturity Model (CMM), a software process management certification, is being increasingly adopted by organizations with software development groups. More than 10 years of data from companies that have implemented the process improvement tool has proven that process discipline has returned on average a minimum of $5 for every $1 invested. By implementing a project measurement system, "Merrill Lynch has saved between $25 million and $30 million over the past year by slowing down or stopping planned initiatives and redirecting project funding faster and more effectively than it used to."[2]

In another case, Belk, Inc., a national retailer, was "forced to adopt productivity metrics as a means of staving off devastating system failures." The company was spending $1.1 million out of a $30-million IT budget on unplanned maintenance. "Belk's batch systems went down an astounding 800 times a month." A year later, after implementing performance measurements, system failures declined to 480 per month and maintenance expenses were reduced by $800,000.[3]

Finally, the importance of implementing a performance measurement program is critical to the success of the CIO. Managing the performance of the unit is obviously the responsibility of the CIO. Not having a program in place is a reflection on the CIO's level of understanding of business management and skills. The performance of the unit will ultimately suffer as will the perceived performance of the CIO.

Value of Measurement

Value from measurement is gained by analyzing the data, taking action, and then improving the operations. Improving the operations of the unit, increases productivity and the return on capital invested in IT. Because cost of implementing a measurement system is not trivial but is typically small compared to the benefits, measurement systems are usually a high return on investment proposition. Information technology investments and operations should not be measured unless the expected benefit of measurement exceeds the costs of data collection, analysis, management, and reporting. In other words, do not measure for the sake of measurement itself; expect a return.

The expected value of measurement is the difference between the expected benefits (both direct and indirect) and the expected costs. The value is derived primarily from the direct benefits that can be obtained from regularly measuring and managing the IT department. These benefits include

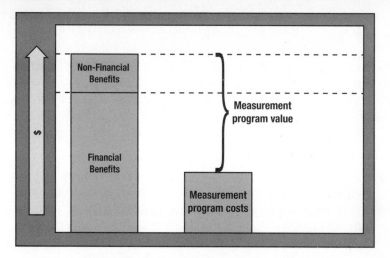

Exhibit 18.1   Value of IT Measurement Program

better allocation of resources, improved system performance, reduction of risks, and improved customer service. Additionally, there are some "hidden" or indirect benefits that include the development of a performance culture, enhanced alignment of IT with the business, and increased transparency of the value of IT throughout the organization.

A critical mistake commonly made during the implementation of IT measurement programs is overcomplicating the program and tracking hundreds of complicated metrics. The error is in tracking every conceivable metric and not differentiating between metrics that are important versus ones that *might* be important. The result is a behemoth report of irrelevant information and untimely data. This approach is both costly and cumbersome. Return on the program is low, it generally dies a slow and painful death, and the effort to maintain the program is greater than the actual use of the data; therefore, benefits are minimal.

As illustrated in Exhibit 18.1, if the measurement program is constructed properly, the value of the program should be considerable.

Benefits of IT Measurement

The key benefits of IT measurement result from *actions* taken in response to its output; they include:

- Improved customer service.
- More efficient allocation of resources.
- Improved system performance and uptime.
- Reduction in risk and unplanned activities.

- Increase in staff productivity (development and support).
- Seeds planted for high performance culture.

IMPROVED CUSTOMER SERVICE. Improved customer service is a result of mutual agreement on service levels and then the meeting or exceeding of those levels. Many of the benefits are interrelated. For example, decreasing unplanned system outages reduces staff work and improves customer service. Increasing staff productivity allows projects to be completed faster, which again increases customer satisfaction.

Typically, there is a disconnect between the true costs of providing IT services to enterprise customers and the price of any actually paid by the customer for the services. Furthermore, there is often no correlation between a business unit's desired service level, the service level received, and what it actually pays for the specific services. Business units do not recognize this directly because they are usually charged for services via ad-hoc overhead allocation rules, instead of paying for differentiated levels of services. This lack of market discipline leads to high costs and potentially over-specified service levels. For example, business unit A may not need desktop support response within 30 minutes. Four hours would potentially suffice. Yet, IT makes an arbitrary decision to have a 30-minute response time, which means more people and more costs.

Years ago, the only company that sold or leased telephones was AT&T. The telephones made were overengineered. They were rugged—made of heavy plastic—and rarely broke. However, they were very expensive; an average phone could cost well over $100. After the market was deregulated, new telephone equipment manufacturers began selling $20 disposable phones. They quickly became popular, and soon everyone was purchasing disposable phones made of cheap plastic that lasted for a year or two. Soon, a huge industry grew to satisfy consumer demand for designer phones. AT&T assumed that everyone needed the same phone at the same price—an incorrect assumption.

The same is true for the uneducated IT department; IT continually makes uninformed assumptions regarding user's desired service levels. The IT department typically sets its level of service to the highest common denominator. However, not every business unit or function requires the highest level of service. Most IT organizations can make tremendous improvements in their effectiveness simply by providing differential services for units willing to pay more for higher levels of service and providing low-cost options for those who do not require premium service.

Benefits accrue through utilization of customer feedback of their expectations and judgment of the department's relative performance across a variety of service areas. The knowledge highlights areas where IT has overinvested resources, as well as areas where additional resources are needed. This inevitably improves customer service as well as utilization of capital and operating expenditures. Since the program enables IT to track and analyze customer service levels, it facilitates genuine discussion of appropriate levels of service and performance.

MORE EFFICIENT ALLOCATION OF RESOURCES. Metrics allow the CIO to move staff to areas in need of improved service levels and divert staff from areas that already exceed service levels. Additionally, project-tracking metrics allow allocation of resources to appropriate projects.

IMPROVED SYSTEM PERFORMANCE AND UPTIME. Another clear benefit to measurement is improved system performance. This performance can be measured in many ways, including capacity utilization, system availability, and speed. Tracking of various system performance metrics can help managers quickly isolate problems before they become serious. Just as warning gauges on a car help the driver maintain the vehicle in high performance, system metrics help a manager keep systems running at peak performance.

REDUCTION IN RISK AND UNPLANNED ACTIVITIES. A benefit that is often hidden from typical analysis is the reduction of risk. Without any tracking or measurement, it is difficult for managers to understand trends in system usage and anticipate potential problems or upgrades required in the future. This can result in major problems creeping up on managers at the most inopportune times. For instance, at one client firm, a large server crashed unexpectedly not because of faulty hardware or a virus, but because a large group of acquired employees had recently started and drove usage that exceeded the system's processing capacity. Instead of methodically planning the system's upgrade in the most cost-effective manner, the IT department was forced to call the vendor to have new hardware shipped overnight. This resulted in additional costs that were both unexpected and exorbitant. In the end, the department still had to pay for the regular systematic upgrade in addition to the "quick patch" costs that were incurred on the day of the damage. This expense does not even include the costs for the firm being without the system for nine hours. There were opportunity costs of lost business, lost goodwill, delayed shipments, and a host of other problems that cascaded from this unexpected event. If the team had been analyzing system metrics over time and planned for the additional employees, they would have known that the system was reaching capacity and could have avoided the large unexpected expense and effort.

INCREASE IN STAFF PRODUCTIVITY (DEVELOPMENT AND SUPPORT). Developing a process and tracking metrics allows the CIO to benchmark personnel. It will establish a baseline of "good" performance for personnel that can then be used in performance reviews. For example, if the total help desk tickets closed per day by employee is tracked, then all help desk personnel can be judged on their performance based on the number of tickets they close each day. Underperforming employees can be spotlighted and counseled for improvement.

HIGH PERFORMANCE CULTURE.   Finally, implementing metrics will cultivate a performance-oriented culture. While this affect cannot be directly measured, it can be an important side-affect of instituting a measurement program. Even without necessarily tying incentive compensation to metrics, instituting a measurement program can often motivate employees and help them develop creative plans for ongoing job performance improvement. Competitive and goal-oriented employees excel in an environment that provides them specific goals and continuous feedback. They tend to succeed in such environments and deliver outstanding results. With an ongoing program of efficient and effective measurement, organizations can develop a performance culture that strives for continuous improvement. Over time, this can improve employee satisfaction and reduce undesired turnover.

The Costs of IT Measurement

While some of the benefits can be relatively difficult to measure, the costs of a program are relatively simple and straightforward. The costs fall into four major categories: planning, measurement, analysis, and management. With the exception of the planning phase, an efficient measurement program should not take significant time to manage, and should be integrated in regular IT processes, just like regular system maintenance.

The planning costs are usually the most significant in an IT measurement program, because they are critical for ensuring that the program is both effective and efficient. The planning costs entail some time of the senior manager (CIO) and one to three full-time employees for a few weeks. These resources are used to establish the goals, estimate the potential benefits of the program, select evaluation metrics, develop measurement processes, set organizational roles, and estimate the overall value of the program.

Measurement costs should be minimal, as the metrics selected should be fairly easy to observe and require minimal resources to capture. The majority of these costs are likely to result from the administration and management. Subjective measurement techniques such as user surveys can't be automated, and thus take the most resources to create and administer.

The analysis costs are high in the early stage of establishing the program, but fall over time with repetition and potential automation of more common analysis tasks. Analysis includes all the tasks needed to translate measured data into useful information that can help in decision making. While some of the raw data may be interesting, it is useless for decision making without framing it within a particular context that provides insight to the CIO. For example, overall IT spending per employee is not useful to a manager by itself, but it can provide some insight into the department's relative efficiency when compared with historical performance and industry benchmarks.

The management costs involve time spent by senior IT management interpreting the information so they can formulate recommended actions. Without any action taken, the measurement program will be of no value, so when considering the costs of a measurement program, these costs must be taken into account.

Developing an IT Measurement Program

Successfully implementing a measurement program is not simple. Almost 80 percent of all IT measurement programs fail. Avoid the common pitfalls such as overcomplicating the system, tracking too many metrics, requiring significant manual recording from workers, and tracking meaningless metrics. All these pitfalls discredit the CIO, lengthen implementation time, and undermine the true objective.

Successful measurement programs have several characteristics in common:

- Recognize that 20 percent of the metrics provide 80 percent of the relevant information needed. Prior to implementing measurement programs, most of the client companies we have assisted collected network statistics, server performance data, and help desk statistics, but found little use in the pages of meaningless data.
- Are broad enough to capture more than just system/IT metrics, for example, capture customer satisfaction.
- Require little effort to track and produce.
- Results are communicated to staff and executives on a standard schedule.

The IT Dashboard

A successful approach we recommend is the *IT dashboard.* This is a practical and simplified snapshot of IT performance. It is similar in concept to the *Balanced Scorecard* developed by Robert S. Kaplan and David Norton, but not as rigorous or strenuous to implement.

The dashboard concept was developed using the metaphor of an automobile dashboard. The gauges describe in real time all the valuable information a driver must know to operate the vehicle safely. The IT dashboard serves the same purpose.

The IT dashboard provides an easy-to-understand framework for measuring and tracking metrics that reveal IT performance. The dashboard provides a nontechnical foundation to share departmental objectives and performance results across the organization and is a significant step toward developing credibility and respect across the business. This framework allows everyone in the organization to understand how IT is measured.

The dashboard is a single page subdivided into sections or gauges. These gauges, composed of three to five key performance indicators (KPIs), can be used to quickly assess IT performance on a regular basis. The KPIs are driven by one or more metrics (objective and/or subjective) and are normalized using a system that is easy to understand. An effective method of reporting KPIs is to represent conditions in green, yellow, and red for respective satisfactory, caution, and needs attention states. An example of an IT dashboard is shown in Exhibit 18.2.

The major areas or gauges of the IT dashboard include the following:

- IT investment; for example, IT spending, capital invested, IT budget variance.
- Investment return.
- Infrastructure and operations.
- Project delivery.
- Customer satisfaction.
- People development.

To develop an effective and efficient IT measurement program, a CIO should follow these steps:

- Evaluate and define metrics that are important to the business.
- Define the IT dashboard by area, and map the associated metrics to each area.
- Define the target performance for each metric.
- Develop a summary IT dashboard as shown in Exhibit 18.2.
- Conduct a baseline survey and modify targets.
- Develop processes for data collection, analysis, synthesis, and reporting.
- Regularly reassess the program's value and adjust goals, metrics, and processes as necessary.

The overall process is outlined in Exhibit 18.3.

Evaluate Metrics

The most critical factor of success in this process is selecting a small set of valuable metrics to track. A framework for selecting those metrics entails the following:

IT INVESTMENT

Cost per seat	H
Cost % of revenue	OK
Cost % of SG&A	H

INVESTMENT RETURN

Benefit Capture	L
ROI	L

INFRASTRUCTURE & OPS

Desktops	OK
Data Center	OK
Midrange	OK
Telecom/Network	OK

PROJECT DELIVERY

Number Completed	OK
Project Quality	L
Value Added	L
Delays	H

CUSTOMER SATISFACTION

Overall Satisfaction	OK
Support	L
Applications	L

PEOPLE DEVELOPMENT

Number of Layers	OK
Average Tenure	OK
Skills Availability	L

H = High   L = Low   OK = Average

Exhibit 18.2   Example IT Dashboard

583

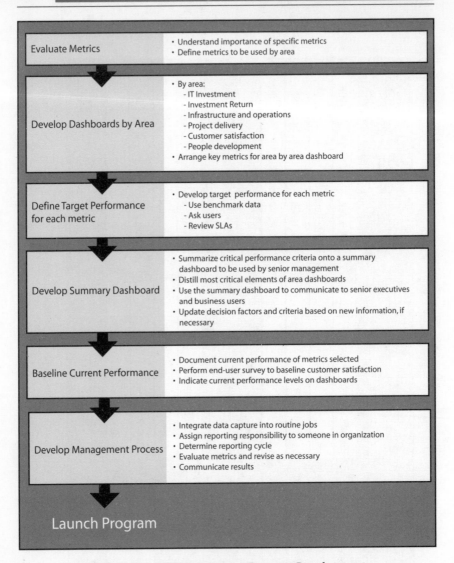

Evaluate Metrics	• Understand importance of specific metrics • Define metrics to be used by area

Develop Dashboards by Area	• By area:
	   - IT Investment
	   - Investment Return
	   - Infrastructure and operations
	   - Project delivery
	   - Customer satisfaction
	   - People development
	• Arrange key metrics for area by area dashboard

Define Target Performance for each metric	• Develop target performance for each metric
	   - Use benchmark data
	   - Ask users
	   - Review SLAs

Develop Summary Dashboard	• Summarize critical performance criteria onto a summary dashboard to be used by senior management • Distill most critical elements of area dashboards • Use the summary dashboard to communicate to senior executives and business users • Update decision factors and criteria based on new information, if necessary
Baseline Current Performance	• Document current performance of metrics selected • Perform end-user survey to baseline customer satisfaction • Indicate current performance levels on dashboards
Develop Management Process	• Integrate data capture into routine jobs • Assign reporting responsibility to someone in organization • Determine reporting cycle • Evaluate metrics and revise as necessary • Communicate results

Launch Program

Exhibit 18.3   IT Measurement Program Development

- Review critical business measures. Understand key metrics tracked by business units and functions, and then translate those metrics into IT metrics that can impact their performance. For example, if sales are measured by new orders sold, determine IT factors that can contribute to the success or failure of the sales process. Gather key metrics from around the company, and begin to analyze the impact that IT can have on those metrics.
- Take each IT area in turn and develop a *sub-dashboard* for that area. This enables the creation of specific metrics, development of summary dashboard, and management of the subareas on a daily basis.

The following is an explanation of key dashboard areas:

- *IT investment:* Metrics that describe how the IT organization is performing against budget. For example, the three most important measures might include: (1) performance against budget, (2) spending as a percent of revenue, and (3) spending as a percent of company gross margin. Other measures of IT investment are listed in the next section.

- *Investment return:* Summarizes results of captured business benefits from projects and system investments. For each business case, track the actual benefits versus the stated benefits, and report the results in this section of the dashboard. For example, track dollars returned versus dollars expected. Other examples include percent of end users adopting standards, percent of users adopting application, amount of green bar paper used (indicator of online reporting adoption), and revenue generated from new online ordering system.

- *Infrastructure and operations:* Critical measures in infrastructure include system and network reliability, support, security, virus protection, and others. Select the critical business measures and translate those measures into IT metrics. System availability may only be critical to business units that manage significant work processes through IT applications. Other measures of infrastructure and operations are listed in the next section.

- *Project delivery:* Summary of execution on projects. Projects should be segmented by size. Every IT project should be rated on four criteria: risk, client satisfaction, time performance, and budget. Risk is a measure of the level of uncertainty in a project. Client satisfaction is how well it is meeting client expectations. Time performance is a measure of how well the team is meeting the time schedule. Budget is a measure of how close to budget the project is running. Give each project a ranking of green, yellow, or red. Green represents a project that is on schedule and budget with little risk and an 80 percent or better client satisfaction score. Yellow represents a project that is within certain tolerances (10 to 20 percent) of time and budget schedules and has moderate risk and 50 percent or better client satisfaction ranking. Red represents a project that is out of these tolerances. The summary dashboard may only display the top two projects in the company, whereas the sub-dashboard for the applications group will show all projects sorted by size or importance.

- *Customer satisfaction:* Relative level of customer satisfaction within the organization; for example, satisfaction with the help desk, escalation procedures, problem resolution, system enhancement requests, availability of IT staff, quality of personnel, and so on. A satisfaction survey is typically the source for customer satisfaction scores.

- *People development:* Represents the degree to which the organization is executing its personnel development plan. Questions are answered as to how the IT organization is developing its people. Are the skills available in-house to execute projects? Is the attrition level average or increasing? Create metrics that are most important to the organization based on current environment. Examples of metrics for this area include attrition, average tenure, training days used versus available, average salary of IT personnel, skills availability, resources available, promotions for the current quarter, bonuses achieved, and number of individual performance objectives achieved.

Develop Dashboards by Area

After developing critical metrics for each IT area, each area should have its own one-page dashboard. These one-page dashboards are used to manage the personnel responsible for each respective area (e.g., operations manager receives the infrastructure and operations dashboard). Providing specific dashboards to the teams helps align their performance to the metrics deemed important by the CIO.

Define Target Performance for Each Metric

For each metric, define *target* performance. There are several ways to determine target performance. For example, is 98 percent uptime a reasonable target or is 99 percent required? There are three ways to set the target. If a service level agreement is already in place with the business users, this is the quickest way to set the target (it may still need to be reassessed). Essentially, begin to measure what was agreed on when the service levels were first negotiated. The second way to determine the target is to gather benchmark statistics about the metric to determine good performance in similar companies. For example, if statistics point to 99.4 percent uptime as average performance for all companies, that may be an appropriate level to achieve. Finally, the third way to determine the target is to negotiate with users. For example, manufacturing may actually need 99.9 percent uptime to meet business requirements. Setting targets based on agreement between the IT organization and the key business units is equivalent to developing a service level agreement.

Gather benchmarks of comparable performance for related companies within the industry from research groups like Gartner Group or Meta who collect and aggregate such information. These benchmarks can provide a guideline for assessing the IT department performance in comparison to companies of the same size and type of business. For example, in areas where the IT department is significantly underperforming other companies, recognize and note the gap, determine potential causes, and develop recommended actions to correct. In areas where the IT department is significantly overperforming other companies, note the overperformance and identify the area as a potential for decreasing the service level if the cost savings are attractive.

Develop Summary Dashboard

After the subdashboards are developed, distill the top two to three metrics for each area to create the summary dashboard. This is called the *IT dashboard* and is communicated to senior management. An example is shown in Exhibit 18.2.

Baseline Current Performance

The next step for the CIO is to document current performance. Objective metric results (hard quantitative metrics) should be collected from the most direct source (e.g., help desk system for help desk metrics).

Subjective metrics should be collected via survey(s) for all representative stakeholder groups. The surveys should include the following:

- Description and purpose of the survey.
- Fields for collecting stakeholder group differences (e.g., IT specialist versus business unit customer).
- Importance rating for each metric on a defined scale (e.g., 1 to 5) indicating the importance of the topic, service, or metric to the stakeholder.
- Performance rating for each metric on the same scale as previous point.

For the subjective measures, the following specific figures should be analyzed for each metric:

- *Mean of importance:* If this is higher than the mean for all metrics combined, the metric has relatively higher importance to the stakeholders. If this is lower than the mean for all metrics combined, the metric has relatively lower importance.
- *Standard deviation of importance:* A low standard deviation indicates agreement throughout the organization on the level of importance. Conversely, a high standard deviation indicates disagreement on the level of importance.
- *Mean of performance:* If this is higher than the mean for all metrics combined, it can be concluded that performance is better than average. If this is lower than the mean for all metrics combined, it can be concluded that performance is below average.
- *Standard deviation of performance:* A low standard deviation indicates agreement throughout the organization on the level of performance. Conversely, a high standard deviation indicates disagreement on the level of performance.
- *Gap of importance is a measure comparing IT personnel's view of importance versus business customer's view of importance for the topic,*

service, or metric: If the gap is low, the IT department has a relatively strong understanding of the customer's priorities. Conversely, if the gap is high, the IT department may not have a full grasp of the business needs.

- *Gap of performance between IT specialists and business customers:* If the gap is low, the IT department has a fairly strong understanding of its current performance. Conversely, if the gap is high, there is a strong disconnect between IT's perception of its performance versus the business community.

Based on these analyses, subjective performance metrics can be prioritized on the relative importance and perceived performance (see Exhibit 18.4). Areas with high importance and low performance indicate critical performance deficiencies and need the highest level of attention. Areas with low importance, but a relatively high level of performance, should receive the next level of priority because there may be some potential for cost savings. The remainder of the metrics can be addressed on a case-by-case basis.

Based on this prioritization, performance targets should be set for metrics in the highest priority problem areas. Targets can be set based on an absolute improvement, absolute percentage improvement, or relative percentage improvement to the average. In addition to high and low targets, specific bands can be set for low, medium, and high ranges for each metric, indicating performance tolerance ranges.

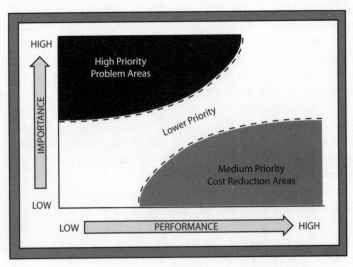

Exhibit 18.4   Subjective Metric Prioritization

Develop Management Process for Data Collection, Analysis, and Reporting

In parallel with the baseline survey, ongoing processes for data collection, analysis, and reporting should be established to ensure that (1) the measurement program is integrated into the IT business process, (2) the program does not become overly burdensome in terms of data collection efforts and costs, and (3) the program is effectively launched and communicated to the rest of the organization.

For all objective metrics, document the data collection process and identify the following:

- Method of collection.
- Frequency of collection.
- Person who performs collection.
- Method of transfer of data to the analyst.
- Duration of history to be preserved.

For subjective metrics, a survey should be designed based on the baseline survey. Care should be exercised developing the survey to ensure that the most appropriate questions are being asked at the right frequency, using the best methods available to capture an accurate response. Surveys should be no longer than absolutely necessary to capture the data needed—generally 5 to 10 minutes in duration for the person filling it out. Pay attention to format and accuracy. Inaccurate responses, at best, hinder the measurement effort and, at worst, make the measurement effort a complete failure. Fortunately, a manager does not need a degree in statistics or survey design to build an effective survey that captures an accurate response. Numerous short papers and books address this topic from a practical and useful standpoint. Many of the IT research houses provide guidance in developing user feedback surveys. Additionally, some firms specialize in conducting these surveys for companies.

Beware of mistakes commonly made with surveys:

1. Not repeating the survey in the frequency stated.
2. Failure to explain the purpose of the survey.
3. Making the survey too long, burdensome, or overcomplicated.
4. Failure to report the results of the survey to all stakeholders.
5. Failure to use statistically scientific approach to surveys.

A single analyst, who is responsible for leading the measurement analysis and reporting, should collect the survey results along with the objective metrics. It should be this person's job to verify and validate the data to ensure that major errors do not creep into the analysis. Following collection, the data need to be analyzed to develop useful information for decision making. There are many methods for digesting and aggregating the data; however, the most basic and effective methods include gap analysis and trend analysis.

Using gap analysis, the analyst examines the absolute difference between the current performance point and the target. Depending on the targets set, the analyst determines whether each particular key performance indicator is within a good, fair, or poor state. Using trend analysis, the analyst can identify how the state is changing over time by referring to data collected on previous survey dates. The trend can also be reflected on the IT dashboard using additional codes or colors.

When performing trend analysis, the following specific figures should also be analyzed for all the subjective (survey) metrics combined into one group for IT personnel and another for business customers:

- *Correlation of importance and performance for business customers:* A high level of correlation indicates a high level of business customer satisfaction. If this figure is dropping over time, there may be changing customer needs, or performance is falling off for the more important needs.
- *Correlation of importance between IT specialists and business customers:* A high level of correlation indicates that IT specialists understand the needs of business customers. If this is decreasing over time, the IT department probably needs to gain more insight into the nature of changing business needs.

Additional analysis techniques include regression analysis, factor analysis, and perceptual analysis. These advanced techniques can be used to develop an in-depth understanding of causal factors, relationships between metrics, and gaps in questioning. These techniques require more advanced training or outside help in statistics and quantitative measures. They are best left to larger organizations that can collect more extensive information and justify the expense of using a statistician or statistics training for the staff for conducting some of the analyses.

The information obtained through the analysis should be entered into an appropriate reporting program such as Microsoft Access or Excel. Significant gaps and trends should be noted and graphs prepared that illustrate the measurements in a simple, yet effective, manner.

A report should be generated on a regular interval as data is collected and analyzed. Depending on the complexity and needs of the organization, the collection and reporting frequency can range from weekly to quarterly. In many cases, the team will set an interval similar to the standard financial reporting cycle. At a minimum, most organizations should measure performance semiannually.

Hard copies of the dashboard should be posted in prominent places in the IT department so that everyone is aware of the current status of the IT organization's performance. Similar to a thermometer used to motivate people during a fund-raising drive, an IT dashboard motivates people in an IT department to improve performance and calls attention to exemplary performance. Soft copies should be distributed to all relevant parties, including:

- IT steering committee members.
- IT organization employees.
- Senior management team.
- Business process managers.
- Any end user who completed a survey.

To encourage communication of the business relevance of information technology throughout the company, some of the key performance indicators and results should be shared via internal newsletters or marketing materials. Finally, a soft copy should be available on the company's intranet for easy viewing by any company employee. Chapter 14 contains additional information on effective communication between IT and the business.

Reassessment of the Measurement Program

While it is important for the CIO to identify particular deficiencies in the organization from the measurement process, it is equally important to include the information in all major decision-making processes. This information should become the baseline for developing and justifying both operating and capital expenditures on a regular basis. After all, if a proposed investment in technology is not going to fulfill a specific business need, why should the investment be made?

The same applies in reverse. If an investment should *obviously* be made, shouldn't the investment's value be reflected in the organization's key performance indicators? The measurement program should be adjusted often enough to ensure that the measurements reflect the needs of the business units but not so often that historical comparisons become impractical. The historical trend of various KPIs is important to understand how changes in the organization are being reflected in the business user's views of importance and performance of various aspects of the IT organization.

The measurement and evaluation program provides a key point in the overall IT planning and management process and should provide critical inputs into the IT planning and budgeting process (see Exhibit 18.5). Feedback from the regular planning and evaluation can help improve the overall efficiency of the IT organization by:

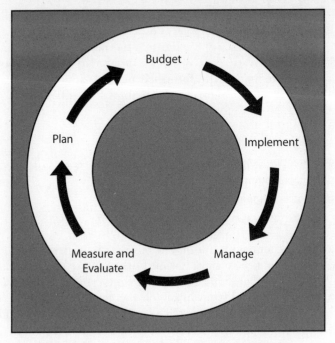

Exhibit 18.5   IT Planning and Management Process

- Identifying projects whose priority has shifted (either higher or lower) since the project was started.
- Identifying projects whose relevance has shrunk so much that elimination may be the best option.
- Helping define required service levels appropriately.
- Helping set appropriate time lines for projects and initiatives.
- Providing guidance when considering whether to buy, build, or outsource particular initiatives.
- Helping identify costs to serve particular populations in the organization and sizing services to cost effectively serve them.

The outputs of measurement and evaluation should help guide the organization in a continuous cycle of improvement—including improvement of the measurement process itself. As the organization grows and changes, so do the needs of various stakeholders of the IT department. To accommodate these changes, re-assess the measurement program to determine where additional information should be collected or to see where existing metrics are inadequate.

Evaluate and Take Action

The CIO will now be in position to take action based on the metrics through the following steps: analyze performance data to develop a snapshot of performance expressed in terms of key performance measures, analyze variance from expected target, and develop understanding into drivers of performance and causal relationships (for overreporting or underreporting, the schedule is the same).

Recognize and reward individuals for positive performance. Address underperformance through remedial action. Update strategy, planning, and budget processes to reflect new information. Raise performance targets to reinforce emerging objectives.

IT Metrics

Depending on the particular situation, some metrics are more relevant than others for improving IT performance. One of the critical components of the dashboard, discussed in the previous section, is selecting the appropriate measures. IT metrics can be categorized as objective metrics or subjective metrics. This section provides a starting point for selecting metrics.

Objective Metrics

Objective metrics are quantifiable facts about an organization that are easily observable or calculated and can be meaningfully compared to those in similar organizations. There are several advantages to including these metrics in a measurement program:

- *Free from bias:* While user satisfaction may be influenced by measurement techniques and nuances of survey questions, hard metrics, like the number of IT employees per IT user, are unbiased.
- *Ease of collection:* These figures are usually collected as part of regular accounting or system management, so they usually involve little additional labor or planning to collect.
- *Comparability:* Most of these figures can be readily compared with similar organizations in other companies or within an industry using benchmarks.

There are literally dozens of objective metrics that can be easily collected and recorded about an IT organization. While many of these metrics may be interesting, there are actually only a few dozen that are useful in achieving the ultimate objective of any program. In the planning stage of instituting a measurement program, it is crucial that the managers select only those metrics that will be useful in helping the manager improve performance. The value of the program can be seriously diluted if time is spent collecting, analyzing, or reporting statistics that do not help in decision making.

The actual metrics for a specific organization depend on the size of the IT group, organizational structure of the company, industry, growth rate, and many other circumstantial variables. Generally, however, we have found that there are some metrics useful in nearly every circumstance. These metrics are listed in Exhibits 18.6 through 18.12.

METRIC	COMPONENTS
I/T spending as percent of revenue	• Total enterprise IT spending divided by same period company revenue.
I/T spending as percent of gross margin	• Total enterprise IT spending divided by same period company gross margin.
I/T operations as a percent of I/T spending	• Spending on I/T operations divided by total enterprise IT spending.
I/T spending per employee	• Total enterprise IT spending divided by total number of employees in the company.
I/T employees as a percent of total employees	• Total I/T employees plus outsourcing employees dedicated to supporting company plus I/T contractors divided by total company employees.
I/T capital budget as a percent of revenue	• I/T capital budget divided by total company revenue.
Administrative costs as percent of total I/T cost	• I/T administration budget plus business support services plus service planning costs divided by total I/T budget.
I/T senior management span	• Number of I/T senior managers divided by total IT employees.
Number of layers	• Average number of layers between an entry-level I/T professional and the I/T Manager or CIO.
Percent of staff with less than 12 months of experience	• Total IT staff with less than 12 months' experience divided by total IT staff.

Exhibit 18.6 Objective Management Metrics

METRIC	COMPONENTS
Total annual cost per seat	• Desktop support staff plus tech support staff plus network connectivity plus printer support plus initial desktop preparation and delivery to user plus one-time purchased software licenses plus basic desktop maintenance (licenses, support, etc.) divided by total end users.
Desktops per employee	• Total number of desktops divided by total number of employees.
Total desktop support ratio (desktops per support FTE)	• Total desktops divided by total number of help desk personnel plus total number of desktop support, install, move/add/change (internal and outsourced) personnel plus total number of tech support staff plus total LAN management and administration staff plus total asset management-related staff.
Help desk staff per seat	• Total number of internal help desk staff plus total number of outsourced help desk staff divided by total end users.

Exhibit 18.7   Desktop Metrics

METRIC	COMPONENTS
First call resolution	• Percentage of calls resolved on the first call.
Average time to resolve trouble ticket	• Average time to resolve a trouble ticket from initial call to problem resolution.
Call queue waiting time	• Average wait on help desk call.
Call abandoned rate	• Percentage of help desk calls abandoned while on queue.
Length of help desk call	• Average time spent by user on a help desk call—includes time on Level 1 and Level 2.
Average reaction time	• Time between first call or message and the time it takes to reach someone live.

Exhibit 18.8   Help Desk Metrics

METRIC	COMPONENTS
Telecom cost per employee (annual)	• Basic telephone service plus equipment plus labor/support plus telephone usage (local/long distance) plus data network divided by total employees.
Telecom as percent of I/T cost	• Basic telephone service plus equipment plus labor/support plus data network plus telephone usage (local/long distance) divided by total enterprise IT spending.
Telecom cost as percent of total revenue	• Basic telephone service plus equipment plus labor/support plus data network plus telephone usage (local/long distance) divided by total revenue.
Network availability	• Total hours network is available divided by total available hours for the period.
Total data cost per user per year	• Call center costs plus calling card costs plus toll-free number costs plus remote access data costs divided by total number of end users.
Data network cost per minute of use	• Communications lines maintenance, support divided by total minutes used.

Exhibit 18.9   Network and Telecommunication Metrics

METRIC	COMPONENTS
Total cost per MIPs	• All costs (hardware, software, labor) for processor, DASD, tape, HSM, mainframe printing, disaster recovery, dedicated software, and services plus cost of production scheduling plus cost of data center operations plus cost of security and availability plus cost of host platform technology plus cost of asset management divided by total MIPs.
Total mainframe FTEs per MIPs	• Total mainframe FTEs including all operations and systems programming/management personnel, including: —Production scheduling. —Data center operations. —Security and availability

Exhibit 18.10   Mainframe Metrics

METRIC	COMPONENTS
	—Host platform technology. —Asset management. • All divided by total mainframe MIPs.
Total operators per MIPs	• Number of operations staff divided by MIPs managed.
System programmers per MIPs	• Number of systems programmers divided by MIPs managed.
Mainframe availability	• Total hours system available divided by total available hours during same period.
Hardware cost per gigabyte	• Total processor costs divided by total gigabytes of storage space.
Cost per printed page	• Total cost for mainframe printing (including application and end-user printing) divided by total printed pages.

Exhibit 18.10 *Continued*

METRIC	COMPONENTS
User support ratio	• Total number of users divided by total midrange support FTEs.
Midrange availability	• Total hours system available divided by total available hours during same period.
Midrange hardware cost per gigabyte	• Total processor costs divided by total gigabytes of storage space.
Applications per processor	• Total applications divided by total server processors.

Exhibit 18.11   Midrange Metrics

METRIC	COMPONENTS
I/T custom application costs	• Application development cost plus application maintenance cost.
Overall applications support percentage	• Total number of IT staff providing application development and maintenance services divided by total number of IT staff.
Application portfolio by age	• Number of applications older than 3 years (set timeframe) divided by total number of applications.
Retirement rate for applications	• Number of applications retired in last 12 months.
Percent of package applications in application portfolio	• Total number of packaged applications divided by total number of applications.
Programmer to lead ratio	• Number of programmers divided by number of team leads.
New application development spend as percent of total application spend	• Cost for development of new applications divided by total cost for development and maintenance of all applications.
Application enhancements as percent of total application spend	• Cost for development of system enhancements divided by total cost for development and maintenance of all applications.
Application support and maintenance as percent of total I/T cost	• Applications support and maintenance cost divided by total enterprise IT budget.
Application maintenance and support as percent of total application spend	• Cost of application maintenance divided by total cost for development and maintenance of all applications.
Application maintenance distribution	• Concentration of maintenance FTEs per application.
Application maintenance support ratio	• Total number of applications maintenance staff divided by total number of applications.

Exhibit 18.12   Application Metrics

Subjective Metrics

Subjective metrics are figures compiled from feedback of stakeholders in the company. The majority of these metrics are used to measure customer satisfaction but also include information to quantify what is sometimes termed as *alignment* between IT and the business units. There are several advantages of using subjective metrics for measuring IT:

- Ability to quantify business needs (e.g., functionality, reliability, responsiveness, system quality, cost effectiveness) and relative priorities of different groups throughout the organization.
- Ability to quantify the department's performance against specific needs.
- Ability to customize specific measures to particular aspects of the business.

There are also some disadvantages to using subjective metrics:

- Not only must subjective surveys be meticulously planned, but the administration and collection of the feedback is laborious.
- Because questions can be specific to each business and usually are heavily customized, there is no reliable way to benchmark the metric results within an industry or across industries.

Subjective metrics should always be measured using two dimensions: expectation and performance. Performance of any service organization is relative to its customers' expectations. It is the differences between expectations and performance where much of the value of measurement can be found.

We generally group subjective measures as follows:

- Suitability, accessibility, reliability, and security of systems.
- Functionality of applications.
- Efficiency of completing projects.
- Service levels.
- Responsiveness to business requirements.

These are typically measured through carefully designed questionnaires, administered by administrators and third parties, and conducted through various media such as the Web, intranet, phone, and paper.

Periodic IT Health Check

In addition to performing regular ongoing measurement of objective and subjective measures to evaluate the performance of the IT organization, a major organizational health assessment should be performed every 12 to 18 months to evaluate the overall fitness and effectiveness of the organization. Additionally, all new CIOs should perform an IT health assessment during the first 90 days in the position. This assessment should cover every major IT area to identify potential problems that may have gone undiscovered through regular measurement or observation. The areas covered should include:

- Organization.
- Infrastructure.
- Applications.
- Budget/costs.
- Vender agreements.
- Operations.
- Processes.
- IT demand management processes.
- Project management practices.
- Communication networks.
- IT standards.
- Financial and risk management practices.
- Measurement and quality control.
- Overall IT planning practices.

For *each* of these areas, the assessment should evaluate:

- Overall health of the area according to objective and subjective benchmarks.
- Adequacy to service the current and future organization.
- Relative position to industry best practices.
- Overall cost effectiveness.

In considering all the areas, the assessment should provide:

- Opportunities for cost-effective service improvements.
- Opportunities for cost savings.
- Recommendations and action plan for improvement.

Generally, the assessment should be performed by a capable analyst or an outside consultant who has expertise in evaluating the IT departments of organizations similar in size and scope. The consultant should follow a standard methodology for performing the assessment while interviewing personnel, auditing systems, examining documentation, and observing functions in the department. Specific time lines should be set for interviews, analysis, and deliverables. At a minimum, deliverables should include:

- *Statement of work:* Explains the areas to be addressed by the assessment, methods to be used, people to be involved, timelines, deliverables, costs, and so on.
- *IT assessment:* Includes the full assessment covering the overall health, cost effectiveness, adequacy, and relative position of each area to best practices.
- *Strategic recommendations:* Describes specific opportunities for service improvements and cost savings and prescribes specific recommendations, along with an action plan for implementing the recommendations over a given period with specific resources.
- *Executive summary:* Summary of the entire assessment and strategic recommendations for the executive leadership team, board of directors, and outside investors.

In addition to performing this study on an annual basis, it should also be performed immediately before or after major events that will significantly affect the structure of the organization, such as a merger, acquisition, spin-off, divestiture, joint venture, restructuring, major geographic expansion, or major project affecting many internal systems (CRM or business process outsourcing).

The study generally takes three to six weeks and involves significantly more resources than the regular ongoing measurement and evaluation program. Therefore, this type of study should be commissioned using the same practices that would be used for purchasing any major professional services project.

At the conclusion of the project, the consultant should conduct a workshop with the IT steering committee to discuss the results and recommendations. This four- to six-hour workshop should provide the management team with a strong understanding of the current effectiveness of the IT department, where it needs to be in the future, and the most cost-effective and timely path for reaching that future point.

The report should then be used by management as the basis for a medium-term IT strategic plan, which may affect every area within IT. Because of this, the strategic plan should be widely distributed and communicated to all stakeholders who are normally involved in the IT measurement and evaluation process.

RESOURCES

Gartner Measurement Services Group. Provides benchmarking data.

International Quality and Productivity Center. www.iqpc.com. Provides practical information on IT metrics.

Kaplan, Robert S., and David P. Norton. *The Balanced Scorecard: Translating Strategy into Action.* Boston: Harvard Business School Publishing, 1996.

META Group. Provides benchmarking data.

Money, Arthur D., Remenyi, and Alan Twite, *Effective Measurement and Management of IT Costs and Benefits,* 2nd ed. Boston: Butterworth-Heinemann, 2000.

NetworkSolutions. www.metricnet.com. Provides benchmarking data.

Tanaszi, Margaret. *IT Value Metrics and Measurement: What's IT Worth to Corporate Success?* Framingham, MA: International Data Corporation, 2002.

Yourdon, Ed. *IT Measurement: Practical Advice from the Experts, International Function Point Users Group.* Reading, MA: Addison-Wesley, 2002.

NOTES

1. Thomas J. Peters and Nancy K. Austin, *Passion for Excellence* (New York: Warner Books, 1986).

2. Thomas Hoffman, "IT Investment Model Wins Converts," *ComputerWorld* (August 5, 2002).

3. Deborah Asbrand, "IT Metrics for Success," *Information Week* (August 17, 1998).

19

IT Governance

Disagreement produces debate but dissent produces dissension. Dissent . . . means originally to feel apart from others. People who disagree have an argument, but people who dissent have a quarrel. People may disagree and both may count themselves in the majority. But a person who dissents is by definition in a minority. A liberal society thrives on disagreement but is killed by dissension. Disagreement is the life blood of democracy, dissension is its cancer.

—Daniel J. Boorstin, U.S. historian[1]

This chapter introduces IT governance and the IT steering committee. IT governance consists of methods corporate management and the CIO employ to ensure the IT department successfully executes an IT strategy and operating philosophy that support the company's strategic and tactical goals. Simply said: IT governance ensures the IT department is working on the right things and doing the right things correctly. One of the most critical components of IT governance is the IT steering committee, a group composed of the CIO and company senior managers who collaborate to ensure IT priorities are aligned with company business priorities. Senior executives and representatives from business units and functions across the company meet regularly to provide input on IT direction; communicate company business objectives; remove impediments to IT success; and approve IT priorities, spending, and projects. The chapter also discusses functions that support IT governance as well as regulations and audit standards for corporations that affect IT.

The chapter is organized in four sections. The first provides background and an overview of IT governance. The second discusses control and audit practices that support IT governance. Third discusses functions that support IT governance. The fourth discusses the IT steering committee concept in depth and explains the purpose of the group, the appropriate membership in the committee, and the committee operations. As with other tools discussed in this book, CIOs should determine the best approach to implement the

603

concept and modify the membership makeup and operating variables to accomplish most effectively the primary objectives in their company.

Why This Topic Is Important

As Daniel Boorstin wrote, "Disagreement is the life blood of democracy, dissension is its cancer." Throughout this book, we emphasize the costs of an ineffective IT department—overspending, failed projects, heterogeneous costly environments, unhappy business users, low morale in IT, poorly run operations and applications, and improper use of scarce corporate resources. The most effective approach for tackling the issues that we have highlighted in this book is a cooperative, communicative relationship between IT and the business units it serves. IT governance and the IT steering committee are the tools through which the communication and cooperation between IT and the business units can be established and perpetuated. The IT steering committee provides a venue in which IT can communicate issues, status, obstacles, and priorities to the company, while the company can ensure that overall corporate investments are flowing to the highest priority initiatives, and that business roadblocks to IT effectiveness are demolished. Most important, the IT steering committee promotes a healthy, cooperative relationship between the business and IT, instead of the backbiting, contentious, finger-pointing, dysfunctional tar pit that is so often encountered.

IT departments suffer from common stereotypes such as self-absorbed, technology-focused introverts with weak communications skills, who are disconnected from the business, its priorities, and the big picture. Accurate or not, this stereotype can naturally lead to defensiveness in IT and promote a hostile, uncooperative attitude. Compounding the issue is the utility nature of IT operations, where performance is only noticed if it is absent. Often, IT managers and staff lack business experience in general, and specific knowledge of their company's business priorities and operations. The CIO may lack the corporate political capital to effectively represent the IT group and sell initiatives to senior executives or defend the IT group when its performance appears to be poor.

On the other hand, staff working in sales, marketing, and other functions and business units are usually not technology experts, and are often disinterested in learning even the basics. Technology can be intimidating, or at best, appear overly complex to nontechnical staff. Some executives still have their assistants print e-mails to read on paper, and users are often impatient when dealing with complex, sophisticated systems. Business users intimidated by technology often translate those feelings to the IT department as aggravation or disinterest. All systems may have worked perfectly for 12 straight months; a sterling performance only to be tarnished by one phone call to the help desk in which the user waited too long on hold and whose question was never answered.

The rapid changes in technology and business priorities that are a natural part of any company only increase the need for discussion and communication. It is easy to understand how the business-IT relationship can become strained.

Most often, there is no set mechanism that forces IT and business to communicate with the appropriate frequency and depth. Typically, the CIO and the corporate officer in charge of IT (e.g., CEO, CFO, COO) meet periodically to review plans and progress. Perhaps once a year at budgeting and strategic planning time, a presentation is made by the CIO to the senior management team. This informal, infrequent, and narrow communication is a major cause of IT departments getting off-track. The business doesn't understand what IT can accomplish and abandons it, or worse, commissions their own duplicate IT department inside their business unit. The steering committee, with its carefully selected membership and frequent, well-planned, structured agenda meetings forces the key business departments and IT to communicate routinely, properly setting priorities and expectations, and provides an effective two-way communication avenue for a traditionally communication-challenged relationship.

Throughout this book, we present substantial evidence supporting the argument that if an organization fails to monitor and supervise information technology investment decisions and operations, it fails to achieve the corporate strategic objectives and, thus, fails to gain competitive advantage through IT. Implementing the ideas in this chapter enhances the communication flow between the business and IT, as well as ensures that the business and IT are together setting IT priorities and investment levels. The result will be the avoidance of many of the IT perils we have covered previously.

IT Governance

IT governance consists of methods corporate management and the CIO employ to ensure the IT department successfully executes an IT strategy and operating philosophy that support the company's strategic and tactical goals. The bottom line is IT must align with the company's objectives and effective IT governance assures this happens. IT governance defines who makes decisions, how they make those decisions, and when. In addition IT governance encapsulates "controls" and audit procedures. Practices such as PMO, CMM, ITIL help manage IT processes better so that governance is not as onerous for the management. These practices have the additional benefit of lowering risk of IT failures. Proper IT governance ensures that all senior management and business unit managers collaborate and prioritize for the good of the company. The most important IT project for the year will be the one that is the most valuable to the company not the one that IT or one executive decides in a vacuum.

Proper governance has a number of benefits for CIOs. First, communication with the business is improved. Governance encourages collaboration and shared decision making. With more executives involved in the IT decision making processes, everyone buys into the decision and owns them; there is a shared commitment. No longer are all fingers pointing at the CIO and IT department with full blame thrown in the most convenient direction. Governance also ensures that appropriate audit and controls are in place. For private companies the audit and controls may not be as stringent. For public companies compliance can be expensive.

Key Activities in Governance
Approving IT Strategy.
- Reviewing and approving the Project Portfolio.
- Assisting with company board of director IT inquiries.
- Reviewing Security practices and controls.
- Ensuring compliance with policies, regulations and controls.
- Assessing IT performance (via SLAs, performance management, etc.).
- Ensuring P&L goals are met.

These topics are covered extensively in this book and the different disciplines should be pulled together to create a comprehensive governance structure. Functions that support IT governance include project management office (Chapter 17), architecture strategy and planning (Chapter 4), and IT service management (Chapters 8 and 9). Controls and audits are another discipline that ensure the IT department and systems are in compliance with laws and generally accepted corporate best practices. Important control laws and bodies that may effect and/or be helpful to an organization include Sarbanes-Oxley Section 404 for public companies, SAS 70 information systems audit and internal control, control objectives for information and related technology (COBIT), and service level agreements (SLAs). Governance strives to answer the following questions:

- What projects are we working on?
- Are the projects important to company objectives?
- Are those projects on schedule, budget, and hitting obstacles?
- Do we have the appropriate technical architecture?
- Are the technologies we are implementing consistent with current architecture strategy?
- Are proper controls in place?
- Are proper security measures being taken to protect systems and data?

If you're part of a private company and have not implemented governance, you can begin relatively quickly. Begin by forming an IT steering committee (outlined later in this chapter) and implement the IT project portfolio management (Chapter 17). This will get you started.

If you have already implemented some forms of IT governance but can't answer these questions, then you need to implement additional forms for governance where there are gaps.

Due to Sarbanes Oxley, most every public company will have already implemented some form of IT governance. The next step for most public company CIOs will be to automate and simplify the governance process so that governance occurs more efficiently with less effort for those involved. There are dozens of software applications that can help streamline each area of governance. Key areas for IT governance software applications include Project Portfolio Management, Regulatory Compliance, and Change Management.

Control and Audit

Control and audit compliance includes the processes and mechanisms companies utilize to comply with laws such as Sarbanes Oxley Section 404 or standards such as COBIT.

The Sarbanes Oxley (SOX) legislation was passed in 2002 to ensure the effectiveness of internal controls for public companies. While SOX is large and companywide, there are a number of provisions that greatly affect the IT department. Section 302 (certification of financial reports), Section 404 (certification of internal controls), and Section 409 (material-event reporting) all have provisions that impact IT. IT governance must ensure that the IT department can comply with the provisions in these sections (provided the company is publicly owned). Key items include the ability of IT to certify that systems are secure and reliable, that controls are in place for password, that access to customer financial information and personal information is restricted, and that there are checks and balances throughout the systems and applications that ensure proper financial controls.

Under SOX, most companies are required to obtain a SAS 70 report from their vendors that stipulates that the vendors have appropriate controls that comply with the client companies required controls. IT service providers in many areas including outsourcing, application hosting, security management will be required by most public companies to obtain a SAS 70.

COBIT is discussed in Chapter 4 but bears some discussion in this chapter. COBIT is a set of best practices for IT governance created by Information Systems Audit and Control Association (ISACA) and the IT Governance Institute (ITGI). COBIT is extensive and details control objectives across major IT processes that IT should ensure are met. Along with COBIT, other disciplines include CMM (discussed in Chapter 10) and ITIL (discussed in Chapter 4).

In general, the larger the company, the more these regulations and practices are going to affect the organization. Small and mid-size companies may manage their own best practices and run into regulations like SOX only minimally. Whereas a public Fortune 500 company is probably going to have to address all of these items. The trick is effectively implementing compliance across these areas in the most efficient manner possible. While there is much good that results in compliance and adherence, there can be significant wasted investments if the implementation of these is not managed appropriately.

Functions Supporting IT Governance

We have discussed extensively major functions that support IT governance including project portfolio management, service level agreements, change control, and change management. One of the most critical functions is the IT steering committee. The IT steering committee is composed of senior IT management and senior business leaders who meet on a regular schedule to review, discuss, prioritize, and resolve IT projects, issues, and strategy. Used properly, the IT steering committee is one of the most effective tools for creating a high-performance IT department. The steering committee conveys business priorities to IT so that IT management can direct resources to the highest value business functions in real time. The committee provides approval, oversight, and high-level steering of projects, as well as finalizes project priorities based on IT demand management analyses. It also reviews proposed operating and capital budgets, IT operations service levels, and IT performance metrics. The committee has the senior level membership and authority to facilitate the resolution of any roadblocks to IT effectiveness. Perhaps the most important responsibility of the committee is to improve communication and relationships between key business personnel and IT managers, and facilitating better informal communication between groups outside of the committee. This chapter outlines the typical charter, responsibilities, membership, and ongoing operations of a properly functioning IT steering committee.

Of note here are internal IT policies. There should be a set of policies published by the IT department for users, vendors, and client partners. These policies should include:

- Security policy.
- Data policy.
- Customer information policy.

- Security incident policy.
- Password policy.
- Internet and mail services usage policy.
- Instant messaging policy.
- General computer usage (include care of desktop or laptop).
- Confidential information policy.
- Acceptable use statement.
- Records management policy.
- Training policies.
- HR policies.

Several other functions that assist in governance include runbooks, project postmortems, and incident reports.

Runbooks are a method of documenting (via online system or paper) the critical aspects of computer systems. This includes login ids, password, support contact information, inventory of systems, configuration layouts and details, end-user contact information, hardware specifications and standards, software license information, escalation procedures, patch history and upgrade information, IP addresses (external), and all application data. There can be no governance or stability in the IT department if this information is not captured and managed correctly. The intelligent classifying of this information is critical for control, policy, and quality processes within the IT department and governance function. Project postmortems discussed in Chapter 18 are critical for the PMO function to understand how well the company is doing at managing projects over time. They are critical information for the governance function to determine the confidence level in project estimates and project management. Incident reporting is analogous to project postmortems but is completed during infrastructure or operations failures. Incident reporting is the key to root cause correction of infrastructure problems. Incident reporting can be fed to the governance function for communication to the business, and planning to improve infrastructure areas.

IT Steering Committee Concept

The IT steering committee is composed of senior IT management and senior business leaders who meet on a regular schedule to review, discuss, prioritize, and resolve IT projects, issues, and strategy. Used properly, the IT steering committee is one of the most effective tools for creating a high-performance IT department. The steering committee conveys business priorities to IT so that IT management can direct resources to the highest value business functions in real time. The committee provides approval, oversight, and high-level steering of projects, as well as finalizes project

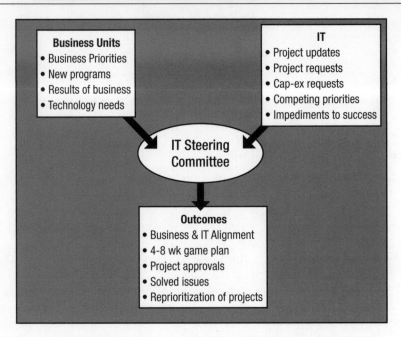

Business Units
- Business Priorities
- New programs
- Results of business
- Technology needs

IT
- Project updates
- Project requests
- Cap-ex requests
- Competing priorities
- Impediments to success

IT Steering
Committee

Outcomes
- Business & IT Alignment
- 4-8 wk game plan
- Project approvals
- Solved issues
- Reprioritization of projects

Exhibit 19.1   IT Steering Committee Communication Flows

priorities based on IT demand management analyses. It also reviews proposed operating and capital budgets, IT operations service levels, and IT performance metrics. The committee has the senior level membership and authority to facilitate the resolution of any roadblocks to IT effectiveness. Perhaps the most important responsibility of the committee is to improve communication and relationships between key business personnel and IT managers, facilitating better informal communication between groups outside of the committee. This chapter outlines the typical charter, responsibilities, membership, and ongoing operations of a properly functioning IT steering committee.

Exhibit 19.1 illustrates the communication flow and outcomes of the committee.

Purpose of an IT Steering Committee

Life without an IT steering committee is tough for both the business and the IT department. There are very few senior-level advocates for the IT department, and the business suffers by not achieving the benefits of an effective IT department. Typically, the IT plan is recreated annually, at which time the CIO presents the IT strategy for the next 12 months. The CIO highlights the initiatives the department has accomplished and will accomplish. The pages are littered with technical project upon technical project. "We must upgrade our desktop virus software; we are upgrading the servers; we are implementing an AR/AP patch" are typical projects listed as a strategic initiative. Senior management listens for an hour, and unless there is a controversial application being implemented, the meeting ends, the CIO goes away, and everyone meets again the following year. Interim meetings are only called in the worst case, when a high-profile application being implemented is behind schedule and hundreds of thousands of dollars over budget. In these meetings, the business managers, entangled in a seemingly endless maze of technical obfuscations, throw up their hands, and ask the IT manager to come back in a month with a comprehensive explanation of all the things that caused the implementation to go awry.

Further, the IT department, while being highly accountable to the senior executive who owns IT, shows very little accountability to the rest of the business. At one of our client companies, IT reported to the CFO, and the accounting department received the undivided attention of the IT department while the vice president of sales and marketing had met with the CIO three times in four years and had no idea if the IT dependent sales initiatives were being driven by IT, or when they would be completed.

In the same company, the executive in charge of distribution logistics felt that the system enhancement request process used by the IT department was confusing and onerous. Additionally, new functions and features for the warehouse system would be developed and demonstrated, but there would be no design input from his team except when creating the original requirements specification. This led to rework when features were not developed that supported the warehouse team properly. When a new stock-keeping-units based work release function was rolled out, several variables for releasing the wave were not available. The developers went back to the drawing board for several weeks to correct the functionality. Most business unit leaders in companies where IT has limited direct accountability to the business have similar tales.

In another client company, a financial services provider, senior management was disappointed by the lack of vision and technology strategy being shown by the IT department. A host of questions were left begging by the IT communications gap: What new technologies need to be rolled out to support customers in the future? What are fast-moving competitors doing with technology to better support their customers and reduce costs? What tools should employees use to improve productivity? Infrequent business-IT strategy planning sessions and a lack of proactive agenda setting by IT are other common symptoms of poor leadership and communication that is solved by the proper implementation of the IT steering committee.

In another client environment, an accounting financial analyst was working on selecting package software to support the accounting function. The analyst had met with five vendors and had them completing request for proposals (RFPs) at considerable vendor expense, conducting system demonstrations, and providing installation and licensing quotes. Simultaneously, the IT department was commissioned to review ERP packages to replace legacy systems, including finance and accounting applications. Neither group realized that the two competing package selection projects were taking place. After we helped senior management inventory the full list of IT-related projects across the company, the duplicate, disconnected effort was discovered.

Implementing an IT steering committee helps IT ensure that they are providing the best value for the business, as well as ensuring that the business is working to remove any obstacles to the success of the IT department within the organization. Working together, IT and the business unit can eliminate the situations described above and throughout this book. The steering committee helps:

- Align technology decisions with business strategy.
- Provide broad inspection and assessment of progress against company IT goals.
- Facilitate communication of business and project priorities.
- Build relationships between IT and business communities.
- Manage overall implications and trade-offs of project priorities and business activities based on business rationale and IT capacity.
- Convert dissention to disagreement.

There are several interesting acid tests to perform in companies experiencing business-IT disconnects. One test involves submitting a contrived help desk request to solve a business mission critical-systems problem. For instance, a salesperson can send a message to the IT help desk to report that a printer is not working and note that it needs to be fixed quickly so that sales can get a quote or proposal out to a waiting customer. The test should measure how rapidly the IT department sends an initial response to repair the printer—in this case, examines the printer and determines that nothing is wrong. If the time elapsed is greater than four hours total for both answers, the company has a prioritization issue in the IT operations area. Clearly, a company cannot drive revenues if salespeople can't get quotes or proposals out the door to customers, and every minute that goes by is at best leading to a dissatisfied client. IT departments that understand the business impact of downtime to various organizations know that attending to customer-impacting problems is a high priority and repair delays mean lost revenue for the company.

Another simple test is to select two business units or functions in the company, and ask the top manager in those units the following questions:

- How often do you meet with the CIO to discuss priorities for your business unit?
- When did you have an informal meeting with the CIO (lunch, dinner, water-cooler conversation)?
- How many projects is IT working on for you at this moment? What is the top project? When will it be completed?

The answer to the first question should be greater than four times per year. Further, the CIO and top managers should be interacting on an informal basis frequently, outside of their formal status and planning meetings. The CIO should also respond to the final question. If the business unit leader and CIO high-value projects don't match, or the completion target dates differ, then there is a clear communication gap between IT and the business.

Benefits to the Company

At the company level, the benefits from implementing an IT steering committee are significant. First, the entire business provides direct and more frequent input into IT decisions, spending, and priorities. Second, increased scrutiny will result in better progress toward long-term goals. Third, the committee builds a team that backs IT and cooperates with IT, instead of blaming and castigating it. Last and foremost, the committee helps ensure that precious corporate effort and capital is not wasted on unnecessary projects or hardware.

Benefits to the Business Units

The business unit and functional department levels gain access and representation on the IT steering committee, which ensures that users from across the business have a voice in IT decision making. Business units also gain an understanding into the priorities of IT and how they are linked to the priorities within each business unit or function. They understand and help correctly set priorities—items that are of significance to the business and not unilateral priorities set by the IT department.

Benefits to IT Management

The CIO benefits by receiving direct, clear feedback from the most important constituencies on the performance of IT on a regular basis. Additionally, the CIO receives focused input in setting priorities, ensuring that the IT team is working on the correct set of projects and issues. It also reduces the occurrence of *canceled project phenomenon.*

The canceled project phenomenon is a result of misalignment in business priorities. For instance, the IT department may decide to implement an expensive terminal server solution, which allows applications to run on a centralized server accessible by cheap desktop computers, thus simplifying end-user desktop support. IT gets internal approval, purchases the hardware and software, and installs the system. To attain approval, IT convinces business users that the system will increase the speed and longevity of their computers. When the system is finally deployed, the inevitable problems are encountered. Because IT has not properly defined and set end-user expectations, the first users see the new product, try it, and hate it because it's slower than anticipated and certain key features are missing. The users complain to management, management complains to senior management, and what could have been a successful project is shut down.

The committee helps ensure that business and IT are in tight linkage throughout any system rollout, and provides a forum for building IT relationships with the business decision makers. When impediments to successful completion of initiatives are encountered, the business and IT will work in partnership to remove them. Finally, it ensures a "no surprise" environment and minimizes potential for negative backlash.

Benefits to the IT Department

Members of the IT department benefit greatly by receiving more frequent and meaningful feedback on initiatives and service levels from senior management. IT teams can be frustrated by the start-and-stop nature of poorly chartered projects. Improved direction setting and feedback that minimizes canceled projects benefit everyone in IT. Periodically, members of the IT department will present information to the steering committee; this provides those individuals with greater exposure to senior executives than they received before. The team will also have a satisfaction and sense of achievement that comes from finishing high-priority, high-return business projects and making a larger impact on the company. Last, it ensures that the team has better representation from influential senior managers in the corporation.

Objective of the IT Steering Committee

The primary responsibility of the steering committee is to provide IT direction setting. At the decision-making level, the IT steering committee is responsible for 12 key activities:

1. Review on an ongoing basis the IT strategic plan to ensure that it is consistent with the overall corporate direction.
2. Review (and approve or reject) all proposals for information systems package implementation or application development that cost more

than a specified amount, depending on company size and authorization guidelines. The IT steering committee prescribes the required format of the information technology proposals, business case format, including a cost/benefit analysis and projects financial value calculation. (See Chapter 17 for details.)

3. Consistent with IT Demand Management principles, manage the information systems project portfolio, set priorities for the development of the business information systems, allocate the necessary resources, and monitor the progress of each project against objectives, time lines, and budgets.

4. Provide guidance and approval for capital expenditures over the CIO's spending authority. Sets authority levels by company size and company economic condition. At one extreme, the level can be set at zero and the ITSC review all capital expenditures. More realistically, the number is several thousand dollars. The committee can then review capex over $10,000 with final authorization provided by the executive with capex authority, given the amount and the recommendation of the steering committee. See Chapter 15 on IT budgeting.

5. Assist with allocation of IT and business unit resources for IT projects.

6. Resolve issues impeding high-priority projects. Key issues that are blocking the progress on projects are discussed in the meeting. Members debate the issues and offer resolutions. If issues cannot be resolved within the committee, the key stakeholders can meet offline and provide a later update.

7. Approve use of all outside technology vendors by all business units. The committee should review new technology vendors and provide approvals.

8. Provide ongoing oversight of key projects (e.g., over $25,000 or longer than a certain duration).

9. Review project change requests requiring $10,000 or more capital. The ultimate responsibility for sign-off of project change orders is the executive who owns IT and the business unit or function involved.

10. Discuss any major business initiatives that may impact systems.

11. Approve IT standards proposed by IT (see Chapter 7).

12. Conduct post-implementation systems reviews and IT effectiveness assessments that are independent of the IT department; the findings and recommendations of the review are presented to the committee with a response from the IT department.

The CIO has the responsibility to make the following preparation before each meeting:

1. Prepare an appropriate agenda that covers the decisions to be made and status updates to be provided.
2. Create project status reports for high-priority projects, including an outline of progress, percent complete versus percent of project budget spent, major issues, and change requests.
3. Aggregate all IT capital expenditures that should be reviewed by the steering committee for delivery to the steering committee prior to meeting.
4. Develop list of key questions or issues to discuss with committee members.
5. Create IT demand management/project prioritization schedule update.

In addition, the CIO's management responsibilities between meetings are as follows:

1. Approve IT projects and all initiatives/projects with an IT component that fall under the steering committee threshold.
2. Aggregate IT capital expenditures, ensuring the steering committee considers viable expenses.
3. Approve and assist with allocation of IT resources to initiatives/projects with an IT component.
4. Resolve minor issues impeding projects or support.
5. Screen projects before they are brought to the steering committee.
6. Evaluate change requests that fall under the steering committee threshold.

Membership of the IT Steering Committee

The IT steering committee is composed of 5 to 10 company managers who can provide the most comprehensive, company-focused input into the IT decision-making process. The committee should be composed of a cross-section of business function and business unit leaders with a high stake in the productivity and effectiveness of IT. The typical committee includes the following members:

- CIO.
- The person CIO reports to (typically the CFO, COO, or CEO). This person chairs the steering committee.
- CEO or COO (if different from above).

- One to three business function leaders or super users (accounting, HR, etc.).
- One to three business unit leaders or super users (influential business unit heads or their direct reports).

Other staff in the IT department should be brought into meetings to present specific project updates, but then leave the meeting; they should not be part of the steering committee.

At some client steering committee meetings, the senior management team intentionally leaves out CEO participation to ensure that his or her participation does not unduly sway decisions or recommendations from the committee. In these cases, the CEO is usually presented summaries of recommended decisions for final approval.

Roles and responsibilities on the ideal steering committee are outlined in the following section.

Structure of the IT Steering Committee

The IT steering committee is composed of a chairperson, secretary, scribe, and members. The chairperson of the IT steering committee is usually the senior executive who ultimately owns the IT function. In most midsize companies, this is the CFO. In larger companies, it may be the COO or CEO. Whoever the CIO or CIO reports to is the *chairperson.* In some large companies, the CIO may be a senior executive at the same level as, for example, the CFO. If that is the case, the CIO should serve as chairperson.

The actual members and member composition change over time according to business requirements and staff changes. Passage and approval of issues/recommendations can be based on the chairperson's decision or a majority vote. Organizations should determine what works best for their specific situation.

Roles and Responsibilities
- *Chair:* The chairperson is the leader of the IT steering committee:
  —Leads the IT steering committee, selects members, and directs the agenda.
  —Manages typical meeting functions—calls meeting to order, arranges for minutes to be taken and distributed before meetings, builds consensus, summarizes results and decisions.
  —Is generally the ultimate arbiter, tie-breaker, and final decision maker, depending on the topic.

- *Secretary:* The secretary is responsible for administration of the group:
  —Produces the agenda.
  —Organizes the meeting (finalizes time and location).
  —Acts as the chair in the chairperson's absence.
  —Records minutes of meeting.
  —Prepares and distributes meeting materials in advance.
  —Distributes minutes after meeting.
  —Monitors and reports status on meeting action items and open issues.
  —Manages time in the meeting.
- *Scribe:* The scribe is responsible for meeting notes (in small committees, this position can be combined with the secretary); often this role is filled by the IT department administrative assistant.
- *Members:* Members are responsible for giving input and comments on issues:
  —Prepares and participates in meetings by reviewing agenda and meeting material before the meeting.
  —Considers issues and implications presented.
  —Participates in meeting discussions and decisions.
  —Represents the business unit or function.

Often busy business unit managers ask a trusted deputy to serve as their proxy on the steering committee. This should be avoided where possible; for the steering committee to have credibility and clout, as well as for the business unit area to be well represented, the committee should be composed of top company decision makers. An alternative approach to suggest is to have the business unit manager deputize his or her proxy, and have that person attend only the meetings that the business unit manager cannot possibly make. In every case, the CEO or COO should be made aware of consistent attendance problems to avoid the above issues.

Operating the IT Steering Committee

The steering committee meets on a regular schedule and covers the following topics at each meeting:

- Reviews critical issues affecting IT productivity.
- Reviews status of projects.
- Approves new projects/capital expenditure requests.
- Assesses IT priorities; re-prioritizes approved projects when appropriate.
- Approves proposed vendor relationships.

Exhibit 19.2 is a sample agenda. Each of the agenda topics is described in more detail in the following sections.

AGENDA ITEM	DESCRIPTION
Review issues	IT director presents priority issues.
Review status on projects	Team members present progress on milestones.
Approve new projects/ Capital expenditures	Business units provide business case. IT director presents capacity.
Assess priorities	Present competing objectives. Allocate resources as appropriate.
Approve proposed vendor relationships	Business unit or IT presents business justification.

Exhibit 19.2   Example IT Steering Committee Agenda

The steering committee, at the outset, may be forced to meet as frequently as once per week to purge the backlog of issues, stalled projects, and project-prioritization work. Over the longer term, the IT steering committee should not have to meet more frequently than once every two weeks. The committee should meet, at a minimum, once per month.

Reviewing Critical Issues

The first item to discuss is the top three to six issues that are hampering or hindering progress in IT. The issues are prepared for the committee to consider, along with potential resolutions and specific actions that IT and business managers can take. Project issues are covered in the next agenda item, so these issues should be non-project issues. For example: Issue 1—the company has been plagued by its third e-mail virus in the past three months. Should IT spend the resources and capital to increase prevention of viruses? It is important that business users on the committee weigh in on this question. If the virus caused no negative impact on the business, why spend the extra resources to get rid of all viruses? On the other hand, if the viruses are causing substantial business interruption, that input will be provided. The committee may then commission the IT department to develop recommendations for correcting the problem.

Often the IT department recommends solutions to issues that the business may not care about. Now the CIO or CFO can understand what issues are causing the largest business impact. The desired outcome is to have for each of the top issues (1) a resolution, (2) an action plan, or (3) a request for additional data.

Reviewing Status of In-Process Projects

The next step is to review the status of current high-priority IT projects (in prioritized order).

- *List of projects:* This lists all IT projects currently underway and includes the following attributes for each project: priority, target completion date, milestones, percent of hours worked as a total of estimated hours, and percent of project complete. Projects can be segmented into red (problem), yellow (caution/warning), or green (no problems or ahead of schedule).
- All red and yellow projects should be discussed; if time permits, the committee can review green project status updates.
- Any existing project in which the scope is changing from the original project plan needs a change request form completed. This form details the modification from original project design specification and allows the committee to determine whether the change is necessary, and any additional implications of the change.
- Existing project and applications should follow these change process steps:
  —Project champion (typically a line of business representative) completes preliminary sections of the change request form and submits it to IT.
  —IT works with the project champion to identify project scope, high-level design, IT requirements, schedule, and business rationale (cost and project financial value).
  —The completed change request form and schedule are submitted to the CIO.
  —The CIO reviews the change request.
  —Action is decided by the CIO depending on threshold limits. If moved to the committee, members may individually review and investigate issues before the meeting.
  —If approved by the CIO, the project champion and IT present the project to the committee using the project change request form and associated material (project schedule, project definition, etc).
  —ITSC discusses project proposal and determines appropriate action.
- *Outcome:* Each discussion on red projects should result in one of the following outcomes: (1) actions to be taken to correct the problem with follow-up at the next IT steering committee meeting, (2) a decision to kill the project, or (3) assignment of an independent resource to validate and verify the project issues and present at the next IT steering committee meeting.

Approve New Projects/Prioritization and Assess Capital Expenditure Requests

New project proposals should be completed and reviewed by the IT steering committee. The key is to prioritize new project proposals relative to existing projects. Each proposal should contain the following information:

- Project champion (typically a line of business representative—the person who completes preliminary sections of the project proposal form and submits it to IT).
- Description of project and scope, business reason for the project, the cost, the team, the time line, and the return on investment anticipated. Appendix items can include high-level design, IT requirements, and project plan.

The process to get project proposals in front of the committee includes having the champion complete the project proposal and submit it to the CIO. The CIO reviews the proposal and may request additional information. The CIO should approve proposals under a certain size in advance. Proposals over a certain threshold should go before committee for approval. After approval, the project will be added to the approved projects list for further prioritization by the committee (see Chapter 17).

- *Outcome:* The IT steering committee should decide for each project proposal to either: (1) approve and move forward with project, (2) decline project, or (3) request additional information and decide at next meeting.

Capital expenditure requests for hardware are also reviewed and approved by the committee. The process is identical to the project proposal requests. The level of IT spending can be increased or decreased by loosening or tightening constraints on approval. Capital expenditure approvals by the IT steering committee help ensure that IT funds are being spent on investments that deliver appropriate value to the business.

Assessing IT Priorities

The committee will assess priorities periodically (at least once a quarter). The IT demand management and prioritization process is detailed in Chapter 17. During this segment of the meeting, review the updated priority list and discuss any issues with the current priorities.

The committee will also approve proposed vendor relationships, discuss proposed new vendors, and approve changes to current vendor contracts or terms.

Summary

The IT steering committee is a critical component of the effective IT department. The process described here increases and improves communication between IT and the business. The IT steering committee ensures buy-in of strategic IT decisions and projects by the business and upper management. Additionally, the discipline helps curb spending on unnecessary technology and IT projects, as well as helps enforce the disciplines and approaches covered throughout this book.

Steering committees can fail if they do not have the right charter, membership (both makeup and skill set), organization (run effectively with support from the culture), authority, processes, and attendance. Therefore, merely going through the motions is not enough. Committee members must be engaged and active to ensure that the steering committee is effective.

Sometimes, the name *committee* alarms the organization and brings out the cynical skeptics who dislike the connotation of the word. If *committee* is a negative term in the organization, the name can easily be changed to advisory group, board, council—any name that is appropriate; the most important step is creating the group and using it effectively.

The initial meetings may run long and seem like there is too much content to discuss; however, after the backlog of issues is cleared, subsequent meetings can focus on only the high-priority IT issues and projects and can be both rapid and successful. Over the long run, the committee can usually take the meeting frequency down to once every two to four weeks.

RESOURCES

K. Doughty, "Auditing the Implementation of the IT Strategic Plan," *EDP Auditing Journal* (New York: Auerbach, 1998).

K. Doughty, "Auditing Project Management for IS Developments," *EDP Audit, Control and Security Newsletter* (New York: Auerbach, 1996).

Mary Hayes, "IT Cuts Boost Productivity," *Information Week* (June 17, 2002).

NOTE

1. Daniel J. Boorstin, *The Decline of Radicalism: Reflections on America Today* (New York: Random House, 1969).

Index

623